68ᵗʰ

Ashbridge

PERSONAL INJURY TITLES
FROM WILEY LAW PUBLICATIONS

ARBITRATING PERSONAL INJURY CLAIMS
John Farrell Fay

AUTOMOTIVE ENGINEERING AND LITIGATION (VOLUMES 1–5)
George A. Peters and Barbara J. Peters

AUTOMOTIVE ENGINEERING AND LITIGATION (VOLUME 6): THE INTERNATIONAL
DIRECTORY OF EXPERTS AND CONSULTANTS IN AUTOMOTIVE ENGINEERING 1993
George A. Peters and Barbara J. Peters

CALIFORNIA WORKERS' COMPENSATION CITATOR
C. Duke Marsh

EMERGENCY MEDICINE MALPRACTICE (SECOND EDITION)
Mikel A. Rothenberg

EVALUATING AND SETTLING PERSONAL INJURY CLAIMS
George M. Gold, Editor

EVALUATING TMJ INJURIES
Reda A. Abdel-Fattah

FIRE LITIGATION SOURCEBOOK (SECOND EDITION)
Alexander J. Patton

HANDLING BIRTH TRAUMA CASES
Stanley S. Schwartz and Norman D. Tucker

LITIGATING HEAD TRAUMA CASES
Arthur C. Roberts

LITIGATING STRESS CASES IN WORKERS' COMPENSATION
Steven Babitsky and James Mangraviti

LITIGATING TMJ CASES
A. Clark Cone and Michael J. McHale

MODERN TORT LIABILITY: RECOVERY IN THE '90S
Terrence F. Kiely

OB/GYN MALPRACTICE
Scott M. Lewis

ATTORNEY'S GUIDE TO ONCOLOGY CASES
Melvin A. Shiffman

ORTHOPEDIC DISABILITY AND EXPERT TESTIMONY (FOURTH EDITION)
Harold F. Goodman

PERSONAL INJURY DAMAGES LAW AND PRACTICE
Edward C. Martin

ATTORNEY'S GUIDE TO ONCOLOGY CASES
VOLUME 1

SUBSCRIPTION NOTICE

This Wiley product is updated on a periodic basis with supplements to reflect important changes in the subject matter. If you purchased this product directly from John Wiley & Sons, Inc., we have already recorded your subscription for this update service.

If, however, you purchased this product from a bookstore and wish to receive (1) the current update at no additional charge, and (2) future updates and revised or related volumes billed separately with a 30-day examination review, please send your name, company name (if applicable), address and the title of the product to:

Supplement Department
John Wiley & Sons, Inc.
One Wiley Drive
Somerset, NJ 08875
1-800-225-5945

For customers outside the United States, please contact the Wiley office nearest you:

Professional and Reference Division
John Wiley & Sons Canada, Ltd.
22 Worcester Road
Rexdale, Ontario M9W 1L1
CANADA
(416) 675-3580
1-800-567-4797
Fax: (416) 675-6599

John Wiley & Sons, Ltd.
Baffins Lane
Chichester
West Sussex, PO19 1UD
UNITED KINGDOM
Phone: (44) (243) 779777

Jacaranda Wiley Ltd.
PRT Division
P.O. Box 174
North Ryde, NSW 2113
AUSTRALIA
Phone: (02) 805-1100
Fax: (02) 805-1597

John Wiley & Sons (SEA) Pte. Ltd.
37 Jalan Pemimpin
Block B # 05-04
Union Industrial Building
SINGAPORE 2057
Phone: (65) 258-1157

ATTORNEY'S GUIDE TO ONCOLOGY CASES
VOLUME 1

MELVIN A. SHIFFMAN, M.D., J.D.

JACK BROOK, M.D.

PIERRE V. HAIG, M.D.

Wiley Law Publications
JOHN WILEY & SONS, INC.
New York • Chichester • Brisbane • Toronto • Singapore

Library of Congress Cataloging-in-Publication Data

ISBN 0-471-11209-7 (Set)
ISBN 0-471-11206-2 (V. 1)
ISBN 0-471-11208-9 (V. 2)

Printed in the United States of America

10 9 8 7 6 5 4 3 2 1

PREFACE

This book is more than a basic text in oncology for plaintiff and defense attorneys. It includes legal considerations regarding medical malpractice, with examples from various legal cases. The purpose is to produce an insight into the diagnosis and treatment of cancer and allied diseases and the legal implications of the failure to care for patients properly.

It is also intended that physicians gain an understanding of the legal pitfalls which may be manifested in medical care and treatment. Probably more important, sufficient time and effort should be spent during medical training to introduce physicians to medical jurisprudence and methods to avoid or reduce opportunities for malpractice litigation. For example, physicians' production of medical records tends to be inadequate and thereby diminishes their opportunity for a proper defense. Establishing rapport and spending time with patients in discussions and explanations both help to avoid misunderstandings and conflicts. Patients have a right to know all that is transpiring and the implications of the various diagnostic and therapeutic methods available.

Being successful in a medical malpractice case depends upon many important factors, any one of which may have an adverse effect:

1. Evaluating the plaintiff's complaints, injuries, and demeanor
2. The attorney's complete review and understanding of the medical facts and legal implications
3. The attorney's preparation to cover all contigencies
4. Selection of expert witnesses who have sufficient understanding of the medical problems involved and the standard of care, plus an influential demeanor
5. Careful selection of a jury
6. Careful consideration of the client's best interests in deciding whether to settle or proceed with arbitration or trial.

July 1994

MELVIN A. SHIFFMAN, M.D., J.D.
Tustin, California
JACK BROOK, M.D.
Anaheim, California
PIERRE V. HAIG, M.D.
Dana Point, California

iii

ACKNOWLEDGMENTS

Thanks to Dee Richardson, Romona Coon, and Jennifer Widzer for their patience and perseverance in placing the handwritten manuscripts on computer, including multitudinous changes and corrections.

ABOUT THE AUTHORS

Melvin A. Shiffman received his M.D. degree from Northwestern University School of Medicine and his J.D. degree from Western State University College of Law. He currently practices in Tustin, California, specializing in surgical oncology with a subspecialty of cosmetic and reconstructive surgery. A former assistant clinical professor of surgery at the University of California, Irvine, Dr. Shiffman's publications consist of over 50 books and papers, including *Medical Malpractice: Handling General Surgery Cases.* He is editor-in-chief of the American Journal of Cosmetic Surgery.

Jack Brook received his M.D. degree from New York Medical College and completed his fellowship in hematology at Mount Sinai Hospital. He founded the Hematology Department at the U.S. Naval Hospital in Portsmouth, Virginia, and the medical oncology training program at the Veterans' Administration Hospital in Long Beach, California. The author of 16 articles about cancer, Dr. Brook is also the recipient of three National Cancer Institute Research Grant awards. He is presently in the private practice of oncology in Anaheim, California.

Pierre V. Haig received his M.D. degree from the University of Southern California. A radiation oncologist for many years, he also served as director of radiation oncology at St. Jude Medical Center from 1970 to 1990. Dr. Haig was a clinical professor at the University of Southern California and has published articles on rare oncologic phenomena. He is presently retired.

SUMMARY CONTENTS

Volume 1

Volume 2

DETAILED CONTENTS

DETAILED CONTENTS

CHAPTER 1

MALPRACTICE LITIGATION AND PROCEDURE

THEORIES OF LIABILITY IN MEDICAL MALPRACTICE

§ 1.1   Negligence

Medical negligence is the breach of a duty to the patient that is the proximate cause of harm or injury to the patient.

§ 1.2   —Duty

Facts must be present that support a finding that a duty exists between the health care provider and the injured patient. In essence, the relationship between the parties must form a legal obligation of one to the other. Statutes, rules, principles, and precedents establish this duty.

In medical practice the duty of due care arising from the physician-patient relationship requires the physician to obtain an adequate medical history, perform a competent physical examination, diagnose the patient, and treat the patient. The physician must perform those tests necessary to reach a reasonable diagnosis, obtain competent and timely consultation when necessary, and make use of the physician's own training and experience to diagnose and treat.

There is a duty in medicine to inform the patient of the diagnosis and/or possible diagnoses and to describe the intended treatment and its material complications as well as alternative treatments and their material or significant complications. Materiality is usually determined by that information necessary for the patient to make a knowledgeable and informed decision as to the treatment to be rendered. The physician also has a duty to see the patient as often as necessary to diagnose and treat the patient properly.

The physician must inform the patient of potential malignancy[1] and of any material facts concerning the patient's bodily condition and the risks created by that condition.[2] When a physician examines a person, even if no doctor-patient relationship exists, there is a duty of good medical care that includes informing the person that there is a dangerous condition and that further medical evaluation and treatment should be sought.[3]

Traditionally the physician's duty has been measured by a community standard if not regulated by statute. There is increased uniformity of medical training throughout the country, and medical organizations, meetings, and publications are more national in character. Continuing education requirements keep physicians informed about changes in medical diagnosis and treatment on a national

---

[1] Jamison v. Lindsay, 166 Cal. Rptr. 443 (Ct. App. 1980).

[2] Gates v. Jenson, 92 Wash. 2d 246, 595 P.2d 919 (1979).

[3] Betesh v. United States, 400 F. Supp. 238 (D.D.C. 1974).

level. The trend is toward increased standardization of care regardless of geographic location. Standard of care in some states such as Colorado, Delaware, Idaho, Kentucky, New York, Oregon, and Vermont follows the *same locality rule*. This rule requires the physician to possess the degree of medical skill that a reasonable practitioner practicing in the same locality would possess. Some states use the *same or similar locality rule,* which makes the standard of care that care a physician would exercise practicing in the same or similar community under the same or similar circumstances. This standard is followed in Arkansas, Indiana, Kansas, New Mexico, North Carolina, North Dakota, Tennessee, and Texas. The *same state standard,* through which the physician is held to the standard of care of a specialist possessing that degree of care and skill exercised in the same specialty throughout the state, is used in Virginia and Washington. A *nationwide standard* of care may be employed in Alabama, Connecticut, Georgia, Idaho, Illinois, Kansas, Louisiana, Maine, Massachusetts, Michigan, Minnesota, Mississippi, Montana, Nevada, Ohio, Oklahoma, Pennsylvania, South Carolina, South Dakota, and Wisconsin.

The duty of the hospital is to maintain the equipment and the physical plant of the hospital for the safety of the patients and visitors. There are judicial and statutory requirements of duty toward patients that must be fulfilled.

The medical staff of the hospital must be competent, and the hospital has a duty to adequately investigate the background and character of the physicians applying for staff privileges. These privileges must be reevaluated every one to two years.

The hospital may be liable under the theory of *respondeat superior* for the acts of its employees. The hospital has the duty both to hire competent nurses and to have adequate numbers of personnel to care for the patients in the facility. There is a responsibility to maintain medical records and to disperse medical reports in a timely fashion.

The nurse's duty to the patient is to use due care and diligence in handling patients and to use training and experience to carry out proper orders from the physician. The nurse has a responsibility to refuse orders that might endanger the health and safety of the patient. If a potentially dangerous problem exists, the nurse has a duty to inform the physician or superiors or both.

Dugger v. Danello.[4]   The court held that the degree of skill and care required was determined by the way in which the majority of competent physicians could have handled the case rather than by a national standard.

Curry v. Summer.[5]   The court determined that the physician owes the duty of due care in treatment of the patient. The plaintiff must prove the duty owed, its breach, and causation.

---

[4] 175 Ga. App. 618, 334 S.E.2d 3 (1985).
[5] 136 Ill. App. 3d 468, 483 N.E.2d 711 (1985).

Jackson v. Bumgardner.[6]   The plaintiff had to allege and prove that the breach of duty to the patient was the cause of the injuries sustained.

Pepe v. United States.[7]   The court stated that the physician must use the degree of skill and care used by the average physician in similar circumstances and must exercise his best judgment.

§ 1.3   —Breach of Duty

There is a standard of conduct under the imposed duty of care, below which an individual may not fall without giving rise to a breach of that duty. In medical malpractice cases the standard of conduct may be that of a reasonable person, a prudent person, or a reasonable physician with a similar patient under similar circumstances. "Negligence is the omission to do something which a reasonable man, guided upon those considerations which ordinarily regulate the conduct of human affairs, would do, or doing something which a prudent and reasonable man would not do."[8]

The breach can consist of an intentional act such as nondisclosure or misrepresentation. More often, though, an unintentional act creates a risk of recognizable damage or injury that may constitute negligence. Even an honest mistake or blunder will not absolve the physician from liability[9] if a reasonable physician would probably anticipate that the injury might occur.

Ordinarily, expert testimony is required to prove the breach was an act outside the standard of care. If, however, the provider's conduct falls within the experience of a layperson, expert testimony is not required.

§ 1.4   —Proximate Cause

Another requirement for a prima facie case of medical negligence is that there be a reasonable connection between the act of omission of the health care provider and the damages suffered by the patient.

The *but for* or *sine qua non* rule established in some jurisdictions states that the provider's conduct is a cause of the event if the event would not have occurred but for that conduct. Other courts have applied the *substantial factor* rule, which states that the defendant's conduct is a cause of the event if it was a material element and substantial factor in bringing it about.[10]

---

[6] 347 S.E.2d 743 (N.C. 1986).

[7] 599 F. Supp. 798 (E.D.N.Y. 1984).

[8] Blyth v. Birmingham Water Works Co., 11 Ex. 781, 784, 156 Eng. Rep. 1046 (1856).

[9] Teepen v. Taylor, 141 Mo. App. 282, 124 S.W. 1062 (1910).

[10] W.P. Keeton et al., Prosser and Keeton on the Law of Torts § 41, at 266–67 (5th ed. 1984).

The mere fact that other events have contributed to the damages a patient may suffer does not absolve the health care provider from liability when the defendant's conduct was a substantial factor in causing the injury. Legal causation in some courts refers only to *foreseeable risks* secondary to the provider's actions or inaction. In other jurisdictions, the scope of liability extends to all *direct* consequences that are foreseeable. Intervening forces that are foreseeable come within the scope of the original risk and thus are deemed the provider's responsibility or negligence. Unforeseeable results of unforeseeable causes are not attributed to the provider's negligence.[11]

§ 1.5   —Damages

As an essential element of the plaintiff's case, damages, consisting of a loss or injury to the patient, must be proved.

The statute of limitations does not begin to run in a negligence action until some damage has occurred. There is a delay in the running of the statute in some jurisdictions under the following circumstances:

1. The provider's duty continues until the physician-patient relationship has ended.

2. There is fraudulent concealment of damages or the cause of damages.

3. The provider is silent when a confidential relationship gives rise to a duty to speak.

4. Foreign objects left in the plaintiff's body have not been discovered or removed (*continuing negligence*).

5. The plaintiff has not yet discovered that she has suffered injury unless by the exercise of reasonable diligence she should have discovered it (*discovery rule*).[12]

§ 1.6   Battery

Battery is defined as a harmful or offensive contact with a person resulting from an act intended to cause the party to suffer such contact. *Assault* is "any act of such a nature as to excite an apprehension of a battery."[13]

The performance of a surgical procedure not within the realm of oral or written consent constitutes a battery. Most often this occurs when a surgeon performs

---

[11] *Id.* § 41, at 268, § 42, at 273, § 43, at 303.

[12] W.P. Keeton et al., Prosser and Keeton on the Law of Torts § 30, at 166 (5th ed. 1984).

[13] W.P. Keeton et al., Prosser and Keeton on the Law of Torts § 9, at 39, § 12, at 43 (5th ed. 1984).

a gratuitous procedure while the patient is under a general anesthetic or a surgeon performs a surgery on the wrong side (for example, performing a right inguinal herniorrhaphy instead of a left inguinal herniorrhaphy for which the consent was signed).

§ 1.7   Intentional Infliction of Emotional Distress

For the plaintiff to have a case for intentional infliction of emotional distress the conduct must be of a flagrant character. Circumstances surrounding the aggravation or extreme misconduct must be more than mere insult, indignity, obscenity, abuse, or annoyance before mental distress is considered genuine. In some jurisdictions the statutes are more lenient and provide an action for "all words which from their usual construction and acceptance are considered as insults, and lead to violence and breach of the peace."[14]

The emotional distress must in fact exist and it must be severe. Except in cases in which the defendant has knowledge of the plaintiff's susceptibility and practices upon it, the distress must be such as would affect a reasonable person *of ordinary sensibilities* under the circumstances. In some cases the conduct may be willful, wanton, or reckless; in such instances there is a high degree of probability that mental distress will follow.

§ 1.8   Contract

The bases for contractual obligations are those representations made under circumstances such that the patient can reasonably regard the statements as an intent to guarantee. A contract is a mutual agreement, upon sufficient consideration, to do or not to do a particular thing. Most contracts between patient and physician are implied contracts.

The statement by a surgeon that "you will have a hairline scar" can be interpreted as a guarantee and therefore the basis for a contractual obligation. A wide or thick scar may then be regarded as a breach of the contract. Recovery by the plaintiff would be either return of the fees paid or return of the cost required to make a thick scar into a hairline scar. There is, in most jurisdictions, no recovery for pain and suffering in a breach of contract action.

Gould v. Concord Hospital.[15]   The court held that a contract action can arise where the physician agrees to effect a cure of the patient.

---

[14] W.P. Keeton et al., Prosser and Keeton on the Law of Torts § 12, at 63 (5th ed. 1984).

[15] 493 A.2d 1193 (N.H. 1985).

Murray v. University of Pennsylvania.[16]   Breach of contract was claimed when there was an express warranty given regarding a tubal ligation. The contracted-for specific result that did not occur was actionable even if the physician exercised the highest degree of care.

§ 1.9   Wrongful Death

Wrongful death statutes provide recourse when death occurs due to any wrongful act, neglect, or failure to act. There is ordinarily no action available for a breach of contract unless the contract was made to assure or enhance the patient's safety and death results from its breach. Intentional as well as negligent acts are covered.[17] The plaintiff in a wrongful death action may be the executor, the administrator of the estate, or the beneficiaries or heirs as designated by statute.

Recoverable damages are compensation for economic loss (out-of-pocket financial loss) as well as benefits that might reasonably have been expected in the form of support, services, or contributions during the remainder of the lifetime of the decedent if death had not occurred. Some jurisdictions base damages on the loss to the dependents or survivors. Living expenses or contributions to the decedent's maintenance absent death are subtracted from the expected lifetime earnings in order to estimate damages.

In some states in which there are both survival acts and death acts, there are then two causes of action following a patient's death. Both may be claimed concurrently.[18] Thus, medical and funeral expenses, pain and suffering, and loss of earnings up to the date of death may be allocated to the survival action (estate),[19] while heirs may recover for loss of affection, comfort, and companionship in a wrongful death action.

The same defenses are available to the defendant as would have been valid prior to the decedent's death. These include comparative fault, contributory negligence, assumption of the risk, and valid consent.

Keys v. Mercy Hospital of New Orleans.[20]   Negligent intubation resulted in the death of the pregnant patient. The husband was awarded $200,000 and the child $150,000 from the hospital and nurse anesthetist.

Any judgment or settlement during the decedent's lifetime is intended to cover all damage and would bar a survival action or wrongful death action in most

---

[16]490 A.2d 839 (Pa. Super. Ct. 1985).

[17]Kling v. Torello, 126 Ky. 685, 102 S.W. 278 (1907).

[18]Koehler v. Wankesha Milk Co., 190 Wis. 52, 208 N.W. 901 (1926).

[19]National Bank v. Norfolk & W. Ry., 73 Ill. 2d 160, 383 N.E.2d 919 (1978).

[20]485 So. 2d 514 (La. Ct. App. 1986).

instances. There are some states that would still allow a wrongful death action, reasoning that there is danger of an improvident settlement by an optimistic person that takes no account of a shortened life expectancy or of the interests of the survivors.

§ 1.10   Survival Actions

A survival action is a cause of action held by the decedent immediately before or at death that is transferred to the decedent's personal representative (the executor or administrator of the estate). The action is subject to the same defenses that could have been urged against the decedent had the decedent lived.

Damages may include lost wages, medical expenses, pain and suffering, and punitive damages. A number of states specifically exclude pain and suffering while some states exclude punitive or exemplary damages.

Under some statutes if death results from the tort, there is no survival action and any claim made on behalf of the heirs or beneficiaries is that of a wrongful death action.

Wheat v. United States.[21]   Applying Texas law, there was failure to repeat a pap smear, biopsy the cervical tumor, and perform necessary diagnostic tests. The physician also failed to disclose to the patient the presence of cancer of the cervix even though the diagnosis was noted in the physician's records. The patient's daughter was awarded $1,000,000 for loss of consortium resulting from the death of her mother.

§ 1.11   Spoliation of Records

Changes in medical records may occur when errors in the recorded information are first noted. It is advisable that each significant change be dated and initialed at the time of the correction.

When these alterations of records or the loss of records appears, after a suit has been filed or in anticipation of a malpractice action, the physician may be suspected of trying to add self-serving information or to lose incriminating evidence. At trial, altered or lost records can be detrimental to the defendant physician's testimony and credibility. In law, bearing chiefly on evidence, there is a maxim that everything most to the spoliator's disadvantage is to be presumed against the spoliator.

---

[21] 630 F. Supp. 699 (W.D. Tex. 1986).

Bondu v. Gurvich.[22]   The plaintiff's negligence action was dismissed for failure to state a cause of action. A new action was filed alleging that the hospital failed to furnish the decedent's records and that this breach caused the plaintiff to lose the medical malpractice lawsuit. The court held that res judicata does not apply and that the hospital had a duty to maintain and furnish such records to a patient or the patient's personal representative upon request (implicit in which is the duty to make such records in the first instance) as found in § 395.202, Florida Statutes (1979). That section provided:

> § 395.202 Patient records; copies; examination, . . .
>
> (1) Any licensed hospital shall, upon request, and only after discharge of the patient, furnish to any person admitted therein for care and treatment or treated thereat, or such person's guardian, curator, personal representative, or anyone designated by such person in writing, a true and correct copy of all records in the possession of the hospital, except progress notes and consultation report sections of a psychiatric nature concerning the care and treatment performed therein by the hospital, provided the person requesting such records agrees to pay a reasonable charge for copying of said records, and further shall allow examination of the original records in its possession, or microfilms or other suitable reproductions of the records, upon such reasonable terms as shall be imposed to assure that the records shall not be damaged, destroyed, or altered.
>
> (2) The provisions of this act shall not apply to any hospital whose primary function is to provide psychiatric care to its patients.[23]

Because Mrs. Bondu alleged that this duty was breached by the hospital when it failed to furnish Mr. Bondu's records to her, and that this breach caused her damage in that she lost "a medical negligence lawsuit when [she] could not provide expert witnesses," her complaint stated a cause of action.[24]

Furlong v. Stokes.[25]   The plaintiff claimed that the defendant was negligent in allowing a hot lamp to shine on the inside left knee during an operation, which resulted in a burn. Res ipsa loquitur was not found to apply because the defendant did not have the right and duty of control of instrumentality causing injury. On readmission to the hospital for a skin graft to the knee the record showed "burn area, 3rd degree left medial thigh (old)." Defendant wrote over this, "ulcer of left knee, medial aspect." The court held that it was apparent that a change was made in the record, but that it was not the same as destroying the record or the same as alteration or erasure intended to obliterate completely that which was there before. This act, therefore, could not be characterized as spoliation.

---

[22] 473 So. 2d 1307 (Fla. Dist. Ct. App. 1984).

[23] Fla. Stat. Ann. § 395.202 (West 1979).

[24] *Id.*

[25] 427 S.W.2d 513 (Mo. 1968).

The plaintiff was found to have failed to carry the burden of making a submissible case for the jury, and the directed verdict for the defendant was upheld.

Hardy v. Fattah.[26] The 18-year-old decedent was admitted to the hospital by the defendant for dyspnea and chest pain. Following discharge his condition became worse, and after readmission a lung scan showed pulmonary emboli. He died shortly thereafter. The defendant alleged that death was due to myocarditis and produced a certificate of death that contained the word *myocarditis*. The defendant claimed that his death certificate was authentic. The official state death certificate produced by the plaintiff was different from the defendant's certificate. The arbitration panel found for the defendant but a later jury trial verdict awarded the plaintiff $400,000.

May v. Moore.[27] The court held that the spoliation of or attempt to suppress material evidence by a party to a suit, favorable to the adversary, is sufficient foundation for an inference of the adversary's guilt or negligence. In *May v. Moore* the defendant failed to perform laboratory tests, other than a blood count, in a newborn infant with central nervous system injury, sepsis, pneumonia, and meningitis. The infant ultimately died after transfer to another hospital. The original hospital medical records had disappeared, and the administrator's copies of the records were different from the defendant's records. Sanctions were granted against the defendant for not producing records requested by court order within the time allowed by the trial court. Testimony by the hospital administrator showing defendant physician's connection with missing records of another of his patients was admitted solely for purposes of impeachment. The attempt to impeach the defendant was based on the prior denial of the defendant that he ever had in his possession any part of the original record of such patient when in fact the hospital administrator produced circumstantial evidence that the defendant did have possession of such record.

Public Health Trust of Dade County v. Valcin.[28] In this case the operative note was missing due to the intentional acts of the physician and hospital. The Florida Supreme Court concluded that if the records were unavailable because of unintentional acts or omissions, a rebuttable presumption of negligence would be imposed upon the defendants if the patient showed that the absence of the records impaired the patient's ability to prove a prima facie case of medical malpractice. This shifted to the defendants the burden of producing evidence that the medical treatment or procedure was performed in a nonnegligent manner. However, if it was determined that the defendants intentionally brought about

---

[26] No. 84-805-PI-1 (Stark County Ohio Ct. C.P. 1984), *reprinted in* 4 Med. Malpractice Verdicts, Settlements & Experts No. 8, at 11 (1988).

[27] 424 So. 2d 596 (Ala. 1982).

[28] 507 So. 2d 596 (Fla. 1987).

the loss or destruction of the critical medical records, the court could impose sanctions under the rules of civil procedure. These sanctions included preventing the defendants from opposing any claims of negligence or rendering against the defendants a judgment of default, which has the effect of conclusive presumption.

Thor v. Boska.[29]   This case involved a missed diagnosis of cancer of the breast. The defendant claimed to have made a more legible copy of the records and to have lost the originals. He did not, however, copy a diagram drawn of the breast when the lump first appeared. The court held that the lost records created a strong inference of consciousness of guilt on his part, and admission of allegations as to one issue out of several did not neutralize the effect of alleged "spoliation." The court, quoting Wigmore, said:

> It has always been understood . . . the inference . . . that a party's . . . suppression of evidence by . . . spoliation . . . is receivable against him as an indication of his consciousness *that his case is a weak or unfounded one;* and from that consciousness may be inferred the fact itself of the cause's lack of truth and merit. The inference . . . operates, indefinitely though strongly, *against the whole mass of alleged facts constituting his cause."* (2 Wigmore (3d ed. 1940) sec. 278, p. 120).

Then, quoting McCormick, the court said the plaintiff should be entitled to an instruction that "the adversary's conduct may be considered as tending to corroborate the proponent's case *generally,* and as tending to discredit the adversary's case *generally"* (McCormick on Evidence (2d ed. 1972) sec. 273, p. 661).

§ 1.12   Res Ipsa Loquitur

Res ipsa loquitur may be available in certain specific situations, whereby the burden of proof shifts to the defendant to prove that the plaintiff's injury was not the result of negligence. To invoke the doctrine of res ipsa loquitur, the following elements must be shown:

1. The injury does not ordinarily occur in the absence of someone's negligence.
2. The injury must be caused by an agency or instrumentality within the exclusive control of the defendant.
3. The injury must not have been a result of any voluntary action or contribution on the part of the plaintiff.
4. In some courts, evidence of the true explanation of the event must be more readily accessible to the defendant than to the plaintiff.

---

[29] 38 Cal. App. 3d 558, 113 Cal. Rptr. 296 (1974).

In South Carolina the doctrine exists under the principle of circumstantial evidence and not as res ipsa loquitur. Most courts regard res ipsa loquitur as one form of showing that the defendant has not exercised reasonable care.

Brown v. Keaveny.[30]   The doctrine of res ipsa loquitur was applied when injuries were suffered by a patient following injection into his hand of a fluid labeled Novocain® but which was in fact not Novocain. The fluid caused swelling and an ulceration of the thumb that required skin grafts. The solution was prepared from procaine crystals, labeled, stored, and dispensed by the hospital. The fact that the crystals and the various other ingredients of the solution were purchased from others was immaterial because, after purchasing the ingredients, the hospital had complete dominion and control over them, and the hospital's own process changed the nature of the ingredients completely and produced the solution, the instrumentality that injured the patient. The hospital furnished all the equipment used in giving the injection, and it had complete control of the solution until it was injected. The physician who gave the injection did nothing to change the solution's character but was merely a conduit through which the solution reached the patient. The hospital was found liable.

Cho v. Kempler.[31]   An injury to the facial nerve occurred during a mastoidectomy. The court concluded that the res ipsa loquitur instruction was needed to protect an injured patient by inducing the physician to explain the reason for the injury or suffer the penalty of adverse inference in the absence of such explanation. This type of accident would not happen in the ordinary course of things if those who had control of the instrumentality used ordinary care. The accident was a type that probably would not have occurred unless someone was negligent.

Hasemeier v. Smith.[32]   Paralysis of the patient's arm occurred following a hysterectomy. The doctrine of res ipsa loquitur was found applicable by the court. Testimony of doctors and nurses showed that paralysis was probably caused by trauma while the patient was under anesthesia either by faulty positioning of the arm, by rotating the patient's arm while extended, by movement of the patient while the table was tilted, or by traction or pressure on the arm or shoulder. The appellate court stated that "to emerge from abdominal surgery with a paralyzed arm is so extraordinary an occurrence within the general observations of mankind as to raise an inference of negligence that requires both explanation and proof of nonnegligence to meet."[33] A judgment for $25,000 was entered against the hospital.

---

[30] 326 F.2d 660 (D.C. Cir. 1963).

[31] 177 Cal. App. 2d 342, 2 Cal. Rptr. 167 (1960).

[32] 361 S.W.2d 697 (Mo. 1962).

[33] *Id.* at 703.

§ 1.13   Loss of Consortium

A cause of action for loss of consortium is brought by the spouse of an injured person to assert the spouse's legal rights to the services, society, sexual intercourse, and conjugal affection (love, companionship, and comfort) of the injured person. Damages may be affixed in the absence of economic loss. Punitive damages may also be awarded.

Varelis v. Northwestern Memorial Hospital.[34]   The patient was given an overdose of magnesium while receiving chemotherapy for leukemia. Cardiac arrest ensued, and as a result the patient was in a permanent vegetative state. The patient was awarded $2 million and his wife awarded $573,500 for loss of consortium.

Vincent v. Bowling Green-Warren County Community Hospital Corp.[35]   A sponge was left in the patient following surgery for a bleeding ulcer. The sponge was removed surgically nine months later. The patient's wife was awarded $12,000 for loss of companionship, assistance, and aid during her husband's illness.

§ 1.14   Loss of Chance

Loss of chance of survival or increased risk of harm is a viable cause of action in many jurisdictions. The cause of action may exist in medical negligence cases in which the patient has lost the opportunity to avoid some physical injury, disease, or death. Typically, there is a failure to diagnose and treat a medical disorder in a timely fashion.

The basic variation in jurisdictional application of the loss of chance action hinges on the issue of causation. Some courts have held that patients who do not have initially at least a 50-percent chance of survival cannot recover because it is more likely than not (a reasonable medical probability) that the patient would not have survived anyway. Therefore, it is not possible to meet the test of sufficient proof of the causal connection between the violation of the standard of care and the injury sustained. The defense may argue that the issue of causation is in the realm of conjecture and not probability.

This raises the issue of insufficiency of proof whenever a patient who does not have more than a 50 percent chance of five-year survival sustains an injury through medical negligence. A decrease in the patient's opportunity for survival,

---

[34] No. 87L 15613 (Ill. Cook County Cir. Ct. 1987), *reprinted in* 5 Med. Malpractice Verdicts, Settlements & Experts No. 4, at 47 (1989).

[35] No. 87-Cl-1011 (Ky. Warren County Cir. Ct. 1987), *reprinted in* 5 Med. Malpractice Verdicts, Settlements & Experts No. 4, at 65 (1989).

no matter how great (1 to 49 percent), would not sustain a cause of action. This would affect all patients with cancer of the stomach, lung, and pancreas or with any disease causing the patient to have a poor chance of survival.

Other courts reason that causation can be proved if the injury sustained was more likely than not a result of a breach in the standard of care. This increased risk must be a substantial factor in producing the resulting harm.

The injury can be a poor result, particular complications, the need for unnecessary alternatives (for example, chemotherapy, radiation therapy, and more extensive surgery), or death. All of these may be compensable under the theory of loss of chance.

Herskovits v. Group Health Cooperative of Puget Sound.[36]   The court held that although the decedent would have had only a 39 percent chance of survival if the negligence had not occurred, the 14 percent reduction of his chance of survival was sufficient evidence of actual causation to allow the causation issue to go to the jury.

Other isolated cases show compensation for loss of chance.[37] Some factual situation involve patients who would have had at least a 50 percent chance of survival but lost a substantial percentage of that chance due to the defendant's negligence.[38]

Misdiagnosis of heart disease and cancer are especially suitable for a loss of chance action because these have fairly accurate estimates for chances of recovery. These illnesses can be detected by new sophisticated methods, and early diagnosis is important in limiting their severity.[39]

Ladner v. Campbell.[40]   The physician's failure to timely diagnose the breast cancer reduced the chance for survival from 62 percent to 32 percent, and this failure constituted negligence.

McKellips v. Saint Francis Hospital, Inc.[41]   The plaintiff decedent was brought into the emergency room with substernal chest pain. He was diagnosed as having gastritis and discharged to go home. Five hours later the decedent suffered a cardiac arrest and was returned to the hospital where he was pronounced dead. The plaintiff's expert testified that if treated promptly the patient's chance of survival would have been significantly improved. The Oklahoma Supreme Court on certiorari from the Court of Appeals stated that health care providers

---

[36] 99 Wash. 2d 609, 664 P.2d 474 (1983).

[37] *See, e.g.,* James v. United States, 483 F. Supp. 581 (N.D. Cal. 1980).

[38] *See, e.g.,* Hamil v. Bashline, 481 Pa. 256, 392 A.2d 1280 (1978).

[39] Wolf, *Playing the Percentages: A Reexamination of Recovery for Loss of Chance,* 26 Santa Clara L. Rev. 429–59 (1986).

[40] 515 So. 2d 882 (Miss. 1987).

[41] 741 P.2d 467 (Okla. 1987).

should not be given the benefit of the uncertainty created by their own negligent conduct and that percentage-probability testimony was not required, thereby adopting the *lost chance of survival* doctrine.

Clark v. Hoerner.[42]   Failure to diagnose and properly treat the child's rare and rapidly progressive lung disease was alleged. A jury question was presented regarding the cause of death and whether the alleged negligence may have increased the risk of harm and decreased the patient's chances of survival.

§ 1.15   Abandonment

The physician has a duty to use reasonable skill and care in treating patients. This duty of care includes attending to the patient until treatment is concluded or providing substitute medical attention during the physician's absence. A physician can terminate care with appropriate notification to the patient. The patient has a duty to inform the physician about any problems that have arisen or any change in symptoms.

Johnston v. Ward.[43]   The court held that the physician could not abandon the patient without appropriate notice in a case in which the patient had ingested a large amount of aspirin. The physician was required to attend the patient as long as necessary depending on the patient's condition. There would be no abandonment, however, if the physician made provisions for other physicians to care for the patient.

Miller v. Greater Southwest Community Hospital.[44]   The court held that there was no abandonment when the patient had no need for immediate medical care and was given by her physician a list of substitute physicians. In fact, the hospital provided necessary medical care until the new physician arrived.

Thompson v. Sun City Community Hospital.[45]   The hospital was held liable for transferring the patient because of the patient's financial ineligibility. The patient had sustained transection of the femoral artery, and experts testified as to the need for immediate emergency care in such cases.

Watkins v. Fromm.[46]   The court held that a physician-patient relationship can end upon withdrawal notice or when the condition no longer requires treatment.

---

[42] 525 A.2d 377 (Pa. Super. Ct. 1987).

[43] 344 S.E.2d 166 (S.C. Ct. App. 1986).

[44] 508 A.2d 927 (D.C. 1986).

[45] 141 Ariz. 597, 688 P.2d 605 (1984).

[46] 488 N.Y.S.2d 768 (App. Div. 1985).

PREFILING ISSUES

§ 1.16 Statute of Limitations

The statute of limitations in a negligence action does not generally begin to run until some damage has occurred. The limitations period protects the defendant against fictitious claims and also against the difficulty of obtaining evidence after a lapse of time.

To allow a more equitable solution for the plaintiff who is not aware of or who does not discover the negligence until a later date, courts have found exceptions to the rule. The negligent treatment may be found to continue until the relationship of physician and patient has ended.[47] The statute of limitations is tolled when there is fraudulent concealment of the damage or its cause[48] or when there is a confidential relationship and the defendant is silent when there is a duty to speak.[49] Continuing negligence may be found when a foreign object such as a sponge or instrument is left in a plaintiff's body.[50] The *discovery rule* has expanded the tolling of the statute of limitations until such time as the plaintiff has in fact discovered that she has suffered injury or by the exercise of reasonable diligence should have discovered it.[51]

Statutes have been enacted to place limits to the time of discovery when there may be great hardship to the defendant. Some of these statutes have been found unconstitutional as in *Kenyon v. Hammer*.[52] In this instance the Arizona Supreme Court held that a state statute that bars most medical malpractice actions not filed within three years of the date of the injury, whether or not the injury could have been discovered, violates the equal protection clause of the state constitution.

Bell v. West Harrison County District.[53] The court held that the two-year medical malpractice statute of limitations was applicable in the case of an injury resulting from the failure to raise bed rails at night and that the six-year general negligence statute did not apply.

Bellmund v. Beth Israel Hospital.[54] The court held that the statute of limitations of two and one-half years had expired when the suit was filed 10 days after

---

[47] Greene v. Greene, 56 N.Y.2d 86, 436 N.E.2d 496, 451 N.Y.S.2d 46 (1982).

[48] Brown v. Bleiberg, 32 Cal. 3d 426, 651 P.2d 815, 186 Cal. Rptr. 228 (1982).

[49] Hardin v. Farris, 87 N.M. 143, 530 P.2d 407 (1974).

[50] Stoner v. Carr, 97 Idaho 641, 550 P.2d 259 (1976).

[51] Rod v. Farrell, 96 Wis. 2d 349, 291 N.W.2d 568 (1980).

[52] 688 P.2d 961 (Ariz. 1984).

[53] 523 So. 2d 1031 (Miss. 1988).

[54] 131 A.D.2d 796, 517 N.Y.S.2d 161 (1987).

expiration of the statute. The limitations period began to run at the last visit and not after expiration of the period recommended for appointment.

Gaines v. Preterm-Cleveland, Inc.[55]   The Ohio Supreme Court held the statute of limitations unconstitutional as it provided plaintiff less than one year to pursue her claim after discovery of injury.

Griggs v. Cherry.[56]   In this case involving an alleged failure to diagnose breast cancer, the suit was dismissed because of the statute of limitations. The patient was examined in January 1982 by the defendant because of a lump in the breast. The physician did not feel a dominant mass and told her to continue monthly self-examination of the breasts. In February 1984 the lump had gotten larger. Biopsy showed infiltrating ductal carcinoma, and a modified radical mastectomy was performed. The patient consulted an attorney in June 1984 but suit was not filed until January 1986. Nebraska had a limitations period of two years or one year from the date of discovery. The defendant's motion for summary judgment was granted.

James v. Buck.[57]   Filing of the case tolled the statute of limitations until 30 days after the claim was no longer pending before the malpractice panel. The panel was to retain jurisdiction of the case by statute no longer than 90 days and the plaintiff then had 30 days in which to file suit. The malpractice panel, in this case, made its decision 125 days after the filing of the claim, and the plaintiff then filed suit within 30 days. A motion for summary judgment by the defendant for expiration of the statute of limitations was granted by the trial court but reversed by the Idaho Supreme Court. The court states that to allow the statute to expire would mean that the panel's jurisdiction automatically ended at 90 days, and this would frustrate the legislative purpose of encouraging settlement and would deprive the parties of the panel's recommendation.

Otto v. National Institutes of Health.[58]   The plaintiff had normal and diseased parathyroid glands, except for one-half of a normal gland, removed for hyperparathyroidism. Because of resultant hypoparathyroidism the plaintiff had parathyroid tissue transplanted on two occasions. A claim was filed less than two years after the last operation but more than three years after the original surgery. The Court of Appeals for the Fourth Circuit reversed the defendant's summary judgment, holding that the cause of action does not accrue until the end of a continuous course of treatment.

---

[55] 514 N.E.2d 709 (Ohio 1987).

[56] No. CV-86-L-92 (Neb. Dist. Ct. 1986), *reprinted in* 4 Med. Malpractice Verdicts, Settlements & Experts No. 11, at 14 (1988).

[57] 727 P.2d 1136 (Idaho 1986).

[58] 815 F.2d 985 (4th Cir. 1987).

Reynolds v. Porter.[59]   The Oklahoma Supreme Court struck down the Oklahoma statute, title 760S, § 18 (1981), that limited the scope of recoverable damages when an action is brought more than three years after the date of injury. The plaintiff alleged negligent hemorrhoidectomy performed on May 17, 1976, and filed her claim on April 27, 1982. Because the class of health care providers described in § 18 of the Oklahoma statute was not affected by an excessively high incidence of losses that might call for special statutory treatment, the claim for damages was not limited to actual medical and surgical expenses.

§ 1.17   Medical Malpractice Arbitration Acts

In an attempt to solve the problems of increasing numbers and costs of medical malpractice suits and to find an alternative to the crowded courts in the malpractice arena, the mechanism of arbitration was selected for resolution of disputes. Some states have general arbitration statutes while others are rule-based.

The essential characteristics of arbitration include the following:

1. A decisional form of dispute resolution
2. An agreement by the parties before the award is known that the decision is to be final and binding
3. The unavailability of the mechanism to the parties absent the mutual agreement of the parties
4. A decision maker with no formal connection with the court system.[60]

Other important aspects of a malpractice arbitration statute include safeguards to ensure that the patient's agreement to arbitrate is voluntary, that the agreement is not a prerequisite to medical care, and that the agreement may be revoked within a reasonable period of time. The agreement must be explained to the patient and an informational booklet must be provided.

In 1975 the Michigan legislature enacted the Medical Malpractice Arbitration Act, which offered a system of arbitration to patients as a way of resolving disputes arising from the furnishing of health care.[61]

Morris v. Metriyakool.[62]   The court held that the statute did not violate the patient's due process rights because of the presence of a physician, hospital, or

---

[59] 760 P.2d 816 (Okla. 1988).

[60] Powsner & Hamermesh, *Medical Malpractice Crisis the Second Time Around: Why Not Arbitrate?,* 8 J. Legal Med. 283–304 (1987).

[61] Bedikian, *Medical Malpractice Arbitration Act: Michigan's Experience with Arbitration,* 10 Am. J. L. & Med. 290 (1984).

[62] 418 Mich. 423, 344 N.W.2d 736 (1984).

medical health provider as part of the three-member arbitration panel. There was no showing that the medical members of the panels had a direct pecuniary interest or that their decision would have any substantial effect on the availability of insurance or insurance premiums.

The courts have found violation of due process in other cases,[63] and some arbitration statutes have been challenged.

Mattos v. Thompson.[64]   The Pennsylvania Supreme Court declared § 309 of the Health Care Services Malpractice Act of Pennsylvania unconstitutional. The statute gave state health care arbitration panels original, exclusive jurisdiction over all malpractice claims. The court showed that this had, in practice, caused oppressive delays in processing malpractice claims that had impermissibly infringed the state constitutional right to a jury trial.

Perea v. Medical Arts Center Hospital.[65]   The medical malpractice panel findings were set aside. When the hearing was convened, a practicing attorney who had been admitted to the bar in 1986 was substituted on the panel in place of the attorney named at the outset. The court held that the attorney member of the panel did not have the statutorily required trial experience.

Carson v. Mauer.[66]   The medical malpractice statute was found unconstitutional in New Hampshire under the plaintiff's right to equal protection. The court struck down a provision that required expert witnesses to have been experts at the time the alleged negligence occurred and held that the trial court should have discretion to determine whether the witness's expertise was close enough in time to the alleged malpractice incident to allow the testimony. The provision for the limitations period to be two years was rejected and the *discovery rule* reinstated. Also reversed was a provision for a 60-day written detailed notice to the defendants before bringing suit, the court holding that the special notice placed additional procedural hurdles in the way of malpractice plaintiffs. The *collateral source rule* was reinstated and a maximum of $250,000 for noneconomic loss was rejected, the court reasoning that the ceiling precluded the most seriously injured malpractice claimants from receiving full compensation for their injuries. Also reversed was a provision for the court to order periodic payments, the court stating that any money judgment awarded became the property of the plaintiff at the time of judgment, and that he or she was therefore entitled to payment of the whole amount. The court also held that an established contingency fee scale for plaintiffs' attorneys in malpractice actions was unjust

---

[63] Jackson v. Detroit Memorial Hosp., 110 Mich. App. 202, 204, 312 N.W.2d 212, 213 (1981).

[64] 491 Pa. 385, 421 A.2d 190 (1980).

[65] 137 Misc. 2d 249, 520 N.Y.S.2d 129 (1987).

[66] 424 A.2d 825 (N.H. 1980).

interference with the freedom of contract and that this was discriminatory and unconstitutional.

A medical malpractice screening tribunal was established in Massachusetts in 1975[67] to discourage frivolous medical malpractice claims. The panel had the task of deciding whether the evidence presented raised a legitimate question of liability appropriate for judicial inquiry. The statute was upheld in *Feinstein v. Massachusetts General Hospital*[68] and in other cases.[69]

Fein v. Permanente Medical Group.[70]   The United States Supreme Court upheld a California statute limiting the amount of noneconomic damages to $250,000 in medical malpractice suits. The Court found this limitation was a reasonable response to the problem of escalating medical malpractice insurance costs.

The United States Supreme Court declined to hear a constitutional challenge to a 1975 California statute limiting the contingency fees that plaintiffs' attorneys can collect in malpractice cases.[71]

STANDARD OF CARE

§ 1.18   Standard of Care Generally

In medical malpractice actions the standard of care has traditionally been that degree of skill and learning commonly possessed by members of the medical profession or subspecialty. The standard may be local or national depending on the jurisdiction.

Shamburger v. Behrens.[72]   The plaintiff's expert testified that board-certified surgeons must meet and comply with national standards to maintain their certification. The court's instruction referred to a national standard. The South Dakota Supreme Court upheld the instruction and specifically adopted a national standard of care for specialists.

---

[67] An Act Relative to Medical Malpractice, 1975 Mass. Acts 362 (codified as Mass. Gen. Laws Ann. ch. 231, § 60B (West Supp. 1979).

[68] 49 U.S.L.W. 2599 (1st Cir. Mar. 10, 1981).

[69] *See* Ossyra, *The Massachusetts Malpractice Plaintiffs' New Hurdles: The Expanding Role of the Medical Malpractice Screening Tribunal,* 8 Am. J. L. & Med. 481 (1983).

[70] 106 S. Ct. 214 (1985).

[71] Roa v. Lodi Medical Group, Inc., 37 Cal. 3d 920, 695 P.2d 164, 211 Cal. Rptr. 77 (1985).

[72] 418 N.W.2d 299 (S.D. 1988).

§ 1.19   Violation of Statute

The standard of care may be regulated by legislative enactment. These statutes provide that under certain circumstances particular acts shall or shall not be done. Once violation of the statute is proved, most jurisdictions will consider the issue of negligence to be thereby conclusively determined, in the absence of sufficient excuse. In some states, violation creates a presumption of negligence, which may be rebutted by a showing of adequate justification.

§ 1.20   Reasonable Prudence

Although standard of care is usually the providence of expert witnesses in medical malpractice cases, there is a tendency for the plaintiff and defense experts to take opposite points of view. Obviously, if the standard of practice in a community is poor, some commonsense evaluation should prevail and the patient should not be made to suffer. There are some cases that are so obvious to a reasonable person that no expert testimony is required to establish the standard of care or its breach by the physician.[73]

Courts have taken a stand in defining what is reasonably prudent rather than allowing an inadequately defined medical standard of care.

Helling v. Carey.[74]   The 23-year-old patient was first seen in 1959 by the defendant in order to get contact lenses. Despite complaints about visual problems and eight visits to the defendant's office, it was not until 1968 that the intraocular pressure was measured and found to be abnormal. The diagnosis of open angle glaucoma was made, but by that time there was vision loss. It was determined that the glaucoma had existed for 10 years. Despite the fact that the ophthalmologic standard of care was not to conduct routine pressure examinations in patients under the age of 40, the court held that reasonable prudence required a standard of care mandating the timely administration of the simple, harmless, definitive, and inexpensive pressure test. Because the failure to perform the test was the proximate cause of the patient's vision loss, the defendant was held liable.

Truman v. Thomas.[75]   In this case the professional standard of care was found inadequate. The plaintiff was first seen by the defendant in 1964 for her second pregnancy. For the next five years the defendant saw the patient intermittently and on numerous occasions recommended a pap smear. The plaintiff consistently refused the test but was not informed of the risks involved in not

---

[73] *See, e.g.,* Thomas v. Corso, 288 A.2d 379 (Md. 1972).

[74] 83 Wash. 2d 514, 519 P.2d 981 (1974).

[75] 27 Cal. 3d 285, 611 P.2d 902, 165 Cal. Rptr. 308 (1980).

undergoing the exam. In 1969, another physician diagnosed an advanced carcinoma of the cervix. The patient died one year later at the age of 30. It was established that if she had undergone a pap smear at any time between 1964 and 1969 the tumor would have been discovered possibly in time to prevent her death. The California Supreme Court reversed the judgment for the defendant, stating that the physician has a duty to advise the patient of all material risks involved in the patient's refusal to undergo a recommended diagnostic test capable of detecting illness that could lead to death or serious complications. Material risks include those that the physician knows or should know would be regarded as significant by a reasonably prudent person in the patient's position when deciding to accept or reject the recommended diagnostic procedure.

INFORMED CONSENT

§ 1.21   Consent Problems

The physician has a positive duty to disclose to the patient significant or material information so that the patient can make a knowledgeable decision.[76] The patient must be informed of all relevant information that might influence the choice of whether to undergo any specific treatment. There is, however, a therapeutic privilege that allows a physician to withhold information for the sake of the patient to prevent a state of shock, depression, or anxiety that would prevent an autonomous choice. In emergency situations that include severe pain or threat of life and limb, there may not be time enough to explain in detail the information necessary to obtain an informed consent. The patient may also waive the right to receive information or make a decision by deferring to the physician.

A consent is adequate when the information given to the patient includes all the positive and negative factors of the treatment that would influence the decision whether to have the proposed treatment. Conversely, those details that would not affect the final decision are not necessary to inform the patient. The positive features are those benefits to be obtained from the treatment. The negative aspects are those complications or aftereffects that might be detrimental or unsatisfactory to the patient. Other negative factors include detrimental aspects of not having the proposed treatment. Finally, there is the need to explain viable alternative treatments. The patient is permitted to make unwise choices provided there is the ability to understand the information about the proposed treatment and the inherent complications.

A surgical consent should include any possible anticipated procedures. At the time of surgery if a condition is found that is an immediate or imminent threat to

---

[76] Shatz, *Autonomy, Beneficence and Informed Consent: Rethinking the Connections; I.*, 4 Cancer Investigation 257 (1986).

the patient's life or if a later surgical procedure would be an urgent life-threatening alternative, the emergency consent doctrine may be invoked, relieving the physician of the need to obtain an actual informed consent.[77]

Disclosure must include the nature and purpose of the proposed treatment, its risks and consequences, the expected benefits, any reasonably available alternatives, and the prognosis if the proposed treatment is not undertaken. The nature and magnitude of the risk, its probability, the personal experience of the provider with the treatment in question, and the relative costs of alternative treatments should also be provided. The physician must not minimize the known dangers for the purpose of inducing the patient's consent.

Spotls v. Reidell.[78]   The plaintiff had a polyp of the rectum that appeared non-malignant on a barium enema and with a biopsy. The general surgeon did not inform the plaintiff of the alternative of snare wire polypectomy but performed a resection of six inches of bowel. Anal stricture and anal incontinence resulted. Monthly digital dilation of the anal stricture was done, which was painful (on at least one occasion the plaintiff fainted from the pain) and which caused excessive bleeding one time that resulted in a temporary hospitalization. Nine months after the original surgery, the surgeon's finger perforated the bowel wall and entered the bladder. A permanent colostomy was required as an emergency procedure. A judgment of $167,000 was awarded because of the surgeon's failure to inform the plaintiff of the alternative, less invasive procedure.

Goodreau v. State.[79]   The plaintiff filed suit, alleging a lack of informed consent after having been diagnosed and treated for lymphocytic lymphosarcoma involving an inguinal node. At trial it was established that this form of cancer, if untreated, can spread rapidly to other areas of the body, and if it reaches the internal organs, the likelihood of successful treatment is substantially reduced and the chances of survival significantly lessened. The appellate division reversed the court of claims finding for the plaintiff, stating that "given the life threatening nature of the illness, it is inconceivable that a prudent person would have declined treatment."

Many patients develop impairment of understanding when faced with a catastrophic illness,[80] especially cancer. The inability to assimilate necessary information and instructions may require repetitious discussions with the patient

---

[77] Kennedy v. Parrott, 243 N.C. 355, 362 S.E.2d 754, 759 (1956).

[78] Civ. Action No. 82-667 (Pa. Ct. C.P. Center County 1982), *reprinted in* 2 Med. Malpractice Verdicts, Settlements & Experts No. 6, at 30 (1986).

[79] 129 A.D.2d 961, 514 N.Y.S.2d 291 (1987).

[80] Carnerie, *Crisis and Informed Consent: Analysis of a Law Medicine Malocclusion,* 12 Am. J. L. & Med. 55 (1987).

(and, at times, the family). In order to obtain an informed consent for any subsequent procedures, the physician must be aware of this cognitive problem.

A language barrier may contribute to similar difficulties and may require the presence of a translator to present the facts. This obstacle affects not only the foreign patient but also the foreign physician who may have difficulties being understood.

The incompetent patient may include those who are unconscious in an emergency situation, mentally retarded, or mentally ill. Consent may be obtained from the next of kin (for example, parent or spouse), guardian, or court. A minor will ordinarily require the consent of a parent or guardian in order to have medical treatment, except in an emergency situation.

Cardwell v. Bechtol.[81] The plaintiff, age 17, had low back pain with a herniated disc that responded to conservative treatment. Five months later, because of recurring back pain, the plaintiff went to her father's chiropractor, the defendant, without her parents' knowledge. After examination she was treated with manipulation of the neck, spine, and legs. Treatment was paid for by the plaintiff with one of her father's blank, signed checks, which had been given to her to be used when she needed money. Later that day she had to be admitted to the hospital for increasing pain and urinary retention. Ultimately, a laminectomy was performed for a herniated disc. The *mature minor* is the exception to the general rule that parental consent is required to treat a minor. In this case the plaintiff was a high school senior with good grades, had been licensed to drive since age 16, carried signed blank checks in lieu of cash, and was permitted substantial discretion by her parents because of her demonstrated maturity. The Tennessee Supreme Court ruled that the consent was sufficient. The requirement of disclosure of every risk no matter how remote was found prohibitive and unrealistic.

One court stated, "Every human being of adult years and sound mind has a right to determine what shall be done with his own body; and a surgeon who performs an operation without his patient's consent commits an assault, for which he is liable in damages."[82] To prove lack of informed consent, the majority of jurisdictions use the *reasonably prudent physician* standard, which is what a practitioner would do under similar facts and circumstances in the same or similar community. In some courts the *reasonably prudent patient* standard prevails. This requires inclusion of information that is material to the decision being made according to what a reasonable person would desire (as determined by the jury).

---

[81] 724 S.W.2d 739 (Tenn. 1987).
[82] Schloendorff v. Society of N.Y. Hosp., 211 N.Y. 125, 105 N.E. 92, 93 (1914).

Largey v. Rothman.[83]   New Jersey adopted a *prudent patient* standard for informed consent cases. A breast biopsy and some axillary lymph nodes were excised for benign disease. Lymphedema of the arm and hand developed from inadequate lymphatic drainage following excision of the lymph nodes. The plaintiff claimed that she was not warned of the risk of lymphedema. The trial court charged the jury that the defendant was required to tell the patient what a *reasonable physician* under the same or similar circumstances would have told the patient. The defense verdict was reversed and the case remanded for a new trial. The New Jersey Supreme Court adopted the prudent patient standard, requiring disclosure of material risks, those to which a *reasonable patient* would be likely to attach significance in deciding whether or not to undergo a proposed treatment.

Garash v. Collum.[84]   The 19-year-old plaintiff had inflammation of the left breast. A consent was signed for incision, drainage, and possible biopsy. The defendant removed two sections of breast measuring 3 cm × 8.5 cm × 9 cm and 1.8 cm × 2.5 cm × 3 cm. The surgery caused the left breast to appear higher and smaller than the right, scarred, and discolored, and the nipple turned in direction. The verdict was $100,000 for lack of informed consent for performing more surgery than a simple biopsy.

Parikh v. Cunningham.[85]   Postoperative complications occurred and the plaintiff claimed a lack of informed consent. A release authorizing treatment had been signed by the plaintiff, stating that the risks and consequences had been explained and that no guarantees or assurances had been made as to the results. The jury was charged that a written consent by a competent person gave rise to a conclusive presumption of informed consent under the state statute. The Florida Supreme Court found the statute constitutional but required that there be more than just a writing introduced as evidence to establish the elements of informed consent.

Medina v. Hickman.[86]   The plaintiff alleged that he had not been informed of the risks and hazards of a hiatal hernia repair. The plaintiff now has episodes of diarrhea and nausea and must remain on a bland diet. The defendant claimed the injuries were known and accepted risks in this type of surgery. The award was for $1 million reduced under a settlement.

---

[83] 540 A.2d 504 (N.J. 1988).

[84] 726 S.W.2d 271 (Ark. 1987).

[85] 493 So. 2d 999 (Fla. 1986).

[86] No. 84-CI-04982 (Tex. Dist. Ct. ___ 1984), *reprinted in* 4 Med. Malpractice Verdicts, Settlements & Experts No. 8, at 50 (1988).

Orellora v. Mejia.[87]   The plaintiff had a subtotal thyroidectomy for hyperthyroidism. She claimed that she was not informed of the risk of hypoparathyroidism, which in fact did develop. The award was for $295,000 reduced to $250,000 under California law.

Jozsa v. Hottenstein.[88]   A directed verdict for the defense was reversed because of lack of informed consent. A carpal tunnel release was performed on the plaintiff, and postoperative severe pain, swelling, and impairment of motion and strength occurred. The evidence established an undisclosed risk; according to the appellate court, whether the omission was material was a question for the jury to decide.

Hospitals are ordinarily not involved in the disclosure of information in order to obtain an informed consent for invasive or surgical procedures. Nevertheless, the theory of *respondeat superior* is available if a physician employed by the hospital does not adequately inform a patient.

Magana v. Elie.[89]   The appellate court found the hospital had a duty to act reasonably to protect the patient when the patient suffered an undisclosed complication inherent in the surgery. The hospital should have required physicians to whom it granted privileges to inform patients of the risks of a proposed procedure.

Because physicians have been reluctant to adequately inform patients of the alternatives to modified radical mastectomy for treatment of cancer of the breast, the California legislature enacted a law requiring the use of a state developed pamphlet. The pamphlet is reproduced in **§ 1.24.** The information contained in the pamphlet is a review of the viable alternatives of care for breast cancer. The patient must have a discussion of the various treatments available for cancer of the breast and be given the state pamphlet. This is considered adequate for informed consent concerning the methods of treatment. The patient may choose a form of treatment that is less optimal than the one advised by the physician. In fact, cancer patients have the right to undergo unorthodox treatment instead of standard methods.[90]

---

[87] No. C491643 (Cal. Norwalk Super. Ct. 1984), *reprinted in* 3 Med. Malpractice Verdicts, Settlements & Experts No. 12, at 58 (1987).

[88] 528 A.2d 606 (Pa. Super. Ct. 1987).

[89] 108 Ill. App. 3d 1028, 439 N.E.2d 1319 (1982).

[90] Hofbauer v. Hofbauer, 47 N.Y.2d 648, 393 N.E.2d 1009, 419 N.Y.S.2d 936 (1979).

§ 1.22 —Intentional Violation

An operation cannot be performed without the patient's implied or express consent. When the surgeon acts knowingly contrary to the patient's consent, a technical battery has occurred. Conversely, malpractice based on negligence is unintentional.

Bakewell v. Kahle.[91] The court applied the theory of negligence despite the fact that the surgeon acted with full knowledge and intent. It was held that an unauthorized operation amounts to malpractice even though negligence was not charged. The court defined malpractice as bad or unskilled practice resulting in injury to the patient and comprising all acts and omissions of a physician that may render the surgeon civilly or criminally liable to the patient.

Woods v. Brunlop.[92] The court applied the concepts of assault and battery but concluded that the conduct was malpractice when the physician intentionally withheld information relating to the risks of electroshock therapy and then assured the patient that no risk was involved. The case concerned the concept of no consent and not lack of due care but was considered malpractice when injury occurred.

Damages are presumed in assault and battery. Professional malpractice insurance does not usually cover assault and battery, and the statute of limitations may differ from that for negligence actions.

§ 1.23 —Unintentional Violation

When a wrong operative procedure is performed or surgery is done on the wrong patient, there is a violation of consent that can be considered an unprivileged touching under the theory of assault and battery. There was in fact the intent, by the surgeon, to do the specific surgery although the surgery was performed in error. Conversely, the surgeon's actions could be considered to have been performed in good faith and be merely unintentional.

Hively v. Higgs.[93] The patient consented to surgery on his nose but in fact had his tonsils removed. The operation performed was considered to be without the patient's consent and, therefore, assault and battery.

---

[91] 125 Mont. 89, 232 P.2d 127 (1957).
[92] 71 N.M. 221, 377 P.2d 520 (1962).
[93] 120 Or. 588, 253 P. 363 (1927).

Hershey v. Peake.[94]   The dentist extracted a healthy tooth instead of the diseased one. The court concluded that the dentist neglected to use proper care and, therefore, was liable under the theory of negligence.

§ 1.24   Sample Informed Consent Language

Breast Cancer Treatment: Summary of Alternative Effective Methods, Risks, Advantages, and Disadvantages (Reprinted December 1986)

This summary is required by SB1893, "The Breast Cancer Informed Consent Law," authored by Senator David Roberti, effective January 1, 1981: Prepared by the [California] State Department of Health Services based on recommendations of the State Cancer Advisory Council. Printed and distributed by the BOARD OF MEDICAL QUALITY ASSURANCE STATE DEPARTMENT OF CONSUMER AFFAIRS. HEALTH AND SAFETY CODE, SECTION 1704.5

California Physicians and Surgeons are required by law to inform patients of all alternative effective methods of treatment for breast cancer. This brochure describes medically viable treatment including surgical, radiological (x-ray), and chemotherapeutic (drugs) treatments or combinations thereof. It has been printed in a form which may be reproduced by physicians for distribution to their patients.

DIAGNOSIS

Diagnosis is the scientific determination of the nature of the lump. It is made by the pathologist who examines the tissue from the breast lump (breast biopsy) under the microscope.

The breast biopsy entails the surgical removal of part or all of the lump under suitable anesthesia. Unless the lump is quite large it is usually removed in one piece (excisional biopsy). (A large lump may be biopsied with a special needle or by surgically removing a small sample.) The tissue removed by biopsy provides material for the definitive test for cancer, namely the examination of tissue under the microscope by the pathologist. If cancerous, part of the fresh tissue may also be studied for receptors for hormones (estrogen and progesterone), which could be important if future treatment decisions become necessary. (Only about 20% of breast biopsies are cancerous; the remainder represent less serious conditions.)

The procedure for obtaining the biopsy should be discussed with you since you must make a decision between two courses of action—the One-Step or Two-Step procedure.

In the One-Step procedure, you and your physician decide beforehand that if the biopsy shows cancer and if surgery will be the treatment of choice, the entire

---

[94] 115 Kan. 562, 223 P. 1113 (1924).

procedure (biopsy, diagnosis by pathologist, and the appropriate surgery) will be completed in one operation.

In the Two-Step Procedure, the biopsy is done under local or general anesthesia and no additional operation is performed at this time. After the pathologist examines and reports on the biopsy, the surgeon reviews the pathology report with you and discusses with you the various treatment options available and effective for your particular case. A decision is then made by you and your physician on which procedure is preferred by you for your individual care.

Prior to the procedure you choose, a general medical evaluation which may include any or all of the following diagnostic procedures is usually done to determine your individual situation:

Your medical history (including family history of cancer)

Physical examination

Blood tests evaluating function of various systems, e.g., liver, kidney, immunity, etc.

X-ray films (chest, bones, etc.)

Breast X-ray films (mammography)

Radioisotope scan (bones, liver, brain, etc.)

Computerized tomographic body scans (specialized x-ray views of any or all internal organs and bones)

Sonograms (pictures of internal organs made with ultrasound waves).

Treatment recommendations are individualized. They are based primarily on the extent (stage) and type of disease present as well as other factors related to your personal health.

INTRODUCTION

You have a treatable disease and are entitled to know about the various medically effective surgical, radiological, and chemotherapeutic treatment procedures available.

This brochure has been developed to assist you to understand what these various treatment procedures are, their advantages, disadvantages, and risks.

The treatment of cancer is quite complex. It must be individualized. The choice of therapy may be difficult to make. It is important for you to have this basic information about the methods of treatment so that you may discuss them more fully with your physician as they apply to your case. This will help you understand what treatment programs may be used and what their effects may be in your individual situation. Using this information as a basis for discussion, you and your physician should be able to make an informed choice.

Because cancer is a serious disease, it may be appropriate for either you or your physician to seek additional opinions if either of you desires. Your consent is required before any treatment is carried out and you have the right to participate in making the final choice of the treatment procedure(s). Your physician has a corresponding right to withdraw from the case if he chooses.

It is very important to take a reasonable amount of time to obtain enough medical information and consultation to make a final and informed decision. But prolonged delay may interfere with the success of your treatment. Making this choice is an important step. Once you and your physician have reached a decision about your treatment, you will have a positive attitude which will be a tremendous help as you and your physician begin and carry out the treatment of your cancer.

MANAGEMENT OF BREAST CANCER

Management of breast cancer is achieved by the cooperation of appropriate specialists in the field: the primary (personal) physician for general support and coordination; the surgeon for diagnosis by biopsy and specific surgical procedure for removal of the breast tumor; the pathologist for gross and microscopic diagnosis; the radiation oncologist for supervising and administering radiation treatment; the medical oncologist for specialized management of the patient's care and administration of chemotherapy. In actual practice these members proceed fairly independently but maintain liaison by telephone and written reporting.

TREATMENT AND ALTERNATIVES: ADVANTAGES, DISADVANTAGES, RISKS

If your diagnosis is breast cancer, it is important for you to understand there is enough time to make a careful decision. Prolonged delay and failure to get adequate treatment may result in the deterioration of your situation. In contrast, the benefits of modern breast cancer therapy far outweigh the risks. This is especially true when treatment is undertaken early. The risk may be small or serious, and its occurrence may vary from frequent to rare. There is a wide range of potential benefits and risks from various treatment procedures for the different stages and kinds of breast cancer. Before deciding on your course of therapy, you should discuss with your physician the particular benefits and risks of the treatment methods suitable for your individual case.

SURGERY

This process involves removal of the tumor, and either a portion of the breast, all of the breast, or all of the breast and some surrounding tissues as well.

RADICAL (HALSTED) MASTECTOMY

The Radical (Halsted) Mastectomy is not commonly used today except in unusual cases. In this procedure, the entire breast, nipple, some of the overlying skin, underlying chest muscles, nearby soft tissue, and lymph nodes extending into the armpit are removed.

Advantages

If cancer has not spread beyond breast or nearby tissue, it can be completely removed. Examination of lymph nodes provides information that is essential in planning future treatment.

Disadvantages

Removes entire breast and underlying chest muscles. Leaves a long scar and a hollow area where the muscles were removed. May result in swelling of the arm, some loss of muscle power in the arm, restricted shoulder motion, and some numbness and discomfort. Reconstructive (plastic) surgery and fitting of breast prosthesis are difficult.

MODIFIED RADICAL MASTECTOMY

Entire breast, nipple, some of overlying skin, nearby soft tissue, and lymph nodes in armpit are removed. Chest muscles are left intact, but overlying covering of muscle is removed.

Advantages

Retains chest muscles and muscle strength of arm. Swelling of arm occurs less frequently and is milder than after radical. Cosmetic appearance is better than with radical. Apparently as effective as radical, but not if cancer is large or has invaded the muscle sheath. Cosmetically effective reconstructive surgery is usually feasible.

Disadvantages

Entire breast and part of overlying skin are removed. In some cases removal of lymph nodes in armpit may be incomplete. Some persons may experience swelling of the arm.

RADIATION THERAPY AS A SUPPLEMENT (ADJUVANT) TO SURGERY

Following surgery, examination of the surgical specimen by the pathologist may show the cancer has spread outside the breast and into armpit lymph nodes or local surrounding areas. Radiation therapy will usually control cancer cells remaining in these areas. The treatment of advanced cancer often requires the consultation and coordinated efforts of the surgeon, radiation oncologist, and the medical oncologist (see below).

Advantages

The goal of radiation therapy is to destroy cancer cells in tissue in the radiation treatment area which improves control of or stops the spread of cancer in the treatment area. Modern equipment gives very precise control of the x-ray treatment. Radiation therapy may be used to treat localized metastases.

Disadvantages

The major side effects are the same as those listed under radiation therapy as a primary treatment. When cancer is treated by radiation therapy as a supplement to surgery, there may be wide variations in the extent of the treatments required depending on the problem or site of disease being treated.

CHEMOTHERAPY

Medical oncologist is the specialist who usually plans and administers the chemotherapy and may coordinate the patient's management with other physicians. Chemotherapy is designed to destroy breast cancer cells that cannot be removed surgically or by radiation or their combination.

In recent years important and effective advances in breast cancer treatment have been made in this area, especially advanced cancer. Different drugs or a combination of drugs are administered orally or by injection. This program is adapted to the individual and may continue at intervals for six months to two years or longer depending on the cancer being treated and the drug program being used.

SUPPLEMENTAL (ADJUVANT) CHEMOTHERAPY

Chemotherapy supplements primary surgical or radiation treatment when it is likely the patient has a cancer which has spread into or beyond nearby lymph nodes. Such patients have a higher risk of recurrence than those whose lymph nodes are found to be free of cancer. Supplemental chemotherapy may reduce this risk considerably.

Advantages

Increases the effectiveness of surgery or radiation therapy and reduces the risk of breast cancer recurrence. Works to stop its growth at distant sites in the body.

Disadvantages

Most chemotherapy drugs have reversible side effects. Some side effects are minimal while others can cause discomfort, including nausea, temporary loss of hair, bone marrow depression (resulting in temporary susceptibility to infection and bleeding tendency), anemia, loss of appetite, and fatigue, and rarely damage to heart muscles. Also may depress reproductive function and cause change of life symptoms. Newer techniques of administration and dosage reduce the side effects of chemotherapy.

CHEMOTHERAPY FOR RECURRENT BREAST CANCER

Anti-cancer drugs, taken alone or in combination with other modalities, can arrest the disease, help to relieve symptoms, and prolong the life of a patient who experiences recurrence of breast cancer.

HORMONAL THERAPY

Many breast cancers are sensitive to female hormones (estrogen and proges-terone) and are partially controlled by them. In many treatment centers, fresh tissue from the tumor (specimen or biopsy) can be tested to measure this hormone sensitivity (estrogen receptor assay). In some breast cancer patients, beneficial effects can be received by adding hormones, removing glands that produce them, or by administering drugs (anti-hormones) that counteract the hormones produced by the body. Hormone therapy often increases significantly the effectiveness of other cancer therapy.

SIMPLE MASTECTOMY

The main breast structure is removed. Underlying chest muscles and often armpit lymph nodes are left in place. Many surgeons remove some of the armpit lymph nodes through a separate small incision under the arm to determine if cancer has spread to nodes. Often followed by radiation therapy.

Advantages

Chest muscles are not removed and strength of arm is not affected. Swelling of arm occurs infrequently. Reconstructive surgery usually feasible.

Disadvantages

Breast is not preserved. If cancer has spread to armpit lymph nodes, it may remain undiscovered unless these nodes are sampled or removed at the time of surgery; adequate treatment could be delayed.

SEGMENTAL MASTECTOMY, PARTIAL MASTECTOMY, AND LUMPECTOMY

If cancer is small and detected early, a segment of the breast containing the tumor is removed. Many surgeons also remove some armpit lymph nodes through a separate incision to check for possible spread of cancer. Most cancer experts feel this type of operation should be followed by radiation therapy and some feel chemotherapy should be used in selected cases as well. These procedures are relatively new and long-term results are being documented.

Advantages

Most of the breast remains. Reconstructive surgery is usually easier if needed at all, loss of muscle strength and swelling of the arm are unlikely to occur. Commonly used as a first step for Radiation Therapy as Primary Treatment in Early Breast Cancer, especially if preservation of the breast is desired.

Disadvantages

Most cancer specialists feel these procedures may be incomplete unless armpit lymph nodes are removed for pathological examination and person is given radiation therapy or a combination of radiation therapy and chemotherapy. Otherwise, spread of cancer into armpit lymph nodes or undetected areas of cancer present elsewhere in breast may go untreated and chance for cure may be lost.

RADIATION (X-RAY) THERAPY

Radiation treatment of local tissues of the body, known as radiotherapy, can destroy cancer cells while producing less injury to surrounding tissues. Radiation for treatment may come from a number of devices, e.g., super voltage x-ray, linear accelerator, Betatron, Cobalt-60, and radioactive isotopes. The source and type of radiation is chosen to suit the requirements of the individual.

RADIATION THERAPY AS PRIMARY TREATMENT IN EARLY BREAST CANCER

This approach has been used for about 10 years in this country and for about 20 years in Europe for the treatment of early breast cancer. After pathologic diagnosis by biopsy and surgical removal of the local tumor, external radiation therapy is used to treat the remainder of the breast, the lymph nodes, and the chest wall. This is then followed by a radiation "boost" to the biopsy site with radioactive sources temporarily introduced into the area of the excision. Sometimes the boost may be given with more external irradiation (or electron beam).

Advantages

The breast is preserved. It may be mildly to moderately firmer. Usually there is minimal or no visible deformity of surrounding tissues. After completion of the treatment, the skin usually regains normal appearance.

In early breast cancer, lumpectomy or segmental resection, with radiation as the primary treatment, has demonstrated results that currently appear equal to long-established surgical procedures.

<u>Disadvantages</u>

A full course of treatment requires daily outpatient visits for four to six weeks. Treatment may produce a skin reaction similar to sunburn and may cause temporary difficulty in swallowing. Radiation therapy can affect bone marrow where blood cells are made. This may limit the dosage and effectiveness of later chemotherapy if it is needed. A small area of scarring, permanently visible on x-ray examination, may develop in the lung, but usually causes no symptoms.

INVESTIGATIVE TREATMENT FOR BREAST CANCER

Clinical trials are new treatments which are not yet generally available. Laboratory or other reliable studies may indicate a new cancer treatment procedure or therapy program could be better than ones in current use. Research to measure effectiveness is conducted in clinical trials by many major cancer treatment groups. The new treatment methods are put to general use only after long-term evaluation by cancer experts when they find the new treatment gives results as good as, or better than, established treatments.

BREAST FORMS

Breast forms (prostheses) are made with a variety of substances such as silicone, foam rubber, silastic, viscous fluid, or glycerin. Fitted individually and worn in brassiere pockets, they can give the form, weight, and appearance of a normal bustline. The right bra for you may very well be the one you've always worn. Your health insurance generally covers a portion of this cost with your physician's prescription.

RECONSTRUCTIVE BREAST PROCEDURES

Reconstructive plastic surgery may effectively restore the form of the breast and adjacent tissues lost at surgery. Implants of breast prostheses or surgical transfer of body tissues may be used. Usually at least two surgeries are required to achieve desired results, but in some cases advance planning can minimize this. The possibility of reconstructive surgery should be discussed with your physician in advance of a definitive surgical treatment procedure. You should investigate the extent of financial coverage available through your health insurance for this procedure.

FOLLOW-UP

The success of cancer treatment depends not only on early detection and effective treatment, but also on a careful, consistent follow-up program to detect cancer recurrence as early as possible if it should occur. Consistent regular visits to the treating physician and monthly self-examination are essential. New methods of detection and treatment are being continually developed and can be used to your advantage.

Many very helpful and thoughtful women who have been through a similar experience can lend you their support and guidance. They can be contacted through your physician, your hospital, your local unit of the American Cancer Society, or the National Cancer Institute's Cancer Information Service.

SUMMARY

This brochure is intended to make you aware of the effective alternative methods of treating breast cancer available in California, and your role in choosing the method to be used in your care. In order to reach a decision on the treatment method, it is important for you to understand the nature of the disease, the extent of your problem, the treatment needed, the method or methods of providing that treatment suitable to your particular situation, and finally the results that may reasonably be expected.

This is best done by having a complete evaluation followed by a thorough discussion with your physician(s). The brochure should assist you to participate in these discussions by providing essential background information so you can ask questions you need answered, and help you understand what your physician is talking about and how the choice of cancer treatment method will affect you and your circumstances.

Many important details are necessarily left out and you should look to your physician for your complete and current information. Being well informed and having thoroughly discussed the alternatives will make it easier to make a knowledgeable decision about your course of treatment. It will give you justified confidence you have made the best choice possible. This will be a tremendous help to you and your physician as you carry out your treatment and establish your follow-up program.

REFUSAL OF MEDICAL TREATMENT

§ 1.25   The Competent Patient

The patient has a right to refuse medical treatment after being informed of the treatment, the complications, and the consequences of lack of treatment. There is a constitutional right to privacy that "is an expression of the sanctity of individual free choice and self determination as fundamental constituents of life."[95] The idea of personal autonomy and the right of a person to decide for herself or himself whether to accept treatment stems from the due process clause of the

---

[95] Superintendent of Belchertown State Sch. v. Sailewicz, 373 Mass. 728, 742, 370 N.E.2d 417, 426 (1977).

Fourteenth Amendment, which protects the right to privacy, bodily integrity, and personal security.[96] In some cases religious freedom may be grounds for refusing, withholding, or withdrawing treatment.[97]

When refusal of treatment is likely to result in death, the patient's rights may not be absolute.

Barling v. Superior Court (Glendale Adventist Medical Center).[98]   The patient had signed a release, a "living will," and a durable power of attorney for health care, confirming his decision to reject artificial life support. Nevertheless, court approval was required to disconnect the ventilator in this patient with pulmonary emphysema, angina, and diffuse arteriosclerosis.

A patient was not found incompetent because she vacillated in her decision regarding amputation of her gangrenous foot, and the court upheld her right to refuse the amputation.[99] Similarly, the New Jersey Superior Court held that amputation of a gangrenous leg would entail an extensive bodily invasion and the state's interest in preserving life was outweighed by the patient's right to privacy.[100]

Occasionally there are compelling state interests in preserving life that outweigh the patient's rights.

Powell v. Columbia Presbyterian Medical Center.[101]   A transfusion was ordered for a Jehovah's Witness because she was the mother of six children. The presence of dependent minor children can be a compelling interest to prevent the creation of wards of the state.

Raleigh Fitkin-Paul Morgan Memorial Hospital v. Anderson.[102]   Transfusions were ordered by the court for a Jehovah's Witness who was 32 weeks pregnant when the court found a state interest in preserving the life of a viable fetus.

Other interests or concerns may be considered, such as whether the patient's refusal infringes on the hospital's, nurse's or attending physician's standards of medical practice or the state's interest in preventing suicide.[103]

---

[96] Rogers v. Okin, 478 F. Supp. 1342, 1365 (D. Mass. 1979).

[97] *In re* Melideo, 88 Misc. 2d 974 390 N.Y.S.2d 523 (Sup. Ct. 1976).

[98] 163 Cal. App. 3d 186, 209 Cal. Rptr. 220 (1984).

[99] Lane v. Candura, 6 Mass. App. Ct. 377, 376 N.E.2d 1232 (1978).

[100] *In re* Quackenbush, 156 N.J. Super. 282, 383 A.2d 785 (Harris County Ct. 1978).

[101] 49 Misc. 2d 215, 267 N.Y.S.2d 450 (Sup. Ct. 1965).

[102] 42 N.J. 421, 201 A.2d 537, *cert. denied,* 377 U.S. 985 (1964).

[103] Swartz, *The Patient Who Refuses Medical Treatment: A Dilemma for Hospitals and Physicians,* 11 Am. J. L. & Med. 147 (1985).

When there is a clear expression of treatment preference that is proved by clear and convincing evidence of a now incompetent patient, that wish must be honored.

Eicher v. Dillon.[104]   The court decided to disconnect a life support system of an incompetent patient when it was shown there was a prior competent expression of refusing extraordinary treatment.

The parens patriae power, under which a person may be hospitalized in New York against his or her will, requires a finding of incompetency before the power can be exerted.[105] In the *substitution of judgment* rule, however, there is a procedural mechanism to determine the incompetent's own preference and these desires are considered fully by the court.[106]

Bourra v. Superior Court.[107]   The California Court of Appeal granted a writ of mandate to compel removal of a nasogastric tube. The 28-year-old patient suffered from cerebral palsy from birth, was a quadriplegic, and had severe, chronic arthritis. She was mentally alert and competent although confined to bed. The court stated that a person's right to refuse medical treatment is a basic and fundamental right of privacy. A patient's decision must be respected, even when the withdrawal of life support equipment will necessarily hasten death. A natural course of events, leading to an earlier death with dignity and peace, is not equivalent to an election to commit suicide.

§ 1.26   The Incompetent Patient

Mental competence to give or refuse consent to medical treatment may be present despite the involuntary commitment to a psychiatric facility.[108] Conversely a person may become incompetent to make a decision regarding medical treatment as a result of physical injury, age, or intoxication.

In re Schiller.[109]   A 67-year-old patient with a gangrenous foot was found incapable of understanding either his condition or the necessity of surgery because of the presence of organic brain syndrome. The court appointed a guardian to consent to the amputation.

---

[104] 52 N.Y.2d 363, 420 N.E.2d 64, 438 N.Y.S.2d 266 (1981).

[105] Winters v. Miller, 446 F.2d 65 (2d Cir.), *cert. denied,* 404 U.S. 985 (1971).

[106] *In re* Spring, 380 Mass. 629, 405 N.E.2d 115 (1980).

[107] 179 Cal. App. 3d 1127, 225 Cal. Rptr. 297 (1986).

[108] Price v. Sheppard, 239 N.W.2d 905 (Minn. 1976).

[109] 148 N.J. Super. 168, 372 A.2d 360 (1977).

In re President & Directors of Georgetown College, Inc.[110]   When physical injury caused blood loss and consequent shock, the court directed the administration of a blood transfusion even though the patient and husband had previously refused the transfusion for religious reasons. The reasoning was that at the time the patient refused treatment she was in shock from blood loss and therefore incompetent.

There are degrees of incompetency such that a legally incompetent patient may have her wishes considered.

In re Ingram.[111]   The patient was found to be demented and delusional but not completely vegetative. The court considered her expressed preference for radiation over surgery to treat cancer of the larynx.

In making treatment decisions on the incompetent patient's behalf, the physician may consider the patient's family's or guardian's decision or require direct court approval. One court has even directed that any required procedure for an incompetent patient should be legislatively mandated.[112]

Some courts have attempted to look into the mind of the patient and determine under the circumstances what the patient, if competent, would have decided. "The goal is not to do what most people would do, or what the court believes is the wise thing to do, but rather what this particular individual would do if she were competent and understood all the circumstances."[113]

For patients who have never been competent there is a *best interests* test whereby the court authorizes withholding or withdrawal of life-sustaining treatment if such action would further the patient's best interests.[114] When the patient has become incompetent and no expression has been made as to treatment, the court's decision "must take place within the context of an analysis which seeks to implement what is in that person's best interests by reference to objectively, societally shared criteria."[115]

---

[110] 331 F.2d 1000 (D.C. Cir. 1964).

[111] 102 Wash. 2d 827, 841, 689 P.2d 1363, 1371 (1984).

[112] *In re* Stoar, 52 N.Y.2d 363, 420 N.E.2d 64, 438 N.Y.S.2d 266 (1980).

[113] *In re* Ingram, 102 Wash. 2d 827, 689 P.2d 1363 (1984).

[114] *In re* Conroy, 98 N.J. 321, 486 A.2d 1209 (1985).

[115] Foody v. Manchester Memorial Hosp., 40 Conn. Supp. 127, 482 A.2d 713 (Super. Ct. 1984).

CASE PREPARATION

§ 1.27   Case Preparation Generally

Most medical-legal cases revolve around the medical records, plaintiff's and defendant's statements, witnesses, and expert testimony. The records include physician's office records, hospital records, x-rays (also CT scans, radioactive studies, sonography, thermography), and pathology slides. It behooves the prudent plaintiff's attorney to obtain a statement from the plaintiff and/or the plaintiff's family concerning the events of alleged malpractice. The complete medical records should be obtained and then reviewed by a medical expert. If, in the opinion of the expert, medical malpractice has occurred, a suit may be filed.

The defendant's attorney needs not only the complete medical records but also a statement from the defendant physician concerning the physician's view of the events surrounding the claimed malpractice. A medical expert's point of view is essential to formulating a defense.

§ 1.28   Attorney's Library

The attorney must have a fundamental knowledge of medical disorders, treatment, and complications. Up-to-date medical texts are helpful. Much information can be obtained from medical experts. Medical journals can supply recent changes in almost any specialty.

The selection of proper books for an attorney's basic library allows easy access to medical terminology and facts. Having references close at hand conserves time and effort in reviewing specific medical problems. The attorney should subscribe to any annual updates because there may be significant annual changes.

Garvey v. O'Donoghue.[116]   The plaintiff alleged that an antibiotic prescribed by the defendant caused tinnitus (ringing of the ears). The appellate court held that the applicable pages of the *Physicians' Desk Reference®* and the package insert for the antibiotic tobramycin were relevant and probative evidence of the medical standard of care for selecting, administering, and monitoring the drug. Further, in a medical malpractice case alleging improper administration, dosage, and monitoring of the drug, the PDR pages and the medication package's insert were admissible as prima facie evidence of both the standard of care and the physician's notice of their contents.

---

[116] 530 A.2d 1141 (D.C. 1987).

Some suggested references include the following:

1. *Physicians' Desk Reference® (PDR)®.* 48th ed. Oradell, N.J.: Medical Economics Company Inc., 1994.

2. Haber, K. *Common Abbreviations in Clinical Medicine.* New York: Raven Press, 1979.

3. Sabiston, D.C., Jr., ed. *Textbook of Surgery: The Biological Basis of Modern Surgical Practice.* 14th ed. Philadelphia: W.B. Saunders Co., 1991.

4. Wyngarden, J.B., and L.H. Smith, Jr., eds. *Cecil Textbook of Medicine.* 19th ed. Philadelphia: W.B. Saunders Co., 1992.

5. *Dorland's Illustrated Medical Dictionary.* 27th ed. Philadelphia: W.B. Saunders Co., 1988.

6. Haskell, C.M., ed. *Cancer Treatment.* 3d ed. Philadelphia: W.B. Saunders Co., 1990.

7. Gray, H. *Anatomy of the Human Body.* 36th ed. Edited by C.M. Goss. Philadelphia: Lea & Febiger, 1980.

8. American College of Surgeons. Committee on Pre and Postoperative Care. *Manual of Preoperative and Postoperative Care.* 3d ed. Philadelphia: W.B. Saunders Co., 1983.

9. Gunz, F.W., and E.S. Henderson, eds. *Leukemia.* New York: Grune & Stratton, Inc., 1983.

10. Attman, A.J., and A.D. Schwartz, *Malignant Diseases of Infancy, Childhood and Adolescence.* Philadelphia: W.B. Saunders, 1983.

11. Helm, F. *Cancer Dermatology.* Philadelphia: Lea & Febiger, 1979.

12. DeSaia, P.J. *Clinical Gynecologic Oncology.* St. Louis: C.V. Mosby Co. Ltd., 1984.

13. Culp, D.A., and S.A. Loening, eds. *Genitourinary Oncology.* Philadelphia: Lea & Febiger, 1985.

14. Skinner, D.G., and G. Liekovsky. *Genitourinary Cancer.* Philadelphia: W.B. Saunders Co., 1988.

15. Henson, R.A., and H. Urich. *Cancer and the Nervous System.* Oxford: Blackwell Scientific Publications, 1982.

16. Pilch, J.H. *Surgical Oncology.* New York: McGraw-Hill Book Co., 1984.

17. DeVita, V.T., Jr., et al., eds. *Cancer: Principles & Practice of Oncology.* 4th ed. Philadelphia: J.B. Lippincott Co., 1993.

18. Copeland, E.M., III, ed. *Surgical Oncology.* New York: John Wiley & Sons, 1983.

19. Reese, A.B. *Tumors of the Eye.* New York: Harper & Row, 1976.

20. Donald, P.J. *Head and Neck Cancer: Management of the Difficult Case.* Philadelphia: W.B. Saunders Co., 1984.

21. Mirra, J.M. *Bone Tumors: Diagnosis and Treatment*. Philadelphia: J.B. Lippincott Co., 1980.

22. Lichtenstein, L. *Bone Tumors*. St. Louis: C.V. Mosby Co. Ltd., 1977.

23. Choi, N.C., and H.C. Grillo, eds. *Thoracic Oncology*. New York: Raven Press, 1983.

24. Van Scoy-Mosher, M.B., ed. *Medical Oncology: Controversies in Cancer Treatment*. Boston: G.K. Hall Medical Publishers, 1981.

25. Roth, J.A., et al. *Thoracic Oncology*. Philadelphia: W.B. Saunders Co., 1989.

26. Sherlock, P., et al., eds. *Precancerous Lesions of the Gastrointestinal Tract*. New York: Raven Press, 1983.

27. Spratt, J.S. *Neoplasms of the Colon, Rectum, and Anus*. Philadelphia: W.B. Saunders Co., 1984.

28. Beahrs, O.H., et al. *Colorectal Tumors*. Philadelphia: J.B. Lippincott Co., 1986.

Reference books that are available for the attorney at the libraries of hospitals and medical schools can be used to supplement other sources of information. Suggested additional books for the lawyer's medical library include the following sources:

1. Netter, F.N. *The Ciba Collection of Medical Illustrations*. Edited by F.F. Yonkwan. Summit, N.J.: CIBA Pharmaceutical Products, Inc.
   Volume 1.   Nervous System
      Part I.   Anatomy and Physiology (1983)
      Part II.   Neurologic and Neuromuscular Disorders (1986)
   Volume 2.   Reproductive System (1965)
   Volume 3.
      Part I.   Upper Digestive Tract (1959)
      Part II.   Lower Digestive Tract (1962)
      Part III.   Liver, Biliary Tract, and Pancreas (1964)
   Volume 4.   Endocrine System (1965)
   Volume 5.   Heart (1969)
   Volume 6.   Kidneys, Ureters, and Urinary Bladder (1973)
   Volume 7.   Respiratory System (1979)

2. Gilman, A.G., and L.S. Goodman. *Goodman and Gilman's The Pharmacological Basis of Therapeutics*. 8th ed. Edited by T.W. Rall and F. Murad. New York: MacMillan Publishing Co., 1990.

3. Miller, R.D., ed. *Anesthesia*. 3d ed. New York: Churchill Livingstone, Inc.,
   _____.

4. Hardy, J.D. *Complications in Surgery and Their Management*. Philadelphia: W.B. Saunders Co., 1985.

5. Kissane, J.M., and W.A.D. Anderson, eds. *Anderson's Pathology.* 3d ed. St. Louis: C.V. Mosby Co. Ltd., 1977.

§ 1.29 Records

Records must be acquired from the defendant physician and all consulting and other treating physicians. These documents should include all records that can be obtained from prior and subsequent treating physicians that may have any relevance whatsoever to the incident involved and any medical or surgical disorders that may have affected the plaintiff at the time of the occurrence of the incident.

The documents that should be obtained from the hospital include, but are not limited to, the following:

1. Complete hospital records and X-rays (including all hospitalizations)
2. Bylaws, rules, and regulations of the medical staff
3. Rules and regulations of the nursing department/service
4. Rules and regulations of the critical care units when applicable
5. Rules and regulations of the medical, surgical and subspecialty departments.

§ 1.30 Case Outline

After gathering all essential records and material, a detailed chronological written outline should be formulated. The sequence of events will enable the experts to review records more quickly and efficiently. The outline can be referred to during the case development for a quick reminder of the details of the suit.

§ 1.31 Case Reviewers

The case should be reviewed by an expert in the field who will agree to testify on behalf of the client. A review may be initiated by a nurse who is able to spot possible problems, thereby reducing initial expenditures.

§ 1.32 Expert Witness

The careful selection of a physician as an expert witness involves consideration of many important factors. Composure, credibility, presentability, clear speech, and ability to present medical subjects in layman's terms are characteristics to be evaluated. The expert should have experience in the field in which she is to be questioned. The expert should also have knowledge of the standard of care in the community in which the event occurred or in a similar community.

A medical university expert witness may add stature to the testimony. However, the ivory tower opinions may not be consistent with the standards of community medical practice.

It is not always necessary for an expert to be board certified in or practicing in the particular field of specialty in order to give an opinion on the standard of care.

Hedgecorth v. United States.[117]   An ophthalmologist and an emergency medicine specialist were expert witnesses on the standard of care in giving a stress test. It was held that the witnesses need only demonstrate to the court's satisfaction their familiarity with the applicable standard of care for the test or procedure at issue. However, an experienced board certified specialist in the particular field of medicine in question may be more influential to a jury.

It is the responsibility of the attorney to supply the expert with all the records that may have even the slightest value in the case at hand. The witness should review the records thoroughly prior to rendering an opinion, before a deposition, and again prior to court testimony. Pathology slides and x-rays may be needed for evaluation. When necessary the plaintiff patient may need to be examined. Depositions of opposing expert witnesses must be reviewed. The testimony of an expert witness is only as good as the facts on which the expert relied. The evidence should rest on the *material* from which the opinion is fashioned and the *reasoning* by which the expert progresses from the material to a conclusion.[118]

Not all cases need an expert witness. When an understanding of the physician's alleged lack of due care or skill requires only common knowledge or experience, expert medical testimony is not required.

Opposing expert witnesses are ordinarily deposed for disclosure and discovery of their testimony and materials. To some extent, the testimony at trial may be limited to the opinions expressed at the deposition by a motion in limine.

The expert witness should be adequately prepared by the attorney just prior to trial. The gist of the expert's proposed questioning and answers should be reviewed so that the lawyer is not surprised by the opinions expressed. The availability of the witness for trial must be established.

In some jurisdictions disclosure of experts may be required prior to trial. Undesignated witnesses can be called for rebuttal purposes but may not contribute opinions.

The need for expert witnesses and some of the issues arising when experts are used are illustrated by the following cases.

---

[117] 618 F. Supp. 627 (E.D. Mo. 1985).
[118] People v. Basset, 69 Cal. 2d 122, 141, 443 P.2d 777, 70 Cal. Rptr. 193 (1968).

Nally v. United States.[119]   Surgery was performed on the wrong lower extremity. The plaintiff's experts' affidavits were conclusory but did not show that the specific standard of care in Delaware was known by the expert.

Coleman v. Garrison.[120]   The court held that plaintiff's expert must be an expert on the issue in question and must demonstrate knowledge of the degree of skill ordinarily employed in Delaware.

Noor v. Continental Casualty Co.[121]   In this case, there was a summary judgment for the defendant. The plaintiff was seen by the defendant for a lump in the left breast, which had first been noted by the patient 14 months earlier. A needle aspiration was attempted but no fluid obtained. The patient was again seen 10 weeks later and the mass was still present. Five months afterward a biopsy was done and a modified radical mastectomy performed. Eleven of 13 lymph nodes showed metastatic cancer. The plaintiff claimed a decreased life expectancy, emotional trauma, and mental anguish. The court found that a decreased life expectancy was purely speculative because there was no expert testimony or affidavit to that particular claim.

Solon v. Godbole.[122]   The defendant performed surgery for a cancer of the lung. A recurrence on the chest wall was not treated for three and a half months. The plaintiff tardily identified her expert and submitted his report rather than an affidavit in response to a defense motion for summary judgment. The court ruled that the report itself was not an affidavit, and that a later affidavit saying the report itself was true and correct was not sufficient. Instead, the report must be sworn or certified and attached to the affidavit, and the affidavit must consist of facts admissible as evidence.

Gualtieri v. Burleson.[123]   In this case the attorney was required to pay the expert fees. The client had been paralyzed following vaccination for the swine flu. The attorney contacted a neuropsychiatrist as an expert and initially stated he was calling the witness on behalf of the client. As the case proceeded, the attorney paid the witness his expenses and agreed to pay the witness's fee at the end of the case. When the case was lost, the attorney refused to pay the $2,800 fee. The court found that the witness had all his dealings and agreements with the attorney, and the attorney personally contracted to pay the fee.

---

[119] No. 84-653-LON (M.O.) (D.D.C. 1984), *reprinted in* 4 Med. Malpractice Verdicts, Settlements & Experts No. 12, at 69 (1988).

[120] 349 A.2d 8 (Del. 1975).

[121] 508 So. 2d 363 (Fla. Dist. Ct. App. 1987).

[122] 163 Ill. App. 3d 845, 516 N.E.2d 1045 (1987).

[123] 353 S.E.2d 652 (N.C. Ct. App. 1987).

Kahn v. Burman.[124]   The plaintiff had originally been sued for malpractice relating to a cardiac catheterization. The defendant was asked to evaluate the merits of the malpractice claim. The defendant wrote two reports criticizing the care by the plaintiff, was identified as an expert witness, and gave a deposition. The plaintiff sued the defendant for negligence, fraudulent and negligent misrepresentation, defamation, and intentional infliction of emotional distress. The district court concluded that the deposition testimony was protected by witness immunity; however, if immunity did not apply to the written reports, the court found that the witness had a duty to the court to provide information, that the witness's subjective opinion was expressed in the reports, that the plaintiff did not rely on those reports, and that there was no showing that the reports were extreme and outrageous. The court concluded, "In the absence of expert review, then, meritless medical malpractice suits will be eradicated less frequently prior to filing. This result is neither desirable nor efficient."[125]

Weekly v. Solomon.[126]   The defendant performed a gastric stapling procedure for morbid obesity. The plaintiff did not lose weight as expected and alleged that she was not informed of this possibility. Plaintiff's expert from Ohio was barred from testifying by the trial court because he was not familiar with the local standard of care. The appellate court reversed, stating that no locality rule is applicable to the issue of informed consent.

Schrantz v. Luancing.[127]   Death due to pulmonary embolus occurred following an automobile accident causing fractured ribs. Plaintiff's expert's opinion was based upon reasonable medical certainty, which the expert concluded was the same as accepted standards of practice. The expert's testimony was struck and the appellate court affirmed, concluding the expert demonstrated that he did not know the standard of care by his own definition.

Thompson v. Webb.[128]   When rectal cancer was misdiagnosed as hemorrhoids, the summary judgment for the defendant was reversed. The plaintiff's expert, who was not licensed to practice in Illinois, testified that the defendant was negligent in failing to locate the tumor of the rectum on digital rectal examination, relying on anoscopy, and failing to perform a sigmoidoscopy on the first visit. The appellate court found that the expert was familiar with the standard of care in similar communities with comparable facilities.

---

[124] 673 F. Supp. 210 (E.D. Mich. 1987), *aff'd,* 878 F.2d 1436 (6th Cir. 1989).

[125] *Id.*

[126] 156 Ill. App. 3d 1011, 510 N.E.2d 152 (1987).

[127] 218 N.J. Super. 434, 527 A.2d 967 (1986).

[128] 138 Ill. App. 3d 629, 486 N.E.2d 326 (1985).

Glover v. Ballhagen.[129]   The defendant was a board certified family practitioner. The plaintiff's experts were a board certified orthopedic surgeon and a board certified internist and infectious disease specialist. The trial court quoted from *Aasheim v. Humberger*[130] that "the standard of care is measured by the skill and learning possessed by other doctors in good standing practicing in the same specialty and who hold the same national board certification." However, the Montana Supreme Court reported that the standard of care must be that practiced by others in the same specialty and certification but not that doctors in the same specialty are the only ones who may testify as to that standard. The Supreme Court held in the instant case that the judge had the discretion to determine whether a witness had the requisite knowledge, skill, experience, training, or education to testify as to the diagnosis and treatment in question and as to the standard applicable to the doctor charged with negligence.

Reasonable medical certainty or *reasonable medical probability* are terms the expert should use in establishing an opinion. *More likely than not* is better than *reasonable medical possibility,* which suggests that there is less than a 50-percent chance for the event to occur and which will not carry the burden of proof.

Erkens v. Tredennich.[131]   Experts proposed alternative points of view regarding the cause of a postoperative eye infection. After a defense verdict, the plaintiff appealed, contending that the testimony of the defendant's expert should have been struck by the trial court because the opinions did not rise to the level of required certainty. It was held that the trial court had the discretion to allow testimony from one expert showing that the facts did not support the opinion of another expert. The testimony had been quite clear as to the basis for finding that suture removal had not caused the infection even though there was no statement of reasonable medical certainty.

Cardwell v. Bechtol.[132]   The defendant, an osteopath, was alleged to have fallen below the standard of care in manipulating the plaintiff when, in fact, the plaintiff had a herniated disc. The plaintiff's experts, an orthopedic surgeon and a neurologist, testified that they were not familiar with an osteopath's standard of care in treating patients but that it was a reasonable medical certainty that the osteopath's actions fell below the standard of care. The trial judge disallowed the testimony of both experts on the issue of alleged malpractice, and the appeals court affirmed.

---

[129] 232 Mont. 427, 756 P.2d 1166 (1988).

[130] 695 P.2d 824 (Mont. 1985).

[131] 509 A.2d 424 (Pa. Super. Ct. 1986).

[132] 724 S.W.2d 739 (Tenn. 1987).

§ 1.33   —Establishing Credentials: Sample Questions

In qualifying a physician as an expert, or in determining the credentials of an expert witness at deposition, the examination should be in detail. It will save time if a curriculum vitae is obtained prior to questioning.

As an example, an expert witness in a case involving gastric stapling for morbid obesity might be questioned as follows:

Q. At what medical school did you receive your medical degree?

Q. What year did you receive your medical degree?

Q. Did you do an internship?

Q. Where did you do your internship?

Q. What years did you do your internship?

Q. Did you do your internship in a specialty?

Q. In what specialty did you do your internship?

Q. Have you done a residency?

Q. Where did you do your residency?

Q. What years did you do your residency?

Q. In what specialty did you do your residency?

Q. Are you board certified?

Q. In what board are you certified?

Q. What year were you board certified?

Q. In what specialty do you practice?

Q. How many years have you practiced in that specialty?

Q. Do you practice in a subspecialty?

Q. How many years have you practiced in that subspecialty?

Q. Do you practice stomach (gastric) surgery involving gastric stapling for the treatment of morbid obesity?

Q. How many years have you performed gastric stapling for morbid obesity?

Q. How many times in the past five years have you performed gastric stapling procedures for morbid obesity?

Q. Have you written any papers on the subject of morbid obesity?

Q. How many papers have you written on morbid obesity?

Q. In what journals were each of the papers on morbid obesity written?

Q. What years were each of the papers on morbid obesity published?

Q. Can you supply a copy of each of the papers written on morbid obesity?

Q. Will you therefore mail a copy of each of the papers on morbid obesity to me? [Will you attach to the deposition a copy of each of the papers you have written on morbid obesity?]

§ 1.34 —Establishing Special Knowledge: Sample Questions

In establishing an expert's knowledge in the surgical procedure being discussed, the following questions may be asked when the case involves cancer of the rectum.

Q. Are there various surgical procedures that may be performed for cancer of the rectum?

Q. What are the various surgical procedures that may be used in the treatment of cancer of the rectum?

Q. What are the indications and contraindications for each of the possible surgical procedures that may be used in the treatment of cancer of the rectum?

Q. Are there viable methods of treating cancer of the rectum in combination with surgery as adjuvant or concomitant treatment?

Q. When can chemotherapy be used in the treatment of primary rectal cancer?

Q. When can radiation therapy be used in the treatment of primary rectal cancer?

Q. Can cancer of the rectum be locally resected, preserving the anal sphincter in order to cure the cancer?

Q. What are the indications and contraindications for local resection of rectal cancer?

Q. How do you have knowledge of the standard of care of general surgeons in the community of [Name of community] and the state of [Name of state]?

§ 1.35 —Questioning an Expert Witness in the Case at Hand

The expert can only answer the questions asked. If the questions are not specific and detailed, the expert's answers may not include all the information desired. In addition, the expert may not be able to remember every single point the attorney wishes to establish.

A foundation must be laid for each area of questioning. A hypothetical question has to include all the facts previously established.

A general question will allow the expert to expound on a subject. The question should not be so broad, however, that the jury becomes bored with the answer. The use of large sheets of paper for drawing diagrams or previously prepared anatomical and graph posters make it easier for a jury to understand what is being described.

The expert should not be expected to memorize all the patient's records. When possible, the specific page of the record being questioned should be shown to the expert prior to requesting an answer, saving time and avoiding errors. Seeing a specific entry may jog the expert's memory to allow a concise and accurate answer.

§ 1.36   Contingency Fees

It is appropriate for an attorney to take a malpractice lawsuit on a contingency fee basis. The basic theory is to allow access to the courts for the underprivileged who would otherwise be unable to afford litigation fees. The lawyer risks the costs of filing suit, discovery procedures, incidentals, experts, and trial against a percentage of the recovery. Because the costs of litigation may be high, there can be a tendency, by the plaintiff's attorney, to find inexpensive experts and to do minimal discovery. The defense attorney, on the other hand, may tend to increase the expenses, especially if an insurance company is involved, by massive amounts of paperwork and discovery proceedings in order to put pressure on the opposition.

It would be inappropriate for an expert witness to charge a contingency fee. If the expert has a stake in the case, there can be suspicion of bias in the expert's testimony. This might be detrimental to the plaintiff's case.

Comments and Cases

There still exists the issue of whether it is appropriate for medical-legal consulting firms to enter contingency fee contracts with plaintiffs. Comments and cases relative to this problem have been published in *Medical Malpractice Verdicts, Settlements and Experts:*[133]

> Henry E. Weil wrote to say that the Maryland Court of Special Appeals has upheld such fees. **Schackow v. Medical Legal Consulting Services, Inc.,** 46 Md. App. 179, 416 A.2d 1303 (1980). . . .
>
> Steven Keyser, J.D., writes: "It was my impression, that you (or someone) had interpreted [ABA Formal Opinion 87-354; November 7, 1987] to preclude a contingent fee to a medico-legal firm.
>
> "It is my opinion and the opinion of our (Medi-Legal Services) counsel that ABA Formal Opinion 87-354 DOES NOT preclude contingent fees to a medicolegal consulting firm. What it apparently does is to further define the circumstances under which a firm can charge a contingent fee and to say that it MAY be necessary in some cases for a determination to be made as to the COMBINED total fees charged by both the attorney handling the case and of the medicolegal consulting service to insure that they are 'reasonable.' What is reasonable will surely vary from state to state and case to case. In the majority of cases, this issue will not even come up.
>
> "In New York the specific issue of what is 'reasonable' regarding the contingent fees to a medicolegal service was addressed by the **New York State Bar Association, Committee on Professional Ethics, Opinion #572 — 11-29-85**

---

[133] 5 Med. Malpractice Verdicts, Settlements & Experts No. 3, at 5–7 (1989). Reprinted by permission. Copyright 1994 Lewis L. Laska.

(9-85) wherein it was determined that a contingent fee was proper under specific circumstances. A fee of 6 to 10% has been suggested as proper, however a figure of 20% or more to a consulting service may be excessive.

"I would like to go on record at this time agreeing with the New York opinion that a contingent fee of 20% or more to a consulting service is clearly excessive and in my mind, outrageous.

"I would like to point [out] that the field of medicolegal consulting is one filled with hard work. It is most difficult to obtain contacts with highly qualified medical experts who have the courage to become involved in medical malpractice cases. As you know, many physicians find peer review most repugnant and refuse to become involved in a malpractice case in any way. As any malpractice attorney knows, maintaining those contacts to insure continuing communication and availability is a never ending task. I think that if you ask any attorney who has employed a reputable medicolegal consulting service whether that service earned its compensation, the overwhelming majority of those attorneys will answer in the affirmative.

"I think that the major issues facing medicolegal consulting firms and the attorneys that call upon these services for assistance involve the assurance that such services provide only honest, objective and professional opinions. These opinions to be provided by non "commercial" experts (less than 5% of their practice commitment in malpractice issues), either in active practice or recently retired with an active license and if practicing in a medical specialty, either board-certified or board-eligible. Further they must have absolutely no criminal or civil blemishes in their background. And, I feel that the owners/operators of such consulting services must also have absolutely 'clean' civil and criminal backgrounds as well as comprehensive knowledge of medicine and the law."

New Jersey Court Rejects Contingency Fee . . . . The agreement between a plaintiff, her attorney, and a medical expert consulting business was rendered void and unenforceable by a New Jersey court, where a contingency fee payment to the consulting business was part of the contract. The court ruled that such an arrangement violates the professional code of ethics applicable to attorneys in that state and ethical guidelines of the medical profession. **Polo v. Gotchel,** 225 N.J. Super. 429, 542 A.2d 947 (1988).

The underlying medical liability action involved a birth injury claim against the obstetrician that delivered the plaintiff. The consulting service, JDMD, Inc., was retained by plaintiff's guardian and her attorney to review medical records, render an opinion, be deposed, and testify at trial, with expert witness fees to be computed at an hourly rate. However, according to the court the method of payment of these hourly fees involved two "service charges." The first was an initial charge of $500.00 due when the identity of the expert located by JDMD, Inc., was disclosed to the plaintiff and her attorney. The second service charge provided for a 6% contingent fee on the gross recovery upon successful disposition of the case by either settlement or verdict. This contingent fee, payable by the client, was in addition to the attorney's own contingent fee. Moreover, the plaintiff's attorney was required by the agreement to act as guarantor of the contingent fee payment to JDMD, Inc.

The action against the obstetrician was ultimately settled. Reviewing the expert witness contingent fee arrangement, the court objected to it on a number of grounds. First, the court determined that it was contrary to the Current Opinions of the American Medical Association's Council on Ethical and Judicial Affairs, which stated that a physician's fee should be calculated only on the value of the medical services provided. The court expressed concern for the danger of a physician "becoming more of an advocate and less of a healer."

Second, the court held that the contract was prohibited by an ethical opinion issued by the New Jersey Advisory Committee on Professional Ethics, which regulates attorney conduct in the state. The opinion reaffirmed that a physician's fee for providing medical-legal consultation should not be based on the outcome of the litigation and stated that attorneys should not assist in fostering a contingent fee arrangement with a doctor.

Third, the court noted that New Jersey's medical practice act prohibited physicians from charging a contingent fee where the medical services involved supporting a legal claim for damages. New Jersey's Supreme Court rules on fee arrangements also manifest a clear intent to prohibit anyone other than an attorney from charging a contingent fee; in addition, attorneys are prohibited from sharing their fee with anyone other than a licensed attorney.

Finally, the court reviewed its duty to safeguard the interests of minor plaintiffs by closely monitoring litigation settlements on their behalf and attendant fee arrangements. As the court stated, if photographers, accident reconstruction experts, investigators, and the like were permitted to charge on a contingent fee basis, only a minuscule portion of a recovery would be left for the injured plaintiff.

For these reasons, the court determined that it was obviously contrary to the public policy of the State of New Jersey and the expectation of its citizens to allow contingent fee agreements for medical expert witness services to stand. Therefore, the fee arrangement of JDMD, Inc., was declared void.

Montana Federal Court Won't Enforce Contingency Fee . . . . Virginia Bock sued Billings Deaconess Hospital and Dr. John Heiser, alleging malpractice in the death of her husband, Joseph, in connection with liver surgery in 1978. Her lawyer, R.P. Ryan, sent Medical Quality Foundation a contract employing their services in obtaining a medical expert. MQF sent a new revised fee agreement calling for 20% of recovery, which Ryan did not return. MQF advised Ryan by phone that there was no evidence of malpractice or negligence in the case. Dr. Thomas Brown, Bock's new husband, pressed the issue with Dr. Barry Jacobs, principal of MQF. MQF thereafter submitted a 16-page report explaining their conclusion of no malpractice.

According to Montana Law Week, Ryan advised MQF that Defendants had offered to settle and that MQF's services were no longer needed. On the same day, unknown to Ryan, Bock called Jacobs requesting his opinion of a $30,000 settlement offer. Jacobs advised her that she should accept. Ryan later negotiated a $70,000 settlement and MQF sought a 20% fee. Bock said Ryan filed this declaratory action, contending that MQF was employed only under the original contract to provide an initial report for no more than $150 and that if MQF agreed that the case was meritorious, experts would be located. MQF contends that they were retained under both contracts and completed an analysis and lengthy report, and that it would be inequitable to let Bock use the benefits of their labors and skills without compensation. The Court finds that the original contract remained in effect, and that under it Bock and Ryan contracted for and received a Work Product Consultant Report of $150. Even assuming that the contract was for more than that report, MQF failed to do more. Rather than retaining "any number of physicians" as experts, they submitted a report outlining their decision that no negligence had occurred. The new fee agreement was never in effect because it was not accepted by Bock and Ryan. It appears that MQF Defendants are on the fringe of practicing law when they advise clients as to appropriate settlement offers. Montana prohibits this type of activity without a valid license and certificate. The court will not compensate them for nonmedical activity performed in this matter. Further, MQF advised Bock to accept the original offer of $30,000. After further negotiations she agreed to $70,000. It would be a windfall to MQF to receive any compensation for an increased settlement award without performing any contracted functions. **Bock v. The Medical Quality Foundation,** U.S. District, Montana (Billings) No. CV-87-96-BLG.

Sample Code of Conduct

The ethics committee of the National Forensic Center has proposed a code of professional and ethical conduct for expert witnesses as follows:[134]

The proposal, developed by the Ethics Committee of the National Forensic Center, is divided into two sections. Section 1 lists basic "Principles" which serve as an outline of the responsibilities of the forensic expert. Section 2 lists certain "Precepts," or standards of performance to meet the responsibilities of being an expert. A third section on enforcement will ultimately be added. The preamble points out that "as an organization with voluntary membership, the National Forensic Center is not and does not intend to be, a regulatory body. Any disciplinary recommendations that evolve from this code will do so from the wishes of the membership and the community it serves."

Scope of the Code
The proposal would apply to all "members," a term intended to include not only members of the National Forensic Center, but "all experts who offer their services in dispute resolution matters." Additionally, the term "dispute resolution matter" is intended to include various so-called "alternative dispute resolution" mechanisms such as arbitration and mediation, as well as the traditional judge and jury trials. Thus to the extent that the Code would apply to experts as an authoritative guide for professional and ethical conduct, its scope is quite broad.

---

[134]"Code of Professional and Ethical Conduct" (proposed), 1 Expert Witness J. 1 (1989) (H.D. Sewall ed.) Reprinted with permission, SEAK, Inc., Legal and Medical Publishers, Falmouth, MA.

Nonetheless, the Code is not intended to supplant any established system of ethical guidelines within the various professions. "The professional, ethical, and regulatory standards attendant to the individual's professional status should take precedence." The Code goes on to say that "Often the various professions are not prepared to address the activities of their members in performing services as forensic experts, and do not provide the needed regulatory support for their members' actions in this forum. Although professional control rests with individual professions, the Center and its members believe that a Code that compliments the professional standards, by addressing the Principles and Rules dealing with the Forensic aspect of the members' work, and the social responsibilities undertaken in the process, will assist in filling this void.

Articles

The Code includes the following excerpted Articles as well as explanatory text after each Article. Only the Articles themselves are reported here.

Article 1: Responsibilities

Forensic Experts should always be mindful of their dual responsibilites [sic]. Not only are they responsible for the judgements [sic] and ethics of their professional activities, they are also responsible for the effect that those activities have on the process of social justice. Forensic experts should accept justice as their foremost responsibility.

Article 2: The Public Trust

Members will perform forensic services in a manner that will serve the public interest. Member's professional activities, and their activities as forensic experts, will honor the public trust at all times.

Article 3: Integrity

Members will perform all aspects of their professional responsibilities as experts, including the dissemination of findings and conclusions, with the highest degree of integrity.

Article 4: Objectivity and Independence

Members should maintain objectivity in all professional dealings. Members should be free from conflicts of interest and possess an independence that will not jeopardize their objectivity. This objectivity and independence should be in fact as well as appearance, and should cover both the work product and the dispute resolution forum in which this work product is being used.

Article 5: Professional Care and Competence

A member should observe the technical and ethical standards of their profession, whether written or implied. They should continually strive to improve the competence and quality of their expertise and discharge that expertise to the best of their ability, consistent with true justice.

Article 6: Scope and Nature of Services

A member should only hold themself out as an expert in matters in which they would be considered expert by their professional peers. In addition, members should offer services as an expert only after consideration has been given to the principles outlined previously.

Precepts

The Precepts give direction and standards of conduct for forensic experts. "They are definitive guides based on the principles that preceded them. Although not intended to be immutable rules, members should be prepared to justify departures from these precepts."

Precept 1 deals with Personal Standards (including independence, integrity, objectivity, and representation). Members who hold themselves out as experts **shall** be independent in "fact and appearance.["] Further, "a member **shall** maintain actual and apparent objectivity in preparing and presenting work product and opinions."

Precept 2 deals with Professional and Technical Standards (professional competence, due professional care, adequate data, methodology, professional criteria, and continuing education and training). Precept 3 involves General Practice Standards, Precept 4 involves Standards of Presentation, and Precept 5 discusses Responsibilities to Fellow Members and Other Experts.

DISCOVERY

§ 1.37   Informal Discovery

The parties to a malpractice action have the right to discovery of any nonprivileged matter that is relevant to the pending suit. Informal exchange of information and material early in the claim may help to resolve the issues before trial. Requests for records and reports promptly honored will save time and expense and may aid in eliminating nonmeritorious cases.

§ 1.38   Formal Discovery

Formal discovery techniques have some uniformity under the federal rules of discovery[135] that are being utilized under many state rules and statutes. Interrogatories, requests for production of documents, requests for admissions, requests to inspect and copy, depositions, and pretrial conferences are within the

---

[135] Fed. R. Civ. P. 26–37.

scope of discovery. Depositions of witnesses, defendants, plaintiffs, and experts can define the boundaries of the disagreement and may prevent surprises at trial.

§ 1.39   Interrogatories

Interrogatories are an inexpensive method for obtaining objective information. The questions posed should be specific and not argumentative. The beginning section should contain a definition of terms to be used in the interrogatories. For example:[136]

> To "identify" a person means to state his name, current address, telephone number and employment both present and at the times material to the occurrences giving rise to the complaint.
>
> To "identify" a document means to describe it sufficiently to be able to later request its production, and to identify the custodian thereof, or to attach a true copy of the document(s) to your answer hereto.
>
> "Injury" means the accident, damage, loss, disfigurement, affliction or injury complained of.
>
> "Including" means including but not limited to.
>
> "Describe" means comprehensive, full, fair, frank, complete, accurate, and detailed description of the matter inquired of.
>
> "Document" means any kind of written, typewritten, printed or recorded material whatsoever, including, but not limited to notes, transcription of notes, memoranda, letters, telegrams, publications, agreements, pictures, schematics, drawings, tape recordings, video recordings, log books, and business records.

§ 1.40   Significant Cases

Shibilski v. St. Joseph's Hospital of Marshfield.[137]   The court held that hospital regulations and reports of hospital committees are discoverable.

Phillips v. District Court.[138]   The court held that, in the absence of a showing of exceptional circumstances, a medical report written by a physician who is not going to testify at trial is not discoverable.

City of Edmond v. Parr.[139]   The records of the hospital's Infectious Disease Committee pertaining to investigation of staph infection among hospital patients was found to be privileged.

---

[136] Dombroff, *Pretrial Proceedings: Discovery and Tactics,* 30 Trial Law. Guide 322 (1986).

[137] 83 Wis. 2d 459, 266 N.W.2d 264 (1978).

[138] 194 Colo. 455, 573 P.2d 553 (1978).

[139] 587 P.2d 56 (Okla. 1978).

Holiday v. Harrows, Inc.[140]   Nonmedical information pertaining to the treatment of patients other than the plaintiff is discoverable as being necessary to establish overall quality of emergency room care.

Seymour v. District Court for El Paso County.[141]   The Director of Nursing was required to answer deposition questions regarding the standard of nursing care as reasonably calculated to lead to discovery of admissible evidence even though the answers would not be admissible at trial.

Argonaut Insurance Co. v. Peralta.[142]   It was held that the court cannot order the defendant to produce medical records and photographs of other patients, not party to the action, who had undergone augmentation mammoplasty.

SETTLEMENT CONFERENCE

§ 1.41   Settlement Conference Generally

The settlement conference is too often a farce where the plaintiff demands an excessive recovery and the defense makes an unreasonably low offer. Most experienced attorneys have a rational idea of the approximate realistic value of the case. The chances of winning or losing the action must be taken into account. The plaintiff and defendant should be informed in some detail of the medical and legal intricacies involved, the possibilities of success or failure in the suit, the costs of going to trial compared to the amount of the possible recovery, the time spent in trial by the client with the concomitant loss of income, and the reasonable amount for settlement. If the client is unrealistic in her decision, the conversation and conclusions should be placed in writing and a copy sent to the client.

Another incentive to settlement is the possibility of losing what appears to be a very strong case because of unforeseen factors. The jury does not always produce, what would appear to be, a proper decision. The client may not make a convincing witness. The expert may concede important points when pressed by the opposing attorney.

The persuasive factors in the client's favor must be presented if settlement is desired. There is a reluctance to introduce these details prior to trial in order to prevent the opposing attorney from learning the proposed strategy. However, by the time discovery has been completed, these aspects of the case are fairly obvious and countermeasures have already been prepared.

---

[140] 458 N.Y.S. 2d 669 (App. Div. 1983).

[141] 116 Colo. 102, 581 P.2d 302 (1978).

[142] 358 So. 2d 232 (Fla. 1978).

Settlement can be mutually agreed upon prior to or even during trial. If unforeseen detrimental information or testimony comes to light during the trial, the client's position should be reconsidered.

TRIAL PREPARATION

§ 1.42   Trial Preparation Generally

The medical malpractice case must be prepared in detail. Detailed preparation requires that counsel have considerable knowledge of medical facts. Accurate anatomic models and diagrams should be studied, especially in relationship to the case facts.

Prior to trial counsel should thoroughly and critically examine the issues involved and all essential matters to be covered, integrating factual issues with legal principles. Familiarity with medical terminology and medical concepts is necessary to this process.

Counsel should review the testimony of witnesses and estimate the duration of time needed on the stand. Counsel should confer with each witness at least one day prior to appearance at the trial.

§ 1.43   Pretrial Hearing

The pretrial hearing allows completion of discovery and reduces delay in the onset of trial. It may obviate the need for authentication of documents or other material that is likely to be offered into evidence. Amendments to pleadings can usually be made before the case is assigned to a judge for final hearing.[143] Feigned issues can be precluded.

§ 1.44   Trial Brief

A trial brief submitted to the court prior to trial will allow the judge to become familiar with the case so that it will proceed more smoothly. The attorney's position on all pertinent medical facts and legal issues should be outlined.

Anatomy, physiology, biochemistry, radiology, and pathology should be simply described and medical terminology defined. A chronological digest of pretrial pleadings and results are included. Plaintiff's and defendant's proposed facts and legal principles are outlined. Evidence of principal witnesses should be

---

[143] Simonelli v. Cassidy, 336 Mich. 635, 59 N.W.2d 28 (1953).

outlined. Excerpts of legal authorities on all substantive and evidentiary legal issues likely to arise in the case are included.

§ 1.45   Trial Notebook

The notebook should contain tabbed sections to include:

1. Trial brief
2. Complete medical records
3. Depositions of all witnesses with appropriate statements marked and tabbed
4. Anticipated motions for self and opposing attorney
5. Copies of opinions, statutes, rules, and regulations likely to be needed during trial
6. Outline of pertinent points to be made in opening statement
7. Anticipated questions for all expected witnesses, expanded as the trial proceeds
8. Outline of closing arguments
9. Instructions to jury.

The case should be kept simple and easily understood by the jury. The more complicated the case, the more likely the jury will find for the defendant. It is presumed that the defendant physician has performed the duty of care in a reasonably competent manner despite an untoward result. A simple error in judgment might not impose liability because a physician cannot guarantee the results of any treatment or procedure.

Defenses to be considered should include the following:

1. Lack of causation between breach of duty and injuries sustained
2. Statute of limitations problems
3. Failure to comply with statutes such as notice statute[144]
4. Failure to prove essential elements of case
5. Emergency situation or assumption of the risk
6. Contributory or comparative negligence.

---

[144] Dougherty v. Oliviero, 427 A.2d 487 (Me. 1981).

§ 1.46   Jury versus Judge

Most juries are sympathetic to defendant physicians because there is, generally, a high regard for the medical profession as a whole. However, the jury is the best tribunal for the plaintiff in cases of medical malpractice. A judge may have idiosyncrasies and preconceived prejudices so that it is worthwhile to know the background and prior actions of the judge selected for the case. A jury will dilute the prejudices of its individuals.

§ 1.47   Jury Selection

With experience, attorneys learn to select the types of jurors that might be sympathetic to their aspect of the case. Intuitive feelings as to favorable or unfavorable responses by each individual are developed. Psychological traits can be exposed on voir dire.

Professional help is available from specialists in jury selection. This can be expensive and time-consuming but many times quite rewarding. Information gathered should include the following:

1. Background investigation of potential jurors
2. Surveys and profiles of jurors with reference to age, sex, racial background, and profession
3. Observation of jurors in court, which includes noting eye contact, posture, body movement, speech patterns, and intelligence
4. Social science analysis of background.

For example, the college-educated female who is politically conservative is potentially a leader but may conflict with males who wield power and influence in the community. The authoritative individual tends to maintain assumptions regardless of contrary evidence but can be influenced by persons of higher professional status and group pressure.

Voir Dire

Most attorneys rely on answers to certain questions and their own intuition in order to select jurors. Intuition is actually a subconscious response to the body language and auditory clues from the potential juror. With experience some attorneys can select sympathetic jurors quite accurately. However, a juror's fitness can be evaluated by observing the individual's response to the lawyers, the judge, and possible controversies involved in the trial.

Anxiety by any individual may be manifested by body and/or vocal actions. A juror may display signs of anxiety regarding the unfamiliar environment of the court with its lawyers, judge, and rules of behavior or from the juror's own attempts to be less than candid or to be actually deceptive. The potential juror's background may give an indication of the reasons for certain reactions, but body language and auditory clues are better indications in specific situations.

Some manifestations of the juror's anxiety are easily recognized by the observant attorney. Increased movements such as wringing of hands, shifting of position, fingers to face or hair, or swinging of foot are attempts to relieve tension. Stiff posture, grasping of the chair arms, and lack of head movement indicate rigidity of the anxious person. Avoiding prolonged eye contact may indicate anxiety, thoughtfulness, or deception. Some people habitually cannot maintain eye contact.

Speech patterns may be indicative of anxiety. Unfinished sentences, interruption in the midportion of sentences, and rapid speech indicate nervousness. Voice tone and pitch tend to change with anxiety. There may be inappropriate laughter that helps to relieve tension.

Eye contact must be evaluated in context with facial expression. Relaxed facial muscles indicate interest or acceptance. Tense facial muscles, such as a frown or squinting, may indicate hostility or aggressiveness.

Body posture can indicate attitude toward the speaker. Folding arms across the chest, crossing the legs, and moving back in the chair may reflect withdrawal or hostility. Facing the speaker and leaning forward are signs of interest and compatibility.

A baseline of anxiety level is established early during the voir dire process. Simple, easy questions are asked to show a baseline, and then changes in body language and vocal clues can be better evaluated. The attorney should note the juror's attitude in response to the judge and opposing legal counsel.

§ 1.48   Opening Statement

The opening statement should be prepared so that the issues of the case can be presented in a succinct and chronological order. This is not a detailed argumentative statement of all contentions to be made during the case. The evidence that is expected to be shown is outlined and should be consistent with all the evidence actually presented at trial.

CHAPTER 2

BASIC CONCEPTS IN CANCER

§ 2.1   Diagnosis and Treatment

The St. Paul Fire and Marine Insurance Company of St. Paul, Minnesota, stated in 1990 that failure to diagnose cancer was the most frequent malpractice allegation reported, making up more than 6 percent of all claims.[1] Expeditious diagnosis and treatment of malignancies can prevent loss of opportunity for cure or effective palliation. Delay in treatment can result in the necessity for more extensive surgery, the need for radiation therapy, and the requirement for chemotherapy, which would have been unnecessary if treatment had been rendered earlier. There may be significant side effects from radiation and chemotherapy.

§ 2.2   Risk Factors

There is still much to be learned about the causes of cancer. However, some hereditary and environmental risk factors are known.

---

[1] 7 Primary Care & Cancer 12 (1990).

Tobacco

Cigarette smoking has a known carcinogenic effect. Cancers associated with smoking include cancers of the lung, bladder, pancreas, lip, mouth, tongue, larynx, esophagus, and kidney. Heavy cigarette smoking (over one pack per day) increases the cancer risk.

Alcohol

Alcohol per se does not cause cancer directly but increases the risk of development of cancer when associated with smoking. The combination is related to cancers of the mouth, tongue, pharynx, and larynx. Primary cancer of the liver is associated with cirrhosis, and alcohol is one of the causes of liver cirrhosis.

Diet

Dietary contents influence the onset of malignancies. Carotenoids and vitamin A protect against cancers of the lung, oral cavity, pharynx, and larynx. Vitamin C inhibits the formation of N-nitroso compounds, which are carcinogenic, from ingested nitrates, and N-nitroso compounds are associated with bowel cancer. Animal fats are linked with increased cancer of the breast, colon, endometrium, and prostate. High dietary fiber tends to protect against colon cancer. Vitamin E and selenium-activated enzymes block damage to cellular DNA from some carcinogens. Pickled, cured, and smoked foods have been indicated in the increased risk of stomach cancer.

Hormones

Estrogens increase the danger of endometrial cancer but have not conclusively been shown to increase breast cancer occurrence. Diethylstilbestrol (DES) taken during pregnancy can cause vaginal adenocarcinoma in the female offspring.

Chemotherapy

Some anticancer drugs are associated with an increased incidence of leukemia and lymphoma. Immunosuppressive drugs used in organ transplant patients are related to the onset of lung cancer, lymphoma, and Kaposi's sarcoma.

Radiation

Ionizing radiation from the sun and radiation therapy are damaging to tissues, especially the cellular DNA. Basal cell carcinoma, squamous cell carcinoma, and melanoma can be precipitated by excessive sun exposure. Small doses of radiation to the head and neck areas in childhood for benign diseases can result in thyroid cancer many years later. Leukemia, bone cancer, chondrosarcoma, breast cancer, stomach cancer, and lung cancer have been reported from excessive radiation.

Heredity

Hereditary factors may encourage the development of cancer. Familial multiple polyposis, Gardner's syndrome, dysplastic nevus syndrome, xeroderma pigmentosum, retinoblastoma, ataxia-telangiectasia, multiple endocrine neoplasia (MEN IIb, MEN III), Wermer's syndrome (MEN I), Sipple syndrome (MEN II, MEN IIa), and some neuroblastomas have hereditary origin with predisposition to malignancy.

Industrial Toxins

Industrial toxins can be causally related to the development of cancer. Known causative toxic substances are 4-aminobiphenyl, arsenic and compounds, asbestos, benzene, benzidine, chlornaphazine, bis(chloromethyl) ether, chromium and compounds, soots, tars, oils, 2-naphthylamine, and vinyl chloride. Those probably carcinogenic to humans include acrylonitrile, benzopyrene, beryllium and compounds, diethyl sulphate, dimethyl sulfate, nickel and compounds, and ortho-tolidine.[2]

Viruses

Certain viruses affect the genetic makeup of cells and can precipitate cancer. The Epstein-Barr virus (EBV) has been linked with Burkitt's lymphoma and nasopharyngeal cancer. Herpes simplex type 2 (HSV2) is associated with cervical cancer. Hepatitis B virus has been implicated in some liver cancers. T-cell leukemia-lymphoma virus (HTLV-J) plays a role in leukemia and lymphoma, whereas HTLV-III causes AIDS with its predisposition to cancers. The human papilloma virus (HPV) causes cervical condylomas, with types 11, 16, and 18 associated with the development of squamous cell carcinoma.[3]

Viruses can cause genetic changes by converting normal cellular genes or proto-oncogenes to oncogenes. Chromosomal alterations have been recognized in leukemia, lymphoma, lung cancer, and renal cell cancer.[4] Malignant melanomas have abnormalities at chromosomes 1, 6, and 7.

---

[2] U.S. Dep't of Health & Human Services, Cancer Rates and Risks (3d ed. NIH Pub. No. 85-691 Apr. 1985).

[3] E. Burghardt, Colposcopy Cervical Pathology 24–30 (1984).

[4] Rowley, *Cancer: A Genetic Disease,* 5 Advances in Oncology 3 (1989).

Magnetic Fields

Exposure to extremely low frequency magnetic fields from electrical installations and power lines is an inevitable fact of everyday living. There may be a carcinogenic effect of the magnetic fields, especially in relationship to childhood cancers.[5]

§ 2.3   Tumor Markers

Biological markers are available to determine the presence or progression of tumors. Virulence or degree of malignancy can also be predicted with the use of tumor markers.

Estrogen and Progesterone Receptors

The presence of positive estrogen and progesterone receptors in breast cancer indicates hormone sensitivity of the tumor cells. Treatment with endogenous hormones, ablation of hormones, or blockage of hormone effect will result in a decrease in tumor growth. The estrogen receptor status is a prognostic indicator for risk of recurrence. There are no consistent data as to the effectiveness of receptor status in predicting the response to cytotoxic therapy.

Estrogen receptors have been found in renal cell carcinoma, melanoma, ovarian tumors, colorectal cancers, and hepatoadenomas. No clinical application of this finding has been determined in these tumors.

Calcitonin

Calcitonin is a hypocalcemic factor produced by the parafollicular cells (C-cells) of the thyroid gland. Medullary carcinoma of the thyroid is a neoplasm of the C-cells that produces calcitonin. Ectopic secretion of calcitonin may occur in carcinoid tumors[6] and malignancies of the lung[7] and breast.[8]

---

[5] Savitz et al., *Case Control Study of Childhood Cancer and Exposure to 60 Hz Magnetic Fields,* 128 Am. J. Epidemiology 21 (1988); Delpizzo, *An Evaluation of the Existing Evidence on the Carcinogenic Potential of Extremely Low Frequency Magnetic Fields,* 12 Australian Phys. Engineering Sci. Med. 55 (1989); Wertheimer & Leeper, *Electrical Wiring Configuration and Childhood Cancer,* 109 Am. J. Epidemiology 273 (1979).

[6] Frolich et al., *The Carcinoid Flush Provocation by Pentogastrin and Inhibition by Somastatin,* 299 New Eng. J. Med. 1055 (1978); Kaplan et al., *Humoral Similarities of Carcinoid Tumors and Medullary Carcinomas of the Thyroid,* 74 Surgery 21 (1973).

[7] Silva et al., *Ectopic Secretion of Calcitonin by Oat-Cell Carcinoma,* 290 New Eng. J. Med. 1122 (1974).

[8] Coombes et al., *Secretion of Immunoreactive Calcitonin by Human Breast Carcinomas,* 2 Brit. Med. J. 197 (1975).

In certain tumors, the level of calcitonin can be helpful in staging or predicting the extent of spread. Serial determinations are used for evidence of therapy-induced remission and preclinical evidence of recurrence.

Prostatic Acid Phosphatase (PAP)

Elevated PAP occurs in localized cancer of the prostate as well as with metastatic disease.[9] The levels are used to monitor efficacy of treatment for patients with stage D prostatic cancer and in evaluating a patient's clinical status. Recurrent disease can be detected early.

Carcinoembryonic Antigen (CEA)

Carcinoembryonic antigen (CEA) may be elevated in gastrointestinal malignancies[10] and in cancers of the breast,[11] lung,[12] and cervix.[13] The more elevated the CEA, the more likely the tumor will recur. Monitoring CEA is useful in detecting residual cancer, in detecting preclinical recurrence, and in monitoring treatment of advanced disease.

Alpha Fetoprotein (AFP)

Alpha fetoprotein (AFP) is elevated in the presence of primary hepatocellular cancer. This factor may aid in the diagnostic distinction of this tumor from metastatic lesions in the liver, although AFP can be elevated in gastric cancer, pancreatic cancer, and teratocarcinoma. Tumor response to therapy can be monitored and early recurrence detected.

---

[9] Lee et al., *Value of New Fluorescent Immunoassay for Human Prostatic Acid Phosphatase in Prostate Cancer,* 15 Urology 338 (1980).

[10] Alexander, Jr., et al., *CEA Levels in Patients with Carcinoma of the Esophagus,* 42 Cancer 1792 (1978); Cooper et al., *A Reappraisal of the Value of Carcinoembryonic Antigen in the Management of Patients with Various Neoplasms,* 66 Brit. J. Surgery 120 (1979); Jubert et al., *Characteristics of Adenocarcinomas of the Colorectum with Low Levels of Preoperative Plasma Carcinoembryonic Antigen (CEA),* 42 Cancer 635 (1978).

[11] Wahren et al., *Carcinoembryonic Antigen and Other Tumor Markers in Tissue and Serum or Plasma of Patients with Primary Mammary Carcinoma,* 42 Cancer 1870 (1978).

[12] Dent et al., *Measurement of Carcinoembryonic Antigen in Patients with Bronchogenic Carcinoma,* 42 (3d Supp.) Cancer 1484 (1978); Ford et al., *Role of Carcinoembryonic Antigen in Bronchial Carcinoma,* 32 Thorax 582 (1977).

[13] Khoo et al., *Carcinoembryonic Antigen and B-2-Microglobulin as Serum Tumor Markers in Women with Genital Cancer,* 16 Int'l J. Gynaecology & Obstetrics 388 (1979); Lindgren et al., *Tissue CEA in Premalignant Epithelial Lesions and Epidermoid Carcinoma of the Uterine Cervix: Prognostic Significance,* 23 Int'l J. Cancer 448 (1979).

DNA Flow Cytometry

The cellular DNA content can be analyzed by flow cytometry to determine the presence of abnormal DNA. Aneuploid tumors often have a poorer prognosis than diploid tumors. Ploidy can correlate with histologic grade with more undifferentiated tumors associated with aneuploidy. Correlation has been found in head and neck cancers,[14] lymphoma,[15] leukemia,[16] meningioma,[17] melanoma,[18] sarcoma,[19] neuroblastoma,[20] and malignancies of the urinary bladder,[21] testicle,[22] uterus,[23] ovary,[24] colon,[25] breast,[26] lung,[27] thyroid,[28] esophagus,[29] stomach,[30] and bone.[31]

[14] Kaplan et al., *Retrospective DNA Analysis of Head and Neck Squamous Cell Carcinoma,* 112 Archives Otolaryngology Head & Neck Surg. 1159 (1986); Kokal et al., *Tumor DNA Content as a Prognostic Indicator in Squamous Cell Carcinoma of the Head and Neck Region,* 7 Proc. Am. Soc'y Clinical Oncology 179 (1988); Rua et al., *Relationship between Histologic Features, DNA Flow Cytometry, and Clinical Behavior of Squamous Cell Carcinomas of the Larynx,* 67 Cancer 171 (1991).

[15] Braylan & Benson, *Flow Cytometric Analysis of Lymphomas,* 113 Archives Pathology & Laboratory Med. 627 (1989).

[16] Kropff et al., *Prediction of Survival and Disease Transformation in Chronic Phase CML by DNA Cytometry,* 185 Pathology Resident Prac. 85 (1989).

[17] Crone et al., *Relationship Between Flow Cytometric Features and Clinical Behavior of Meningiomas,* 23 Neurosurgery 720 (1988).

[18] Sondergaard et al., *DNA Ploidy—Characteristics of Human Malignant Melanoma Analyzed by Flow Cytometry and Compared with Histology and Clinical Course,* 42 Virchows Archives 43 (1983).

[19] Alvegard et al., *Cellular DNA Content and Prognosis of High-Grade Soft Tissue Sarcoma: The Scandinavian Sarcoma Group Experience,* 8 J. Clinical Oncology 538 (1990).

[20] Look et al., *Cellular DNA Content as a Predictor of Response to Chemotherapy in Infants with Unresectable Neuroblastoma,* 311 New Eng. J. Med. 231 (1984).

[21] Coon et al., *Flow Cytometry of Deparaffinized Nuclei in Urinary Bladder Carcinoma: Comparison with Cytogenetic Analysis,* 57 Cancer 1594 (1986).

[22] Oosterhuis et al., *Karyotyping and DNA Flow Cytometry of Mature Residual Teratoma after Intensive Chemotherapy of Disseminated Nonseminomatous Germ Cell Tumor of the Testis: Report of 2 Cases,* 22 Cancer Genetics & Cytogenetics 149 (1986).

[23] Iverson, *Flow Cytometric Deoxyribonucleic Acid Index: A Prognostic Factor in Endometrial Carcinoma,* 155 Am. J. Obstetrics & Gynecology 770 (1986).

[24] Rodenburg et al., *Tumor Ploidy as a Major Prognostic Factor in Advanced Ovarian Cancer,* 59 Cancer 317 (1987).

[25] Wersto et al., *Variability in DNA Measurements in Multiple Tumor Samples of Human Colon Carcinoma,* 67 Cancer 106 (1991).

[26] Thorud et al., *Primary Breast Cancer: Flow Cytometric DNA Pattern in Relation to Clinical and Histopathologic Characteristics,* 57 Cancer 808 (1986).

[27] Volm et al., *Five Year Follow-up Study of Independent Clinical and Flow Cytometric Prognostic Factors for the Survival of Patients with Non-small Cell Lung Carcinoma,* 48 Cancer Res. 2923 (1988).

[28] Joensuu & Klemi, *Comparison of Nuclear DNA Content in Primary and Metastatic Differentiated Thyroid Carcinoma,* 89 Am. J. Clinical Pathology 35 (1988); McLeod, *The Measurement*

S-phase indicates the rapidity of cellular division. High S-phase occurs in more rapidly growing tumors and is a poor prognostic factor.

Other Tumor Markers

Other tumor markers related to prognosis are:

HER 2 Neu (C-Erb B-2):[32] breast

Ki-67:[33] gastric lymphoma

Collagen IV:[34] colorectal cancer

Epidermal Growth Factor (EGF):[35] squamous cell carcinoma

CA 125:[36] ovary cancer, lung cancer

Lipid-bound Sialic Acid (LASA):[37] lung cancer, leukemia, breast cancer, head and neck cancer

Urinary Gonadotropin Peptide (UGP): ovary cancer

N-myc:[38] neuroectodermal tumors

---

of DNA Content and Ploidy Analysis in Thyroid Neoplasms, 23 Otolaryngology Clinics N. Am. No. 2, at 271 (1990).

[29] Sugimachi et al., *Comparative Data on Cytophotometric DNA in Malignant Lesions of the Esophagus in the Chinese and Japanese,* 59 Cancer 1947 (1987).

[30] Czerniak et al., *DNA Distribution Patterns in Early Gastric Carcinomas,* 59 Cancer 113 (1987).

[31] Xiang et al., *Flow Cytometric Analysis of DNA in Bone and Soft-Tissue Tumors Using Nuclear Suspensions,* 59 Cancer 1951 (1987).

[32] Slamon et al., *Human Breast Cancer: Correlation of Relapse and Survival with Amplification of the HER-2/Neu Oncogene,* 235 Sci. 177 (1987); Tandon et al., *HER-2/Neu Oncogene Protein and Prognosis in Breast Cancer,* 7 J. Clinical Oncology 1120 (1989).

[33] Villar et al., *Immunophenotyping in the Management of Gastric Lymphoma,* 161 Am. J. Surg. 171 (1991).

[34] Offerhaus et al., *The Value of Immunohistochemistry for Collagen IV Expression in Colorectal Carcinomas,* 67 Cancer 94 (1991).

[35] Yano et al., *Immunohistologic Detection of the Epidermal Growth Factor Receptor in Human Esophageal Squamous Cell Carcinoma,* 67 Cancer 91 (1991).

[36] Diez et al., *Evaluation of Serum CA 125 as a Tumor Marker in Non-small Cell Lung Cancer,* 67 Cancer 150 (1991); Onetto et al., *Evaluation of the Ovarian Cancer Antigen, CA 125 as a Tumor Marker,* 46 Oncology 117 (1989).

[37] Lyston et al., *Glycoproteins and Human Cancer: I. Circulating Levels and Disease Status,* 43 Cancer 1766 (1979); Patel, *Serum Glycoconjugates in Patients with Anemia and Myeloid Leukemia,* 74 Tumori 639 (1988); Patel et al., *Significance of Serum Sialoglycoproteins in Patients with Lung Cancer,* 36 Neoplasms 53 (1989).

[38] Rouah et al., *N-myc Amplification and Neuronal Differentiation in Human Primitive Neuroectodermal Tumors of the Central Nervous System,* 49 Cancer Res. 1797 (1989).

Cathepsin D:[39] breast cancer

Cathepsin B:[40] breast cancer, gynecologic tumors

CA 549:[41] breast cancer

CA 15-3:[42] breast cancer

§ 2.4   Immunologic Treatment of Cancer

Immunology is the production of antibodies in response to antigenic challenge. The immunoglobulin molecule (antibody) has a specific amino acid sequence that interacts only with and destroys the antigen that induced its synthesis or an antigen closely related to it. Subpopulations of tumor cells may express a mutated form of the antigen or lack the surface antigen altogether (termed *heterogeneity*) and are unreactive to antigen. Antibody reactivity may be lost because of mutations of cells causing inability to translate the target protein gene and to transcribe message, glycosylate, or expression of the cell surface cytoplasmic protein or because of antibody-mediated reversible loss of surface antigen or modulation.

Immunologic Therapies[43]

I.   Active Immunotherapy
  A.   Specific
    1.   Inactivated Tumor Vaccines
    2.   Humor Tumor Hybrids
    3.   Monoclonal Tumor Antibodies
  B.   Nonspecific
    1.   Chemical Immunostimulants: Levamisole hydrochloride, Picabanyl, Cimetidine
    2.   Biologic Immunostimulants: Bacille Calmette-Guérin (BCG), Methanol Extracted Residue of BCG (MER), Cyclophosphamide, C. Parvum, OK 432

---

[39] Tandon et al., *Cathepsin D and Prognosis in Breast Cancer,* 322 New Eng. J. Med. 297 (1990).

[40] Krepela et al., *Cathepsin B in Human Breast Tumor Tissue and Cancer Cells,* 36 Neoplasms 41 (1989); Tandon et al., *Cathepsin D and Prognosis in Breast Cancer,* 322 New Eng. J. Med. 297 (1990).

[41] Beveridge et al., *A New Biomarker in Monitoring Breast Cancer: CA 549,* 6 J. Clinical Oncology 1815 (1988).

[42] Hayes et al., *Comparison of Circulating CA 15-3 and Carcinoembryonic Antigen Levels in Patients with Breast Cancer,* 4 J. Clinical Oncology 1542 (1986).

[43] Lotze & Rosenberg, *The Immunologic Treatment of Cancer,* 38 Ca-A Cancer J. for Clinicians 69 (1988).

   3. Cytokines: Interferon, Interleukin-2 (IL-2), Tumor Necrosis Factor (TNF)

   4. Chemotherapy: Cyclophosphamide, Melphalan, Cisplatin, Doxorubicin hydrochloride, Vinca Alkaloids

II. Passive Immunotherapy

   A. Specific

      1. Heterologous Antiserum

      2. Monoclonal Antibodies

      3. T lymphocytes

      4. Monoclonal Lymphocytes

      5. Allogenic Bone Marrow Transplants

   B. Nonspecific

      1. Lymphokine-Activated Killer Cells (LAK)

      2. Activated Macrophages: Interferon, Phorbol Esters

      3. Cytostatic or Cytotoxic Cytokines: Interferon, Tumor Necrosis Factor

Bacille Calmette-Guérin (BCG)

BCG has been used, with some success, as intralesional therapy[44] or adjuvant immunotherapy for regional lymph node metastases[45] in melanoma. Prolonged survival or disease-free survival has not been proved.

Interferon

There are three types of interferon, which include *alpha* (derived from leukocytes), *beta* (derived from fibroblasts), and *gamma* (immume-lymphocyte-derived). Some effectiveness of alpha interferon has been shown in epidemic Kaposi's sarcoma,[46] chronic myelogenous leukemia,[47] hairy cell leukemia,[48]

---

[44] Rosenberg & Rapp, *Intralesional Immunotherapy of Melanoma with BCG,* 60 Med. Clinics N. Am. 419 (1976).

[45] Eiber et al., *Adjuvant Immunotherapy with BCG in Treatment of Regional-Lymph-Node Metastases from Malignant Melanoma,* 294 New Eng. J. Med. 237 (1976).

[46] Volberding & Mitsuyasu, *Recombinant Interferon Alpha in the Treatment of Acquired Immune Deficiency Syndrome-Related Kaposi's Sarcoma,* 12 Seminars in Oncology 2 (1985).

[47] Bergsagel et al., *Interferon Alfa-2b in the Treatment of Chronic Granulocytic Leukemia,* 13 Seminars in Oncology 29 (1986); Talpaz et al., *Leukocyte Interferon-Induced Myeloid Cytoreduction in Chronic Myelogenous Leukemia,* 62 Blood 689 (1983).

[48] Groopman, *Therapeutic Options in Hairy-Cell Leukemia,* 12 Seminars in Oncology 30 (1985); Quesada et al., *Alpha Interferon for Induction of Remission in Hairy-Cell Leukemia,* 310 New Eng. J. Med. 15 (1984).

non-Hodgkin's lymphoma,[49] cutaneous T-cell lymphoma,[50] melanoma,[51] multiple myeloma,[52] and renal cell carcinoma.[53] Gamma interferon decreases cellular proliferation, enhances cell surface major histocompatibility (MHC) expression and may have a synergistic effect with lymphokine, tumor necrosis factor (TNF), or cachectin. Cancers that may be affected by gamma interferon include melanoma, hepatoma, other solid tumors, and hematologic malignancies.

Interleukin

Interleukin-2 (IL-2) causes lymphoid proliferation and reversal of immune deficiency, and activates lymphokine-activated killer (LAK) cells and cytolytic T cells. IL-2 enhances the immune effects of LAK or specific antitumor T cells. Therapeutic responses have been reported in patients with melanoma and renal cell carcinoma.[54]

The toxicity of high dose IL-2 consists of fever, nausea, vomiting, diarrhea, anemia, and marked cutaneous erythema. Fluid retention may cause weight gain, and there may be hepatic and renal dysfunction.

Monoclonal Antibodies

Monoclonal antibodies are specific and have well-characterized binding specificity, avidity, and isotype. The potential mechanisms for immune destruction of tumor cells by antibodies include activation of complement through opsinization or through antibody-dependant cellular cytotoxicity. Clinical improvement has

---

[49] Canellos, *Interferon in the Treatment of Malignant Lymphoma*, 12 Seminars in Oncology 25 (1985); Foon et al., *Alpha Interferon Treatment of Low-Grade B-cell Non-Hodgkin's Lymphomas, Cutaneous T-cell Lymphomas, and Chronic Lymphocytic Leukemia*, 13 Seminars in Oncology 35 (1986).

[50] Bunn, Jr., & Foon, *Therapeutic Options in Advanced Cutaneous T-cell Lymphomas: A Role for Interferon Alpha-2a (Roferon-A)*, 12 Seminars in Oncology 18 (1985).

[51] Kirkwood & Ernstoff, *Potential Applications of the Interferons in Oncology: Lessons Drawn from Studies of Human Melanoma*, 13 Seminars in Oncology 48 (1986).

[52] Cooper & Welander, *Interferons in the Treatment of Multiple Myeloma*, 13 Seminars in Oncology 334 (1986).

[53] Krown, *Therapeutic Options in Renal-Cell Carcinoma*, 12 Seminars in Oncology 13 (1985); Quesada et al., *Renal-Cell Carcinoma: Antitumor Effects of Leukocyte Interferon*, 43 Cancer Res. 940 (1983).

[54] Lotze et al., *High-Dose Recombinant Interleukin-2 in the Treatment of Patients with Disseminated Cancer: Responses, Treatment-Related Morbidity, and Histologic Findings*, 256 JAMA 3117 (1986); Rosenberg et al., *A Progress Report on the Treatment of 157 Patients with Advanced Cancer Using Lymphokine-Activated Killer Cells and Interleukin-2 or High Dose Interleukin-2 Alone*, 316 New Eng. J. Med. 889 (1987).

been noted in B-cell[55] and T-cell[56] lymphomas, melanoma,[57] neuroblastoma,[58] gastrointestinal[59] and pancreatic[60] malignancies, acute lymphoblastic leukemia,[61] chronic lymphocytic leukemia,[62] and acute myelogenous leukemia.[63]

Intravenous monoclonal antibody infusions may be associated with symptoms of toxicity consisting of chills, fever, nausea, vomiting, urticaria, wheezing, dyspnea, and hypotension.

§ 2.5   Staging

The extent of cancer at a particular point in time is called *staging*. The purpose of staging is to define the tumor so that comparisons can be made in terms of prognosis and treatment. The apparently arbitrary groupings allow better definition of the patient's outlook, usually in terms of five-year survival. Comparisons can then be made as to the results of various treatment modalities. The staging of cancer facilitates exchange of information between physicians.

The stage of a cancer is determined when it is first diagnosed and worked up. This process is called *clinical staging*. When the tumor has been surgically treated and the extent of the malignancy determined microscopically, it is called *pathologic staging*. The pathology examination is more accurate than the clinical stage.

---

[55] Miller et al., *Treatment of B-cell Lymphoma with Monoclonal Anti-Idotype Antibody,* 306 New Eng. J. Med. 517 (1982).

[56] Miller & Levy, *Response of Cutaneous T-cell Lymphoma to Therapy with Hybridoma Monoclonal Antibody,* 2 Lancet 226 (1981).

[57] Goodman et al., *Pilot Trial of Murine Monoclonal Antibodies in Patients with Advanced Melanoma,* 3 J. Clinical Oncology 340 (1985); Irie & Morton, *Regression of Cutaneous Metastatic Melanoma by Intralesional Injection with Human Monoclonal Antibody to Ganglioside GD2,* 83 Proc. Nat'l Acad. Sci. 8694 (1986); Spitler et al., *Therapy of Patients with Malignant Melanoma Using a Monoclonal Antimelanoma Antibody-ricin A Chain Immunotoxin,* 47 Cancer Res. 1717 (1987).

[58] Cheung et al., *Ganglioside GD2 Specific Monoclonal Antibody 3F8: A Phase I Study in Patients with Neuroblastoma and Malignant Melanoma,* 5 J. Clinical Oncology 1430 (1987).

[59] Sears et al., *Effects of Monoclonal Antibody Immunotherapy on Patients with Gastrointestinal Adenocarcinoma,* 3 J. Biologic Response Modification 138 (1984).

[60] Sindelar et al., *Trial of Therapy with Monoclonal Antibody 17-1A in Pancreatic Carcinoma: Preliminary Results,* 5 Hybridoma S125 (1986).

[61] Ritz et al., *Serotherapy of Acute Lymphoblastic Leukemia with Monoclonal Antibody,* 58 Blood 141 (1981).

[62] Dillman et al., *Toxicity and Efficacy of 24 Hour Infusions of T101 Monoclonal Antibody in Chronic Lymphocytic Leukemia and Cutaneous T cell Lymphoma,* 4 Proc. Am. Soc'y Clinical Oncologists 230 (1985); Foon et al., *Effects of Monoclonal Antibody Therapy in Patients with Chronic Lymphocytic Leukemia,* 64 Blood 1085 (1984).

[63] Ball et al., *Monoclonal Antibodies to Myeloid Differentiation Antigens: In Vivo Studies of Three Patients with Acute Myelogenous Leukemia,* 62 Blood 1203 (1983).

§ 2.6 — TNM System

The division into tumor size, regional nodal involvement, and presence of metastasis is termed *TNM staging*. When a tumor spreads to regional nodes, the prognosis ordinarily is worse than when there is no nodal involvement. In the presence of metastases, the longevity is reduced and most tumors can no longer be cured.

To standardize the staging process, the American Joint Committee on Cancer (AJCC) was formed and published the groupings to be used.[64] In certain specific cancers, other more accurate methods than TNM staging are available. Melanoma is best identified by the depth of invasion using Breslow's measurements of depth and Clark's levels. In cancer of the colon and rectum, Duke's as well as Astler and Coller's staging are available.

§ 2.7   Doubling Time

The length of time it takes for a malignant tumor to double its number of cells is useful in estimating the duration of the disease prior to diagnosis and in understanding the clinical course of the disease. The concepts of chemotherapy are based on tumor cell kinetics and doubling time.[65] The relationship of early exponential growth of a tumor and later linear growth is expressed in the Gompertzian curve, shown in **Figure 2–1**.[66]

The factors involved in slowing the growth rate of a tumor as it increases in size include:

1. Diminished blood supply to the central portion of the tumor
2. Necrosis of the central portion of the tumor from loss of blood supply
3. Increased number of cells in a resting state (rather than in a dividing mode)
4. Compression from surrounding tissues.

As the tumor increases in size (over approximately 0.5 cm in diameter), it enters an almost linear growth pattern. Any objective tumor measurements at two different times allow an estimate of tumor doubling time. From this information, the size of the neoplasm can be determined at any point in time in the linear phase.

---

[64] American Joint Committee on Cancer, Manual for Staging of Cancer (3d ed. 1988).

[65] C.M. Haskell, Cancer Treatment 33–34 (2d ed. 1985).

[66] R.B. Livingston, *Tumor Cell Biology and Kinetics, in* Surgical Oncology 108–14 (Y.H. Pilch ed., 1984).

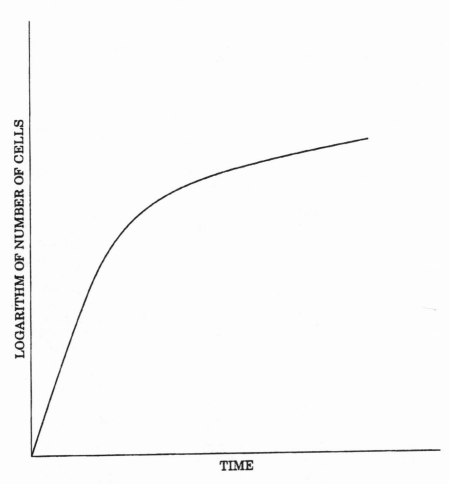

Figure 2–1. Gompertzian curve.

Using the standard of one billion cells in one centimeter diameter of mass of malignancy, tables of tumor size versus number of tumor cells can be formulated. The volume of a sphere is $4/3\pi r^3$ while the volume of an ovoid or cylindrical mass is $4/3\pi a^2 b$, $4/3\pi ab^2$, or $4/3\pi abc$, as shown in **Tables 2–1** and **2–2.**

An expert witness, knowledgeable in doubling times, can provide valuable data concerning tumor size at various intervals of time. The mass in relationship to the TNM categories can also furnish information to estimate survival statistics at different times of the malignancy growth.

Table 2–1

Relationship of Spherical Tumor Diameter to Volume $(4/3\pi r^3)$
and Number of Cells

Diameter (cm)	Radius (cm)	Volume (cc)	Number of Cells
0.0	0.00	0.000	0
0.1	0.05	0.001	1,000,000
0.2	0.10	0.004	8,000,000
0.3	0.15	0.014	27,000,000
0.4	0.20	0.034	64,000,000
0.5	0.25	0.065	125,000,000
0.6	0.30	0.113	216,000,000
0.7	0.35	0.180	343,000,000
0.8	0.40	0.268	512,000,000
0.9	0.45	0.382	729,000,000
1.0	0.50	0.524	1,000,000,000
1.1	0.55	0.697	1,331,000,000
1.2	0.60	0.905	1,728,000,000
1.3	0.65	1.150	2,197,000,000
1.4	0.70	1.437	2,744,000,000
1.5	0.75	1.767	3,375,000,000
1.6	0.80	2.145	4,096,000,000
1.7	0.85	2.572	4,913,000,000
1.8	0.90	3.054	5,832,000,000
1.9	0.95	3.591	6,859,000,000
2.0	1.00	4.189	8,000,000,000
2.1	1.05	4.849	9,261,000,000
2.2	1.10	5.575	10,648,000,000
2.3	1.15	6.371	12,167,000,000
2.4	1.20	7.238	13,824,000,000
2.5	1.25	8.181	15,625,000,000
2.6	1.30	9.203	17,576,000,000
2.7	1.35	10.306	19,683,000,000
2.8	1.40	11.494	21,952,000,000
2.9	1.45	12.770	24,389,000,000
3.0	1.50	14.137	27,000,000,000
3.1	1.55	15.599	29,791,000,000
3.2	1.60	17.157	32,768,000,000
3.3	1.65	18.817	35,937,000,000
3.4	1.70	20.580	39,304,000,000
3.5	1.75	22.449	42,875,000,000
3.6	1.80	24.429	46,656,000,000
3.7	1.85	26.522	50,653,000,000
3.8	1.90	28.731	54,872,000,000
3.9	1.95	31.059	59,319,000,000
4.0	2.00	33.510	64,000,000,000
4.1	2.05	36.087	68,921,000,000
4.2	2.10	38.792	74,088,000,000
4.3	2.15	41.630	79,507,000,000
4.4	2.20	44.602	85,184,000,000

Table 2–1 *(continued)*

Diameter (cm)	Radius (cm)	Volume (cc)	Number of Cells
4.5	2.25	47.713	91,125,000,000
4.6	2.30	50.965	97,336,000,000
4.7	2.35	54.362	103,823,000,000
4.8	2.40	57.906	110,592,000,000
4.9	2.45	61.601	117,649,000,000
5.0	2.50	65.450	125,000,000,000
5.1	2.55	69.456	132,651,000,000
5.2	2.60	73.622	140,608,000,000
5.3	2.65	77.952	148,877,000,000
5.4	2.70	82.448	157,464,000,000
5.5	2.75	87.114	166,375,000,000
5.6	2.80	91.953	175,616,000,000
5.7	2.85	96.967	185,193,000,000
5.8	2.90	102.161	195,112,000,000
5.9	2.95	107.536	205,379,000,000
6.0	3.00	113.098	216,000,000,000
6.1	3.05	118.847	226,981,000,000
6.2	3.10	124.789	238,328,000,000
6.3	3.15	130.925	250,047,000,000
6.4	3.20	137.259	262,144,000,000
6.5	3.25	143.794	274,625,000,000
6.6	3.30	150.533	287,496,000,000
6.7	3.35	157.480	300,763,000,000
6.8	3.40	164.637	314,432,000,000
6.9	3.45	172.007	328,509,000,000
7.0	3.50	179.595	343,000,000,000
7.1	3.55	187.402	357,911,000,000
7.2	3.60	195.433	373,248,000,000
7.3	3.65	203.689	389,017,000,000
7.4	3.70	212.175	405,224,000,000
7.5	3.75	220.894	421,875,000,000
7.6	3.80	229.848	438,976,000,000
7.7	3.85	239.041	456,533,000,000
7.8	3.90	248.475	474,552,000,000
7.9	3.95	258.155	493,039,000,000
8.0	4.00	268.083	512,000,000,000
8.1	4.05	278.263	531,441,000,000
8.2	4.10	288.696	551,368,000,000
8.3	4.15	299.388	571,787,000,000
8.4	4.20	310.340	592,704,000,000
8.5	4.25	321.556	614,125,000,000
8.6	4.30	333.039	636,056,000,000
8.7	4.35	344.792	658,503,000,000
8.8	4.40	356.819	681,472,000,000
8.9	4.45	369.122	704,969,000,000
9.0	4.50	381.704	729,000,000,000
9.1	4.55	394.570	753,571,000,000
9.2	4.60	407.721	778,688,000,000
9.3	4.65	421.161	804,357,000,000

Table 2–1 *(continued)*

Diameter (cm)	Radius (cm)	Volume (cc)	Number of Cells
9.4	4.70	434.894	830,584,000,000
9.5	4.75	448.922	857,375,000,000
9.6	4.80	463.248	884,736,000,000
9.7	4.85	477.876	912,673,000,000
9.8	4.90	492.808	941,192,000,000
9.9	4.95	508.049	970,299,000,000
10.0	5.00	523.600	1,000,000,000,000
10.1	5.05	539.466	1,030,301,000,000
10.2	5.10	555.649	1,061,208,000,000
10.3	5.15	572.152	1,092,727,000,000
10.4	5.20	588.979	1,124,864,000,000
10.5	5.25	606.132	1,157,625,000,000
10.6	5.30	623.616	1,191,016,000,000
10.7	5.35	641.433	1,225,043,000,000
10.8	5.40	659.585	1,259,712,000,000
10.9	5.45	678.077	1,295,029,000,000
11.0	5.50	696.912	1,331,000,000,000
11.1	5.55	716.092	1,367,631,000,000
11.2	5.60	735.620	1,404,928,000,000
11.3	5.65	755.501	1,442,897,000,000
11.4	5.70	775.736	1,481,544,000,000
11.5	5.75	796.330	1,520,875,000,000
11.6	5.80	817.285	1,560,896,000,000
11.7	5.85	838.605	1,601,613,000,000
11.8	5.90	860.292	1,643,032,000,000
11.9	5.95	882.349	1,685,159,000,000
12.0	6.00	904.781	1,728,000,000,000
12.1	6.05	927.589	1,771,561,000,000
12.2	6.10	950.778	1,815,848,000,000
12.3	6.15	974.350	1,860,867,000,000
12.4	6.20	998.308	1,906,624,000,000
12.5	6.25	1022.656	1,953,125,000,000
12.6	6.30	1047.397	2,000,376,000,000
12.7	6.35	1072.533	2,048,383,000,000
12.8	6.40	1098.069	2,097,152,000,000
12.9	6.45	1124.006	2,146,689,000,000
13.0	6.50	1150.349	2,197,000,000,000
13.1	6.55	1177.100	2,248,091,000,000
13.2	6.60	1204.263	2,299,968,000,000
13.3	6.65	1231.841	2,352,637,000,000
13.4	6.70	1259.836	2,406,104,000,000
13.5	6.75	1288.252	2,460,375,000,000
13.6	6.80	1317.093	2,515,456,000,000
13.7	6.85	1346.360	2,571,353,000,000
13.8	6.90	1376.058	2,628,072,000,000
13.9	6.95	1406.190	2,685,619,000,000
14.0	7.00	1436.758	2,744,000,000,000
14.1	7.05	1467.767	2,803,221,000,000
14.2	7.10	1499.218	2,863,288,000,000

Table 2–1 *(continued)*

Diameter (cm)	Radius (cm)	Volume (cc)	Number of Cells
14.3	7.15	1531.115	2,924,207,000,000
14.4	7.20	1563.461	2,985,984,000,000
14.5	7.25	1596.260	3,048,625,000,000
14.6	7.30	1629.514	3,112,136,000,000
14.7	7.35	1663.227	3,176,523,000,000
14.8	7.40	1697.402	3,241,792,000,000
14.9	7.45	1732.042	3,307,949,000,000
15.0	7.50	1767.150	3,375,000,000,000
15.1	7.55	1802.729	3,442,951,000,000
15.2	7.60	1838.783	3,511,808,000,000
15.3	7.65	1875.314	3,581,577,000,000
15.4	7.70	1912.325	3,652,264,000,000
15.5	7.75	1949.821	3,723,875,000,000
15.6	7.80	1987.803	3,796,416,000,000
15.7	7.85	2026.276	3,869,893,000,000
15.8	7.90	2065.242	3,944,312,000,000
15.9	7.95	2104.704	4,019,679,000,000
16.0	8.00	2144.666	4,096,000,000,000
16.1	8.05	2185.130	4,173,281,000,000
16.2	8.10	2226.100	4,251,528,000,000
16.3	8.15	2267.579	4,330,747,000,000
16.4	8.20	2309.570	4,410,944,000,000
16.5	8.25	2352.077	4,492,125,000,000
16.6	8.30	2395.101	4,574,296,000,000
16.7	8.35	2438.648	4,657,463,000,000
16.8	8.40	2482.719	4,741,632,000,000
16.9	8.45	2527.317	4,826,809,000,000
17.0	8.50	2572.447	4,913,000,000,000
17.1	8.55	2618.110	5,000,211,000,000
17.2	8.60	2664.311	5,088,448,000,000
17.3	8.65	2711.053	5,177,717,000,000
17.4	8.70	2758.337	5,268,024,000,000
17.5	8.75	2806.169	5,359,375,000,000
17.6	8.80	2854.550	5,451,776,000,000
17.7	8.85	2903.484	5,545,233,000,000
17.8	8.90	2952.974	5,639,752,000,000
17.9	8.95	3003.024	5,735,339,000,000
18.0	9.00	3053.635	5,832,000,000,000
18.1	9.05	3104.812	5,929,741,000,000
18.2	9.10	3156.558	6,028,568,000,000
18.3	9.15	3208.876	6,128,487,000,000
18.4	9.20	3261.768	6,229,504,000,000
18.5	9.25	3315.239	6,331,625,000,000
18.6	9.30	3369.291	6,434,856,000,000
18.7	9.35	3423.927	6,539,203,000,000
18.8	9.40	3479.150	6,644,672,000,000
18.9	9.45	3534.964	6,751,269,000,000
19.0	9.50	3591.372	6,859,000,000,000

Table 2–1 *(continued)*

Diameter (cm)	Radius (cm)	Volume (cc)	Number of Cells
19.1	9.55	3648.377	6,967,871,000,000
19.2	9.60	3705.982	7,077,888,000,000
19.3	9.65	3764.190	7,189,057,000,000
19.4	9.70	3823.005	7,301,384,000,000
19.5	9.75	3882.429	7,414,875,000,000
19.6	9.80	3942.465	7,529,536,000,000
19.7	9.85	4003.117	7,645,373,000,000
19.8	9.90	4064.388	7,762,392,000,000
19.9	9.95	4126.282	7,880,599,000,000
20.0	10.00	4188.800	8,000,000,000,000

Table 2–2

Number of Cells in Each Tumor Doubling

Doublings	No. of Cells	Doublings	Number of Cells
0	1	25	33554432
1	2	26	67108864
2	4	27	134217728
3	8	28	268435456
4	16	29	536870912
5	32	30	1073741824
6	64	31	2147483648
7	128	32	4294967296
8	256	33	8589934592
9	512	34	17179869184
10	1024	35	34359738368
11	2048	36	68719476736
12	4096	37	137438953472
13	8192	38	274877906944
14	16384	39	549755813888
15	32768	40	1099511627776
16	65536	41	2199023255552
17	131072	42	4398046511104
18	262144	43	8796093022208
19	524288	44	17592186044416
20	1048576	45	35184372088832
21	2097152	46	70368744177664
22	4194304	47	140737488355328
23	8388608	48	281474976710656
24	16777216		

§ 2.8   Cytogenetics of Neoplasms

Benign and malignant neoplasms are a result of chromosomal abnormalities, some of which have only recently been identified. Genetic manipulation may play a part in future cancer treatment.

§ 2.9   —Chromosomal Abnormalities

Banding techniques have been established to identify individual chromosomes and subchromosomal structure and changes.[67] Consistent chromosomal abnormalities have been identified in various malignant diseases. Genes or gene products are responsible for the regulation of growth and differentiation of cells. There appears to be a relationship between chromosomal abnormality and the induction of neoplasms from uncontrolled growth of specific cells.

There is a hypothesis for the origin of childhood cancer that requires that two mutations occur.[68] In the hereditary form, patients who inherit one mutation as a germinal (*prezygotic*) event need only one additional mutation to induce malignancy. The nonhereditary form results from two somatic (*postzygotic*) mutations in a single cell with a tumor-specific gene resulting from the first somatic mutation.

Each neoplasia may be associated with a primary chromosomal change. Secondary changes may have a profound influence on the biologic behavior and clinical course of the tumor.

Chromosomal Abnormalities

Cancer is the result of chromosomal abnormalities. Some of the chromosome changes include:

Bladder Cancer

Translocation chromosome 18 to chromosome 15

Deletion chromosome 8p

Isochromosome: i (16q)

Isochromosome: i (5p)

---

[67] Caspersson et al., *Differential Banding of Alkylating Fluorochromes in Human Chromosomes,* 60 Experimental Cell Res. 315 (1970); Pardue & Gall, *Chromosomal Localization of Mouse Satellite DNA,* 168 Science 1356 (1970); Yunis, *Comparative Analysis of High-Resolution Chromosome Techniques for Leukemic Bone Marrows,* 7 Cancer Genetics & Cytogenetics 43 (1982).

[68] Knudson, Jr., *The Genetics of Childhood Cancer,* 35 Cancer 1022 (1975); Knudson & Meadows, *Developmental Genetics of Neuroblastoma,* 57 J. Nat'l Cancer Inst. 675 (1976).

Deletion chromosome 9q

Deletion chromosome 11p

Addition chromosome 7

Breast Cancer

Addition chromosome 1q (trisomy)[69]

Cervical Cancer

Trisomy chromosome 1q[70]

Deletion chromosome 5q

Deletion chromosome 11q

Colon Cancer

Deletion chromosome 12q

Addition chromosome 7

Addition chromosome 8

Addition chromosome 12

Deletion chromosome 17p (p53 gene)

Deletion chromosome 18g (DCC gene)

Deletion chromosome 5q21 (familial adenomatous polyposis, Gardner's syndrome)

Deletion chromosome 2p15-16 (hereditary nonpolyposis colorectal cancer)

Kidney Cancer

Deletion chromosome 3: del (3) (p21)

Leukemia

Chromosome 1[71]

Chronic Myelocytic Leukemia (CML)

Ph (Philadelphia chromosome) translocation from chromosome 22 to chromosome 9 [t(9;22) (q34;q11)][72]

---

[69] Cruciger et al., *Human Breast Carcinomas: Marker Chromosome Involving 1q in Seven Cases,* 17 Cytogenetics & Cell Genetics 231 (1976); Kovacs, *Abnormalities of Chromosome No. 1 in Human Solid Malignant Tumors,* 21 Int'l J. Cancer 688 (1978).

[70] Atkin & Baker, *Chromosome 1 in 26 Carcinomas of the Cervix Uteri. Structural and Numerical Changes,* 44 Cancer 604 (1979); Sandberg, *Solid Tumors and Metastatic Cancer, in* The Chromosomes in Human Cancer and Leukemia 458–565 (1980).

[71] Morse et al., *Chromosome 1 Abnormalities in Relapse and Terminal Stages in Childhood Leukemia,* 7 Med. Pediatric Oncology 9 (1979).

[72] A.A. Sandberg, The Chromosomes in Human Cancer and Leukemia (1980).

Isochromosome for long arm of chromosome 17:i(17q)[73]

Deletion chromosome 22q

Chronic Lymphocytic Leukemia: B-cell (CLL)

Translocation chromosome [t(6;12) (q15;p13)][74]

Acute Nonlymphocytic Leukemia (ANLL)

Acute Myeloblastic Leukemia

Translocation chromosome [t(8;21) (q22;q22)][75]

Deletion chromosome 5q

Deletion chromosome 7q

Acute Monocytic Leukemia

Deletion chromosome 11q

Acute Promyelocytic Leukemia (APL)

Translocation chromosome [t(15;17) (q24;q21)][76]

Acute Myelomonocytic Leukemia

Deletion chromosome 11q

Acute Monoblastic Leukemia (AMoL)

Translocation chromosome [t(9;11) (p21;q23)][77]

Acute Lymphoblastic Leukemia (ALL)

Translocation chromosome [t(4;11) (q21;q23)]

Translocation chromosome 22 (Philadelphia chromosome) to chromosome 9 [t(9;22) (q34;q11)]

Translocation chromosome [t(8;14) (q23;q32)]

Deletion chromosome 6q

---

[73] Sadamori et al., *Therapeutic and Prognostic Value of Initial Chromosomal Findings at the Blastic Phase of Ph-Positive Chronic Myeloid Leukemia*, 61 Blood 935 (1983).

[74] Salamori et al., *Possible Specific Chromosome Change in Prolymphocytic Leukemia*, 62 Blood 729 (1983).

[75] Rowley, *Identification of a Translocation with Quinacrine Fluorescence in a Patient with Acute Leukemia*, 16 Annals Genetics 109 (1973); Sakurai et al., *8-21 Translocation and Missing Sex Chromosomes in Acute Leukaemia*, 2 Lancet 227 (1974); Trujillo et al., *Clinical Implications of Aneuploid Cytogenetic Profiles in Adult Acute Leukemia*, 33 Cancer 824 (1974).

[76] Testa et al., *Hypergranular Promyelocytic Leukemia (APL): Cytogenetic and Ultrastructural Specificity*, 52 Blood 272 (1978).

[77] Hagemeijer et al., *Translocation (9;11) (p21;q23) in Three Cases of Acute Myeloblastic Leukemia*, 5 Cancer Genetics & Cytogenetics 95 (1982).

Deletion chromosome 9p (T-cell variety)

Addition chromosome 14q

Addition chromosome 21

Lymphoma

Translocation chromosome [t(8;14) (q23;q32)]

Deletion chromosome 6q

Burkitt's Lymphoma

Translocation chromosome[78] [t(8;14)(q23;q32)] or to chromosome 2 [t(8;2) (q23;q12)] or to chromosome 22 [t(8;22)(q23;q11)]

Lung Cancer

Deletion chromosome 3p (p14–p23)

Melanoma

Chromosome 1 (deletion 1p)[79]

Isochromosome: i(6p)

Deletion chromosome 6: del (6) (q11;q27)

Meningioma

Chromosome 1p

Chromosome 22 (deletion 22q)[80]

Nephroblastoma

Chromosome 11p (deletion of short arm)[81]

Neuroblastoma

Chromosome 1 (short arm deletion p32-1 pter)[82]

---

[78] Abe et al., *North American Burkitt-type ALL with a Variant Translocation t(8;22)*, 7 Cancer Genetics & Cytogenetics 185 (1982).

[79] Kakati et al., *Chromosomes and Causation of Human Cancer and Leukemia. XIX. Common Markers in Various Tumors*, 40 Cancer 1173 (1977); McCulloch et al., *Common and Individually Specific Chromosomal Characteristics of Cultured Human Melanoma*, 36 Cancer Res. 398 (1978).

[80] A.A. Sandberg, *Solid Tumors and Metastatic Cancer*, *in* The Chromosomes in Human Cancer and Leukemia 458–565 (1980).

[81] Riccardi et al., *Chromosome Imbalance in the Aniridia-Wilms Tumor Association: 11p Interstitial Deletion*, 61 Pediatrics 604 (1978).

[82] Brodeur et al., *Chromosomal Aberrations in Human Neuroblastomas*, 40 Cancer 2256 (1977); Hayashi et al., *Cytogenetic Findings and Prognosis in Neuroblastoma with Emphasis on Marker Chromosome 1*, 63 Cancer 126 (1989).

DM (Double Minute Chromosomes)[83]

HSR (Homogeneously Staining Region)[84]

Chromosome 17[85]

Ovarian Cancer

Serous Cystadenocarcinoma

Translocation chromosome [t(6;14)(q21;24)]

Trisomy chromosome 1q[86]

Parotid Gland Cancer

Addition chromosome 14b

Translocation chromosome [t(3;8)(p25;q21)]

Translocation chromosome [t(9;12)(p13-22;q13-15)]

Polycythemia Vera

Deletion chromosome 20q

Prostate Cancer

Deletion chromosome 10: del (10) (q24)

Retinoblastoma

Chromosome 13 (deletion of long arm)[87]

Sarcoma

Ewing's sarcoma

Translocation chromosome [t(11;22)(q24;q12)]

Liposarcoma

Translocation chromosome [t(12;16)(q13;q11)]

---

[83] Balaban-Malenbaum & Gilbert, *Double Minute Chromosomes and the Homogeneously Staining Regions in Chromosomes of a Human Neuroblastoma Cell Line,* 198 Science 739 (1977).

[84] Balaban-Malenbaum & Gilbert, *The Proposed Origin of Double Minutes from Homogeneously Staining Region (HSR)-Marker Chromosomes in Human Neuroblastoma Hybrid Cell Lines,* 2 Cancer Genetics & Cytogenetics 339 (1980).

[85] Gilbert et al., *Human Neuroblastoma and Abnormalities of Chromosome 1 and 17,* 44 Cancer Res. 5444 (1984).

[86] Atkin & Pickhtall, *Chromosome 1 in 14 Ovarian Cancers. Heterochromatin Variants and Structural Changes,* 38 Hum. Genetics 25 (1977); Vander Riet-Fox et al., *Chromosome Changes in 17 Human Neoplasms Studied with Banding,* 44 Cancer 2108 (1979).

[87] Knudson et al., *Chromosomal Deletion and Retinoblastoma,* 295 New Eng. J. Med. 1120 (1976); Yunis & Ramsay, *Retinoblastoma and Subband Deletion of Chromosome 13,* 132 Am. J. Diseases Childhood 161 (1978).

Rhabdomyosarcoma

   Translocation chromosome [t(2;13)(q37;q14)]

Synovial sarcoma

   Translocation chromosome [t(x;18)(p11.2;q11.2)]

Testical Cancer

   Trisomy chromosome 1q[88]

   Deletion chromosome 12p

   Isochromosome: i(12p)

Uterine Cancer

   Deletion chromosome 1p

   Isochromosome: i(1q)

Wilms Tumors

   Deletion chromosome: del (11) (p13)

§ 2.10   —Gene Therapy

The National Institutes of Health (NIH) plans investigation into gene therapy for cancer patients. This treatment consists of inserting the gene for tumor necrosis factor (TNF) into tumor-infiltrating lymphocytes (TIL) and then transfusing the cells.[89] Theoretically, TIL targets the tumor and TNF destroys the cells.

---

[88] Wang et al., *Nonrandom Abnormalities in Chromosome 1 in Human Testicular Tumors*, 40 Cancer Res. 796 (1980).

[89] National Institutes of Health, *Gene Therapy Study for Cancer Patients Is Approved by FDA*, 2 NIH Observer No. 1, at 1 (1991).

CHAPTER 3

SURGICAL ONCOLOGY

§ 3.1   Surgical Oncologist

The various surgical specialties are trained in the diagnosis and treatment of malignancies within their own fields. There is now special additional training for the general surgeon in surgical oncology and the gynecologist in gynecologic oncology. Some surgeons such as the head and neck surgeon or the surgical oncologist have restricted their practices to the treatment of cancer.

To treat cancer, the surgeon must understand tumor biologic behavior, diagnostic techniques, available surgical procedures, and the role of chemotherapy and radiation therapy. There should be a coordinated consultative relationship between the surgeon, medical oncologist, radiation oncologist, radiologist, and pathologist.

§ 3.2   Responsibilities

All surgical procedures have some risk of complications. Even local anesthesia has a risk of drug reaction. The patient must be properly evaluated in order to minimize problems. The surgical procedure itself must be explained to the patient so that the patient knows what is being done, the reasons for the procedure, the expectations of results, any material risks of the operation, any viable alternatives, and the risks of the alternatives (including the risk of doing nothing).

Whether he or she admits it, the cancer patient will almost always have some psychological problems that consist of anxieties of various types and extent. There can be fear of the unknown, of surgery, of chemotherapy or radiation, and of death, and worries about business, finances, and family. Cancer can be a very expensive disease with the costs of drugs, tests, and hospitalizations and the loss of earning power.

The surgeon may be responsible only for the short-term care of the patient. However, as a physician, the surgeon should be willing to listen to the patient's problems and help to support the patient by a concerned and sympathetic attitude. The surgeon must refer patients to appropriate specialists for a team approach to the care of the cancer problem. The medical oncologist and the radiation oncologist are an integral part of proper care of most cancers.

§ 3.3   Perioperative Surgical Problems

The surgeon performing operative procedures for cancer must be aware of complicating preoperative medical disorders such as diabetes mellitus, heart disease, kidney disease, endocrine aberrations, pulmonary abnormalities, and electrolyte disturbances. Preoperative preparation includes treatment of nutritional deficiencies with hyperalimentation, correction of anemia with transfusions, and the use of intravenous fluids for hydration and improving electrolyte abnormalities. Perioperative transfusions should be avoided in treating colon[1] and lung[2] cancer because of the reduction in cure rates.

Decisions must be made as to the need for blood pressure monitoring, Swan-Ganz pulmonary pressure monitoring, and central venous line. The insertion of a gastric or jejunal feeding tube for postoperative nutrition may have to be considered. Nutrition is also available by hyperalimentation through a central venous catheter.

With major surgery, especially in elderly patients, postoperative problems are likely to occur. Patients must be monitored adequately and complications avoided or treated early. Hemorrhage, breakdown of intestinal anastomosis, pneumonia, pulmonary embolus, shock, sepsis, and abscess are serious disorders that the surgeon must keep in mind when the postoperative course is not running smoothly.

---

[1] Foster et al., *Adverse Relationship Between Blood Transfusions and Survival after Colectomy for Colon Cancer,* 55 Cancer 1195 (1988); Hom et al., *Recurrence of Colorectal Cancer and Perioperative Blood Transfusion,* 33 Diseases of Colon & Rectum 127 (1990).

[2] Little et al., *Perioperative Blood Transfusion Adversely Affects Prognosis of Patients with Stage I Non-Small-Cell Lung Cancer,* 160 Am. J. Surgery 630 (1990).

§ 3.4   Diagnostic Procedures

Tissue analysis is necessary for the definitive diagnosis of cancer. Microscopic visualization of tumor tissue, although the most important, is not the only study that can be performed. Hormone analysis (estrogen and progesterone receptors), tissue characteristics, staining (of, for example, mucin or keratin), cytogenic chemotherapy sensitivity, and immunohistologic techniques are studies that can be performed on tissue specimens to aid in diagnosis and treatment.

A variety of surgical diagnostic procedures are available. The specific method utilized depends on the type and location of the tumor.

Cytologic examination of abraded cells can be accomplished by direct scraping (of, for example, the cervix), through endoscopic brushings (of the lungs, stomach, or bladder) or washings, or aspiration of peritoneal pleural fluid. Cellular morphology is examined for characteristics of malignancy.

Interpretation of results from skinny needle aspiration of tumor cells requires an experienced cytopathologist. Superficial tumors (of, for example, the thyroid or breast) are easily reached with a needle, while some deeper tumors may be aspirated using guidance with sonography (for example, tumors of the prostate or liver) or computerized tomography (for tumors of the lung or liver or for retroperitoneal tumors).

Needle biopsy can usually be performed under the same circumstances as needle aspiration. The core biopsy supplies a larger piece of tissue that allows better identification of the type of malignancy. Tumors of the breast, liver, prostate, and pancreas (transduodenal during surgery) are some examples of tumors for which needle biopsy may be utilized.

Incisional biopsy takes a piece of tissue from a large mass, which allows tissue analysis prior to formulating therapeutic options. Large melanomas, basal or squamous cell carcinomas of the skin, sarcomas, and breast tumors may be handled in this manner.

Excisional biopsy not only removes tissue for examination but at the same time may be curative for certain malignancies. All the characteristics of the cancer can then be analyzed for possible need for further treatment such as chemotherapy, radiation therapy, or more extensive surgery.

§ 3.5   Staging of Cancer

Clinical staging of cancer is accomplished, following physical examination, biopsy, and tissue diagnosis, and by laboratory and radiologic techniques. Treatment options and prognosis are dependent on the stage of the disease. Pathologic staging requires the surgical removal of the neoplasm with the regional lymph nodes and/or biopsies of possible metastatic areas. This process is a more accurate means of determining tumor extent than is clinical staging.

§ 3.6   Biological Behavior of Cancer

The biological behavior of neoplasms determines the therapeutic approach to the tumor. There is a tendency for each specific type of tumor to act in a particular manner, having its own method of local and distant spread, rapidity or slowness of growth, and response to chemotherapy and/or radiation therapy. Some specific examples follow.

Papillary-follicular carcinoma of the thyroid is slow growing and tends to remain confined to the neck lymph nodes for a long period of time (20 to 30 years).

Malignant melanoma metastasizes by vascular channels as readily as lymphatic channels, and the chance of metastasis increases in direct relation to the measured depth of the primary tumor.

Hodgkin's disease tends to spread to contiguous lymph nodes in the progression of the tumor. It responds readily to radiation therapy.

Non-Hodgkin's lymphoma tends to involve lymph nodes in multiple noncontiguous areas of the body early in the course of the disease.

Squamous cell carcinoma and **basal cell carcinoma** of the skin rarely metastasize.

Hypernephroma (adenocarcinoma) of the kidney, sarcoma, or colon carcinoma may involve single metastasis to the liver or lung.

Melanoma of the eye does not usually metastasize.

Small cell carcinoma of the lung metastasizes early in the course of the disease, and its spread to the brain is common.

Patients with breast cancer that spreads only to bone live longer than those with spread only to the viscera.

Residual ovarian cancer under 2 cm in diameter responds to curative chemotherapy much more readily than when over 2 cm in diameter.

Oral carcinoma spreads to cervical (neck) lymph nodes long before metastasizing to the lung.

Mixed (pleomorphic) tumors of the parotid have a false capsule with tumor cells extending through the capsule.

Sarcomas generally metastasize by the bloodstream.

Carcinomas of the left side of the colon usually cause obstructive symptoms whereas right colon tumors bleed and are associated with anemia.

§ 3.7   Palliation

When a malignancy cannot be cured, there is the possibility of preventing complications, decreasing pain, prolonging life, and improving the quality of the remaining life span with the use of palliative techniques.

Chemotherapy and radiation therapy, when not used for adjuvant therapy or cure, can increase survival time and quality of life in certain situations. Surgical reduction of tumor bulk and intestinal bypass procedures may be used for palliation. Resection of a colon cancer in the presence of metastatic disease will prevent obstruction and bleeding. Choledochojejunostomy will relieve jaundice in an unresectable carcinoma of the pancreas. Resection of the bulk of an incurable breast cancer may relieve local tumor ulceration and bleeding as well as reduce the tumor burden for chemotherapy and/or radiation therapy.

§ 3.8   Basic Surgical Principles

Certain fundamental surgical principles apply in the treatment of malignancies. Experimentation and clinical experience have established the bases for these standards. To disregard these principles in the treatment of cancer may be detrimental to the health and survival of the patient. Of course, there are always exceptions to the rule involving cancer.

Never Cut Across Cancer

The admonition "never cut across cancer when attempting to perform curative surgery" sounds like a commonsense recommendation. When a malignancy in the thorax or abdomen is transected, there is a reasonable medical probability of spreading cancer cells by sponges, instruments, gloves, and the oozing of blood and/or secretions. These cells can seed and grow on pleural (chest), peritoneal (abdomen), and serosal surfaces as well as anastomotic edges, tubular (bowel and bronchi) or solid organs, or any incised surface such as the incisional wound.

However, procedures such as needle aspiration, needle biopsy, or open biopsy may be necessary for definitive diagnosis prior to a surgical procedure. These procedures have a minimal chance of causing spread if performed properly. Excisional biopsy is the best procedure in many instances. In the lung, excisional biopsy requires at least a wedge resection or lobectomy in order to avoid cutting the tumor. Breast biopsies may be excisional or incisional (taking a piece of the tumor). When definitive surgery of the breast is undertaken after incisional biopsy, the incision site and all previously incised tissue must be completely removed.

Skin cancer, oral cavity tumor, and even primary malignant melanoma can have partial excision without the potential for spread. Sarcoma can be incised for biopsy outside body cavities as long as the site of biopsy is totally removed when curative surgery is performed.

Needle biopsies of tumors of the lung, thorax, kidney, liver, thyroid, brain, bone, and retroperitoneum are performed regularly without risk of spread. Tumors of the head of the pancreas, during exploratory laparotomy, are best biopsied by inserting the needle first through the duodenum because the duodenum is removed for definitive surgery.

Tubular organs can have a piece of tissue removed by endoscopy. Large bowel, stomach, duodenum, bronchi, larynx, and bladder tumors are handled in this manner. Radiosensitive malignancies, such as lymphoma or neuroblastoma, can be biopsied as long as radiation therapy encompasses the biopsy site. Tumors that cannot be completely extirpated surgically are biopsied and may be treated with chemotherapy and/or irradiation.

Perform En-bloc Resection

Where possible, malignant neoplasms should have an *en-bloc* resection for curative surgery. The whole tumor and all involved organs or portions of organs are removed, keeping the incisions in normal tissues to avoid cutting any portion of the malignancy.

Regional lymph nodes may need to be removed in continuity with the primary site when possible. Tumors of the larynx and oral cavity can have a radical neck dissection, including portions of the mandible, en-bloc with the primary site. Malignant melanoma can have regional lymph node dissection if the nodes are suspicious for metastases and are close enough to the primary. Intestinal malignancies have the lymph nodes resected with the mesentery wedge supplying the blood supply to the involved bowel.

In some instances, the lymph node drainage site is too far from the primary or technically too difficult to remove with the tumor for a true en-bloc resection. This situation occurs with lung cancer and mediastinal node dissection, ovarian or uterine cancer with retroperitoneal node resection, and lip cancer with neck dissection.

Avoid Luminal Spread of Cancer

It has been shown that malignant cells disseminated into the bowel lumen may implant in the intestinal anastomosis. Large bowel cancers require occlusion of the lumen on each side of the tumor, usually with ligatures, prior to handling of the malignancy to prevent intraluminal spread. This single maneuver has markedly reduced anastomotic recurrences.

Avoid Vascular Spread of Cancer

The manipulation of malignant tumors during surgical extirpation has been shown to disseminate tumors into the venous and lymphatic drainage areas. Malignancies of the kidney, breast, bowel, and lung should not be handled excessively at any time. Ligation of the major veins is performed early in the surgical dissection. A testicular mass requires ligation of all the cord structures before manipulating the tumor.

Large ovarian tumors may prevent visualization of the vessels in the confined space of the pelvis until the tumor has been dissected free. Retroperitoneal sarcomas do not usually have a distinct simple vascular supply that can be tied off before manipulating the tumor.

Avoid Instrument Spread of Cancer

The primary tumor should not have hemostats or other instruments applied to the malignancy itself. A good habit in cancer surgery is to discard all hemostats from the surgical table after a single use. These instruments can be resterilized during surgery for further use. Scissors and forceps, unfortunately, cannot be discarded because of the limited supply. The assistant surgeon must be conscious of the need to avoid tumor handling.

§ 3.9   Tumor Board

Most hospitals handling large numbers of cancer patients have tumor boards that consist of multispecialty consultants. The cancer patient's case is presented to the board with the history, physical, and laboratory results. The radiologist presents and interprets the X-rays and scans, while the pathologist shows and interprets the histologic findings. The surgical specialist, medical oncologist, and radiation oncologist discuss the findings, diagnosis, and various forms of treatment. Other specialists at the meeting may ask questions and add comments. Usually, there is a consensus as to the preferred method or methods of further workup or treatment, but this is often not unanimous.

The purpose of the tumor board is to give the patient's attending physician an opportunity to hear all possible aspects of diagnosis and treatment. The physician may follow any course of action she feels is appropriate and may or may not follow the specific recommendations of the board. The tumor board is only as good as its participating specialists, and the conclusions reached are not necessarily the best way to proceed with the particular patient.

The board also acts as a teaching mechanism. The physicians attending on a regular basis will be educated regarding the multiple facets of handling cancer patients. A variety of problems with each type of malignancy will give the attendee a better idea of what diagnostic and therapeutic procedures are available and a better concept of their usefulness.

MEDICAL ONCOLOGY

§ 4.1   Tumor Markers

Certain cancers can be detected by abnormalities in a variety of serum substances such as enzymes, hormones, antigens, and proteins. Abnormal elevations in these tumor markers may be used to diagnose specific malignancies, to determine the response of a tumor to therapy, or to detect early recurrences of the neoplasm. The incidence of elevation in various malignancies determines the marker's area of usefulness.

Carcinoembryonic Antigen (CEA)[1]

    Colorectal, breast, bronchogenic, pancreatic

---

[1] M.A. Heirera et al., *Carcinoembryonic Antigen (CEA) as a Prognostic and Monitoring Test in Clinically Complete Resection of Colorectal Carcinoma,* 183 Annals Surgery 5 (1976); J.P.

Useful to detect early recurrences

Alphafetoprotein (AFP)[2]

Hepatocellular, testicular (teratocarcinoma, embryonical cell cancer), metastases to liver, hepatoblastoma

Used for diagnosis of hepatoma; detects early recurrences

Pancreatic Oncofetal Antigen (POA)[3]

Pancreas

May be used in diagnosis

Prostate-Specific Antigen (PSA)[4]

Prostate

Used in diagnosis; detects early recurrences

Prostate Acid Phosphatase (PAP)[5]

Prostate

Used for diagnosis; elevation correlates with stage

Mach et al., *Detection of Recurrence of Large Bowel Carcinoma by Radioimmunoassay of Circulating Carcinoembryonic Antigen (CEA)*, 2 Lancet 535 (1974); A.M. Mackay et al., *Role of Serial Plasma CEA Assays in Detection of Recurrent and Metastatic Colorectal Carcinoma*, 4 Brit. Med. J. 382 (1974); E.W. Martin et al., *The Use of CEA as an Early Indicator for Gastrointestinal Tumor Recurrence and Second-Look Procedures*, 39 Cancer 440 (1977).

[2] R. Beach et al., *Production of Human Chorionic Gonadotropin by Hepatoblastoma Resulting in Precocious Puberty*, 37 J. Clinical Pathology 734 (1984); N. Javadpour & S. Bergman, *Recent Advances in Testicular Cancer*, 15 Current Probs. Surgery 1 (1978); N. Javadpour et al., *The Role of Radioimmunoassay of Serum Alphafetoprotein and Human Chorionic Gonadotropin in the Intensive Chemotherapy and Surgery of Metastatic Testicular Tumors*, 119 J. Urology 759 (1978); P. Lo Gerfo & H.G. Barker, *Immunologic Tests for the Detection of Gastrointestinal Cancers*, 52 Surgical Clinics N. Am. 829 (1972); A. Nakagawara et al., *Hepatoblastoma Producing Both Alphafetaprotein and Human Chorionic Gonadotropin*, 56 Cancer 1636 (1985); D. Trichopoulos et al., *Alphafetoprotein Levels of Liver Cancer Patients and Controls in a European Population*, 46 Cancer 736 (1980).

[3] O. Banwo et al., *New Oncofetal Antigen for Human Pancreas*, 1 Lancet 643 (1874); K. Nishida et al., *Enzyme Immunoassay of Pancreatic Oncofetal Antigen (POA) as a Marker of Pancreatic Cancer*, 26 Gut. 450 (1985); H. Oguchi et al., *A Pancreatic Oncofetal Antigen (POA): Its Characterization and Application for Enzyme Immunoassay*, 7 Cancer Detection & Prevention 51 (1984); R.A.B. Wood & A.R. Moosa, *The Prospective Evaluation of Tumour-Associated Antigens for the Early Diagnosis of Pancreatic Cancer*, 64 Brit. J. Surgery 718 (1977).

[4] C.S. Killian et al., *Prognostic Importance of Prostate-Specific Antigen for Monitoring Patients with Stages B_2 to T_1 Prostate Cancer*, 45 Cancer Res. 886 (1985); M. Kuriyama et al., *Use of Human Prostate-Specific Antigen in Monitoring Prostate Cancer*, 41 Cancer Res. 3874 (1981).

[5] J.F. Cooper, *The Radioimmunochemical Measurement of Prostatic Acid Phosphatase: Current State of the Art*, 7 Urologic Clinics N. Am. 653 (1980); J.F. Cooper et al., *Combined Serum and Bone Marrow Radioimmunoassays for Prostatic Acid Phosphatase*, 122 J. Urology 498 (1979);

Human Chorionic Gonadotropin (HCG)[6]

   Trophoblastic neoplasms

   Used for diagnosis, correlates with stage; detects early recurrence

Alkaline Phosphatase, Bone[7]

   Osteogenic Sarcoma

   Correlates with prognosis

Human Placental Lactogen (HPL)[8]

   Trophoblastic neoplasms

   May be used for diagnosis, correlates with treatment

Calcitonin[9]

   Medullary carcinoma of thyroid

   Used for diagnosis

CA-125[10]

   Ovarian

   Useful to detect early recurrences

A.G. Foti et al., *Detection of Prostatic Cancer by Solid-Phase Radioimmunoassay of Serum Prostatic Acid Phosphatase*, 297 New Eng. J. Med. 1357 (1977); D.E. Johnson et al., *Clinical Significance of Serum Acid Phosphatase Levels in Advanced Prostatic Carcinoma*, 8 Urology 123 (1976).

[6] K.D. Bagshaur et al., *Markers in Gynecological Cancer*, 229 Archives Gynecology 303 (1980); N. Javadpour, *The National Cancer Institute Experience with Testicular Cancer*, 122 J. Urology 657 (1978); N. Javadpour, *The Value of Biologic Markers in Diagnosis and Treatment of Testicular Cancer*, 6 Seminars in Oncology 37 (1979); J.J. Lokich, *Tumor Markers: Hormones, Antigens, and Enzymes in Malignant Disease*, 35 Oncology 54 (1978).

[7] A.M. Levine & S.A. Rosenberg, *Alkaline Phosphatase Levels in Osteosarcoma Tissue are Related to Prognosis*, 44 Cancer 2291 (1979); W.P. Thorpe et al., *Prognostic Significance of Alkaline Phosphatase Measurements in Patients with Osteogenic Sarcoma Receiving Chemotherapy*, 43 Cancer 2178 (1979).

[8] S.W. Rosen et al., *Placental Proteins and Their Subunits as Tumor Markers*, 82 Annals Internal Med. 71 (1975); B.N. Saxena et al., *Serum Placental Lactogen Levels in Patients with Molar Pregnancy and Trophoblastic Tumors*, 102 Am. J. Obstetrics & Gynecology 115 (1968); B.D. Weintraub & S.W. Rosen, *Ectopic Production of Human Chorionic Somatomammotropin by Nontrophoblastic Cancers*, 32 J. Clinics Endocrinology & Metabolism 94 (1971).

[9] R.A. DeLillis et al., *Calcitonin and Carcinoembryonic Antigen as Tumor Markers in Medullary Thyroid Carcinoma*, 70 Am. J. Clinical Pathology 587 (1978); R.L. Richardson et al., *Tumor Products and Potential Markers in Small Cell Lung Cancer*, 5 Semin. Oncol. 253 (1978); J.C. Stevenson & C.J. Hillyard, *Tumor Markers*, 73 Recent Results Cancer Res. 60 (1980).

[10] R.C. Bast, Jr., et al., *A Radioimmunoassay Using a Monoclonal Antibody to Monitor the Course of Epithelial Ovarian Cancer*, 309 New Eng. J. Med. 883 (1983).

CA 19-9[11]

Colorectal

Useful to detect early recurrences

CA 15-3

Breast

Used to detect early recurrences

Neuron Specific Enolase[12]

Neuroblastoma, small cell carcinoma of lung

Used for diagnosis, levels associated with survival

Immunoglobulins[13]

Multiple myeloma

Useful in diagnosis

Adrenocorticotropic Hormone (ACTH)[14]

Bronchogenic carcinoma, ovary, islet cell, carcinoid, thymoma, pheochromocytoma

Ectopic secretion may be used for monitoring treatment.

§ 4.2   Immunohistochemistry

Pathologic identification of a tumor is important because of different methods of treatment (surgery, chemotherapy, radiation therapy, hormonal therapy, or

---

[11] H. Koprowski et al., *Specific Antigen in Serum of Patients with Colon Carcinoma,* 212 Science 53 (1981); W.H. Schmiegel et al., *Multiparametric Tumor Marker (CA 19-9, CEA, AFP, POA) Analysis of Pancreatic Juices and Sera in Pancreatic Disease,* 32 Hepatogastroenterology 141 (1985); H.J. Staab et al., *The Clinical Validity of Circulating Tumor-Associated Antigens CEA and CA 19-9 in Primary Diagnosis and Follow-Up of Patients with Gastrointestinal Malignancies,* 63 Klinische Wochenschrift 106 (1985).

[12] Y. Ariyosha et al., *Evaluation of Serum Neuron-Specific Enolase as a Tumor Marker for Carcinoma of the Lung,* 74 Gann. 219 (1983); E.H. Cooper et al., *Evaluation of a Radioimmunoassay for Neuron Specific Enolase in Small Cell Lung Cancer,* 52 Brit. J. Cancer 333 (1985); T. Notoni et al., *Radioimmunoassay Development for Human Neuron-Specific Enolase: With Some Clinical Results in Lung Cancers and Neuroblastoma,* 6 Tumor Biology 57 (1985); S. Pahlman et al., *Neuron-Specific Enolase as a Marker for Neuroblastoma and Small-Cell Carcinoma of the Lung,* 5 Tumour Biol. 119 (1984).

[13] J.M. Paredes & B.S. Mitchell, *Multiple Myeloma: Current Concepts in Diagnosis and Management,* 64 Med. Clinics N. Am. 729 (1980).

[14] I. Lichter & N.E. Sirett, *Serial Measurement of Plasma Cortisol in Lung Cancer,* 30 Thorax 91 (1975); L.H. Rees et al., *ACTH as a Tumor Marker,* 297 Ann. N.Y. Acad. Sci. 603 (1977).

immunotherapy) of specific malignancies. The pathologist must attempt to predict the basic tumor type (carcinoma, lymphoma, or sarcoma), the subclassification as to the particular line of differentiation, and the probable site of origin. Poorly differentiated or highly undifferentiated (anaplastic) malignancies are particularly difficult to identify. Immunohistochemical methods are available that aid in diagnosis, although there are limitations as to specificity and interpretation.

Table 4–1 shows some of the basic histochemical markers.

Table 4–1

Histochemical Markers

Marker	Tumor Type
Alpha Lactalbumin	Breast carcinoma
Alphafetoprotein (AFP)	Embryonal carcinomas, yolk sac tumors
Calcitonin	Medullary thyroid carcinoma
Carcinoembryonic Antigen (CEA)	Carcinoma
Casein	Breast carcinoma
Chromogranin A	Neuroendocrine
Cytokeratin (CYK)	Carcinoma, sarcoma, germ cell tumors
Desmin (DES)	Sarcoma with evidence of muscle differentiation
Epithelial Membrane Antigen (EMA)	Carcinoma
Human Chorionic Gonadotropin (HCG)	Germ cell tumors, carcinoma
Leu 7	Neural, neuroendocrine
Leukocyte Common Antigen (LCA, T200 protein)	Lymphoma
Neuron-Specific Enolase (NSE)	Neuroendocrine
Placental Alkaline Phosphatase (PLAP)	Germ cell tumors, carcinoma
Prostate Acid Phosphatase (PAP)	Prostate carcinoma
Prostate-Specific Antigen (PSA)	Prostate carcinoma
S-100	Melanoma, tumors of Schwann cell origin
Secretory Protein-I (SP-I)	Neuroendocrine, parathyroid
Surfactanyl-Associated Apoproteins	Bronchogenic carcinoma
Thyroglobulin	Thyroid
Vimentin (VIM)	Lymphoma, melanoma, sarcoma

§ 4.3   The Cell Cycle

Antineoplastic therapy may depend on the drug effect during specific phases of cellular reproduction. A normal and neoplastic cell life cycle starts with mitosis (cell division). After cell division, the G_1 (*gap*) phase begins, in which protein synthesis and doubling of the cellular content occurs. The more rapid the tissue growth, the shorter the G_1 phase. In the synthesis (S) phase, there is DNA synthesis and replicating chromosomes. Further protein and RNA synthesis occurs in the G_2 phase. Cellular division proceeds in the mitotic (M) phase. A resting period may occur in the G_1 phase, or a prolonged resting period may be seen in the G_0 phase, as shown in **Figure 4–1.**

§ 4.4   DNA Analysis

Analyzing deoxyribonucleic acid (DNA) by means of flow cytometry in malignancies may be useful as a means of determining prognosis.

Ploidy

Nuclear DNA can be evaluated to determine ploidy characteristics. Diploid or euploid are normal chromosomal elements, whereas aneuploid is abnormal and usually means a poor prognosis.

S Phase

The more rapidly growing tumors have a larger percentage of cells progressing toward mitosis (division) in the cell cycle. The S (synthesis) phase fraction can be analyzed, with a *high S phase* meaning a larger fraction in a growth mode, which may be a poor prognostic sign.

   DNA flow cytometry is frequently used in breast cancer to help formulate decisions as to adjuvant therapy, especially in Stage I malignancy. Disease-free

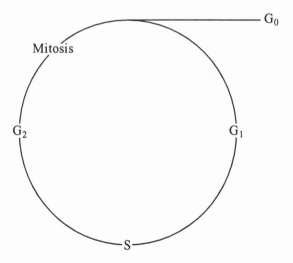

Figure 4–1. The cell cycle.

survival rates are better in euploid tumors than aneuploid in malignant melanoma. DNA as an indicator of prognosis has been used in colorectal cancer,[15] carcinoma of the esophagus,[16] prostate cancer,[17] and renal cell carcinoma.

§ 4.5   Chemotherapy

Anticancer (chemotherapeutic) agents have become a basic necessity treating most advanced malignancies, some early malignancies, and as adjuvant therapy for various tumors treated by other means (surgery, radiation therapy). These drugs are toxic to normal growing tissues as well as cancer cells. The highly proliferating cells are most affected by the chemotherapeutic agents, and there is only a narrow margin between killing normal cells and malignant cells.

The drugs may be administered orally, intramuscularly, intravenously, intra-arterially, intrapleurally, or intraperitoneally. There is a blood-brain barrier that prevents the effective use of some chemotherapy for tumors affecting the central nervous system. The medication may, however, be instilled directly into the cerebrospinal fluid in these instances.

§ 4.6   —Principles

Certain basic principles are inherent when determining the dosage, frequency, and duration of chemotherapeutic agents.

1.   The higher the tumor cell burden, the lower the growth fraction. The higher the tumor cell burden, the higher the probability of drug-resistant cell sublines. Therefore, the lower the tumor burden at the onset of chemotherapy, the more likelihood of curing the affected cells.

2.   The cell kill from a chemotherapeutic agent is directly related to the growth fraction of neoplastic cells and the presence of drug-resistant malignant cells.

3.   The major tumor burden is most often present in the primary neoplasm. If the primary neoplasm is destroyed by surgery or radiation, chemotherapy may be more effective because of a higher growth fraction in micrometastases and a smaller number of drug-resistant malignant cells.

---

[15] Armitage, *The Influence of Tumor Cell DNA Abnormalities on Survival in Colorectal Patients,* 72 Brit. J. Surgery 828 (1985).

[16] Matsuura, *Malignant Potentiality of Squamous Cell Carcinoma of the Esophagus Predictable by DNA Analysis,* 57 Cancer 1810 (1986).

[17] Frankfort, *Relationship Between DNA Ploidy, Glandular Differentiation and Tumor Spread in Human Prostate Cancer,* 45 Cancer Res. 1418 (1985).

4. Some chemotherapeutic agents are phase-specific and are effective only during a particular phase of the cell cycle. Phase-nonspecific agents have a prolonged action and are independent of the cell cycle phase.

5. Small tumors grow more rapidly than large tumors and have a larger proportion of cells in the replication cycle. The early growth rate is exponential as in the Gompertzian growth curve.[18]

6. In the *log cell kill hypothesis,* at any given exposure to chemotherapeutic agents, a variable fraction of the cells are killed.[19] Expressed in logarithmic terms, a single exposure of tumor cells to an antineoplastic agent achieves between two and five logs of cell kills. The treatment must be repeated multiple times to achieve control. The normal immune system eliminates 10^4 malignant cells, but not 10^6 cells. The immunologic treatment of cancer, therefore, may be ineffective against larger tumors.

§ 4.7 — Alkylating Agents

Alkylating agents produce antitumor effects by alkylation of nucleic acids, primarily DNA. This produces a break in the DNA molecule and cross-links its twin strands, which interferes with DNA replication and the transcription of RNA.

The five chemical classes of alkylating agents include the following:

Nitrogen Mustard Derivatives

Mechlorethamine (Mustargen®).   A potent vesicant (blistering agent) that causes severe local tissue injury when infiltrated under the skin. This should be injected into the tubing of a rapidly flowing intravenous solution. Toxicity consists of myelosuppression, nausea, vomiting, diarrhea, and diaphoresis (sweating). There is a possibility of delayed carcinogenesis.

Cyclophosphamide (Cytoxan®).   Requires activation in the liver prior to systemic effects and is excreted through the kidneys. Toxicity includes marrow suppression, nausea, vomiting, mucosal ulcerations, alopecia, hemorrhagic cystitis, and inappropriate water retention. Immunosuppression, fetal damage, cardiac damage, pulmonary fibrosis, and possible delayed carcinogenesis are other side effects.

---

[18] See **Ch. 2.**

[19] H.E. Skipper et al., *Experimental Evaluation of Potential Anticancer Agents XIII. On the Criteria of Kinetics Associated with "Curability" of Experimental Leukemia,* 35 Cancer Chemotherapy Rep. 1 (1964).

Chlorambucil (Leukeran®).   May cause myelosuppression, immunosuppression, nausea, vomiting, and hepatotoxicity. This has been implicated in carcinogenesis, especially acute myeloblastic leukemia.[20] Total dose over 6.5 mg/k risks permanent bone marrow damage.

Melphalan (Alkeran®).   Toxicity includes marrow suppression, nausea, immunosuppression, and alopecia. This has known potential carcinogenesis.

Ethylenamine Derivatives

Triethylenethiophosphoramide (Thiotepa).   This may cause immunosuppression, but seldom causes nausea.

Alkyl Sulfonates

Busulfan (Myleran®).   Toxicity includes myelosuppression, impotence, amenorrhea, pulmonary fibrosis, ocular cataracts, nausea, vomiting, diarrhea, and hyperpigmentation. This has potential carcinogenicity[21] and may cause gynecomastia.

Triazine Derivatives

Dacarbazine (DTIC-Dome®).   This is minimally immunosuppressive, but may cause nausea, vomiting, and marrow suppression. This has potential teratogenic and carcinogenic effects.[22]

Nitrosoureas

Carmustine (BCNU), Lomustine (CCNU), Semustine® (Methyl CCNU). These are excreted primarily by the kidneys, although excretion is assisted by the liver. They cross the blood-brain barrier easily. Toxicities include nausea, vomiting, and marrow suppression. Rarely, pulmonary fibrosis, alopecia, and stomatitis may occur. These may be mutagenic, teratogenic, and carcinogenic.[23]

---

[20] D. Fiere et al., *Acute Myeloid Leukemia Following the Administration of Chlorambucil. Two Cases,* 7 Nouvelle Presse Medecin 756 (1978).

[21] J.F. Peyzimenti et al., *Erythroleukemia-Like Syndrome Due to Busulfan Toxicity in Polcythemia Vera,* 38 Cancer 2242 (1976); S.M. Sieber & R.H. Adamson, *Toxicity of Antineoplastic Agents in Man, Chromosomal Aberrations, Antifertility Effects, Congenital Malformations, and Carcinogenic Potential,* 22 Advances Cancer Res. 57 (1975).

[22] S.M. Sieber & R.H. Adamson, *Toxicity of Antineoplastic Agents in Man, Chromosomal Aberrations, Antifertility Effects, Congenital Malformations, and Carcinogenic Potential,* 22 Advances Cancer Res. 57 (1975).

[23] *Id.*

§ 4.8 —Antimetabolites

The antineoplastic action of antimetabolites is through interaction with cellular enzymes and thereby damaging cells. The agent may substitute for a metabolite causing abnormal function, compete successfully for the catalytic site of an enzyme, or compete with a metabolite that acts at an enzyme regulatory site to alter the catalytic rate of an enzyme.

Methotrexate (MTX)

Methotrexate blocks tetrahydrofolate synthesis by competing for the folate binding site of an enzyme. The toxic effects are stomatitis, diarrhea, myelosuppression, renal and hepatic dysfunction, and immunosuppression. Leucovorin (*leucovorin rescue*) is used to overcome the cytotoxic effects.

5-Fluorouracil (5-FU), Floxuridine (FUDR)

These are metabolized by the liver and cause bone marrow suppression, ulceration of buccal mucosa, anorexia, nausea, diarrhea, alopecia, somnolence, and cerebellar ataxia. These drugs are immunosuppressive and have been reported to cause cardiac ischemia.

Cytosine Arabinoside (Cytosar, Ara-C)

This is an S phase-specific antineoplastic agent. Toxicity consists of nausea, vomiting, diarrhea, abdominal pain, and marrow suppression. It is potentially mutagenic, teratogenic, and carcinogenic.[24]

6-Thioguanine, 6-Mercaptopurine (Purinethol®)

These act as purine antagonists and are excreted by the kidneys. Toxic side effects include myelosuppression, nausea, anorexia, vomiting, stomatitis, and liver dysfunction.

§ 4.9 —Vinca Alkaloids

Antineoplastic action is through binding of microtubular contractile proteins of the mitotic spindle of the dividing cells.

---

[24] *Id.*

Vincristine (Oncovin®)

Intravenous administration must be done carefully because of severe tissue destruction from extravasation. The toxicity causes mixed motorsensory and anatomic neuropathy. The Achilles tendon reflex becomes depressed, parasthesias of the fingers and toes appear, and then weakness, muscle pain, and sensory impairment develop. Constipation and ileus results from autonomic dysfunction. Occasionally alopecia, marrow suppression, stomatitis, nausea, and the symptom of inappropriate antidiuretic hormone secretion may occur.

Vinblastine (Velban®)

This is primarily excreted via the liver into the bile. It can cause bone marrow suppression, nausea, vomiting, constipation, abdominal pain, alopecia, malaise, and weakness.

§ 4.10   —Antibiotics

The cytotoxic effects are through intercalation or other forms of binding causing DNA damage. Use of these antibiotics inhibits DNA and RNA synthesis.

Doxorubicin (Adriamycin®), Daunomycin

These are transformed by the liver into active metabolites and are excreted in the bile. They cause severe marrow suppression, alopecia, stomatitis, vomiting, and cardiac toxicity. The maximum lifetime dose of doxorubicin is 550 mg/m^2 (less if treated with mediastinal irradiation or alkylating agents). The maximum lifetime dose of daunomycin is 600 mg/m^2. These are severely irritating to tissues if extravasation occurs; can cause delayed radiation reactions.

Dactinomycin (Cosmegen®)

Toxicity includes vomiting, alopecia, stomatitis, glossitis, diarrhea, rashes, and marrow suppression. It is a radiosensitizing drug and can cause delayed radiation reactions (*recall phenomenon*). It causes severe tissue inflammation and necrosis with extravasation.

Bleomycin (Blenoxane®)

This is excreted primarily by the kidneys. It rarely causes marrow suppression, but it causes pulmonary dysfunction in 10 percent of patients and may progress to fatal pulmonary fibrosis in one percent of patients. Extreme care must be taken when administering anesthetics to use room air and not concentrated oxygen, which can result in pulmonary fibrosis even years after the use of bleomycin. Other toxicities include systemic sclerosis, mucositis, and alopecia. The drug is mutagenic and probably teratogenic.[25] A rare fulminant reaction with high fever, hypotension, cardiorespiratory collapse, and death has been reported.

Mithramycin (Mithracin®)

Toxicities include hemorrhagic diathesis, arterial occlusions, fever, malaise, vomiting, headache, lethargy, stomatitis, and hepatorenal dysfunction. This can be used in treating hypercalcemia. Because reactions are unpredictable and may be severe, hospitalization for administration of the drug is recommended.

Mitomycin (Mitomycin-C®)

Myelosuppression is the most common toxicity, but alopecia, stomatitis, rash, and pulmonary, hepatic, and renal dysfunction may be seen. Local tissue necrosis can occur with extravasation.

§ 4.11   —Miscellaneous Agents

Cisplatin (Cis-DDP)

This forms an activated complex that interacts with a nucleophilic site on DNA, RNA, or protein. It requires hydration because of nephrotoxicity. It causes nausea, vomiting, myelosuppression, neuropathy, and progressive hearing loss. It is both mutagenic and carcinogenic.

Hydroxyurea (Hydrea®)

This causes marrow suppression, nausea, stomatitis, alopecia, and neurologic problems. Hydroxyurea is teratogenic.

Procarbazine (Matulane®)

This freely crosses the blood-brain barrier and is excreted by the kidneys. Toxicity includes anorexia, nausea, vomiting, marrow suppression, somnolence, depression, agitation, psychosis, and peripheral neuropathies. Ataxia, rash, and

---

[25] R.H. Blum et al., *A Clinical Review of Bleomycin—A New Antineoplastic Agent,* 31 Cancer 903 (1973).

pleuropulmonary reactions have been reported. It is immunosuppressive, mutagenic, teratogenic, and carcinogenic.

Mitotane (Lysodren®)

This causes destruction of adrenal cortical tissues. Toxicity includes nausea,
vomiting, rash, hypotension, hematuria, drowsiness, lethargy, and vertigo.

L-Asparaginase (Elspar®)

This may cause allergic reactions, depression of clotting factors, nausea, vomiting, immunosuppression, liver dysfunction, and nervous system dysfunction.

§ 4.12   —Complications

Each chemotherapeutic drug has a number of side effects that can be found in
the *Physicians' Desk Reference* (PDR).[26] Hematopoietic toxicity is the most
common side effect and may require delay in subsequent drug doses or a reduction in the dosage. Gastrointestinal (mucositis, anorexia, nausea, vomiting, and
diarrhea), renal, and hepatic toxicities, cutaneous reactions, and neurologic
effects can be significant problems. Pulmonary and cardiac toxicities may limit
antineoplastic drug doses and are serious concerns to the medical oncologist.

Many of the agents sensitize tissues to radiation therapy, and, when given concomitantly, both may have to be reduced in dosage. Doxorubicin can cause a
recall phenomenon with acute radiation toxic symptoms occurring when radiation therapy previously has been given.

Some drugs have been implicated in fetal loss from occupational exposure to
chemotherapeutic agents during the first trimester of pregnancy.[27] Cyclophosphamide, doxorubicin, and vincristine show statistically significant problems.
Pregnant medical personnel should avoid administering antineoplastic drugs.
The patient with cancer who has a pregnancy must be forewarned of the possible
effects of abnormal growth and development, as well as death, of the fetus with
the use of chemotherapy. Antineoplastic treatment may be refused, or the patient
may wish to terminate the pregnancy.

Secondary malignancies including leukemia, bladder tumors, and multiple
myeloma have been reported following treatment with chemotherapy. The drugs
themselves are thought to be a causative agent.[28]

---

[26] Medical Economics Co., Inc., Oradell, N.J. 07647 (1991).

[27] Selevan, *A Study of Occupational Exposure of Antineoplastic Drugs and Fetal Loss in Nurses,*
313 New Eng. J. Med. 1173 (1985).

[28] May & Costanzi, *Acute Leukemia Following Combination Chemotherapy for Cancer of the
Lung,* 38 Oncology 134 (1981).

Extravasation

Chemotherapeutic medications are frequently given intravenously. The usual method is to place a needle in a peripheral vein of the upper extremity and inject the drug as a bolus or in an intravenous drip. Thrombosis of these small veins, from irritation to the vein wall due to high drug concentrations and frequent needle sticks, occurs ultimately.

The agents that extravasate may cause severe damage to surrounding tissues. Pain, swelling, and ulceration, followed by necrosis of the tissues, can occur. Doxorubicin, dactinomycin, mithramycin, and daunorubicin are likely to cause severe, extensive necrosis, and when leakage occurs, the local injection of steroids and/or sodium bicarbonate might help. Vinblastine and vincristine are ulcerogenic and can be treated by injecting hyaluronidase diluted with steroids and hot or cold packs. Nitrogen mustard requires using sodium thiosulfate locally for extravasation.[29]

Prevention is the best protection against the injuries due to extravasation. Using a plastic catheter instead of a metal needle may limit the opportunity for dislodgment. When chemotherapy is expected to be used over a long period of time, a Hickman cutaneous catheter or implantable catheter and port allow access to large central veins which dilute the medications more readily. These catheters essentially eliminate the problem of drug leakage.

§ 4.13   —Commentary and Significant Cases

The side effects and complications of chemotherapy vary with each drug given. Great care must be taken in deciding drug combinations and dosages. Errors can occur in amounts of medication given. Intravenous chemotherapy that extravasates may cause extensive tissue damage.

Colasanto v. Memorial Sloan Kettering Hospital.[30]   The settlement for this case was $350,000. The plaintiff had treatment of bladder cancer with BCG, an experimental treatment, by inserting it into the bladder. After the first course of therapy, he developed chills, fever, and other abnormalities of the lungs, liver, and bone marrow. He recovered after plasmapheresis eight months later. The diagnosis of hypersensitivity reaction was made. The plaintiff alleged that the BCG was administered improperly, traumatizing the urethra in inserting the catheter, thus providing a pathway for the BCG to enter the bloodstream.

---

[29] Rudolph & Larson, *Etiology and Treatment of Chemotherapeutic Agent Extravasation Injuries: A Review,* 5 J. Clinical Oncology 1116 (1987).

[30] No. 88 CIV 3556 (N.Y. 1990), *reprinted in* 6 Med. Malpractice Verdicts, Settlements & Experts No. 6, at 53 (1990).

Hamza v. Scripps Clinic and Research Foundation.[31]   The 63-year-old plaintiff was given the chemotherapeutic agent ARA-C for the treatment of leukemia. High doses of the drug were used, resulting in neurotoxicity, which caused debilitation. The plaintiff contended that ARA-C was given in excess of the protocol, and that he should have received and obtained an informed consent. The drug was given when the decedent's leukemia was in remission. He later died from the myeloblastic leukemia. The case was settled for $195,000.

Howard v. Strum.[32]   The plaintiff was given adjuvant chemotherapy for Duke's C colon cancer. Mitomycin-C, a vesicant drug, was administered on four separate occasions. Pain and swelling of the hand developed. Ultimately, the hand was debrided several times, and a rotation flap with split thickness skin graft was used to close the defect. The plaintiff contended that the injury was from extravasation of Mitomycin-C. The settlement was for $86,318.

Lathan v. Southwest Detroit Hospital.[33]   Chemotherapy was administered through a needle placed in the left hand of the plaintiff. The chemotherapy agent went subcutaneously, causing chemical burns to the tissues of the left hand, including the tendons, requiring multiple plastic surgical procedures. The plaintiff alleged failure to treat her hand after the incident. The nurse had instructed the plaintiff to soak her hand in hot water. The settlement was for $500,000 with 5 percent comparative negligence assessed against the plaintiff.

Lefler v. Yardmian.[34]   There was a defense verdict following injury from extravasation of chemotherapy drugs. An enormous area of tissue ulceration appeared on the left arm, and the tendons were affected. The defendant alleged that the plaintiff was negligent in causing her own injuries.

Mackintosh v. Winokur.[35]   A defense verdict resulted after chemotherapy was given to the decedent for testicular cancer. The treatment reduced the granulocytes in the blood and he developed clostridium septicum infection which produced gas gangrene. He underwent multiple amputations and finally died. The defendants contended that patients undergoing chemotherapy are at risk for

---

[31] No. 607750 (Cal.), *reprinted in* 6 Med. Malpractice Verdicts, Settlements & Experts No. 11, at 45 (1990).

[32] No. C629814 (Cal.), *reprinted in* 4 Med. Malpractice Verdicts, Settlements & Experts No. 9, at 41 (1988).

[33] No. 88-807313-NH (Mich. 1990), *reprinted in* 7 Med. Malpractice Verdicts, Settlements & Experts No. 7, at 45 (1991).

[34] No. 83-14700 (Fla.), *reprinted in* 3 Med. Malpractice Verdicts, Settlements & Experts No. 7, at 35 (1987).

[35] No. D-21386/D-33574 (Tex. 1989), *reprinted in* 6 Med. Malpractice Verdicts, Settlements & Experts No. 6, at 53–54 (1990).

infection and the decedent developed an infection so lethal that his death could not have been prevented even if antibiotic therapy had been instituted at the moment of onset.

Markley v. Albany Medical Center.[36]   The nine-month-old patient had a malignant tumor resected. Treatment was started using chemotherapy including the drug Adriamycin. The child was admitted to the hospital for her fourth treatment and was given an overdose of Adriamycin by the resident pursuant to orders from the hospital's oncology department. There was summary judgment, the court finding that the defendant hospital owed no duty of care because they neither undertook to supervise the chemotherapy nor exercised control over it.

Metcalfe v. Baylor University Medical Center.[37]   An injection of 10 times the recommended dosage of oncovin by a nurse was alleged to have caused the patient's death. There was a $100,000 settlement.

Newman v. Geschke.[38]   A $450,000 settlement was the result when an overdose of vincristine caused decreased short-term memory, blurry vision, decreased muscular strength, bowel and bladder incontinence, decreased hearing, hand and arm tremors, and depression. The defendant prescribed 1.5 mg of the medication, but a much larger dose was given. The defendant and his professional corporation were liable under the theory of respondeat superior.

Skinner v. Clay.[39]   A $200,000 settlement resulted from extravasation of Adriamycin given as adjuvant chemotherapy for breast cancer. Tissue damage required extensive reconstructive surgery and skin grafting.

Wray v. All Saints Episcopal Hospital.[40]   The 45-year-old decedent was treated for kidney cancer in 1983 with nephrectomy. In January 1984, metastasis to the lung was diagnosed and chemotherapy started. In May 1984, the hospital pharmacist misunderstood a prescription given orally, and seven times the usual dose of Velban, an anticancer drug, was given. The hospital nurse did not check the written prescription against the dispensed drug as hospital procedure required. The patient died from infections and bleeding brought on by the lethal

---

[36] 558 N.Y.S.2d 688 (App. Div. 1990).

[37] No. 85-8306 (Tex.), *reprinted in* 4 Med. Malpractice Verdicts, Settlements & Experts No. 5, at 42 (1988).

[38] No. A8609-05800 (Or.), No. 8608-05800 (Or. 1986), *reprinted in* 4 Med. Malpractice Verdicts, Settlements & Experts No. 4, at 44 (1988).

[39] No. E85-0180L (S.D. Miss.), *reprinted in* 3 Med. Malpractice Verdicts, Settlements & Experts No. 5, at 35 (1987).

[40] No. 86-243 (N.D. Tex.), *reprinted in* 4 Med. Malpractice Verdicts, Settlements & Experts 41 (1988).

dose of medication, which destroyed his immune system. The $11 million settlement was approved by the judge.

§ 4.14 Hormones

Manipulating the hormonal system can be used to influence the growth of neoplasms. For steroid hormones, there is a binding of specific receptor proteins in the cytoplasm with translocation through the nuclear membrane ultimately binding with DNA. Other hormones may react with membrane-bound nucleotide cyclase systems, stimulating conversion of nucleosides, which interact with appropriate cellular sites.

Estrogens have been used to treat carcinoma of the prostate by blocking the effects of androgens. Cancer of the breast may be suppressed by estrogens or antiestrogens (tamoxifen, Nolvadex®), especially for patients with positive estrogen receptors. Progestins, such as medroxyprogesterone acetate (Provera®), hydroxyprogesterone caproate (Delalutin®), and megestrol acetate (Megace®) have been used in treating breast cancer and endometrial carcinoma.

Corticosteroids cause metabolic changes, inhibit inflammation, and have immunosuppressive effects. Prolonged usage may be associated with water retention, potassium loss, psychosis, peptic ulceration, osteoporosis, glaucoma, hypertension, impaired wound healing, and aseptic necrosis of bone. Treating leukemias, lymphomas, multiple myeloma, breast cancer, and prostate cancer may necessitate using corticosteroids. Symptoms from cerebral edema associated with metastatic or primary malignancy of the brain can be controlled by using dexamethasone.

§ 4.15 Immunotherapy

Cancer patients are capable of forming humoral antibodies against a variety of antigenic agents even in the presence of advanced disease. Cell-mediated immune reactions, however, are impaired in lymphoreticular neoplasia and localized or advanced solid malignancies. There is a clinical correlation between the course of the malignant disease and impaired cell-mediated immunity. Resection of the tumor can result in a return of the immunologic competence of patients with sarcomas.

Nonspecific immunotherapy with bacille Calmette-Guérin (BCG) or Corynebacterium parvum can activate patient defense mechanisms. BCG has been used as intralesional injections into metastatic malignant melanoma[41] and breast

---

[41] C.M. Balch et al., *A Randomized Prospective Comparison of BCG Versus C Parvum Adjuvant Immunotherapy in Melanoma Patients with Resected Metastatic Lymph Nodes,* 3 Am. Soc'y

carcinoma.[42] BCG has been instilled in the bladder to reduce recurrence of superficial bladder cancers,[43] while colorectal carcinoma,[44] ovarian cancer,[45] soft tissue sarcomas,[46] and lung carcinoma[47] have been treated with BCG as adjuvant immunotherapy. Corynebacterium parvum has been tested in treating disseminated malignant disease.[48] DNCB (dinitrochlorobenzene) and TEIB (triethylene iminobenzoquinone) have caused regression of basal cell and squamous cell carcinomas in previously sensitized patients.[49] Early vaginal cancer,[50] metastatic melanoma, and breast cancer have responded to DNCB immunotherapy.

Levamisole is a synthetic antihelminthic drug that stimulates immune responses in immunodepressed patients. Levamisole has been utilized in treating lung cancer,[51] breast carcinoma,[52] colorectal carcinoma, and head and neck cancers.

Clinical Oncology 263 (1984); F.R. Ellier et al., *Adjuvant Immunotherapy with BCG in Treatment of Regional-Lymph-Node Metastases from Malignant Melanoma*, 294 New Eng. J. Med. 237 (1976).

[42] A.V. Buzdar et al., *Intensive Postoperative Chemoimmunotherapy for Patients with Stage II and Stage III Breast Cancer*, 41 Cancer 1064 (1978); E. Klein et al., *Immunotherapy for Accessible Tumors Utilizing Delayed Hypersensitivity Reactions and Separated Components of the Immune System*, 60 Med. Clinics N. Am. 389 (1976); G.V. Smith et al., *Immunotherapy of Patients with Cancer*, 74 Surgery 59 (1973).

[43] D. Eidinger & A. Morales, *Discussion Paper: Treatment of Superficial Bladder Cancer in Man*, 277 Ann. N.Y. Acad. Sci. 239 (1976).

[44] G.M. Mavligit et al., *Adjuvant Immunotherapy and Chemotherapy in Colorectal Cancer (Duke's Class C): Prolongation of Disease-Free Interval and Survival*, 40 Cancer 2726 (1977).

[45] D.S. Alberts, *Ovarian Cancer, in* Adjuvant Therapy of Cancer 327 (S.S. Salmon & S.E. Jones eds., 1977).

[46] C.M. Townsend, Jr., et al., *Skeletal and Soft Tissue Sarcomas. Treatment with Adjuvant Immunotherapy*, 236 JAMA 2187 (1976).

[47] M.F. McKneally et al., *Regional Immunotherapy of Lung Cancer with Intrapleural B.C.G.*, 1 Lancet 377 (1976); M.F. McKneally et al., *Intrapleural B.C.G. Immunostimulation in Lung Cancer*, 1 Lancet 593 (1977).

[48] A.L. Lipton et al., *Corynebacterium Parvum Versus Bacille Calmette-Guérin Adjuvant Immunotherapy of Stage II Malignant Melanoma*, 9 J. Clinical Oncology 1151 (1991).

[49] E. Klein, *Tumors of the Skin. X. Immunotherapy of Cutaneous and Mucosal Neoplasms*, 68 N.Y. St. J. Med. 900 (1968); W.R. Levis et al., *Topical Immunotherapy of Basal Cell Carcinomas with Dinitrochlorobenzene*, 33 Cancer Res. 3036 (1973).

[50] D. Guthrie & S. Way, *Immunotherapy of Nonclinical Vaginal Cancer*, 2 Lancet 1242 (1975).

[51] J.F. Holland & J.G. Bekesi, *Immunotherapy of Human Leukemia with Neuraminidase-Modified Cells*, 60 Med. Clinics N. Am. 539 (1976); R.L. Powles et al., *Immunotherapy for Acute Myelogenous Leukemia*, 28 Brit. J. Cancer 365 (1973); F.C. Sparks et al., *Immunology and Adjuvant Chemoimmunotherapy of Breast Cancer*, 111 Archives Surgery 1057 (1976); H. Takita & A. Brugarolas, *Adjuvant Immunotherapy for Bronchogenic Carcinoma: Preliminary Results*, 4 Cancer Chemotherapy Rep. 293 (1973); C.M. Townsend, Jr., et al., *Skeletal and Soft Tissue Sarcomas. Treatment with Adjuvant Immunotherapy*, 236 JAMA 2187 (1976).

[52] W.A. Amery, *Double-Blind Levamisole Trial in Resectable Lung Cancer*, 277 Ann. N.Y. Acad. Sci. 260 (1976).

Allogenic tumor vaccines have been tested as adjuvant immunotherapy in lung cancer, breast carcinoma, malignant melanoma, leukemia, and sarcoma.[53]

Adoptive cellular immunotherapy involves activating (outside the body) cancer patients' blood mononuclear cells with biologic response modifiers. The activated monocytes have an antitumor cytotoxic effect and have been tried in various cancers,[54] but they need further investigation.

§ 4.16   Karnofsky Performance Status Scale

The Karnofsky scale[55] is used as a standard of comparing responses to therapy. **Table 4-2** shows the Karnofsky scale percentages.

Table 4-2

Karnofsky scale percentages

Percentage	Condition
100	Normal, no complaints, no evidence of disease
90	Minor signs or symptoms of disease, able to carry on normal activity
80	Normal activity with effort, some signs or symptoms of disease
70	Cares for self, unable to carry on normal activities or do active work
60	Requires occasional assistance, but is able to care for most personal needs
50	Requires considerable assistance and frequent medical care
40	Disabled, requires special care and assistance
30	Severely disabled, hospitalization is indicated, death not imminent
20	Very sick, active supportive treatment, and hospitalization is necessary
10	Moribund, fatal processes rapidly progressing
0	Dead

---

[53] A.F. Rojas et al., *Levamisole in Advanced Human Breast Cancer,* 1 Lancet 211 (1976).

[54] A. Fradji et al., *Phase I Study of Liposomal MTP-PE-Activated Autologous Monocytes Administered Intraperitoneally to Patients with Peritoneal Carcinomatosis,* 9 J. Clinical Oncology 1251 (1991); H.C. Stevenson et al., *Ex Vivo Activated Monocytes and Adoptive Immunotherapy Trials in Colon Cancer Patients,* 211 Progress Clinical & Biological Res. 75 (1986); H. Stevenson et al., *The Treatment of Cancer with Activated Leukocyte Subsets,* 12 Artificial Organs 128 (1988).

[55] D.A. Karnofsky & J.H. Burchenal, *Performance Status, in* Evaluation of Chemotherapeutic Agents 191 (C.M. MacLeod ed., 1949).

CHAPTER 5

RADIATION ONCOLOGY

§ 5.1   Biological Basis

The therapeutic use of radiation is based on the difference in radiation sensitivity between well-differentiated and less-differentiated tissues, the less-differentiated (which include cancers) being more sensitive or vulnerable. The effects produced by radiation are the result of the ionization of tissues. Electrons are ejected from the molecules of the cells struck by the rays. The free radicals thus created produce the chemical changes responsible for radiation effects. For most forms of radiation, the hydroxyl (OH) radical is the one responsible for the greater portion of the radiation reaction. Neutron radiation is an exception. It is not mediated by radicals, but acts directly on the deoxyribonucleic acid (DNA) in the nucleus of the cell.

Oxygenation

Oxygen is an important factor in modifying radiosensitivity with the better oxygenated tissues more susceptible to radiation. Tumors have a property not shared by normal tissues. Their sensitivity to radiation can increase during the course of radiation therapy through a process of reoxygenation. Oxygen diffusion into the tumor from the blood vessels in the tumor is limited to small areas around the blood vessels. As the better oxygenated tumor cells are killed, oxygen becomes more accessible to the remaining tumor cells as the tumor contracts, thereby making them more radiosensitive. The importance of oxygen is demonstrated by the concept of the oxygen enhancement ratio (OER). This is the ratio between the doses of radiation needed to produce the same biologic effect in the presence of molecular oxygen versus the absence of oxygen. In experimental tests, the ratio is three. In other words, in the absence of oxygen, three times as much radiation is needed to equal the effect produced in the oxygenated environment. Larger tumors require larger doses of radiation because of the presence of a larger volume of hypoxic cells. The first attempts at oxygenation of hypoxic tumors were made by placing patients in hyperbaric oxygen chambers to increase the circulating oxygen in the blood, but this method proved to be impractical. Another approach has been to sensitize hypoxic cells independently of oxygen by prescribing certain drugs. The best known of these medications is misonidazole. The dosage of misonidazole to sensitize hypoxic cells unfortunately is neurotoxic.

Radiosensitivity and Radiocurability

Radiosensitivity is sometimes regarded incorrectly as synonymous with radiocurability. Radiosensitivity refers to the rapidity and completeness with which a tumor disappears under radiation. A radiosensitive tumor may indeed be easy to eradicate in the field of irradiation, but radiosensitive tumors often have a tendency to metastasize early and widely. A radiosensitive tumor with distant metastases therefore will not be radiocurable, however gratifying the results of local radiation may be. On the other hand, a moderately radioresistant tumor that regresses slowly may, given time, be radiocurable if it has not spread beyond the field of irradiation. It becomes apparent that the stage of a tumor is a more important factor in radioocurability than its precise radiosensitivity. Seminomas and lymphomas are radiosensitive tumors, epidermoid carcinomas are moderately resistant, and soft tissue sarcomas and melanomas are more resistant. The amount of residual tumor at the completion of radiation therapy does not correlate in every case with its ultimate curability. Postirradiation biopsies to determine the *viability* of residual tumors are a pathologic myth. The only proof of radiation failure is evidence of the tumor's regrowth.

Fractionation

Radiation becomes an effective method of treating tumors by exploiting the difference in sensitivity between normal tissues and malignant tissues through the principle of fractionation. The difference in susceptibility between normal and malignant tissues is sufficiently small that a lethal dose of radiation given to a cancer in a single treatment would be extremely damaging, if not lethal, to the normal tissues as well. By dividing the total dose into a series of small fractions, the malignant tissue is killed, but the normal tissues sustain only minor to moderate changes. This result is possible because of the greater repairability of the normal tissues during the rest periods between the dose fractions. In the case of the tumor, fractionation allows time for the tumor to become more vulnerable through reoxygenation and through progression of the more resistant cells into the more vulnerable segments of the mitotic cell cycle. Special fractionation strategies exist such as hyperfractionation and accelerated fractionation. In hyperfractionation, two treatments are given daily instead of one, as in conventional fractionation, but the treatment is completed in the same number of weeks as in conventional fractionation. The two treatments per day are given at least four hours apart. The total of the two doses is slightly greater than the single conventional dose to compensate for the small individual fractions. The final total dose is 15 to 20 percent greater than the conventional dose. The intent of hyperfractionation is to decrease the acute radiation effects (though not necessarily the late effects) and to improve control of rapidly repopulating tumors. Accelerated fractionation involves no increase in the total dose and no increase in the number of fractions, but by giving two full treatments a day and thereby doubling the daily dose, the treatment is completed much sooner. The acute reaction is more severe and may require interruption of the treatment. The intent of accelerated fractionation is to get better control of rapidly repopulating tumors.

Voltage

Radiation is used with a variety of energies. High energy (megavoltage) radiation is for deep tumors, while low energy (kilovoltage) radiation is used to treat skin cancers. Megavoltage radiation has the advantage of producing less reaction in the superficial tissues it traverses to reach a deep tumor. The ions that are produced in the collisions between the radiation and the molecules in the tissues are scattered in all directions, and themselves produce additional ions by colliding with other molecules. The higher the energy of the radiation beam, the greater the forward scatter of the ions. At a particular point under the skin, depending on the energy of the radiation, the accumulation of ions reaches a maximum. Beyond this point of maximum radiation, the levels of radiation decrease as the radiation is absorbed. At the energy levels commonly used in radiation therapy, the level of maximum radiation ranges from the surface of the skin with kilovoltage radiation to about 3 cm below the surface with 18 million volt radiation.

Dosage

Dosage in radiation has been expressed in different ways over the years. The initial standardized unit, adopted in 1937, was the *roentgen* (R), defined as the quantity of radiation that produced ions carrying a total of one electrostatic unit of electricity in one cubic centimeter of air under standard conditions. The unit was named after Wilhelm Konrad Roentgen, the discoverer of X-rays. The *rad* (radiation absorbed dose) was adopted as the unit of radiation in 1953. It was defined as the amount of absorbed radiation equal to 100 ergs of energy per gram of absorbing medium. In studying old radiation records, one might wish to convert roentgens to rads. The conversion factor varies with the energy of the radiation and the type of absorbing medium, for example, muscle or fat. Usually, roentgens convert to a smaller number of rads; that is, 100 roentgens becomes a number of rads greater than 90, but less than 100. The radiation unit in current use is the *Gray*. One Gray equals 100 rads. One centiGray (cGy) equals one rad.

Types of Rays

The ionizing radiations used in radiation therapy consist of a variety of rays. X-rays and gamma rays are electromagnetic (noncorpuscular) waves. There is no difference between them, but they are defined according to their source. X-rays are generated by machine, while gamma rays are emitted as a result of nuclear decay in radioactive elements. Electromagnetic waves have no mass, no electrical charge, and travel with the speed of light. Other rays, which are in the corpuscular category, include electrons, protons, and neutrons, all of which have mass. Electrons are negatively charged, light-weight particles that are accelerated by betatrons or linear accelerators to the high energies needed for radiation therapy. Protons are positively charged heavy particles that also are accelerated for radiation therapy. Neutrons, which are generated in cyclotrons, are heavy particles like protons, but carry no electrical charge.

Treatment

With the foregoing varieties of radiation and strategies of fractionation, tumors are watched and measured as treatment progresses. After delivering a standard dose (such as 6000 cGy) and observing substantial regression of the well-oxygenated periphery of a tumor, a shrinking field may be used to irradiate the still hypoxic remnant of a tumor to 7000 cGy or more to obtain a biologic effect equivalent to that obtained at the periphery with the lesser dose. An alternative approach to remnants of a tumor is the employment of intracavitary or interstitial radioisotopes for the boost in dosage.

Linear Energy Transfer

Linear energy transfer (LET) describes the average energy deposited locally per unit length along the path of the radiation beam. The patterns vary with different kinds of radiation and account for differing radiation effects. *Relative biologic effect* (RBE) is the concept derived from these facts. If different kinds of radiation are used, the biologic effects differ because of differing LETs, even though the doses are identical. In other words, the pattern of radiation deposition alters the radiation effect even though the total dose is the same in identical volumes of tissue. In reality, RBE is a complex entity subject to alteration by such variables as dose per fraction, dose rate, oxygen, cell type, and the total dose. In general, lower energy radiations have more densely localized LETs and have greater biologic effects than higher energy radiations of the same type. Neutrons differ substantially from X-rays because of lower oxygen enhancement ratios (OERs), less reparable damage, and less variability in sensitivity to neutrons of different cell types and different segments of the cell cycle. Neutron RBE values are increased in slowly growing tumors.

Radiation with Heat

The combination of radiation with heat (hyperthermia) can increase the number of complete tumor regressions and the duration of such regressions. There are several mechanisms by which heat contributes to tumor regression. Heat selectively kills the radioresistant S-phase cells and hypoxic cells. Heat selectively damages the blood vessels in tumors more than the blood vessels in normal tissues. This increases the temperature in the tumor more than the temperature in normal tissues, which is protective for the normal tissues. Another mechanism is selective inhibition of damage repair as a consequence of selective heating.

The methods of heating are with microwaves or ultrasound. Ultrasound is more effective in the absence of interference from air cavities and bone, while microwaves are more effective on shallow tumors. It may be inferred that hyperthermia can present complicated challenges. The most effective use of hyperthermia is with interstitial radiation therapy where the heating elements are placed in the same needle tracks as the radioisotopes.

Cytotoxic Drugs

Certain cytotoxic drugs used in cancer chemotherapy (bleomycin, dactinomycin, doxorubicin, 5-fluorouracil, and methotrexate)[1] increase the acute and late effects of radiation. Radiation in combination with cancer chemotherapy can increase the cure rate in some cancers. A cytotoxic drug does not have to be one of those that enhances the side effects of radiation to be effective in combination with radiation.

§ 5.2   Machine Maintenance

Machine maintenance requires the services of a qualified physicist who is certified by the American Board of Radiology or an equivalent organization. Among the physicist's essential instruments is the thimble ion chamber for measuring radiation exposure rates. The accuracy of this instrument first must be assured by a calibration made during the previous two years at a facility traceable to the National Institute of Standards. The ion chamber is a cavity with a central electrode and outer shell. When exposed to a radiation beam, the gas in the cavity is ionized. The electrical charges are collected and measured by a meter. This information is translated into a statement of the radiation output of the machine in centiGray (cGy) per minute. The beam is further measured for its penetrability by placing various thicknesses of an absorbing medium between the radiation beam and the ion chamber. The amount of radiation that emerges is the *percentage depth dose,* an indication of the energy of the radiation. The energy also may be described as the *half value layer* (hvl) of the beam, namely, the thickness of absorbing material that reduces the amount of radiation by one-half. Each machine must have its own tables of measured depth doses. It is not advisable to use standard generic tables in place of the machine's own tables. Other dose determinations required include the amount of radiation lost or absorbed in transit through lucite trays used to hold beam shaping devices, scattered radiation from the collimator jaws and beam shaping blocks, and the amount of X-ray contamination in the electron beams.

Radiation treatments are set up by creating a light field that simulates the radiation field. There must be exact alignment between the light field and the

---

[1] See **Ch. 4.**

radiation beam it simulates. The alignment is tested by exposing X-ray film on which both the light field and radiation field are superimposed.

Laser lights projected from the walls of the room facilitate alignment of the patient's body in exactly the same position on each treatment day. The laser alignment with the machine isocenter is maintained with an accuracy of one millimeter. Additionally, all the light devices need to checked for off-center parallax errors.

An optical range finder that shows the distance between the radiation source and the patient's skin must give correct readings.

Various movements of the machine must not deviate from a fixed point in space, the *isocenter*. The movements relate to the rotation of the table on which the patient lies, the rotation of the gantry that swings the radiation source around the patient, and the rotation of the collimators that limit the size of the radiation beam.

To assure more homogeneous irradiation, the physicist checks the flatness and symmetry of the radiation beam. *Flatness* refers to the uniformity of the radiation dose across the face of the beam. Neither the flatness nor the radiation output should change when the gantry is set at different angles.

The meters on the machine's control panel must record the dose per unit time and the dose per monitor setting accurately. The field size readings on the collimators must be correct.

The physicist varies the frequency with which tests are done depending on the established behavior of the machine. Variations in testing usually are in the direction of more frequent rather than less frequent testing. Minimum requirements call for a comprehensive calibration every two years for X-ray machines, but once a year for 60-cobalt machines because the radiation source in cobalt machines decays at the rate of about one percent per month. Additional calibrations must be done when machine modifications or repairs may change the radiation output or characteristics of the beam. Spot checks of radiation output rates are required once a week for machines operating at 500 kV or higher and once a month for machine energies of less than 500 kV. In actual practice, it is not uncommon to have spot checks of radiation output daily as well as numerous other daily checks that include the lasers, optical distances, field sizes, and "beam off" buttons that terminate the treatment immediately when treatment must be interrupted. Items such as meter accuracy, beam flatness, focal spot size, light and X-ray field alignment, and energy constancy may be checked monthly. Kilovoltage machines may have their half-value layers checked twice a year.

Irrespective of machine maintenance protocols, every new electron field needs a measurement of the scatter radiation factor if 40 percent or more of the field is blocked. In some clinics, all the new electron fields, particularly the small ones, have this measurement.

Written records must be kept of all testing. Treatment factors for which calibrations do not exist must not be used by making approximations.

§ 5.3   Treatment Planning

Treatment planning starts with a consultation that includes a complete history and physical examination and analysis of previous records that will influence the conduct of radiation therapy. The laboratory tests and imaging procedures are reviewed. The imaging procedures include radiographs, radioisotope scans, computerized tomography (CT), magnetic resonance imaging (MRI), and sonograms that help delineate the volume and location of the tumor under consideration. If an operation has been done, the surgical report is reviewed. The histologic diagnosis is confirmed. Having established the tumor's location, size, invasion of adjacent tissues, and presence or absence of metastases, the staging is recorded.

If radiation is a preferred option, its possible combination with surgery, chemotherapy, and hyperthermia is determined. The options are presented to the patient, who makes a choice and gives an informed consent.

With respect to radiation, the objective is stated: cure versus palliation. The objective of palliation should be specific: to relieve pain, obstruction, or neurologic dysfunction; to stop bleeding; to prevent fracture; to facilitate healing of fracture when the fracture is due to a weakening of the bone by metastases; and to prolong life by reducing tumor volume.

The available forms of radiation are evaluated in order to choose methods that deliver enough radiation to eliminate the tumor cells with as little radiation as possible to the surrounding normal tissues and critical organs. The available forms of radiation are external radiation, intracavitary or interstitial brachytherapy, intraoperative radiation, and systemic radiation with radioisotopes.

The date to begin radiation is then set. Time may be allowed for healing a surgical wound or for recovering from a low leukocyte or platelet count following chemotherapy.

For external radiation, the energy of the radiation is selected based on the depth of the tumor, with the higher energies applied to the deeper tumors. The number of fields, their angles, and points of entry and exit are established. Based on the size and stage of the tumor, the size and shape of the radiation fields are determined by a process called *simulation*. A special machine, the simulator, is used. A simulator is an exact geometrical facsimile of the therapy machine and all its movements, but a diagnostic X-ray tube is substituted for the radiation therapy source. With high-quality radiographs and fluoroscopy, very accurate therapy fields are delineated. The fields are outlined on the patient's skin with marking fluid or with tiny India ink tattoos.

The basic fields are squares or rectangles. Irregular fields require the fabrication of custom blocks. Styrofoam molds are designed. A low melting point alloy is poured into the molds. The alloy solidifies into the desired shapes.

Following simulation, the patient is moved to the therapy machine and positioned. Patient movement during treatment can be a significant source of error.

Positioning and immobilization of the patient with supports, special pillows, straps, and molds are an important part of treatment planning. A bite block attached to the table is useful for positioning the head. The laser beams projected from the walls of the room are particularly valuable for daily reproducible positioning. Verification films are made to confirm the accurate duplication of the plan produced on the simulator. A photograph of the properly positioned patient and the skin markings is made a permanent part of the record.

Additional planning involves the choice of the total radiation dose to be delivered, the fractionation, and the overall duration of the course of treatment. The dosage calculations can be made manually or can be generated by computer from CT or MRI images. Accuracy requires that the CT and MRI images be made with the patient's body in the treatment position. For example, the therapy table is flat, while imaging tables may be concave. A board must be inserted to flatten the patient's body into the therapy configuration. Computerized dosimetry from CT images has the increased accuracy of translating inhomogeneities in tissue density into deflections and variations in the standard isodose displays. From these displays, the radiation patterns can be further adjusted by inserting wedges, boluses, and compensating filters into the radiation beam. Radiation beams can be mixed in advantageous ways. Photon beams of 4 and 6 meV may be combined with 18 meV photons, or photon beams can be combined with electron beams to shift locations of maximum dose areas and reduce dosage to critical organs.

Computerized dosimetry is important for ascertaining the volume of a critical organ exposed to radiation. In assessing potential injury to a critical organ, the dose is important, but the exposed volume may be equally important. A high dose to a small portion of an organ might not result in a clinically detectable injury.

§ 5.4 Radioisotopes

Radioisotopes may be divided into the naturally occurring radioactive elements and the artificially produced radioisotopes of the elements. The radioisotopes used in medicine may produce one or more of three kinds of radiation that are emitted: alpha, beta, and gamma rays. Alpha rays are positively charged helium nuclei. Beta rays are negatively charged electrons. Gamma rays are uncharged electromagnetic waves (photons), which are identical to X-rays. Radioisotopes decay at a constant rate, and the term *half-life* is an expression of the rate of decay.

Alpha rays result when the nucleus of an atom emits a combination of two protons and two neutrons, that is, a helium nucleus. Beta rays are emitted when a neutron in the nucleus changes to a proton by losing its electron. Gamma rays are emitted from the nucleus when the energy level of the nucleus drops from a higher to a lower level.

Activity in reference to radioisotopes deals with the intensity of the disintegration and emitted radiation per unit of time. The unit of activity is the Curie (Ci). It represents 3.7×10^{10} disintegrations per second.

The first radioisotopes used in medicine were the naturally occurring elements radium (226-Ra) and radon (222-Rn). Radon is no longer used, and radium is seldom used. They were employed in intracavitary and interstitial brachytherapy as sources of gamma rays. Their high average energy (0.83 meV) gave greater exposure to personnel handling them than artificial radioisotopes of lower energy currently available. Radium is used in the form of a salt. Fractures of the tubes and needles housing the radium powder can cause major contamination problems with the 1600-year half-life, making the contamination permanent. A contaminated room would have to be demolished. Radon is a gaseous product of radium decay. The gas emitted from a radium source was captured in small gold tubes called *seeds*. The seeds were injected into tumors. With its short half-life of 3.83 days, radon did not present the contamination danger of radium, but there was always concern about the quality control of the seeds, because of the gaseous nature of the element.

In the 1950s, the advent of the artificial radioisotope 60-cobalt was welcomed. It was a high-energy (1.17 and 1.33 meV) source of gamma rays. Small cobalt spheres were encased in tubes and needles. If the spheres accidentally escaped, they could be vacuumed without causing the contamination problems of powdered radium. The short half-life of 60-cobalt (5.26 years) required constant lengthening of treatment times as it decayed, and the frequent replacement of the sources was disadvantageous. Also, personnel exposure was not reduced with 60-cobalt.

Radium was used in milligram quantities in tubes and needles. Gram quantities of radium needed for external machine therapy (*teletherapy*) were prohibitively expensive and unavailable, but large quantities of cheap, reactor-produced 60-cobalt made it possible to develop megavoltage machine therapy using cobalt. Technological developments in medical linear accelerators brought about the replacement of cobalt machines beginning in the 1960s. The tiny focal spots in linear accelerators produced sharply defined X-ray beams that gave less radiation to normal tissues adjacent to tumors. The relatively large radioactive cobalt wafers gave gamma ray beams with undesirably large penumbras.

137-cesium replaced 60-cobalt in tubes and needles in the 1960s and is still widely used in intracavitary brachytherapy. 137-cesium has the advantages of a 30-year half-life, requiring infrequent replacement and a 0.662 meV gamma ray giving less exposure to personnel because of its lesser penetrability. Briefly, 137-cesium machine radiation was in vogue, but quickly was abandoned because of slow treatment times due to low radiation output and large penumbras due to large source sizes.

Other radioisotopes available in the form of seeds are 198-gold (half-life 2.7 days, energy 0.412 meV gamma rays), 125-iodine (half-life 60.2 days, average energy 0.028 meV gamma rays), and 192-iridium (half-life 74.2 days, average energy 0.38 meV gamma rays).

60-cobalt, 125-iodine, 192-iridium, and 90-strontium (half-life 28.9 years, energy 0.54 and 2.27 meV beta rays) are available as plaques for surface applications.

192-iridium and 182-tantalum (half-life 115 days, energy 0.18 to 0.514 meV beta rays and average energy 0.67 gamma rays) are available as wire.

Liquid radioisotopes ingested or infused for systemic therapy are 131-iodine (half-life 8 days, energy 90 percent 0.25 to 0.61 meV beta rays and 10 percent 0.364 meV average energy gamma rays) and 32-phosphorus as sodium radio-phosphate (half-life 14.3 days, energy 1.71 meV beta rays). In addition, 32-phosphorus and 198-gold can be prepared as colloidal solutions for injecting into body cavities.

§ 5.5   Interstitial Implants

The principle of *fractionation*,[2] which is indispensable for external radiation therapy, is not practical or may not be possible when radioactive materials are inserted into the body. The classical adjustment to the unavailability of fractionation is *protraction*. Protraction in brachytherapy (short distance therapy) involves the application of smaller amounts of radioactive material for longer periods of time to produce less reaction in normal tissues. Brachytherapy does have the advantage of delivering a high dose to a limited area with low doses to adjacent areas.

Interstitial implantation involves the insertion of radioactive materials directly into the tissues, in contrast to intracavitary implantation that places radioactive material into the cavities of hollow organs. Most brachytherapy requires anesthesia.

Interstitial implants can be divided into permanent implants and temporary implants. The choice is based on the half-life of the isotope selected. Isotopes with intermediate half lives can be used either as permanent or temporary implants. In the early years of radiation therapy, radium needles (half-life 1600 years) were used as temporary implants, the desired dose of radiation being achieved in a calculated number of hours. Radon seeds (half-life 3.83 days) were permanent implants, the desired dose being achieved with the complete decay of the radon. The "dead" gold seeds in which the radon had been encased remained in the tissues as permanent foreign bodies and were visible on radiographs.

Other seeds that are implanted permanently are 198-gold (half-life 2.7 days) and 125-iodine (half-life 60.2 days). The very low energy and 60.2-day half-life of 125-iodine make it a good permanent implant for low-grade tumors.

---

[2] See § **5.1.**

192-iridium seeds (half-life 74.2 days) are inserted temporarily. Their greater intensity makes them preferable to 125-iodine for high-grade tumors. To be removable, the iridium seeds are carried in plastic tubes or ribbons that are threaded into tumors. The ribbons, with their seeds, can be pulled out when the correct treatment time has elapsed.

192-iridium and 182-tantalum (half-life 115 days) are used in the form of wires for temporary implants.

In addition to radium, other isotopes in needle form for temporary implantation are 60-cobalt (half-life 5.26 years) and 137-cesium (half-life 30 years).

Interstitial brachytherapy owed its early development to the use of radium needles and radon seeds in oral cancers, and later in many other organ systems. The subsequent approaches to using needles, seeds, and wires of all the other isotopes are derived from the experience gained from radium and radon. Computerized dosimetry has added substantial precision to treating given volumes of tumor by furnishing information about the activity of the radioisotopes to be used, the spacing of the radiation sources, and the duration of the radiation exposure. The implantation can last one to three days. The quantity of radioisotopes used may be expressed in two ways: the total number of millicuries or the total amount of radium equivalent milligrams. Due to the vast previous experience with radiation, oncologists prefer to use the newer radioisotopes in terms of their radium equivalence. The dose in centiGray can be calculated from the total exposure in millicurie hours or radium equivalent milligram hours.

In the brachytherapy of temporary implantations, the counterpart to the simulation for external radiation is the insertion of inactive "dummy" sources into the tumor for radiography to be used to get correct spacing and to make other calculations prior to inserting the radioactive sources. This technique is called *afterloading*. One representative afterloading method involves inserting hollow metal guides into the tumor. The dummies are fed into the guides. The guides are removed. When the manipulation of the dummies is completed, they are replaced by the active sources. The afterloading technique allows operators to work without haste to position the sources carefully and make more complex arrangements without rushing to avoid exposure to radiation. The spacing usually places the sources one centimeter apart. Implantations are made in one or more planes depending on the thickness of the tumor.

§ 5.6 Intracavitary Implants

Intracavitary implants have had their greatest use in gynecologic cancers. As with interstitial implants, the techniques were developed using radium. Similarly, radium was followed by the use of 60-cobalt and more recently by 137-cesium. For these procedures, the isotopes are encased in metal tubes, which can be placed in a variety of applicators that fit the anatomic areas to be irradiated.

In cervical carcinoma, a rod containing cesium tubes in tandem arrangement is placed in the cervical and uterine canal. Small cylinders (colpostats) containing cesium are placed upright in each lateral vaginal fornix. In endometrial carcinoma, single cesium tubes are placed in individual metal capsules and inserted into the uterine canal until the uterine cavity is filled. In vaginal carcinoma, plastic cylinders with cesium in tandem arrangement are placed lengthwise in the vagina. These are representative examples of ways in which intracavitary implantations can be used in gynecologic cancers. Afterloading techniques can be used as with interstitial implants. Computerized dosimetry is necessary to avoid overdosage to the bladder and rectum.

The peritoneal cavity can be treated by infusing colloidal solutions of 32-phosphorus and 198-gold in ovarian carcinoma and when peritoneal washings show tumor cells in endometrial carcinoma.

Radioactive elements can be attached to custom-made molds for intracavitary irradiation. Molds can be used postoperatively in the paranasal sinuses and nasal fossa.

Radioactive elements in catheters can be used to irradiate the bladder, esophagus, bile ducts, bronchi, and nasopharynx.

§ 5.7   Complications

The term *radiation complication* is frequently misapplied. The common reactions that accompany radiation are not complications any more than an incision is a complication of surgery. Complications need correct definition. The acute side effects of radiation generally are not complications unless they persist long after they should subside. Radiation-related conditions that appear for the first time months or years following radiation therapy may be complications.

Complications due to poorly administered radiation are avoidable, but biologic variability among individuals means that a small number of patients will have problems regardless of how perfectly the radiation has been delivered. Complications up to 5 percent and sometimes even 10 percent can be expected with good radiation therapy.

Complications are not necessarily the direct result of radiation. They may be triggered at any time during the follow-up period by infection, chemical or physical trauma, and normal aging (arteriosclerosis) of the previously irradiated tissues.

The side effects that are not complications are both systemic and local, the systemic effects being common to all radiation, and the local effects being confined to the area irradiated. Not all patients have side effects. Fatigue is a systemic side effect. It usually appears toward the end of the course of treatment and lasts several weeks.

Other systemic reactions are reductions in white blood cells and platelets, loss of appetite, nausea, and vomiting. The severity of systemic reactions is related to the volume of tissue irradiated, the organs irradiated, and the amount and rate of irradiation.

Confusion arises when reports of fatal radiation accidents reveal amounts of radiation exposure far less than the doses used to treat cancer. An instantaneous 400 cGy dose of total body radiation is fatal in a few weeks in 50 percent (Lethal Dose 50) of exposed individuals who are not given intensive treatment to combat marrow suppression and infection. Intensive medical care will about double the Lethal Dose 50. 1000 cGy is fatal within days due to loss of the intestinal mucosa, yet 6000 cGy of well-fractionated circumscribed radiation to a tumor is easily tolerated because of volume and dose rate considerations.

Prolongation of treatment (*protraction*) reduces the intensity of acute reactions, but will not have the effect on delayed complications that fraction size has. Fractions of 300 cGy or more are well-tolerated in a variety of situations, but can be considered a source of complications in others.

Mutagenesis is a phenomenon found in the experimental laboratory, but there is no human data showing that patients receiving therapeutic radiation are affected by it.

Carcinogenesis has occurred in people ranging from radiation workers to A-bomb survivors. In therapeutic radiology, carcinogenesis has occurred in children and adults irradiated for benign diseases. Carcinoma of the thyroid has been notable in children, and leukemia (not chronic lymphatic leukemia) has been notable in adults. The incidence of leukemia is higher when radiation and chemotherapy are combined.

The overall incidence of a second tumor in an irradiated field is not over 1 percent and should not be a basis for declining radiation. In pediatric tumors, the development of regimens with progressively lower radiation dose totals is expected to reduce the incidence of second tumors.

Surgery on irradiated tissues requires meticulous handling to reduce the possibilities of infection, wound separation, fistulas, necrosis of skin flaps, and carotid artery rupture.

§ 5.8   —Orbit

In the orbital region, the lens should be shielded whenever it can be protected without jeopardizing adequate irradiation of the tumor. Otherwise, a radiation cataract must be accepted. A single dose of 200 cGy can produce a cataract. Divided doses may require two or three times as much radiation.

In the treatment of carcinoma of the eyelid, loss of eyelashes is a normal sequela, not a complication. When the carcinoma involves the inner canthus of the eyelids, lacrimal duct stenosis and tearing of the eye is an unavoidable complication, if it occurs, and the patient must be aware of the possibility. An unavoidable consequence of irradiation of lacrimal gland tumors is a dry eye. Keratinization of the cornea can cause conjunctival irritation.

In plaque therapy of eye tumors, the optic nerve and large retinal vessels can be damaged if the plaque is placed too close to them. Vitreous and retinal hemorrhage can occur. Diplopia may result from cut muscles. Glaucoma may be secondary to uveitis or vitreous hemorrhage.

Irradiation of orbital tumors in children can result in hypopituitarism.

§ 5.9   —Head and Neck

In irradiation of the head and neck, necrosis of the sphenoid, temporal, and maxillary bones might occur, but necrosis of the mandible from irradiation of oral cancers is seen more often. Osteoradionecrosis of the mandible is a complication that can occur despite all preventative precautions, but all preventative measures should be recorded as having been taken. Previously, all teeth were extracted prior to radiation, but now only broken, carious, and infected teeth are extracted, sockets smoothed, and jagged bone fragments removed. A week to 10 days is allowed for healing. For the remaining teeth, dental trays should be constructed for daily self-administered fluoride gel treatments to prevent caries that could be followed by infection and necrosis of the mandible. To further reduce the risk of mandibular necrosis, a one-centimeter gap should be left between an interstitial implant and the mandible. A stent can be placed over the gingiva to push the implant away from the mandible.

If caries occur due to radiation, they are typically at the neck of the tooth. Eventually, the tooth breaks off. If any benefit derives from living with false teeth, it accrues to the person who develops oral cancer.

If necrosis of the mandible occurs and is painless, the best management is to keep the exposed mandible clean and observe the area until it heals by sequestration and extrusion of the necrotic bone. This results in less loss of mandibular bone. If the osteonecrosis is quite painful, surgical resection is the alternative.

Necrosis of the maxillary sinus seldom requires more than establishing dependent drainage for healing.

The patient's responsibility in preventing mandibular and maxillary necrosis includes telling every dentist she visits that her jaws have been irradiated. The patient should have antibiotic coverage, and any dental work should consist of the least traumatic option.

Radiation mucositis appearing about the tenth day of treatment and loss of taste occurring earlier are normal side effects of oral and pharyngeal irradiation. The taste returns, but there can be one or two foods for which it does not become entirely normal. Other acute side effects are oral pain, thickened saliva, dysphagia, and hoarseness. Xerostomia is a frequent permanent sequela. Patients with xerostomia should maintain good oral hygiene to avoid monilial infection in the mouth.

In laryngeal carcinoma, severe edema in the postradiation period can require a tracheostomy. The edema can result from residual cancer or to excessive radiation given too rapidly through fields that were too large.

Aside from necrosis of the suprahyoid epiglottis, which is relatively harmless, necrosis of the laryngeal cartilages is a critical development. It can be due to tumor invasion, infection, or excessive radiation. The symptoms are pain, fever, pneumonia, and respiratory obstruction. Prompt surgical intervention is needed.

Conduction deafness due to swelling of the eustachian tubes is a common side effect of pharyngeal irradiation. Decongestants are useful. If the deafness does not clear spontaneously, a stent may be placed through the ear drum to equalize the air pressure.

§ 5.10   —Thorax

The heart is subject to incidental irradiation during treatment of most thoracic tumors. Doses exceeding 4000 cGy cause pericarditis and myocarditis due to capillary damage.

When carcinoma of the lung invades the esophagus, a tracheoesophageal fistula can be expected. Radiation therapy in this situation can accelerate the development of the fistula.

The irradiation of lung tumors results in variable degrees of pulmonary fibrosis. The possibility of more severe respiratory disability needs to be assessed in patients with preexisting emphysema or pneumoconiosis.

Curative irradiation of a lung tumor can result three months later in a pneumonitis with cough, dyspnea, pain, and sometimes fever. The condition clears with no more than the fibrosis expected with the same amount of radiation in the absence of significant pneumonitis.

§ 5.11 —Breast

Edema of the arm can result from axillary surgery for breast carcinoma. The incidence of edema increases when axillary radiation is added to the surgery.

Slight amounts of fibrosis (induration), tanning, and telangiectasia are to be expected following irradiation of the breast. The fibrosis is more noticeable in larger breasts in which the irradiated volume is large. A complication is present when there is marked subcutaneous fibrosis causing swelling and pain in the breast.

Pneumonitis, as described in connection with direct irradiation of the lung, occasionally develops about three months following irradiation of the breast, despite the use of tangential fields to reduce pulmonary irradiation.

Spontaneous fractures of the ribs underlying the irradiated breast may occur several years later.

§ 5.12   —Gastrointestinal Tract

Irradiation of esophageal tumors may result in sufficient fibrosis to constrict the esophagus and require dilatations. This is not a preventable complication.

Ulceration of the stomach is possible with doses exceeding 4500 cGy. It can be treated medically or surgically.

Ulceration and stenosis of the small intestine become risks with doses exceeding 4500 cGy. The risk reaches 10 percent at 5000 cGy. This dosage can be unavoidable due to the location of the tumor. The risk of small intestinal injury from the presence of adhesions is greater in postoperative radiation than in preoperative radiation. Surgical adhesions fix the bowel so it is no longer a moving target that can shift out of the field of radiation from time to time. For pelvic irradiation, an omental curtain is sometimes constructed to keep the small bowel out of the pelvis. A barium X-ray examination determines if the attempt has been successful. Diarrhea, cramping, and vomiting that may occur during the second or third week of abdominal or pelvic irradiation is a side effect, not a complication. At a later date, the same symptoms occurring as a result of ulceration or stenosis of the small bowel are due to a complication.

Proctitis, both an acute side effect and a chronic complication, produces diarrhea, tenesmus, and bleeding. If rectal bleeding in the later follow-up period is due to telangiectasia, it can be controlled with laser treatment. Rectal inflammation, ulceration, and stenosis may be treated medically or by surgical intervention.

§ 5.13   —Pancreas

With doses exceeding 4000 cGy in pancreatic irradiation, the risk of duodenal ulceration and bleeding must be accepted. Renal failure can occur if the kidneys are not adequately excluded from the external radiation fields.

Abscess formation and anastomotic leaks are complications of 125-iodine implants in the pancreas.

§ 5.14   —Liver and Biliary Tract

Liver failure can occur if most of the liver is included in a radiation field delivering over 3000 cGy.

The dosage needed to irradiate biliary carcinomas is in the risk area for duo-denal ulceration and bleeding.

§ 5.15   —Prostate

Complications from the irradiation of prostatic carcinoma are less than 10 per-cent. Complications of interstitial implantations can be urethral-rectal and vesico-rectal fistulas, bladder neck obstruction, abscess, chronic proctitis and cystitis, and hematuria. Complications of external radiation are bladder neck obstruction and chronic cystitis and proctitis. Impotence in 50 percent of the patients is not a complication. On the contrary, the preservation of potency in 50 percent of patients is a benefit of radiation.

§ 5.16   —Urinary Tract

Acute cystitis in irradiation of the bladder is not a complication. Chronic symp-toms of dysuria, bleeding, and frequency occurring a number of months after-wards can be caused by complications such as fibrosis, ulceration, and contraction of the bladder.

The irradiation of abdominal tumors often places the kidneys in the radiation field. Excessive irradiation of the kidneys results in hypertension and/or kidney failure. Hypertension can occur several years after doses exceeding 1500 cGy. Renal failure can occur with doses exceeding 2400 cGy.

§ 5.17   —Gynecologic Tumors

Urethral stricture from irradiation of gynecologic tumors is managed by periodic urethral dilatations. Any substantial pelvic irradiation causes amenorrhea and sterilization in women. Surgical attempts can be made to move the ovaries nar-rowly outside the radiation fields, but there is no guarantee that fertility will be preserved. The majority of women will get amenorrhea with 500 cGy to the ovaries.

Hydronephrosis due to ureteral obstruction has been described as a complica-tion of radiation therapy for carcinoma of the cervix, but it is rare. Urethral obstruction is nearly always due to recurrent carcinoma.

Irradiation of carcinomas of the cervix and vagina and doses of 6000 cGy to the bladder and rectum result in 5 percent incidence of chronic cystitis or procti-tis. Excessive radiation to the bladder and rectum can occur from slippage of the intracavitary brachytherapy applicators due to inadequate packing to hold them in place or because confused patients pull the packing out. Other causes of over-dosage can be a retroflexed uterus or a narrow vagina. Radiographs confirm, at least at the beginning of the application, that the location of the radioactive sources in relation to the bladder and rectum is correct. Sometimes brachyther-apy results in small bowel injury because a loop of small bowel is adherent to the uterus as a result of previous surgery or infection.

Radiation therapy for carcinoma of the cervix during the third trimester of pregnancy is injurious to fetuses that are expected to survive. Attempts to pro-tect the fetus by limiting the radiation to brachytherapy cannot be considered acceptable.

Vaginal stenosis and edema of the vulva can occur from irradiation of gyneco-logic tumors. Permanent epilation of the pubic hair must be expected. Vesico-vaginal and rectovaginal fistulas can be caused by radiation, but in the great majority of cases they are due to residual tumors.

When external radiation and brachytherapy are combined, the plethora of vari-ables such as fractionation, protraction, rest periods, dose rate, and dose distri-bution prevent exact precision in predicting the outcomes of particular regimens.

Ischemic necrosis of the femoral head and neck can occur following pelvic irradiation in older women. Ischemic necrosis can be avoided by limiting the radiation dose to the hip joints to 3000 cGy.

§ 5.18   —Testis

Sterilization also can occur in men from scattered radiation despite the fact that the testes are outside the pelvis. These occurrences are not complications. Aspermia can develop in several weeks in men receiving 600 cGy to the testes. Patients must be informed about sterilization. Men can bank their sperm before the radiation treatments if they wish.

§ 5.19   —Neurologic

Transverse myelitis is a grave complication of spinal cord overexposure to radia-tion. The cord is at risk in the treatment of any tumor in which the radiation passes through the cord. 4000 cGy in four weeks to a segment of spinal cord not exceeding 10 cm in length is considered a safe dose.

Neuropsychologic dysfunction may develop from irradiation of the brain with large fractions such as 300 cGy per treatment.

Brachytherapy regimens that supplement or re-treat brain tumors after exter-nal radiation can result in localized necrosis of the brain. Resection of the necrotic tissue relieves pressure.

§ 5.20   —Skin

A number of skin changes are normal side effects of radiation. Lower doses of radiation cause increased pigmentation of the skin resulting in long-lasting tanning. High doses, particularly treatment for skin cancer, can kill the melanocytes so that patchy achromia results. Other acute side effects are erythema and dry or moist desquamation.

Acute ulceration in the treatment of skin cancer is not a complication. Necrosis of the skin can be initiated when the patient does not take sufficient care to avoid trauma, infection, or sunburn.

Epilation is expected and is not a complication. Irradiation of the scalp can result in partial or complete loss of hair. If the hair grows back, it is often a darker color.

Total body radiation regimens can cause loss of the fingernails or toenails if they are not shielded.

Erythema multiforme is a rare complication that begins in the field of radiation and spreads like a sunburst to the entire body. It is said to be the result of autosensitization to the tissue products of radiation. However, after the erythema multiforme subsides, additional radiation has been given without reproducing the condition.

§ 5.21   —Soft Tissue Sarcoma

Irradiation of soft tissue sarcomas in extremities, also bone tumors, can result in chronic edema. The records should show an effort to prevent chronic edema by shielding a strip of soft tissue along the extremity.

§ 5.22   —Pediatric Tumors

Disturbances in bone growth are an inevitable consequence of irradiation of pediatric tumors and are not the products of badly administered radiation.

§ 5.23   Commentary and Significant Cases

The radiation therapist has to be wary of details in planning and performing treatments. Correct ports for therapy and dosages are critical. Minor errors lead to major complications. Patient sensitivity to radiation often cannot be predicted.

Bewley v. Long Beach Memorial Hospital.[3]   A defense verdict was reached in which the 52-year-old patient died in 1981 from erosion of an artery of the neck, causing exsanguination. She had been given radiation therapy for Hodgkin's disease from March until September 1966.

Brown v. Comerford.[4]   A directed verdict for the defense was affirmed. The plaintiff was treated for cancer by the defendant radiation oncologist. Because the equipment used in the therapy was incorrectly calibrated, the plaintiff received 14 percent more radiation than the amount prescribed. The plaintiff argued that because radiation therapy has the potential for destroying healthy as well as malignant cells and sometimes produces injuries, complications, and fatalities, it is ipso facto abnormally dangerous. The court held that unavoidable danger inherent in accepted methods of medical treatment does not render it an abnormally dangerous activity as required to impose a strict liability on the physician who treated a patient, but was not involved in miscalibration of the machine.

Brown v. Sklaroff.[5]   The plaintiff had a diagnosis of Hodgkin's disease in 1967 at the age of 15. She remained symptom-free until 1970, when she began to complain of pain in the L5-S1 region of the back. Metastasis of the previous malignancy to the lumbar and/or sacral area was not demonstrated. In 1971, the plaintiff began a course of radiation therapy and chemotherapy despite negative bone scans and lack of histologic confirmation of metastasis. The plaintiff alleged that the unnecessary and improper course of treatment resulted in neurologic impairment, paresthesia, difficulty in walking, and pain and weakness of both lower extremities. The suit was settled.

Deceglia v. Nassau County.[6]   Blindness occurred in the 55-year-old plaintiff following radiation therapy for a grade II astrocytoma brain tumor. The treatment consisted of 5580 rads, but the plaintiff contended that radiation to the optic chiasm should have been shielded from rads over 5000. There was a verdict for $747,000.

---

[3]No. C-413, 143 (L.A. County Super. Ct.), *reprinted in* 4 Med. Malpractice Verdicts, Settlements & Experts No. 1, at 42 (1988).

[4]99 Or. App. 60, 781 P.2d 857 (1989).

[5]No. 8-82-2460 (Phila. C.P. Dec. 19, 1986), *reprinted in* 3 Med. Malpractice Verdicts, Settlements & Experts No. 9, at 39 (1987).

[6]No. 14793/84 (Nassau County N.Y. Sept. 1990), *reprinted in* 6 Med. Malpractice Verdicts, Settlements & Experts No. 12, at 60 (1990).

Doherty v. Hellman.[7]   The plaintiff was treated for breast cancer after lumpectomy by means of radiation therapy and iridium implants. The radiation therapist defendant recommended and administered the plan of therapy devised by Dr. Hellman (another defendant). The plaintiff developed radiation necrosis with debilitating complications and disfigurement. The court granted summary judgment for Dr. Hellman, rejecting the plaintiff's assertion that one who "pioneers" a new therapy is thereby liable for unfavorable results suffered by patients who follow the new therapy with their own physicians.

Duke v. Morphis.[8]   Excessive radiation to the spinal cord resulted from radon seeds implanted in the supraclavicular area for cancer. The plaintiff suffered myelopathy and paralysis. The defendant claimed the injuries were due to the cancer's closeness to the spinal cord. A verdict of $266,700 was returned.

Euston v. Braun.[9]   The decedent was diagnosed with a malignant thymoma. The tumor was unresectable, stage III, with a five-year survival rate of less than 20 percent. Chemotherapy was given which resulted in partial regression of the tumor, and this treatment was followed by 4000 rads of radiation to an area including the heart. A booster dose of 2000 rads was administered through a smaller field. Constructive pericarditis developed with symptoms of chest pain and shortness of breath. Pericardiectomy was performed, but a bronchopleural fistula and pneumonia developed. The decedent died from pneumonia and sepsis. The plaintiff alleged that excessive radiation was administered. The case was settled for $550,000.

Giacco v. DiDominica.[10]   The plaintiff was diagnosed as having endometrial adenocarcinoma and underwent a total hysterectomy. She was then given a course of radiation of 4500 rads over a five-week period, following which a cerium disk was implanted vaginally for an additional 4000 rads over a period of three days. Two hours before the end of the three-day exposure period, the disk position shifted and the patient immediately notified the hospital staff. The disk was not removed for approximately one-half hour. She subsequently suffered chronic pain and discomfort, chronic bleeding, and rectal incontinence (must wear diapers). The plaintiff claimed excessive radiation and failure to remove cerium disk promptly, resulting in burns to areas that never should have been exposed to radiation. A $750,000 settlement resulted.

---

[7] 547 N.E.2d 931 (Mass. 1989).

[8] No. 352-62434-80 (Tarrant County Tex.), *reprinted in* 4 Med. Malpractice Verdicts, Settlements & Experts No. 1, at 43 (1988).

[9] No. EAC55513 (L.A. County Super. Ct.), *reprinted in* 7 Med. Malpractice Verdicts, Settlements & Experts No. 3, at 40 (1991).

[10] No. 17044/86 (Bronx County Sup. Ct.), *reprinted in* 5 Med. Malpractice Verdicts, Settlements & Experts No. 12, at 36 (1989).

Golstein v. Superior Court.[11]   There was a $500,000 settlement, but the parent's claim for emotional distress was denied. The nine-year-old decedent was diagnosed with cancer in November 1987. Data for radiation therapy dosages were supplied by a computer facility. The decedent received too much radiation and died in August 1988 from radiation toxicity. The court held that for emotional distress theory or recovery, the "bystander" rule requires that the plaintiff must be present at the scene of the injury-producing event when it occurs and be aware that it is causing injury to the victim.

Nerigstad v. United States.[12]   A $250,000 settlement resulted when the 74-year-old plaintiff was treated with radiation therapy for prostate cancer and developed sciatic nerve damage with paralysis of the legs. The plaintiff contended that the radiation therapy was given in too high a dosage over too large an area.

Mays v. United States.[13]   The decedent, who had been suffering from voice loss and a cough, had a chest X-ray in January 1977 that showed a 4-cm lung lesion. The decedent was neither advised of the X-ray findings nor of the need to return for a follow-up examination. A repeat chest X-ray was performed in March 1977, and again, the decedent was not notified of the findings. In May 1978, further chest X-rays showed the lesion to be five and one-half centimeters in size. Radiation therapy was administered, but three months later, she developed numbness and tingling in the legs, loss of sensation, and loss of bladder control that progressed to complete paralysis below the midchest level. The diagnosis was radiation-induced transverse myelitis. She died in January 1982 of cancer. The court, applying Colorado law, found that the husband was entitled to recover damages for reduction in his wife's chance of survival, and that the radiation therapy administered was below the applicable standards of the community.

Meachum v. United States.[14]   Cancer of the left anterior tonsillar pillar was diagnosed. The patient was given radiation therapy over several months. Excessive amounts of radiation caused damage to the skin and tissues of the face and neck. This also predisposed the patient to future malignancies. The suit was settled for $400,000.

---

[11] 223 Cal. App. 3d 1415, 273 Cal. Rptr. 270 (1990).

[12] No. C89-276TB (W.D. Wash. 1989), *reprinted in* 6 Med. Malpractice Verdicts, Settlements & Experts No. 8, at 44 (1990).

[13] 608 F. Supp. 1476 (D. Colo. 1985).

[14] No. M-84-2471 (D. Md.), *reprinted in* 3 Med. Malpractice Verdicts, Settlements & Experts No. 10, at 34 (1987).

Nelson v. Patrick.[15]   The plaintiff claimed that the defendants failed to adequately inform her of the known hazards of radiation therapy and thereby did not obtain her informed consent for the radiation treatment. Medical malpractice based on lack of informed consent is governed by the three-year statute of limitations applicable to negligence actions.[16] The court held that voluntary dismissal of a claim of negligent treatment did not result in dismissal of the claim for failure to obtain informed consent.

Newell v. Richards.[17]   The plaintiff was treated with radiation therapy for cancer that was ultimately cured. Bowel complications developed that the plaintiff alleged were the result of improper use of radiation. The court held that the statute of limitations had run, and found for the defendant.

Rudman v. Beth Israel Medical Center.[18]   Excessive radiation to the spine was given for nasopharyngeal cancer and progressive paralysis resulted. The defense stated that this was an inherent risk of the procedure that was necessary to save the plaintiff's life. The plaintiff alleged that a pilot film, which is standard procedure for safely plotting the portals of entry for the radiation beams, had not been made before the patient was radiated. There was a $2 million settlement.

Teschner v. Mirenda.[19]   The plaintiff alleged that following laryngectomy surgery for cancer, excessive radiation doses were given in some areas and inadequate doses in other areas. Ulceration of the skin and a recurrence of cancer in the stoma site (tracheostomy) resulted, with eventual death. The jury found for the defendants on medical malpractice, but awarded the decedent's spouse $28,000 for loss of consortium.

Tse v. Willis.[20] The plaintiff was suffering from terminal colon cancer and was given radiation therapy to prevent cancer recurrence and possible bowel obstruction. Injuries of weight loss, nausea, and radiation burns were claimed. The defendant contended that the radiation was proper and necessary. The jury brought a defense verdict.

---

[15] 293 S.E.2d 829 (N.C. App. 1982).

[16] N.C. Gen. Stat. § 90-21.13(a)(3).

[17] No. 86-CG-3346 (Baltimore County Cir. Ct.), *reprinted in* 6 Med. Malpractice Verdicts, Settlements & Experts No. 12, at 43 (1990).

[18] No. 4764/86 (N.Y. County Sup. Ct. May 13, 1988), *reprinted in* 4 Med. Malpractice Verdicts, Settlements & Experts No. 7, at 46 (1988).

[19] No. 842-5669 (St. Louis, Div. no. 7), *reprinted in* 4 Med. Malpractice Verdicts, Settlements & Experts No. 10, at 39 (1988).

[20] No. A8508-04906 (Multnomah County, Or.), *reprinted in* 3 Med. Malpractice Verdicts, Settlements & Experts No. 12, at 42 (1987).

Wilkinson v. Vesey.[21]   In 1951, the plaintiff had a chest X-ray that showed a "shadow," interpreted as probably a lymphoma or possibly a substernal thyroid. Without benefit of a biopsy, radiation therapy was started. After 11 days, a repeat X-ray showed shrinkage of the shadow. The defendant concluded that the plaintiff had a malignant tumor and continued therapy. In 1955, the skin of the chest area broke down and multiple surgeries, including skin grafts and removal of ribs, clavicle, and sternum, were necessary for radiation damage from the earlier treatments. Expert testimony showed that the accepted community standard was not to recommend radiation therapy unless convinced that the patient had cancer. The court held that failure to use all scientific facilities available so that the best factual data could be obtained can be considered negligence. A directed verdict for the defendants was reversed.

---

[21] 110 R.I. 606, 295 A.2d 676 (1972).

CHAPTER 6

ORBIT NEOPLASMS

MELANOMA

§ 6.1   Staging and Classification

Melanoma of Eyelid

TNM: American Joint Committee on Cancer.[1]

---

[1] American Joint Committee on Cancer, Manual for Staging of Cancer. 218 (3d ed. 1988).

The TNM system is not ordinarily utilized, whereas Breslow's thickness and Clark's level are related to prognosis.

Melanoma of Conjunctiva

TNM: American Joint Committee on Cancer.[2]
The prognosis relates to tumor depth and to the extent of conjunctiva involvement.

Melanoma of Uvea

TNM: American Joint Committee on Cancer.[3]
The prognosis of melanoma involving the iris or the ciliary body is related to the local extent of the tumor, whereas in the choroid tumor, dimension and elevation are significant as to prognosis.

§ 6.2   Etiology

Malignant melanoma arises from melanocytes (mature melanin-producing cells) within the normal eye tissues, the surrounding tissues, or in congenital acquired melanocytic lesions (such as benign nevi).[4]

There is evidence of familial tendency for ocular melanomas.[5] This can be an autosomal dominant trait.[6] An association of uveal melanomas with von Recklinghausen's disease has been shown.[7]

§ 6.3   Clinical Manifestations

Malignant melanoma of the skin of the eyelids are similar to other skin melanomas. A change in any pigmented lesion (pink, brown, red, white, blue, or

---

[2] *Id.* at 228.

[3] *Id.* at 232.

[4] G. Smolin, *Malignant Change of a Benign Melanoma; Report of a Case,* 61 Am. J. Ophthalmology 174 (1966); M. Yanoff & L.E. Zimmerman, *Histogenesis of Malignant Melanomas of the Uvea. III. The Relationship of Congenital Ocular Melanocytosis and Meurofibromatosis to Uveal Melanomas,* 77 Archives Ophthalmology 331 (1967).

[5] D.E. Anderson et al., *Hereditary Aspects of Malignant Melanoma,* 200 JAMA 741 (1967); S.F. Bowen, Jr., et al., *Malignant Melanoma of Eye Occurring in Two Successive Generations,* 71 Archives Opthalmology 805 (1964); R.C. Davenport, *A Family History of Choroidal Sarcoma,* 11 Brit. J. Ophthalmology 443 (1927).

[6] H.T. Lynch et al., *Heredity and Intraocular Melanoma: Study of Two Families and Review of Forty-Five Cases,* 21 Cancer 119 (1968).

[7] J. Nordmann & A. Brini, *Von Recklinghausen's Disease and Melanoma of the Uvea,* 54 Brit. J. Ophthalmology 641 (1970).

black) with darkening of color, nodularity, pruritus, ulceration, or bleeding can indicate malignancy. Conjunctival pigmented lesions are ordinarily benign.

A pigmented area of the iris associated with distorted pupil, neovascularization, ectropion uvea, elevation of intraocular pressure, and local cataract formation is the usual presentation of melanoma of the iris. Ciliary body pigmented lesions with extension into the iris root, choroid, or episclera can indicate malignancy. Melanoma of the choroid appears as an elevated gray-to-brown subretinal mass with retinal detachment. Choroidal melanomas at the posterior retina cause loss of normal vision.

§ 6.4 Diagnosis

Direct and indirect ophthalmoscopy visualizes the characteristics of a melanoma of the ciliary body and choroid.[8] Tumor detail can be analyzed with the biomicroscope and the Goldmann three-mirror contact lens. Visual fields should be tested. The other eye should be examined for vision and evidence of any suspicious lesions.

Indirect ophthalmoscopy, fluorescein angiography, and ultrasonography establish the diagnosis in ocular melanomas. Growth is documented by serial fundus photographs. There should be a positive p^{32} test,[9] because neoplastic tissues take up the injected radioactive phosphorus preferentially. Other diagnostic procedures available for orbital tumors include:

1. X-rays of the skull, orbits, optic foramina and canals, sphenoid ridges, paranasal sinuses
2. CT scanning with and without contrast
3. Ultrasonography (A and B modes)
4. Orbital venography (to rule out inflammatory diseases)
5. Contrast orbitography
6. Pleuridirectional polytomography
7. Cerebral angiography
8. Magnetic resonance imaging (MRI).

Conjunctival and eyelid lesions must be biopsied for definitive diagnosis. Incisional biopsy is not associated with tumor spread or decreased survival.

---

[8] J.A. Shields, *Current Approaches to the Diagnosis and Management of Choroidal Melanoma,* 21 Surgical Ophthalmology 443 (1977).

[9] J.A. Shields, *Accuracy and Limitations of the P Test in the Diagnosis of Ocular Tumors. An Analysis of 500 Cases,* 85 Ophthalmology 950 (1978).

§ 6.5 Surgical Treatment

A wide local excision with resection of regional lymph nodes is performed for melanomas of the eyelid skin. Conjunctival melanoma requires wide local resection, but large lesions can require orbital exenteration.[10]

Choroidal Melanoma

Choroidal melanomas can have little or no potential to cause local tissue damage or to metastasize. Xenon arc photocoagulation or argon lasers can be used in lesions not exceeding 10 mm in diameter or 3 mm in thickness as measured by A-scan ultrasonography.

A tumor that shows evidence of growth that is greater than 6 mm in diameter and 3 mm in elevation and is less than 15 mm in diameter and 8 mm in elevation can be treated with cobalt plaque radiotherapy.[11]

Periscleral choroid tumors can require sclerochorioretinal resection (full-thickness eye wall resection).[12] The tumor should not exceed 8 mm in diameter and 6 mm in thickness, the vitreous must be clear to allow preoperative photocoagulation, and there should be minimal retinal detachment.

Iris Melanoma

Most melanomas of the iris are relatively benign and slow growing. If there is definite evidence of growth, sector iridectomy can be performed. For tumors involving the iris and ciliary body, a segmental iridocyclectomy is performed.

Uvea Melanoma

Enucleation is indicated for a diffuse iris melanoma producing severe secondary glaucoma and that is too large to surgically resect, a ciliary or choroidal melanoma associated with significant visual loss and too large to treat with radiation or surgical resection, or any posterior or uveal melanoma that has total retinal detachment, dense cataract, and secondary glaucoma.

Orbital exenteration may be indicated when there is extrascleral extension of melanoma.[13]

---

[10] A.B. Reese, Tumors of the Eye (1976).

[11] J.A. Shields, *Surgical and Nonsurgical Management of Intraocular Tumors, in* Ophthalmic Surgery: Principles and Practice 728 (G.L. Spaeth ed., 1982).

[12] G.A. Peyman et al., *Full-Thickness Eye Wall Resection in Primates. An Experimental Approach to the Treatment of Choroidal Melanoma,* 89 Archives Ophthalmology 410 (1973).

[13] H.C. Shammas & F.C. Blodi, *Orbital Extension of Choroidal and Ciliary Body Melanomas,* 95 Archives Ophthalmology 2002 (1977).

§ 6.6   Chemotherapy Treatment

Hematogenous spread to the liver can occur with extraocular extension or during enucleation by too vigorous manipulation of the organ. This development can be followed by metastases to other sites. Metastatic melanoma is incurable, and treatment with chemotherapy is similar to the treatment of metastatic integument melanomas.[14]

§ 6.7   Radiation Therapy Treatment

Selected melanomas of the choroid can be treated successfully with radiation with preservation of the eye. They can be further classified by size as small, medium, and large. The medium range is 10 to 15 mm in diameter and 2.1 to 5 mm in elevation. The medium ones are those suitable for radiation, provided they are at least 2 mm away from the optic nerve. Brachytherapy is the method of treatment. Cobalt-60 or iodine-125 radioactive plaques are sutured to the eyeball over the tumor. Because of the rapid fall-off of the radiation in brachytherapy, a tumor dose of 10,000 cGy can be given with a low incidence of radiation injury to the eye. Iodine-125 is often the preferred modality because its fall-off is even greater than that of cobalt-60. The immediate complications of the treatment can be hemorrhage due to the breakup of the tumor or double vision from cutting an eye muscle to position the plaque. In these selected cases, the cure rate is as good as surgical enucleation of the eye.

Large tumors in which surgical enucleation of the eye is the treatment of choice can be given a preoperative dose of 2000 cGy with external radiation to reduce the incidence of metastases following surgery.

§ 6.8   Significant Litigation

Callahan v. Burton.[15]   The defendant ophthalmologist had been examining the plaintiff's eyes over a period of 11 years, during which time her left eye gradually changed color from blue to hazel to brown. The last examination was in November 1966. She failed to pass the driver's visual acuity test in April 1969, following which a melanoma of the ciliary body was diagnosed and enucleation performed. The court held that the plaintiff failed to establish that the malignant melanoma was in a diagnosible state during the time of the defendant's treatment, and dismissed the case.

---

[14] See **Ch. 17** regarding chemotherapy of malignant melanoma.
[15] 157 Mont. 513, 487 P.2d 515 (1971).

CARCINOMA

§ 6.9   Staging and Classification

Carcinoma of Eyelid

TNM: American Joint Committee on Cancer.[16]
  Tumor size and involvement of tarsal plate is related to prognosis.

Carcinoma of Conjunctiva

TNM: American Joint Committee on Cancer.[17]
  The prognosis relates to tumor size and involvement of contiguous structures.

Carcinoma of Lacrimal Duct

TNM: American Joint Committee on Cancer.[18]
  Tumor size and involvement of contiguous structures are related to prognosis.

Epithelial Orbit Tumors[19]

Tumors of the eye are classified histologically to distinguish one from another. Various classifications follow.

Eyelid, conjunctiva, cornea

  Basal cell carcinoma

  Squamous cell carcinoma

  Adenoid epithelial tumors

    Trichoepithelioma

    Adenoid cystic epithelioma

    Syringoma

  Benign calcified epithelioma

  Intraepithelial epithelioma (Bowen's disease)

---

[16] American Joint Committee on Cancer, Manual for Staging of Cancer 214 (3d ed. 1988).

[17] *Id.* at 224.

[18] *Id.* at 246.

[19] A.B. Reese, *Tumors of the Eye and Adnexa, in* Atlas of Tumor Pathology § X, fascicle 38, at 11 (1956).

Uveal tract

   Benign epithelial tumor (benign epithelioma, adenoma)

   Carcinoma (malignant epithelioma)

Medulloepithelioma

   Embryonal type (diktyoma)

   Adult type

   Mixed type

Epithelial Tumors of Lid, Conjunctiva, Cornea, and Lacrimal Sac[20]

Basal cell type

   Adnexal tumors

      Hair follicle tumors

         Folliculoma

         Trichoepithelioma

      Pilomatrixoma (benign calcifying epithelioma of Malherbe)

      Sweat gland tumors (glands of Moll)

         Syringoma

         Syringocystadenoma

         Cylindroma

      Sebaceous gland tumors (Meibomian glands, Zeis glands)

         Epithelioma

         Carcinoma

   Basal cell carcinoma

Squamous cell type

   Intraepithelial tumors (Bowen's disease)

   Squamous cell carcinoma

Epithelial Tumors of the Uvea[21]

Retinal pigment epithelium tumors

Neuroepithelium tumors of ciliary body

---

[20] A.B. Reese, *Epithelial Tumors of the Lid, Conjunctiva, Cornea, and Lacrimal Sac, in* Tumors of the Eye 38 (1976).

[21] A.B. Reese, *Epithelial Tumors of the Uvea, in* Tumors of the Eye 64 (1976).

Congenital

  Glioneuroma

  Medulloepithelioma (diktyoma)

    Benign

    Malignant

  Teratoid medulloepithelioma (diktyoma)

    Benign

    Malignant

Acquired

  Pseudoadenomatous hyperplasia

  Adenoma (benign epithelioma)

  Adenocarcinoma

Iris pigment epithelium tumors

Lacrimal Gland Tumors[22]

Benign mixed tumor

Malignant mixed tumor

  Adenocystic carcinoma

  Adenocarcinoma

  Undifferentiated carcinoma

  Squamous cell carcinoma

§ 6.10   Clinical Manifestations

Periorbital epidermal malignancies appear as a form nodule, ulceration, or ery-thematous thickening. Lacrimal gland tumors occur as a swelling in the lateral aspect of the upper portion of the orbit. Ulceration can occur in large tumors.

    Conjunctival lesions are pearly white and elevated, and there tends to be a predilection for the limbus. Diffuse lesions appear as a chronic infective process. Unilateral chronic conjunctivitis resistant to treatment, punctate keratitis, and diffuse thickening and inflammation of the tarsal plate should raise the suspicion of malignancy.[23]

---

[22] A.W. Forrest, *Lacrimal Gland Tumors. in* Diseases of the Orbit 355 (I.S. Jones & F.A. Jakobiec eds., 1979).

[23] F.H. Theodore, *Conjunctival Carcinoma Masquerading as Chronic Conjunctivitis,* 46 Eye Ear Nose & Throat Monthly 1419 (1967).

§ 6.11   Diagnosis

Biopsy should be performed for periorbital tumors before total resection when cosmetically acceptable reconstruction is necessary. Lacrimal gland tumors require biopsy if locally invasive; otherwise, total excision can be done for diagnosis.[24]

Cytologic smears of conjunctival scrapings for tumors involving the conjuctiva have been recommended to aid in the diagnosis. Biopsy of the lesion can be done.

§ 6.12   Surgical Treatment

Small lesions of the lid can be excised with reconstruction. The chemosurgery technique of Mohs also can be used for smaller tumors. Large fungating lesions of the lid sometimes require a combination of surgery and radiation. The projecting portion is excised down to the skin level prior to irradiation. Exenteration of the orbit is performed for lesions of the lid extending into the orbit.

Localized tumors of the conjunctiva can be excised. Heat cautery or cryotherapy can be applied at the sulcus between the cornea and sclera after excision to prevent recurrence. Enucleation is necessary when there is invasion of the sclera.

Uveal tumors require enucleation or orbital exenteration with resection of involved contiguous structures.

Lacrimal gland mixed tumors must have the entire gland removed with the overlying periorbital tissue. Adenoid cystic carcinoma of the lacrimal gland requires exenteration with radical removal of bone.

Complications of orbital surgery include bleeding, damage to muscles and nerves, infection, visual loss, injury to the lacrimal gland, enophthalmus, ptosis, strabismus, and dural defects.

§ 6.13   Radiation Therapy Treatment

Carcinoma of the Eyelid

Basal cell and squamous cell carcinomas of the eyelids can be irradiated with a high likelihood of cure and superior functional and cosmetic results. The irradiation technique involves inserting a lead shield under the eyelids to protect the cornea and lens. Low energy X-rays or electrons are used. The X-ray energies can range from 100 kV to 250 kV, the higher of these energies being used for the

---

[24] P.C. Dykstra & B.A. Dykstra, *The Cytologic Diagnosis of Carcinoma and Related Lesions of the Ocular Conjunctiva and Cornea,* 73 Trans. Am. Acad. Ophthalmology & Otolaryngology 979 (1969).

larger tumors. The number of treatments can range from 1 to 30, and the total dose can range from 2500 cGy to 6000 cGy. The larger the tumor, the greater the number of treatments required and the higher the total dose.

The occasional treatment failures will be apparent within three years. Radiation does not confer immunity against additional cancers. Another carcinoma in the same area after three years is most likely a new cancer.

Epilation of the irradiated eyelashes is a normal side effect of the doses required to cure a carcinoma. Patients have a tendency to develop ectropion as they grow older. This development should be recorded if present, so that the abnormality is not attributed to the radiation at a later date inasmuch as radiation itself is known to cause ectropion from excessive scarring. Similarly, tissue destruction resulting from the carcinoma should be noted in advance of the treatment because tissue loss caused by the cancer is not restored by the radiation, and such tissue loss should not be called the result of radiation necrosis. Radiation therapy in the area of the inner canthus can produce stenosis of the lacrimal duct that drains the tears. The stenosis is manifested by excess tearing. The condition can be treated by dilation of the lacrimal duct.

Carcinoma of the Conjunctiva

This carcinoma is often a very superficial one that can be treated by beta radiation given with a radioactive strontium-90 applicator. Strontium-90 gives very little radiation below a depth of 2 mm, so the possibility of injury to the eye is very slight. Six treatments of 1500 cGy given at weekly intervals for a total of 9000 cGy is a representative course of treatment.

For thicker tumors, superficial X-rays in the range of 50 kV to 100 kV or 4 meV electrons are used. Fractions of 200 cGy each for a total dose of 5000 cGy in five weeks can be given.

Carcinoma of the Lacrimal Gland

Carcinomas of the lacrimal gland are irradiated following radical surgery. If the resection appears complete, 5000 cGy in five weeks can be given. If obvious gross tumor has been left, 6000 cGy in six weeks is an appropriate dose. Protective devices are used to the greatest extent possible to shield the eye from radiation, but not to the extent that would leave any portion of the tumor unirradiated.

A sequela of lacrimal gland irradiation when the gland is intact is a dry eye due to decreased tear production. Using artificial tears protects the eye as much as possible from corneal damage. Radiation given after radical resection of the gland, however, has nothing to do with dryness of the eye if the eye has not been enucleated.

Carcinoma of the Lacrimal Duct and Sac

Carcinomas of the lacrimal duct and sac can be irradiated with techniques using the same energies of radiation employed on the eyelids, but with total doses more consistently in the range of 5000 cGy to 5600 cGy in five or six weeks.

ANGIOMATOUS TUMORS

§ 6.14   Classification

Vascular tumors of the orbit are distinguished by histologic and clinical characteristics according to the following classifications.[25]

Benign

    Capillary hemangioma (benign hemangioendothelioma)

    Cavernous hemangioma

    Kimura's disease (angiolymphoid hyperplasia with eosinophilia)

    Pseudosarcomatous endothelial proliferation

    Vascular leiomyoma

    Angioma serpiginosum

    Sturge-Weber syndrome

Malignant

    Malignant hemangioendothelioma

    Hemangiopericytoma

    Kaposi's sarcoma

§ 6.15   Clinical Manifestations

Angiomatous tumors usually occur in children. The periorbital or eyelid skin can be involved with a red, raised, dimpled lesion consistent with capillary hemangioma. These must be distinguished from the flat, purplish-red port wine stain or nevus flammeus of the Sturge-Weber syndrome. Involvement of the orbit causes bluish suffusion of the lids conjunctiva, and a soft spongy feeling when palpated

---

[25] F.A. Jakobiec & I.S. Jones, *Vascular tumors, malformations, and degenerations, in* Diseases of the Orbit 269 (1979).

and compressed. There is the possibility of misalignment of the eye, ptosis, or amblyopia.

Cavernous hemangiomas cause proptosis, extraocular motility difficulties, and visual problems. There can be a noticeable increase in growth during pregnancy. It is possible to have a concomitant cavernous hemangioma of the facial skin.

With hemangiopericytoma, moderate swelling of the eyelids occurs with dysplopia. Proptosis can follow.

Kaposi's sarcoma can occur in the periorbital skin as red or brown raised papules. The conjunctiva may become involved.

§ 6.16   Diagnosis

B-scan ultrasonography is helpful in diagnosing hemangioma. Hemangiopericytoma appears as a solid tumor on A-scan ultrasonography. Computerized tomography (CT scan) can be beneficial. X-rays of the orbit do not usually show bony erosion.

Biopsy of periorbital lesions can be necessary for the diagnosis of hemangiopericytoma or Kaposi's sarcoma.

§ 6.17   Surgical Treatment

Angiomatous lesions are treated by light coagulation, cryotherapy, diathermy, or electrosurgery. Complications of light coagulation include hemorrhage, retinal detachment, and yellow retinal exudation. Localized telangiectasis can be treated similarly.

Orbital hemangiomas can be excised. Choroidal hemangioma requires enucleation in the presence of pain or blindness, although early lesions can respond to cryosurgery, radiation therapy, or light coagulation. Polymorphous hemangiomas of the lid, conjunctiva, and orbit tend to regress spontaneously and are treated when distortion causes disfigurement. Cryotherapy, sclerosing solutions, irradiation, or surgical excision can be utilized.

Hemangiopericytoma of the orbit requires excision, malignant hemangioendothelioma needs wide resection, and lymphangiomas can require repeated excisions.

CHAPTER 7

HEAD AND NECK NEOPLASMS

LIP

§ 7.1   Staging and Classification

TNM: American Joint Committee on Cancer.[1]

Tumors of the lip 2 cm or less (T1) have a better prognosis than tumors that range from 2 cm to 4 cm (T2). A neoplasm over 4 cm has a poor outlook (T3). Nodal involvement is of prognostic significance and is related to the size of the nodes and fixation to surrounding tissues.

Cancer of the lip is predominantly squamous cell carcinoma. The more undifferentiated the tumor, the less favorable the prognosis.

Tumors of the Lip[2]

Hemangioma

Fibroma

Cyst

Keratoacanthoma

Squamous cell carcinoma

Basal cell carcinoma

§ 7.2   Etiology

Patients with light-colored skin and prolonged exposure to sunlight are more susceptible to lip cancer than those with darker skin. Smoking probably plays a role in the onset of lesions of the lip.

Poor dental hygiene associated with jagged teeth, poorly fitting dentures, and chronically infected gingiva results in lip irritation with evolution of malignancy. Chronic alcoholism was present in 47 percent of patients with carcinoma of the lip.[3]

Lip cancer has been reported in patients with chronic immunosuppression following renal transplantation.[4]

---

[1] American Joint Committee on Cancer, Manual for Staging of Cancer 29 (3d ed. 1988).

[2] R.R. Million et al., *Cancer in the Head and Neck, in* Cancer: Principles & Practice of Oncology 503 (1989).

[3] L. Molnar et al., *Carcinoma of the Lip: Analysis of the Material of 25 Years,* 29 Oncology 101 (1974).

[4] H.M. Berger et al., *Epidermoid Carcinoma of the Lip after Renal Transplantation: Report of Two Cases,* 128 Archives Internal Med. 609 (1971).

§ 7.3   Clinical Manifestations

A raised lesion or thickened area of lip that ulcerates and can bleed occurs with squamous cell carcinoma of the lip. A white plaque (leukoplakia) can develop slowly with scab formation and incomplete healing. Erythema of the perioral skin suggests lymphatic involvement by tumor. The lesion feels firm and indurated. Nerve invasion causes anesthesia or paresthesia of the skin of the lip.

§ 7.4   Diagnosis

Biopsy of suspicious lesions of the lip is the only method to assure diagnosis. Any persistent undiagnosed lesion of the lip must be biopsied. X-rays of the mandible can indicate bone or mental nerve involvement.

§ 7.5   Surgical Treatment

Leukoplakia is treated by local resection or vermilionectomy (lip shave). Excision of a malignancy can be combined with the lip shave.

For malignancies up to 2 cm in diameter that do not involve the commissure, wide, through-and-through resection is performed. Simple closure has good cosmetic and functional results. Larger lesions can require reconstruction following excision, usually with an Abbe or similar flap from the opposite lip. Irradiation should be considered for lesions over 2 cm in diameter, for lesions involving the commissure, and for high-grade carcinomas.

Large lesions involving bone can require massive resection with reconstruction. Advanced lesions, high-grade malignancies, and recurrent tumors need to be considered for elective neck dissection or nodal irradiation.

Complications of performing surgery include microstomia (small mouth opening), drooling, and cosmetic deformity. There also can be difficulties inserting dentures if the oral opening is too small.

§ 7.6   Chemotherapy

Squamous cell carcinoma of the head and neck, which includes primary neoplasms of the lip, tongue, floor of the mouth, buccal mucosa, hypopharynx, nose, sinuses, nasopharynx, tonsils, and larynx, is responsive to chemotherapy.

Induction chemotherapy prior to any other treatment can reduce tumor bulk allowing resection of otherwise unresectable tumors. Complete tumor regression occurs in 20 to 50 percent of patients, and significant tumor regression occurs in 70 to 90 percent of patients. Response rates increase through at least three cycles of induction therapy. Complete response is associated with optimal local control and improves survival rates. Combinations of cisplatin, bleomycin, 5-fluorouracil, methotrexate, cyclophosphamide, and vincristine sulfate have been effective.[5]

Chemotherapy can be given as adjuvant therapy alone or synchronous with radiation therapy. Antineoplastic agents can potentiate the cytotoxic effects of radiation, especially using cisplatin, 5-fluorouracil, bleomycin, or mitomycin-C.[6]

Regional intra-arterial chemotherapy can gain short-term control of the neoplasms, but does not increase long-term survival.[7]

Advanced or metastatic disease can be controlled by using methotrexate, bleomycin, cisplatin, 5-fluorouracil, cyclophosphamide, or doxorubicin.[8] Combination chemotherapy studies do not show an improved duration of response or survival time.

---

[5] T.J. Ewin et al., *An Analysis of Indiction and Adjuvant Chemotherapy in the Multidisciplinary Treatment of Squamous-Cell Carcinoma of the Head and Neck,* 5 J. Clinical Oncology 10 (1987); C. Haas et al., *Randomized Neo-Adjuvant Study of 5-Fluorouracil (FU) and Cis-Platinum (DDP) for Patients. (PTS) with Advanced Resectable Head and Neck Squamous Carcinoma (ARHNSC),* 27 Proc. Am. Ass'n Cancer Res. 185 (1986); P.Y. Hologe et al., *Randomized Study of Adjuvant Chemotherapy for Head and Neck Cancer,* 93 Head & Neck Surgery 712 (1985); C. Jacobs et al., *Chemotherapy as a Substitute for Surgery in the Treatment of Advanced Resectable Head and Neck Cancer. A Report from the Northern California Oncology Group,* 60 Cancer 1178 (1987); M. Martin et al., *Neo-Adjuvant Polychemotherapy of Head and Neck Cancer: Preliminary Results of a Randomized Study,* 5 Proc. Am. Soc'y Clinical Oncology 141 (1986); M.N. Spaulding, *Adjuvant Chemotherapy in Head and Neck Cancer: An Update,* 144 Am. J. Surgery 432 (1982).

[6] M. Abe et al., *Combined Use of Bleomycin with Radiation in the Treatment of Cancer,* 63 Recent Results Cancer Res. 169 (1978); D.J. Adelstein et al., *Combined Modality Therapy (CMT) with Simultaneous 5-Fluorouracil (5-FU), Cis-platinum (DDP) and Radiation Therapy (RT) in the Treatment of Squamous Cell Cancer of the Head and Neck,* 4 Proc. Am. Soc'y Clinical Oncology 131 (1985); K. Birter, *Postoperative Chemotherapy Versus Postoperative Cobalt 60 Radiation in Patients with Advanced Oral Carcinoma: Report on a Randomized Study,* 3 Head & Neck Surgery 264 (1981); K.K. Fu et al., *Combined Radiotherapy and Chemotherapy with Bleomycin and Methotrexate for Advanced Inoperable Head and Neck Cancer: Update of a Northern California Oncology Group Randomized Trial,* 5 J. Clinical Oncology 1410 (1987); A.T. Huang et al., *Adjuvant Chemotherapy after Surgery and Radiation for Stage III and IV Head and Neck Cancer,* 200 Annals Surgery 195 (1984); J.T. Johnson et al., *Adjuvant Chemotherapy for High-Risk Squamous-Cell Carcinoma of the Head and Neck,* 5 J. Clinical Oncology 456 (1987); G.J. Richards & R.G. Chambers, *Hydroxymia: A Radiosensitizer in the Treatment of Neoplasms of the Head and Neck,* 105 Am. J. Roentgenology, Radium & Thermonuclear Med. 555 (1969).

[7] G. Arcangeli et al., *Combined Radiation and Drugs: The Effect of Intra-Arterial Chemotherapy Followed by Radiotherapy in Head and Neck Cancer,* 1 Radiotherapy & Oncology 101 (1983); S.K. Carter, *The Chemotherapy of Head and Neck Cancer,* 4 Seminars Oncology 413 (1977); M.A. Goldsmith & S.K. Carter, *The Integration of Chemotherapy into a Combined Modality Approach to Cancer Therapy. V. Squamous Cell Cancer of the Head and Neck,* 2 Cancer Treatmet Rep. 137 (1975).

[8] L. Basauri et al., *Carboplatin, an Active Drug in Advanced Head and Neck Cancer,* 70 Cancer Treatment Rep. 1173 (1986); R.C. De Conti & D. Schoenfeld. *Randomized Prospective Comparison of Intermittent Methotrexate, Methotrexate with Leucovorin, and a Methotrexate*

§ 7.7   Radiation Therapy

Cure rates are about the same for radiation therapy and surgery. The cosmetic and functional result is a basis for considering radiation therapy when the tumor requires resection of one-third or more of the lip.

Radiation usually is given through lead cutouts shaped to the outline of the tumor plus a margin of surrounding normal tissue. A lead shield is placed behind the lip to protect the gums and teeth.

The energy of the radiation is selected according to the size and thickness of the tumor. X-rays of 100 to 300 kV can be used, or 4 or 6 meV electrons can be used.

Other decisions involve fractionation and time-dose factors. Fractions can range from 200 to 400 cGy. Total doses can be 4400 to 6000 cGy, the higher total doses being due to the longer courses of therapy resulting from using smaller fractions.

In the interest of completing treatment quickly, removable brachytherapy interstitial implants also have been used: 226-radium and 137-cesium needles, and 192-iridium seeds and wire. Interstitial implants can result in more fibrosis and tenderness of the lip than external radiation, and the uniformity of dosage is less certain than with external radiation therapy. Gamma ray molds have the same possibility of nonuniform dosage.

In Stages III and IV, the regimen is more likely to be a combination of radiation and surgery rather than either one alone. A large primary tumor can be irradiated. If the primary tumor invades bone, surgery is indicated followed by radiation. Lymph node metastases are most often managed by a neck dissection followed by radiation. In follow-up radiation, 4 or 6 meV X-rays can be used to deliver 5000 cGy in five and one-half weeks with 180 cGy fractions. In all head and neck neoplasms involving a combination of surgery and radiation, there are advocates for preoperative instead of postoperative radiation. Preoperative radiation does have a definite place in fixed metastatic lymph nodes to make them more resectable.

In high-grade tumors, large tumors, or recurrent tumors, the neck can be irradiated *electively* (irradiated in the absence of detectable metastases in the knowledge that occult metastases are likely to be present).

Recurrent tumors after surgery can be treated with further surgery or with radiation. Tumors that recur after radiation are treated surgically.

Combination in Head and Neck Cancer, 48 Cancer 1061 (1981); W.E. Grose et al., *Comparison of Methotrexate and Cisplatin for Patients with Advanced Squamous Cell Carcinoma of the Head and Neck Region: A Southwest Oncology Group Study,* 69 Cancer Treatment Rep. 577 (1985); S.F. Taylor et al., *A Randomized Comparison of High-Dose Infusion Methotrexate Versus Standard-Dose Weekly Therapy in Head and Neck Squamous Cancer,* 2 J. Clinical Oncology 1006 (1984); W.R. Vogler et al., *Methotrexate Therapy With or Without Citrovorum Factor in Carcinoma of the Head and Neck, Breast, and Colon,* 2 Cancer Clinical Trials 227 (1979).

FLOOR OF THE MOUTH

§ 7.8   Staging and Classification

TNM: American Joint Committee on Cancer.[9]

Like the lip prognosis of tumors, tumors of the floor of the mouth are related to tumor size (T1 = 2 cm or less, T2 = 2 cm to 4 cm, and T3 = more than 4 cm) and nodal involvement.

Carcinoma of the floor of the mouth is predominantly squamous cell carcinoma. The more undifferentiated the neoplasm, the less favorable the prognosis.

§ 7.9   Etiology

Smoking and chronic irritation from poorly fitting dentures are problems that can be involved in the onset of floor of the mouth cancer.

§ 7.10   Clinical Manifestations

Red or white slightly elevated lesions can occur. Thickening or nodularity becomes evident. Soreness appears when eating or drinking, and this can be confused with canker or denture sores.

As the lesion enlarges, there can be complaints of dentures fitting improperly. Pain, bleeding, loose teeth, and speech changes can become prominent symptoms.

§ 7.11   Diagnosis

Oral examinations, frequently done first by the dentist, identify early lesions. Occlusive (dental) X-ray views establish early bone involvement. Panorex X-ray examination of the mandible can be helpful to show bone destruction. Computerized tomography is more accurate in determining invasion of bone and the extent of local spread.

---

[9] American Joint Committee on Cancer, Manual for Staging of Cancer 29 (3d ed. 1988).

Discrete lesions under 5 mm in diameter can be excised. All other lesions should be biopsied for diagnosis.

§ 7.12   Surgical Treatment

Localized areas of leukoplakia can be excised. More extensive involvement needs cryotherapy or laser treatment. All smoking must be stopped, and oral hygiene must be improved.

Malignancies up to 4 cm in diameter can be treated by local resection with a rim of mandible if the lesion is near the bone or mandibular resection if bone is involved. Advanced lesions can require radical resection including lymph node dissection with reconstruction.

Complications include speech defects, difficulties eating, and problems replacing dentures. If radical lymph node dissection has been performed en bloc with the intraoral resection, neck infection and/or salivary fistula can occur.

§ 7.13   Chemotherapy

Chemotherapy is the same for squamous cell carcinoma arising in any area of the head and neck (see § 7.6).

§ 7.14   Radiation Therapy

Complete agreement is lacking for treating oral and pharyngeal cancers. Generally, there are two philosophies: surgery with adjuvant or salvage radiation, and radiation with salvage surgery.

Carcinomas of the floor of the mouth that are not attached to the mandible or invading it are the ones usually considered suitable for radiation therapy. The greater risk of osteoradionecrosis in tumors attached to the mandible is the factor for preferring surgery in these cases. In small moveable tumors, curability is the same with either radiation or surgery. Radiation can be considered preferable, however, for tumors of the floor of the mouth encroaching on the tongue.

Radiation can be given entirely with external lateral fields directed at the mouth and upper neck lymph nodes supplemented by treatment through an intraoral cone of kilovoltage X-rays or electrons. More often, however, the supplemental radiation consists of an interstitial implant of 226-radium, 137-cesium, or 192-iridium, as well as permanent 198-gold seed implants. The external lateral field irradiation can consist of 4 or 6 meV X-rays given up to a total dose of 4000 to 5000 cGy in four or five weeks. The supplemental radiation adds 2000 to 2500 cGy.

Advanced Stage III and IV tumors are likely to be treated by a combination of surgery and radiation. Postoperative radiation can consist of 5000 cGy given in five and one-half weeks in 180 cGy fractions. Generally, managing lymph nodes in tumors of the floor of the mouth and pharyngeal tumors consists of preoperative or postoperative radiation.

BUCCAL MUCOSA

§ 7.15   Staging and Classification

TNM: American Joint Committee on Cancer.[10]

Buccal mucosal tumors are prognostically related to the size of the tumor (T1 = 2 cm or less, T2 = 2 to 4 cm, T3 = more than 4 cm) as well as nodal involvement.

The neoplasm is usually squamous cell carcinoma and the more undifferentiated the tumor, the less promising the prognosis.

§ 7.16   Etiology

Chronic irritation from smoking, poorly fitting dentures, and jagged sharp teeth can be associated with malignancy of the buccal mucosa.[11]

Using betel leaves (Piper betel), areca nut (Areca catechu), and shell lime have been reported as a cause of buccal cancer.

Precursors

Leukoplakia.   The thickened white patches of leukoplakia is common in smokers. Carcinomatous changes can occur.[12]

Queyrat's Erythroplasia.   Erythroplasia of Queyrat consists of reddish papular lesions that are squamous cell carcinoma in situ. Seen most often on the soft palate, anterior tonsillar pillars, and buccal mucosa, invasive malignancy can develop.

---

[10] American Joint Committee on Cancer, Manual for Staging of Cancer 29 (3d ed. 1988).

[11] M.K. Nair et al., *Evaluation of the Role of Radiotherapy in the Management of Carcinoma of the Buccal Mucosa,* 61 Cancer 1326 (1988).

[12] C.A. Waldron & W.G. Shafer, *Leukoplakia Revisited,* 36 Cancer 1386 (1975).

Erythroplakia.   Erythroplakia is a combination of erythroplasia and leukoplakia. Severe dysplasia is present frequently with carcinoma in situ and microinvasive carcinoma.[13]

§ 7.17   Clinical Manifestations

Leukoplakia (white patches) are common. Small malignancies are usually
asymptomatic and feel like a nodule (usually felt by the tongue). Pain can occur
and can be referred to the ear. Involvement of Stensen's duct (parotid duct) produces parotid enlargement. Trismus (pain with opening the mouth) results from
infiltration into the surrounding muscles.

§ 7.18   Diagnosis

Multiple biopsies can be necessary to make the diagnosis. X-rays of the mandible and maxilla are used to determine extension into the bone.

§ 7.19   Surgical Treatment

Leukoplakia can be excised if localized. Large areas can be treated with cryotherapy or laser therapy. Small malignancies are locally resected.
   Extensive malignancies through the cheek are widely excised and recon-
structed with a myocutaneous flap. With bone involvement, a portion of the
mandible or maxilla has to be resected.

§ 7.20   Chemotherapy

Chemotherapy is the same for squamous cell carcinoma arising in any area of
the head and neck (see § 7.6).

§ 7.21   Radiation Therapy

The tumors suitable for radiation therapy are the early ones that do not invade
the jaws or the pterygoid area. The early tumors most suitable for radiation are
those invading the oral commissure. Salvage surgery can cure residual or recurrent tumors following radiation.

---

[13] W.G. Shafer & C.A. Waldron, *Erythroplakia of the Oral Cavity,* 36 Cancer 1021 (1975).

External megavoltage radiation is used. Electron therapy can be advantageous because of the laterality of the tumor and the lack of any necessity to irradiate to the midline of the oral cavity. Interstitial therapy with needles has advocates. Intraoral cone therapy is possible in edentulous patients who can open their mouths widely.

The advanced tumors can be resected and followed by radiation. Advanced tumors submitted for radiation therapy rather than surgery receive external megavoltage radiation supplemented by interstitial implantation in tumor remnants. The lymph nodes should be irradiated in advanced tumors whether or not there is evidence of tumor involvement in them. The radiation dose totals are similar to those for the floor of the mouth (see § 7.14).

ANTERIOR TONGUE

§ 7.22   Staging and Classification

TNM: American Joint Committee on Cancer.[14]

The prognosis of malignancies of the anterior tongue is related to tumor size (T1 = 2 cm or less, T2 = 2 to 4 cm, T3 = more than 4 cm) as well as involvement of nodes.

The neoplasm is usually squamous cell carcinoma. The more undifferentiated the tumor, the more unfavorable the prognosis.

§ 7.23   Etiology

Tertiary syphilis is associated with interstitial glossitis. These patients have a high incidence of lingual (tongue) cancer, especially on the dorsum of the tongue.[15]

Dentures causing chronic irritation, broken carious teeth, and cigarette smoking are associated with malignancy of the tongue. Heavy alcohol use is seen in many patients.

§ 7.24   Clinical Manifestations

The usual complaint is mild irritation with a feeling of soreness. Pain first occurs with eating or drinking, but gets progressively worse. As the tumor infiltrates

---

[14] American Joint Committee on Cancer, Manual for Staging of Cancer 29 (3d ed. 1988).

[15] N. Trieger et al., *Cirrhosis and Other Predisposing Factors in Carcinoma of the Tongue,* 11 Cancer 357 (1958).

deeper, the tongue on that side protrudes incompletely, and there are difficulties in speaking and swallowing.

§ 7.25   Diagnosis

Palpation of the lesion reveals firmness and induration. Examination may have to be performed under anesthesia in the painful posterior lesion.

§ 7.26   Surgical Treatment

Wide local excision is performed for lesions under 2 cm in diameter. Larger lesions require glossectomy (partial or total anterior tongue) and possibly mandibulectomy. Reconstruction should be attempted.

§ 7.27   Chemotherapy

Chemotherapy is the same for squamous cell carcinoma arising in any area of the head and neck (see § 7.6).

§ 7.28   Radiation Therapy

Most radiation therapy for the anterior tongue consists of external radiation supplemented by interstitial radiation. Sometimes small tumors are treated entirely with interstitial radiation. A combination of external radiation and intraoral coned radiation also is used.

External radiation is given to the tongue through lateral fields with megavoltage X-rays to 5000 cGy in five to five and one-half weeks in 180 to 200 cGy fractions. After a one- or two-week rest, interstitial gamma ray therapy, consisting of 2000 cGy, is given in two days with needles or with seeds in ribbons. 192-iridium ribbons are preferable at times because their flexibility permits better conformation to the shape of the tongue.

Using an intraoral cone can be quite successful if a large enough cone can be directed at an accessible tumor. After 4500 cGy is given through lateral external fields, supplemental radiation is given with 10 (300 cGy) fractions of kilovoltage X-rays through the intraoral cone.

If the primary tumor is treated exclusively with interstitial radiation, a representative course of treatment is a total of 6000 cGy over six or seven days.

In advanced infiltrating carcinomas, surgery and radiation are combined using a total dose of 5000 cGy in 180 cGy fractions postoperatively or preoperatively.

The neck cannot be ignored in carcinoma of the tongue. Depending on the size and location of the primary tumors, one-third to two-thirds of patients, with no evidence of lymph node metastases at the time of diagnosis, develop metastases at a later date if the neck is left untreated. Whether the tongue is treated with radiation or treated surgically, the entire neck should be electively (*prophylactically*) irradiated. The upper neck is treated through lateral opposing fields. The lower neck is treated through an anterior field with a midline block to shield the spinal cord and larynx. A total dose of 5000 cGy is given in 180 to 200 cGy fractions.

Radiation combined with surgery can be utilized for clinically detectable metastatic lymph nodes.

BASE OF TONGUE AND HYPOPHARYNX

§ 7.29   Staging and Classification

TNM: American Joint Committee on Cancer.[16]

Base of the tongue and hypopharynx malignancies are prognostically related to the extent of the tumor and involvement of contiguous structures as well as nodal involvement.

Squamous cell carcinoma is the predominant histologic malignancy, and the more undifferentiated the lesion, the less favorable the prognosis.

§ 7.30   Clinical Manifestations

Early lesions are asymptomatic. As the tumor grows, there is a mild sore throat or irritated throat and intolerance to rough or hot foods. There can be dysphagia and increasing pain becoming worse with coughing or swallowing. With tongue fixation, there are marked difficulties in swallowing and speaking.

§ 7.31   Diagnosis

Manual palpation of the tongue, floor of the mouth, oropharynx, and hypopharynx is the best means of assessing the extent of the tumor. Indirect (with a mirror) and direct (with a laryngoscope) pharyngolaryngoscopy with tumor biopsy establishes the diagnosis.

Soft tissue X-rays show the tumor mass. Laryngograms disclose the extension of the tumor into the hypopharyngeal and laryngeal areas.

---

[16] American Joint Committee on Cancer, Manual for Staging of Cancer 34–35 (3d ed. 1988).

§ 7.32   Surgical Treatment

Lesions under 2 cm in diameter can be locally resected by the lateral pharyngo-tomy or medial labiomandibular glossotomy approach. Subtotal supraglottic laryngectomy following preoperative irradiation can be performed at times.[17]

Larger lesions can require total glossectomy with or without laryngectomy and neck dissection. There remains a significant functional defect with remov-ing the tongue, and therefore reconstruction with a flap or preferably a free mus-culocutaneous graft is essential.

§ 7.33   Chemotherapy

Chemotherapy is the same for squamous cell carcinoma arising in any area of the head and neck (see § 7.6).

§ 7.34   Radiation Therapy

Superficial exophytic T1 and T2 tumors of the base of the tongue can be treated successfully with radiation alone. Infiltrating tumors at the posterior extremity of the base of the tongue are better treated with surgery and postoperative radia-tion. Surgery for infiltrating tumors farther forward in the base of the tongue requiring total glossectomy is less likely to be acceptable to the patient. Radia-tion is used as needed in these cases with salvage surgery.

The primary tumor in the base of the tongue and the neck are irradiated with the same techniques employed for the anterior tongue (see § 7.28). The base of the tongue is not accessible to an intraoral cone, but the radiation "boost" can be given with an external submental electron beam or with reduced lateral X-ray fields.

If surgery is chosen as the initial treatment, postoperative radiation is given to the area of the primary tumor and to the entire neck using the postoperative regi-men already described. Three or four weeks are allowed for the healing of any graft before starting radiation.

If the radiation is given preoperatively, surgical complications can be severe. Preoperative radiation is likely to be limited to cases with fixed metastatic lymph nodes that could be rendered resectable with preliminary radiation.

In the hypopharynx, superficial exophytic tumors at the upper rim of the pyri-form sinus are curable with radiation. Tumors at the base (apex) of the pyriform sinus invade the larynx and epiesophageal tissues and are seldom curable.

---

[17] J.H. Ogura & R.W. Mallen, *Conservation Surgery for Cancer of the Epiglottis and Hypophar-ynx, in* Cancer of the Head and Neck 407–22 (J. Conley ed., 1967).

Doses of 6500 to 7000 cGy given in fractions during the six and one-half to seven weeks are needed for maximum success. In combined regimens, postoperative radiation is preferred because of the severity of complications attending surgery after preoperative radiation. Modified preoperative radiation regimens designed to reduce complications can be utilized. One plan gives a dose of 2000 cGy in one week. Another plan gives a dose of 5000 cGy and delays surgery for four weeks. As with other tumors in these regions, preoperative radiation can be given to make questionably resectable tumors resectable.

Radiation techniques are similar to those used in the adjacent regions, bilateral fields for the primary site and the upper neck and anterior fields for the lower neck. The junction between the upper and lower fields should not be through the primary tumor or through a metastatic nodal mass.

Treating carcinomas of the posterior pharyngeal wall is governed by the principles adopted for the remainder of the hypopharynx, except that radiation fields are extended superiorly to the base of the skull because of the extensive submucosal infiltration of posterior wall cancers.

Postcricoid carcinomas are the hypopharyngeal tumors least likely to be cured. Radiation is essentially palliative.

TONSILS

§ 7.35   Staging and Classification

TNM: American Joint Committee on Cancer.[18]

Tumor size is of prognostic significance in cancer of the tonsils (T1 = 2 cm or less, T2 = 2 to 4 cm, T3 = more than 4 cm) as well as nodal involvement.

The tumor is predominantly squamous cell carcinoma, and the more undifferentiated the neoplasm, the less promising the prognosis.

§ 7.36   Etiology

Alcohol, smoking, nutrition, and local irritation have been implicated as factors in the origin of tonsillar cancer. Textile factory dust, especially wool, has been reported as a possible factor.[19]

---

[18] American Joint Committee on Cancer, Manual for Staging of Cancer 34 (3d ed. 1988).

[19] E. Moss & W.R. Lee, *Oral and Pharyngeal Cancers in Textile Workers,* 32 Brit. J. Cancer 248 (1975).

§ 7.37   Clinical Manifestations

Most small tumors are asymptomatic. A persistent sore throat or irritated throat can ensue and dysphagia, the feeling of a mass in the throat, otalgia (earache), or trismus can occur.

§ 7.38   Diagnosis

Examination of the throat shows a sessile, indurated, ulcerated mass in the tonsillar region. The extent of tumor can be determined by indirect and direct nasopharyngoscopy. X-rays of the bone and soft tissues as well as computerized tomography can be helpful in determining the areas of involvement. Transoral biopsy is necessary for definitive diagnosis. Tonsillar tissue removed from adults following tonsillectomy should always be examined microscopically by the pathologist, because rare instances of tonsillar carcinoma might be found.

§ 7.39   Surgical Treatment

Tonsillar resection is adequate for a small lesion. When the tumor is exceptionally large or resistant to radiation therapy, radical resection with reconstruction is needed.[20]

§ 7.40   Chemotherapy

Chemotherapy for tonsils is the same for squamous cell carcinoma arising in any area of the head and neck (see § 7.6).

§ 7.41   Radiation Therapy

Variations in treating carcinoma of the tonsil are numerous. Generally, external radiation alone is as effective as anything else in T1 and T2 tumors. Large bilateral fields are used to treat the primary tumor and upper cervical lymph nodes with 4 or 6 meV X-rays to a total dose of 5000 cGy. Small fields are then applied to the gross tumor, and an additional 1500 to 2000 cGy boost is delivered in fractions of 180 to 200 cGy. Delivering the boost with ipsilateral high-megavoltage (18 meV) X-rays has the advantage of moving the zone of maximum dosage beyond the mandible and reducing the risk of mandibular necrosis. Interstitial radiation also is widely used for the boost. Special attention

---

[20] J. Conley, *Concepts in Head and Neck Surgery* 109 (1970).

is paid to the base of the tonsillar fossa, where the tumor can extend into the adjacent tongue. This is a common site for residual or recurrent tumor.

The lymph nodes in the neck are given a minimum of 5000 cGy. If there are no palpable lymph nodes in the neck, only the nodes exposed in the fields for the primary tumor receive this dose. The fields for the primary tumor, however, are extended posteriorly to include the posterior upper cervical nodes. Irradiation of this extension is terminated at 4500 cGy to stop further exposure of the spinal cord. The dose to the nodes in this area can be brought to 5000 cGy with an electron boost.

If there is palpable adenopathy in the upper neck, the lower neck also is treated with a dose up to 5000 cGy with an anterior field. If the palpable adenopathy is not going to be treated surgically, the dose to the adenopathy must be extended beyond 5000 cGy to the same high doses given to the primary tumor.

T3 and T4 primary tumors that are treated surgically receive the usual postoperative radiation for these regions.

NOSE, PARANASAL SINUSES, AND NASOPHARYNX

§ 7.42   Staging and Classification

Nasopharynx

TNM: American Joint Committee on Cancer.[21]

Prognosis is related to invasion of surrounding structures as well as lymph node involvement. The tumor is primarily squamous cell carcinoma. The more undifferentiated the lesion, the more unfavorable the prognosis.

Maxillary Sinus

TNM: American Joint Committee on Cancer.[22]

The prognosis of maxillary sinus tumors relates to involvement of surrounding structures and the presence of nodal involvement or metastases. The tumor is usually squamous cell carcinoma and the more undifferentiated the tumor, the less promising the prognosis.

Table 7–1[23] lists the tumors of the nose, nasopharynx, and paranasal sinuses.

---

[21] American Joint Committee on Cancer, Manual for Staging of Cancer 34–35 (3d ed. 1988).

[22] *Id.* at 46.

[23] J.C. Goldstein & G.A. Sisson, *Tumors of the Nose, Paranasal Sinuses, and Nasopharynx, in* Otolaryngology in Head and Neck 2087 (M.M. Paparella & D.A. Shumrick eds., 1980). Reprinted with permission of W.B. Saunders Co.

Table 7–1

Tumors of the Nose, Nasopharynx, and Paranasal Sinuses

I. BENIGN
  A. *Soft Tissue*
    1. Epithelium
      a. Papilloma
        (1) Squamous
        (2) Epithelial
      b. Adenoma
      c. Mixed tumor (pleomorphic adenoma)
      d. Adenoids
    2. Connective tissue
      a. Nasal glioma
      b. Meningioma
      c. Neurofibroma
      d. Neurilemoma
      e. Ganglioma
      f. Ganglioneuroma
      g. Paraganglioma
      h. Nevus
      i. Fibroma
      j. Myxoma
      k. Hemangioma
      l. Lymphangioma
      m. Chondroma
      n. Lipoma
  B. *Osseous*
    1. Primary osseous (nonodontic)
      a. Osteoma
      b. Exostoses (torus)
      c. Osteoid osteoma
      d. Giant cell lesions
        (1) Giant cell tumor
        (2) Giant cell reparative granuloma
        (3) Osteitis fibrosa cystica
        (4) Cherubism
      e. Cysts
        (1) Median (fissural)
        (2) Globulo maxillary (lateral fissural)
        (3) Nasopalatine (nonfissural)
        (4) Simple (unicameral)
        (5) Aneurysmal bone cyst
    2. Odontic (odontogenic)
      a. Epithelium
        (1) Cysts
          (a) Follicular

II. INTERMEDIATE
  A. *Soft Tissue*
    1. Epithelium
      a. Inverted papilloma
      b. Leukoplasia
    2. Connective tissue
      a. Angiofibroma
      b. Chordoma
      c. Plasmacytoma
      d. Teratoma (dermoid, teratoid, teratoma, epignathus)
      e. Rathke's pouch tumors
      f. Hemangioendothelioma
      g. Hemangiopericytoma
      h. Kaposi's sarcoma
      i. Hand-Schüller-Christian complex
  B. *Fibro-osseous Disorders*
III. MALIGNANT
  A. *Soft Tissue*
    1. Epithelium
      a. Basal cell carcinoma
      b. Squamous cell carcinoma
      c. Transitional cell (lymphoepithelioma)
      d. Spindle cell and clear cell carcinoma
      e. Adenocarcinoma
      f. Minor salivary glands (for example, adenoid cystic)
      g. Olfactory neuroepithelioma
      h. Undifferentiated
      i. Malignant melanoma
    2. Connective tissue
      a. Wegener's granulomatosis
      b. Fibrosarcoma
      c. Rhabdomyosarcoma
        (1) Embryonal (sarcoma botryoides
        (2) Alveolar
        (3) Pleomorphic
      d. Hemangioendotheliosarcoma
      e. Malignant lymphoma
      f. Myxosarcoma
      g. Reticulum cell sarcoma
      h. Chondrosarcoma
    3. Osseous
      a. Osteogenic sarcoma

Table 7–1 *(continued)*

(1) Primordial (simple follicular)	b. Ewing's sarcoma
(2) Dentigerous	IV. TUMORLIKE LESIONS
(b) Radicular (periodontal)	1. Mucocele
(1) Apical	2. Pyocele
(2) Lateral	3. Pyogenic granuloma
(3) Residual	4. Rhinoscleroma
(2) Ameloblastoma (adamantinoma)	5. Sarcoidosis
	6. Amyloidosis
(a) Adenoameloblastoma	7. Polyps
(b) Pindborg	8. Choanal polyp
b. Mesodermal	9. Infections
(1) Myxoma	a. Tuberculosis
(2) Fibroma (odontogenic fibroma)	b. Syphilis
	c. Fungi
(3) Dentinoma	(1) Actinomycosis
(4) Cementoma	(2) Blastomycosis
(5) Cementifying fibroma	(3) Rhinosporidiosis
c. Mixed	(4) Mucormycosis
(1) Odontoma	(5) Sporotrichosis
(a) Complex composite	(6) Aspergillosis
(b) Compound composite	(7) Moniliasis (candidiasis)
(2) Ameloblastic fibroma	(8) Histoplasmosis and coccidioidomycosis
(3) Ameloblastic odontoma	
(4) Ameloblastic hemangioma	
(5) Ameloblastic neurilemoma	

§ 7.43   Etiology

Many patients with cancer of the paranasal sinuses have a history of sinus or nasal surgery, especially multiple removals of nasal polyps. Long-standing fistulas resulting from dental extractions and chronic sinusitis can be related to the onset of sinus cancer. Smoking, dust particles, and chemicals employed in cabinetmaking can be inciting factors in sinus malignancy.

§ 7.44   Diagnosis

The nasopharynx can be examined indirectly with a small mirror. It is possible to visualize the nasopharynx directly by using a soft palate retractor or a fiberoptic nasopharyngoscope. Biopsy can be accomplished by an appropriate instrument passed through the nose or mouth.

Biopsy of the sinuses requires opening the bone overlying the sinus through exploratory antrostomy. Sinus X-rays with tomography or computerized tomography reveal the tumor extent.

§ 7.45   Surgical Treatment

Maxillectomy is performed for T1 and T2 lesions. Larger tumors might need radiation therapy followed by resection (radical maxillectomy). A craniofrontoethmoid approach might be necessary if intracranial extension is suspected.

§ 7.46   Chemotherapy

Chemotherapy is the same for squamous cell carcinoma arising in any area of the head and neck (see § 7.6).

§ 7.47   Radiation Therapy

Aside from tumors of the nasal vestibule, the tumors of the nasal cavity are treated like tumors of the paranasal sinuses. The tissue inside the vestibule is similar to skin, and its tumors can be irradiated like carcinoma of the skin with a total dose of 6000 cGy given in 200 cGy fractions. Tumors chosen for radiation are likely to be those that would require nasal reconstruction if they were resected.

Most oncologists favor combined radiation and surgery for carcinomas of the paranasal sinuses and nasal fossa. Preoperative or postoperative radiation reduces the high rate of local recurrence with surgery alone. The narrow clearances by which injuries to the eyes, nerves, and brain have to be avoided as well as the irregular tissue contours and tissue inhomogeneities make the radiation treatment plans very complex. Postoperative radiation has the advantage of permitting the concentration of radiation in particular spots based on the pathologic information obtained from surgery. Standard treatment is an anterior external radiation field along with one or two lateral wedged fields. To a large extent, however, radiation fields have to be customized by using specially shaped fields, electron beams, and brachytherapy molds.

The dose in postoperative therapy should be 6000 cGy in 180 to 200 cGy increments. The incidence of occult lymph node metastases is not sufficiently great for elective radiation to the nodes.

In early ethmoid sinus carcinoma, the preponderance of opinion can favor using radiation without surgery, but the number of cases is too small to recommend standard regimens.

In paranasal sinus and nasal fossa tumors not treated surgically, the tumor dose is raised to a total of 6500 or 7000 cGy. In maxillary sinus tumors, dependent drainage should be established surgically before starting radiation.

Sphenoid sinus carcinomas are difficult to differentiate from nasopharyngeal carcinomas and should be treated like the latter.

Radiation is the primary treatment for nasopharyngeal carcinoma. Large fields are needed because some recurrences in the past have been due to fields that were too small. Radiation is given from the base of the skull to the clavicles. The fields cover the nasopharynx, retropharyngeal lymph nodes, all the cervical lymph nodes, sphenoid and posterior maxillary and ethmoid sinuses, and the posterior nasal cavity. X-rays of 4 or 6 meV are used in 180 to 200 cGy fractions.

The initial fields expose the brain, pituitary, optic nerves, and spinal cord to radiation that must not exceed 4500 to 5000 cGy before they are reduced to exclude these tissues from further radiation. Small fields are then used to bring doses to gross tumor masses to a total of 6500 cGy in the nasopharynx and to as much as 7000 cGy to metastatic lymph nodes. The areas in the neck with no adenopathy receive a minimum dose of 5000 cGy. The supplemental doses through small fields can be given in part through anterior fields.

Recurrences in the nasopharynx are not amenable to surgery. They have been reirradiated successfully in some instances with small fields. Osteonecrosis has occurred in these cases, but it has been reasonably well-tolerated. Residual or recurrent lymph node metastases can be treated surgically.

LARYNX

§ 7.48   Staging and Classification

TNM: American Joint Committee on Cancer.[24]

The prognosis of laryngeal malignancies relates to the site of tumor origin (supraglottic, glottic, or infraglottic), involvement of surrounding or contiguous structures, and the presence of nodal metastases.

The tumor is primarily a squamous cell carcinoma, and the more undifferentiated the tumor, the less promising the prognosis.

§ 7.49   Etiology

Smoking has been implicated in the origin of laryngeal cancer. There is a high incidence of lung cancer in these patients, which also is a disease associated with smoking. Other agents possibly related to the onset of cancer of the larynx include chronic infections, irradiation, air pollution, and herpes simplex infection.

---

[24] American Joint Committee on Cancer, Manual for Staging of Cancer 40–41 (3d ed. 1988).

Occupational exposure to asbestos, metal processing, mustard gas, sulfuric acid, and textile fiber can be associated with laryngeal malignancies.[25]

Leukoplakia and hyperkeratosis can be prodromal findings prior to the onset of cancer. Keratosis with atypia is particularly significant. These disorders are associated with smoking and voice abuse.

§ 7.50   Clinical Manifestations

Hoarseness of the voice with a rough, grating, low-pitch voice is the most common symptom. Sore throat can occur. Dyspnea, dysphagia, stridor, and cough appear with more advanced tumors. Weight loss, laryngeal pain, and hemoptysis are other possible symptoms.

§ 7.51   Diagnosis

Indirect (with a mirror) and direct (with a flexible fiberoptic or rigid laryngoscope) show the laryngeal lesion and delineate the extent of tumor. Vocal cord mobility should be assessed. Biopsies are taken for definitive diagnosis.

Soft tissue X-rays, laryngogram, and computerized tomography can be utilized to determine tumor margins, especially in the subglottic and supraglottic areas.

§ 7.52   Surgical Treatment

Leukoplakia and hyperkeratotic lesions of the vocal cords can be treated by vocal cord stripping. Small cancers of the cord need excision either by scalpel or laser.

Where the vocal cord is mainly involved with minimal extension, it is possible to preserve the voice and airway by means of cordectomy from an anterior translaryngeal approach or by hemilaryngectomy. Supraglottic localized malignancies can have a supraglottic laryngectomy, which preserves the airway and voice.

Vocal cord fixation requires at least a near-total laryngectomy. Extension of glottic tumor to the infraglottic or supraglottic area necessitates total laryngectomy with a permanent tracheotomy. Speech therapy is necessary to learn esophageal speech or a mechanical external device can be used for speaking.

---

[25] C.E. Cann et al., *Epidemiology of Squamous Cell Cancer of the Head and Neck,* 18 Otolaryngology Clinics N. Am. 367 (1985).

§ 7.53   Chemotherapy

Chemotherapy is the same for squamous cell carcinoma arising in any area of the head and neck (see § 7.6).

§ 7.54   Radiation Therapy

The objective of radiation therapy alone or in combination is to utilize the regimens that give the highest cure rates with the best preservation of the voice. Promises for voice preservation must not be excessive. The pitch of the voice can be lower, and vocalists might not be able to sing the same as before the therapy.

Carcinoma in situ can be managed with close follow-up treatment after vocal cord stripping, but some favor a full course of radiation therapy following the stripping, believing that routine pathologic assessment can miss foci of invasive carcinoma.

T1 and T2 superficial carcinomas of the vocal cord can be treated with 4 or 6 meV X-rays through small bilateral fields that cover only the larynx. A total dose of 6000 or 6500 cGy can be given in six to eight weeks in 200 cGy fractions. Occult lymph node metastases are unlikely. The lymph nodes are not irradiated electively.

Larger tumors with or without some impairment of vocal cord mobility are irradiated to doses of 6500 to 7000 cGy.

Tumors with transglottic spread can be irradiated, and 50 percent of them can be cured. Half of the failures can be cured by salvage laryngectomy. Three-fourths of the patients, therefore, are cured by this sequence, which is the same cure rate obtained with primary laryngectomy, except that two-thirds of the irradiated patients retain their voices.

In advanced carcinomas treated initially by laryngectomy, the incidence of occult metastases is sufficiently great that the neck should be irradiated regardless of whether a neck dissection has been done. The dose to the nodes are 5000 to 6000 cGy.

Small superficial supraglottic tumors are treated with radiation to 6500 cGy. The risk of occult metastases to the lymph nodes warrants irradiation of the neck to 5000 cGy. Large tumors and infiltrating tumors with fixation of the arytenoids are treated surgically and given postoperative radiation to the tumor bed and neck. Another approach to large supraglottic tumors is induction chemotherapy. If tumor regression is less than 50 percent, laryngectomy and adjuvant radiation are performed. If regression is 50 percent or more, radiation is given followed by salvage surgery as needed.

Preoperative radiation in laryngeal carcinoma is in the range of 4000 to 4500 cGy.

ORAL MANIFESTATIONS ASSOCIATED
WITH INTERNAL MALIGNANCY

§ 7.55   Acanthosis Nigricans

Acanthosis nigricans is a brown or black warty epidermal hyperplasia affecting the axilla, neck, groin, nipples, and umbilicus. In adults, the tongue and lips can have small, grayish, papillomatous, warty lesions, and the buccal mucosa can have edematous, grayish, granular, rough lesions. Internal malignancy is associated with acanthosis nigricans.[26]

§ 7.56   Oral Pigmentation

Brown pigmentation of the oral mucosa has been noted in patients with lung disease and bronchogenic carcinoma.[27] Peutz-Jeghers syndrome is an association of melanin spots of the oral mucosa, lips, and fingers with generalized intestinal adenomatous polyps. Malignancy of the colon or stomach can occur. Pigmentation of the lips and oral mucosa can be a manifestation of neurofibromatosis (von Recklinghausen's disease), which has a 5 to 10 percent incidence of malignant change of the neurofibromas.

§ 7.57   Gingival Hyperplasia

In acute and chronic leukemia, the gingiva can become swollen, ulcerated, and hyperplastic. Necrosis and hemorrhage secondary to granulocytopenia and thrombocytopenia can appear.

---

[26] G. Bang, *Acanthosis Nigricans Maligna,* 29 Oral Surgery, Oral Med. & Oral Pathology 370 (1970); A. Navaratnam & G.A. Hodgson, *Acanthosis Nigricans with Carcinoma of the Stomach,* 89 Brit. J. Dermatology Supp. 9 at 46 (1973).

[27] H.W. Merchant, *Oral Pigmentation Associated with Bronchogenic Carcinoma,* 36 Oral Surgery, Oral Med. & Oral Pathology 675 (1973); H.W. Merchant et al., *Soft-Palate Pigmentation in Lung Disease, Including Cancer,* 41 Oral Surgery, Oral Med. & Oral Pathology 726 (1976).

§ 7.58   Mucosal Bullae

Bullae (blisters) of the oral mucous membranes occur with various disorders. Malignancy has been reported in association with pemphigus vulgaris,[28] bullous pemphigoid,[29] and benign mucous membrane pemphigoid.[30]

§ 7.59   Gardner's Syndrome

Osteomas of the mandible and maxilla as well as impactions of supernumerary teeth are signs of Gardner's syndrome, which is a dominant hereditary disorder consisting of multiple familial colon polyposis, hard tissue (bone) tumors, and soft tissue tumors. There is a high incidence of intestinal malignancy in this disorder.[31]

§ 7.60   Mycosis Fungoides

Erythematous raised lesions of the oral cavity, which can ulcerate, can be seen in mycosis fungoides, a chronic malignant lymphoreticular neoplasm of the skin. This lymphomatous malignancy can involve the lymph nodes and viscera.

§ 7.61   Polycythemia Vera

Polycythemia vera is a neoplastic condition of the erythropoietic system, which may have a deep red purplish color of the tongue, gingiva, and oral mucosa. Edema of the gingiva and petechial hemorrhages also can occur.

---

[28] E. Calo, *Considerazione su un Caso de Stomatite Perfigosa in Soggetto Affetto de Lenamia Linfatica Cronica,* 7 Mondo Odontostomatologico 247 (1965); L. Krain. *The Association of Pemphigus with Thymoma or Malignancy: A Critical Review.* 90 Brit. J. Dermatology 397 (1974).

[29] L. Bohatka & G. Alfoldy, *Oral Manifestations in the Paraneoplastic Syndrome,* 44 Oral Surgery, Oral Med. & Oral Pathology 684 (1977); J.M. Marks, *Pemphigoid with Malignant Melanoma,* 54 Proc. Royal Soc'y Med. 225 (1961); R.L. Parsons & J.A. Savin, *Pemphigoid and Malignancy,* 22 Brit. J. Cancer 669 (1968); N.M. Sarkia et al., *A Case of Bullous Pemphigoid and Figurate Erythema in Association with Metastatic Spread of Carcinoma,* 88 Brit. J. Dermatology 331 (1973); I.B. Sneddon, *The Skin and Visceral Cancer,* 135 Royal C. Surgery, Edinburgh 300 (1968).

[30] M.E. Foster & F.F. Nally, *Benign Mucous Membrane Pemphigoid (Cicatricial Mucosal Pemphigoid),* 44 Oral Surgery, Oral Med. & Oral Pathology 697 (1977); P.E. Kilby, *Carcinoma of the Pancreas Presenting with Benign Mucous Membrane Pemphigoid,* 18 Cancer 847 (1965); A. Polliack, *Benign Mucous Membrane Pemphigoid with Laryngeal Stenosis in a Patient with Thyroid Carcinoma,* 86 Archives Pathology 48 (1968).

[31] P.H. McFarland et al., *Gardner's Syndrome: Report of Two Families,* 26 J. Oral Surgery 632 (1968).

§ 7.62   Regional Enteritis (Crohn's Disease)

Small oral nodules, vesicles, or ulcerations can be seen in regional enteritis. This disorder has a known association with intestinal malignancy.

SALIVARY GLAND TUMORS

§ 7.63   Staging and Classification

TNM: American Joint Committee on Cancer.[32]

The size of salivary tumors (T1=2 cm or less, T2=2 to 4 cm, T3=4 cm or more), local extension, nodal involvement, and metastases are related to prognosis.

Prognosis is related to histopathologic type. The World Health Organization classification of salivary gland tumors includes the following:

Acinic cell carcinoma

Adenoid cystic carcinoma (cylindroma)

Adenocarcinoma

Squamous cell carcinoma

Carcinoma in pleomorphic adenoma (malignant mixed tumor)

Mucoepidermoid carcinoma

   Well differentiated (low-grade)

   Poorly differentiated (high-grade)

Other.

Distinguishing benign from malignant tumors, as in the following five classifications, helps in determining the type of therapy.

Epithelial Tumors[33]

Benign Variant

   Adenoma (tubular solid)

   Acinic cell adenoma

---

[32] American Joint Committee on Cancer, Manual for Staging of Cancer (3d ed. 1988).

[33] R.W. Evans & A.H. Cruikshank, *Epithelial Tumours of the Salivary Glands, in* Major Problems in Pathology 21 (1970).

Adenolymphoma

Basal cell adenoma

Clear cell adenoma (glycogen-rich)

Clear cell adenoma (nonglycogen-containing variant of acinic cell tumor and sometimes present in parts of mixed tumors)

Mixed tumor

Mucinous cyst

Mucoepidermoid tumor

Oncocytoma

Sebaceous adenoma

Sebaceous lymphoma

Papilloma intraduct

Malignant Variant

Acinic cell carcinoma

Carcinomatous behavior of the epithelial element has been reported (rare)

Adenocystic carcinoma (cylindroma)

Malignant basal cell tumor (sometimes occurs as a hybrid neoplasm)

Carcinoma

Malignant mixed tumor (very rare)

Carcinoma ex mixed tumor

Mucoepidermoid tumor

Sebaceous carcinoma.

Major Salivary Gland Tumors: AFIP[34]

Mixed tumors:

   Benign mixed tumors

   Malignant mixed tumors

Mucoepidermoid tumors:

   Low-grade tumors

   High-grade tumors

Squamous cell carcinomas

---

[34] F.W. Foote & E.L. Frazell, *Tumors of the Major Salivary Glands, in* Atlas of Tumor Pathology § 4, p. II, at 8 (1954).

Adenocarcinomas

   Adenoid cystic

   Miscellaneous forms

      Trabecular or solid; anaplastic, mucous cell, or with pseudoadamantine
      pattern

   Acinic cell

Papillary cystadenomata lymphomatosa

Oxyphil adenoma

Sebaceous cell adenoma

Benign lymphoephithelial lesions

Unclassified tumors.

Epithelial Tumors of Parotid and Submaxillary Glands[35]

Adenomas

   Pleomorphic adenoma (mixed tumor)

   Monomorphic adenoma

      Adenolymphoma (papillary cystadenoma lymphomatosum, Warthin's
      tumor)

      Oxyphilic adenoma (onkocytic adenoma)

      Other types of adenoma:

         Tubular adenoma

         Clear cell adenoma

         Basal cell adenoma

         Trabecular adenoma

         Sebaceous adenoma

Mucoepidermoid tumors

Acinic cell tumors

Carcinomas

   Adenoid cystic carcinoma (cylindroma)

   Adenocarcinoma

   Epidermoid carcinoma

---

[35] C.M. Eneroth, *Salivary Gland Tumors in the Parotid Gland, Submandibular Gland, and the Palate Region,* 27 Cancer 1415 (1971); A.C. Thackray & R.B. Lucas, *Tumors of the Major Salivary Glands, in* Atlas of Tumor Pathology, fascicle 10, at 14 (1974).

Undifferentiated carcinoma

Carcinoma in pleomorphic adenoma (malignant mixed tumor).

Classification of Epithelial Salivary Gland Tumors[36]

Benign

Mixed tumor (pleomorphic adenoma)

Papillary cystadenolymphomatosum (Warthin's tumor)

Oncocytoma-oncocytosis

Monomorphic adenomas

Basal cell adenoma

Glycogen-rich adenoma

Clear cell tumor

Myoepithelioma

Others

Sebaceous adenoma

Sebaceous lymphadenoma

Papillary ductal adenoma (papilloma)

Benign lymphoepithelial lesion

Malignant

Carcinoma from pleomorphic adenoma (carcinoma arising in or from a mixed tumor)

Malignant mixed tumor

Mucoepidermoid carcinoma

Low-grade

Intermediate-grade

High-grade

Adenoid cystic carcinoma

Acinic cell carcinoma (acinic carcinoma)

Adenocarcinoma

Mucus-producing adenopapillary and nonpapillary carcinoma

Salivary duct carcinoma (ductal carcinoma)

---

[36] Otolaryngology in Head and Neck 2229 (M.M. Paparella & D.A. Shumrick eds., 1980).

Oncocytic carcinoma (malignant oncocytoma)

Clear cell carcinoma (nonmucinous and glycogen-containing or nonglycogen-containing)

Primary squamous cell carcinoma

Hybrid basal cell adenoma/adenoid cystic carcinoma

Epithelial/myoepithelial carcinoma of intercalated ducts

Undifferentiated carcinoma

Miscellaneous (including sebaceous tumors, Stensen's duct tumors, melanoma, and carcinoma from lymphoephithelial lesion)

Metastatic.

Tumors of the Salivary Glands[37]

Blastomas of Epithelial Sector

Benign

  Adenoma

    Oxyphilic adenoma

    Basal cell adenoma

    Sebaceous adenoma

    Acinic cell adenoma

    Mucoepidermoid adenoma

    Pleomorphic adenoma

    Adenolymphoma (cystadeno-lymphoma)

Malignant

  Carcinoma

    Undifferentiated (solid undifferentiated carcinoma)

    Trabecular

    Tubular (adenocarcinoma)

    Epidermoid (squamous cell carcinoma)

    Adenocystic (cylindroma)

    Mucoepidermoid

    Pleomorphic adenoma (cancerous)

---

[37] J. Yoel, *Pathology and Surgery of the Salivary Glands* 394 (1975).

Cystadenolymphoma (cancerous)

Sebaceous

Adenomatous (acinic cell adenocarcinoma)

Malignant basal cell tumor (basalioma)

Blastomas of Reticuloendothelial Sector

Benign

Histiocytoma

Malignant

Reticulosarcoma

Blastomas of Connective and Vascular Tissue Sector

Benign

Lipoma

Fibroma

Hemangioma

Lymphangioma

Leiomyoma

Rhabdomyoma

Branchial cyst

Malignant

Sarcoma

Fibrosarcoma

Leiomyosarcoma

Rhabdomyosarcoma

Lymphosarcoma

Blastomas of Neuroglial Sector

Benign

Neurinoma (Schwannoma, Neurilemmoma)

Neuroma

Neurofibroma

Malignant

Neurosarcoma.

§ 7.64   Etiology

Most masses of the salivary glands are inflammatory in origin. Cysts or swelling associated with sialolithiasis (stones in the duct) can occur. In the parotid and submandibular areas, lymph node enlargement can mimic salivary gland tumor, especially because there can be intraparotid lymph nodes.

Normal salivary gland tissue can be found ectopically in the lymph nodes of the neck.[38] This is more common in the upper cervical region. The major salivary glands are the parotid and submandibular glands. The minor salivary glands are found in the oral cavity in the sublingual area, palate, and buccal regions.

Radiation can cause malignancy of the salivary glands.[39] In Japan, an increased number of neoplasms have been reported in survivors of the atomic bomb in comparison to nonirradiated groups.[40]

§ 7.65   Clinical Manifestations

A painless mass is the most common presentation of salivary gland malignancies. The tumor can be present for many years before appearing to grow rapidly. Occasional tumors are large enough in the parotid area to form significant cosmetic deformity. The parotid gland is intimately associated with the facial nerve (seventh cranial nerve), and malignancies can invade the nerve, causing facial paralysis. Trismus (pain on opening the mouth), skin adherence, and pain can occur with extensive parotid tumors.

Warthin's tumor (papillary cystadenoma lymphomatosum) involving the parotid occurs bilaterally in 5 to 10 percent of cases.

§ 7.66   Diagnosis

Biopsy of a mass in the salivary gland is not usually performed except with large, extensive tumors. Seventy-five percent of the benign neoplasms are mixed tumors (pleomorphic tumor), which have extensions through a false capsule and

---

[38] A.C. Thackray & R.B. Lucas, *Tumors of the Major Salivary Glands, in* Atlas of Tumor Pathology, Fascicle 10, at 2 (1974).

[39] H.R. Maxon et al., *Radiation-Associated Carcinoma of the Salivary Glands: A Controlled Study,* 90 Annals Otolaryngology 107 (1981); B. Modan et al., *Radiation Induced Head and Neck Tumors,* 1 Lancet 277 (1974).

[40] J.L. Belsky et al., *Salivary Gland Tumors in Atomic Bomb Survivors, Hiroshima-Nagasaki, 1957 to 1970,* 219 JAMA 864 (1972).

can seed the biopsy site with tumor cells even along the tract of a needle biopsy. Most tumors are removed with a wide excision before a pathologic diagnosis is made.

Sialogram is sometimes helpful to show destruction of ducts that is consistent with malignancy. Bone destruction can show bony erosion from tumors.

§ 7.67   Surgical Treatment

Wide excision of all tumors of the parotid gland should be performed with preservation of the facial (seventh cranial) nerve. The superficial parotid is removed following complete exposure and dissection of the facial nerve branches. The facial nerve is sandwiched between the superficial and deep lobes. A tumor of the deep lobe requires dissection of the nerve fibers off the deep lobe and retraction of the nerve to approach the deep portion.

When malignancy involves the facial nerve, sacrificing the whole nerve or a branch can be necessary. Reconstruction of the nerve can be done by removing a portion of the posterior auricular nerve (sensory nerve) and anastomosing the segment to the cut ends of the facial nerve.

Radical neck dissection is usually reserved for evidence of lymph node metastases. Some of the more aggressive malignancies, such as high-grade mucoepidermoid carcinoma or malignant mixed tumor, should have prophylactic upper cervical nodes resected.

Removal of parotid tumors is frequently followed by temporary paralysis of the facial muscles. The patient must be forewarned of this potential problem. Permanent paralysis follows facial nerve resection, but a portion of the muscles can have resumption of function after a prolonged period of time if nerve reconstruction is performed. When the ophthalmic branch is sacrificed, the eye cannot close. Frequent instillation of wetting solutions, eyelid taping, and protective eye coverings are necessary to prevent corneal ulcerations and loss of sight.

Submandibular tumors are almost always malignant and need extensive local resection. Intraoral neoplasms are usually small and require local removal. Palate lesions rarely involve the bone, but when this involvement occurs, the bone may have to be resected. Closure of palate mucosal defects can necessitate split thickness skin graft.

§ 7.68   Chemotherapy

Significant regression of salivary tumors occurs with the use of chlorambucil, hydroxyurea, hexamethylmelamine, daunorubicin, and cisplatin, singly or in combination.[41] Another useful combination includes mitomycin-C, methotrexate, bleomycin, and vincristine.[42]

§ 7.69 Radiation Therapy

Radiation is not the primary treatment for salivary gland tumors unless they are inoperable, or surgery is refused. Postoperative radiation is generally indicated for carcinomas. Treatment considerations are more complex in parotid carcinoma. The parotid carcinomas in which radiation can be omitted are the well-differentiated localized carcinomas of the superficial lobe that are totally resected. For radiation to be omitted, they must not involve the facial nerve or be closely adherent to it; they must not invade the deep lobe, muscle, bone, and perineural lymphatics; and they must not have lymph node metastases. Reexcised recurrent tumors are irradiated regardless of their grade or location.

Radiation is given in about the same manner as for other carcinomas of the upper aerodigestive region. Megavoltage radiation, including electrons, is given in 180 to 200 cGy fractions. The field includes the entire surgical scar to forestall implantation metastases. If the perineural lymphatics are involved, the field extends to the base of the skull. For gross tumors, 6000 cGy are required, with boosts to the residual tumor to 6500 or 7000 cGy. Postoperative radiation to the parotid bed for microscopic tumor and elective radiation to the neck can range from 5000 to 6000 cGy. After exposure of the brain and spinal cord to 4500 cGy, electron beams or changes in direction can be employed to terminate the exposure of those tissues. In high-grade tumors, recurrent tumors, and tumors with lymph node metastases in the upper neck, the entire neck on the same side is irradiated. Contralateral neck irradiation is not needed.

§ 7.70 Commentary and Significant Cases

Damage to the facial nerve (seventh cranial nerve) during parotid surgery is usually avoidable. The facial muscle paralysis from injury to the nerve leaves a very

---

[41] E.T. Creagan et al., *Cis-Platinum (P) by 24-Hour Infusion in Upper Aerodigestive Cancer (ADC),* 22 Proc. Am. Soc'y Clinical Oncology 533 (1981); R.O. Johnson et al., *Infusion of 5-Fluorouracil in Cylindroma Treatment,* 79 Archives Otolaryngology 625 (1964); R. Rentschler et al., *Chemotherapy of Malignant Major Salivary Gland Neoplasms. A 25-Year Review of M.D. Anderson Hospital Experience,* 40 Cancer 619 (1977); I.F. Tannock & D.J. Sutherland, *Chemotherapy for Adenocystic Carcinoma,* 46 Cancer 452 (1980).

[42] G.T. Budd & C.W. Groppe, *Adenoid Cystic Carcinoma of the Salivary Gland: Sustained Complete Response to Chemotherapy,* 51 Cancer 589 (1983); A.P. Venook et al., *Cisplatin, Doxorubicin, and 5-Fluorouracil Chemotherapy for Salivary Gland Malignancies: A Pilot Study of the Northern California Oncology Group,* 5 J. Clinical Oncology 951 (1987).

noticeable deformity. The muscles contort the face with smiling or laughing, there may be drooling from the mouth, and the eye might not close, resulting in irritation of the eye.

Shalom v. Beth Israel Medical Center.[43]   Injury to the seventh facial nerve resulted in total paralysis of one side of the face. The patient had had three prior surgeries for removal of a benign tumor and its recurrences prior to the surgery in 1976, when nerve damage occurred. The defendant contended that the surgery was required to prevent massive growth of tumorous tissue, and that the nerves could not be identified by electrical stimulation because of extensive scar tissue in the area caused by the prior surgeries. Another surgical excision had to be done in 1985. A defense verdict was the outcome.

THYROID

§ 7.71   Staging and Classification

TNM: American Joint Committee on Cancer.[44]

The TNM system is not ordinarily used. Prognosis relates to histologic classification, nodal involvement, and presence of metastases.

Classifying neoplasms according to histopathologic type allows the differentiation of slow-growing from fast-growing types.

Histopathologic type

   Papillary carcinoma

   Follicular carcinoma

   Mixed papillary-follicular carcinoma

   Medullary carcinoma

   Undifferentiated (anaplastic) carcinoma

   Unclassified malignant tumor.

Staging allows tumors to be classified as their prognosis worsens and the stage advances.

---

[43] No. 15615-80 (N.Y.), *reprinted in* 4 Med. Malpractice Verdicts, Settlements & Experts No. 1, at 55 (1988).

[44] American Joint Committee on Cancer, Manual for Staging of Cancer 58–59 (3d ed. 1988).

Surgical and Pathologic Staging in Thyroid Carcinoma[45]

Stage I

A—Confined to one lobe

B—Bilateral, multicentric, or in isthmus

Stage II

Primary as in Stage I-A or Stage I-B with metastases in lymph nodes

A—Unilateral lymph nodes

B—Bilateral lymph nodes, lymph nodes in mediastinum, or midline lymph nodes

Stage III

Invasion of other tissues or structures in neck or adjacent mediastinum with or without lymph nodes

Stage IV

Distant metastases.

Distinguishing benign from malignant tumors, as in the following two classifications, allows a determination as to the course of therapy.

Thyroid Tumors[46]

Tumor-like lesions

Anomalous and ectopic thyroid tissue

Struma ovarii

Thyroglossal duct cysts

Intrathyroidal cysts

Adenomatous goiter

Graves' disease

Thyroiditis

Subacute thyroiditis

Struma lymphomatosa

Riedel's struma

Nonspecific chronic thyroiditis

---

[45] M.E. Smedal et al., *The Value of 3 mv. Roentgen-Ray Therapy in Differentiated Thyroid Carcinoma.* 99 Am. J. Roentgenology 352 (1967).

[46] W.A. Meissner & S. Warren, *Tumors of the Thyroid Gland, in* Atlas of Tumor Pathology, Fascicle 4 at 7 (1969).

Hamartomatous adiposity

Amyloid goiter

Squamous metaplasia

Benign tumors

Adenoma

Follicular adenoma

Embryonal adenoma

Fetal adenoma

Simple adenoma

Colloid adenoma

Oxyphil adenoma

Atypical adenoma

Papillary adenoma

Benign teratoma of the thyroid and thyroid region

Other benign tumors

Malignant tumors

Carcinoma

Papillary adenocarcinoma

Follicular carcinoma

Clear cell carcinoma

Oxyphil carcinoma

Medullary carcinoma

Undifferentiated carcinoma

Small cell carcinoma

Giant cell carcinoma

Epidermoid carcinoma

Other malignant tumors

Lymphoma

Sarcoma

Malignant teratoma

Secondary tumor.

Thyroid Tumors[47]

I.   Epithelial tumors

   A.   Benign

      1.   Follicular adenoma

      2.   Others

   B.   Malignant

      1.   Follicular carcinoma

      2.   Papillary carcinoma

      3.   Squamous cell carcinoma

      4.   Undifferentiated (anaplastic) carcinoma

         a.   Spindle cell type

         b.   Giant cell type

         c.   Small cell type

      5.   Medullary carcinoma

II.   Nonepithelial tumors

   A.   Benign

   B.   Malignant

      1.   Fibrosarcoma

      2.   Others

III.   Miscellaneous tumors

      1.   Carcinosarcoma

      2.   Malignant hemangioendothelioma

      3.   Malignant lymphomas

      4.   Teratomas

IV.   Secondary tumors

V.   Unclassified tumors

VI.   Tumor-like lesions.

---

[47] C. Hedinger, *Histological Typing of Thyroid Tumors, in* International Histological Classification of Tumours, No. 11 (1974).

§ 7.72   Etiology

Irradiation to the neck is associated with a high incidence of thyroid cancer. A prevalence of malignancy of the thyroid was noted in survivors of Hiroshima and Nagasaki.[48] Prior irradiation for benign diseases of the neck, especially in infancy or childhood, is associated with cancer of the thyroid.[49] Malignancy of the thyroid can result from radiation therapy for malignancy of the neck, especially Hodgkin's disease.[50]

Gardner's syndrome has been reported as associated with thyroid malignancy in siblings.[51]

Diseases of the thyroid having a high incidence of thyroid cancer include hyperplasia of the thyroid epithelium, adenomatous goiter, benign adenoma, and thyroiditis.[52]

§ 7.73   Clinical Manifestations

A discrete, slow-growing mass can be a benign or malignant tumor. Hyperthyroidism is rare in thyroid malignancies. Thyroiditis causes soreness in the neck and tenderness of the thyroid gland. A history of radiation to the neck is associated with a high incidence of thyroid carcinoma.

The most common malignancies are the papillary, follicular, and mixed papillary-follicular tumors. These tend to remain confined to the neck for long periods of time, although follicular carcinoma can metastasize to the lungs. Local lymph node enlargement of the ipsilateral side is indicative of metastases. Occasionally, the first sign of thyroid cancer is the presence of enlarged cervical nodes without a palpable mass in the thyroid. A large multinodular goiter can cause lateral displacement of the trachea and esophagus.

---

[48] R.J. Sampson et al., *Thyroid Carcinoma in Hiroshima and Nagasaki: 1. Prevalence of Thyroid Carcinoma at Autopsy,* 209 JAMA 65 (1969).

[49] L.J. DeGroot, Radiation-Associated Thyroid Carcinoma (1977); M.J. Favus et al., *Thyroid Cancer Occurring as a Later Consequence of Head-and-Neck Irradiation,* 294 New Eng. J. Med. 1019 (1976); R.A. Prunz et al., *Prior Irradiation and the Development of Coexistent Differentiated Thyroid Cancer and Hyperthyroidism,* 48 Cancer 874 (1982).

[50] E.P. G'etaz et al., *Anaplastic Carcinoma of the Thyroid Following External Irradiation,* 43 Cancer 2248 (1979); I.R. McDougall et al., *Thyroid Carcinoma after High-Dose External Radiotherapy for Hodgkin's Disease,* 45 Cancer 2056 (1980).

[51] M.R. Camiel et al., *Association of Thyroid Carcinoma with Gardner's Syndrome in Siblings,* 278 New Eng. J. Med. 1056 (1968).

[52] W.A. Meissner & S. Warren, *Tumors of the Thyroid Gland, in* Atlas of Tumor Pathology, Fascicle 4 at 60 (1969).

§ 7.74   Diagnosis

A chest X-ray can show mediastinal extension of the gland or mediastinal lymph node involvement. A thyroid scan most often discloses a *cold* (nonfunctioning) nodule in the gland. Ultrasound can distinguish a cyst from a solid tumor, although cancer can be present in a cystic mass.

The incidence of malignancy is 5 percent in a gland with multiple cold (nonfunctioning on radioactive iodine uptake scan) nodules, 10 percent in an adult with a single cold nodule, and over 30 percent in children with a single cold nodule.

Needle aspiration or needle biopsy can diagnose thyroiditis and, at times, malignancy. Negative pathology requires surgical exploration.

Thyroid function tests, including thyroid stimulating hormone (TSH) level, can distinguish the presence of hyperthyroidism. Antithyroid antibody (antimicrosomal or antithyroglobulin) measurement distinguishes chronic lymphocytic thyroiditis from other disorders. Serum calcitonin and histaminase levels are elevated in patients with medullary thyroid carcinoma.

§ 7.75   Surgical Treatment

Initial treatment with suppressive doses of thyroid hormone over several months can allow resolution of the thyroid nodule. This indicates the benign nature of the mass. Recurrence or incomplete dissolution of the tumor suggests the possibility of malignancy.

A persistent nodule of the thyroid is treated by thyroid lobectomy for diagnosis. If malignancy is present, near-total resection of the contralateral lobe removes the frequently present intrathyroid metastases or concomitant primary malignancies. Lesser surgical resections are performed to prevent injury to the parathyroids and recurrent laryngeal nerves, but are associated with more-frequent recurrence of the malignancy. Modified radical neck dissection is necessary for metastatic disease to the cervical lymph nodes.

Malignancy of the thyroid is associated with a pheochromocytoma and/or parathyroid tumors, which also require surgical removal.

Tumor recurrences might not occur for at least 10 to 20 years because of the slow growth. Radioactive iodine destroys the residual thyroid gland. Thyroid hormone replacement acts to suppress growth of the malignancy. Some thyroid cancers can grow rapidly and require extensive local resection. These do not respond well to radioactive iodine or thyroid hormone.

Nerve Injury

Recurrent laryngeal nerve injury causing paresis of the recurrent laryngeal nerve can occur because of exposure and manipulation of the nerve during surgery. Permanent paralysis is expected when a malignancy involves the nerve and must be resected. Bilateral nerve injury in a total or near-total thyroidectomy can require a temporary tracheostomy until function of one or both nerves returns. Nerve grafts can be attempted, but are not usually successful.

Hypoparathyroidism

The parathyroids are small glands (two on each side) posterior to the thyroid that control the blood calcium levels. When all the glands lose their function, the drop in serum calcium causes tingling of the extremities and circumoral area. Spasm of the hand and feet occur. Intravenous calcium corrects the symptoms, and oral calcium and vitamin D can then be used.

Hypoparathyroidism is usually temporary. However, following total thyroidectomy, especially with bilateral lymph node resection, the disorder can be permanent. Identification and preservation of at least one of these glands is essential in thyroid surgery for malignancy or hyperthyroidism.

§ 7.76 Chemotherapy

Locally extensive or metastatic thyroid cancer that does not respond to other modalities of treatment might respond to doxorubicin; doxorubicin and cisplatin; bleomycin; or doxorubicin, bleomycin, vincristine, and melphalan.[53]

§ 7.77 Radiation Therapy

Radioactive iodine (131-I), administered orally, has a major role in the treatment of well-differentiated papillary, follicular, and papillary-follicular carcinomas of the thyroid; it is given following surgery. When only a lobectomy has been done, it is frequently recommended in the event of a delayed final diagnosis of carcinoma, that the patient have another operation to complete a near-total thyroidectomy for two reasons: (1) the possibility of multifocal carcinoma in the remaining lobe; and (2) to achieve subsequent ablation of the residual thyroid tissue with a lower cumulative dose of 131-I. The radioiodine is given six weeks after the thyroidectomy to develop a high-circulating TSH level in reaction to the depletion of the body's endogenous thyroid hormone. The higher the TSH level, the more efficient the radioiodine uptake in the thyroid tissue to be treated.

---

[53] T. Marada et al., *Bleomycin Treatment for Cancer of the Thyroid,* 122 Am. J. Surgery 53 (1971); K. Shimaoka et al., *A Randomized Trial of Doxorubicin Versus Doxorubicin Plus Cisplatin in Patients with Advanced Thyroid Cancer,* 59 Cancer 2155 (1985); S.D. Williams et al., *Phase II Evaluation of Doxorubicin Plus Cisplatin in Advanced Thyroid Cancer. A Southeastern Cancer Study Group Trial,* 70 Cancer Treatment Rep. 405 (1986).

To decrease the period of clinical hypothyroidism, triiodothyronine can be given during the first four weeks of the waiting period. The TSH reaches the same high level two weeks after discontinuation of triiodothyronine as it does after six weeks without thyroxine.

The dosages recommended for ablation range from 30 mCi to 100 mCi. An initial dose of 100 mCi might require fewer repeat doses to complete the ablation, and therefore result in a lower final cumulative dose. A total body scan is performed 48 hours or longer after the treatment, whenever the background radiation dissipates sufficiently for good imaging. At this point, it is highly unlikely that anything will show other than the residual normal thyroid tissue. Tumor cells, if present, do not compete with normal thyroid tissue for iodine. They begin picking up radioiodine after the normal tissue is gone. After the scan, thyroxine is started in gradually increasing doses. If a near-total thyroidectomy has not been done, and the patient has one lobe intact, an ablative dose of radioiodine can result in acute thyroiditis. This condition subsides promptly with prednisone. The patient is advised to chew gum during the waking hours of the week of treatment. Iodine is secreted in the saliva, and chewing gum promotes salivary flow, thus reducing the possibility of sialoadenitis and/or a dry mouth.

After three months, or some prefer six to twelve months, a scan is done with 1 mCi to 10 mCi of 131-I after stopping thyroxine for six weeks and triiodothyronine for two weeks. Thyroid tissue disclosed outside the thyroid bed is metastatic carcinoma. There is no way to tell, however, whether uptake in the thyroid bed is carcinoma or residual normal tissue. If carcinoma is diagnosed, the next dose of 131-I is 150 to 200 mCi. This therapeutic dose can show additional foci of thyroid tissue that a tracer dose might not show.

The circulating thyroglobulin also indicates the presence of thyroid tissue in the body without differentiating between benign and malignant tissue. However, very high levels do suggest metastatic carcinoma. Thyroglobulin is a more sensitive indicator than the radioiodine scan, but sometimes the scan shows thyroid tissue in the absence of thyroglobulin elevation. Both tests should be used.

The total cumulative dosage of 131-I over time can be stopped at 500 to 1000 mCi. The limits are imposed by the risk of bone marrow depression and the slight possibility of leukemia. Radioiodine has been highly effective in treating pulmonary metastases, but treating miliary metastases can result in pulmonary fibrosis. Lower therapeutic doses can reduce this risk. Fertility problems and congenital abnormalities do not occur with radioiodine therapy, but women should be advised not to become pregnant for six months after radioiodine therapy. Men are advised to avoid procreation for three months.

Papillary, follicular, and papillary-follicular carcinomas are treated effectively with external radiation. They have been called radioresistant in the past due to insufficient regard for their slow regression that can last over a year. While radioiodine is most successful in treating microscopic carcinoma, the presence of gross carcinoma requires the concomitant use of external radiation. External radiation also should be used when a microscopic tumor does not respond to radioiodine. Various treatment plans can be used. A good plan uses an anterior electron field that spares the spinal cord. After 4000 cGy is given to the entire area at risk in four or five weeks using 180 to 200 cGy fractions, a 1000 cGy boost can be given to areas of identified tumor. In quite large, unresectable tumors, the field should cover all the cervical and superior mediastinal lymph nodes. The basic dose can be 5000 cGy, with the boost going to 6500 cGy. For metastases to bone or brain and superior vena caval obstruction, external radiation is given to 4000 or 5000 cGy.

Medullary carcinomas do not pick up radioiodine, but 131-I can be given postoperatively to ablate thyroid remnants. Contiguous C cells and medullary tumor might be eliminated indirectly by the radiation from a dose of 150 cGy given to the adjacent normal thyroid tissue. If the medullary carcinoma is known to be incompletely resected, lymph node metastases are present, or if calcitonin levels remain high postoperatively, the thyroid bed and all the lymph nodes from the base of the skull to the central mediastinum should be irradiated to 5000 cGy with boosts to suspected residuals to 6000 cGy. These tumors have been called radioresistant erroneously for the same reason as papillary and follicular carcinomas. Calcitonin testing is used for follow-up tests, and there is no value in using thyroglobulin levels in medullary carcinoma.

Anaplastic carcinoma can develop with no antecedent disease in the thyroid or can develop from dedifferentiation of low-grade carcinomas existing for many years. There is no evidence that the dedifferentiation is due to prior radiation. The prognosis is poor, and 5000 or 6000 cGy is essential for palliative radiation. In efforts to achieve better results, a variety of treatment regimens can exist such as hyperfractionation, large fraction therapy, and radiation therapy combined with doxorubicin. Radioiodine is not picked up, and thyroglobulin testing is of no value.

§ 7.78   Commentary and Significant Cases

Injury to the recurrent laryngeal nerve is avoidable unless malignancy involves the nerve itself. The parathyroid glands are small (less than 1 cm) and have a yellow-brown color that becomes more yellow with aging. These glands can be mistaken for a lymph node or fatty tissue. The parathyroids have variable positions in relationship to the thyroid gland, and they also have been found along the carotid sheath and in the upper anterior mediastinum. The surgeon must be familiar with parathyroid vascular supply, color, and shape as well as variations in location to prevent permanent injury.

Bailey v. Lowery.[54]   The defendant performed a total thyroidectomy and severed both recurrent laryngeal nerves to the vocal cords. Speech and respiratory

---

[54] No. 86-2205 (Escambia County, Fla. Oct. 1987), *reprinted in* 4 Med. Malpractice Verdicts, Settlements & Experts No. 3, at 55 (1988).

impairment ensued. The pathology report indicated that the extensive surgery had been necessary. The jury awarded $1,200,000.

Gruidl v. Schell.[55]   The patient saw her physician for a lump on the left side of her neck. A thyroid scan revealed a tumor in the left side of the thyroid. She was admitted to the hospital, and the surgeon could not palpate a mass. She was discharged without surgery, but in June 1985, a biopsy showed a medullary carcinoma. Radiation therapy was not successful and death ensued. The jury awarded a net $187,560 for survival and wrongful death, which included 40 percent contributory negligence of the decedent.

Lupton v. Bartley.[56]   A near-total thyroidectomy was performed. Persistent hoarseness, numbness, twitching of the extremities, and spasms of the hands and feet resulted. The plaintiff alleged that the thyroidectomy was unnecessary and excessive for chronic lymphocytic thyroiditis, that there was failure to identify and protect the recurrent laryngeal nerves and parathyroids, and failure to obtain appropriate consultations before and during surgery to prevent injury. The award was for $163,500.

HEAD AND NECK NODULES

§ 7.79   Differential Diagnosis

Masses in the neck without obvious primary source are a diagnostic challenge. The location of the nodule gives a clue as to its origin. The neck lymph nodes are divided into five levels for more accurate assessment (see **Figure 7–1**). Tumors in the lower third of the anterior cervical triangle or under the lower third of the sternocleidomastoid muscle (level IV) are usually metastatic malignancies originating from below the diaphragm (lung, esophagus, bowel, testes, ovary, or pancreas), thyroid gland, and, rarely, the pyriform sinus. Masses in the midanterior cervical triangle or under the midsternocleidomastoid muscle (Level III) can be a benign branchial cleft cyst or a metastatic malignancy of the thyroid or nasopharynx. When nodules are in the upper third of the neck (Level II), the nasopharynx, oropharynx, tongue, and larynx, primaries are suspect. Branchial cleft cyst occurs in this area, but tends to lie under the sternocleidomastoid muscle. Carotid body tumors lie at the junction of the common carotid artery with the internal and external carotid arteries. This is a pulsating mass. The posterior cervical triangle (Level V) can contain tumor metastases from thyroid or nasopharynx. Cystic hygroma occurs in this area. Level I, submandibular, mass can

---

[55] 166 Ill. App. 3d 276, 519 N.E.2d 963 (1988).

[56] No. 85-8356 (Hillsborough County, Fla.), *reprinted in* 3 Med. Malpractice Verdicts, Settlements & Experts No. 9, at 59–60 (1987).

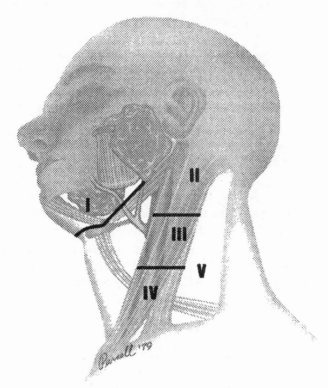

Figure 7–1. Lymph node levels in the cervical region. *Head and Neck Oncology* 265. Edited by Kagan & Miles. G.K. Hall Medical Publishers, 1981. By permission of Mosby-Year Book, Inc.

be a tumor of the submaxillary gland or metastasis from the lip or anterior tongue.

Masses appearing in the suprahyoid area can be primary submaxillary gland tumors or metastases from the anterior tongue, oral cavity, gingiva, buccal mucosa, or lips. Midline tumors in this region can be a hyperplastic node or dermoid tumor.

Nodules in the neck posterior to the mandible can be nasopharyngeal metastasis or primary parotid gland tumor. A common mistake is to assume this is a lymph node and remove the mass without preparing to do a superficial parotidectomy.

Midline masses inferior to the hyoid bone can be thyroid or thyroglossal duct cyst. Tuberculous adenitis tends to have matted masses of nodes in the internal jugular region. Lymphoma can occur in any lymph node of the neck. Metastatic melanoma can appear in any lymph node of the neck that drains the skin area of the primary. Sarcoidosis and infectious mononucleosis are associated with multiple enlarged cervical lymph nodes. Skin infections can cause enlarged neck nodes. Neurofibromas of von Recklinghausen's disease and other neurologic tumors can occur in the neck.

§ 7.80   Diagnosis

Careful examination of the head and neck area by visualization of skin areas and palpation of the neck followed by oral, nasal, and nasopharyngeal exam (both visual and palpation), and indirect and direct laryngoscopy diagnose the source of most head and neck nodules. Chest X-ray is essential and should be followed by CT scan of the head and neck area if the diagnosis is in doubt.

Endoscopic studies by esophagogastroscopy, colonoscopy, and bronchoscopy can be valuable. Upper gastrointestinal X-ray series, barium enema, and computerized tomography (CT) of the abdomen are used to evaluate for possible intraabdominal primary malignancies.

A relatively simple method to evaluate a neck mass for possible malignancy is aspiration using a skinny needle. Excisional biopsy gives a definitive diagnosis.

Metastatic adenocarcinoma to the neck on biopsy signifies a primary from the thyroid, lung, breast, bowel, kidney, or pancreas. Positive mucin stains indicate origin from the bowel or pancreas. Metastatic squamous cell carcinoma on biopsy can be from the oropharynx, nasopharynx, sinuses, larynx, lungs, or esophagus. Positive melanin staining indicates melanoma.

§ 7.81   Surgical Treatment

When a thorough workup has not indicated a source for the metastatic malignancy to the neck, radical neck dissection or radiation therapy is indicated. See § 7.84. With this form of treatment, a fair percentage of patients live over five years without evidence of recurrent tumor. Continued regular reevaluation is essential to search for the elusive primary tumor.

§ 7.82   Chemotherapy

If metastatic squamous cell carcinoma to the neck nodes from an unknown primary is diagnosed, treatment with chemotherapy is reserved for recurrent nonresectable or distant metastatic disease. The agents used are the same as those for a primary head and neck squamous cell carcinoma (see § 7.6).

§ 7.83   Radiation Therapy

Opinions vary on the best way to manage a metastatic tumor in the neck from a primary source that remains unknown after intensive investigation.

It is known that 25 or 30 percent of squamous cell carcinomas that are treated with a radical neck dissection never develop a primary tumor. Traditionally, after five years without the appearance of a primary tumor, it has been postulated retrospectively that the tumor in the neck was a primary branchial cleft carcinoma. Presently, immunologic mechanisms are hypothesized as causing spontaneous disappearance of the primary tumor.

Because you cannot know which one out of four cases will be cured by a neck dissection alone, additional management decisions need to be implemented for all of them, usually involving radiation therapy.

One option has been to avoid the unpleasant radiation aftereffect of xerostomia by withholding radiation after a radical neck dissection until a primary tumor becomes apparent. The traditional objection to this method is that the extirpation of the normal lymphatic channels has opened the gate to widespread incurable cutaneous metastases. Administering radiation immediately after the radical neck dissection is a partial solution, but it does not answer the traditional objection to treating metastases before treating the primary when a cure is still the objective.

A second option is simply to excise the tumor in what amounts to a debulking procedure and to follow up with radiation therapy.

A third option is to give radiation preferably after a needle biopsy or an incisional biopsy if the diagnosis cannot be made with a needle. A radical neck dissection can follow the radiation for any persisting metastases.

The elective areas to be irradiated can be given a total dose of 5000 cGy in 180 to 200 cGy fractions with boosts to areas of gross tumor to 7000 cGy using megavoltage X-rays and electrons. A strip of skin along the anterior aspect of the neck should be kept out of the radiation field to avoid or reduce chronic submental and facial edema.

Carcinomas of the posterior cervical triangle and other carcinomas in the middle and upper thirds of the neck should be treated by irradiating all the lymph nodes on both sides of the neck, as well as the pharynx from the nasopharynx to the pyriform sinuses, to eradicate an occult primary tumor.

Supraclavicular carcinomas come from primary tumors of the breast, thorax, or abdomen. Radiation is palliative, and, if needed, is given only to the obvious metastases.

§ 7.84   Radical Neck Dissection Generally

Cervical lymph node metastases from cancers of the head and neck region or carcinoma without evidence of a primary lesion can be treated with radical neck dissection. Known primary lesions should be controlled surgically or with radiation therapy.

§ 7.85   —Surgical Procedure

In radical neck dissection, the deep cervical lymphatics from the mandible to the clavicle and trapezius muscle to the midline are resected. This procedure includes removing the sternocleidomastoid muscle, omohyoid muscle, submaxillary gland, and frequently the spinal accessory (eleventh cranial) nerve.

Injury to the following nerves must be avoided:

1. Trigeminal nerve (fifth cranial): The lingual nerve, sensory to the tongue, lies in the neck superior to the submaxillary gland. The chorda tympani nerve (branch of facial nerve) to the submaxillary gland, following the lingual nerve, is sacrificed.

2. Facial nerve (seventh cranial): This nerve supplies the facial musculature. The mandibular branch that courses anteriorly to the mandible is the most often injured. The cervical branch to the platysma muscle is sacrificed.

3. Glossopharyngeal nerve (ninth cranial): This nerve provides sensory and motor fibers to the tongue and pharynx. It is most often injured when transecting the internal jugular vein at its highest point.

4. Vagus nerve (tenth cranial): This nerve provides auricular sensory and motor fibers to pharyngeal muscles and larynx (recurrent laryngeal nerve), and visceral sensory and motor fibers to the heart, bronchi, bowel, kidney, liver, pancreas, and spleen. It is most often injured at the highest point of transection of the internal jugular vein.

5. Hypoglossal nerve (twelfth cranial): This is the motor nerve of the tongue. It is most susceptible to injury at the high point of the internal jugular vein or as it crosses anteriorly to the carotid vessels. A branch of the first cervical nerve (descending hypoglossal nerve) following the hypoglossal, plus the descending cervical nerve (from second and third cervical nerves), both of which supply the omohyoid muscle, are sacrificed.

6. Phrenic nerve: This nerve originates from the third, fourth, and fifth cervical nerves, and it supplies the diaphragm. It is usually injured in the lower third of the neck when transecting the major sensory cervical nerves.

7. Brachial plexis: This nerve bundle originates from the fourth, fifth, sixth, and seventh cervical nerves and the first thoracic nerve. It is the motor and sensory supply to the arm, shoulder, scapula, serratus anterior muscle, and latissimus dorsi muscle. It can be injured in the lower neck dissection.

Elective tracheostomy is added to the procedure if tongue or laryngeal edema is anticipated. If the anterior portion of the mandible is resected, tracheostomy should be considered to allow airway maintenance during and following surgery.

Suction catheters are placed under the skin flaps to prevent hematoma. Antibiotics are given if the oral cavity has been entered or if laryngectomy or pharyngeal resection has been performed.

§ 7.86   —Complications

In radical neck disssection, hemorrhage as a hematoma or bleeding through the suture line can occur from major arterial branches. Surgical exploration with ligation of bleeders and evacuation of the hematoma must be performed.

Airway obstruction can be caused by edema or hematoma. Endotracheal intubation handles the emergency problem of hypoxia. At times, tracheostomy is necessary.

Pneumothorax is precipitated by entering the dome of the pleural cavity at the lowest area of the neck dissection. Dyspnea, restlessness, or chest pain can indicate this problem. A chest X-ray establishes the diagnosis. Significant pneumothorax (over 15 percent) is treated with a chest tube placed in underwater drainage.

Chylous fistula is the accumulation of whitish fluid in the neck wound. This condition is caused by an unrecognized injury to the thoracic duct near its entry into the junction of the internal jugular vein and subclavian vein at the base of the left neck. There can be enlarged lymph channels in the lower aspect of the right neck that can be transected, but this situation is less usual. Compression dressings and cessation of oral feeding helps resolve the problem. If drainage continues, surgical ligation should be accomplished.

Skin necrosis can appear, especially, at the triangular junction of closure in the midneck, which happens more often if the neck has been previously irradiated. Debridement and wet dressings help the wound to heal. Erosion into the carotid with massive bleeding can follow infection and skin breakdown with exposure of the artery.

Wound infection is more likely when the surgery has entered the oral cavity, pharynx, or esophagus. The wound has to be opened and drained. Appropriate antibiotics are given.

Salivary fistula must be recognized early to prevent dissection under the skin flaps. The possibility of a fistula arises when the oral cavity, pharynx, or esophagus has been entered. Draining secretions from resection of the inferior aspect of the parotid gland extending into the neck is possible.

§ 7.87   —Commentary and Significant Cases

Surgery in the neck area is fraught with danger of injury to vital structures, especially nerves. A physician performing a surgical procedure in the neck must have expert knowledge of the anatomy and take due care in incising and cutting any of the tissues.

Parotid gland surgery risks injury to the facial (seventh cranial) nerve, which is avoidable unless malignant tumor involves the nerve. Facial muscle paralysis that ensues with nerve injury results in significant facial deformity. The muscles control the face with smiling or laughing, there can be drooling from the mouth, and the eye might not close resulting in irritation of the eye.

Thyroid surgery risks injury to the recurrent laryngeal nerve with voice hoarseness. Damage is avoidable unless malignancy involves the nerve. Removal or impingement to the local supply of the parathyroid glands can result in hypoparathyroidism with depressed serum calcium and muscle cramps and spasm. This result is avoidable except in the presence of malignancy, for which bilateral neck dissection is required. Identifying the small parathyroid supply is an essential part of thyroid surgery.

Block v. McVay.[57]   The plaintiff had a hard lump noted in the anterior right lower neck in April 1959. The defendant advised the plaintiff that the lump might be malignant and that it should be removed. The mass was removed through a small incision, and it was then discovered that the tumor base had been attached to the brachial plexus. Neurofibroma was diagnosed on pathology. Neurologic deficit occurred with numbness and pain of the right arm and thumb. The court held that absent expert testimony that the manner of performing the operation for removing the tumor was unsuccessful or for showing that such surgery should be performed only by a neurosurgeon, the surgeon could not be held liable for poor results resulting from the mistaken belief that the tumor was malignant, whereas it was a benign nerve tumor.

Bois v. United States.[58]   The plaintiff developed a cancer of the right pyriform sinus in 1979. This condition was treated with laser surgery followed by radiation therapy. In 1985, he complained of huskiness of the voice and difficulty with swallowing. A biopsy was performed in August 1985. The symptoms continued, and an ulceration was noted in the pyriform sinus in January 1986. A total laryngectomy was performed. The plaintiff's expert testified that the lesion would have been observable in August 1985, that invasive carcinoma was present in November 1985, and that local excision could have been done in August 1985 instead of laryngectomy.

Grimes v. Webb.[59]   The plaintiff had a biopsy of a lymph node located in the right side of the neck. During the procedure, the defendant cut the spinal accessory nerve. The biopsy was negative. Despite repeated complaints postoperatively, the defendant failed to diagnose the injured nerve. Another physician diagnosed the injury and reconnected the nerve. There was a $250,000 settlement.

---

[57] 80 S.D. 469, 126 N.W.2d 808 (1964).

[58] No. 88-2418-Mc (D. Mass.), *reprinted in* 7 Med. Malpractice Verdicts, Settlements & Experts No. 1, at 49–50 (1991).

[59] No. 89-05586-CA (Duval County, Fla.), *reprinted in* 6 Med. Malpractice Verdicts, Settlements & Experts No. 6, at 65 (1990).

Hardy v. Southern Pacific Employees Ass'n.[60]   There was a verdict for $45,000. The plaintiff had spilled creosote on his lower lip in January 1964, and a lesion developed on the lip. He was referred to the defendant in July 1964 "to rule out carcinoma." Pain in the lip continued despite local treatment. A lump developed next to the sore on the lip, and a biopsy was performed in September 1965. Cancer was diagnosed and excised. Further surgery to eliminate the lip cancer was necessary in November 1966. The court held the award was not excessive when the plaintiff was disfigured by operations, was subjected to pain and suffering, and was required to seek new employment that would not necessitate being out of doors.

Holloway v. Chaudhary.[61]   There was a $475,000 settlement. The 47-year-old plaintiff complained to the defendant of sore throat on several occasions early in 1986. In November 1986, another physician diagnosed her as having a T3 squamous cell carcinoma of the larynx, necessitating total laryngectomy with permanent tracheostomy. The plaintiff contended that the defendant should have diagnosed the cancer or referred her to a specialist by April or May 1986 when the tumor was probably in an earlier stage and treatable by radiation therapy alone.

Joynt v. Barnes.[62]   The 28-year-old decedent had a chest X-ray taken in October 1973 that disclosed a right paratracheal mass, and a bronchoscopy or a scalene node biopsy was recommended. He was seen by the defendant, who ordered further chest X-rays and laminograms. These were interpreted as negative. The decedent complained of dyspnea, loss of voice, chest pains, and fatigue in January 1974. He was diagnosed as having pleurisy and pneumonia. Hemoptysis (coughing up blood) occurred and bronchoscopy was performed in February 1974. An adenocarcinoma of the trachea was found. He was treated with radiation and chemotherapy and died in January 1979. The court held that there was failure to properly diagnose the cancer by failing to perform a bronchoscopy when X-rays indicated a possible abnormality. The verdict for the plaintiff was affirmed.

Kilburn v. United States.[63]   The plaintiff was diagnosed in October 1982 with cancer of the tongue with metastasis to a neck lymph node. Radiation therapy was administered, and the plaintiff was instructed in oral hygiene. The plaintiff

---

[60] 10 Ariz. App. 464, 459 P.2d 743 (1969).

[61] No. 86-2-18558-5 (King County, Wash. Nov. 1989), *reprinted in* 6 Med. Malpractice Verdicts, Settlements & Experts No. 5, at 17 (1990).

[62] 71 Ill. App. 3d 187, 388 N.E.2d 1298 (1979).

[63] No. 87-328 (E.D. Ky. July 1990), *reprinted in* 6 Med. Malpractice Verdicts, Settlements & Experts No. 12, at 43 (1990).

did not use the daily fluoride treatment and did not return to the dental clinic. In 1984, his teeth were extracted because of dental decay, and osteoradionecrosis was diagnosed in February 1986. He was started on hyperbaric oxygen therapy and advised not to smoke. He continued to smoke and the mandible had to be removed in August 1986. The plaintiff alleged that his teeth should have been removed prior to radiation therapy. The court found that removing the teeth would not have prevented the osteoradionecrosis.

Meyer v. United States.[64]   The six-year-old patient had a lump in the left side of the neck associated with fever in April 1975. He was seen at the Andrew Radar Army Clinic and at Walson Army Hospital Pediatric Clinic several times. In April 1976, enlarged cervical nodes were noted, which persisted until a biopsy was done in January 1977. A diagnosis of toxoplasmosis was made by the pathologist. Medication for that disorder caused an adverse reaction requiring hospitalization. A repeat biopsy was done in October 1977 at a private facility, and Stage II-A Hodgkin's disease was diagnosed. Radiation and chemotherapy was given. The court awarded $26,063.95 for pain and suffering and special medical damages.

Nichols v. Phillips.[65]   There was a $150,000 verdict for the misdiagnosis of a cytology specimen from a benign neck tumor as squamous cell carcinoma. The patient unnecessarily underwent radical neck dissection, sustaining loss of motion and strength of the right shoulder, numbness in the neck, and drooping of the right lower lip.

O'Brien v. Stover.[66]   Applying Iowa law, the court held that the $50,000 award was not excessive for failing to diagnose cancer by performing a tissue biopsy. The decedent had a toothache, and she went to the dentist defendant in May 1967. Abscess or infection was diagnosed, and the tooth was extracted. X-rays revealed partial destruction of the bone underlying the tooth, and there was intermittent bleeding from the unhealed friable tissues in the socket. After multiple visits to the defendant, a cytologic smear was taken in August 1967 and was interpreted as negative. The disorder was treated as chronic osteomyelitis with antibiotics. In October 1967, another physician performed a biopsy that disclosed poorly differentiated epidermoid cancer. Despite surgery and radiation, the patient died in August 1968.

---

[64] No. 79-CV-637 (N.D. N.Y. Oct. 9, 1986), *reprinted in* 4 Med. Malpractice Verdicts, Settlements & Experts No. 11, at 53 (1988).

[65] No. 336219-1 (Fresno County Super. Ct.), *reprinted in* 4 Med. Malpractice Verdicts, Settlements & Experts No. 6, at 46–47 (1988).

[66] 443 F.2d 1013 (8th Cir. 1971).

Rolfson v. Clements.[67]   The decedent underwent surgical removal of a tumor in the neck. Pathologic examination was determined as benign. He was advised that no further treatment was necessary. In 1987, the decedent was diagnosed as having cancer, which ultimately caused his death. Review of the pathology slides disclosed cancer. The case settled for $500,000.

Santos v. United States.[68]   The plaintiff was seen at the United States Public Health Service Hospital in June 1980 with hoarseness of the voice and a lump in the left neck. He had a history of heavy smoking for 28 years. The diagnosis of inflammation of the throat was made, and there was no referral to a specialist. The diagnosis of Stage 4 squamous cell carcinoma of the larynx was made at another hospital in January 1981. Chemotherapy was given, and then a total laryngectomy with left radical neck dissection was performed. Applying Massachusetts law, the court held that the plaintiff failed to prove that the negligent delay in treatment was a proximate cause of his undergoing more extensive surgery with its attendant negative impact on the plaintiff.

Schwartz v. United States.[69]   There was an award of $725,000 when cancer of the maxillary sinus occurred following installation of thorotrast into the sinus. The plaintiff was treated for sinusitis at the Naval Hospital in 1944. X-ray of the sinus was performed with a radioactive contrast dye, thorotrast (umbrathor), which remained in the sinus being visualized on X-rays at the Veterans Administration Clinic in 1947, 1948, and 1953. He was treated for allergic rhinitis in 1948. Headaches, burning throat, and discharge of pus and blood occurred in 1953 and again in 1955. No treatment was given. A tooth extraction in October 1956 resulted in a persistent drainage of bloody secretion. A biopsy in 1957 was diagnosed as squamous cell carcinoma of the left maxillary sinus. Radical surgery including removal of the left eye was performed in February 1957. The court, applying Pennsylvania law, held that the government knew or should have known about carcinogenic properties of thorotrast, which were documented and reported in the 1940s. The government doctors should have reviewed the records of all patients to whom thorotrast had been given and warned them of the danger of its retention in their bodies. The past medical history should have been inserted in the current treatment folders of the Veterans Administration Clinic. There was negligent failure to remove the thorotrast from the patient's sinus when he was in the clinic for treatment in 1948 and 1953.

---

[67] No. 88-7360-B (Dallas County, Tex.), *reprinted in* 6 Med. Malpractice Verdicts, Settlements & Experts No. 11, at 52 (1990).

[68] 603 F. Supp. 417 (D. Mass. 1985).

[69] 230 F. Supp. 536 (E.D. Pa. 1964).

Shalom v. Beth Israel Medical Center.[70]   Injury to the seventh facial nerve resulted in total paralysis of one side of the face. The patient had had three prior surgeries for removal of a benign tumor and its recurrences prior to the surgery in 1976, when the nerve damage occurred. The defendant contended that the surgery was required to prevent massive growth of tumorous tissue and that the nerves could not be identified by electrical stimulation because of extensive scar tissue in the area caused by the prior surgeries. Another surgical excision had to be done in 1985. A defense verdict was the outcome.

---

[70] No. 15615-80 (N.Y.), *reprinted in* 4 Med. Malpractice Verdicts, Settlements & Experts No. 1, at 55.

THORACIC NEOPLASMS

§ 8.27 Chemotherapy

§ 8.28 Radiation Therapy

LUNG TUMORS

§ 8.1 Staging and Classification

TNM: American Joint Committee on Cancer (AJCC).[1]

Prognosis is related to tumor size (T1=3 cm or less, T2=more than 3 cm, T3=invasion of surrounding structures or within 2 cm distance from the carina), nodal involvement (especially mediastinal), and metastases.

Table 8–1 shows the International Union Against Cancer (UICC) stage grouping.[2]

Table 8–1

UICC Stage Grouping

Stage	Tumor	Node	Metastasis
Occult Cancer	TX	N0	M0
Stage IA	T1	N0	M0
	T2	N0	M0
Stage IB	T0, T1	N1	M0
Stage II	T2	N1	M0
Stage III	T3	N0, N1	M0
	Any T	N2	M0
Stage IV	Any T	Any N	M1

Histopathologic Types[3]

Squamous cell carcinoma

Adenocarcinoma

Bronchioalveolar carcinoma (alveolar cell)

Large cell carcinoma

Neuroendocrine carcinoma

　　Carcinoid

　　Well-differentiated cell type

---

[1] American Joint Committee on Cancer, Manual for Staging of Cancer 118 (3d ed. 1988).

[2] The TNM Classification of Malignant Tumors 41–45 (M.H. Harmen ed., 3d ed. 1978).

[3] V.E. Gould & W.H. Warren, *Epithelial Neoplasms of the Lung, in* Thoracic Oncology 77 (J.A. Roth, et al. eds., 1989).

Intermediate cell type

Small cell type

Giant cell carcinoma

Adenosquamous carcinoma

Spindle cell carcinoma

Carcinosarcoma

Salivary gland type

Mucous gland adenoma.

§ 8.2   Etiology

Tobacco smoke contains carcinogenic initiating and promoting substances. N-nitrosamines from nicotine and tobacco alkaloids, catechols, aldehydes (including formaldehyde), and peroxides are found in tobacco smoke, and they act as carcinogens or cocarcinogens and tumor promoters. Lung cancer is directly related to the duration of smoking. Even passive exposure to cigarette smoke increases the risk of lung neoplasms.[4]

There is an increased risk of lung cancer in vitamin A-deficient individuals.[5] The intake of carotene, but not retinol, is inversely related to the incidence of lung cancer.[6]

Ras genes encode proteins (designated as p21) and are located on the cell membrane. Alterations in the c-ras gene (altered p21 ras) has reportedly been responsible for the transforming potential in lung cancer.[7] All three classes of the ras gene (c-k-ras, c-H-ras, and W-ras) have been detected in human lung tumor cell lines and/or fresh lung tumor. When activated, the ras genes have oncogenic capabilities.

---

[4]D.C. Janerick et al., *Lung Cancer and Exposure to Tobacco Smoke in the Household,* 323 New Eng. J. Med. 632 (1990); D.P. Sandler et al., *Cumulative Effects of Lifetime Passive Smoking on Cancer Risk,* 1 Lancet 312 (1985).

[5]E. Bjelke, *Dietary Vitamin A and Human Lung Cancer,* 15 Cancer 561 (1975).

[6]R.B. Shekelle, *Dietary Vitamin A and Risk of Cancer in the Western Electric Study,* 2 Lancet 1185 (1981).

[7]C.J. Der et al., *Transforming Genes of Human Bladder and Lung Carcinoma Cell Lines are Homologous to the Ras Genes of Harvey and Kirsten Sarcoma Virus,* 79 Proc. Nat'l Acad. Sci. USA 3637 (1982); E. Santos et al., *T 24 Human Bladder Carcinoma Oncogene Is an Activated Form of the Normal Human Homologue of BALB- and Harvey-MSC Transforming Genes,* 298 Nature 343 (1982); E. Taparowsky et al., *Structure and Activation of the Human N-Ras Gene,* 34 Cell 581 (1983).

Amplifying and/or expressing the c-myc gene correlates with the variant subset of small cell lung cancer (SCLC), suggesting a role in the phenotype conversion and malignant behavior of this SCLC phenotype.[8] Some variant SCLC cell lines were amplified by the N-myc or L-myc gene. The c-myc gene is assigned to chromosome 8, the N-myc is assigned to chromosome 2, and the L-myc to chromosome 1p (near 1p32).[9]

One SCLC cell line was amplified for and expressed the myb oncogene. A possible role was suggested for c-myb transcription in expressing the SCLC phenotype, because a significant difference existed in the levels of transcription of this oncogene in the four major histologic phenotypes of lung cancer.[10]

Other oncogenes that affect lung tumors or cell lines include p53 (a protein), c-raf gene, fes or fps (cytoplasmic location), fms (located in plasma membrane and cytoplasm), and fos (a nuclear oncogene).[11]

A specific chromosomal deletion 3p(14-23) is found in SCLC, suggesting that there is a genetic defect present.

§ 8.3   Clinical Manifestations

In most cases, there is a gradual development of a persistent cough wrongly attributed to upper respiratory infection, bronchitis, pneumonia, or cigarette cough. There can be weight loss, dyspnea (shortness of breath), wheezing, chest pain, hemoptysis (coughing of blood), fever, malaise, or bone pain. The presenting signs and symptoms are related to the location of the primary tumor.

§ 8.4   —Superior Vena Cava Syndrome (SVC)

Superior vena cava syndrome (SVC) with headache, chest pain, cough, or other symptoms associated with facial edema, dilated neck veins in the sitting position, proptosis, conjunctival suffusion, or papilledema occurs with obstruction of the superior vena cava (see **Chapter 12**).

---

[8] C.D. Little et al., *Amplification and Expression of the c-myc Oncogene in Human Lung Cancer Cell Lines,* 306 Nature 196 (1983).

[9] M.M. Nau et al., *L-myc: A New Myc-Related Gene Amplified and Expressed in Human Small Cell Lung Cancer,* 318 Nature 69 (1985); M. Schwab et al., *Chromosome Localization in Normal Human Cells and Neuroblastomas of a Gene Related to c-myc,* 308 Nature 288 (1984); R. Taub et al., *Translocation of the c-myc Gene into the Immunoglobulin Heavy Chain Locus in Human Burkitt Lymphoma and Murine Plasmacytoma Cells,* 79 Proc. Nat'l Acad. Sci. USA 7837 (1982).

[10] M. Vinocour & J.O. Mina, *Cellular and Molecular Biology of Lung Cancer,* in Thoracic Oncology 46 (J.A. Roth et al. eds., 1989).

[11] D.J. Salmon et al., *Expression of Cellular Oncogenes in Human Malignancies,* 224 Science 256 (1984); M. Vinocour & J.D. Minna, *Myc and p53 Expression in Human Lung Cancer Cell Lines,* 46 Fed. Proc. 740 (1987).

§ 8.5 —Superior Sulcus Tumor
(Pancoast's Syndrome)

A tumor originating in the superior sulcus (apex of the lung) occurs in 4 percent of lung cancer patients.[12] Pain in the shoulder and ulnar nerve portion of the arm with this neoplasm is called *Pancoast's syndrome.*[13] Involvement of the sympathetic nerve results in Horner's syndrome, consisting of enophthalmos, ptosis, meiosis, and anhidrosis.

§ 8.6 —Paraneoplastic Syndromes

Some lung tumors are associated with the production of biologically active substances resulting in paraneoplastic syndromes, as shown in **Table 8–2.**

Table 8–2
Paraneoplastic Syndromes

Syndrome	Signs and Symptoms
Ectopic Parathyroid Hormone[14]	Irritability, confusion, lethargy or coma, anorexia, constipation, nausea, cardiac arrhythmias, polyuria, polydypsia
Inappropriate Antidiuretic Hormone (SIADH)[15] [seen in small cell carcinoma of the lung]	Anorexia, nausea, vomiting, confusion, lethargy, psychotic behavior, seizures, coma
Cushing's Syndrome (ectopic adrenocorticotropic hormone [ACTH] or corticotropin-releasing factor [CRF]) [seen in small cell lung cancer]	Hypokalemic alkalosis, muscle weakness, muscle wasting, hyperglycemia, hyperpigmentation
Carcinoid Syndrome [seen in small cell lung cancer][16]	Flushing, episodes of tachycardia, wheezing, diarrhea, facial edema, weight loss, anorexia

---

[12] L. Hyde & C.I. Hyde, *Clinical Manifestations of Lung Cancer,* 65 Chest 299 (1974).

[13] D.L. Paulson, *Carcinoma in the Superior Pulmonary Sulcus,* 70 J. Thoracic Cardiovascular Surgery 1095 (1975).

[14] W.P.L. Myers, *Differential Diagnosis of Hyper-calcemia and Cancer,* 27 Ca: Cancer J. Clinicians 258 (1977).

[15] W.D. Odell & A.R. Wolfsen, *Humoral Syndromes Associated with Cancer,* 29 Annals Rev. Med. 379 (1978).

[16] K.L. Melmon et al., *Distinctive Clinical and Therapeutic Aspects of the Syndrome Associated with Bronchial Carcinoid Tumors,* 39 Amer. J. Med. 568 (1965).

Table 8–2 *(continued)*

Syndrome	Signs and Symptoms
Gynecomastia (ectopic gonadotropin production)[17]	Swelling of the breasts, galactorrhea, testicular atrophy

§ 8.7 —Neurologic and Myopathic Syndromes

Neurologic and myopathic syndromes are known to be associated with lung neoplasms,[18] as shown in **Table 8–3**.

Table 8–3

Neurologic and Myopathic Syndromes

Syndrome	Signs and Symptoms
Subacute cerebellar degeneration	Symmetric cerebellar failure often with dementia, dysarthria
Limbic encephalitis	Dementia
Optic neuritis	Decrease in visual acuity, papilledema; unilateral or bilateral
Subacute necrotic myelopathy	Rapid ascending motor and sensory paralysis to thoracic level
Sensory neuropathy	Sensory loss including deep tendon reflexes, with normal strength and normal motor conduction velocity
Sensorimotor peripheral neuropathy	Distal weakness and wasting, areflexia, distal sensory loss
Autonomic and gastrointestinal neuropathy	Orthostatic hypotension, neurogenic bladder, intestinal pseudo-obstruction
Dermatomyositis and polymyositis	Progressive muscle weakness
Myasthenic syndrome (Eaton-Lambert syndrome)	Weakness and fatigue of proximal muscles, especially pelvic girdle and thigh; dryness of mouth, dysphagia, dysarthria, and peripheral paresthesias

[17] M.R. Blackman et al., *Ectopic Hormones,* 23 Advances Internal Med. 85 (1978).

[18] P.B. Croft & M. Wilkinson, *Carcinomatous Neuromyopathy: Its Incidence in Patients with Carcinoma of the Lung and Breast,* 1 Lancet 184 (1965); P.A. Bunn & J.D. Minna, *Paraneoplastic Syndromes, in* Cancer: Principles and Practice of Oncology 1913 (V.T. DeVita et al. eds., 1989).

§ 8.8   —Dermatologic Disorders

Various dermatologic lesions are associated with lung cancer,[19] as shown in **Table 8–4.**

Table 8–4

Dermatologic Disorders

Disease	Signs and Symptoms
Acanthosis nigricans	Hyperkeratosis and pigmentation, especially of axillae, neck, flexures, and anogenital region
Acquired ichthyosis	Generalized dry, cracking skin, hyperkeratotic palms and soles, rhomboidal scales
Bazex's disease	Erythema, hyperkeratosis with scales and pruritus predominantly on palms and soles
Dermatomyositis	Purplish-pink erythema, especially on eyelids, neck, and hands
Erythema gyratum repens	Rapidly changing and advancing gyri with scaling and pruritus
Lanuginosa acquisita	Rapid development of fine, long, silky hair, especially on ears and forehead, and can involve the entire body
Leser-Trelat syndrome	Sudden appearance of large numbers of seborrheic (wart-like) keratoses
Pachydermoperiostitis	Thickening of skin and creation of new folds; thickened lips, ears, and lids; macroglossia; thick forehead and scalp; clubbing; excessive sweating

---

[19] P.A. Bunn & J.D. Minna, *Paraneoplastic Syndromes, in* Cancer: Principles and Practice of Oncology 1924 (V.T. DeVita et al. eds., 1989).

§ 8.9   Diagnosis

Early diagnosis of lung cancer should result in an increased number of surgically resectable cases and improved survival. It would be prudent to perform chest X-ray screening on high-risk patients who are cigarette smokers and who are 50 years of age or older.[20] Sputum cytology is another simple method for screening and can detect lung cancer at an occult stage.

Chest X-ray is the usual means of identifying a lung malignancy. Any previous chest X-rays must be obtained and evaluated. Thoracic computerized tomography (CT scan) establishes the extent of the lesion, shows involvement of surrounding structures, and evaluates lymph node enlargement.

Bronchoscopy with irrigation and/or brushing cytology is valuable in diagnosing malignancy of a lung mass. Biopsy of visible lesions should be performed. Transthoracic needle aspiration or biopsy can be performed with CT guidance in peripheral lesions.

Preoperative assessment requires evaluation of pulmonary functions, although no single test can absolutely contraindicate surgery.[21] Severe ventilation impairment can influence the decision to perform a pneumonectomy.

Mediastinoscopy with biopsy, or cervical or parasternal mediastinal lymph node biopsy are available staging procedures. With small cell carcinoma, a liver-spleen scan or CT, bone scan, CT of brain, or bone marrow aspiration, in combination with biopsy, is essential.

When a paraneoplastic syndrome is suspected, appropriate hormone studies must be performed. Adrenocorticotropic hormone (ACTH) or corticotropin-releasing factor (CRF) are evaluated with Cushing's syndrome. Antidiuretic hormone (ADH) is elevated in the syndrome of inappropriate antidiuretic hormone (SIADH). Serotonin (5-hydroxytryptamine), bradykinins, or 5-hydroxytryptophan (5-HIAA) can be increased in the carcinoid syndrome. Urinary 5-HIAA is usually elevated. With gynecomastia, the beta subunit of human chorionic gonadotropin (beta-hCG) and human placental lactogen (hPL) should be elevated. Serum calcium and parathormone levels are abnormally high when there is ectopic parathyroid hormone secretion.

Hematologic abnormalities can be present in lung cancer. A normochromic, normocytic anemia,[22] secondary erythrocytic, or acute hemolytic anemia (AHA) can occur. Leukoerythroblastosis changes with myeloblasts, or neutrophilic myelocytes can develop with malignant involvement of the bone marrow.[23]

---

[20] N. Martini et al., *Early Diagnosis of Carcinoma of the Lung, in* Thoracic Oncology 136 (J.A. Roth et al. eds., 1989).

[21] G.D. Gass & G.N. Olsen, *Preoperative Pulmonary Functions Testing to Predict Postoperative Morbidity and Mortality,* 89 Chest 127 (1986).

[22] S. Zucker et al., *Bone Marrow Erythropoiesis in the Anemia of Infection, Inflammation and Malignancy,* 53 J. Clinical Investigation 1132 (1974).

[23] D.C. Ihde et al., *Bone Marrow Metastases in Small Cell Carcinoma of the Lung: Frequency, Description and Influence on Chemotherapeutic Toxicity and Prognosis,* 53 Blood 677 (1979).

Thrombocytosis,[24] idiopathic thrombocytopenic purpura (ITP),[25] and disseminated intravascular coagulation (DIC)[26] have been reported. Migratory venous thrombosis (Trousseau's syndrome) can occur.[27]

DNA flow cytometry of nonsmall cell carcinoma can be informative concerning prognosis. Aneuploid tumors and high S-phase cells are more likely to have metastases and a shorter survival.[28]

§ 8.10   Surgical Treatment

Small cell carcinoma is rapid growing and usually disseminated at the time of diagnosis.[29] Lobectomy or pneumonectomy has been performed at times,[30] but the preferred treatment is chemotherapy.

Segmental resection can be used for small, localized carcinomas that are not small cell, especially in patients with restricted lung capacity. Lobectomy is used for peripheral tumors, and pneumonectomy is used for any other resectable tumors. Addition of mediastinal lymphadenectomy has not increased survival.

Invasion of the chest wall by a tumor can require en bloc resection with a portion of the chest wall. This procedure can be necessary in superior sulcus neoplasms.

---

[24] S.E. Silvis et al., *Thrombocytosis in Patients with Lung Cancer,* 211 JAMA 1852 (1970).

[25] H.D. Kim & D.R. Boggs, *A Syndrome Resembling Idiopathic Thrombocytopenic Purpura in 10 Patients with Diverse Forms of Cancer,* 67 Am. J. Med. 371 (1979).

[26] C.A. Owen & E.J. Bowie, *Chronic Intravascular Coagulation Syndromes: A Summary,* 49 Mayo Clinic Proc. 673 (1974).

[27] R.B. Byrd et al., *Bronchogenic Carcinoma and Thromboembolic Disease,* 202 JAMA 1019 (1967); G.H. Sack et al., *Trousseau's Syndrome and Other Manifestations of Chronic Disseminated Coagulopathy in Patients with Neoplasms,* 56 Medicine 1 (1977).

[28] T.P.M. Ten Velde et al., *Flow Cytometric Analysis of DNA Ploidy Level in Paraffin-Embedded Tissue of Non-Small Cell Lung Cancer,* 24 Eur. J. Cancer & Clinical Oncology 455 (1988); M. Volm et al., *Prognostic Significance of DNA Patterns and Resistance—Predictive Tests in Non-Small Cell Lung Carcinoma,* 56 Cancer 1396 (1985); M. Volm et al., *DNA Distribution in Non-Small Cell Lung Carcinomas and Its Relationship to Clinical Behavior,* 6 Cytometry 348 (1985); M. Volm et al., *DNA and S-Phase Distribution and Incidence of Metastasis in Human Primary Lung Carcinoma,* 9 Cytometry 183 (1988).

[29] D. Bergsagel & R. Feld, *Small Cell Lung Cancer Is Still a Problem,* J. Clinical Oncology 1189 (1984); S. Davis et al., *Long Term Survival in Small Cell Carcinoma of the Lung: A Population Experience,* 3 J. Clinical Oncology 80 (1985).

[30] W. Fox & J.G. Scadding, *Medical Research Council Comparative Trial of Surgery and Radiotherapy for Primary Treatment of Small Celled or Oat Celled Carcinoma of Bronchus. Ten Year Follow Up,* 2 Lancet 63 (1973); M.N. Kirsh & H. Sloan, *Mediastinal Metastases in Bronchogenic Carcinoma: Influence of Postoperative Irradiation, Cell Type, and Location,* 33 Annals Thoracic Surgery 459 (1982).

§ 8.11　Chemotherapy

Non-Small Cell Lung Cancer

Adjuvant chemotherapy with cisplatin-based drug combinations has led to an improved one-year survival rate, but it is still being investigated. The combinations include cisplatin, cyclophosphamide, and doxorubicin (CAP); cisplatin and etoposide; and cisplatin, mitomycin, and vinblastine sulfate.[31] BCG and levamisole immunotherapy has not been as successful. The five-year survival rates are unknown. There may be some improvement in survival with the addition of radiation therapy. Cyclophosphamide, doxorubicin, methotrexate, and procarbazine combination has been used with irradiation with some success.

Preoperative (neoadjuvant) chemotherapy has been performed to shrink tumor bulk, improve operability, sterilize micrometastases, and minimize hematogenous spread or local seeding during surgical manipulation. Increased morbidity and mortality from surgery can be a hazard. Cisplatin and etoposide; cisplatin and 5-fluorouracil; mitomycin, vinblastine sulfate or vindesine, and cisplatin (MVP); and cisplatin with etoposide have shown response with increased survival.[32]

Patients with metastatic non-small cell carcinoma who show response to combination chemotherapy survive longer than those who do not show a response. Although response has occurred with single agents such as cisplatin, Ifosfamide, mitomycin, vindesine, vinblastine sulfate, and etoposide, there is no increase in survival. Combinations that have shown tumor regression include cyclophosphamide, doxorubicin, methotrexate and procarbazine (CAMP); methotrexate, doxorubicin, cisplatin, and CCNU (MACC); cisplatin, doxorubicin, and cyclophosphamide; vindesine and cisplatin; etoposide and cisplatin; mitomycin, vinblastine, and cisplatin; VP16 and cisplatin; and Ifosfamide with cisplatin. There is no standard regimen or chemotherapy combination for treating metastatic non-small cell lung cancer. Significant treatment-related toxicities exist, including death.[33]

---

[31] R.T. Eagan et al., *Platinum-Based Poly-Chemotherapy Versus Dianhydrogalacitol in Advanced Non-Small Cell Lung Cancer,* 61 Cancer Treatment Rep. 1339 (1977); R. Fram et al., *Combination Chemotherapy Followed by Radiation Therapy in Patients with Regional Stage III Unresectable Non-Small Cell Lung Cancer,* 69 Cancer Treatment Rep. 587 (1985); J.C. Ruckdeschel et al., *Chemotherapy for Metastatic Non-Small Cell Bronchogenic Carcinoma: EST 2575, Generation V: A Randomized Comparison of Four Cisplatin-Containing Regimens,* 3 J. Clinical Oncology 72 (1985); H. Wagner et al., *Treatment of Locally Advanced Non-Small Cell Lung Cancer (NSLC) with Mitomycin C, Vinblastine, and Cisplatin (MVP) Followed by Radiation Therapy. An ECOG Pilot Study,* 4 Proc. Am. Soc'y Clinical Oncology 183 (1985).

[32] D.C. Finkelstein et al., *Long Term Survivors in Metastatic Non-Small Cell Lung Cancer: An Eastern Cooperative Group Study,* 4 J. Clinical Oncology 702 (1986); N. Martini et al., *The Effects of Preoperative Chemotherapy on the Resectability on Non-Small Cell Lung Carcinoma with Mediastinal Lymph Node Metastases (N2M0),* 23 Proc. Soc'y Thoracic Surgery 28 (1987).

[33] H.H. Hansen, *Advanced Non-Small Cell Lung Cancer: To Treat or Not to Treat?,* 5 J. Clinical Oncology 1711 (1987).

Newer drugs presently under investigation that show some effect are taxol, navelbine, and EDAM (10-ethyl-deaza-aminopterin, Edatrexate).

Chemotherapy without radiation therapy is not recommended for the superior vena cava syndrome from non-small cell lung cancer because the drugs have a slow and upredictable response.

Small Cell Lung Cancer

Small cell lung cancer has an aggressive clinical course, but it is responsive to chemotherapy and irradiation. Single agents such as cyclophosphamide, mechlorethamine (nitrogen mustard), doxorubicin, methotrexate, hexamethylmelamine, etoposide, vincristine, carboplatin, and tenoposide (VM-26) have shown at least a 30-percent response rate, but less than 5 percent experience a complete response.

Aggressive combination chemotherapy gives the best response rates and longer survival time. These combinations include cyclophosphamide, methotrexate, and CCNU; cyclophosphamide and CCNU; cyclophosphamide, doxorubicin, and DTIC; methotrexate, cyclophosphamide, vincristine, and procarbazine; cyclophosphamide and methotrexate; cyclophosphamide, methotrexate, CCNU, and vincristine; and etoposide with cisplatin. Late-dose intensification does not improve survival and can require autologous bone marrow infusions.

Chemotherapy should be administered for four to six months because survival is improved with longer administration and toxicity is minimized.

Spinal cord and leptomeningeal metastases can be treated by intrathecal chemotherapy, but only in patients with a life expectancy of at least three months. The spinal fluid status must be monitored during treatment.

§ 8.12   Immunotherapy

Levamisole has no effect on non-small cell lung cancer, and other immunotherapy agents have shown no consistent benefit.

Immunotherapy with BCG or thymosin fraction V (modulator of T-cell function) for small cell lung cancer has shown no improvement in survival.

§ 8.13   Radiation Therapy

Surgery is the primary treatment for non-small cell carcinoma of the lung, but radiation, either definitive or palliative, is part or all of the treatment plan in at least 90 percent of the cases. The other cases are operable tumors (Stage I) with no extension beyond the lung and no lymph node metastases. These are not candidates for postoperative radiation, although about half of them need radiation at a later date.

Definitive radiation is administered to early non-small cell carcinomas that are inoperable for medical reasons and to operable cases that are found to have metastases: in the chest wall, pericardium, hilar, and/or mediastinal lymph nodes. Radiation is given to this group regardless of whether the metastases appear to be completely resected. Definitive radiation is given to locally extensive inoperable tumors that can be encompassed in a single radiation field, but the tumor must be confined to only one lung.

Small cell carcinomas are treated primarily with chemotherapy. After several courses of chemotherapy, radiation is given to the original area of the tumor to prevent its recurrence, even though the tumor might no longer be visible on X-rays.

Radiation is the alternative when patients with small cell carcinoma refuse chemotherapy, or if they have operable non-small cell carcinomas and refuse surgery.

Radiation is aimed at effecting cures or at least prolonging life. Palliative radiation is used in widespread incurable cancers to relieve symptoms such as cough, hemoptysis, dyspnea from atelectasis, chest pain, pain from bone metastases, neurological dysfunctions due to brain metastases, superior vena caval obstruction, and esophageal constriction.

The timing of the radiation in relation to other therapeutic modalities is variable. Recently, preoperative radiation has been limited mainly to superior sulcus (apical) tumors. Radiation otherwise is given postoperatively, after chemotherapy, or as primary treatment without intent to combine it with other modalities.

The radiation technique involves irradiation of all known tumors plus adjacent sites likely to be involved. The fields are specially shaped with custom-made blocks to shield the uninvolved areas of the lung. Generally, irradiation of tumors in both lungs results in excessive loss of functioning lung tissue. The radiation field should cover the primary tumor, hilum of the lung, and at least enough of the mediastinum to include the subcarinal lymph nodes. In lower lobe carcinomas, the mediastinal field is extended inferiorly beyond the subcarinal lymph nodes to the diaphragm. Opinions vary regarding routine treatment of the supraclavicular lymph nodes in one or both sides of the neck, because the incidence of supraclavicular metastases is low from some areas of the lungs. Irradiation of both supraclavicular areas can be recommended. The morbidity from including them in the field of treatment is negligible and can prevent treatment failure in the neck. When atelectasis is present and opacifies the lung, the margins of the tumor can be obscured. Prudent therapy requires using a large field. X-rays are taken at 1000 cGy intervals, looking for reaeration of the lung that permits better visualization of the tumor and reduces the field size.

Treatment planning with computerized tomography (CT) is essential before undertaking treatment. CT shows the extent of the tumor far better than X-rays of the chest. Because it is not unusual to discover silent metastases in the liver and adrenals, CT should include the upper abdomen. Enlargements of the adrenal can be due to benign adenomas and should therefore not be misinterpreted as metastases and establish a false basis for foregoing definitive radiation to the lung. CT of the brain also should be done to look for silent metastases. Complete regression from radiation is more likely with small silent metastases in the brain than with large symptomatic ones.

In carcinomas of the lung treated primarily with radiation, the highest control rates are achieved with 5500 to 7000 cGy, using appropriate fractions and field reductions as higher dose levels are attained. Radiation is given from multiple directions to avoid doses in excess of 4500 cGy to the spinal cord and to exclude as much of the heart as possible from doses exceeding 4000 cGy. This order of radiation can result in five-year cure rates of 5 to 12 percent and local control in 60 percent.

A special situation exists in patients with emphysema and poor respiratory function. Radiation might have to be confined only to the outline of the known tumor.

An important reason for recurrence of the primary tumor in small cell carcinoma is using a small radiation field, that is, failure to irradiate the original volume of the tumor as it was presented prior to chemotherapy. Chemotherapy combined with adequate radiation doubles the two-year survival rate. Adequate radiation, in addition to the choice of the correct volume, is the delivery of about 5000 cGy.

Preoperative radiation has been a standard treatment for superior sulcus tumors. The dosage has been 3000 to 4000 cGy in two to four weeks, followed by surgery in four to six weeks. Recently, apical tumors can be cured equally well with a complete course of radiation alone, which is 5500 to 6500 cGy. A disadvantage of preoperative radiation is that the tumor might be found to be inoperable at the subsequent exploratory surgery, in which case part of the patient's radiation tolerance has been expended, and further radiation postoperatively cannot be taken to an effective level. A cure by radiation requires that the entire course of radiation be given in continuity without significant interruption. If surgery is to be done at all, it reasonably can be done first, so it can be followed by a full course of aggressive radiation therapy when indicated. In addition to the site of the primary tumor, the radiation field includes the mediastinum down to the carina and the opposite supraclavicular area. For postoperative irradiation, the total dose is 5000 cGy with an additional 1000 cGy through small fields to known areas of residual tumor.

Prophylactic irradiation of the brain is a commonly employed regimen in cancer of the lung. *Prophylaxis* is a misnomer. Radiation does not prevent metastases. Radiation is given to eradicate occult, clinically undetectable metastases that are already present. Better terminology is *elective* radiation. The doses for elective radiation are 2000 to 3000 cGy in two to four weeks. Elective radiation has been controversial because some patients develop neuropsychologic disabilities, and statistics do not confirm increased survival. Statistics do indicate, however, that there is a lower incidence of signs and symptoms of brain metastases. Despite lack of statistical proof from population analyses, there is no doubt about the increased survival of some individuals with diagnosable brain metastases who have had complete remissions and have lived for 5 or 10 years. The neuropsychologic problems can be avoided by reducing the fractions to 160 to 180 cGy per treatment and not concurrently using chemotherapeutic agents with a potential for neurotoxicity. The incidence of brain metastases is sufficiently high to warrant elective radiation in all cases except squamous cell carcinomas.

Palliative radiation is a major component of the management of widespread incurable lung cancer. Painful bone metastases can be treated effectively with 80 percent of the patients getting relief of pain. Doses of 3000 to 4000 cGy can be given in two to four weeks. Definitive irradiation of the primary tumor is not justified in widespread cancer, but palliative radiation can be used at the 4000 cGy level to relieve symptoms of cough, chest pain, and hemoptysis. In cases with esophageal constriction, the obstruction can be relieved if it is due to extrinsic pressure. When frank tumor invasion of the esophagus is present, radiation is not indicated. Radiation can cause a tracheoesophageal fistula that would be harmful rather than palliative.

Cancer of the lung is the commonest cause of superior vena caval obstruction. Radiation can be effective in the treatment of the superior vena cava syndrome (see § **8.4** and **Chapter 18**).

Palliative, rather than elective, radiation for established brain metastases can consist of 4000 cGy with 160 to 180 cGy fractions. The entire brain is irradiated. Pinpoint irradiation of individual metastases is futile. New metastases will develop in adjacent unirradiated areas of the brain.

Endobronchial brachytherapy is a form of palliative radiation. A catheter is placed at an appropriate level in a bronchus. Radioactive iridium 192 is inserted in the catheter and gives very localized radiation that can be used to arrest hemorrhage or relieve obstruction. This option is available in recurrent endobronchial carcinoma in previously irradiated patients who cannot tolerate further external radiation through large fields.

§ 8.14   Commentary and Significant Cases

Most often, litigation concerning lung cancer occurs because of the radiologist's failure to note a significant abnormality on the chest X-ray that would require further investigation, or the report of a possible lung cancer is either lost or not seen by the attending physician. Because lung cancer is a life-threatening disease, the consultant radiologist must make some effort to contact the physician beyond simply mailing out a report. The consultant radiologist must make sure the physician receives the necessary information. Oral communication either in person or by telephone is the easiest method, but even using a certified or registered letter to send the report is a means of alerting the physician to the importance of the communication. Delay in diagnosing and treating lung cancer can result in a decreased opportunity for the patient to survive.

Alessio v. Crook.[34]   Judgment for defense was affirmed. The plaintiff had a cancer of the palate treated with irradiation and surgery in 1969. A throat cancer was excised in April 1978. A chest X-ray at that time showed a density in the right lower lung, but the report was not placed on the chart until after the plaintiff was discharged from the hospital. The defendant did not see the X-ray report until November 1978. Because of enlarged hilan nodes, a total pneumonectomy was performed. The plaintiff asserted that a lobectomy would have been done and the lung would not have been totally removed if the diagnosis had been made in May 1978. No expert could state to a certainty whether or not the entire right lung might have had to be removed in May 1978.

Dennis v. St. Peters Hospital.[35]   The court granted summary judgment for defense. The plaintiff complained of weight loss and fatigue present for six weeks. The white blood count showed a mass in the upper lobe of the left lung. Bronchoscopy was inconclusive as to diagnosis. Exploratory surgery disclosed a hard, baseball-sized mass as well as multiple abscesses in the lung. Total pneumonectomy was performed based on the size of the mass. Organizing pneumonia was found on pathology. The court held that a physician is not negligent when there is preliminary diagnosis of cancer and the mass, whether cancer or pneumonia, had to be removed. Under the plaintiff's circumstances, this could not be accomplished without removing the entire lung.

Green v. Walker.[36]   Summary judgment for the defendant was reversed when a chest X-ray was taken for an annual physical examination and the defendant reported the decedent as employable without restriction. One year later, lung cancer was diagnosed and resected, but the patient ultimately died. The plaintiff alleged failure to diagnose lung cancer. Applying Louisiana law, the court held that a physician has a duty to conduct tests and diagnose in a manner exercising the level of care consistent with the physician's training and expertise, and to take reasonable steps to make the information available in a timely manner to the examinee of any findings that pose an imminent danger to his physical or mental well being.

Herskovits v. Group Health Cooperative of Puget Sound.[37]   The court held that a 14 percent reduction, from 39 percent to 25 percent, in chance for survival

---

[34] 633 S.W.2d 770 (Tenn. Ct. App. 1982).

[35] 558 N.Y.S.2d 304 (App. Div. 1990).

[36] 910 F.2d 291 (5th Cir. 1990).

[37] 99 Wash. 2d 609, 664 P.2d 474 (1983).

was sufficient evidence of causation to allow the jury to consider the possibility that the physician's failure to diagnose illness in a timely manner was the proximate cause of the patient's death. The decedent had complaints of pain and coughing in early 1974. Chest X-rays showed an infiltrate in the left lung. Chest pain and cough continued, and occasional chest X-rays were performed. The decedent saw another physician in July 1975, and his lung was removed for cancer. He died 20 months later.

Hope v. Seahorse, Inc.[38]   The 39-year-old decedent was examined in September 1979 because of complaints of pain in the chest, back, and shoulder following a fall. A chest X-ray disclosed an increased density in the right lung. He was treated for pneumonia. In April 1980, a repeat chest X-ray showed a nodular density in the same area of the right lung. Tomograms were diagnostic for lung cancer. A bronchoscopy performed in July 1980 was negative for cancer. Chest pain continued. Mediastinoscopy in March 1981 was positive for cancer in the lymph nodes. The lung cancer was inoperable. Radiation therapy and chemotherapy were administered. The patient died in July 1982. Applying Texas law, the court awarded $1,045,948, including $100,000 for the spouse's loss of consortium and $200,000 for the minor child's loss of companionship and loss of society, advice, and counsel.

James v. United States.[39]   The plaintiff had a chest X-ray in December 1976 as a part of his preemployment examination. The report of a suspected tumor, through clerical error, was not brought to the attention of the attending physician. In October 1978, because of chest pain, cough, and shortness of breath, a chest X-ray was taken and revealed a large mass in the right lung. A biopsy showed a large cell indifferentiated carcinoma that was inoperable. Radiation therapy was given. Applying California law, the court held that the plaintiff would have benefited from early treatment and was thus entitled to $60,000 damages for loss of opportunity for earlier treatment, mental suffering, and anguish.

Jenoff v. Gleason.[40]   The decedent had a chest X-ray taken in September 1980 preoperatively for wrist surgery. The X-ray reports reflected the presence of a 2 cm nodule in the left lower lobe suggesting possible bronchogenic carcinoma. The report was placed on the chart after the decedent was discharged. The X-ray report was reviewed by the insurance company in November 1980, and new chest X-rays were ordered. Mediastinoscopy revealed that the tumor had spread to the lymph nodes and was inoperable. Radiation therapy and chemotherapy were administered, but the patient died in September 1982. The court held that

---

[38] 651 F. Supp. 976 (S.D. Tex. 1986).
[39] 483 F. Supp. 581 (N.D. Cal. 1980).
[40] 215 N.J. Super. 349, 521 A.2d 1323 (App. Div. 1987).

the communication of an unusual finding in an X-ray, so that it can be benefi-
cially utilized, is as important as the finding itself. Communication through
administrative personnel can be adequate, but it does not justify lack of communication with a primary care physician, and direct contact with the treating
physician is necessary in certain situations. The method of communicating a
radiologist's findings concerning a patient in a hospital is not a matter peculiarly
within the knowledge of trained medical experts. The finding for the defense
was reversed in part, and the case was remanded for a new trial.

La Bieniec v. Baker.[41]   A directed verdict for the defense was upheld when the
plaintiff did not establish a causal relationship between the failure to diagnose
lung cancer and the injury claimed. In June 1981, routine chest X-rays were
taken and showed an area of questionable haziness. The plaintiff collapsed in
July 1981, and chest X-rays were taken. Biopsy disclosed carcinoma of the lung.
Computerized tomography of the brain showed metastasis from the lung cancer.
Radiation therapy was given. The court held that the evidence failed to remove
the deceased's chance of successful treatment theory from the realm of speculation.

Peterson v. St. Cloud Hospital.[42]   The plaintiff's chest X-ray revealed a nodule
of the lung in November 1986. A needle biopsy was performed and reported as
"suggestive of small cell carcinoma." Chemotherapy and radiation therapy were
begun in December 1986. The tumor did not respond as expected, and therefore
bronchial biopsy was performed. The tumor was diagnosed as bronchial carcinoid, which is ordinarily treated by surgery or observation. Summary judgment
for the defendant on the statute of limitations was reversed, the court holding
that the cause of action accrued in December 1986 on the date of the first treatment.

Ratcliffe v. National Pathology Laboratories, Inc.[43]   There was a $45,000 set-
tlement for an incorrect diagnosis of cancer when an improper piece of cancerous tissue was accidentally placed on a slide. After the removal of the lobe of the
patient's lung, a diagnosis of coccidioidomycosis was made.

Sawka v. Prokopowycz.[44]   Verdict for the defendants was reversed and the case
was remanded for new trial. The plaintiff had an annual chest X-ray taken in
September 1972. The X-ray report indicated that nothing "alarming" was found.

---

[41] 11 Conn. App. 199, 526 A.2d 1341 (1987).

[42] 460 N.W.2d 635 (Minn. Ct. App. 1990).

[43] No. 87-2966-0 (Dallas County, Tex.), *reprinted in* 4 Med. Malpractice Verdicts, Settlements &
Experts No. 11, at 53 (1983).

[44] 104 Mich. App. 829, 306 N.W.2d 354 (1981).

In 1974, a chest X-ray did not indicate the presence of a tumor. The court held that instructions combined with admission of evidence as to patient's failure to return for follow-up examination and continued smoking could be considered erroneously by the jury as contributory negligence and as a factor in determining whether an action in malpractice existed.

Stager v. Schneider.[45]   A chest X-ray was taken in March 1980 prior to foot surgery. A slightly increased density was noted in the apex of the right lung. Comparison with previous films or follow-up films were recommended. Neither the plaintiff nor attending physician was notified of the findings. Surgery was canceled by the patient and she was not subsequently operated on for the foot problem. A routine chest X-ray taken in December 1980 disclosed a tumor of the right lung, which was removed in February 1981. The court, applying District of Columbia law, reversed the judgment for the defendant and remanded for a new trial. The cause of action does not accrue until the plaintiff knew or by due diligence should have known of the injury. Due care required notifying the patient and/or her physician directly of the finding on the X-ray of her lungs.

Tappan v. Florida Medical Center, Inc.[46]   The court held that the widow could not maintain a malpractice action under the Wrongful Death Act when the defendant's alleged negligence in failing to diagnose lung cancer was not a cause-in-fact of the death, and the plaintiff could not prove that with proper diagnosis and treatment it was more likely than not that the decedent would have survived. A malpractice action against the chiropractor could be maintained for failure to diagnose lung cancer under the survival statute when it was alleged that the decedent would have lived six or eight months longer had he received proper diagnosis and treatment of lung cancer, but whose condition was incurable even with proper treatment.

Van Vleet v. Pfeifle.[47]   Because the patient was coughing up blood, a chest X-ray was taken in April 1976, and was reported as negative. Bronchoscopy was suggested in the medical record, but not performed. Recurrent bleeding from the nose was treated by reconstructive nasal surgery in July 1976. Coughing up blood recurred in April 1977 and a chest X-ray showed an abnormality. Bronchoscopy disclosed a malignant lung tumor. The court held that the plaintiff's allegations that bronchoscopy should have been performed in a timely manner in 1976 was a material issue of fact to be tried by the jury or court. The doctors could not escape liability for failure to discover the patient's cancer and thereby hastening and prematurely causing his death simply because the cancer would eventually have resulted in the patient's death, even if it were discovered sooner.

---

[45]494 A.2d 1307 (1985).

[46]488 So. 2d 630 (Fla. Dist. Ct. App. 1986).

[47]289 N.W.2d 781 (N.D. 1980).

Waffen v. United States.[48]   There was a verdict for the defense when the plaintiff did not prove a loss of substantial possibility of survival despite a seven-month delay in acting on an abnormal chest X-ray that showed a cancer of the lung. The 38-year-old plaintiff had a chest X-ray taken in April 1981 that was interpreted as having a mass 4 cm in diameter in the right upper lobe. The report was misplaced. A chest X-ray taken in October 1981 disclosed a lung mass that on biopsy was diagnosed as malignant. The tumor was resected and measured 5 × 6 cm. Metastases appeared in October 1983.

Weiner v. Memorial Hospital.[49]   There was a $2,320,000 verdict, plus $500,000 to the patient's husband for loss of services, when a bronchoscopic biopsy specimen slide was confused with another patient's slide, an improper diagnosis of cancer was made, and a portion of normal lung was removed. The plaintiff alleged cancerphobia and deterioration of family relationships.

Weiss v. Bigman.[50]   An accelerated judgment for the defendant on the statute of limitations was reversed and remanded for a new trial. In September 1972, the decedent had a chest X-ray taken that showed a lesion in the apex of the right lung. The defendant treated her for tuberculosis. Further X-rays were taken in March 1973 and August 1973. In February 1974, the decedent was told she had carcinoma of the lung with metastases to the brain. She died on July 19, 1976. The court held that an action arises at the time the defendant discontinues treatment or when the plaintiff discovers or should have discovered the existence of the claim.

PLEURAL TUMORS

§ 8.15   Classification

Histopathologic Types (see **Table 8–5**)

    Benign mesothelioma (fibroma)

    Localized malignant mesothelioma (fibrosarcoma)[51]

    Diffuse malignant mesothelioma.

---

[48] 799 F.2d 911 (4th Cir. 1986).

[49] Nos. 16172-81, 24712-81 (N.Y.), *reprinted in* 3 Med. Malpractice Verdicts, Settlements & Experts No. 11, at 43 (1987).

[50] 84 Mich. App. 487, 270 N.W.2d 5 (1978).

[51] P.M. McCormack et al., *Surgical Treatment of Pleural Mesothelioma,* 84 J. Thoracic & Cardiovascular Surgery 834 (1982).

Table 8–5

Pathologic Staging of Mesothelioma[52]

Stage	Definition
Stage I	Tumor confined within the capsule of the parietal pleura, that is, involving only ipsilateral pleura, lung, diaphragm, and external surface of pericardium within the pleural reflection.
Stage II	Tumor invading chest wall or mediastinal tissues or structures, for example, esophagus, trachea, great vessels. Lymph node involvement inside the chest.
Stage III	Tumor penetrating diaphragmatic muscle to involve peritoneum or the retroperitoneal space. Tumor penetrating pericardium involving its internal surface or involving the heart. Involvement to the opposite pleura. Lymph node involvement outside the chest.
Stage IV	Distant blood-borne metastases.

§ 8.16   Etiology

Asbestos exposure is not related to the onset of localized benign or malignant mesothelioma.[53] However, diffuse malignant mesothelioma is definitely related to asbestos exposure.[54] There is a latent interval between asbestos exposure and onset of tumor that ranges from 15 to 50 years.[55]

---

[52] E.G. Butchart, *Surgery of Mesothelioma of the Pleura, in* Thoracic Oncology 568 (J.A. Roth et al. eds., 1989).

[53] J.L. Kovarik, *Primary Pleural Mesothelioma,* 38 Cancer 1816 (1976); D.A. Taryle et al., *Pleural Mesotheliomas—An Analysis of 18 Cases and Review of the Literature,* 55 Med. 153 (1976).

[54] T. Ashcroft, *Epidemiological and Quantitative Relationships Between Mesothelioma and Asbestos Exposure,* 26 Thorax. 6 (1971); D.O.B. Hourihane, *The Pathology of Mesotheliomata and an Analysis of Their Association with Asbestos Exposure,* 19 Thorax 268 (1964); S.S. Legha & F.M. Muggia, *Therapeutic Approaches in Malignant Mesothelioma,* 4 Cancer Treatment Rev. 13 (1977); M.L. Newhouse & H. Thompson, *Mesothelioma of the Pleura and Peritoneum Following Exposure to Asbestos in the London Area,* 22 Brit. J. Indus. Med. 261 (1965); I.J. Selikoff et al., *Relation Between Exposure to Asbestos and Mesothelioma,* 272 New. Eng. J. Med. 560 (1965); J.C. Wagner et al., *Diffuse Pleural Mesothelioma and Asbestos Exposure in the North Western Cape Province,* 17 Brit. J. Indus. Med. 260 (1960).

[55] P.C. Elmes, *The Epidemiology and Clinical Features of Asbestosis and Related Diseases,* 42 Postgraduate Med. J. 623 (1966); I.J. Selikoff et al., *Latency of Asbestos Disease Among Insulation Workers in the United States and Canada,* 46 Cancer 2736 (1980); F. Whitwell & R.M. Rawcliffe, *Diffuse Malignant Pleural Mesothelioma and Asbestos Exposure,* 26 Thorax 6 (1971).

The mineral zeolite, found in Turkey, also has been implicated in the origin of mesothelioma.[56]

§ 8.17   Clinical Manifestations

Localized mesothelioma is asymptomatic in 40 percent of patients. Symptoms, when they occur, include cough, chest pain, dyspnea, pulmonary osteoarthropathy, hemoptysis, night sweats, pleural effusion, weight loss, and hypoglycemia.[57]

Diffuse malignant mesothelioma's initial clinical symptoms depend on the presence or absence of a pleural effusion. "Dry" mesotheliomas present with heaviness or mild aching discomfort in the chest associated with some dyspnea. In the presence of pleural effusion, shortness of breath is the predominant complaint. Nonproductive cough and general malaise can appear. Severe localized chest pain and dysphagia (difficulties swallowing) from esophageal involvement are indicative of extension of the disease.

§ 8.18   Diagnosis

Benign mesothelioma is most often found on routine chest X-rays. Diffuse malignant mesothelioma can present on chest X-rays as unexplained pleural effusion, especially in a patient with a history of asbestos exposure. Unilateral pleural thickening is usually found on chest X-rays.

Computerized tomography is an effective means of examining for pleural thickening, chest wall contraction, interlobar fissure thickening, and asbestos hyaline pleural plaques.

Pleural fluid cytology is not often diagnostic. Pleural biopsy, closed or open, is more accurate and rewarding. Special staining techniques are necessary to distinguish diffuse malignant mesothelioma (DMM) from metastatic pleural adenocarcinoma. See **Table 8–6.**

---

[56] Y.I. Baris et al., *Environmental Mesothelioma in Turkey,* 330 Annals N.Y. Acad. Sci. 423 (1979).

[57] M. Briselli et al., *Solitary Fibrous Tumors of the Pleura: Eight New Cases and Review of 360 Cases in the Literature,* 47 Cancer 2678 (1981).

Table 8–6

Histologic Staining

Histologic Staining	DMM	Adenocarcinoma
CEA[58]	−	+
BerEP	−	+
HBME	+	−
Keratins	+	+
Leu M	−	+
Mucin	−	+
Hyaluronic Acid	+	−

§ 8.19 Surgical Treatment

Diffuse malignant mesothelioma can be treated by radical pleuropneumonectomy, including the ipsilateral hemidiaphragm and pericardium in Stage I
disease.[59] This radical surgical procedure can be associated with serious complications including hemorrhage, respiratory failure, arrhythmias, bronchial stump
fistula, esophagopleural fistula, empyema, chylothorax, cardiac dislocation,
ascites, herniation of abdominal contents, and tension pneumoperitoneum.

Palliative surgical procedures are more often necessary for diffuse malignant
mesothelioma.[60] Debulking tumor mass can aid in improving the response to
chemotherapy or radiation therapy. Suction drainage of pleural effusion and
intrapleural sclerosing agents help relieve symptoms.

Benign mesothelioma and localized malignant mesothelioma can be treated
by local resection, including portions of the chest wall when applicable in the
presence of chest wall invasion.

§ 8.20 Chemotherapy

Diffuse malignant mesothelioma responds occasionally to single dose chemotherapy with doxorubicin, detorubicine, cyclophosphamide, mitomycin, dacarbazine

---

[58] D. Whitaker & K.B. Shilkin, *Carcinoembryonic Antigen in Tissue Diagnosis of Malignant Mesothelioma,* 1 Lancet 1369 (1981).

[59] E. Allica et al., *Pleuropneumonectomia Allargata Nei Mesothelioma Maligna Diffusi della Pleura,* 37 Archives Monaldi 319 (1982); E.G. Butchart et al., *Pleuropneumonectomy in the Management of Diffuse Malignant Mesothelioma of the Pleura,* 31 Thorax. 15 (1976); G.A. DeLaria et al., *Surgical Management of Malignant Mesothelioma,* 26 Annals Thoracic Surgery 375 (1978).

[60] J. Aisner & P.H. Wiernik, *Malignant Mesothelioma: Current Status and Future Prospects,* 74 Chest 438 (1978); S.S. Legha & F.M. Muggia, *Therapeutic Approaches in Malignant Mesothelioma,* 4 Cancer Treatment Rev. 13 (1977).

(DTIC), and 5-fluorouracil. Combination chemotherapy is more effective, with up to a 40-percent response rate from regimens containing doxorubicin or cisplatin. Combined agents that showed response include 5-azacytidine and doxorubicin; cisplatin and doxorubicin; cyclophosphamide, vincristine, and doxorubicin; cyclophosphamide, dacarbazine, vincristine, and doxorubicin; cyclophosphamide, methotrexate, vincristine, VP-16, and doxorubicin; cyclophosphamide, vincristine, 5-fluorouracil, and methotrexate; cisplatin and mitomycin; and cisplatin with a high dose methotrexate.[61]

Intracavitary administration of chemotherapy can be valuable in delivering a high concentration of agents to enhance local control.

§ 8.21   Radiation Therapy

Radiation therapy is of doubtful value in affecting the course of mesothelioma. Radiation doses of 4000 to 5000 cGy can be helpful in controlling pain.

§ 8.22   Significant Litigation

Migues v. Nicolet Industries, Inc.[62]   The court found a $3 million verdict excessive and reduced it to $1.5 million, less a $400,000 settlement by the other defendants. This industrial court litigation resulted when 14 defendants marketed asbestos products, knowing the risks inherent to the insulation worker. The decedent died from mesothelioma as a result of constant exposure to asbestos-containing products.

---

[61]K. Antman et al., *Multimodality Therapy for Mesothelioma Based on a Study of Natural History,* 68 Am. J. Med. 356 (1980); A.P. Chakinian et al., *Diffuse Malignant Mesothelioma: Prospective Evaluation of 69 Patients,* 96 Annals Internal Med. 746 (1982); H. Dhingra et al., *Combined Modality Treatment for Mesothelioma with Cytoxan (CTX), Adiamycin (ADR), and DTIC (CYADIC) and Adjuvant Surgery,* 2 Proc. Am. Soc'y Clinical Oncology 205 (1983); H. Lerner et al., *Malignant Mesothelioma: The Eastern Cooperative Oncology Group (ECOG) Experience,* 52 Cancer 1981 (1983); M. Samson et al., *Randomized Comparison of Cyclophosphamide, DTIC and Adriamycin (CIA) Versus Cyclophosphamide and Adriamycin (CA) in Patients with Advanced Malignant Mesothelioma. A Sarcoma Intergroup Study,* 4 Proc. Am. Soc'y Clinical Oncology 128 (1985).

[62]493 F. Supp. 61 (E.D. Tex. 1980).

THYMUS NEOPLASMS

§ 8.23   Staging and Classification

The histogenetic cell origin of neoplasms of the thymus determines the histologic character of the tumor.

Histopathologic Type

  Thymoma

  Thymic carcinoid

  Oat cell carcinoma

  Germ cell tumors

    Seminoma

    Nonseminomatous tumor

  Lymphoma

    Hodgkin's disease

    Non-Hodgkin's lymphoma.

Tables 8–7 and **8–8** describe two systems for staging related to thymoma.

Table 8–7

Bergh Staging System for Thymoma[63]

Stage	Definition	Proportion of Cases (%)
I	Intact capsule or growth within the capsule	40
II	Pericapsular growth into the mediastinal fat tissue	19
III	Invasive growth into the surrounding organs and/or intrathoracic metastases	41

---

[63] N.P. Bergh et al., *Tumors of the Thymus and Thymic Region: I. Clinicopathologic Studies on Thymomas,* 25 Annals Thoracic Surgery 91 (1978).

Table 8–8

Japanese Staging System for Thymoma[64]

Stage	Definition
I	Macroscopically, completely encapsulated; microscopically, no capsular invasion
IIa	Macroscopic invasion into surrounding fatty tissues or mediastinal pleura
IIb	Microscopic invasion into the capsule
III	Macroscopic invasion into a neighboring organ (pericardium, great vessels, or lung)
IVa	Pleural or pericardial dissemination
IVb	Lymphogenous or hematogenous metastases

§ 8.24   Clinical Manifestations

Most patients with thymus neoplasm have an asymptomatic anterior superior mediastinal mass on chest X-ray. Vague symptoms of cough, dysphagia, fever, chest pain, weight loss, and anorexia can occur.[65]

Thymoma can appear with a variety of autoimmune or endocrine disorders. A mediastinal mass associated with myasthenia gravis, hypogammaglobulinemia, or red cell aplasia is diagnostic of thymoma. Leukopenia and thrombocytopenia can occur. Polymyositis, systemic lupus erythematosus, rheumatoid arthritis, thyroiditis, Sjogren's syndrome, ulcerative colitis, and hyperthyroidism have been reported. Cushing's syndrome can occur, but is more common with thymic carcinoid.

Myasthenia gravis involves weakness of voluntary muscles due to circulatory antibodies to the acetylcholine receptor. The patient usually has weakness of the eye muscles and complains of dyplopia (double vision). There are difficulties swallowing (deglutition) and possibly weakness of the arms and legs.

---

[64] A. Masaoka et al., *Follow-Up Study of Thymomas with Special Reference to Their Clinical Stages,* 48 Cancer 2485 (1981).

[65] J.V. Souadjian et al., *The Spectrum of Disease Associated with Thymoma,* 134 Archives Internal Med. 374 (1974).

§ 8.25   Diagnosis

Thymic tumors are usually encountered on routine chest X-rays. Computerized tomography (CT scan) identifies the extent and position of the tumor. Biopsy is usually not necessary.

The Tensilon test, which consists of administering Tensilon® (edrophonium chloride), markedly decreases the muscle weakness in myasthenia gravis most noticeably by improvement in ptosis (eyelid droop) and extraocular muscle abnormalities (range of eye motion).

§ 8.26   Surgical Treatment

Myasthenia gravis must be controlled prior to any surgical procedure. Acetyl-choline esterase inhibitors, such as pyridostigmine or corticosteroids, are administered.

Complete surgical removal of the mediastinal mass should be accomplished. Advanced disease can require pericardectomy, resection of the left innominate vein, resection of the superior vena cava, or sacrifice of the phrenic nerve.

§ 8.27   Chemotherapy

Using corticosteroids has resulted in regression of some unresectable thymomas that do not respond to radiotherapy. Single agents such as alkylating agents, cis-platin, and doxorubicin have had some success.[66] Combination chemotherapy can be more effective. A 56-percent response rate was reported with the use of vincristine, cyclophosphamide, lomustine, and prednisone.[67]

§ 8.28   Radiation Therapy

A distinction is made between invasive malignant thymoma and encapsulated, noninvasive malignant thymoma. The noninvasive thymoma is not given postoperative radiation unless there is doubt that the patient can be depended upon to submit to 10 years of follow-up treatment for possible recurrence. The invasive

---

[66] B. Boston, *Chemotherapy of Invasive Thymoma,* 38 Cancer 49 (1976); A.E. Papatestas et al., *Prognosis in Occult Thymomas in Myasthenia Gravis Following Transcervical Thymectomy,* 122 Archives Surgery 1352 (1987).

[67] G. Daugaard et al., *Combination Chemotherapy for Malignant Thymoma,* 99 Annals Internal Med. 189 (1983).

malignant thymomas are given postoperative radiation or primary radiation if they have metastases and are inoperable.

If the resection is incomplete, metal clips can be placed in areas of residual tumor for localization. The entire mediastinum and the hila of both lungs are irradiated. The field should be adjusted to include pleural implants and metal clips, if any. The radiation doses are 4500 to 6000 cGy in 160 to 180 cGy fractions with appropriate field reductions and angulations to avoid excessive irradiation of the spinal cord and heart.

Old medical records of thymomas associated with myasthenia gravis might show preoperative radiation to control the myasthenia gravis to reduce the surgical risk.

CHAPTER 9

BREAST NEOPLASMS

§ 9.1   Staging and Classification

TNM: American Joint Commission on Cancer.[1]

Breast cancer prognosis relates to tumor size (T1=2 cm or less, T2=2 to 5 cm, T3=more than 5 cm), involvement of surrounding structures, nodal involvement, and metastases. Recent studies have shown that prognosis differs with tumors of 1 cm as compared to 2 cm in size.

---

[1] American Joint Committee on Cancer, Manual for Staging of Cancer 146 (3d ed. 1988).

Breast Cancer Classification[2]

Invasive carcinoma

    Ductal carcinoma

    Medullary carcinoma with lymphoid infiltration

    Mucinous (colloid) carcinoma

    Papillary carcinoma

    Invasive lobular carcinoma

    Tubular, or well-differentiated, adenocarcinoma

Noninvasive carcinoma

    Intraductal carcinoma

    Lobular carcinoma in situ

Rare types of invasive carcinoma

    Epidermoid carcinoma

    Adenocystic carcinoma

    Sudoriferous carcinoma

    Carcinoma with cartilaginous and osseous metaplasia.

Tumors of the Breasts[3]

Paget's disease

Carcinoma of mammary ducts

    Noninfiltrating duct tumors

        Duct papilloma

        Noninfiltrating papillary carcinoma

        Noninfiltrating solid or comedocarcinoma

        Intracystic carcinoma

    Infiltrating duct carcinomas

        Infiltrating papillary carcinoma

        Infiltrating duct carcinoma with productive fibrosis

        Infiltrating comedocarcinoma

        Colloid carcinoma

---

[2] W.L. Donegan & J.S. Spratt, Cancer of the Breast 158 (1979).

[3] R.W. McDivitt et al., *Tumors of the Breast, in* Atlas of Tumor Pathology 7, fascicle 2 (1968).

Medullary carcinoma

Circumscribed infiltrating duct carcinoma

Carcinoma of mammary lobules

In situ lobular carcinoma

Infiltrating lobular carcinoma

Rare carcinomas

Sweat gland carcinoma

Tubular carcinoma

Adenoid cystic carcinoma

Metaplastic lesions

Cartilaginous metaplasia

Spindle cell

Squamous metaplasia

Inflammatory carcinoma

Breast sarcomas

Cystosarcoma phyllodes

Stromal sarcoma

Liposarcoma

Angiosarcoma

Lymphoma

Benign breast lesions

Sclerosing adenosis

Subareolar duct papillomatosis

Juvenile hypertrophy

Fibroadenoma

Granular cell tumor.

Prognosis Related to Pathologic Type

Favorable prognosis

Mucinous carcinoma[4]

Papillary carcinoma

---

[4] H.S. Gallagher, *Pathologic Types of Breast Cancer: Their Prognoses,* 53 Cancer 623 (1984).

Tubular carcinoma[5]

Medullary carcinoma[6]

Adenoid cystic carcinoma[7]

Secretory carcinoma[8]

Unfavorable prognosis

Metaplastic carcinoma[9]

Sarcomatoid carcinoma

Inflammatory carcinoma.[10]

§ 9.2 Etiology

A very controversial aspect in the causation of breast cancer is the administration of female hormones. The evidence has been neither consistent nor convincing. Oral contraceptives are known to reduce the incidence of benign breast diseases, including fibrocystic disease and fibroadenoma.[11] Some studies show no increased risk of breast cancer,[12] whereas other studies do indicate an increased incidence,[13] especially after prolonged use of the oral contraceptive.

---

[5] G.N. Peters et al., *Tubular Carcinoma of the Breast: Clinical Pathologic Correlations Based on 100 Cases,* 193 Annals Surgery 138 (1981).

[6] H.J.G. Bloom et al., *Host Resistance and Survival in Carcinoma of Breast: A Study of 104 Cases of Medullary Carcinoma in a Series of 1411 Cases of Breast Cancer Followed for 20 Years,* 3 Brit. Med. J. 181 (1970).

[7] B.A. Friedman & H.A. Oberman, *Adenoid Cystic Carcinoma of the Breast,* 54 Am. J. Clinical Pathology 1 (1970).

[8] F.A. Tavassoli & H.J. Norris, *Secretory Carcinoma of the Breast,* 45 Cancer 2404 (1980).

[9] M.W. Kaufman et al., *Carcinoma of the Breast with Pseudosarcomatous Metaplasia,* 53 Cancer 1908 (1984).

[10] F.V. Lucas & C. Perez-Mesa, *Inflammatory Carcinoma of the Breast,* 41 Cancer 1595 (1978).

[11] Boston Collaborative Drug Surveillance Programme, *Oral Contraceptives and Venous Thromboembolic Disease. Surgically Confirmed Gallbladder Disease, and Breast Tumors,* 1 Lancet 1399 (1973); J.L. Kelsey et al., *Oral Contraceptives and Breast Disease. An Epidemiologic Study,* 107 Am. J. Epidemiology 236 (1978); A. Nomura & G.W. Comstock, *Benign Breast Tumor and Estrogenic Hormones. A Population-Based Retrospective Study,* 103 Am. J. Epidemiology 439 (1979); B. Ravnihar et al., *An Epidemiologic Study of Breast Cancer and Benign Breast Neoplasias in Relation to the Oral Contraceptive and Estrogen Use,* 15 Eur. J. Cancer 395 (1978); M. Vessey et al., *Oral Contraceptives and Breast Neoplasia: A Retrospective Study,* 3 Brit. Med. 719 (1972).

[12] Boston Collaborative Drug Surveillance Programme, *Surgically Confirmed Gallbladder Disease, Venous Thromboembolism in Relation to Postmenopausal Estrogen Therapy,* 290 New Eng. J. Med. 15 (1974); J. Casagrande et al., *Exogenous Estrogens and Breast Cancer in Women with Natural Menopause,* 56 J. Nat'l Cancer Inst. 839 (1976); R. Hertz, *The Problem of*

Certain benign breast disorders are associated with an increased risk for the subsequent development of breast cancer. Atypical duct hyperplasia[14] and large duct hyperplasia[15] are considered important risks.

The College of American Pathologists held a consensus meeting in 1985 and estimated the following relative risks for invasive breast carcinoma based on the pathologic examination of benign breast tissue.[16]

Slightly Increased Risk (1.5 to 2 Times)

Women with any lesion specified below in a biopsy specimen are at slightly increased risk for invasive breast carcinoma relative to comparable women who have had no breast biopsy:

Hyperplasia, moderate or florid, solid or papillary

Papilloma with fibrovascular core

Moderately Increased Risk (5 Times)

Women with a lesion specified below in a biopsy specimen are at moderately increased risk for invasive breast carcinoma relative to comparable women who have had no breast biopsy:

Atypical hyperplasia (borderline lesion)

   Ductal

   Lobular

Possible Effects of Oral Contraceptives on Cancer of the Breast, 24 Cancer 1140 (1969); H.P. Leis et al., *The Pill and the Breast,* 16 J. Reproductive Med. 5 (1976); H.M. Lemon, *Abnormal Estrogen Metabolism and Tissue Estrogen Receptor Proteins in Breast Cancer,* 25 Cancer 423 (1970); H. Ory et al., *Oral Contraceptives and Reduced Risk of Benign Breast Disease,* 294 New Eng. J. Med. 419 (1976); P.E. Sartwell et al., *Exogenous Hormones, Reproductive History, and Breast Cancer,* 59 J. Nat'l Cancer Inst. 1589 (1977); M.P. Vessey et al., *Oral Contraceptives and Breast Cancer. Progress Report of an Epidemiological Study,* 1 Lancet 941 (1975).

[13] M.M. Black & H.P. Leis, Jr., *Mammary Carcinogenesis: Influence of Parity and Estrogens,* 72 N.Y. State J. Med. 1601 (1972); E. Fasal & R.S. Paffenbarger, Jr., *Oral Contraceptives as Related to Cancer and Benign Lesions of the Breast,* 55 J. Nat'l Cancer Inst. 767 (1975); R. Hoover et al., *Menopausal Estrogens and Breast Cancer,* 295 New Eng. J. Med. 401 (1976); B.E. Henderson et al., *An Epidemiologic Study of Breast Cancer,* 53 J. Nat'l Cancer Inst. 609 (1974); R.M. Kretzschmar, *Oral Contraceptives and Cancer,* 28 CA-A Cancer J. for Clinicians 118 (1978); A.L. Lees et al., *Oral Contraceptives and Breast Disease in Premenopausal Northern Albertan Women,* 22 Int'l J. Cancer 700 (1978); E.F. Lewison, *The Pill, Estrogens, and the Breast,* 28 Cancer 1400 (1971).

[14] M.M. Black et al., *Association of Atypical Characteristics of Benign Breast Lesions with Subsequent Risk of Breast Cancer,* 29 Cancer 338 (1972); C.M. Karpas et al., *Relationship of Fibrocystic Disease to Carcinoma of the Breast,* 162 Annals Surgery 1 (1965); W.H. Kern & R.N. Brooks, *Atypical Epithelial Hyperplasia Associated with Breast Cancer and Fibrocystic Disease,* 24 Cancer 668 (1969).

[15] L.J. Humphrey & M.A. Swerdlow, *Large Duct Epithelial Hyperplasia and Carcinoma of the Breast,* 97 Archives Surgery 592 (1968).

[16] College of American Pathologists, *Is Fibrocystic Disease of the Breast Precancerous?,* 110 Archives Pathology & Laboratory Med. 171 (1986).

There is a familial incidence in the occurrence of breast cancer.[17] These malignancies occur in the younger age group[18] and are frequently bilateral.[19] Klinefelter's syndrome is a disorder due to chromosomal polysomy and involves spermatogenesis, gynecomastia, and long arm span, which can have an excessive incidence of breast cancer.[20]

In patients who have cancer in one breast, there is a 10 percent possibility of cancer developing in the opposite breast. Other primary neoplasms of different sites are frequently noted in breast cancer patients, especially in the uterus, ovary, and colon. Cancer of the breast can occur in patients who have previously had cancer of the ovary, endometrium, major salivary glands, or Hodgkin's disease.

There is an increased risk of breast cancer in patients who have a first birth after age 34. This risk can be four times the normal population rate.[21] Early menarche can be a risk factor in developing malignancy of the breast.[22] Late menopause also is a consideration in the more frequent occurrence of breast cancer.

There can be an association with the administration of reserpine and breast cancer.[23]

---

[17] J. Clemmensen, *Statistical Study in the Aetiology of Malignant Neoplasms—I, Review of Results*, 1 Acta Pathologica Microbiologica Scandinavica 543 (Supp. 174, 1965); G.K. Lokuhate, *Morbidity and Mortality Among Offspring of Breast Cancer Mothers*, 89 Am. J. Epidemiology 139 (1969); M.T. Macklin, *Comparison of the Number of Breast Cancer Deaths Observed in Relatives of Breast-Cancer Patients and the Number Expected on the Basis of Mortality Rates*, 22 J. Nat'l Cancer Inst. 927 (1959); M.J. Tendler, *Heredity in Cancer of the Breast*, 31 S. Med. J. 602 (1938); H.J. Vanderberg, *Can Cancer Be an Inherited Family Disease?*, 495 Mich. Med. Soc'y 1185 (1950); W.V. Wate & H.W. Trout, Jr., *The Heredity Factor in Cancer of the Breast*, 90 Am. J. Surgery 434 (1955).

[18] D.E. Anderson, *Some Characteristics of Familial Breast Cancer*, 28 Cancer 1500 (1971); E. Papadrianos et al., *Cancer of the Breast as a Familial Disease*, 165 Annals Surgery 10 (1967).

[19] F. DeWaard & E.A. Baanders-Van Halewijn, *The Bimodal Age Distribution of Patients with Mammary Carcinoma; Evidence for the Existence of 2 Types of Human Breast Cancer*, 17 Cancer 141 (1964).

[20] G.M. Coley et al., *Multiple Primary Tumors Including Bilateral Breast Cancer in situ in a Man with Klinefelter's Syndrome*, 27 Cancer 1476 (1971); A.W. Jackson et al., *Carcinoma of Male Breast in Association with Klinefelter Syndrome*, 1 Brit. Med. J. 223 (1965); M.C. Robson et al., *Bilateral Carcinoma of the Breast in a Patient with Klinefelter's Syndrome*, 28 J. Clinical Endocrinology & Metabolism 897 (1968).

[21] Am. College of Obstetrics & Gynecology, Technical Bulletin, No. 54 (Oct. 1979).

[22] D. Apter & R. Vihko, *Early Menarche, a Risk Factor for Breast Cancer, Indicates Early Onset of Ovulatory Cycles*, 575 Clinical Endocrinology Med. 82 (1983); B. McMahon et al., *Age at Menarche, Probability of Ovulation and Breast Cancer Risk*, 29 Int'l J. Cancer 13 (1982).

[23] B. Armstrong et al., *Retrospective Study of the Association Between the Use of Rauwolfia Derivatives and Breast Cancer in English Women*, 2 Lancet 672 (1974); Food & Drug Administration, *Reserpine Reported to Increase Incidence of Breast Cancer*, FDA Drug Bull. (Sept. 1974); O.P. Heinonen et al., *Reserpine Use in Relation to Breast Cancer*, 2 Lancet 675 (1974).

Dietary factors have been implicated in the causation of carcinoma of the breast, especially the high intake of fat.[24]

Ionizing radiation is known to have a carcinogenic effect. Low-dose mammography on a routine yearly screening basis for a prolonged period of time does not have a significant effect in the causation of breast malignancy. Higher-dose radiation is related to an increase in the incidence of breast cancer.[25]

Hair dyes contain chemicals that are carcinogenic,[26] and these dyes can be absorbed into the general circulation and produce systemic effects. Breast malignancy has been reported as significantly related to the use of hair dye.[27]

Oncogene alterations and/or overexpression have been associated with more aggressive cancers. The genetic alterations involve protooncogenes, which are involved in the malignant transformation of cells. In breast cancer, amplification has been noted in some patients in c-myc,[28] c-erb B-2 (HER-21 neu),[29]

[24] D. Kritchevsky, *Nutrition and Breast Cancer*, 66 Cancer 1321 (1990); E.L. Wynder & D.P. Rose, *Diet and Breast Cancer*, 19 Hosp. Prac. 73 (1984).

[25] J.D. Boice, Jr., & R.R. Monson, *Breast Cancer in Women after Repeated Fluoroscopic Examinations of the Chest*, 59 J. Nat'l Cancer Inst. 823 (1977); N.G. Hildreth et al., *The Risk of Breast Cancer after Irradiation of the Thymus in Infancy*, 321 New Eng. J. Med. 1281 (1989); G.R. Howe et al., *Estimated Benefits and Risks of Screening for Breast Cancer*, 124 Can. Med. Ass'n 124 (1981); C.E. Land & D.H. McGregor, *Breast Cancer Incidence Among Atomic Bomb Survivors: Implications for Radiobiologic Risk at Low Doses*, 62 J. Nat'l Cancer Inst. 17 (1979); I. Mackenzie, *Breast Cancer Following Multiple Fluoroscopies*, 19 Brit. J. Cancer 1 (1965); A.B. Miller et al., *Mortality from Breast Cancer after Irradiation During Fluoroscopic Examinations in Patients being Treated for Tuberculosis*, 321 New Eng. J. Med. 1285 (1989); J.A. Myrden & J.E. Hiltz, *Breast Cancer Following Multiple Fluoroscopies During Artificial Pneumothorax Treatment of Pulmonary Tuberculosis*, 100 Can. Med. Ass'n 1032 (1969); R.E. Shore et al., *Breast Neoplasms in Women Treated with X-rays for Acute Postpartum Mastitis*, 59 J. Nat'l Cancer Inst. 813 (1977).

[26] B.N. Ames et al., *Carcinogens as Frameshift Mutagens: Metabolites and Derivatives of 2-Acetylaminofluorene and Aromatic Amine Carcinogens*, 69 Proc. Nat'l Acad. Sci. 3128 (1972); B.N. Ames et al., *An Improved Bacterial Test System for the Detection and Classification of Mutagens and Carcinogens*, 70 Proc. Nat'l Acad. Sci. 782 (1973).

[27] R.B. Shafer & R.W. Shafer, *Potential Carcinogenic Effects of Hair Dyes*, 76 N.Y. State J. Med. 394 (1976).

[28] C. Escot et al., *Genetic Alteration of the c-myc Proto-oncogene (MYC) in Human Primary Breast Carcinomas*, 83 Proc. Nat'l Acad. Sci. 4834 (1986); J.L. Whittaker et al., *Differential Expression of Cellular Oncogenes in Benign and Malignant Human Breast Tissue*, 38 Int'l J. Cancer 651 (1986).

[29] J. Advane et al., *Proto-oncogene Amplification and Human Breast Tumor Phenotype*, 4 Oncogene 1389 (1989); I.U. Ali, *Amplification of C-Erb B-2 and Aggressive Human Breast Tumors?*, 240 Sci. 1795 (1988); S. Park et al., *Pathologic Findings from the National Surgical Adjuvant Breast and Bowel Project: Prognostic Significance of Erb B-2 Protein Overexpression in Primary Breast Cancer*, 8 J. Clinical Oncology 103 (1990); D.J. Slamon et al., *Human Breast Cancer: Correlation of Relapse and Survival with Amplification of the HER-2/neu Oncogene*, 235 Sci. 177 (1987); D.J. Slamon et al., *Studies of HER-2/neu Proto-oncogene in Human Breast and Ovarian Cancer*, 244 Sci. 707 (1989).

hst/int-2,[30] c-ras-Ki,[31] EGFr (epidermal growth factor receptor),[32] c-myb, and c-ras-Ha. New prognostic factors include the somatostatin receptor (SSR) and pS2 protein.[33] Galactosyl hydroxylysine has been found to be a predictor of bone metastases in breast cancer.[34]

Tumor suppressor genes have been identified for breast cancer.[35] Loss of heterozygosity has been noted in the long arm of chromosome 17q, which is associated with estrogen receptor-negative tumors and the long arm of chromosome 18q, which is clinically correlated with a more malignant microscopic appearance.

§ 9.3 Clinical Manifestations

Breast problems can manifest themselves as pain, nipple discharge, a mass, or eczema. Various disorders can manifest these symptoms.

§ 9.4 —Nipple Discharge

A spontaneous discharge of yellow, brown, or red liquid from the nipple can indicate the presence of an intraductal papilloma. The discharge is intermittent and tends to stain the brassiere or nightgown. Vigorous squeezing of the nipples by middle-aged women will produce a grayish discharge of no real significance. Bloody discharge can occur during pregnancy and can be an exaggerated proliferation of mammary epithelium.[36] Malignancy can cause a thin, watery, or bloody nipple discharge.[37] Other known causes of various types of discharge

---

[30] R. Lidereau et al., *Amplification of the Int-2 Gene in Primary Human Breast Tumors,* 2 Oncogene Res. 285 (1988); C. Theillet et al., *Amplification of FGH-Related Sequences in Human Tumors: Possible Involvement of HST in Breast Carcinomas,* 4 Oncogene 915 (1989); D.-J. Zhou et al., *Amplification of Human Int-2 in Breast Cancers and Squamous Carcinomas,* 2 Oncogene 279 (1988).

[31] D.-J. Zhou et al., *Proto-Oncogene Abnormalities in Human Breast Cancer: C-Erb-2 Amplification Does Not Correlate with Recurrence of Disease,* 4 Oncogene 105 (1989).

[32] J.R.C. Sainsbury et al., *Epidermal-Growth-Factor Receptor Status as a Predictor of Early Recurrence of and Death from Breast Cancer,* 1 Lancet 1398 (1987).

[33] J.G.M. Klijn et al., *The Somatostatin Receptor (SSR) and pS2 Protein (pS2): Two New Prognostic Factors in Primary Breast Cancer,* 9 Proc. Am. Soc'y Clinical Oncology 51 (1990).

[34] E. Galligioni et al., *Galactosyl Hydroxylysine (GH) Is Highly Predictive for Bone Metastases in Breast Cancer Patients,* 9 Proc. Am. Soc'y Clinical Oncology 33 (1990).

[35] M.J. Cline et al., *Proto-Oncogene Abnormalities in Human Breast Cancer: Correlations with Anatomic Features and Clinical Course of Disease,* 5 J. Clinical Oncology 999 (1987).

[36] C.D. Haagenson et al., Breast Carcinoma: Risk and Detection 152 (1981).

[37] E.F. Lewison & R.G. Chambers, *Clinical Significance of Nipple Discharge,* 147 JAMA 295 (1951).

include adenosis (bloody), gross cystic disease (serous, bloody), duct ectasia (serous, bloody), and multiple papilloma (serous, bloody).[38]

Lactation (white nipple discharge) is normally associated with pregnancy, but also can be seen in certain other conditions such as:

Trauma to chest wall (including surgical)[39]

Pituitary necrosis from severe obstetrical hemorrhage (Sheehan's syndrome, Chiari-Frommel syndrome)[40]

Pituitary neoplasms[41]

Hypothyroidism[42]

Drugs (phenothiazines, reserpine, methyldopa)[43]

Hormonal contraceptives.[44]

§ 9.5   —Breast Mass

Fibrocystic Disease (Chronic Cystic Mastitis)

The subtle changes of fibrocystic disease can begin in the young adult and consists of soreness of the breasts around the time of menses and can progress to persistent breast soreness and tenderness during the remainder of the menstrual cycle. Diffuse nodularity of the breast tissue appears, and a dominant mass can occur. This tumor can be a conglomeration of fibrocystic disease, extensive adenosis (sclerosing adenosis), or a gross cyst. A solitary papilloma can form a

---

[38] C.D. Haagensen et al., Breast Carcinoma: Risk and Detection 1653 (1981).

[39] R.L. Berger et al., *Lactation after Incision on the Thoracic Cage,* 274 New Eng. J. Med. 1493 (1966); S. Grossman et al., *Idiopathic Lactation Following Thoracoplasty,* 10 J. Clinical Endocrinology 729 (1950); D. Salkin & E.W. Davis, *Lactation Following Thoracoplasty and Pneumonectomy,* 18 J. Thoracic Surgery 580 (1949).

[40] H.J. Levine et al., *Persistent Lactation,* 243 Am. J. Med. Sci. 118 (1962).

[41] D. Krestin, *Spontaneous Lactation Associated with Enlargement of the Pituitary,* 1 Lancet 928 (1932); M.E. Levin, *Persistent Lactation Associated with Pituitary Tumor and Hyperadrenal Corticism,* 27 Am. J. Med. 172 (1959).

[42] D.M. Brown et al., *Study of Composition of Milk from Patient with Hypothyroidism and Galactorrhea,* 25 J. Clinical Endocrinology 1225 (1965).

[43] F.J. Ayd, Jr., *Thorazine and Serpasil Treatment on Private Neuro-Psychiatric Patients,* 113 Am. J. Psychiatry 16 (1956); J.H. Hooper et al., *Abnormal Lactation Associated with Tranquilizing Therapy,* 178 JAMA 506 (1961); H.W. Johnson et al., *Lactation with Phenothiazine Derivative (Temaril),* 80 Am. J. Obstetrics & Gynecology 124 (1960); J. Mendels, *Thioproperazine Induces Lactation,* 121 Am. J. Psychiatry 109 (1964).

[44] W.I. Gregg, *Galactorrhea after Contraceptive Hormones,* 274 New Eng. J. Med. 1432 (1966); S.H. Schachner, *Galactorrhea Subsequent to Contraceptive Hormones,* 275 New Eng. J. Med. 1138 (1966).

mass in the subareolar area and multiple intraductal papillomas can cause a peripheral mass.

A tumor from fibrocystic disease occurs usually in women between ages 35 to 55, but can be noted at almost any age. Gross cysts are associated with a higher incidence of cancer than patients with other forms of fibrocystic disease. Multiple papillomatosis predisposes to cancer.

Fibroadenoma

Fibroadenoma occurs in a younger age group (usually ages 20 to 35) and increases in size very slowly. The most significant diagnostic technique is *ballottement,* which involves gently squeezing one side of the tumor between two fingers until it pops away from the fingers and then falls back to its original position, hitting the tips of the fingers. This response does not occur with other tumors.

Although fibroadenoma is a benign condition, in rare instances the neoplasm can convert into a rapidly growing cystosarcoma phyllodes.

Carcinoma

The typical breast cancer is hard and irregular. The malignancy can be semifirm or feel like an area of thickening with poorly defined borders. Cancer appears in women most often after the age of 55, but is seen in the younger age group although very rarely under the age of 20. Cases have been reported in children and juveniles. One percent of breast cancers occur in males.

As the tumor increases in size, there can be attachments to the skin, through Cooper's ligaments, resulting in skin dimpling. Nipple retraction and *peau d'orange* (edema of the skin with accentuation of the pores like an orange peel) are indications of probable malignancy. Nipple inversion is a form of nipple retraction, but it is sometimes present in normal individuals, or can occur from duct ectasia. Tumor extensions can cause fixation of the mass to the underlying muscle (pectoralis major muscle or serratus anterior muscle) or a rib. The skin can ulcerate and satellite subcutaneous nodules form in advanced disease. Palpable or visible axillary node enlargement may be an early manifestation, although it is most often seen in the later stages of the disease.

Malignancy of the breast is usually painless, but an early sign can be short episodes of pain, usually sharp in character, in the region of the tumor. In advanced disease, pain is more common, especially with ulceration. Bone pain, most often in the low back, can be an indication of bony metastases.

Inflammatory carcinoma is a highly malignant form of breast cancer and includes redness of the skin of at least one third of the breast (frequently with peau d'orange), a rapidly growing mass (occurring over days or weeks), and containing subdermal lymphatic tumor invasion on microscopic examination.

Some cancers of the breast can become inflamed with redness of the skin, but are not inflammatory carcinoma.

Abscess in a nonlactating breast is extremely rare and must be considered a possible cancer until proven otherwise. Breast infection or inflammation occur from trauma or in fibrocystic disease, but will respond rapidly to antibiotics and local heat with resolution of the skin redness and mass. Infection of the glands of Montgomery, present along the periphery of the areola, is a benign disorder. There can be a persistent infection under the edge of the areola with persistent drainage that defies treatment and frequently requires adequate resection.

§ 9.6   —Paget's Disease

Paget's disease is an eczematoid weeping, inflamed dermatitis of the nipple. There are itching and burning sensations with oozing or bleeding. This disorder contains nests of tumor cells within the lining and ducts of the nipple and is associated with an underlying malignancy of the breast. The condition is to be distinguished from a dermatitis of the areola not involving the nipple, which is a benign disorder. An associated breast lump is present in 60 percent of cases.

§ 9.7   Diagnosis

Every physician is taught how to do a complete physical examination, including a proper breast exam. There should be adequate lighting to visualize the breasts. The flat portions of the fingers (not the tips) are used to palpate the breasts with the patient supine; in addition, bimanual palpation can be done with the patient in a sitting position. The axillary areas also are palpated. The arms should be elevated over the head with the patient sitting and the skin and nipples observed for retraction or dimpling. This exam is repeated with the palms pressed together, tensing the pectoralis major muscles.

The American Cancer Society suggests the following guidelines for asymptomatic women for the detection of breast cancer:[45]

1. Women 20 years of age and older should perform breast self-examination every month.

2. Women 20 to 40 years old should have a physical examination of the breasts every three years, and women over 40 years old should have a physical examination of the breasts every year.

---

[45] G.D. Dodd, *American Cancer Society Guidelines from the Past to the Present*, 72 Cancer 1429 (1993); American Cancer Society, *Mammography Guidelines 1983: Background Statement and Update of Cancer-Related Check-Up Guidelines for Breast Cancer Detection in Asymptomatic Women Age 40–49*, 33 CA-A Cancer J. for Clinicians 255 (1983).

3. Women 40 to 49 years old should have a mammogram every one to two years.

4. Women 50 years old and over should have a mammogram every year.

5. Women with personal or family histories of breast cancer should consult their physicians about the need for more frequent examinations.

Breast Imaging

Thermography detects heat differences between normal and abnormal tissues. The technique is not to be used without other more accurate means of imaging because early malignancy can be missed.[46]

Mammography is the most accurate means of detecting breast cancer for early nonpalpable tumors and should be performed on all patients with pain, mass, or nipple discharge. The technique depends on a cooperative patient and an experienced technologist to obtain high-quality radiographs. In 10 to 20 percent of cases, cancer will not be visualized on the mammogram.[47] Therefore, when a tumor is palpable, the mammography is only a secondary tool in confirming the presence of the mass and possible malignancy, but it is more useful to detect tumors in the remaining areas of the breast or in the opposite breast.

There are specific abnormalities on a mammogram that require either a follow-up mammogram every three to six months for two and one-half years or excisional biopsy.[48] A poorly defined border of a mass in any of the views on an X-ray can indicate malignancy. Grouped microcalcifications are suspicious if there are three or more calcifications.[49] These can appear punctate or linear. There is some controversy as to whether at least three or at least five calcifications must be present to indicate the possibility of malignancy. With excision of the area, however, approximately 20 percent are actually cancer. Although breasts are usually somewhat asymmetric, the appearance of significant densities that appear asymmetric from the opposite breast, especially in a patient over 55, should alert the radiologist and clinician for the possibility of malignancy. Densities that are stellate in appearance are usually cancer.

Breast ultrasound can usually distinguish a cyst from a solid mass. A cyst with smooth borders is benign. In pregnant patients, ultrasonography is the preferred method of examination if the physician is adverse to mammography,

---

[46] M. Moskowitz et al., *Lack of Efficacy of Thermography as a Screening Tool for Minimal and Stage I Breast Cancer*, 295 New Eng. J. Med. 249 (1976).

[47] M.J. Homer, *Analysis of Patients Undergoing Breast Biopsy: The Role of Mammography*, 2435 JAMA 677 (1980); J.E. Martin et al., *Breast Cancer Missed by Mammography*, 132 Am. Radiology 737 (1979).

[48] M.J. Homer, *Breast Imaging: Pitfalls, Controversies, and Some Practical Thoughts*, 23 Radiology Clinics N. Am. 459 (1985).

[49] N. Sadowsky & D.B. Kopans, *Breast Cancer*, 21 Radiology Clinics N. Am. 51 (1983).

because the breasts can appear very dense on mammography. In very young patients, ultrasound can be used in preference to an X-ray examination.

Xeromammography, although now used less often, is another means of examining the breast using low dose radiography and is nearly as accurate as the mammogram. Low dose X-rays are now utilized for mammography, which is preferred by most radiologists.

Patients with silicone gel implants from mammary augmentation can have some of the breast tissue obscured on an X-ray.[50] Small cancers can be missed. Even saline implants can obscure the tissue on mammography. A new organic polymer filler that is somewhat radiotranslucent has been developed under the name of Misti Gold™ (Bioplasty, Inc.), but even this material does not allow adequate mammograms. The pinch technique, which displaces the prosthesis,[51] is the best method of evaluating the augmented breast and is capable of displaying 90 to 95 percent of the breast tissue. In the presence of capsule contracture, however, the technique does not work and extra views of the breast are necessary.

Breast Mass

Every patient with a dominant mass in the breast that is present for over four weeks in the premenopausal patient (through at least one menstrual cycle) or over two weeks in a postmenopausal patient should have an adequate and complete investigation to rule out a cancer. Diagnostic mammography is essential, but it should not be relied upon exclusively. Ultrasound can distinguish a cyst from a solid tumor.

If a cyst is suspected, needle aspiration should be performed and the fluid sent for analysis. Solid masses can be examined by thin needle aspiration and cytology[52] or by means of needle biopsy.[53] Needle aspiration has a significant incidence of false positive or false negative findings. Extreme care must be taken in interpretation of the cytology results. Negative findings for malignancy on needle aspiration or needle biopsy should be followed by open biopsy or excision. A large mass might need an incisional biopsy before resection is attempted.

---

[50] M.J. Silverstein et al., *Breast Cancer in Women after Augmentation Mammoplasty,* 123 Archives Surgery 681 (1988).

[51] G.W. Eklund et al., *Improved Imaging of the Augmented Breast,* 151 Am. J. Radiology 469 (1988).

[52] C.S. Grant et al., *Fine-Needle Aspiration of the Breast,* 61 Mayo Clinic Proc. 377 (1986); M.P. Kahky et al., *Needle Aspiration Biopsy of Palpable Breast Masses,* 156 Am. J. Surgery 450 (1988); F.A. Sheikh et al., *Final Diagnosis by Fine-Needle Aspiration Biopsy for Definitive Operation in Breast Cancer,* 154 Am. J. Surgery 470 (1987).

[53] A.D. Baildem et al., *Extended Role for Needle Biopsy in the Management of Carcinoma of the Breast,* 76 Brit. J. Surgery 552 (1989).

Excisional biopsy is the most reliable means for diagnosis. All masses should be considered potentially malignant and must be excised with an adequate margin of normal tissue. The patient should *never* be told not to worry about the mass and to return if it gets larger. The physician has a duty to reexamine the patient at regular intervals.

Mammographic Abnormality Without Palpable Mass

Excision must be performed when the mammogram reveals either a solid tumor, the borders of which are not all well defined and smooth, or a stellate lesion. Both grouped punctate or linear calcifications consisting of three to five calcium deposits and smooth-walled solid masses can be followed by repeat mammograms every three to six months for at least two and one-half years.[54] If any change occurs, such as tumor growth or increased number of grouped calcifications, excision must be performed.

Paget's Disease

Any dermatitis involving the nipple must be biopsied to rule out Paget's disease. Because more than 30 percent of patients with Paget's disease do not have a palpable breast mass, an early diagnosis is essential. This disorder must be considered as always being associated with underlying breast cancer and mammography must be performed.

§ 9.8   Surgical Treatment

Nipple Discharge

The duct of origin must be localized by pressure on the breast and areola to reproduce the discharge. A probe can be placed in the duct at the time of surgery so that it can be identified. The duct is transected at the nipple and a wedge of breast tissue associated with the duct is removed.

Breast Mass

A fibroadenoma can be removed by enucleation because the capsule is thick and the tumor is benign. All other tumors are removed with a wide margin of normal

---

[54]R.J. Brenner & E.A. Sickles, *Acceptability of Periodic Follow-Up as an Alternative to Biopsy for Mammographically Detected Lesions Interpreted as Probably Benign,* 171 Radiology 645 (1989); M.J. Homer, *Nonpalpable Mammographic Abnormalities: Timing the Follow-Up Studies,* 1356 Am. J. Radiology 923 (1981); J.N. Wolfe et al., *Xeroradiography of the Breast: Overview of 21,057 Consecutive Cases,* 165 Radiology 305 (1987).

breast tissue, preferably 1 cm in width. If malignancy is present and the margins of the specimen are clear of cancer, then an adequate wedge resection has been performed. If neoplasm is close to any margin or if more than 25 percent of the specimen contains intraductal carcinoma (*carcinoma in situ*), a further resection is necessary for adequate lumpectomy.

Lumpectomy

When considering the type of surgery to be performed for breast cancer, the patient must receive adequate information as to the viable alternatives of care and their results and complications. Early breast cancer can be treated effectively by lumpectomy (wedge resection, quadrant resection) as long as the tumor is totally removed along with a margin of normal tissue. The lumpectomy is followed by axillary node dissection (at least 10 lymph nodes, but not complete radical resection) and then postoperative radiation therapy.

Contraindications to lumpectomy are a tumor over 5 cm in diameter, multiple primary tumors in the same breast, or a large breast. Radiation therapy of a large breast can result in a painful shrunken breast that may have to be resected.

Modified Radical Mastectomy

A viable alternative to lumpectomy is the modified radical mastectomy, which consists of mastectomy (removal of the breast) and regional lymph node dissection (at least 10 nodes). The preservation of the pectoralis major muscle allows better reconstruction with an implant. A segment of the lateral aspect of the muscle can be resected if there is tumor attachment in that area.

Radical Mastectomy

There are still some advocates of radical mastectomy as the primary treatment for breast cancer.[55] The surgery involves mastectomy with en bloc resection of the pectoralis major and pectoralis minor muscles and axillary node dissection. This technique allows adequate removal of the interpectoral nodes (between the muscles) in the rare instance of metastases to these nodes. Large tumors and tumors involving the pectoralis major muscle are best treated by this radical procedure.

---

[55] J. Hayward, *The Significance of Local Control in the Primary Treatment of Breast Cancer,* 122 Archives Surgery 1244 (1987).

Mammographic Abnormality Without Palpable Mass

Preoperative needle localization by the radiologist is usually necessary for excision of nonpalpable lesions noted on mammography.[56] The needle is inserted under mammographic visualization, and when it is in position near the abnormality, a blue dye is injected. A hooked wire is placed through the needle and the needle is then removed. The wire is more stable and less likely to be moved out of position during the surgical excision.

Intraductal Carcinoma (Carcinoma in Situ)

When an area of abnormal tissue is removed and contains extensive intraductal carcinoma, there are a variety of possible surgical procedures that can be performed. Wider local resection is adequate if it encompasses the whole involved area with a margin of normal tissue. Minimal axillary node dissection is used to stage the disease in case there is any area of invasive malignancy. This procedure is followed by radiation therapy to the remainder of the breast.

Because other regions of the breast can contain intraductal carcinoma, some physicians advocate simple mastectomy or modified radical mastectomy.

Invasive ductal carcinoma of the breast can be associated with intraductal carcinoma. When the intraductal component comprises more than 25 percent of the specimen in a lumpectomy, local wider resection is essential to be sure that all malignant areas are removed and to decrease local recurrence if modified radical mastectomy is not planned.

Lobular Carcinoma in Situ

Lobular carcinoma or lobular carcinoma in situ can be treated in a similar fashion as intraductal carcinoma; however, there is a high potential for malignancy in the opposite breast. A mirror-image wide resection can be performed in the contralateral (opposite) breast for diagnostic purposes. Some physicians prefer to perform a simple mastectomy in the contralateral breast. The patient must be informed of the problem of another malignancy, the alternatives of care, and their possible complications, including careful observation of the opposite breast over a long period of time in preference to an immediate surgical approach. Invasive lobular carcinoma, however, does not show as a mammographic abnormality, and it does not tend to occur as a palpable mass. When large enough, the neoplasm feels like firmness or induration.

---

[56] D.D. Dershaw, *Nonpalpable, Needle-Localized Mammographic Abnormalities: Pathologic Correlation in 219 Patients,* 4 Cancer Investigation 1 (1986); H.P. Leis et al., *Breast Biopsy and Guidance for Occult Lesions,* 70 Int'l Surgery 115 (1985); C.H. Rusnak et al., *Preoperative Needle Localization to Detect Early Breast Cancer,* 157 Am. J. Surgery 505 (1989).

Breast Reconstruction

The forms of breast reconstruction following mastectomy include immediate or delayed insertion of an implant, or skin expander or musculocutaneous flap prior to placing the implant. Multiple procedures are usually required and capsule contracture can be a significant complication. With the newer textured implants, capsule contracture can be minimized. The majority of patients that prefer no reconstruction are those in the older age group, those that fear multiple further surgical procedures, and those that fear the implants can obscure early diagnosis of local recurrence.

Recurrence Following Wedge Resection

Repeat wedge excision, as an alternative to mastectomy, can be used for isolated breast recurrences that are 2 cm or smaller in diameter, without signs of rapid growth, without fixation to skin or chest wall, without tumor associated erythema or edema, without clinically positive axilla, and without severe radiation changes due to prior therapy.[57] Axillary dissection should be carried out if not done at the primary procedure.

§ 9.9 Chemotherapy

Independent risk factors are considered when contemplating adjuvant chemotherapy following lumpectomy. The following factors indicate a high risk for metastasis:

Negative estrogen receptors[58]

Negative progesterone receptors

Undifferentiated carcinoma[59]

Vascular (blood or lymphatic) invasion[60]

---

[57] J.M. Kurtz, *Results of Wide Excision for Mammary Recurrence after Breast-Conserving Therapy,* 61 Cancer 1969 (1988).

[58] R. Croton et al., *Oestrogen Receptors and Survival in Early Breast Cancer,* 283 Brit. Med. J. 1289 (1981); D.W. Kinne et al., *Estrogen Receptor Protein in Breast Cancer as a Predictor of Recurrence,* 47 Cancer 2364 (1981); A. Singhakowinta et al., *Clinical Application of Estrogen Receptor in Breast Cancer,* 46 Cancer 2932 (1980).

[59] E.R. Fisher et al., *The Pathology of Invasive Breast Cancer. A Syllabus Derived from Findings of the National Surgical Adjuvant Breast Project (Protocol No. 4),* 36 Cancer 1 (1975).

[60] K.C. Arthur et al., *Prognostic Significance of Peritumoral Lymphatic and Blood Vessel Invasion in Node-Negative Carcinoma of the Breast,* 8 J. Clinical Oncology 1457 (1990); R. Bettelheim et al., *Prognostic Significance of Peritumoral Vascular Invasion in Breast Cancer,* 50 Brit. J. Cancer 771 (1984); B.W. Davis et al., *Prognostic Significance of Peritumoral Vessel Invasion*

Skin dimpling

Axillary node metastasis[61]

Aneuploid DNA flow cytometry[62]

High S-phase fraction in DNA flow cytometry[63]

Large tumor size.[64]

H-thymidine labeling index has recently been noted to have prognosis significance.[65]

Some patients with negative axillary nodes, Stage I, are at increased risk for
relapse, according to the National Institute of Health consensus development
conference on adjuvant chemotherapy for breast cancer, held in 1985.[66] Patients
at high risk

> may be identified by large tumor size, negative hormone receptors, and cell differ-
> entiation pattern, including high degree of anaplasia, high thymidine labeling
> index, and aneuploidy. For patients at high risk who cannot be entered into an
> ongoing trial, chemotherapy may be considered, but the decision to institute adju-
> vant therapy rests with each individual patient and her physician.[67]

---

in Clinical Trials of Adjuvant Therapy for Breast Cancer with Axillary Lymph Node Metastasis,
16 Hum. Pathology 1212 (1985); P.P. Rosen, Tumor Emboli in Intramammary Lymphatics in
Breast Carcinoma: Pathologic Criteria for Diagnosis and Clinical Significance, 18 Pathology
Ann. 215 (p. 2, 1983).

[61] F.F. Parl et al., Prognostic Significance of Estrogen Receptor Status in Breast Cancer in Relation to Tumor Stage, Axillary Node Metastasis, and Histopathologic Grading, 54 Cancer 2237
(1984).

[62] K. Christov et al., DNA Aneuploidy and Cell Proliferation in Breast Tumors, 64 Cancer 673
(1989); C.J. Comelisse et al., DNA Ploidy and Survival in Breast Cancer Patients, 8 Cytometry
225 (1987).

[63] G.M. Clark et al., Prediction of Relapse or Survival in Patients with Node-Negative Breast
Cancer by DNA Flow Cytometry, 320 New Eng. J. Med. 627 (1989); W.L. McGuire & L.G.
Dressler, Emerging Impact of Flow Cytometry in Predicting Recurrence and Survival in Breast
Cancer Patients, 75 J. Nat'l Cancer Inst. 405 (1985).

[64] C.L. Carter et al., Relationship of Tumour Size, Lymph Node Status and Survival in 24,740
Breast Cancer Cases, 63 Cancer 181 (1989); S.M. O'Reilly et al., Node-Negative Breast Cancer: Prognostic Subgroups Defined by Tumor Size and Flow Cytometry, 8 J. Clinical Oncology
2040 (1990).

[65] R. Silvestrini et al., Prognostic Implications of Labeling Index Versus Estrogen Receptors and
Tumor Size in Node-Negative Breast Cancer, 7 Breast Cancer Res. Treatment 161 (1986); R.
Silvestrini et al., 3H-Thymidine-Labeling Index as a Prognostic Indicator in Node-Positive
Breast Cancer, 8 J. Clinical Oncology 1321 (1990).

[66] National Cancer Institute, Early Breast Cancer Treatment Choice Between Doctor, Patient, 1
NIH Observer No. 5, at 1 (1980).

[67] Id.

The 1990 consensus panel of the National Cancer Institute (see § **9.15**) concluded that there are important prognostic factors associated with tumor recurrences:[68]

1. The risk of recurrence increased with tumor size
2. Positive estrogen and progesterone receptors have a better prognosis than receptor negative tumors
3. High nuclear grade is associated with higher rates of relapse
4. Measurement of cellular proliferation correlates well with outcome
5. High levels of cathepsin D are associated with an unfavorable prognosis
6. Tubular, colloid, and papillary histologic subtypes have a favorable prognosis.

There is no indication for chemotherapy or hormone therapy in patients with intraductal (in situ) or in situ lobular carcinoma.

Stage I tumors less than 1 cm in size that have favorable histologic types such as medullary, mucinous, papillary, or tubular, or diploid tumors with less than 10 percent of the cells in S phase probably will not benefit from adjuvant chemotherapy.[69]

Patients with Stage I neoplasms measuring from 1.1 to 2.0 cm have a decreasing 20-year disease-free survival rate (88 percent survival at 1 cm to 59 percent survival at 1.7 to 2.0 cm)[70] and deserve serious consideration for adjuvant chemotherapy in estrogen receptor negative patients and tamoxifen in estrogen receptor positive patients.[71] Combination chemotherapy is more effective than single-drug regimens. Cytoxan, methotrexate, and 5-fluorouracil (CMF), and sequential methotrexate and 5-fluorouracil are being used.

---

[68] National Cancer Institute, *New Tumor Suppressor Genes Associated with Breast Cancer,* 1 NIH Observer No. 5, at 4 (1990).

[69] B. Fisher et al., *Systemic Therapy in Patients with Node-Negative Breast Cancer; a Commentary Based on Two National Surgical Adjuvant Breast and Bowel Project (NSABP) Clinical Trials,* 111 Annals Internal Med. 703 (1989); P.P. Rosen et al., *Pathological Prognostic Factors in Stage I (T1NoMo) and Stage II (T1N1Mo) Breast Carcinoma: A Study of 644 Patients with Median Follow-Up of 18 Years,* 7 J. Clinical Oncology 1239 (1989).

[70] P.P. Rosen & S. Groshen, *Factors Influencing Survival and Prognosis in Early Breast Carcinoma (T1NoMo–T1N1Mo): Assessment of 644 Patients with Median Follow-up of 18 Years,* 70 Surgery Clinics N. Am. No. 4, at 937 (1990).

[71] A.R. Bianco et al., *Adjuvant Therapy with Tamoxifen in Operable Breast Cancer: 10 Year Results of the Naples (GUN) Study,* 2 Lancet 1095 (1988); B. Fisher et al., *A Randomized Clinical Trial Evaluating Sequential Methotrexate and Fluorouracil in the Treatment of Patients with Node-Negative Breast Cancer Who Have Estrogen-Receptor-Negative Tumors,* 320 New Eng. J. Med. 473 (1989); B. Fisher et al., *A Randomized Clinical Trial Evaluating Tamoxifen in the Treatment of Patients with Node-Negative Breast Cancer Who Have Estrogen-Receptor-Positive Tumors,* 320 New Eng. J. Med. 479 (1989); E.G. Mansour et al., *Efficacy of Adjuvant Chemotherapy in High-Risk Node-Negative Breast Cancer: An Intergroup Study,* 320 New Eng. J. Med. 485 (1989).

The presence of axillary lymph node metastases (Stage II) is a poor prognostic factor. Neoadjuvant preoperative chemotherapy can be utilized to reduce tumor size to allow breast conservation surgical procedures. If patients have favorable histology or if tumors are diploid with a low S phase, the option for no adjuvant therapy may exist. In patients with estrogen receptor positive tumors, tamoxifen alone or in combination with chemotherapy prolongs disease-free survival. If the neoplasm is estrogen receptor negative, an effective chemotherapy regimen should be administered.

Stage III breast cancer can be either operable (Stage III A) or inoperable (Stage III B) from locally advanced disease. Sequential therapy frequently includes surgery, radiation therapy, and chemotherapy. Combination chemotherapy with or without hormonal therapy is indicated because of the high risk of recurrence.

Multiagent therapy includes the following:

1. Cyclophosphamide, methotrexate, and 5-fluorouracil (CMF)
2. Cyclophosphamide, doxorubicin, and 5-fluorouracil (CAF)
3. Cyclophosphamide, methotrexate, 5-fluorouracil, and prednisone (CMFP)
4. Cyclophosphamide, methotrexate, 5-fluorouracil, vincristine, and prednisone (CMFVP)
5. Cyclophosphamide and doxorubicin (CA)
6. Melphalan and 5-fluorouracil
7. Melphalan, 5-fluorouracil, and prednisone.

Doxorubicin is potentially cardiotoxic, a factor to consider in selecting chemotherapeutic agents for any particular patient. Bispiperazinedione (ICRF-187) can have a protective effect against the cardiotoxicity of doxorubicin.[72] Continuous infusion of doxorubicin also can reduce cardiotoxicity.[73]

Stage IV (metastatic) breast cancer and inflammatory breast cancer are responsive to the same chemotherapy regimens used for Stage III.

§ 9.10   Hormone Therapy

Breast cancer can respond to both additive or ablative hormone therapy. Patients with negative estrogen receptors are less likely to respond to hormone manipulation than patients with positive hormone receptors. Tamoxifen, oophorectomy,

---

[72] J.L. Speyer et al., *Protective Effect of the Bispiperazinedione ICRF-187 Against Doxorabicin-Induced Cardiac Toxicity in Women with Advanced Breast Cancer,* 319 New Eng. J. Med. 745 (1988).

[73] G.N. Hortobayi et al., *Decreased Cardiac Toxicity of Doxorubicin Administered by Continuous Intravenous Infusion in Combination Chemotherapy for Metastatic Breast Carcinoma,* 63 Cancer 37 (1989).

progestins, aminoglutethimide, estrogens, adrenalectomy, and hypophysectomy have shown equivalent responses. Adrenalectomy and hypophysectomy are associated with the most side effects.

In premenopausal and postmenopausal patients, tamoxifen is the treatment of choice. As adjuvant therapy, tamoxifen is administered at a dose of 10 mg twice daily for at least two years and usually up to five years if there is no recurrence. It is questionable if there is an increased incidence of endometrial carcinoma in patients receiving tamoxifen.[74] Ovarian ablation can be utilized in premenopausal patients with metastatic breast cancer.

Premenopausal patients, after response to tamoxifen, can be treated sequentially with oophorectomy, progestins, and then aminoglutethimide. Postmenopausal patients can be treated secondarily with progestins, aminoglutethimide, and then estrogens. Combination endocrine therapy has been utilized with tamoxifen and fluoxymesterone; tamoxifen with diethylstilbestrol; tamoxifen and aminoglutethimide; tamoxifen and medroxyprogesterone; and tamoxifen with aminoglutethimide and danazol.

Endocrine therapy can cause an exacerbation of symptoms from the cancer shortly after the onset of therapy, but these symptoms usually subside within a month. Pain or aching can occur in sites of known metastases, erythema or swelling can appear around skin or soft tissue lesions, hypercalcemia can occur, and the serum carcinoembryonic antigen (CEA) can transiently increase.

Luteinizing-hormone-releasing hormone (LHRH) analogues, buserelin and leuprolide, are presently being tested for breast cancer patients.[75]

§ 9.11   Radiation Therapy

Combinations of radiation and surgery have been used in treating breast neoplasms since the beginning of radiation therapy nearly a century ago. The trend today, whenever possible, is to preserve the breast with limited surgery followed by definitive radiation.

The curability of carcinoma of the breast with radiation alone decreases with the increasing size of the tumor. Consequently, when definitive radiation therapy is elected, a lumpectomy or other limited excision precedes radiation to increase the cure rate substantially. Among the factors playing a role in the choice of therapy is the size of the breast. In a large pendulous breast, the delivery of a larger amount of radiation for a tumor at a greater depth can result in fibrosis and a rather firm breast that detracts from a good cosmetic result. At the other

---

[74] M.A. Killackey et al., *Endometrial Adenocarcinoma in Breast Cancer Patients Receiving Antiestrogens,* 69 Cancer Treatment Rep. 237 (1985).

[75] R.D. Harvey et al., *Medical Castration Produced by the GrRH Analogue Leuprolide to Treat Metastatic Breast Cancer,* 3 J. Clinical Oncology 1068 (1985); J.G.M. Klijn & F.J. de Jong, *Treatment with a Leuteinising-Hormone-Releasing-Hormone Analogue,* 1 Lancet 1213 (1982).

extreme, the excision of a tumor from a very small breast can result in sufficient deformity that conservation of the breast with radiation offers no cosmetic advantage. It can be noted, however, that even in cases with a good proportion between the breast and the tumor, a poorly designed incision can contribute as much to an unsatisfactory cosmetic result as inadequate radiation. The lumpectomy-radiation regimen is not indicated when there is tumor invasion of the skin, fixation of the tumor to the chest wall, a tumor larger than 5 cm in diameter, or multiple tumor masses in the breast.

Surgical excision and radiation therapy are performed in noninvasive intraductal carcinoma and in lobular carcinoma in situ, although in the latter, this treatment is more controversial and has advocates for observation only. Radiotherapy is not contraindicated in the presence of extensive intraductal tumor, multiple microcalcifications, and subareolar locations.

Excision and radiation therapy are performed in Stage I and Stage II carcinomas. The addition of chemotherapy in Stage II and in high-risk Stage I cases is preferred in a sequential fashion. Normal tissue reaction can be severe with concurrent radiation and chemotherapy.

The technique of treatment involves irradiation of the entire breast through tangential fields to minimize irradiation of the lung and heart. The most homogeneous dose pattern is selected from computerized isodose plans obtained with various wedges placed in the radiation beam that modify the radiation absorption patterns in the breast. Five thousand cGy can be given with 4 to 6 meV X-rays over a period of five or six weeks. Treatment is given five times per week, using fractions not exceeding 200 cGy. A 1000-cGy boost may then be given to the site of the primary tumor in Stage I and II cancers. The boost can be given equally well with X-rays, electrons, or a radioactive implant. Some radiation oncologists do not give the boost if the tumor has been excised with clear margins. Others believe the boost is required because tumor cells that might be left in the scar, despite the clear margins, are hypoxic and more radioresistant.

A decision must be made about irradiation of the regional lymph nodes. Noninvasive carcinomas and Stage I carcinomas of the outer quadrants do not require irradiation of the lymph nodes. Stage I carcinomas that are centrally located or in the inner quadrants should have irradiation of the internal mammary and paraclavicular lymph nodes to 5000 cGy. The paraclavicular nodes are treated with a direct anterior field. The medial tangential breast field can be adjusted to include the internal mammary nodes, or these nodes can be treated with a direct 10 to 12 meV electron field.

Regardless of the quadrant of the breast involved, Stage II carcinomas with metastatic axillary lymph nodes receive radiation to the axillary apex, paraclavicular, and internal mammary lymph nodes. An outer quadrant Stage II carcinoma with a T2 tumor but no axillary metastases also can have lymph node irradiation.

Lumpectomy-radiation regimens require close follow-up with physical examination and mammograms to detect early local recurrences, because mastectomy is exceptionally successful in the treatment of early recurrences confined to the breast.

Definitive mastectomy as the treatment of choice is not followed routinely by radiation therapy. Radiation is indicated when there are significant risks of local and regional failure. These risks are a residual tumor, more than four metastatic axillary lymph nodes, lymphatic permeation of tumor in the breast, primary tumors in the 3 to 5 cm range, tumor invasion of the skin, tumor fixation to the chest wall, multiple primary tumors, and central and inner quadrant carcinomas.

The widespread belief that postmastectomy radiation does not increase survival or disease-free survival is contradicted by those who believe meticulous radiation therapy does both. In either case, the reduction in local and regional recurrence with radiation is well established and necessary for the psychological well-being of the patient. The most demoralizing metastases are the visible and palpable metastases on the chest wall. With radical surgery, the local-regional recurrence rate ranges from 15 to 40 percent in advanced operable tumors. Radiation to the subclinical metastases remaining after surgery reduces recurrences more than 90 percent.

Techniques of postoperative radiation are essentially the same as for lumpectomy. Irradiation of the chest wall consists of 5000 cGy through tangential fields. No boosts are necessary. A dose of 5000 cGy also is given to the paraclavicular and internal mammary lymph nodes. Chemotherapy usually follows mastectomy in cases with axillary metastases or high-risk primary tumors. The radiation is usually given after completion of the chemotherapy.

It is sometimes proposed that radiation be deferred until a local or regional recurrence develops so the radiation can be given only to those who need it. However, eradicating gross disease means higher doses, more complications, and less success. Such delay in radiation is not justified. In any medical treatment based on percentage phenomena, there is always an undefinable group of patients who might not have needed the treatment.

Preoperative radiation has generated good statistics, sometimes better than postoperative radiation, but it is not used much. Disease-free survivals have occurred in patients who received preoperative radiation for tumors of doubtful operability. This is the greatest advantage of preoperative radiation. The dosages range from 3500 to 5000 cGy to the breast and 4500 cGy to the regional nodes. The disadvantage of routine preoperative radiation is that regression of the tumor interferes with the pathologic assessment that would determine the future course of therapy. There also can be problems with healing of the surgical wound.

Stage IIIA carcinomas are treated surgically, then by radiation to the chest wall and all the regional lymph nodes, and finally with chemotherapy.

Stage IIIB carcinomas are given radiation to the breast and all the regional lymph nodes, and also are treated with chemotherapy. Surgery can be used to resect residual tumor.

The technique of radiation is similar to that used in lower stages, except that the boosts can carry the total dose in selected areas to 7000 cGy.

Inflammatory carcinoma is a Stage IIIB carcinoma with a notably poor prognosis, but disease-free intervals are being achieved with combinations of radiation and chemotherapy, and surgery when necessary. An advantageous radiation regimen is hyperfractionation, consisting of two 120 cGy treatments a day.

The role of radiation in Stage IV carcinomas is palliative. Radiation of 3000 to 4000 cGy in three to four weeks is especially effective in healing ulcerated tumors and relieving pain in bone metastases. The bone can recalcify and fracture can be avoided. Brain metastases can be treated with 4000 cGy over a five-week period of time.

In previously unirradiated cases, local or regional recurrences following mastectomy are given intensive radiation. Disease-free survivals are possible. Radiation should not be limited to the recurrence alone. The chest wall and the regional nodes should be irradiated to 5000 cGy and the area of recurrent tumor to 6000 cGy or more.

Axillary dissection and radiation sometimes result in edema of the arm. The patient must be aware of this possibility. Other aftereffects can be edema of the breast, fibrosis, tanning of the skin, telangiectasia, pneumonitis, and, occasionally, fracture of a rib. Using the large treatment fractions needed for three-times-a-week treatment regimens adds to the complications and is discouraged. The concurrent use of radiation and chemotherapy also adds to the incidence of complications.

§ 9.12   Treatment of Early-Stage Breast Cancer

In 1990, the National Institutes of Health (NIH) had a panel of experts evaluate the available scientific information in an attempt to resolve the safety and efficacy of issues related to biomedical technology.[76]

§ 9.13   Informed Consent: State Statutes

California Health and Safety Code

1704.5 Breast cancer; failure of physician and surgeon to warn patient of alternative methods of treatment; unprofessional conduct, standardized written summary.

---

[76]National Institutes of Health, *Treatment of Early-Stage Breast Cancer, in* 8(6) NIH Consensus Development Conference Consensus Statement (June 18–21, 1990) *reprinted in* 265 JAMA 371 (1991). See § **9.15.**

The failure of a physician and surgeon to inform a patient by means of a standardized written summary, as developed by the department on the recommendation of the Cancer Advisory Council, in layman's language and in a language understood by the patient of alternative efficacious methods of treatment which may be medically viable, including surgical, radiological, or chemotherapeutic treatments or combinations thereof, when the patient is being treated for any form of breast cancer constitutes unprofessional conduct within the meaning of Chapter 5 (commencing with Section 2000) of Division 2 of the Business and Professions Code.

A standardized written summary in layman's language and in a language understood by the patient, to be developed by the department on the recommendation of the Cancer Advisory Council and printed and made available by the Medical Board of California to physicians and surgeons, informing the patient of the advantages, disadvantages, risks and descriptions of the procedures with regard to medically viable and efficacious alternative methods of treatment, which is given to the patient shall constitute compliance with the requirements of this section.

Prior to performance of a biopsy, the physician and surgeon shall note on the patient's chart that he or she has given the patient the written summary required by this section.

Maine Revised Statutes Annotated

2905-A. (1989) Informed consent for breast cancer

1. Duty of physician. Notwithstanding section 2905, a physician who is administering the primary treatment for breast cancer shall inform the patient as provided in this section, orally and in writing, about alternative efficacious methods of treatment of breast cancer, including surgical, radiological or chemotherapeutic treatments or any other generally accepted medical treatment and the advantages, disadvantages and the usual and most frequent risks of each.

2. Written information. The duty to inform the patient in writing may be met by giving the patient a standardized written summary or brochure as described in subsections 3 and 4.

3. Standardized written summary. The standardized written summary may be developed by the Bureau of Health after consultation with the Cancer Advisory Committee.

4. Brochure. The brochure must be one which is approved or made available through the National Cancer Institute, the American Cancer Society, the American College of Surgeons or any other recognized professional organization approved by the Bureau of Health.

5. Signed form. A form, signed by the patient, indicating that the patient has been given the oral information required by this section and a copy of the brochure or the standardized written summary shall be included in the patient's medical records.

6. Extent of duty. A physician's duty to inform a patient under this section does not require disclosure of information beyond what a reasonably well-qualified physician licensed under Title 32 would know.

7. Actions barred. A patient who signs a form described in subsection 5 is barred from bringing a civil action against the physician, based on failure to obtain informed consent, but only in regard to information pertaining to alternative forms of treatment of breast cancer and the advantages, disadvantages, and risks of each method.

8. Application of this section to common law rights. Nothing in this section restricts or limits the rights of a patient under common law.

Pennsylvania Consolidated Statutes title 35

§ 5641. (1986) Consent for treatment of breast disease

Before a physician operates on a patient for a tumor of the breast a consent form shall have been executed with includes the following:

CONSENT FOR TREATMENT OF BREAST DISEASE

Sign option (a) or option (b), or option (a) and option (b).

(a) _____ Breast Biopsy Side (right or left)

_____

Patient's Signature

(b) If it is determined that I have a malignant tumor in my breast or other breast abnormality requiring surgery, then I authorize Dr _____ to perform such operations or procedures, including breast removal, which are deemed necessary. I have been informed of the current medically accepted alternatives to radical mastectomy.

Procedure:

_____

_____

Patient's Signature

§ 9.14   Commentary and Litigation

The most common litigation in cancer cases involves delay in diagnosing the breast cancer. A patient complaining of a lump in the breast should have a mammogram. However, the mammogram is inaccurate at least 20 percent of the time, with false negative and false positive results. Any dominant mass in the breast that persists more than two to four weeks should be biopsied, despite a negative mammogram. If biopsy is not recommended, the patient must be checked at regular, appropriate intervals.

Delay in diagnosing breast cancer is inevitable if the physician merely reassures the patient that the mass is benign. The patient should seek another opinion if the mass persists or gets larger, although whether the patient does so depends on her confidence in the physician and prior experience with delay in treatment.

Errors in pathologic examination of biopsy tissue and poorly taken or improperly interpreted mammograms can contribute to a missed diagnosis

Amsler v. Verrilli.[77]   In May 1980, the plaintiff discovered a lump in the left breast. Mammogram was performed and interpreted by the defendant and radiologist as negative. In October 1980, however, a modified radical mastectomy was performed for cancer of the breast. The plaintiff's radiologist expert stated in an affidavit that the defendant fell below the requisite standard of care by not examining the plaintiff and not taking adequate views on the X-rays. The court held that the affidavit failed to state that the departure from the standard of care caused the plaintiff's injuries, and therefore summary judgment for the defendant was affirmed.

Barenbrugge v. Rich.[78]   In February 1979, the plaintiff, complaining of pain and a lump in the left breast, was seen by Dr. Rich. The doctor detected a lump or thickening in the breast that she thought was normal tissue. The plaintiff was seen in July 1979 and January 1980 again because of pain and a lump in the left breast. The plaintiff was referred in January 1980 to Dr. Gunn, who noted that the left breast was 25 percent larger than the right breast, and that prominent veins were evident in the left breast. No mammogram was ordered. In May 1981, the plaintiff was examined by Dr. Rich and a suspicious mass noted in the left breast. Dr. Gunn biopsied a supraclavicular node in June 1981, which on frozen section was reported as benign, but on permanent sections was found to be malignant. Radical mastectomy was performed without benefit of the report on the permanent sections. The plaintiff's expert testified that her chance of cure in February 1979 would have been 95 percent and that her cancer could have been detected by mammography. Survival chances decreased with the passage of time until, by the date she was diagnosed, her prognosis was very grave. Dr. Gunn settled for $900,000 and the jury found Dr. Rich liable for $2,099,500. Judgment on the verdict was affirmed by the appeals court. The plaintiff died during the trial.

Beckcom v. United States.[79]   The decedent was 29 years old when seen by the defendant, Dr. Bloomberg, in November 1976 with complaints of thickening in the left breast and two lumps in the right breast. Dr. Bloomberg refused to allow the decedent to explain her history and failed to perform a visual examination of the breasts. Fibrocystic disease was diagnosed, and she was instructed to return in three months. She was examined in March 1977 for multiple breast lumps, including a hard lump in the right breast and nipple retraction. Dr. Bloomberg refused to order a mammogram and, after examination, concluded

---

[77] 119 A.D.2d 786, 501 N.Y.S.2d 41 (1986).

[78] 141 Ill. App. 3d. 1046, 490 N.E.2d 1368 (1986).

[79] 584 F. Supp. 1471 (N.D.N.Y. 1984).

that the lumps were cysts. She was instructed to return in six months. In July 1977, she was examined by a nurse practitioner, who noted in the records that there were no problems other than fibrocystic disease of the breast. The masses in the right breast increased in size and she began to experience pain. In October 1977, a general surgeon examined her and noted lumps in the right breast and right axilla. Biopsy showed cancer, and a right radical mastectomy was performed. In November 1977, a mammogram showed a dominant mass in the left breast and biopsy disclosed cancer. A subcutaneous mastectomy rather than radical mastectomy was performed because of the decedent's emotional state. She died in May 1988. The court, applying New York law, awarded $800,000 for the patient's conscious pain and suffering and $150,000 for the husband's loss of consortium, based on the doctor's failure to take an adequate history, to examine properly, to follow up at appropriate intervals of time, and to biopsy or perform mammograms.

Bullock v. Newman.[80]   There was an 87-day delay between the time the physician learned of the patient's breast cancer and the time he actually notified her so that treatment could begin. In January 1982, the plaintiff saw the defendant for bleeding from the nipple of her left breast. Mammogram results were negative. Bleeding continued, associated with pain, and the plaintiff finally convinced the defendant to do a breast biopsy. The biopsy was performed on April 30, 1982. Despite a number of telephone calls, no diagnosis was forthcoming. Because of severe pain, the plaintiff insisted on being seen and on August 13, 1982, the defendant told her she had cancer. A modified radical mastectomy was performed. The court held that a genuine issue of fact existed as to whether the delay in notifying the patient and beginning treatment and thereby eliminating the pain amounted to a compensable injury.

Burke v. United States.[81]   The plaintiff was seen at the National Naval Medical Center in Bethesda, Maryland in April 1981, complaining of a lump in the left breast. The mass was 2 1/2 cm in diameter. A biopsy was performed and reported as benign. In November 1981, the patient noted enlargement of a residual mass, but after examination was reassured that it was fibrocystic disease. Because of breast and arm pain, she was again seen in September 1982. The mass had increased to 4 × 5 cm in diameter. A mammogram was suggestive of carcinoma. A biopsy showed cancer and a modified radical mastectomy was performed. Eight of 14 lymph nodes contained metastatic tumor. A review of the slides from the April 1981 biopsy disclosed infiltrating ductal carcinoma. Chemotherapy and radiation therapy were administered. Despite positive estrogen and progesterone receptors, the chance of recurrence was estimated to be 80 to 85 percent. If her cancerous condition had been properly diagnosed in April

---

[80]378 S.E.2d 562 (N.C. Ct. App. 1989).

[81]605 F. Supp. 981 (D. Md. 1985).

1981, there would have been a 90-percent chance of survival. Applying Maryland law, the court held that shortened life expectancy could be considered in determining the seriousness of the injury sustained and the physical and mental pain the plaintiff had suffered and would suffer in the future. Other factors to be considered in awarding damages include the effect such injuries have on the overall physical and mental health and well-being of the plaintiff in enjoyment of life during the plaintiff's lifetime, disfigurement, humiliation and embarrassment associated with such disfigurement, medical expenses, and loss of earnings.

Curier v. Mann.[82]   The defendant failed to biopsy a dominant mass in the plaintiff's breast and failed to initiate follow-up procedures. One year later, a biopsy showed cancer, and the malignancy had spread by metastasis to the ribs. The patient was deemed incurable with minimal chance of surviving five years. The defendant contended that palpation alone was an acceptable alternate method of practice, and that the plaintiff's failure to return for a scheduled follow-up visit was the sole cause of her unfortunate circumstances. A net verdict of $1.6 million reflected the plaintiff's negligence of 20 percent.

Daily v. Patt.[83]   An undisclosed settlement occurred from a missed diagnosis of breast cancer. In May 1982, the patient complained of a tender knot in her left breast. A physician examined her and recommended a repeat exam within two weeks and aspiration if no abatement of the symptoms occurred. The patient went to see the defendant, who obtained a mammogram that did not show a malignancy. No biopsy was done. The patient visited another physician in November 1982, and biopsy showed a malignancy. She ultimately died of breast cancer.

Danker v. Brubson.[84]   A lump was noted in the patient's breast in February 1985. A mammogram showed fibrocystic disease. The defendant saw the patient regularly until July 1985, when a biopsy showed cancer. The malignancy was found to have spread to the lymph nodes. Ultimately, the cancer spread throughout her body. The plaintiff contended that the mammogram is 80 to 90 percent accurate, and, if symptoms persist, a biopsy or referral to a specialist is indicated. It also was claimed that a timely diagnosis would have given the plaintiff an 80- to 90-percent chance of survival. The verdict was for $1.1 million.

---

[82] No. 85-6062 (Washoe County, Nev.), *reprinted in* 4 Med. Malpractice Verdicts, Settlements & Experts No. 11, at 18 (1988).

[83] No. Y 86-774 (D. Md.), *reprinted in* 4 Med. Malpractice Verdicts, Settlements & Experts No. 11, at 21 (1988).

[84] No. 3-37-86 (Knox Circuit, Tenn.), *reprinted in* 4 Med. Malpractice Verdicts, Settlements & Experts No. 1, at 29 (1988).

DeBurkarte v. Louvar.[85]   The plaintiff was first seen by the defendant in August 1981 for a lump in the breast. The mammogram ordered was negative for malignancy. The patient was examined multiple times until June 1982, when she finally was referred to a surgeon. Biopsy showed cancer and a mastectomy was performed. In June 1983, the cancer had spread to the bones. She was treated with radiotherapy and her ovaries were removed. The judgment was $405,000 for the patient and $40,000 for the husband's loss of consortium.

Fleming v. Wedd.[86]   In October 1984, the patient saw the defendant because of a lump in the breast. A diagnosis of fibrocystic disease was made without the benefit of a mammogram and the patient was not referred to a surgeon. Breast pain and arm pain occurred, and the patient was referred to an orthopedic surgeon and neurosurgeon, neither of whom examined the breast. The defendant treated the patient until May 1985, and the patient died of metastatic breast cancer in May 1986. Despite the contention by the defendant that the patient refused a mammogram, $282,592.28 was awarded.

Friedman v. Radiology Group, PC.[87]   A routine mammogram was performed in April 1984 and again in April 1985. Both were interpreted as normal by the radiology group. In June 1985, a mammogram was done at another facility and found to be suspicious for malignancy. Biopsy showed a cancer, and two of twelve nodes were found positive after mastectomy. Radiation therapy and tamoxifen were given. The plaintiff's expert indicated that the 1984 mamogram was improperly read, because a carcinoma actually existed. The tumor had increased from 1.5 cm in 1984 to 2.0 cm in 1985. Settlement for $200,000 resulted.

Geary v. Aratow.[88]   In January 1985, the plaintiff was examined by the defendant, who performed a pelvic and breast examination. She started estrogen therapy, even though there was no indication of an estrogen deficiency. In March 1986, the patient found a 6-cm mass in her breast, and a radical mastectomy was performed for cancer of the breast involving one lymph node. The plaintiff claimed that the defendant failed to adequately examine her breasts and failed to perform a mammogram. There was a $200,000 settlement.

---

[85] 393 N.W.2d 131 (Iowa 1986).

[86] No. 1137-86 (Chesterfield Circuit, Va.), *reprinted in* 4 Med. Malpractice Verdicts, Settlements & Experts No. 1, at 19 (1988).

[87] Civ. No. 86 311242NM (Oakland County, Mich. July 17, 1987), *reprinted in* 3 Med. Malpractice Verdicts, Settlements & Experts No. 9, at 54 (1987).

[88] No. WEC 112450 (Santa Monica, Cal.), *reprinted in* 4 Med. Malpractice Verdicts, Settlements & Experts No. 8, at 17 (1988).

Green v. Goldbert.[89]   There was a directed verdict for the defendant on the wrongful death action for delayed diagnosis of breast cancer. The plaintiff was examined by the defendant for complaints of small, painful lumps. After a negative examination and a negative mammogram, the patient was told to return in three months. At reexamination, the lumps had increased in size. Biopsy showed cancer, and a modified radical mastectomy was performed.

Ippolito v. HIP of Greater New York.[90]   A 48-year-old mother of five was found to have a breast lump. A mammogram showed no evidence of malignancy. Although the written report advised that a biopsy be performed, the defendant physician claimed that he had received a phone report, but no written report. He advised the patient that the lump was benign and to return in three to four months. Five months later, a biopsy revealed a malignancy. Brain metastases had developed by the time of trial. The plaintiff patient was awarded $1.5 million and her spouse $600,000 for loss of services. The liability was divided: 65 percent to the physician and 35 percent to the hospital.

Johnson v. Kaiser Georgetown Community Health Plan, Inc.[91]   The patient was seen by the defendant in June 1984 for discomfort in the left breast. Mammograms showed fibrocystic disease. In December 1984, the patient returned because of a lump in the right breast. The patient complained of tenderness of the right breast in January 1985, and then tenderness under the right arm in March 1985. Mammograms in April 1985 showed a lesion suspicious for carcinoma. Surgery in May 1985 disclosed cancer of the breast that had spread to other parts of the body. The patient was given chemotherapy. Because of the loss of chance of survival, there was a settlement of $350,000.

Katz v. Tischler.[92]   There was a defense verdict, despite a failure to diagnose breast cancer. The patient was examined by the defendant in August 1983, and a mass palpated in the left breast. Mammograms were obtained, and the lump diagnosed as benign. In November 1984, the mass had grown and the patient again saw the defendant. Further mammograms were obtained and the lump was diagnosed as benign. When the plaintiff sought the services of another physician, a mastectomy was done for breast cancer. The plaintiff claimed that because the defendant had failed to seek a second opinion and had failed to

---

[89] No. 85-1189 (Palm Beach County, Fla.), *reprinted in* 4 Med. Malpractice Verdicts, Settlements & Experts No. 11, at 18–19 (1988).

[90] No. 8704/82 (Queens Sup. Ct., N.Y.), *reprinted in* 2 Med. Malpractice Verdicts, Settlements & Experts No. 8, at 8 (1986).

[91] No. 6181-86 (D.C. Super. Ct. Feb. 1988), *reprinted in* 4 Med. Malpractice Verdicts, Settlements & Experts No. 7, at 14 (1988).

[92] No. 86-CV-3060 (E.D.N.Y.), *reprinted in* 4 Med. Malpractice Verdicts, Settlements & Experts No. 11, at 16 (1988).

perform further diagnostic tests, such as aspiration or biopsy and pathologic examination of the tissues, she suffered permanent injury and her survival chances were lessened.

***Ouzounian v Varakian.*[93]**　　The 32-year-old plaintiff consulted the defendant for a small lump in the breast in April 1984. No mammogram or biopsy was done. The physician told the plaintiff she had nothing to worry about. Eleven months later, when the lump in the breast had grown, she consulted the defendant, who referred her to a surgeon. Breast cancer was diagnosed and the patient underwent a radical mastectomy. Chemotherapy was given postoperatively for one year. The case was settled for $415,000, which included $15,000 punitive damages assessed to the defendant.

***Perry v. Northwest Suburban Gynecological Associates.*[94]**　　Plaintiff's decedent complained of a lump in the breast while nursing after delivery. A mammogram was done but was difficult to read. The lump got larger, but the defendant told her not to worry because it was only a galactocele. Almost four months later, an inflammatory breast carcinoma was diagnosed and the patient ultimately died. The case was settled for $975,000.

***Powell v. Erickson.*[95]**　　The plaintiff was examined in 1982, and two mammograms were ordered. One mammogram was incorrectly read by the radiologist and one was misread by the rheumatologist consultant. The patient died of metastatic breast cancer. The radiologist and the consultant settled, paying $50,000 each.

***Roach v. United States.*[96]**　　A claim of loss of chance resulted in a $195,000 settlement. In April 1983, the plaintiff had a breast cancer treated by mastectomy. She complained to the defendant of pain in her low back and hip area, and in November 1985 a bone scan came back as abnormal, showing increased uptake in the sacroiliac area. In June 1986, a CEA level was finally taken, and was slightly elevated at 13.4. A repeat bone scan in July 1986 was abnormal. All of this indicated a recurrence of the malignancy. Treatment was started when the patient consulted another physician after November 1986. The defendant maintained that an earlier diagnosis would not have made any difference in the course

[93] No. C574,425 (L.A. County), *reprinted in* 4 Med. Malpractice Verdicts, Settlements & Experts No. 11, at 14 (1988).

[94] No. 85-L-11633 (Cook County, Ill.), *reprinted in* 4 Med. Malpractice Verdicts, Settlements & Experts No. 9, at 22 (1988).

[95] No. 85-2-07262-1 (Pierce Super. Ct., Wash.), *reprinted in* 4 Med. Malpractice Verdicts, Settlements & Experts No. 1, at 20 (1988).

[96] No. EP-87-CIV AC-214 (W.D. Tex. Mar. 1988), *reprinted in* 4 Med. Malpractice Verdicts, Settlements & Experts No. 11, at 20 (1988).

of the disease. The plaintiff alleged failure to diagnose and treat the cancer and claimed loss of chance of survival.

Schriftman v. Jaurigue.[97]   A xeromammogram was negative when ordered in August 1984 for a mass in the left breast. The defendant informed the patient she had fibrocystic disease and should be monitored by semiannual checkups. In November 1984, there was a visible lump the size of a walnut in the left breast. A biopsy was performed in March 1985 and showed cancer, which ultimately metastasized. The settlement was for $675,000.

Wolchok v. Buckman.[98]   An action alleging failure to diagnose a breast cancer resulted in a defense verdict. The patient had been treated for fibrocystic disease for years, and when seen by the defendant in March 1977, a diagnosis of cyst was made, but no mammogram was ordered. Cancer was diagnosed in July 1977 and a modified radical mastectomy performed. The defendant contended that, even if cancer had been diagnosed in March 1977, a mastectomy would have been the treatment of choice, not lumpectomy.

§ 9.15   NIH Consensus Development Conference Consensus Statement (June 1990)

Introduction

Carcinoma of the breast is the most common malignancy in women in the United States. As a cause of cancer death in women, breast cancer is exceeded only by lung cancer. The incidence of breast cancer has been rising steadily over the past decade. In the 1990's, more than 1.5 million women will be newly diagnosed with this disease; nearly 30 percent of these women will ultimately die from breast cancer. The increased number of reported cases may be partially attributable to their detection following more widespread use of screening mammography. Most of the increase has been in patients with smaller primary breast tumors. In 1982, approximately 12,000 women were diagnosed with tumors less than 2 centimeters in diameter and negative axillary lymph nodes. That number had risen to 32,000 by 1986. For those patients with axillary node positive breast cancer, there has been a less dramatic increase in tumors less than 2 centimeters (3,000 in 1982 to 7,000 in 1986) while there has been a decrease in the number presenting with tumors larger than 5 centimeters. Of the 150,000 new patients diagnosed with invasive breast cancer in 1990, 75 to 80 percent will have clinical Stage I or II disease, and approximately two-thirds of these will have no involvement of the axillary lymph nodes.

---

[97] No. 8510-3790 (Pa. C.P. Phila. County Jan. 15, 1987), *reprinted in* 4 Med. Malpractice Verdicts, Settlements & Experts No. 1, at 22 (1988).

[98] No. 549-80 (N.Y.), *reprinted in* 4 Med. Malpractice Verdicts, Settlements & Experts No. 1, at 19 (1988).

Traditional concepts through most of the 20th century held that breast cancer was a local/regional disease best managed by radical mastectomy. Over the past 20 years, there have been several clinical trials worldwide that have compared less extensive breast resections with standard radical mastectomy. These have included comparisons of total mastectomy (with and without radiation therapy of axillary lymph node dissection) with radical mastectomy. Subsequent studies have compared different approaches to breast conservation surgery with total mastectomy. At present, breast conservation therapy is used in a minority of patients. The appropriate use of breast conservation involves a variety of clinical, biological, and psychosocial factors that merit public debate.

Adjuvant therapy has become the standard of care for the majority of breast cancer patients with axillary lymph node involvement. More recently, several randomized trials from North America and Europe have shown an improvement in disease-free survival for node negative breast cancer patients receiving adjuvant therapy.

Absence of metastasis to the axillary lymph nodes has traditionally been considered a favorable biologic condition for patients with invasive breast cancer. However, all patients with node negative breast cancer are at risk for disease recurrence. Intensive efforts to define individual patient's risk of recurrence have produced a plethora of potential prognostic factors, from patient characteristics to histologic, biochemical, and molecular characteristics of the tumor. The importance of these various prognostic factors has been the subject of controversy.

To evaluate the developing results of breast conservation, adjuvant therapy of node negative breast cancer, and clinical prognostic factors, the National Cancer Institute and the Office of Medical Applications of Research of the National Institutes of Health convened a Consensus Development Conference on the Treatment of Early-Stage Breast Cancer on June 18–21, 1990.

After 2 days of presentations by experts and discussion by the audience, a consensus panel drawn from specialists and generalists from the medical profession and related scientific disciplines, clinical investigators, methodologists, and public representatives considered the evidence and agreed on answers to the following key questions:

What are the roles of mastectomy versus breast conservation in the treatment of early-stage breast cancer?

What are the optimal techniques for breast conservation?

What is the role of adjuvant therapy for patients with node negative breast cancer?

How should prognostic factors be used in the management of node negative breast cancer?

What are the directions for future research?

What are the Roles of Mastectomy Versus Breast Conservation in the Treatment of Early-Stage Breast Cancer?

Breast conservation treatment (also referred to as lumpectomy, segmental mastectomy, or partial mastectomy) is an appropriate method of primary therapy for the majority of women with Stage I and II breast cancer and is preferable because it provides survival equivalent to total mastectomy and axillary dissection while preserving the breast.

In general, primary therapy for Stage I and II breast cancer consists of breast conservation treatment or total mastectomy. Breast conservation treatment is defined as excision of the primary tumor and adjacent breast tissue, followed by radiation therapy. Total mastectomy is an appropriate primary therapy when breast conservation treatment is not indicated or selected. Both surgical therapies are accompanied by axillary dissection, which provides important prognostic information.

Prospective randomized trials comparing breast conservation treatment with total mastectomy with maximum followup of 17 years have demonstrated equivalent results as measured by overall patient survival. Important considerations in the choice of therapy for women with Stage I and II breast cancer include clinical criteria, factors that influence local/regional tumor control, cosmetic results, psychosocial issues and patient preferences for treatment method.

Patient Selection

In the selection of women for breast conservation treatment or mastectomy, certain women are not candidates for breast conservation treatment:

Women with multicentric breast malignancies, including those with gross multifocal disease or diffuse microcalcifications detected by mammography.

Patients for whom breast conservation treatment would produce an unacceptable cosmetic result. Examples include women whose tumors are large relative to breast size and those with certain collagen vascular disease.

Certain pathologic and clinical factors may influence treatment selection because of their potentially adverse impact on local recurrence after breast conservation treatment. Controversy exists about these factors, examples of which include the presence of extensive intraductal carcinoma within and adjacent to the primary tumor, extensive lymphatic involvement and young age (under 35–39 years). Prospective studies comparing primary therapies have included women whose primary tumors were usually less than or equal to 4 centimeters in diameter.

Local Control

Local control is a major goal of breast conservation treatment. The incidence of local recurrence is low in appropriately selected patients receiving optimal breast conservation treatment. Results of randomized trials have suggested that the use of adjuvant chemotherapy or hormonal therapy further reduces the rate of local recurrence after breast conservation treatment.

Cosmetic Result

A goal of primary breast cancer treatment is to produce the best cosmetic result consistent with achievement of local/regional control. In clinical trials, the majority of patients achieve good to excellent cosmetic results after breast conservation treatment. Optimal long-term results require integration of careful surgical excision and precise radiotherapy techniques. When mastectomy is indicated or selected, breast reconstruction should be considered to improve the cosmetic result.

Psychosocial Factors

Women should be educated about treatment choices and clinical trial options in order to make an informed decision in consultation with their physicians. A variety of factors have a major influence on a woman's choice of primary therapy. These include logistic and emotional considerations, personal financial issues, and proximity and access to appropriate medical care. A woman's body image and her beliefs and concerns may determine her preference for breast conservation treatment or mastectomy.

What are the Optimal Techniques for Breast Conservation?

The objective of breast conservation is to obtain a high probability of local control, with survival at least equivalent to that obtained with total mastectomy and axillary dissection, combined with maximal cosmetic results and maintenance of normal function. The most widely used treatment that achieves these goals is the combination of local surgical excision, axillary dissection, and postoperative radiation therapy. Although this treatment approach produces survival equivalent to mastectomy, with a high likelihood of good cosmesis and function, further studies are required to refine certain treatment details. The following recommendations define the treatment details deemed optimal based on the available data.

Surgical Recommendations

The diagnosis should be established by fine needle aspiration cytology, limited incisional biopsy (particularly for larger lesions,), or definitive wide local excision.

The type and placement of incisions can influence greatly the quality of cosmesis. Arcuate incisions with thick flaps, centered over the lesion, are superior to radial incisions, particularly for upper quadrant lesions. Routine excision of overlying skin is unnecessary except for very superficial lesions. Careful hemostasis is essential and drains are rarely necessary. In most instances, suture reapproximation of mammary tissue should be avoided.

It is appropriate to excise the primary lesion with a normal tissue margin of approximately 1 centimeter. The intent of the recommendation is to achieve a surgical margin that is grossly and microscopically uninvolved with tumor. To obtain adequate pathological evaluation, it is necessary to mark the specimen for proper orientation and to ink the resection margins. When margins are grossly involved with tumor, further resection is indicated. Available data are inadequate to determine whether focal microscopic involvement of a margin increases the risk of local failure after optimal radiation therapy. Because cosmetic result is related to the amount of tissue excised, unnecessary wide margins (>2 cm) should be avoided.

Because nodal status is the most important available prognostic factor, a Level I–II axillary dissection should be routine both for staging and for prevention of axillary recurrence. Separate incisions should usually be employed for the primary tumor excision and the axillary dissection to enhance functional and cosmetic results.

Radiation Therapy Recommendations

Megavoltage radiation therapy to the whole breast (to a dose of 4,500 to 5,000 cGy per fraction) should be routinely used. Boost irradiation has been used in the majority of trials to date. However, the precise indications are not well defined. In the reported trials, the patients with focal microscopic involvement of margins have been treated with boost irradiation or mastectomy. There are no current data to support lesser treatment for these patients. Treatment planning should be done to minimize radiation exposure to lung and heart and to achieve uniform dosage to the treatment volume. Boost irradiation should be delivered by electron beam or implantation to doses of 1,000 to 1,500 cGy. Higher doses produce a greater incidence of cosmetic impairment.

If a Level I–II axillary dissection has been performed, axillary nodal irradiation is not routinely indicated.

No data indicate any increased risk of secondary malignancies or contralateral breast cancers resulting from breast irradiation. Longer follow up of this population is necessary to resolve this issue fully.

Although local control can be obtained in some patients with local excision alone, no subgroups have been identified in which radiation therapy can be avoided.

In patients receiving adjuvant chemotherapy, no precise recommendations regarding the sequence and timing of radiation therapy and chemotherapy can be made. A small percentage of patients will develop a local recurrence following breast conservation therapy. Total mastectomy is effective salvage therapy for a substantial percentage of these patients. This is in contrast to the poor prognosis associated with local chest wall recurrence following mastectomy. Hence, in patients treated with breast conservation, long-term careful breast monitoring with physical examination and mammography is essential for early detection and treatment of local recurrence.

What is the Role of Adjuvant Therapy for Patients with Node Negative Breast Cancer?

The majority of patients with node negative breast cancer are cured by breast conservation treatment or total mastectomy and axillary dissection.

There is clear evidence that the rate of local and distant recurrence is decreased by both adjuvant combination cytotoxic chemotherapy and by adjuvant tamoxifen.

Data from the 10 randomized trials reviewed show that adjuvant systemic therapy reduces the rate of recurrence by approximately one-third, with a broad range. For example, among a group of women with a 30 percent risk of recurrence adjuvant therapy would decrease that risk to about 20 percent. The role of these treatments in improving overall survival and other important parameters such as quality of life is still being defined.

The completed studies are not large enough, nor is the followup long enough, to estimate with acceptable precision the interactions between menopausal status or steroid receptor positivity and the effects of adjuvant therapy in node negative patients. Although all patient subsets experience lower rates of recurrence, relatively few patients with estrogen receptor-negative tumors have been included in tamoxifen studies. At the present time, reduced mortality is seen in nearly all trials but is not statistically significant in most. However, the rate of death in node negative patients is low, so a clinically important reduction in mortality may require a long followup to achieve statistical significance.

For chemotherapy, more benefit is seen in trials in which antimetabolites (methotrexate and 5-fluorouracil) are administered intravenously than in trials in which they are given orally. For tamoxifen, studies using the drug for more than 2 years (usually 5 years) seem to result in greater reductions in the rate of recurrence than studies using shorter courses.

In prospective studies in node negative patients, tamoxifen reduces the clinical incidence of contralateral primary breast cancer. The overall benefits from tamoxifen in postmenopausal patients clearly outweigh any toxicities currently described. In premenopausal patients, the administration of tamoxifen may cause endocrine abnormalities with uncertain long-term consequences. Although there does not appear to be an excess number of cases of endometrial carcinoma in tamoxifen-treated premenopausal patients, the followup durations are too short to predict confidently whether or not this will occur. The influence of tamoxifen on the developing fetus is unknown. There are no data now available concerning the effects of combination chemotherapy plus tamoxifen in node negative patients. Trials addressing this issue are under way.

Recommendations

The many unanswered questions in the adjuvant systemic treatment of node negative breast cancer make it imperative that all patients who are candidates for clinical trials be offered the opportunity to participate.

The following recommendations apply only to patients who are not candidates for such trials or who refuse participation.

All node negative patients should be made aware of the benefits and risks of adjuvant systemic therapy. The decision to use adjuvant treatment should follow a thorough discussion with the patient regarding the likely risk of recurrence without adjuvant therapy, the expected reduction in risk with adjuvant therapy, toxicities of therapy and its impact on quality of life. Some degrees of improvement may be so small that they are outweighed by the disadvantages of therapy.

Adjuvant therapy should consist of either combination chemotherapy or tamoxifen (20 mg/day for at least 2 years).

No completed studies have directly compared tamoxifen with chemotherapy (with or without tamoxifen) in node negative patients. Tamoxifen has less acute toxicity than chemotherapy, but no statement is possible regarding chronic toxicity or comparative efficacy. The results of current and future trials concerning the safety of tamoxifen in premenopausal patients must be followed carefully.

How Should Prognostic Factors Be Used in the Management of Node Negative Breast Cancer?

Prognostic factors should be used to provide an estimate of risk of recurrence in women with early-stage breast cancer. Although no individual patient can be assured that she has no risk of recurrence, the majority of women will be cured with local/regional therapy.

A useful prognostic factor has the following characteristics:

It has significant and independent predictive value that has been validated by clinical testing.

Its determination must be feasible, reproducible, and widely available, with quality control.

It must be readily interpretable by the clinician and have therapeutic implications.

Prognostic Factors

Tumor Size. There is a strong correlation between tumor size and risk of recurrence. Even within the T-1 category, there is variation in risk. Tumors less than or equal to 1 centimeter have a particularly good prognosis (e.g., <10 percent recurrence at 10 years) relative to tumors 1.1 to 2 centimeters in diameter. In general, the risk of recurrence increases with increasing tumor size. The pathologist should perform a careful gross examination with documentation of tumor size.

Estrogen and Progesterone Receptors Status. Patients with receptor-positive tumors have a better prognosis than those with receptor-negative tumors. However, the difference in recurrence rates at 5 years is only 8 to 10 percent.

Nuclear Grade. This is a well-documented factor. When determined by experienced pathologists, it discriminates favorable and unfavorable prognostic groups. High nuclear grade is associated with a higher rate of recurrence. Nuclear grade is not currently part of the routine pathologic review of breast cancer specimens. The pathology community should adopt a uniform grading system and routinely use this discriminant.

Histologic Type. Several well-characterized histologic subtypes impart a favorable prognosis, although they are a distinct minority of all breast cancer cases. These subtypes include tubular, colloid (mucinous), and papillary types.

Proliferative Rate. Measurements of cellular proliferation in breast cancer specimens using a variety of techniques have shown a strong correlation with outcome. DNA flow cytometry has become widely available for the determination of S-phase fraction as well as ploidy status. S-phase fraction does correlate with prognosis, but ploidy status alone is not of clear prognostic value. Up to 25 percent of specimens are not evaluable by flow cytometry because of methodologic problems. Because of the complexity of the technology, quality control is especially critical. Although S-phase fraction has been shown to be an independent prognostic factor in some studies, its clinical value is being defined.

Other Factors. High levels of the protease cathepsin D are associated with an unfavorable prognosis. Data for HER-2/neu, epidermal growth factor receptor, and stress-response (heat shock) proteins are of interest, but further investigation is required before reaching any conclusion about their clinical value.

Estimating Individual Risk

Currently available prognostic factors are associated with a broad range of risk of recurrence in node negative breast cancer patients. There are extremes of high and low risk where it is possible to make recommendations about adjuvant systemic therapy. For example, outside of clinical trials, it is reasonable not to treat patients with tumors less than or equal to 1 cm in diameter because their chance of recurrence is less than 10 percent at 10 years. With increasing tumor diameter, other prognostic factors should be weighted in the decision to use adjuvant treatment. A major goal is the development of risk profile systems with sufficient accuracy and reproducibility to estimate prognosis in the individual patient.

What are the Directions for Future Research?

To refine existing prognostic factors by:

—reassessing the predictive value of the tumor categories in the American Joint Committee on Cancer Tumor/Node/Metastasis staging system.

—standardizing a nuclear grading system.

—exploring relationships between individual prognostic factors and resistance to systemic therapy.

—developing and using new and existing tissue and clinical data banks for the study of prognostic factors.

To develop risk factor profile systems with sufficient accuracy and reproducibility allow identification of subgroups that:

—may be treated with surgical excision without irradiation.

—do not require axillary node dissection.

—do not require systemic therapy.

To improve systemic chemotherapy regimens through:

—investigation of dose intensity, timing and duration.

—introduction of new agents.

—evaluation of chemotherapy and hormonal therapy combinations.

—evaluation of preoperative (neoadjuvant) chemotherapy.

To gather further data concerning tamoxifen, including:

—safety of prolonged use in premenopausal patients,

—optimal duration of therapy.

—efficacy in patients with steroid receptor-negative tumors.

—comparison and combination with gonadotropin-releasing hormone agonists.

To assess quality-of-life parameters in future clinical trials.

To determine the optimal margin for local primary excision in the presence and absence of extensive intraductal cancer.

To determine whether boost irradiation is required in patients with pathologically negative margins and whether boost irradiation produces a high probability of local control in patients with microscopic involvement of margins.

To determine the optimal sequence and timing for radiation therapy and systemic adjuvant therapy.

Conclusions and Recommendations

Breast conservation treatment is an appropriate method of primary therapy for the majority of women with Stage I and II breast cancer and is preferable because it provides survival equivalent to total mastectomy and axillary dissection while preserving the breast.

The recommended technique for breast conservation treatment includes:

—local excision of primary tumor with clear margins

—Level I–II axillary node dissection

—breast irradiation to 4,500–5,000 cGy with or without a boost

The many unanswered questions in the adjuvant systemic treatment of node negative breast cancer make it imperative that all patients who are candidates for clinical trials be offered the opportunity to participate.

The majority of patients with node negative breast cancer are cured by breast conservation treatment or total mastectomy and axillary dissection.

The rate of local and distant recurrence following local therapy for node negative breast cancer is decreased by both adjuvant combination cytotoxic chemotherapy and by adjuvant tamoxifen. The decision to use adjuvant treatment should follow a thorough discussion with the patient regarding the likely risk of recurrence without adjuvant therapy, the expected reduction in risk with adjuvant therapy, toxicities of therapy, and its impact on quality of life.

While all node negative patients have some risk for recurrence, patients with tumors less than or equal to 1 centimeter have an excellent prognosis and do not require adjuvant systemic therapy outside of clinical trials.

CHAPTER 10

GASTROINTESTINAL NEOPLASMS

ESOPHAGUS

§ 10.1   Staging and Classification

TNM: American Joint Committee on Cancer.[1]

The depth of invasion of esophageal cancer is of prognostic significance, as is the presence of nodal involvement, invasion of contiguous structures, or distant metastases. T1 lesions invade the lamina propria, T2 lesions invade the muscularis propria, T3 lesions invade adventitia, and T4 lesions invade adjacent structures.

The histologic type is squamous cell carcinoma or adenocarcinoma.

---

[1] American Joint Committee on Cancer, Manual for Staging of Cancer 64 (3d ed. 1988).

Histopathology of Esophageal Tumors[2]

Benign

    Leiomyoma

    Polyp

    Lipoma

    Hemangioma

    Fibroma

    Papilloma

    Adenoma

    Neurofibroma

    Cyst

    Inclusion cyst

    Retention cyst (mucocele)

    Duplication cyst

Malignant

    Squamous cell carcinoma

    Adenocarcinoma

    Adenoacanthoma

    Mucoepidermoid carcinoma

    Malignant melanoma

    Leiomyosarcoma

    Rhabdomyosarcoma

    Carcinosarcoma.

---

[2] S.C. Ming, *Tumors of the Esophagus and Stomach, in* Atlas of Tumor Pathology 17 (1982).

§ 10.2   Etiology

Alcohol

There is an increased risk of esophageal cancer in patients with heavy alcohol intake[3] or occupational exposure to alcohol.[4] Ethanol injures the esophageal mucosa and, when associated with nutritional deficiency, which causes damage to mucosal integrity, enzymatic and metabolic cellular dysfunction, and immunosuppression, it can act as a cocarcinogen.[5]

Tobacco

Tobacco is a known carcinogen and has been associated with esophageal cancer, especially in areas where the residue is chewed, such as South Africa and India.[6] In combination with alcohol, smoking tobacco increases the risk of esophageal carcinoma.[7]

Opium

Smoking opium is associated with a high risk of esophageal malignancy, and this incidence is dose-related.[8] The products of opium pyrolysis are mitogenic.

Diet

Diet has been implicated as a causative factor in the development of esophageal cancer.[9] Nitrosammes, such as N-nitro-N-methylbenzylamine, sodium nitrate, and diethyl nitrosamine, experimentally cause esophageal malignancies in animals. N-nitro compounds are formed by the breakdown of ingested nitrates that

---

[3] T. Hirayama, *Diet and Cancer,* 1 Nutrition Cancer 67 (1979); A.J. Tuyns et al., *Esophageal Cancer and Alcohol Consumption: Importance of Type of Beverage,* 23 Int'l J. Cancer 443 (1979).

[4] E.L. Wynder & I.J. Bross, *A Study of Etiological Factors in Cancers of the Esophagus,* 14 Cancer 389 (1961).

[5] D. Schottenfeld, *Alcohol as a Cofactor in the Etiology of Cancer,* 43 Cancer 1962 (1979).

[6] D.J. Jussawalla, *Epidemiological Assessment of Aetiology of Esophageal Cancer in Greater Bombay, in* International Seminar on Epidemiology of Esophageal Cancer 20, Bangalore, India (Monograph No. 1 1971).

[7] E.L. Wynder & I.J. Bross, *A Study of Etiological Factors in Cancers of the Esophagus,* 14 Cancer 389 (1961).

[8] T. Hewer et al., *Ingested Mutagens from Opium and Tobacco Pyrolysis Products and Cancer of the Oesophagus,* 2 Lancet 494 (1978); J. Kmet, *Opium and Oesophageal Cancer in Iran,* 2 Lancet 1371 (1978).

[9] C.S. Yang, *Research on Esophageal Cancer in China: A Review,* 40 Cancer Res. 510 (1955).

are found at high levels in pickled vegetables and cured meats. Molybdenum deficiency in soil leads to increased amounts of nitrates in the crops. Zinc deficiency increases nitrosamine-induced esophageal cancer.[10]

Tylosis-Esophageal Cancer

Tylosis (*keratosis palmaris et plantaris*) consists of hyperkeratosis of the palms and soles and can be associated with squamous cell carcinoma. This syndrome is inherited as an autosomal dominant trait.[11] Some of these patients have oral leukoplakia.[12] There also can be an increased risk for esophageal cancer in spouses of these patients, suggesting exposure to common environmental factors.[13]

Plummer-Vinson Syndrome (sideropenic dysphagia, Paterson-Kelly syndrome)

The Plummer-Vinson syndrome is the association of sideropenia (iron deficiency) with dysphagia (difficulties swallowing). A hypochromic anemia can be present as well as riboflavin, thiamin, and pyridoxine deficiencies.[14] There is a high incidence of esophageal and hypopharyngeal cancer in this syndrome.[15]

Celiac Disease

Esophageal cancer has an increased incidence in patients with celiac disease,[16] which is a familial malabsorptive disorder of the small bowel. These patients

---

[10] L.Y.Y. Fong & P.M. Newberne, *Zinc Deficiency and Methylbenzylnitrosamine-Induced Esophageal Cancer in Rats*, 61 J. Nat'l Cancer Inst. 145 (1978).

[11] A.W. Howel-Evans et al., *Carcinoma of the Oesophagus with Keratosis Palmaris el Plantaris (Tylosis): A Study of Two Families*, 27 Q. J. Med. 413 (1958); S.I. Magalini & E. Serascia, Dictionary of Medical Syndromes 820 (1981).

[12] S.B. Ritter & G. Peterson, *Esophageal Cancer, Hyperkeratosis and Oral Leukoplakia: Occurrence in a 25-Year-Old Patient*, 235 JAMA 1723 (1976); W.R. Tyldesdley, *Oral Leukoplakia Associated with Tylosis and Oesophageal Carcinoma*, 3 J. Oral Pathology 62 (1974).

[13] S.N. Nasipov, *Esophageal Cancer Morbidity as Evidenced by the Genealogy of Patients Registered in the Guryev Province*, 23 Vop. Onkol. 81 (1977).

[14] A. Jacobs & I.A.J. Cavill, *Pyridoxine and Riboflavin Status in the Patterson-Kelly Syndrome*, 14 Brit. J. Haematology 153 (1968); E.L. Wynder et al., *Environmental Factors in Cancer of the Upper Alimentary Tract. A Swedish Study with Special Reference to Plummer-Vinson (Patterson-Kelly) Syndrome*, 10 Cancer 470 (1957).

[15] H.E. Ahlbom, *Simple Achlorhydric Anaemia, Plummer-Vinson Syndrome and Carcinoma of the Mouth, Pharynx and Oesophagus in Women*, 2 Brit. Med. J. 331 (1936).

[16] O.D. Harris et al., *Malignancy in Adult Coeliac Disease and Idiopathic Steatorrhea*, 42 Am. J. Med. 899 (1967); G.K.T. Holmes et al., *Coeliac Disease, Gluten-Free Diet, and Malignancy*, 17 Gut 612 (1976).

can have zinc deficiency, which also can be associated with esophageal malignancy.[17]

Achalasia

Achalasia is a peristaltic motor disorder of the esophagus that can be caused by a neurotropic virus. These patients have a 5- to 10-percent incidence of squamous cell carcinoma of the esophagus.[18]

Cicatricial Strictures

Ingestion of corrosive substances, usually lye, causes cicatricial strictures of the esophagus. Squamous cell carcinoma of the esophagus can occur in patients with these strictures.[19]

Dysplasia

Dysplasia can result from atrophy of the esophageal mucosa from chronic esophagitis. The dysplastic changes can precede the formation of esophageal cancer.[20]

Crohn's Disease

Crohn's disease is a chronic granulomatous disorder of the small intestine. Cancer of the esophagus has been reported in association with this disease.[21]

Barrett's Esophagus

Barrett's esophagus is an anomalous developmental abnormality of the esophageal mucosal lining consisting of columnar cells in contradistinction to the

---

[17] H.J. Lin et al., *Zinc Levels in Serum, Hair and Tumours from Patients with Oesophageal Cancer,* 15 Nutrition Report Int'l 625 (1977).

[18] S. Cohen, *Motor Disorders of the Esophagus,* 301 New Eng. J. Med. 184 (1979).

[19] P. Applequist & M. Salmo, *Lye Corrosion Carcinoma of the Esophagus,* 45 Cancer 2655 (1980); E.B. Benedict, *Carcinoma of the Esophagus Developing in Benign Stricture,* 224 New Eng. J. Med. 408 (1941); M.R. Lawler et al., *Carcinoma of the Esophagus,* 58 J. Thoracic & Cardiovascular Surgery 609 (1969).

[20] N. Munoz & M. Crespi, *High-Risk Conditions and Precancerous Lesions of the Oesophagus, in* Precancerous Lesions of the Gastrointestinal Tract 60 (B. Sherlock et al. eds., 1983).

[21] T.S. Gyde & R.N. Allan, *Colorectal Cancer and Malignancy in Fistulae Complicating Crohn's Disease, in* Precancerous Lesions of the Gastrointestinal Tract 282 (B. Sherlock et al. eds., 1983).

normal stratified squamous epithelium. There is a prevalence for the development of esophageal adenocarcinoma in the presence of Barrett's esophagus[22] and, therefore, is considered to be a premalignant condition.

Genetics

In esophageal adenocarcinoma, from Barrett's epithelium, chromosomal rearrangement at 11p13-15 has been reported.[23] Gene amplification, which is involved in the etiology and progression of tumors, has been noted in esophageal carcinoma. The amplified oncogenes include HER-2/neu[24], 24 int-2, hst-1,[25] and c-erb B (epidermal growth factor receptor gene).[26]

§ 10.3   Clinical Manifestations

Dysphagia (difficulty in swallowing) is the most prominent symptom and occurs first with solid foods and then progresses to difficulties ingesting liquids. In advanced stages, there can be pain and trouble swallowing saliva. Extension of the tumor into the tracheobronchial tree can cause *stridor* (harsh, high-pitched breathing sounds), and if tracheoesophageal fistula develops, coughing, choking, and aspiration pneumonia can result. Invasion of the recurrent laryngeal nerve results in vocal cord paralysis with a harsh, weak voice.

§ 10.4   Diagnosis

Definitive diagnosis tends to occur late in the disease when over 60 percent of the esophageal circumference is infiltrated with cancer and dysphagia has become severe enough to prompt the patient to seek medical attention.

A barium esophagram shows an irregular ragged mucosal lining with luminal narrowing. Computerized tomography of the chest can show evidence of

---

[22] A.J. Cameron et al., *The Incidence of Adenocarcinoma in Columnar-Lined (Barrett's) Esophagus,* 313 New Eng. J. Med. 857 (1985); R. Siewert et al., *Endobrachyoesophagus and Adenocarcinoma der Speiserohre,* 50 Chirurg. 675 (1979); S.J. Spechler et al., *Adenocarcinoma and Barrett's Esophagus. An Overrated Risk?,* 87 Gastroenterology 927 (1984).

[23] E. Rodriguez et al., *11p13-15 Is a Specific Region of Chromosomal Rearrangement in Gastric and Esophageal Adenocarcinomas,* 50 Cancer Res. 6410 (1990).

[24] J. Houldsworth et al., *Gene Amplification in Gastric and Esophageal Adenocarcinoma,* 50 Cancer Res. 6417 (1990).

[25] T. Tsuda et al., *High Incidence of Coamplification of hst-1 and int-2 Genes in Human Esophageal Carcinomas,* 40 Cancer Res. 5505 (1989).

[26] M.C. Hollstein et al., *Amplification of Epidermal Growth Factor Receptor Gene but no Evidence of ras Mutations in Primary Human Esophageal Cancers,* 48 Cancer Res. 5119 (1988).

mediastinal lymph node involvement and extension through and around the esophageal wall.

Esophagoscopy with brush cytology and biopsy usually confirms the diagnosis. Bronchoscopy can be necessary to establish the presence of tracheobronchial
involvement. Palpably enlarged cervical nodes should be biopsied to see if metastatic lymph node involvement is present.

§ 10.5   Surgical Treatment

Cervical Esophagus (Upper Third)

Lesions in the cervical esophagus that are not fixed to the spine, do not invade
major vessels, and do not have fixed cervical lymph node metastases should
have a total esophagectomy with reconstruction using the stomach.[27] Laryngectomy is performed in the presence of tracheal invasion or vocal cord paralysis.[28]
Because microscopic invasion of the trachea can occur, laryngectomy has been
suggested for most cervical esophagus carcinomas.[29] En bloc bilateral lymph
node dissection also is necessary. Operative mortality varies from 4.3 to 10 percent.[30]

Thoracic Esophagus (Middle Third)

Tumors that do not extend completely through the esophagus and do not have
extensive lymph node involvement can be curably resected by total esophagectomy with reconstruction and removal of adjacent lymph nodes. Palliation can
still be achieved in patients who do have extension through the esophageal wall,
but whose cure is unlikely.

---

[27] J.D. Beatty et al., *Carcinoma of the Esophagus: Pretreatment Assessment, Correlation of
Radiation Treatment Parameters with Survival, and Identification and Management of Radia-
tion Treatment Failure,* 43 Cancer 2254 (1979); C.F. Colin & R.H. Spiro, *Carcinoma of the
Cervical Esophagus. Changing Therapeutic Trends,* 148 Am. J. Surgery 460 (1984).

[28] I.L. Kron et al., *Blunt Esophagectomy and Gastric Interposition for Tumors of the Cervical
Esophagus and Hypopharynx,* 52 Am. Surgery 140 (1986).

[29] T.R. DeMeester & A.P. Barlow, *Surgery and Current Management for Cancer of the Esophagus and Cardia: Part II, in* 25 Current Probs. Surgery 553 (1988).

[30] J.W. Baker, Jr. & G.L. Schecter, *Management of Paraesophageal Cancer by Blunt Resection
Without Thoracotomy and Reconstruction with Stomach,* 203 Annals Surgery 491 (1986); T.R.
DeMeester & E.R. Lafontaine, *Surgical Therapy, in* Cancer of the Esophagus, 141–97 (T.R.
DeMeester & B. Levin eds., 1985); T. Kakegawa et al., *Analysis of Surgical Treatment for
Carcinoma Situated in the Cervical Esophagus,* 97 Surgery 150 (1985).

Lower Esophagus (Lower Third)

En bloc resection of the total esophagus, cardia of the stomach, and lymph nodes with reconstruction is necessary for attempts to cure esophageal cancer in this area.[31] Stomach material can be used for reconstruction, but colon material is more applicable when a large portion of the cardia of the stomach is removed. Operative mortality is 1.4 to 11 percent.

Palliation

Esophagectomy with reconstruction is the best palliative procedure when applicable. In the presence of advanced disease or debilitation of the patient, this extensive procedure might not be possible. Removing the primary tumor reduces the problems of pain, dysphagia, bleeding, and perforation.

Dilatation with bougies (dilators) relieve dysphagia for a period of time. Repeated dilatations are usually necessary. There is a small risk of perforation of the esophagus.

Tubes with internal diameters of 10 to 12 mm can be placed into the strictured esophagus to allow passage of food. These tubes are usually polyvinyl (Macklin® or Cellestin® tubes), rigid, and have an upper funnel shape. Complications are not uncommon and include operative mortality, perforation of the esophagus,[32] and obstruction of the lumen of the tube by food or tumor.

Subcutaneous, substernal, or transpleural surgical bypass of the esophagus with segments of colon, jejunum, or stomach is effective for palliation. Operative mortality, however, is 16 to 42 percent.[33] The complications include anastomotic breakdown, fistulae, and reflux of gastric or intestinal contents.

Feeding gastrostomy or feeding jejunostomy allows intake of nutrition when there is no other effective means. These are simple procedures with low morbidity and mortality.

Tumor obstruction of the esophagus can be relieved with electrical coagulation or by laser therapy.[34]

---

[31] H. Akiyama et al., *Principles of Surgical Treatment for Carcinoma of the Esophagus: Analysis of Lymph Node Involvement*, 194 Annals Surgery 438 (1981); A. Logan, *The Surgical Treatment of Carcinoma of the Esophagus and Cardia*, 43 J. Thoracic & Cardiovascular Surgery 150 (1903); D.B. Skinner, *En bloc Resection for Neoplasms of the Esophagus and Cardia*, 85 J. Thoracic & Cardiovascular Surgery 59 (1983).

[32] A.L. Ogilvie et al., *Palliative Intubation of Oesophagogastric Neoplasms at Fiberoptic Endoscopy*, 23 Gut 1060 (1982).

[33] W.J. Burdette, *Palliative Operation for Carcinoma of Cervical and Thoracic Esophagus*, 173 Annals Surgery 714 (1971); K.H. Lam et al., *Intrathoracic Gastric Bypass for Carcinoma of Oesophagus Found Unresectable at Exploration*, 69 Brit. J. Surgery 71 (1982); G.B. Ong, *The Kirshner Operation: A Forgotten Procedure*, 60 Brit. J. Surgery 221 (1973); J. Wong et al., *Results of the Kirshner Operation*, 5 World J. Surgery 547 (1981).

[34] D. Fleischer & F. Kessler, *Endoscopic Nd:YAG Laser Therapy for Carcinoma of the Esophagus. A New Form of Palliative Treatment*, 85 Gastroenterology 600 (1983); J.J. Pietrafitta &

§ 10.6   Chemotherapy Treatment

Preoperative chemotherapy with or without radiation therapy has resulted in tumor shrinkage.[35] Effective single agents include bleomycin, mitomycin C, doxorubicin, cisplatin, and 5-fluorouracil. Clinical remission and relief of esophageal obstruction can be obtained. Definitive surgery also can be made easier.

Combination chemotherapy has been more effective than single agents. Response rates are between 15 and 80 percent, with complete response rates from 0 to 20 percent. Combinations being used include: cisplatin and bleomycin; cisplatin, bleomycin, and vindesine; cisplatin, bleomycin, and methotrexate; cisplatin, vindesine, and mitoquazone (MGBG); cisplatin, mitoquazone, methotrexate, and bleomycin; and cisplatin, 5-fluorouracil, and doxorubicin.[36]

Chemotherapy with radiation therapy can be used without surgery. The median survival is 12 months, which is two months less than with surgery.

§ 10.7   Radiation Therapy Treatment

Curative radiation is used most often in the upper esophagus because it is more successful in that region and because of the surgical problems associated with the upper esophagus.

Long anterior and posterior fields are used to cope with the undetectable submucosal infiltration typical of esophageal carcinoma. With a 5-cm margin of normal esophagus covered at each end of the tumor, radiation often exposes the entire esophagus to treatment. The fields should be wide enough to cover the mediastinal lymph nodes. In addition, the supraclavicular lymph nodes are irradiated with upper esophageal tumors. The gastric lymph nodes are irradiated

---

R.M. Dwyer, *Endoscopic Laser Therapy of Malignant Esophageal Obstruction,* 121 Archives Surgery 395 (1986).

[35] R.W. Carey et al., *Esophageal Carcinoma: Long Term Follow-Up of Patients Treated by Neo-Adjuvant Chemotherapy, Surgery and Possible Postoperative Radiation and/or Chemotherapy,* 9 Proc. Am. Soc'y Clinical Oncology 105 (1990); L.R. Coia et al., *Nonsurgical Management of Esophageal Cancer: Report of a Study of Combined Radiotherapy and Chemotherapy,* 5 J. Clinical Oncology 1783 (1987); A.A. Forastierre et al., *Concurrent Chemotherapy and Radiation Therapy Followed by Transhiatal Esophagectomy for Local-Regional Cancer of the Esophagus,* 8 J. Clinical Oncology 119 (1990); D.P. Kelsen et al., *Preoperative Therapy for Esophageal Cancer: A Randomized Comparison of Chemotherapy versus Radiation Therapy,* 8 J. Clinical Oncology 1352 (1990); J.A. Roth et al., *Randomized Clinical Trial of Preoperative and Postoperative Adjuvant Chemotherapy with Cisplatin, Vindesine, and Bleomycin for Carcinoma of the Esophagus,* 96 J. Thoracic & Cardiovascular Surgery 242 (1988).

[36] C. Gisselbrecht et al., *Fluorouracil, Adriamycin and Cisplatin Chemotherapy of Advanced Esophageal Carcinoma,* 52 Cancer 974 (1983); D.P. Kelsen et al., *Cisplatin, Vindesine and Bleomycin Combination Chemotherapy of Local-Regional and Advanced Esophageal Carcinoma,* 75 Am. J. Med. 645 (1983); S.E. Vogel et al., *Chemotherapy for Esophageal Cancer with Mitoquazone, Methotrexate, Bleomycin and Cisplatin,* 69 Cancer Treatment Rep. 21 (1985).

with upper esophageal tumors. Megavoltage radiation is used with daily fractions of 160 to 180 cGy. After 4000 cGy, oblique or lateral fields can be used to avoid further irradiation of the spinal cord and heart, ultimately reaching 6000 cGy as a total dose.

In postoperative radiation, the dose is more likely to be limited to 5000 cGy. Postoperative radiation is given for questionable surgical margins and metastatic mediastinal lymph nodes whether or not they have been resected.

Preoperative radiation varies from 2000 cGy in one week to 4000 cGy or more in four weeks or longer.

Intracavitary brachytherapy is another available regimen. 192-Iridium ribbons can be placed in the esophagus through a nasogastric tube.

Due to the poor outlook in esophageal carcinoma, a variety of investigative treatment regimens include chemotherapy concurrently or before radiation, surgery preceded by chemotherapy and radiation, and surgery after chemotherapy and before radiation.

In incurable cases, radiation has palliative value in relieving dysphagia.

§ 10.8   Significant Cases

Carthen v. Jewish Hospital.[37]   A verdict for $2.5 million was affirmed. The plaintiff experienced difficulties in swallowing and a burning sensation in the chest in November 1979. Upper gastrointestinal series revealed a hiatus hernia. Endoscopy was performed and an inflamed, ulcerated, strictured area of the esophagus was biopsied. The pathologic diagnosis, which was agreed on by several pathologists, was adenocarcinoma. In December 1979, esophagogastrectomy was done. No cancer was found in any of the slides. A gastric resection had to be performed in June 1980 because of bile and pancreatic juice reflux. The plaintiff's expert testified that the biopsy slides showed focal ulceration with chronic esophagitis and no evidence of cancer. The plaintiff continued to suffer from belching, diarrhea, anemia, difficulty keeping food down, constant pain, nausea, difficulty swallowing, fainting, low blood pressure, and loss of appetite.

Chester v. United States.[38]   Applying Pennsylvania law, the court rendered a judgment for $45,988.10 under the Wrongful Death Act and $14,986.86 under the Survival Act for failure to diagnose and treat the decedent's esophageal cancer. In June 1972, the decedent complained of weight loss, fatigue, loss of energy, decreased exercise tolerance, and intermittent pain under left rib. Regurgitation, difficulties swallowing, and increasing pain were present in August 1972. He went to another physician in November 1972, and X-rays showed that

---

[37] 694 S.W.2d 787 (Mo. Ct. App. 1985).

[38] 403 F. Supp. 458 (W.D. Pa. 1975).

he had a hiatal hernia. Actually, the X-rays showed an obstruction of the cardioesophageal junction consistent with esophageal carcinoma. In March 1973, the X-rays were examined, and the cancer was diagnosed. It was too late by then to resect the cancer, and a gastrostomy tube was inserted to provide sustenance. The patient died in November 1973. The court held that if the decedent's cancer had been resected during the period from August through November 1972, he would have had a better chance of survival.

STOMACH

§ 10.9   Staging and Classification

TNM: American Joint Committee on Cancer.[39]

The TNM system is not usually utilized for stomach cancer. Prognosis depends upon the type of cancer (localized or diffuse), invasion of contiguous structures, and the presence of lymph node involvement.

The usual histology is adenocarcinoma. The more undifferentiated it is, the worse the prognosis will be.

Histopathologic Classification[40]

Benign

   Polyp

   Hyperplastic adenomatous polyp

   Papillary adenoma (villous adenoma)

   Familial polyposis

   Hamartomatous polyp

      Heterotopic adenomatous polyp (Brunner gland adenoma)

      Mucosal nodule

   Hemangioma

   Glomus tumor

   Lymphangioma

Malignant

   Adenocarcinoma

   Carcinoid

---

[39] American Joint Committee on Cancer, Manual for Staging of Cancer 70 (3d ed. 1988).

[40] S-C Ming, *Tumors of the Esophagus and Stomach, in* Atlas of Tumor Pathology 82 (1982).

Leiomyosarcoma

Rhabdomyosarcoma

Lymphoma

  Plasmacytoma

  Kaposi's disease

  Adenoacanthoma (adenocarcinoma with squamous metaplasia)

  Squamous cell carcinoma

  Leiomyoblastoma

  Hemangiopericytoma

  Carcinosarcoma.

§ 10.10   Etiology

Diet

The incidence of gastric cancer is lower in North America, Western Europe, and Australia than in Japan, China, Eastern Europe, and portions of South and Central America. Children of migrants to the United States from high incidence areas have an incidence similar to native-born Americans.[41] This statistical fact shows that environmental factors are associated with the incidence of gastric cancer. Although diet has been suggested as a cause, there is no definite proven relationship.[42]

Immunodeficiency

Immunodeficiency has been associated with the occurrence of gastric cancer.[43] A genetic mediated autoimmune gastritis has been postulated from a genetic defect in T lymphocytes in familial gastric malignancy.[44] Ataxia-Telangiectasia

---

[41] R. Doll, *The Geographical Distribution of Cancer,* 23 Brit. J. Cancer 1 (1969); J.V. Juossens & J. Geboers, *Nutrition and Gastric Cancer,* 2 Nutrition Cancer 251 (1981).

[42] H. Thomason et al., *Impaired Gastric Function in Experimental Malnutrition,* 34 Am. J. Clinical Nutrition 1278 (1981).

[43] P.E. Hermans et al., *Idiopathic Late-Onset Immunoglobulin Deficiency: Clinical Observations in 50 Patients,* 61 Am. J. Med. 221 (1976); B.D. Spector et al., *Genetically Determined Immunodeficiency Diseases (GDID) and Malignancy: Report from the Immunodeficiency-Cancer Registry,* 11 Clinical Immunology & Immunopathology 12 (1978).

[44] F.T. Creagen & J.F. Fraumeni, Jr., *Familial Gastric Cancer and Immunologic Abnormalities,* 32 Cancer 1325 (1973); J.J. Twomey, *Immunological Dysfunction with Atrophic Gastritis and Gastric Malignancy, in* Gastrointestinal Tract Malignancies 83–117 (M. Lipkin & R.A. Good eds., 1978).

(Louis-Bar syndrome) is an inherited autosomal recessive disorder with reported incidents of gastric cancer.[45]

Atrophic Gastritis

Severe atrophic fundic gastritis associated with achlorhydria, low vitamin B, low intrinsic factor levels, and immunological alterations such as high serum gastrin with parietal cell and intrinsic factor antibodies (termed *type A-gastritis*) is a precursor to gastric cancer.[46] Atrophic gastritis of this type is genetically determined.[47] A relationship has been noted between low serum pepsinogen activity, achlorhydria, and gastric carcinoma.[48]

Pernicious Anemia

Pernicious anemia is associated with atrophic gastritis (can be type A-gastritis). Achlorhydria in this disorder results in intragastric bacteria that generates nitrite from nitrate resulting in increased carcinogenic N-nitrosocompounds.[49] There is a high risk of gastric cancer in patients with pernicious anemia.[50]

---

[45] M.B. Daly & M. Swift, *Epidemiological Factors Related to the Malignant Neoplasm in Ataxia-Telangiectasia Families,* 31 J. Chronic Diseases 625 (1978); A.F. Haerer et al., *Ataxia-Telangiectasia with Gastric Adenocarcinoma,* 210 JAMA 1884 (1969).

[46] M. Suirala et al., *Studies of Patients with Atrophic Gastritis—A 10-15 Year Follow-Up,* 1 Scandinavian J. Gastroenterology 40 (1966); R.G. Strickland & I.R. Mackay, *A Reappraisal of the Nature and Significance of Chronic Atrophic Gastritis,* 18 Am. J. Digestive Disorders 426 (1973).

[47] E. Fodor et al., *Hydrochloric Acid Secretion Capacity of the Stomach as an Inherited Factor in the Pathogenesis of Duodenal Ulcer,* 13 Am. J. Digestive Disorders 260 (1968); K. Varis, *A Family Study of Chronic Gastritis: Histological Immunological and Functional Aspects,* 6 Scandinavian J. Gastroenterology 1 (1971).

[48] J.O. Pastore et al., *Serum Pepsin and Tubeless Gastric Analysis as Predictors of Stomach Cancer,* 286 New. Eng. J. Med. 279 (1972).

[49] W.S.J. Ruddell et al., *Pathogenesis of Gastric Cancer in Pernicious Anaemia,* 1 Lancet 521 (1978).

[50] H.S. Kaplan & L.G. Rigler, *Pernicious Anemia and Carcinoma of the Stomach—Autopsy Studies Concerning Their Interrelationship,* 139 Acta Medica Scandinavica 472 (1951); G.G.R. Kuster et al., *Gastric Cancer in Pernicious Anemia and in Patients With and Without Achlorhydria,* 175 Annals Surgery 783 (1972); J. Mosbech & A. Videbaek, *Mortality from and Risk of Gastric Carcinoma Among Patients with Pernicious Anemia,* 2 Brit. J. Med. 390 (1950); N. Zamchek et al., *Occurrence of Gastric Cancer among Patients with Pernicious Anemia at the Boston City Hospital,* 252 New Eng. J. Med. 1103 (1955).

Blood Groups

There is a 20-percent increased risk of gastric cancer in blood group A (ABO blood grouping) patients in comparison to the general population.[51] The reason for the association is unknown.

Polyps

Polyps of the stomach are either hyperplastic polyps without malignant potential or adenomatous polyps that have the potential to become malignant.[52]

Familial Disorders

Patients with Peutz-Jegher's syndrome[53] and familial multiple polyposis[54] have been reported with associated gastric cancer.

Dysplasia

Dysplasia in the stomach lining is an abnormal proliferation with cellular abnormalities and organizational derangements. Severe dysplastic changes have a propensity for malignant transformation.[55]

---

[51] I. Avid et al., *A Relationship Between Cancer of the Stomach and the ABO Blood Groups,* 1 Brit. Med. J. 799 (1953); R.B. McConnell, *The Genetics of Carcinoma of the Stomach, in* Racial and Geographical Factors in Tumour Incidence 107–13 (A.M. Shivas ed., 1967); R.G.A. Wayjen & H. van Linschoten, *Distribution of ABO and Rhesus Blood Groups in Patients with Gastric Carcinoma, with Reference to its Site of Origin,* 65 Gastroenterology 877 (1973).

[52] A. Johansen, *Gastric Polyps: Pathology and Malignant Potential, in* Precancerous Lesions of the Gastrointestinal Tract 185 (P. Sherlock et al., eds., 1983); T. Nagayo, *Precursors of Human Gastric Cancer: Their Frequencies and Histological Characteristics, in* Pathology of Carcinogenesis in Digestive Organs 151–61 (E. Farber et al. eds., 1977).

[53] B.A. Payson & B. Moumgis, *Metastasizing Carcinoma of the Stomach in Peutz-Jeghers Syndrome,* 165 Annals Surgery 145 (1967); B. Cochet et al., *Peutz-Jeghers Syndrome Associated with Gastrointestinal Carcinoma,* 20 Gut 169 (1979).

[54] T. Iowa & H. Watanabe, *Report of Familial Adenomatous Coli Associated with Gastric Cancer,* 13 Stomach & Intestine 1105 (1978).

[55] S-C. Ming et al., *Gastric Dysplasia: Significance and Pathologic Criteria,* 54 Cancer 1794 (1984).

Ménétrier's Disease (giant hypertrophic gastritis)

Ménétrier's disease consists of large gastric folds with protein loss. Cancer of the stomach can occur.[56]

Genetic

Chromosomal rearrangement at 11p13-15 has been noted in gastric adenocarcinoma.[57] Genetic alterations by gene amplification are believed to be involved in the etiology and progression of tumors. Amplification of specific protooncogenes such as HER-2/neu,[58] erb B-2,[59] c-myc,[60] c-yes-1,[61] and ki-ras[62] have been reported in gastric carcinoma.

§ 10.11   Clinical Manifestations

Gnawing epigastric discomfort or a change in character of ulcer symptoms can indicate gastric malignancy. Early symptoms tend to be subtle. Anorexia, weight loss, weakness, dysphagia, or obstruction are likely to follow. Anemia can result from slow oozing of blood from the tumor. Hematemesis (vomiting of blood) and melena (black, tarry stools) occur from more massive bleeding.

---

[56] E.L. Chusid et al., *Spectrum of Hypertrophic Gastropathy,* 114 Archives Internal Med. 621 (1964); P. Ménétrier, *Des Polyadenomes Gastriques et des Leurs Rapport avec le Cancer de L'estomac,* 1 Arch. Physiol. Norm. Pathol. 32 (1888).

[57] E. Rodriguez et al., *11p13-15 Is a Specific Region of Chromosomal Rearrangement in Gastric and Esophageal Adenocarcinomas,* 50 Cancer Res. 6410 (1990)

[58] J. Houldsworth et al., *Gene Amplification in Gastric and Esophageal Adenocarcinoma,* 50 Cancer Res. 6417 (1990).

[59] J.B. Park et al., *Amplification, Overexpression, and Rearrangement of the erb B-2 Protooncogene in Primary Human Stomach Carcinomas,* 49 Cancer Res. 6605 (1989); J. Yokota, *Genetic Alterations of the c-erb B-2 Oncogene Occur Frequently in Tubular Adenocarcinoma of the Stomach and Are Often Accompanied by Amplification of the v-erb A Homologue,* 2 Oncogene 283 (1988).

[60] M. Shibuya et al., *Amplification and Expression of a Cellular Oncogene (c-myc) in Human Gastric Adenocarcinoma Cells,* 5 Molecular & Cellular Biology 414 (1985).

[61] T. Seki et al., *Amplification of c-yes-1 Protooncogene in a Primary Human Gastric Cancer,* 76 Japan J. Cancer Res. 907 (1985).

[62] J.L. Boo et al., *A Human Gastric Carcinoma Contains a Single Mutated and an Amplified Normal Allele of the ki-ras,* 14 Nucleic Acids Res. 1209 (1986).

§ 10.12   Diagnosis

Upper gastrointestinal X-ray series ordinarily distinguish a gastric malignancy. However, 10 percent of benign-appearing gastric ulcers are malignant. A benign-appearing ulcer can be treated medically with Tagamet® or Zantac®, but if the ulcer does not heal *completely* within six weeks or the ulcer recurs, malignancy must be considered.

The gastroscopic appearance of the tumor is characteristic. Brushings with exfoliative cytology and biopsies help confirm the diagnosis. Sometimes these examinations are inconclusive and must be repeated.

§ 10.13   Surgical Treatment

Some surgeons believe that the presence of any lymph node metastases, even locally, results in essentially no cure for surgically resected stomach cancer. Others are more optimistic and resect gastric malignancies even in the presence of palpable local lymph node enlargement. Cancers of the distal stomach can be excised leaving a cuff of proximal stomach and performing a gastrojejunostomy in the form of a Billroth I or II procedure. When the proximal stomach is involved with malignancy, a portion of the distal esophagus and the spleen need to be removed with most, if not all, of the stomach. The stomach can be replaced by forming a small bowel pouch or doing a jejunoesophagostomy. Excision of portions of involved organs or structures should be attempted when applicable, such as resection of colon or pancreas.

Single metastasis to the liver is rare and, therefore, total resection of a liver metastasis is not indicated. Infiltrating malignancy of the stomach, designated linitis plastica, usually requires total gastrectomy to get completely around the tumor. Exophytic gastric malignancies are more likely to be cured and might not require radical forms of gastric resection.

Complications of gastric surgery include anastomotic breakdown, bleeding, sepsis, ileus, wound infection, intraabdominal abscess (including pelvic, subhepatic, and subphrenic), duodenal stump blowout, wound dehiscence or evisceration, obstruction, pulmonary embolus, pneumonia, and fistula. A nasogastric tube can be placed in the residual stomach pouch, but it can cause regurgitation or pneumonitis. Feeding jejunostomy is helpful in the elderly or debilitated patient so that nutritional intake can be resumed at an early time after surgery.

§ 10.14 Chemotherapy Treatment

Chemotherapy can be used in combination with radiation therapy for un-resectable localized disease with some benefit.[63] For recurrent unresectable metastatic stomach cancer, single agents that have shown responses include 5-fluorouracil, mitomycin C, doxorubicin, hydroxzyurea, epidoxorubicin, ftora-fur, methotrexate, cisplatin, triazinate, chlorambucil, BCNU, and mechlorethane. Combination chemotherapy results usually show better response rates, but survival might not be prolonged. Drug combinations include: 5-fluorouracil, doxorubicin, and methotrexate (FAMtx); 5-fluorouracil, doxorubicin, and methyl-CCNU (FAMe); 5-fluorouracil, doxorubin, and cisplatin (FAP); 5-fluorouracil, mitomycin C, and cytosine arabinoside; FAM plus trazinate; FAM plus BCNU; FAM plus methyl-CCNU; and 5-fluorouracil, doxorubicin, and BCNU.[64]

§ 10.15 Radiation Therapy Treatment

Radiation is not an alternative to surgery. Radiation therapy can be given postop-eratively for residual carcinoma or metastatic lymph nodes whether resected or not. Megavoltage radiation is given in 160 cGy to 180 cGy fractions. With total doses exceeding 4500 cGy, the risk of gastric necrosis increases.

Generally, the value of radiation in carcinoma of the stomach is questionable. Combinations of radiation and chemotherapy are used based on some observations that combinations increase survival a few months compared to single modality treatments.

In carcinoma of the cardia of the stomach, radiation can be of palliative value in relieving dysphagia due to obstruction at the gastroesophageal junction.

§ 10.16 Commentary and Significant Cases

Gastric malignancies are accessible for diagnosis through X-rays and endoscopy. The early symptoms can mimic other disorders. Awareness of the possibility of cancer when symptoms do not respond to medical treatment within six weeks should lead to a more detailed workup.

---

[63] D.S. Childs et al., *Treatment of Unresectable Adenocarcinomas of the Stomach with a Combi-nation of 5-Fluorouracil and Radiation,* 102 Am. J. Radiology 1252 (1968).

[64] E. Cazap et al., *Phase II Trials of 5-FU, Doxorubicin, and Cisplatin in Advanced, Measurable Adenocarcinoma of the Lung and Stomach,* 70 Cancer Treatment Rep. 781 (1986); H. Doug-lass et al., *An Eastern Cooperative Oncology Group Evaluation of Combinations of Methyl-CCNU, Mitomycin C, Adriamycin, and 5-Fluorouracil in Advanced Measurable Gastric Cancer,* 2 J. Clinical Oncology 1372 (1984); G. Jamieson & P. Gill, *A Prospective Trial of 5-FU and BCNU in the Treatment of Advanced Gastric Cancer,* 5 Austl. & N.Z. J. Surgery 16

Booth v. United States.[65]   The decedent was a civilian employee of the United States War Department. He had suffered stomach trouble for over 15 years when seen in May 1946 by a medical officer for stomach complaints. In July 1946, X-rays of the upper gastrointestinal tract and gallbladder performed were read as normal. The pain continued, and X-rays by a private physician in December 1946 showed an enlargement of the lining of the stomach. Hemorrhage from the stomach began in February 1947 and a diagnosis of probable stomach cancer was made. Phrenicotomy was performed to relieve the pain, and in March 1947, exploration of the abdomen disclosed the cancer. He died one week later. The court held that the physician must exercise that degree of skill and care exercised by the medical profession in similar cases, but does not have to exercise extraordinary skill and care or the highest degree of skill and care, nor is the physician liable for a mistake in diagnosis.

Thomas v. Group Health Cooperative.[66]   Failure to diagnose a gastric leiomyosarcoma in a 16-year old patient resulted in a $460,000 settlement. The patient was suffering from anemia and was treated by the defendant with oral iron tablets. The physician claimed he performed one hemoccult test, but this test was not documented in the record. Subtotal gastrectomy was performed, and metastasis to one lymph node was discovered. The patient underwent chemotherapy. The plaintiff's expert stated that the delay in diagnosis led to the metastasis and that the prognosis was extremely poor.

Valtean v. Calonje.[67]   There was a $365,000 settlement for the misinterpretation of an upper gastrointestinal series of X-rays as normal, resulting in a seven-month delay in the diagnosis of cancer of the stomach. The malignancy was inoperable by that time, and the patient died one year later.

(1981); J. Levi et al., *Analysis of a Prospective Randomized Comparison of Doxorubicin versus 5-Fluorouracil, Doxorubicin and BCNU in Advanced Gastric Cancer: Implications for Future Studies,* 4 J. Clinical Oncology 1348 (1986); E. Robinson et al., *Phase II Trials in the Treatment of Advanced Gastric Cancer,* 4 Proc. Am. Soc'y Clinical Oncology 77 (1985).

[65] 140 Ct. Cl. 145, 155 F. Supp. 235 (1957).

[66] No. 86-2-01168-2 (Snohomish County Feb. 8, 1988), *reprinted in* 4 Med. Malpractice Verdicts, Settlements & Experts No. 8, at 10 (1988).

[67] No. 86-845 (Med. Rev. Panel, New Orleans June 23, 1987), *reprinted in* 3 Med. Malpractice Verdicts, Settlements & Experts No. 9, at 55 (1987).

SMALL INTESTINE

§ 10.17   Classification

Small Intestine Tumor Classification[68]

Benign
  Adenoma
  Adenoma of Brunner's glands
  Polypoid adenomatosis
  Myoepithelial hamartoma
  Pancreatic adenoma
  Fibroma
  Lipoma
  Leiomyoma
  Hemangioma
    Cavernous hemangioma
    Capillary hemangioma
    Hemangioendothelioma
    Hemangiomatosis
    Hemangiopericytoma
  Lymphangioma
  Neurofibroma
  Neurilemoma
  Ganglioneuroma
Malignant
  Adenocarcinoma
  Carcinoid
  Lymphoma
  Leiomyosarcoma
  Angiosarcoma

---

[68] D.A. Wood, *Tumors of the Intestines, in* Atlas of Tumor Pathology 23 § VI, fascicle 22 (1967).

Liposarcoma

Fibrosarcoma.

§ 10.18   Precancerous Conditions of the Small Intestine

Adult Coeliac Disease

Adult coeliac disease is a chronic malabsorption syndrome with steatorrhea. Atrophy of intestinal villae occur with associated iron deficiency anemia and/or folic acid deficiency. Some patients develop osteomalacia or neuropathy. Lymphoma[69] and carcinoma[70] have been reported in association with coeliac disease. Speculation as to the cause of malignancy has included loss of immune surveillance and viral oncogenesis.

Alpha Chain Disease

Alpha chain disease is a malabsorption disorder with plasma cell or lymphoplasmacytic proliferation in the lamina propria that proceeds to malignant lymphoma.[71] The plasma cells contain alpha-heavy chain immunoglobulin. There can be a relationship between Mediterranean lymphoma and alpha chain disease.[72] Mediterranean lymphoma is a syndrome of chronic diarrhea, abdominal

---

[69] W.I. Austad et al., *Steatorhoea and Malignant Lymphoma. The Relationship of Malignant Tumours of Lymphoid Tissue and Coeliac Disease,* 12 Am. J. Digestive Disorders 475 (1967); H.R. Gough et al., *Intestinal Reticulosis as a Complication of Idiopathic Steatorrhoea,* 3 Gut 232 (1962); O.D. Harris et al., *Malignancy in Adult Coeliac Disease and Idiopathic Steatorrhoea,* 42 Am. J. Med. 899 (1967); P. Isaacson & D.H. Wright, *Intestinal Lymphoma Associated with Malabsorption,* 1 Lancet 67 (1978).

[70] A. Bryechwa-Ajdukiewicz et al., *Carcinoma, Villous Atrophy and Steatorrhea,* 7 Gut 572 (1966); G.K.T. Holmes et al., *Adenocarcinoma of the Upper Small Bowel Complicating Coeliac Disease,* 21 Gut 1010 (1980).

[71] T. Al-Saleem & I.M. Zardani, *Primary Lymphomas of the Small Intestine in Iraq: A Pathological Study of 145 Cases,* 3 Histopathology 89 (1979); K. Henry & G. Farrer-Brown, *Primary Lymphomas of the Gastrointestinal Tract. 1. Plasma Cell Tumors,* 1 Histopathology 53 (1977); V.H. Nassar et al., *Mediterranean Abdominal Lymphoma or Immunoproliferative Small Intestine Disease,* 41 Cancer 1346 (1978).

[72] W.F. Doe, *Alpha Chain Disease—Clinicopathological Features and Relationship to So-Called Mediterranean Lymphoma,* 31 Brit. J. Cancer 350 (Supp. 1975); K.R. Gallian et al., *Pathological Study of Alpha Chain Disease with Special Emphasis on Evaluation,* 39 Cancer 201 (1976); K.J. Lewin et al., *Primary Intestinal Lymphoma of "Western" and "Mediterranean" Type Alpha Chain Disease and Massive Plasma Cell Infiltration,* 38 Cancer 2511 (1976); J.C. Rambaud & C. Natuchansky, *Alpha Chain Disease: Pathogenesis and Relation to Mediterranean Lymphoma,* 1 Lancet 1430 (1973).

pain, clubbing of the fingernails, and diffuse lymphoplasmacytic lymphoma of the upper small intestine.

Crohn's Disease (Regional Enteritis)

Crohn's disease is a chronic granulomatous inflammatory disease involving the terminal ileum, but can involve any area of the gastrointestinal tract. Dysplasia, with nuclear pleomorphism and hyperchromatism, mitoses, disorderly architecture, cytoplasmic basophilia, and loss of cellular polarity has been observed. Carcinoma has been reported in the colon,[73] small bowel,[74] and fistulae[75] in association with regional enteritis. Lymphoma also has been reported.[76]

Peutz-Jeghers Syndrome (Hutchinson-Weber-Peutz syndrome, Peutz-Touraine syndrome)

Peutz-Jeghers syndrome is a disorder involving melanotic pigmentation of the lips, oral mucosa, cheek, nose, extremities, or abdominal area associated with multiple adenomatous polyps in the small bowel, stomach, and colon. The polyps are actually hamartomas that consist of an overgrowth of mature cells and tissues. The syndrome is from a pleiotropic gene inherited as an autosomal dominant trait. Small bowel carcinoma may occur in patients with Peutz-Jeghers syndrome.[77]

---

[73] S.N. Gyde et al., *Malignancy in Crohn's Disease,* 21 Gut 1024 (1980).

[74] J.D. Cantwell et al., *Adenocarcinoma Complicating Regional Enteritis: Report of a Case and Review of the Literature,* 54 Gastroenterology 599 (1968); P.E. Collier et al., *Small Intestinal Adenocarcinoma Complicating Regional Enteritis,* 55 Cancer 516 (1985); D. Fresko et al., *Early Presentation of Carcinoma from the Small Bowel in Crohn's Disease (Crohn's Carcinoma),* 82 Gastroenterology 783 (1982); B. Korelitz, *Carcinoma of the Intestinal Tract in Crohn's Disease: Results of a Survey Conducted by the National Foundation for Ileitis and Colitis,* 78 Am. J. Gastroenterology 44 (1983); M.E. Richards et al., *Crohn's Disease-Associated Carcinoma: A Poorly Recognized Complication of Inflammatory Bowel Disease,* 209 Annals Surgery 764 (1989); G.F.D. Tyers et al., *Adenocarcinoma of Small Intestine and Other Malignant Tumors Complicating Regional Enteritis: Case Report and Review of the Literature,* 169 Annals Surgery 510 (1969); A. Valdes-Dapona et al., *Adenocarcinoma of the Small Bowel in Association with Regional Enteritis,* 37 Cancer 2938 (1976).

[75] H. Thompson, *Precancerous Conditions of the Small Intestine, in* Precancerous Lesions of the Gastrointestinal Tract 213 (P. Sherlock et al. eds., 1983).

[76] G.B. Lee et al., *Lymphosarcoma in Crohn's Disease,* 20 Diseases Colon & Rectum 351 (1977); R.C.N. Williamson et al., *Adenocarcinoma and Lymphoma of the Small Intestine: Distribution and Etiologic Associations,* 199 Annals Surgery 172 (1983).

[77] B. Cochel et al., *Peutz-Jeghers Syndrome Associated with Gastrointestinal Carcinoma. Report of Two Cases in a Family,* 20 Gut 169 (1979); W.J. Dodds et al., *Peutz-Jeghers Syndrome and Gastrointestinal Malignancy,* 115 Am. J. Roentgenology 374 (1972); R.R. Dozois et al., *The Peutz-Jeghers Syndrome—Is There a Predisposition to the Development of Intestinal Malignancy?* 98 Archives Surgery 509 (1969); J.P. Williams & A. Knudsen, *Peutz-Jeghers Syndrome with Metastasizing Duodenal Carcinoma,* 6 Gut 179 (1965).

Familial Multiple Polyposis

Familial multiple polyposis is an inherited disorder with multiple polyps of the colon that can involve the stomach and small bowel. Cancer of the small intestine has been reported in association with multiple polyposis.[78]

Adenoma

Villous adenoma, tubular adenoma, and tubulo-villous adenoma are found infrequently in the small intestine. These adenomas must be differentiated from the polyps found in Peutz-Jeghers syndrome. Adenomas can develop dysplasia and evolve into carcinoma.

§ 10.19   Clinical Manifestations

The symptoms manifested by neoplasms of the small bowel include colicky abdominal pain from partial bowel obstruction, occult bleeding or acute hemorrhage, and occasionally anorexia, malaise, and weight loss. Complete bowel obstruction with abdominal distention, cramping pain, nausea, and vomiting can occur. Intussusception or volvulus can be associated with small bowel tumors.

§ 10.20   Diagnosis

Upper gastrointestinal X-rays with small bowel follow-through frequently discloses the tumor. Small neoplasms, however, can be very difficult to detect. A retrograde barium enema can visualize tumors in the distal ileum. Visceral angiography identifies tumors and also areas of bleeding.

Gastroduodenoscopy is most useful for lesions in the duodenum, but more distal endoscopy is difficult, although possible to do.[79]

---

[78] W.F. Capps, Jr. et al., *Carcinoma of the Colon, Ampulla of Vater and Urinary Bladder Associated with Familial Multiple Polyposis,* 11 Diseases Colon & Rectum 298 (1968); J.M. McDonald et al., *Gardner's Syndrome and Periampullary Malignancy,* 113 Am. J. Surgery 425 (1967); L.G. Phillips, *Polyposis and Carcinoma of the Small Bowel and Familial Colonic Polyposis,* 24 Diseases Colon & Rectum 478 (1981); J.E. Ross & J.E. Mara, *Small Bowel Polyps and Carcinoma in Multiple Intestinal Polyposis,* 108 Archives Surgery 736 (1974).

[79] M. Tada & K. Kawai, *Small Bowel Endoscopy,* 102 Scandinavian J. Gastroenterology 39 (1984).

§ 10.21   Surgical Treatment

Large sections of small bowel can be excised with impunity without causing physiologic changes. A cancer of the small intestine is widely resected including the vascular supply to the area in a wide wedge of mesentery. Contiguous involved structures or portions of organs also can be resected.

Malignancies of the duodenum require duodenectomy with partial pancreatectomy because of the proximity of the pancreas and the common vascular supply to the duodenum. Pancreatoduodenectomy (Whipple procedure) appears to be a radical operation for small cancers involving the second portion of the duodenum or ampulla of Vater but is still the procedure of choice. Reconstruction with a gastrojejunostomy and Roux-en-Y nonfunctional limb for the choledochojejunostomy and pancreaticojejunostomy can be performed but there is a significant incidence of anastomotic breakdown, pancreatic fistula, wound infection, bleeding, sepsis, pneumonia, and intraabdominal abscess.

§ 10.22   Chemotherapy Treatment

Adenocarcinoma of the small bowel can be treated with chemotherapy with improved survival rates in some patients. Combination chemotherapy has improved response rates compared with single agents. Regimens utilized include 5-fluorouracil, methyl-CCNU, doxorubicin, and mitomycin-C.[80]

Chemotherapy for sarcoma of the small intestine can be used for palliation. Responses can be obtained with combinations of doxorubicin, cyclophosphamide, vincristine, and midazole carboxamide. Adjuvant chemotherapy following surgical resection has been advocated to reduce local recurrence and distant metastatic disease.

Extensive unresectable or recurrent lymphoma of the small bowel would benefit from chemotherapy with agents such as methotrexate, vincristine, cyclophosphamide, and 6-mercaptopurine.

§ 10.23   Radiation Therapy Treatment

Radiation therapy has no established use in carcinoma of the small intestine.

---

[80] P.A. Bunn et al., *5-Fluorouracil, Methyl-CCNU, Adriamycin, and Mitomycin-C in the Treatment of Advanced Gastric Cancer*, 62 Cancer Treatment Rep. 1287 (1978); J.E. Dorman et al., *Malignant Neoplasms of the Small Bowel*, 113 Am. J. Surgery 131 (1967); L. Reyes & R.W. Talley, *Primary Malignant Tumors of the Small Intestine*, 54 Am. J. Gastroenterology 30 (1970); J.M. Wilson, *Primary Malignancies of the Small Bowel: A Report of 96 Cases and Review of the Literature*, 180 Annals Surgery 175 (1974).

COLORECTAL

§ 10.24   Staging and Classification

TNM: American Joint Committee on Cancer.[81]
The TNM system is not ordinarily used for colorectal cancer.

Evolution of Duke's Classification

Classification of colorectal carcinoma by means of Duke's criteria has evolved to the most frequently used category, which is the Astler-Coller, classification, as shown in **Figure 10–1.**

Large Intestine Tumor Classification[82]

Benign

   Adenoma

      Polypoid adenoma

      Papillary adenoma

      Mixed semipapillary adenoma

      Familial adenomatosis (hereditary polyposis, multiple polyposis)

Malignant

   Adenocarcinoma

   Mucoid adenocarcinoma

   Adenoacanthoma (adenocarcinoma with squamous cell metaplasia)

   Squamous cell carcinoma.

§ 10.25   Etiology

Diet

Although there is no direct causal relationship between diet and colorectal cancer, there appears to be a higher incidence of colorectal cancer in patients with

---

[81] American Joint Committee on Cancer, Manual for Staging of Cancer 77 (3d ed. 1988).

[82] D.A.Wood, *Tumors of the Intestines, in* Atlas of Tumor Pathology 121 § VI, fascicle 22 (1967).

COMPARISON OF STAGING SYSTEMS FOR CARCINOMA OF THE COLON AND RECTUM

CATEGORIES	CLASSIFICATION
A B_1 B_2 C_1 C_2	Dukes 1929/30-(rectum)
A A A B C C C C	Dukes 1932 (rectum)
A A A B C_1 C_1 C_1 C_2	Dukes 1935 (rectum)
A B_1 B_1 B_2 C C C C	Kirklin et. al. 1949 (rectum & sigmoid)
A B_1 B_1 B_2 C_1 C_2 C_2	Astler-Coller 1953 (rectum & colon)
A A A B C C C C D	Turnbull et. al. 1967 (colon)

ANATOMIC EXTENT of NEOPLASM

← mucosa
← muscularis mucosae
← submucosa
← muscularis propria
← serosa (colon only)
← lymph nodes (any)
← lymph nodes (apical)
→ not removable,
→ adjacent organs,
→ distant sites,

Figure 10–1. The evolution of staging systems based on the Duke's classification. Enker, W.E., Carcinoma of the Colon and Rectum; St. Louis, 1978, Mosby-Year Book, Inc.

diets high in meat or its component animal protein and fat,[83] and high in calorie intake.[84] There is an association of fecal concentrations of bile acids (deoxycholic acid) and large bowel cancer.[85]

Peutz-Jeghers Syndrome

Peutz-Jeghers syndrome has been associated with malignancies of the colorectum.[86] A similar disorder, juvenile polyposis, which is an autosomal dominant trait associated with gastrointestinal polyposis and various congenital defects, also has been reported to undergo dysplastic and neoplastic intestinal changes.[87]

---

[83] M.J. Hill, *Metabolic Epidemiology of Large Bowel Cancer, in* Gastrointestinal Cancer 187–226 (J. DeCosse & P. Sherlock eds., 1981); H.L. Newmark et al., *Colon Cancer and Dietary Fat, Phosphate and Calcium: A Hypothesis,* 72 J. Nat'l Cancer Inst. 1325 (1984).

[84] K.W. Heaton, *Dietary Factors,* 5 Topics Gastroenterology 29 (1977).

[85] M.J. Hill et al., *Bacteria and Aetiology of Cancer of Large Bowel,* 1 Lancet 95 (1971).

[86] G. Monga et al., *Adenomatous and Carcinomatous Transformation in Hamartomatous Polyps (Peutz-Jeghers Type) of the Large Bowel, in* International Symposium on Precancerous Conditions of the Gastrointestinal Tract 100, Fondazione Internazional Menarini, Bologna, Italy, 1981.

[87] Z.D. Goodman et al., *Pathogenesis of Colonic Polyps in Multiple Juvenile Polyposis. Report of a Case Associated with Gastric Polyps and Carcinoma of the Rectum,* 43 Cancer 1906 (1979); T.J. Stemper et al., *Juvenile Polyposis and Gastrointestinal Carcinoma: A Study of a Kindred,* 83 Annals Internal Med. 639 (1975).

Familial Multiple Polyposis (familial adenomatous polyposis, familial polyposis coli)

Familial multiple polyposis is inherited as an autosomal dominant trait and consists of multiple polyps of the colon that can involve the stomach and small intestine. The adenomas in this syndrome are precursors of malignancy. Almost 100 percent of patients with familial multiple polyposis develop cancer of the colon by the age of 50.

Gardner's Syndrome

Gardner's syndrome is a variant of familial multiple polyposis associated with osteomas (skull and mandible), epidermoid cysts, dental abnormalities, and areas of increased fibroblastic reaction (desmoid tumors). There is a similar propensity for cancer of the colon in this disorder.

Adenomas

Adenomatous polyps of the colon can occur singly or in multiples without any indication of a hereditary characteristic. The colonic adenoma can develop dysplasia and carcinoma. Villous adenomas have a greater propensity for malignant degeneration than simple adenomas.

Hereditary Nonpolyposis Colorectal Cancer

Hereditary nonpolyposis colorectal cancer is an autosomal dominant trait with a predisposition to early onset of multiple colorectal cancers.[88] Thus far, no genetic defect in a chromosome has been detected.

Hereditary Flat Adenoma Syndrome

Families have been reported with genetic transmission of flat adenomas predominantly in the right colon and associated with onset of colorectal cancer at a later age than familial multiple polyposis or hereditary nonpolyposis colorectal cancer.[89]

---

[88] H.T. Lynch, *Frequency of Hereditary Nonpolyposis Colorectal Carcinoma (Lynch Syndromes I and II),* 90 Gastroenterology 486 (1986); H.T. Lynch et al., *Hereditary Nonpolyposis Colorectal Cancer—Lynch Syndromes I and II,* 17 Gastroenterology Clinics N. Am. 679 (1988).

[89] H.T. Lynch et al., *Phenotype Variation in Colorectal Adenoma Cancer Expression in Two Families: Hereditary Flat Adenoma Syndrome,* 66 Cancer 909 (1990).

Dysplasia

Severe dysplasia changes in colonic mucosa or in adenomatous or villous polyps are associated with a significant malignant potential. Severe dysplasia has been equated with carcinoma in situ.[90]

Ulcerative Colitis

Ulcerative colitis is a chronic ulcerative disease of the colon associated with crypt abscesses. The rate of malignancy of the colon increases with prolonged symptomatic ulcerative colitis. Colectomy is recommended in the presence of dysplasia or after 10 years of symptomatic disease to prevent cancer.

Crohn's Disease (Regional Enteritis)

A chronic granulomatous disease of the small intestine, Crohn's disease also can involve the large bowel. Cancer of the esophagus, stomach, small bowel, and colon[91] have been reported. Malignancy can develop in fistulae including ileo-rectal and rectovaginal fistula.[92]

Industry

Although colorectal cancer is not ordinarily thought of as an occupational disease, there have been reports that suggest a link between certain occupations and colorectal malignancy. There is increased risk of development of large bowel cancer in synthetic fiber manufacture,[93] asbestos workers,[94] rubber industry,[95]

---

[90] B.C. Morson, *The Pathogenesis of Colorectal Cancer, in* 10 Major Problems in Pathology (B.C. Morson ed., 1978).

[91] A.J. Greenstein et al., *Patterns of Neoplasia in Crohn's Disease and Ulcerative Colitis*, 46 Cancer 403 (1980); S.N. Gyde et al., *Malignancy in Crohn's Disease*, 21 Gut 1024 (1980); D.D. Weedon et al., *Crohn's Disease and Cancer*, 289 New Eng. J. Med. 1099 (1973).

[92] S. Simpson et al., *The Histologic Appearance of Dysplasia (Precarcinomatous Change) in Crohn's Disease of the Small and Large Intestine*, 81 Gastroenterology 492 (1981); H. Thompson et al., *Colorectal Cancer and Malignancy in Fistulae Complicating Crohn's Disease, in* Precancerous Lesions of the Gastrointestinal Tract 284–85 (P. Sherlock et al. eds., 1983).

[93] J. Vobecky et al., *Risk of Large Bowel Cancer in Synthetic Fiber Manufacture*, 54 Cancer 2537 (1984).

[94] I.J. Selikoff et al., *Asbestos Exposure and Neoplasia*, 188 JAMA 142 (1964).

[95] A.J. McMichael et al., *Cancer Mortality Among Rubber Workers: An Epidemiologic Study*, 271 Annals N.Y. Acad. Sci. 125 (1976).

metallurgy workers handling chlorinated oil, weavers, firefighters, manu-
facturers of transport equipment,[96] coke byproduct workers,[97] and copper
smelters.[98]

Vitamin D

According to the geographic distribution of sunlight and the incidence of colorectal cancer, an inverse association of sunlight and colon malignancy has been
discovered. Most vitamin D is produced endogenously from sunlight, and the
reduction of vitamin D in areas receiving less sunlight is proposed as a cause of
colorectal cancer.[99]

Nitrosamines

Nitrosamines are well known to be potent carcinogens. Bacteria in the colon
convert dietary nitrates and secondary amines to tryptophan metabolites and
nitrosamines.

§ 10.26   Clinical Manifestations

Tumor size and location determine the symptoms. Tumors of the right colon
tend to be associated with bleeding, sometimes occult, and weight loss. Large
bulky tumors can cause vague pain, but rarely bowel obstruction. Left colon
lesions are more likely to have symptoms of obstruction with "gas pains" and
cramping discomfort. Changes in bowel habits can occur (increased constipation
or diarrhea). Decreased stool calibre can be described when the tumor is in the
rectum or rectosigmoid.

§ 10.27   Diagnosis

To detect colorectal cancer in asymptomatic persons, the American Cancer Society recommends a digital rectal examination every year after the age of 40. A

---

[96] J.W. Berg & M.A. Howell, *Occupation and Bowel Cancer,* 1 J. Toxicology & Env'tl Health 75
(1975).

[97] C.K. Redmond et al., *Cancer Experience among Coke By-Product Workers,* 271 Annals N.Y.
Acad. Sci. 102 (1976).

[98] S. Tokudome & M. Kuratsune, *Alcohol Study on Mortality from Cancer and Other Causes
Among Workers at a Metal Refinery,* 17 Int'l J. Cancer 310 (1976).

[99] C.F. Garland & F.C. Garland, *Do Sunlight and Vitamin D Reduce the Likelihood of Colon
Cancer?,* 9 Int'l J. Epidemiology 227 (1980); C.F. Garland et al., *Dietary Vitamin D and Calcium and Risk of Colorectal Cancer: A 19 Year Prospective Study in Men,* 1 Lancet 307
(1985).

stool occult blood test should be done every year over the age of 50. Sigmoidoscopy should be performed over the age of 50 every three to five years, after two negative exams one year apart.[100]

Proctosigmoidoscopy diagnoses lesions within 25 cm of the anal verge. Polyps can be removed, and malignant lesions can be biopsied. The flexible sigmoidoscope reaches up to 60 cm from the anal verge, and the colonscope reaches up to 160 cm from the anal verge.

A barium enema defines polyps and malignant tumors. Tumors can be localized so that endoscopic biopsy can be performed.

Abdominal computerized tomography (CT scan) identifies the extent of lesions in the rectum and sigmoid, including involvement of contiguous structures. Involved retroperitoneal lymph nodes and liver metastases can be visualized.

Radioactive scanning to localize cancers of the colon has been successful using Indium 111-labeled LICRLON M8 (a mouse monoclonal antibody),[101] antibody Tc-99m (technitium),[102] and Indium 111-labeled anticarcinogenic antigen (for recurrent colorectal cancer and occult metastases).[103]

§ 10.28   Surgical Treatment

Colon Polyps

Colon endoscopy with the proctosigmoidoscope (25 cm in length), flexible sigmoidoscope (60 cm in length), and colonoscope (160 cm in length) is an effective means of visualizing, diagnosing, and treating polyps. Colonic polyps under 1 cm in diameter have less than 1 percent incidence of cancer. These polyps can be examined endoscopically on a yearly basis. All polyps over 1 cm in diameter should be removed.

Almost any pedunculated polyp can be removed by an experienced endoscopist using a snare (wire loop). Transection should be performed at the neck of the stalk, close to the head. Sessile (flat) polyps can be removed from the rectum or sigmoid, but serious consideration must be given to sessile polyps in other parts of the colon, especially in the thin-walled ascending colon. Factors to

---

[100] *Guidelines for the Cancer-Related Checkup: Recommendations and Rationale,* 30 Cancer Colon & Rectum 208 (1980).

[101] C-Y Yiu et al., *Immunoscintigraphy of Colorectal Cancer with an Antibody to Epithelial Membrane Antigen (EMA),* 33 Diseases Colon & Rectum 122 (1990).

[102] L.C. Swayne, *The Clinical Implications of Diagnostic Imaging Using ImmuRAID CEA-Tc-99m in Colorectal Cancer,* 1 On Target 2 (1990).

[103] Y.Z. Patt et al., *Imaging with Indium-Labeled Anticarcinogenic Antigen Monoclonal Antibody ZCE-025 of Recurrent Colorectal or Carcinoembryonic Antigen Producing Cancer in Patients with Rising Serum Carcinoembryonic Antigen Levels and Occult Metastases,* 8 J. Clinical Oncology 1246 (1990).

be evaluated are the patient's age, medical condition, and clinical setting. The sessile polyp can be removed through multiple small bites with the biopsy instrument.

Polyps that are suspicious for malignancy should only be biopsied and not totally removed. This method allows accurate surgical resection, because a portion of the tumor can still be palpated or localized by open endoscopy at the time of surgery. Indications of possible malignancy include ulceration or other surface irregularity, areas of hardness, fixation of the polyp to the underlying submucosa, or a thick *pseudopedicle.*[104]

Complications of endoscopic polypectomy are less than 2.5 percent and include hemorrhage and perforation.[105] Combustible gases in the colon during colonoscopy also can cause rupture of the bowel.[106] Transmural thermal injury of the bowel can result in the postpolypectomy coagulation syndrome, which includes abdominal pain, fever, signs of localized peritonitis, and leucocytosis without free air on abdominal X-ray examination.[107] The patient usually recovers if treated with bowel rest, intravenous antibiotics, and close observation. However, it might be necessary to perform a temporary diverting colostomy for perforation and peritonitis.

Colonoscopy fails to identify 10 percent of colonic polyps.[108] Colonoscopic examination after polypectomy should be repeated within one year to exclude the presence of other polyps and at regular intervals thereafter.

Colorectal Cancer

Cancer of the colon is treated by wide resection of the bowel en bloc with the draining lymphatics (within the mesentery) and excision of involved organs or structures. The colon is a large redundant organ and can be widely resected without changing bowel physiology. Some surgeons feel that colon malignancy should be treated by subtotal resection to limit the occurrence of new primaries. There is no reason to transect the bowel close to a malignant tumor (5 cm or less), except under very limited circumstances such as:

---

[104] J.D. Wayne et al., *An Endoscopic Determinant of the Need for Subsequent Surgery in the Malignant Polyp,* 31 Gastrointestinal Endoscopy 150 (1985).

[105] E.M. Livstone & M.D. Kerstein, *Serosal Tears Following Colonoscopy,* 111 Archives Surgery 88 (1976); B.H. Rogers et al., *Complications of Flexible Fiberoptic Colonoscopy and Polypectomy,* 22 Gastrointestinal Endoscopy 73 (1975).

[106] J.H. Bond, Jr. & M.D. Levitt, *Factors Affecting Concentration of Combustible Gases in the Colon During Colonscopy,* 68 Gastroenterology 1445 (1975); H. Ragins et al., *The Explosive Potential of Colonic Gas During Colonoscopic Electrosurgical Polypectomy,* 138 Surgical Gynecology & Obstetrics 554 (1974).

[107] J.D. Wayne, *The Postpolypectomy Coagulation Syndrome,* 27 Gastrointestinal Endoscopy 184 (1981).

[108] J.D. Waye & S. Braunfeld, *Surveillance Intervals after Colonoscopic Polypectomy,* 14 Endoscopy 79 (1982).

1. For palliative purposes
2. Astler-Coller or Dukes Stage A, such as carcinomatous changes in a polyp
3. In rectal malignancy when there is limited bowel distal to the malignant lesion and anal preservation is desired.

The extent of colon resection is determined by the position of the cancer and the major blood supply (see **Figures 10–2** through **10–8**). It is well known that ligation of the lumen of the bowel on each side of the tumor prior to handling of the tumor and resection prevents a high incidence of recurrence at the line of anastomosis. Cutting across tumor or lymphatics containing tumor at the line of resection almost always results in recurrence locally in the bowel or mesentery, in the peritoneal cavity, or in the abdominal wall incision. Manipulating the primary cancer prior to ligating the major venous drainage vessels can cause sprays of tumor cells into the blood stream with an opportunity for metastatic implantation, but this has not been definitely proven.

Metastasis to the ovary is a poor prognostic sign. Previously, removing the ovaries as part of the primary resection for sigmoid and rectosigmoid cancers in female patients was thought to be necessary. Reports now show that survival time is not improved by removing the ovaries, probably due to the fact that metastases are in other widespread areas once the ovary is involved. Direct

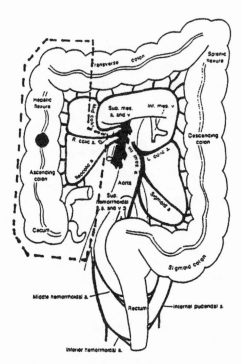

Figure 10–2. Resection for malignancies involving cecum and ascending colon.

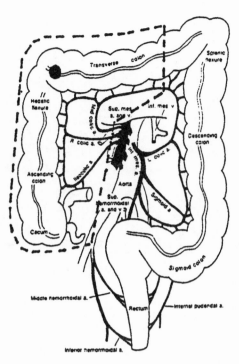

Figure 10–3. Resection for malignancies involving hepatic flexure.

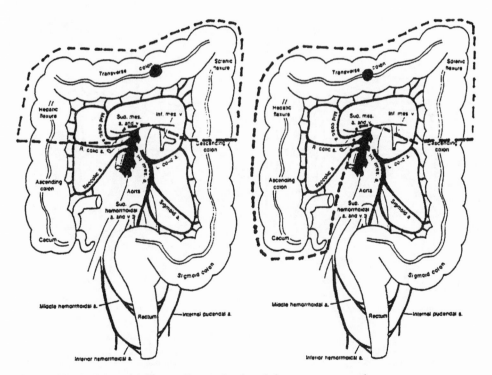

Figure 10–4. Resection for malignancies involving transverse colon.

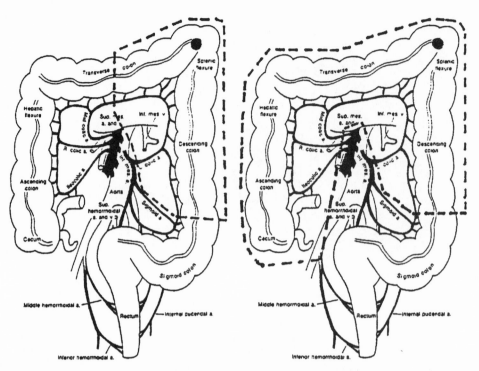

Figure 10–5. Resection for malignancies involving splenic flexure.

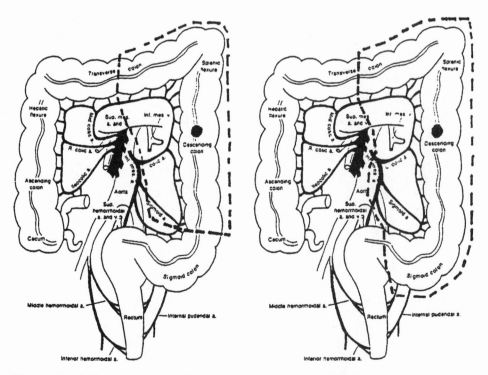

Figure 10–6. Resection for malignancies involving descending colon.

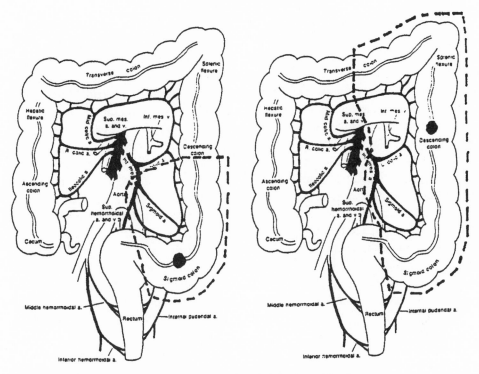

Figure 10–7. Resection for malignancies involving sigmoid colon.

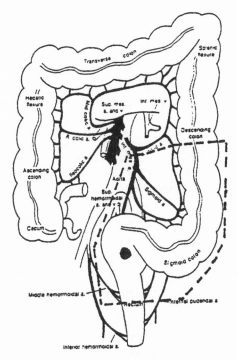

Figure 10–8. Resection for malignancies involving rectosigmoid or rectum.

extension to the ovary does require en bloc removal of the ovary with the primary resection.

In the case of a resectable primary and a single or localized multiple liver metastases or a lung metastasis, an attempt should be made to remove the primary site adequately for cure and then resect the metastatic deposit. When there are multiple metastases, and cure is not possible, palliation can be achieved by removing the primary bowel tumor by limited resection to prevent obstruction, perforation, and/or bleeding.

Rectal or rectosigmoid tumors can be removed by low anterior resection (removing tumor and reanastomosing the bowel low in the pelvis) when the primary neoplasm is at least 10 cm from the anal verge. Tumors located lower in the rectum (5 cm from the dentate line) can still be resected and bowel reanastomosed by using special stapling instruments (EEA) or by using the trans-sacral (Kraske) approach. To preserve the anus, a pull-through operation[109] or anal mucosa stripping with transanal anastomosis[110] can be performed. Anal incontinence is a possible complication. The standard treatment for low rectal cancer is the Mile's abdominoperineal resection with the formation of a permanent end colostomy. Male patients should be warned of the probability of loss of ability to ejaculate.

Minimally invasive rectal carcinomas can be treated by local resection.[111] Patients must be selected carefully because increased local recurrence and decreased survival occurs with positive surgical margins, poorly differentiated histology, and increasing depth of bowel wall invasion. Excision can be performed through transanal,[112] transsacral,[113] or transsphincteric[114] approaches.

Patients must be informed of the various possible procedures and their complications to decide what type of surgery is preferred.

Patients having preoperative blood transfusions in treating colorectal cancer have been associated with a poorer survival than patients who did not have transfusions.[115] Immunosuppression has been suggested as a causative factor.

---

[109] B.M. Black & J.T. Wells, *Combined Abdominoendorectal Resection: Reappraisal of a Pull-Through Procedure,* 47 Surgical Clinics N. Am. 977 (1967); W.O. Kirwan et al., *Pull-Through Operation with Delayed Anastomosis for Rectal Cancer,* 65 Brit. J. Surgery 695 (1978).

[110] A.G. Parks & J.P. Percy, *Resection and Sutured Colo-anal Anastomosis for Rectal Carcinoma,* 69 Brit. J. Surgery 301 (1982).

[111] R.A. Graham et al., *Local Excision of Rectal Carcinoma,* 160 Am. J. Surg. 306 (1990).

[112] M.W. Stearns et al., *Treatment Alternatives: Localized Rectal Cancer,* 54 Cancer 2691 (1984).

[113] P.H. O'Brien, *Kraske's Posterior Approach to the Rectum,* 142 Surgery Gynecology & Obstetrics 412 (1976).

[114] A.Y. Mason, *Trans-Sphineteric Approach to Rectal Lesions,* 9 Surgery Annals 171 (1977).

[115] M. Agarwal & N. Blumberg, *Colon Cancer Patients Transfused Perioperatively Have an Increased Incidence of Recurrence,* 23 Transfusion 421 (1983); L. Burrows & P. Tartter, *Blood Transfusions and Colorectal Cancer Recurrence: A Possible Relationship,* 23 Transfusion 419 (1983); R.S. Foster et al., *Adverse Relationship Between Blood Transfusions and Survival after Colectomy for Colon Cancer,* 55 Cancer 1195 (1985).

The complications for which observation is necessary for include wound infection, intrabdominal abscess (including pelvic, subhepatic, and subphrenic), anastomotic breakdown with peritonitis or abscess formation, sepsis, bleeding, bowel obstruction, pneumonia, pulmonary embolus, ileus, fistula, and wound dehiscence or evisceration.

The remaining portion of the colon should be examined on a yearly basis by colonoscopy and/or barium enema to detect recurrence or new primary cancers early. Carcinoembryonic antigen (CEA) and lipid bound sialic acid (LASA) should be followed on a six- to twelve-month basis, because these monoclonal antibodies can detect recurrent cancer before clinical findings are evident. Fecal occult blood should continue to be examined on a regular basis.

In patients with familial multiple polyposis or Gardner's syndrome, the colon should be subtotally resected soon after the diagnosis is made, and there should be an attempt to evaluate as many members of the family as possible. In the presence of prolonged ulcerative colitis (over 10 years) or when biopsy shows atypical mucosal changes on biopsy, subtotal colectomy should be carried out. Patients with acute ulcerative colitis (approaching 10 years) must have yearly colonoscopy and multiple biopsies searching for atypical changes.

Electrocoagulation of perineal unresectable recurrences of rectal carcinoma can give effective palliation. Laser therapy of locally recurrent unresectable colon carcinoma has been used by endoscopic means to relieve obstruction, bleeding and/or diarrhea, or debulking of rectal recurrences. It is possible to treat primary malignancies of the rectum with multiple electrocoagulation sessions.[116]

§ 10.29   Chemotherapy Treatment

Prior to 1989, there had been many controlled studies of adjuvant therapy in treating colorectal cancer using various chemotherapeutic agents, namely 5-fluorouracil alone or in combination with other agents. Despite these large studies, no significant evidence of improvement was documented. In 1989, the North Central Cancer Treatment Group (NCCTG)[117] reported a possible benefit from using levamisole either alone or in combination with fluorouracil as adjuvant therapy for Stages C and B2 colon cancer. In 1990, Moertel[118] reported a definite reduced risk of cancer recurrence by 41 percent with a reduction in the

---

[116] J.L. Madden & S.I. Kandalaft, *Long-Term Evaluation of Electrocoagulation as a Primary Preferred Method in the Treatment of Cancer of the Rectum, in* Colorectal Tumors 199 (O.H. Beahrs et al. eds., 1986).

[117] J.A. Laurie et al., *Surgical Adjuvant Therapy of Large-Bowel Carcinoma: An Evaluation of Levamisole and the Combination of Levamisole and Fluorouracil: The North Central Cancer Treatment Group and the Mayo Clinic,* 7 J. Clinical Oncology 1447 (1989).

[118] C.G. Moertel et al., *Levamisole and Fluorouracil for Adjuvant Therapy of Resected Colon Carcinoma,* 322 New Eng. J. Med. 352 (1990).

overall death rate by 33 percent in patients with Stage C disease treated with flu-orouracil and levamisole based on a study of 1296 patients. The study also showed a possible improvement in those patients with Stage B2 treated with the same drugs. These preliminary studies continue.

The National Institute of Health (NIH) held a Consensus Development Con-ference on adjuvant therapy for patients with colon and rectal cancer in April of 1990. A consensus opinion[119] (see § **10.39**) was developed by the surgeons, medical oncologists, radiation oncologists, gastroenterologists, and other health care providers at this meeting. The panel recommended that patients with Stage III colon cancer receive adjuvant chemotherapy with 5-FU and levamisole. Spe-cific adjuvant therapy was not recommended for Stage II colon cancer patients outside of clinical trials at this time.

Stage I disease of the colon, which is described as tumor invasion of the sub-mucosa and muscularis propria only, should not be treated with adjuvant chemotherapy. In stage IV colon cancer (metastatic), chemotherapy is recom-mended using 5-FU preceded by leucovorin factor. Levamisole is also given in the usual manner for three days every 15 days.

For the treatment of rectal carcinoma the Gastrointestinal Tumor Study Group[120] developed a trial that randomized patients to surgery alone or surgery and local radiation therapy versus surgery and 5-fluorouracil and methyl-CCNU. The recurrence rate was highest among the patients who had surgery alone and was lowest in the patients receiving chemotherapy and radiation therapy.

In April 1990, the National Institute of Health (NIH) Consensus Development Conference on adjuvant therapy (see § **10.39**) recommended that adjuvant ther-apy combining chemotherapy and radiation therapy improves local control and survival for Stage II and III patients. The most effective combination presently appears to be 5-fluorouracil, methyl-CCNU, and high-dose pelvic irradiation. Using methyl-CCNU outside of clinical trials was discouraged because of docu-mented toxicities. The panel also concluded that patients with Stage I rectal can-cer are at low risk of recurrence and do not warrant adjuvant therapy.

The National Cancer Institute (NCI) published a clinical announcement on the adjuvant therapy of rectal cancer in March 1991.[121] See § **10.40.** The report restated the data suggesting that a sequential regimen of 5-fluorouracil (5-FU) based chemotherapy and radiation therapy can reduce overall tumor recurrence rates, substantially reduce local recurrence, and prolong patient survival. Such a regimen can be recommended as therapy for individuals with resected TNM Stage II (Duke's B2,3) and III (Duke's C) rectal cancer, while previous clinical trials utilized a combination of postoperative radiation therapy to the pelvis plus

---

[119] NIH Consensus Development Conference, *Adjuvant Therapy for Patients with Colon and Rec-tum Cancer,* 8 Consensus Statement No. 4, at 1 (1990).

[120] Gastrointestinal Tumor Study Group, *Prolongation of Disease-Free Interval in Surgically Treated Rectal Carcinoma,* 312 New Eng. J. Med. 1465 (1985).

[121] National Cancer Institute, Adjuvant Therapy of Rectal Cancer (clinical announcement Mar. 14, 1991).

5-FU and the investigational drug, methyl-CCNU, current preliminary information suggests that substantial treatment benefits can be achieved using irradiation and standard doses of 5-FU. This combination avoids the potential risks of leukemia and chronic renal insufficiency associated with the protracted administration of methyl-CCNU.

§ 10.30   Radiation Therapy Treatment

The adjuvant use of megavoltage radiation therapy is well established for reducing local and regional recurrence in rectal and rectosigmoid carcinomas that extend through the wall of the bowel or have lymph node metastases.

Both preoperative and postoperative radiation have advocates. Preoperative evaluation of a tumor cannot be as complete as postoperative evaluation. To avoid preoperative irradiation of low risk tumors that will not benefit from radiation, certain criteria are observed. Preoperative radiation is reserved for tumors larger than 4 cm, that involve the entire circumference of the bowel, and that are ulcerated, fixed, or poorly differentiated. Anterior, posterior, and lateral fields are used giving 4500 to 5000 cGy in 160 to 200 cGy fractions. Field sizes vary, proponents of larger fields extending the radiation up to the level of the midlumbar spine.

When postoperative radiation is contemplated, procedures to reduce small bowel radiation injury are initiated. Attempts can be made to keep the small bowel out of the pelvis by constructing an omental curtain or retroverting the uterus. Metal clips identifying the areas at greatest risk permit maximum reductions in field size for boost doses. Barium examination during treatment planning discloses the exact location of the small bowel in relation to the radiation fields. The dose is 4500 to 5000 cGy to large fields with boosts to 5500 to 6000 cGy with small fields if they do not irradiate the small bowel. When abdominoperineal resections are done, a direct perineal field can be added to irradiate the surgical perineal scar as well as the pelvis.

Small, superficial exophytic rectal tumors are curable with intracavitary 50 kV "contact" X-ray therapy, in which the X-ray tube is inserted into the rectum. Treatments of 2000 to 3000 cGy are given at one- to two-week intervals to total doses of 10,000 cGy or greater. These large fractions and high total doses do not cause necrosis of the bowel because of the very low energy of the radiation.

Interstitial brachytherapy with 192-iridium ribbons also can be used.

In large tumors that are not treated surgically, 5000 to 6000 cGy of megavoltage radiation gives excellent palliative relief of pain and bleeding. In a few cases, palliation results in cure.

Reduced local recurrence rates are cited as the basis for postoperative megavoltage radiation in carcinomas of the proximal colon. The tumor site and adjacent nodal area are irradiated. Dosage can be limited to 4500 cGy because small bowel irradiation seldom can be avoided.

§ 10.31 Commentary and Significant Cases

The diagnosis of colorectal malignancy requires alertness that unexplained anemia, rectal bleeding, or changes in bowel habits can indicate cancer. X-rays must be read accurately, and radiologic reports must adequately describe the possible diagnoses. The attending physician must read all X-ray reports and follow up on any significant abnormalities.

Agard v. Eaton Avenue Medical Group.[122] There was a defense verdict when cancer of the colon was diagnosed 15 months after the defendant examined patient for stomach pain and blood in stool. The defendant contended that he had asked the patient to return 10 days after the exam, but she did not do so.

Badon v. Butler.[123] The 75-year-old patient presented with anemia in August 1979. She was treated with iron sulfate without work-up for anemia and without checking the stool for blood. Colon cancer was diagnosed in March 1986, and the patient died in August 1986. The case was settled for $75,000.

Banta v. Horton.[124] Failure to detect and remove a suspicious area of the bowel during surgery resulted in an award of $606,000 against the surgeon. The plaintiff had chronic constipation and was seen by his physician, who ordered a barium enema. The X-rays in June 1984 showed a polyp in the descending colon and an area of narrowing further distally that was called spasm or aganglionosis, but which should have been called possible neoplasm. The defendant operated only on the polypoid area, where he found nothing, and did not examine the narrowed area. He did not perform, preoperatively, sigmoidoscopy or colonoscopy in June 1985. Cancer of the narrowed area that had metastasized to the liver was diagnosed in September 1985. There was a defense verdict for the radiologist, and the defendant surgeon was found 45 percent negligent.

Bennett v. Raag.[125] There was a summary judgment for the defendants. The plaintiff was seen in November 1974 with complaints of anal and rectal pain. Hemorrhoids and an adenocarcinoma of the rectum were diagnosed. The defendant testified that a colostomy would have to be performed. He explained the extent of the surgery and possible resulting impotence. The plaintiff claimed that he was not told that the colostomy was permanent, that he was not told of any

---

[122] No. 196371 (San Joaquin County, Cal.), *reprinted in* 5 Med. Malpractice Verdicts, Settlements & Experts No. 5, at 19 (1989).

[123] No. SWC 90062 (L.A. Super. Ct.), *reprinted in* 3 Med. Malpractice Verdicts, Settlements & Experts No. 9, at 12 (1987).

[124] No. NEC42447 (L.A. County, Norwalk Super. Ct. Dec. 12, 1987), *reprinted in* 4 Med. Malpractice Verdicts, Settlements & Experts No. 2, at 56 (1988).

[125] 103 Ill. App. 3d 321, 431 N.E.2d 48 (1982).

alternative treatment nor of any effect on his impotency. The court found that the plaintiff failed to present expert testimony to prove the standard of care.

Bradley v. Mackenzie.[126]   The plaintiff complained to the defendant of passing mucous and blood from 1983 to January 1988. Rectal examination was first performed in January 1988. Proctosigmoidoscopy disclosed an 8-×-10 cm villous adenoma with atypia and adenocarcinoma. Abdominoperineal resection with permanent colostomy was required. The plaintiff alleged failure to investigate complaints properly and failure to diagnose. A verdict of $150,000 resulted.

Durkan v. West Side District Hospital.[127]   There was a $345,000 settlement for failure to diagnose colon cancer. The decedent was worked up for bowel symptoms by the defendant and diagnosed as having ulcers. Ten months later, a workup for colon cancer was started. Because of severe pain, surgery was performed and a cancerous growth in the colon was discovered. Six days later, the decedent suffered septic shock, and a diverting ileostomy had to be performed by another physician. The patient died five months later.

Harty v. Gillerbain.[128]   There was a $414,000 verdict in favor of a patient diagnosed as having inoperable colon cancer. The patient had been under another physician's care for 15 years for ulcerative colitis. There was expert testimony that ulcerative colitis patients with involvement of more than 75 percent of the colon for over 10 years have an increased risk of cancer, that the standard of care for such patients requires a sigmoidoscopy every one to two years, and that proper observation would have permitted removing the colon had cancer been detected at an early stage.

Huwe v. Bayer.[129]   Motion for summary judgment in an action seeking damages for intentional infliction of emotional distress was denied as to the parents and granted as to the 18-year-old patient. The facts indicated that the patient underwent an appendectomy for abdominal pain. The defendant reported to the parents that he had to excise an 8- to 10-inch segment of inflamed and possibly cancerous tissue. No test was ever done on the tissue, although the defendant reported that the results were negative. The court held that substantial bodily injury caused by emotional distress is not essential, but it is sufficient that the conduct produces emotional distress, which is severe. The defendant told the

---

[126]No. 89-3S26-12 (Pinellas County, Fla.), *reprinted in* 6 Med. Malpractice Verdicts, Settlements & Experts No. 5, at 15 (1990).

[127]No. 185360 (Kerr County, Cal.), *reprinted in* 2 Med. Malpractice Verdicts, Settlements & Experts No. 8, at 7 (1986).

[128]No. L-075767-85MM (N.J. Super. Ct. Law Div. Apr. 1988), *reprinted in* 4 Med. Malpractice Verdicts, Settlements & Experts No. 8, at 17 (1988).

[129]157 N.J. Super. 310, 428 A. 2d 966 (1981).

parents that their child was suffering from a rare disease that might be cancerous, knowing that the patient had nothing more than a mildly inflamed appendix.

Knight v. Vastola.[130]   The nurse plaintiff, who died during the course of litigation, alleged that the defendant failed to diagnose colon cancer properly. The plaintiff had been treated by the defendant for over eight years and, despite complaints of rectal bleeding and positive occult blood tests of the stool, no further tests were performed. The plaintiff alleged emotional trauma in apprehending her own premature death as a separate element of damages, although this is usually an implied component of recovery for pain and suffering. There was a settlement for $135,000.

Marquis v. Nuss.[131]   A right hemicolectomy was performed on the plaintiff for a sessile mass found on barium enema. Pathologic examination disclosed a normal right colon. The postoperative course was uneventful. The plaintiff claimed failure to diagnose and properly treat, that surgery was performed when not indicated, and that it was done without her informed consent. The court affirmed the defense verdict.

Mason v. Haug.[132]   The plaintiff was treated from June 1979 to April 1983 by the defendants for rectal bleeding and abdominal pain. No rectal examination had been done, and the patient was given therapy for hemorrhoids. In December 1984, the plaintiff was found to have advanced colorectal cancer. The verdict was for $688,400.

Regal v. Davidson.[133]   The decedent complained of constipation and intermittent diarrhea throughout her pregnancy. Two months after giving birth, the symptoms were still persisting and colonoscopy was performed. A rectal cancer with metastases to other organs was diagnosed. Surgical resection followed by radiation therapy and chemotherapy followed, but she died two years later. There was a settlement for $775,000 for failure to diagnose the rectal cancer in a timely manner.

Richoux v. Metropolitan Gastroenterology.[134]   A verdict for the defense was affirmed. The decedent consulted the defendant in 1975 for rectal bleeding that

---

[130]No. 86CV5163 (Dane County Cir. Ct., Wis.), *reprinted in* 7 Med. Malpractice Verdicts, Settlements & Experts No. 3, at 13 (1991).

[131]451 N.W.2d 833 (Iowa 1990).

[132]Nos. 2822, 2870 (Pa. C.P. Phila. County Oct. 22, 1987), *reprinted in* 4 Med. Malpractice Verdicts, Settlements & Experts No. 2, at 13 (1988).

[133]No. 965/85 (N.Y. 1989), *reprinted in* 5 Prof. Negl. L. Rep. No. 6, at 90 (1990).

[134]522 So. 2d 677 (La. Ct. App. 1988).

was diagnosed as anal fissures. Blood-streaked stool occurred in July 1983. Following digital exam and proctoscopy, internal hemorrhoids were diagnosed. A hemoccult test was negative. In May 1984, the bleeding was worse, and the patient consulted the defendant in June 1984 with pain and bloody stool. Anoscopy, barium enema, and hemoccult were negative. The patient saw another physician, who found a rectal cancer after digital exam and proctoscopy. Colostomy was performed, and the tumor was treated with cesium radiation implants. The court held that the defendant was not negligent in failing to discover the decedent's rectal cancer and that expert testimony supported the finding that she would have required the same treatment she eventually received even if her tumor had been discovered on her initial visit to the defendant.

Steinbach v. Barfield. [135] Judgment for the defendant was affirmed. The plaintiff was seen by the defendant in June 1974 for complaints of abdominal pain, nausea, weakness, and pain when she urinated. Following physical examination, the diagnosis of diverticulitis and urinary tract infection was made. In July 1974, because of continued abdominal pain, nausea, and vomiting, a barium enema was done. The X-rays were reported as normal except for a large filling defect at the iliocecal valve, which probably represented lipomatous infiltration. Another barium enema in December 1974 disclosed a cancer in the cecal region of the colon. A portion of the tumor was resected, but it was too extensive to cure. Chemotherapy was administered, but the patient died in September 1976. The court held that expert testimony is necessary to prove standard of care, and the physician is not required to advise the patient of every conceivable possibility and eventuality that can stem from the treatment, but must inform as to those that can be reasonably anticipated.

Thompson v. Webb. [136] Summary judgment for the defendant based on the application of the *locality rule* was reversed. The decedent was treated by the defendant in January 1981 for rectal bleeding. Digital examination and anoscopy were done, and the decedent was treated for hemorrhoids. Several months later, he was admitted to a veterans hospital, and a rectal cancer was diagnosed and removed. The plaintiff died in June 1983. The plaintiff's expert testified that the standards of medical or surgical practice varies throughout the country, but the standard for examination and diagnosis of rectal cancer does not vary. The court held that locality has no precise meaning and varies with the facts of the particular case, and the plaintiff's expert had sufficient familiarity with the standard of care in similar communities to provide a foundation for his opinion.

---

[135] 428 So. 2d 915 (La. Ct. App. 1983).
[136] 138 Ill. App. 3d 629, 486 N.E.2d 326 (1985).

Walters v. Leff.[137]   The defendant admitted that during removing a colon cancer he severed both of the plaintiff's ureters. He fell below the standard of care when he failed to detect that he had severed the ureters before closing the surgical incision. Complications resulted in the loss of one of the kidneys. The award was for $75,000 to the plaintiff and $25,000 to the plaintiff's wife for loss of consortium.

Watry v. Smigielski.[138]   There was a $335,000 settlement when the physician failed to do a rectal examination. The plaintiff had complained of discomfort and diarrhea for three to four years before colorectal cancer was diagnosed. Surgery was performed with permanent colostomy followed by radiation therapy. The prognosis was uncertain, although the defense claimed that the surgery cured the plaintiff.

Zinda v. The Medical Protective Co.[139]   An undisclosed settlement was made for a missed diagnosis of cancer of the colon. The patient complained of abdominal problems and bloody diarrhea in September 1982. A barium enema was done and was interpreted as spasm of the transverse colon, but it did not include carcinoma of the colon as a possibility. The plaintiff was placed on a balanced high-fiber diet. During 1983 and 1984, the patient had progressive weakness and loss of energy. A diagnosis of colon cancer was made in April 1984, and colon resection was performed. Recurrence of the malignancy at the anastomosis site was found later in 1984, and further resection was done. The cancer metastasized and the plaintiff died in December 1986.

ANAL AND PERIANAL

§ 10.32   Staging and Classification

American Joint Committee on Cancer.[140]

Prognosis of a tumor in the anal canal is related to the size and invasive depth of the tumor. A neoplasm under 2 cm has a better outlook than a tumor between 2 and 5 cm, which in turn is more favorable than those over 5 cm. Invasion of

---

[137]No. 87-14505 (Maricopa County, Ariz.), *reprinted in* 4 Med. Malpractice Verdicts, Settlements & Experts No. 12, at 64 (1988).

[138]No. CV738846 (Milwaukee County, Wis.), *reprinted in* 7 Med. Malpractice Verdicts, Settlements & Experts No. 3, at 12–13 (1991).

[139]No. 86-CV-1821 (Waukesha County, Wis.), *reprinted in* 3 Med. Malpractice Verdicts, Settlements & Experts No. 12, at 15 (1987).

[140]American Joint Committee on Cancer, Manual for Staging of Cancer 82 (3d ed. 1988).

surrounding organs, metastases to regional lymph nodes, or distant metastases have a worse prognosis.

Anus Tumor Classification[141]

Benign

Adenoma

Papilloma

Condyloma acuminatum

Malignant

Intraepidermal carcinoma (Bowenoid type)

Squamous cell carcinoma

Basaloid squamous cell carcinoma

Adenocarcinoma (adenoacanthoma)

Epidermatropic carcinoma (extramammary Paget's disease)

Melanocarcinoma.

Histopathic Classification of Anal Tumors[142]

Nonkeratinizing

Basaloid carcinoma (cloacogenic transitional cell carcinoma)

Bowen's disease

Paget's extramammary disease

Basal cell carcinoma

Keratinizing

Squamous cell carcinoma (epidermoid carcinoma).

---

[141]D.A. Wood, *Tumors of the Intestines, in* Atlas of Tumor Pathology 199 § VI, fascicle 22 (1967).

[142]J.L. Sawyers, *Current Management of Carcinoma of the Anus and Perianus,* 43 Am. Surgery 424 (1977).

§ 10.33   Etiology

Disorders associated with anal carcinoma include fistula in ano,[143] anal fissure,[144] leukoplakia,[145] hemorrhoids,[146] abscess,[147] and certain venereal diseases (condylomata and lymphogranuloma).[148] Squamous cell and basal cell carcinoma also have been reported to occur in pilonidal sinuses.[149]

Bowen's disease appears as a dermatosis involving the anal and perianal areas. This disorder is actually a slow-growing intraepidermal squamous cell cancer that has a minimal propensity to invade and metastasize. There is a definite association with visceral cancers.[150]

§ 10.34   Clinical Manifestations

Squamous cell carcinoma of the anal or perianal region is associated with pruritis (itching) and bleeding. Constipation occurs when the tumor is large. The

---

[143] O.H. Beahrs & S.M. Wilson, *Carcinoma of the Anus,* 184 Ann. Surgery 422 (1976); J.T. Brennan & C.F. Stewart, *Epidermoid Carcinoma of the Anus,* 176 Ann. Surgery 787 (1972); J.F. O'Grady et al., *Squamous Cell Carcinoma of the Anus,* 16 Dis. Colon & Rectum 39 (1973).

[144] O.H. Beahrs & S.M. Wilson, *Carcinoma of the Anus,* 184 Ann. Surgery 422 (1976); J.T. Brennan & C.F. Stewart, *Epidermoid Carcinoma of the Anus,* 176 Ann. Surgery 787 (1972); A.F. Cortese, *Surgical Approach for Treatment of Epidermoid Anal Carcinoma,* 36 Cancer 1869 (1975); J.F. O'Grady et al., *Squamous Cell Carcinoma of the Anus,* 16 Dis. Colon Rectum 39 (1973).

[145] O.H. Beahrs & S.M. Wilson, *Carcinoma of the Anus,* 184 Ann. Surgery 422 (1976); J.F. O'Grady et al., *Squamous Cell Carcinoma of the Anus,* 16 Dis. Colon & Rectum 39 (1973).

[146] O.H. Beahrs & S.M. Wilson, *Carcinoma of the Anus,* 184 Ann. Surgery 422 (1976); J.T. Brennan & C.F. Stewart, *Epidermoid Carcinoma of the Anus,* 176 Ann. Surgery 787 (1972); A.F. Cortese, *Surgical Approach for Treatment of Epidermoid Anal Carcinoma,* 36 Cancer 1869 (1975); J.F. O'Grady et al., *Squamous Cell Carcinoma of the Anus,* 16 Dis. Colon & Rectum 39 (1973).

[147] J.T. Brennan & C.F. Stewart, *Epidermoid Carcinoma of the Anus,* 176 Ann. Surgery 787 (1972); J.F. O'Grady et al., *Squamous Cell Carcinoma of the Anus,* 16 Dis. Colon & Rectum 39 (1973).

[148] O.H. Beahrs & S.M. Wilson, *Carcinoma of the Anus,* 184 Ann. Surgery 422 (1976); J.T. Brennan & C.F. Stewart, *Epidermoid Carcinoma of the Anus,* 176 Ann. Surgery 787 (1972); A.F. Cortese, *Surgical Approach for Treatment of Epidermoid Anal Carcinoma,* 36 Cancer 1869 (1975); J.F. O'Grady et al., *Squamous Cell Carcinoma of the Anus,* 16 Dis. Colon & Rectum 39 (1973); M.L. Prasad & H. Abrarian, *Malignant Potential of Perianal Condyloma Acuminatum,* 23 Dis. Colon & Rectum 191 (1980).

[149] B.R. Cleveland & W.O. Green, Jr., *Squamous Cell Carcinoma Arising in a Pilonidal Sinus,* 55 Surgery 381 (1964); S. Gupta et al., *Pilonidal Sinus Epidermoid Carcinoma: A Clinicopathologic Study and a Collective Review,* 38 Current Surgery 374 (1981).

[150] R.J. Strauss & V.W. Fazio, *Bowen's Disease of the Anal and Perianal Area, a Report and Analysis of Twelve Cases,* 137 Am. J. Surg. 231 (1979).

tumor can ulcerate and there can be pain, tenesmus, rectal mass, or fullness in the rectum.

Extramammary Paget's disease of the perianal skin can indicate a large bowel malignancy. A complete workup for colorectal carcinoma must be done.

§ 10.35   Diagnosis

Careful digital examination and proctosigmoidoscopy is necessary for adequate evaluation of the extent of tumor. Inguinal lymph nodes must be palpated. Biopsy of the lesion distinguishes Bowen's disease (carcinoma in situ) and Paget's disease (extramammary) from squamous cell carcinoma, cloacogenic carcinoma, and malignant melanoma. Perianal irritation from hemorrhoid disease can mimic early malignancy, but it should clear up with local therapy.

§ 10.36   Surgical Treatment

Abdominoperineal resection has been the main form of therapy. This radical procedure is being replaced by definitive radiation therapy followed by biopsy, and then surgery is performed only if there is residual tumor. Small, early perianal malignancies with superficial invasion can be carefully resected.[151] Recurrences require radical surgery.

Metastases to inguinal lymph nodes can occur. When groin nodes are enlarged, radical inguinal lymphadenectomy is indicated. The synchronous occurrence of an untreated primary tumor and inguinal lymph node metastases indicates a poor five-year prognosis.

Paget's disease, without underlying invasive malignancy, and Bowen's disease can be treated with wide local resection.[152] Careful follow-up is essential, and occasionally multiple excisions are necessary.

§ 10.37   Chemotherapy Treatment

Stage I (less than 2 cm in diameter) and Stage II (over 2 cm in diameter) can be treated preoperatively with the combination of chemotherapy and radiation therapy. Tumor size and bulk can be reduced, and abdominoperineal resection with end colostomy may be avoided. 5-fluorouracil combined with mitomycin C has been effective.

---

[151] B.M. Boman et al., *Carcinoma of the Anal Canal—A Clinical and Pathologic Study of 188 Cases,* 54 Cancer 114 (1983).

[152] S.H.Q. Quan, *Cancer of the Anus,* Colorectal Tumors 220 (O.H. Beahrs et al. eds., 1986).

Stage III A (spread to perirectal nodes or adjacent organs) and stage III B (involvement of internal iliac or inguinal nodes or spread to adjacent organs or perirectal lymph nodes) can experience improved survival if preoperative radiation therapy and chemotherapy are administered.[153] Postoperative adjuvant chemotherapy can be effective if chemotherapy is not used preoperatively.

Metastatic anal carcinoma can be treated with chemotherapy resulting in short periods of time of remission. Drugs utilized include cisplatin; doxorubicin; bleomycin, vincristine, and high-dose methotrexate; cisplatin, bleomycin, and vinblastine or vindosine; cisplatin, 5-fluorouracil, and mitomycin C; and cisplatin, mitomycin C, doxorubicin, and bleomycin or lomustine (CCNU).[154]

§ 10.38   Radiation Therapy Treatment

The treatment of anal carcinoma is evolving, and a variety of regimens is currently used. The objective is to employ the regimen that gives the highest cure rate together with the likelihood of preserving the anus and avoiding an end colostomy.

Superficial low grade tumors less than 2 cm in diameter located at the anal verge or distal anal canal can be treated expeditiously by local excision. If treated by radiation, they can be cured by radiation alone in doses of 6000 cGy in six weeks given directly to the perineum.

For tumors larger than 2 cm, no direct comparison has been made between radiation alone and combined chemotherapy-radiation, but an accumulation of separate reports suggests that the combined treatment is probably superior not only from the standpoint of cure (fewer metastases) but also by using lower radiation dosage so that less corrective surgery might be needed for anal fibrosis and necrosis.

Megavoltage radiation is given to the pelvic lymph nodes as well as to the primary tumor in carcinomas larger than 2 cm. Anterior and posterior fields are used. In large tumors, the inguinal lymph nodes also can be irradiated electively with an extended anterior field, the dose being boosted later with electron fields, because the posterior field is not contributing to the inguinal irradiation. With

---

[153] B. Cummings et al., *Results and Toxicity of the Treatment of Anal Canal Carcinoma by Radiation Therapy or Radiation Therapy and Chemotherapy,* 54 Cancer 2062 (1984); L. Leichman et al., *Cancer of the Anal Canal: Model for Preoperative Adjuvant Combined Modality Therapy,* 78 Am. J. Med. 211 (1985); J. Papillon et al., *A New Approach to the Managment of Epidermoid Carcinoma of the Anal Canal,* 51 Cancer 1830 (1983); B. Sischy, *The Use of Radiation Therapy Combined with Chemotherapy in the Management of Squamous Cell Carcinoma of the Anus and Marginally Resectable Adenocarcinoma of the Rectum,* 11 Int'l J. Radiation & Oncology 1587 (1985).

[154] W. Fisher et al., *Metastatic Cloacogenic Carcinoma of the Anus. Sequential Responses to Adriamycin and Cis-dichlorodiamineplatinum (II),* 62 Cancer Treatment Rep. 91 (1978); P. Salem et al., *Effectiveness of Cisplatin in the Treatment of Anal Squamous Cell Carcinoma,* 69 Cancer Treatment Rep. 891 (1985).

the most commonly used drugs, mitomycin C and 5-fluorouracil, the pelvic and inguinal doses are 4000 cGy in four or five weeks. The dose for the primary tumor is then boosted to 5000 cGy. The boost can be given with small anterior and posterior fields, a direct perineal field, or interstitial 192-iridium brachytherapy. Standard treatment also consists of combined therapy in which the radiation to the pelvis and primary tumor does not exceed 3000 cGy, therefore requiring no boosts.

If chemotherapy is not used, the pelvis and inguinal doses will be 4500 cGy and the dose to the primary tumor 6000 cGy. Salvage surgery is the back-up here, as well as in the combined therapy cases.

Inguinal metastases respond to radiation just as well as the primary tumor. If palpable inguinal metastases are present, the dose should be carried to the same level as the dose to the primary tumor.

For tumors 5 cm or larger, the best of the various regimens, if independently confirmed, appears to be a split course of combined therapy: two courses of mitomycin C, 5-fluorouracil, and 2500 cGy of radiation one month apart.

If abdominoperineal resection has been chosen as the definitive treatment, any of the combined chemotherapy-radiation regimens can be used preoperatively or postoperatively.

§ 10.39   NIH Consensus Development Conference Consensus Statement (April 1990)

NIH Consensus Development Conferences are convened to evaluate available scientific information and resolve safety and efficacy issues related to a biomedical technology. The resultant NIH Consensus Statements are intended to advance understanding of the technology or issue in question and to be useful to health professionals and the public.

NIH Consensus Statements are prepared by a nonadvocate, non-federal panel of experts, based on: (1) presentations by investigators working in areas relevant to the consensus question during a 1-1/2 day public session; (2) questions and statements from conference attendees during open discussion periods that are part of the public session; and (3) closed deliberations by the panel during the remainder of the second day and morning of the third. This statement is an independent report of the panel and is not a policy statement of the NIH or the Federal Government.

Copies of this statement and bibliographies prepared by the National Library of Medicine are available from the Office of Medical Applications of Research, National Institutes of Health, Building 1, Room 260, Bethesda, MD 20892.

For making bibliographic reference to the consensus statement from this conference, it is suggested that the following format be used, with or without source abbreviations, but without authorship attribution:

Adjuvant Therapy for Patients with Colon and Rectum Cancer, NIH Consens Dev. Conf. Consens. Statement 1990 Apr. 16–18; 8(4).

Introduction

Colorectal cancer is a major public health problem in the United States. The annual incidence of colorectal cancer is more than 150,000, with approximately 110,000 new cases of colon cancer (tumors above the peritoneal reflection or more than 12 cm proximal to the anal verge) and 45,000 new cases of rectal cancer each year. Over the past 30 years, the population-adjusted incidence has remained constant at approximately 47 cases per 100,000, and thus the number of cases has increased due to population growth. These tumors are predominantly of a single histologic type, adenocarcinoma. The average age at presentation is 60 to 65 years. About 75 percent of the individuals with these cancers will have a primary surgical resection with the hope of complete tumor eradication. Recently, mortality from colorectal cancer has decreased overall, more for rectal than for colon tumors. Despite the high resectability rate and a general improvement in therapy, nearly half of all patients with colorectal cancer still die from metastatic tumor.

Adjuvant therapy is administered in addition to surgical treatment of the primary colorectal cancer with the intent to improve outcome. Adjuvant therapy options include chemotherapy, radiation therapy, and immunotherapy that are administered before or after curative intent surgery (i.e., surgery with negative microscopic margins). Over the past three decades, many clinical studies have failed to demonstrate benefits from adjuvant therapy. Claims of efficacy have been viewed with skepticism. Recently, new data from several studies have demonstrated delays in tumor recurrence and increases in survival for specific groups of patients.

Five general principles underlie adjuvant therapy:

1. There may be occult, viable tumor cells in circulation (intravascular, intralymphatic, or intraperitoneal) and/or established, microscopic loci of tumor cells locally, at distant sites, or both.

2. Therapy is most effective when tumor burden is minimal and cell kinetics are optimal.

3. Agents with proven effectiveness against the tumor are available.

4. Cytotoxic therapy shows a dose-response relationship and, therefore, must be administered in maximally tolerated doses, and the duration of therapy must be sufficient to eradicate all tumor cells.

5. The risk-to-benefit ratio for therapy must be favorable for individuals who may remain asymptomatic for their natural life expectancy after tumor resection.

Numerous staging systems, including those of Dukes', Kirklin, Astler-Coller, the Gastrointestinal Tumor Study Group (GITSG), and the Tumor/Node/Metastasis (TNM) system jointly agreed to by the International Union Against Cancer (UICC) and American Joint Committee on Cancer (AJCC), have been used to classify colorectal cancers. Although the modified Astler-Coller Dukes' system (MAC) is probably the most commonly used in the United States, the current TNM staging system should be utilized to accurately translate other systems into a standard format and will be used throughout this consensus statement (see tables 1 and 2).

Patients with Stage II (T3–4, N0, M0 or MAC B_{2-3}) and Stage III (T1–4, N1–3, M0 or MAC C_{1-3}) cancers have limited disease that may be resected with curative intent but remain at high enough risk for tumor recurrence that they may benefit from additional treatment. Adjuvant therapy, as previously defined, is not applicable to metastatic disease (Stage IV) patients. Individuals with Stage I disease (T1,2 N0 or MAC A or B_1) colorectal cancer have a 5-year survival with surgery alone of greater than or equal to 80 to 90 percent. With such a high probability of cure after surgery alone, the risk:benefit ratio for most presently available adjuvant therapy favors no further treatment for this group. Additional factors that may identify subsets within these early-stage patients most at risk for tumor recurrence are being sought, but currently TNM (or MAC) staging remains the only proven prognostic method. Thus, the approximate number of new patients in the United States each year in the conventionally defined high-risk group is 55,000 colon cancer patients and 20,000 rectal cancer patients. Roughly half of these individuals will die from recurrent colorectal cancer. The goal of adjuvant therapy is to reduce the expected 35,000 to 40,000 deaths per year.

Although the history of adjuvant therapy for colorectal cancer has spanned 30 years, only in the past 5 to 8 years have a number of clinical trials yielded reproducible positive results. To evaluate this recent information and resolve issues regarding adjuvant therapy for patients with colon and rectal cancer, the National Cancer Institute and the Office of Medical Applications of Research of the National Institutes of Health convened a Consensus Development Conference on April 16–18, 1990. After a day and a half of presentations by experts and discussion by the audience, a consensus panel drawn from specialists and generalists from the medical profession and related scientific disciplines, clinical investigators, and public representatives considered the evidence and agreed on answers to the following key questions:

1. Who is at risk for recurrence after colon and rectal cancer resection?

2. Is there effective adjuvant therapy for patients with colon cancer?

3. Is there effective adjuvant therapy for patients with rectal cancer?

4. What are the directions for future research?

TABLE 1 TUMOR/NODE/METASTASIS (TNM) STAGING

TX . . . Primary tumor cannot be assessed
T0 . . . No evidence of primary tumor
Tis . . . Carcinoma in situ
T1 . . . Tumor invades submucosa
T2 . . . Tumor invades muscularis propria
T3 . . . Tumor invades through the muscularis propria into the subserosa, or into nonperitonealized pericolic or perirectal tissues
T4 . . . Tumor perforates the visceral peritoneum or directly invades other organs or structures
NX . . . Regional lymph nodes cannot be assessed
N0 . . . No regional lymph node metastasis
N1 . . . Metastasis in 1-3 pericolic or perirectal lymph nodes
N2 . . . Metastasis in 4 or more pericolic or perirectal lymph nodes
N3 . . . Metastasis in any lymph node along the course of a named vascular trunk
MX . . . Presence of distant metastasis cannot be assessed
M0 . . . No distant metastasis
M1 . . . Distant metastasis

TABLE 2 TNM STAGING

				Dukes'
Stage 0	Tis	N0	M0	
Stage I	T1	N0	M0 — A	
	T2	N0	M0 ⎫	
Stage II	T3	N0	M0 ⎬ B	
	T4	N0	M0 ⎭	
Stage III	Any T	N1	M0 ⎫ C	
	Any T	N2,N3	M0 ⎭	
Stage IV	Any T	Any N	M1	

Who Is at Risk for Recurrence after Colon and Rectal Cancer Resection?

Surgery remains the critical modality in the treatment of colon and rectal cancer. Negative surgical margins, including radial margins in the rectum and retroperitoneal margins for selected sites within the colon, must be as wide as anatomically possible. Classic oncologic principles must be followed in removal of the primary tumor, the associated vascular arcade, and draining lymph nodes. No-touch techniques are not essential. The goal of any colorectal resection must be to achieve negative margins.

Clarifying the role of adjuvant therapy for colon and rectal cancer and maximizing benefit of adjuvant regimens require identifying those individuals most likely to develop recurrent disease. As a first step, patients should undergo evaluation of the remainder of the large bowel for synchronous lesions. The presence of inflammatory bowel disease, familial adenomatous polyposis, hereditary nonpolyposis colorectal cancer, or more subtle familial associations should be assessed. An abdominal computerized tomographic (CT) scan for liver metastases and a preoperative carcino-embryonic antigen (CEA) level should be obtained. In patients presenting with emergent perforation or obstruction, or those explored without complete preoperative assessment, these studies should be done postoperatively. Pelvic CT and magnetic resonance imaging (MRI) are neither specific nor sensitive enough to alter the surgical approach to a rectal lesion but may add useful preoperative data. Transrectal ultrasound appears promising in defining depth of penetration preoperatively but needs to be studied further.

At laparotomy, a complete surgical exploration is mandatory. Colon lesions should be resected with contiguous and regional lymph nodes. Lesions adherent to contiguous organs should be resected in continuity rather than dissected free. Adequate radial margins must be obtained to minimize local recurrence in rectal lesions.

The surgical pathologist should specify the gross and microscopic extent of all surgical margins, the depth of gross and microscopic penetration, the number of nodes removed, the number involved, and whether the apical node (highest level) is positive. The disease should be defined by TNM stage.

Characteristics such as venous or lymphatic invasion, perineural invasion, histologic subtype, and grade should be stated.

In assessing risk of recurrence after a potentially curative resection of a colorectal adenocarcinoma, we considered the usefulness of several possible prognostic factors in defining subgroups of patients at low, intermediate, and high risk for recurrence. These included stage of disease, site of disease, marker status, histologic features, host response parameters, and cellular and molecular characteristics.

Pathologic stage is the most important determinant of risk of recurrence and survival probability after primary surgical resection of colon or rectal cancer. The degree of penetration of the primary lesion, the presence or absence of lymph node involvement, and the number of involved nodes are all significant independent risk factors. Several recent retrospective reviews and prospective trials of surgery alone for Stage I and II colon cancer or Stage I rectal cancer indicate that prognosis is favorable. In contrast, the prognosis for patients with more advanced stages is poor. Local recurrence after rectal cancer resection also correlates with TNM staging.

There are clear differences in natural history and patterns of failure between colon and rectal cancer that mandate testing distinct adjuvant strategies for lesions in the two sites. Therefore, separate consideration of adjuvant approaches for colon and rectal cancers is appropriate. The impact of site within the colon or within the rectum on recurrence risk and survival is less significant and will not be addressed in this consensus statement.

Elevation of a preoperative CEA (>5 ng/ml) is an indicator of increased risk for recurrence. CEA elevations correlate with stage and histology. A normal preoperative CEA does not obviate the need for adjuvant therapy in node positive patients. However, an elevated CEA may determine a high-risk subset of patients with Stage II colon cancer appropriate for study of adjuvant therapy compared with an observation-only control.

Pathologic features such as grade, colloid or signet ring histology, venous or lymphatic invasion, perineural invasion, and perforation have been reported to be significant in unvariate analysis. However, in multivariate models where stage is included, many or all of these characteristics lose independent prognostic significance for recurrence or survival.

Pathologic findings suggesting host response such as mononuclear cell infiltration of the primary or reactive regional lymphadenopathy are not reproducible prognostic features. These findings may be of greater interest in the context of current or future adjuvant vaccine trials or studies of tumor infiltrating lymphocytes (TIL)/infiltrating mononuclear cells as adjuvant therapy.

It is premature to use certain cellular or molecular characteristics as standard determinants of recurrence risk or survival in colorectal cancer. Ploidy status and S phase fraction have not consistently correlated with overall recurrence and survival. With refinement and standardization of the methodology, these biologic features may help to determine Stage II subsets at high risk for recurrence.

At a molecular level, the Ki-ras-2 allele is frequently mutated in colon and rectal cancers, but there is thus far no clear correlation between the presence of this mutation and tumor phenotype or clinical course. Deletions of p53 on chromosome 17p and "DCC" on chromosome 18q have recently been documented and may be critical to mechanisms of tumor progression. The effects of transforming oncogenes and potential suppressor genes are highly pleiotropic. Even in the most well-defined systems of viral oncogenesis, hundreds of gene sequences change in expression, all with the potential of contributing to the final tumor phenotype. Data from several investigators suggest similar complexity of changes in gene expression and/or structure in colon and rectal cancer. Data from colorectal tumor cell lines well characterized as poorly, moderately, or well differentiated suggest that production and interaction of growth factors correlate with the degree of differentiation. The clinical significance of these findings remains to be elucidated.

Pursuit of these and future laboratory observations represents critical opportunities for companion studies to current and future clinical trials of adjuvant therapy in colon and rectal cancer. Strategies must be implemented for obtaining optimal tissue and prioritizing assignment of available specimens to studies defining the biological and clinical significance of these cellular and molecular characteristics in relation to etiology, mechanisms of progression, and clinical behavior of colorectal cancer.

Is There Effective Adjuvant Therapy for Patients with Colon Cancer?

Adjuvant therapy for colon cancer should be considered as separate from that for rectal cancer. Patterns of failure differ significantly with local pelvic failure common in rectal cancer because of narrow radial margins defined by the anatomic limits of dissection. Colon cancer, because far fewer limits exist in the extent of surgical resection and margins obtainable, tends to fail in the peritoneal cavity, the liver, or in distant sites with only a small component of isolated local failure. Thus, while a local modality such as radiotherapy may have an important role in the rectum, it is limited to special situations in the colon. Systemic chemotherapy or immunotherapy is the dominant adjuvant modality in colon cancer at this time.

In our identification of effective adjuvant therapies for patients with colon and rectal cancers we have relied exclusively on data derived from prospectively randomized trials. Comparisons using historical controls are subject to bias especially considering the changing prognosis stage for stage of these patients over time. Several aspects contribute to the usefulness of trial results in making consensus recommendations for patient care. First and foremost, an adequate number of patients must be accrued to detect treatment effects that are considered to be worthwhile but realistic. A clinical trial that fails to provide a statistically significant result might be too small to provide sufficient evidence either for or against a specific therapy. Estimates of the magnitude of treatment effects with confidence intervals to reflect the statistical uncertainty of the observed trial results are recommended. The level of statistical significance (p-value) alone is a poor measure of the magnitude of a treatment effect as it is influenced by the sample size of the data being evaluated.

In our deliberations, we attached credibility to high-quality studies, that is, studies with a low percentage of randomized patients excluded from analysis, a large sample size, good treatment compliance, and adequate duration of followup. We gave relatively low credibility to retrospective subset analyses in the absence of confirmatory studies. We regarded overall survival as the primary end point for evaluating treatment effectiveness. In addition, disease-free survival was an important end point. Analyses that weigh the benefits of delaying symptoms of recurrent disease against toxic effects of adjuvant therapy are important for assessing overall treatment gains considering quality of life.

Because individual trials may not be large enough to provide convincing evidence of small but worthwhile treatment effects, meta-analyses have been performed to increase the precision for estimating such treatment effects. These evaluations of data from randomized clinical trials are also useful for putting individual trial results within the context of other available data. Although there are potential methodologic problems with such analyses that relate to the selection and variability of the studies included, these analyses can provide a global summary of treatment effects. For the recommendations made by this panel, we relied on results from individual, well-conducted trials and used the meta-analyses to provide confirmatory evidence.

In the 1960's fluorodeoxyuridine (FUDR) and 5-fluorouracil (5-FU) were given as adjuvant agents for varying periods postoperatively with a wide range of dosage schedules. Activity was demonstrable but not convincing statistically in individual trials. A recent meta-analysis suggested some benefit with the use of 5-FU.

Levamisole alone was first tested in the adjuvant setting in a small group of non-randomized colorectal cancer patients reported by Verhaegen. Despite the failure of this agent to produce a response either alone or with chemotherapy in metastatic disease, an improvement in survival was noted in this series.

The North Central Cancer Treatment Group (NCCTG) and Mayo Clinic, encouraged by Verhaegen's findings, designed a clinical trial that tested the combination of 5-FU and levamisole in the adjuvant therapy of resectable colorectal cancer patients with Stage II and Stage III lesions. Quality control of data acquisition and analysis was excellent. The data are mature at a median followup of 7 years. The 5-FU plus levamisole combination significantly reduced recurrence. Subset analysis for Stage III patients treated with 5-FU and levamisole showed a significant improvement in overall survival. These results were considered sufficiently encouraging to recommend a confirmatory trial.

An intergroup study was designed with the same methodology with two exceptions: patients with Stage II disease were randomized to observation or to 5-FU plus levamisole and those with Stage III disease were randomized to the three arms of observation, levamisole alone, and 5-FU plus levamisole; only patients with colon carcinoma were studied.

This trial was well performed. Median followup is 3 years. Levamisole alone produced no significant effect. A dramatic effect of 5-FU and levamisole relative to surgery alone on disease-free survival and overall survival was demonstrated for Stage III patients. Therapy with 5-FU and levamisole reduced the risk of cancer recurrence by 41 percent and the overall death rate by 33 percent. Overall survival percentages at 3-1/2 years were estimated to be 71 percent versus 55 percent for the control group. Analysis failed to demonstrate an outcome difference in Stage II patients, but 1 to 2 years of additional observation is needed. Side effects from this combination were well tolerated and primarily associated with 5-FU.

There are potential pitfalls in interpreting these results. The mechanism of action of levamisole is not understood. The positive results seen in the NCCTG/Mayo Clinic study were based on a relatively small number of patients and a subset analysis. The short followup is a concern for the interpretation of results from the intergroup study. At this time, however, these studies are the most compelling investigations demonstrating a statistically significant improvement in disease-free survival and overall survival in the adjuvant setting for Stage III patients. Longer followup will hopefully strengthen the conclusion that adjuvant 5-FU/levamisole for Stage III patients should be the control arm for ongoing clinical trials and should be offered to similarly staged patients for trial unless medical or psychosocial contraindications exist.

If subsequent analysis of 5-FU/levamisole demonstrates significant benefit for Stage II patients, identical recommendations for trial or nontrial patients would pertain. However, the high survival rates observed in node-negative patients without adjuvant therapy would require a close examination of risk and benefit if this subset of patients were to be treated outside of clinical trials. It is noteworthy to observe the high response rates in metastatic colon cancer with the use of 5-FU and leucovorin. This combination, with or without levamisole, is under current clinical trial investigation.

The National Surgical Adjuvant Breast and Bowel Project (NSABP) protocol C01 demonstrated a significant, although modest, improvement in disease-free survival at a median followup of 7 years using a combination of methyl-chloroethyl-cyclohexly-nitrosourea (methyl-CCNU), vincristine, and 5-FU. This effect seems to be diminishing with time. A major concern, demonstrated in other studies as well, is the leukemogenic effect and renal toxicity of methyl-CCNU.

The GITSG protocol 6175 failed to demonstrate any benefit for the adjuvant use of methyl-CCNU/5-FU, methanol extracted residue of BCG (MER) or methyl-CCNU/5-FU plus MER for similarly staged node-positive and node-negative colon cancer patients.

Recognition that the liver is the most common site of tumor recurrence has led to multiple controlled and uncontrolled studies to evaluate portal vein infusion as adjuvant therapy in high-risk patients. One study combined systemic infusion with hepatic irradiation. All of these studies sought to demonstrate an improvement in regional control of hepatic metastases. Although some have reported significant improvement in disease-free survival and overall survival (presumed to be secondary to systemic effect), none, with the exception of the original study by Taylor et al., have succeeded in reducing liver metastases. This form of regional adjuvant therapy remains investigational. In view of the improved overall survival results, other approaches for using short duration intraoperative or immediate postoperative (perioperative) chemotherapy might be investigated.

Whenever a new therapy is found to be effective in a clinical trial, it is always difficult to determine how to advise other patient groups not precisely identical to the clinical study group. Although the available clinical trial data demonstrate benefit for patients who receive their therapy within 6 weeks of surgery, there is no evidence that patients who receive therapy after that period benefit significantly. Because there is no appropriate way to design a prospective trial that intentionally delays therapy beyond 6 weeks, this question cannot be answered by existing data or by subsequent clinical trial. The decision to begin adjuvant chemotherapy in appropriate patient groups later than 6 weeks after surgery must be left to individual decisions between the patient and doctor.

Is There Effective Adjuvant Therapy for Patients with Rectal Cancer?

Oncologic principles of surgical removal of the primary and draining lymph nodes apply to rectal cancer as well as to colon cancer. In general, two standard surgical approaches, abdominoperineal resection and low anterior resection, have been used in these trials. In contrast to colon cancer, there is a significant risk of symptomatic local-regional failure as the only or first site of recurrence in patients with curatively resected rectal cancer. In node-negative patients, local recurrence may be as low as 5 to 10 percent for Stage II tumors. In patients with Stage III tumors, local recurrence rates increase to 50 percent or more for more invasive tumors. The principal reason for local recurrence in resected rectal cancer appears to be related to the anatomic constraints in obtaining wide radial margins, even though the proximal and distal margins are adequate. Thus, in addition to the standard treatment outcomes of overall and disease-free survival, local-regional control should be considered in patients with rectal cancer. Clearly, this is not only an academic issue because local recurrence is associated with significant morbidity and often not effectively palliated by local treatment (surgery and/or radiation therapy) or by systemic chemotherapy at the time of recurrence.

Patients with locally invasive rectal cancer are at high risk for systemic relapse similar to patients with locally advanced colon cancer. The systemic risk for node-negative rectal cancer patients also appears comparable to similarly staged colon cancer patients.

By definition, "effective" adjuvant therapy of surgically resected rectal cancer should address both the local and systemic relapse potential of the disease. Over the past 10 to 15 years, the use of adjuvant radiation therapy has been evaluated in several randomized studies in both the preoperative and postoperative setting. An important variable in the studies of preoperative irradiation has been the total dose ranging from a single 5 Gray (Gy) fraction within 24 hours before surgery to high-dose fractionated (35–50 Gy in 4–7 weeks) irradiation over several weeks before surgery. Overall, there appears to be a significant decrease in local recurrence rates in patients receiving moderate to high dose (>35 Gy) preoperative irradiation (10 to 20 percent versus 25 to 50 percent in controls), usually without any impact on survival.

More recently, randomized trials in patients with resected rectal cancer have assessed the impact of postoperative irradiation. This approach allows for accurate pathological staging and inclusion of only high-risk patients in the study. An improvement in local control is found in most studies where postoperative irradiation (40–50 Gy) is compared to surgery alone. However, similar to preoperative irradiation, no significant benefits in terms of disease-free or overall survival are evident.

In light of a minimal, if any, impact of adjuvant radiation therapy alone on survival, it is evident that systemic treatment is necessary to improve the prognosis of surgically resected rectal cancer patients. Several large, well-designed randomized trials employing systemic therapy in at least one study arm were updated at the consensus conference. The GITSG 7175 and 7180 studies, the NSABP R-01 study, and the NCCTG-Mayo 794751 study were reviewed in detail and form the principal basis for our recommendations.

The major evidence in favor of the use of chemotherapy for systemic disease control comes from these trials. All relevant trials demonstrate an advantage for chemotherapy using 5-FU and methyl-CCNU with or without radiotherapy for overall survival, disease-free survival, or both. The second GITSG study (7180) compared the effects of radiation therapy with 5-FU or 5-FU/methyl-CCNU. Preliminary analysis documented no differences in recurrence rates, suggesting that methyl-CCNU may be unnecessary. Unfortunately, early termination of this trial makes a definitive answer difficult. In the first GITSG trial (7175), the combination of 5-FU and methyl-CCNU with radiotherapy continues to show significant improvement in local control and survival with 10-year followup compared with surgery alone and somewhat better than either modality on its own. In the NCCTG study with a median. followup of 6 years, the same combination is shown to be superior to radiotherapy alone (using DFS as the end point, overall survival is only marginally significant). In both studies, combined modality treatment yields local failure rates about one-half of single modality therapy. In the NSABP study, a combination of 5-FU, methyl-CCNU, and vincristine is significantly better than surgery alone but local failure remains high (23 percent). The one trial that does not fit this pattern is a European Organization for Research on Treatment on Cancer (EORTC) study (40741), where the addition of only 5-FU during preoperative radiotherapy had an apparently adverse effect on survival.

Overall, these results are strongly suggestive that the best current adjuvant therapy for rectal cancer involves postoperative treatment with both chemotherapy and radiotherapy. However, the absolute necessity for radiotherapy for survival benefits is by no means convincingly demonstrated at this time, and we must await the completion of current trials for clarification of this issue. Likewise, the presence of methyl-CCNU in most of the successful chemotherapy regimens is problematic in view of its demonstrated leukemogenesis and nephrotoxicity. It should be noted that the NCCTG study that documents benefits from combined modality therapy utilized only two doses of methyl-CCNU compared with seven doses in the NSABP and GITSG studies. Thus, if methyl-CCNU is found to be essential it may be possible to deliver fewer doses. We are optimistic about the likely effectiveness of combined modality therapy, but we recognize the need to study the effectiveness of combinations that do not include methyl-CCNU, such as 5-FU and leucovorin or related combinations in concert with radiotherapy for local control.

As with the colon carcinoma trials, the majority of the adjuvant treatments in rectal carcinoma were initiated within 6 weeks of surgery. It is not known whether therapy initiated after that point would be beneficial. The decision to begin adjuvant chemotherapy later than 6 weeks after surgery must be decided individually between the patient and the doctor.

The administration of adjuvant therapy must be balanced against the possible deleterious side effects that might negate any beneficial effect. Chronic radiation effects, although infrequent, can be severe, including radiation enteritis and bowel obstruction, because tumoricidal doses (45–55 Gy) of radiation are necessary.

Clearly, careful attention to the technical details of radiation therapy, including CT-assisted, contrast-enhanced treatment planning to exclude small bowel and the use of multiple radiation fields, can reduce acute and chronic radiation side effects. Additionally, surgical attention should be directed to preventing small intestine loops from entering the pelvis, using either natural structures or synthetic mesh. Chemotherapy should be administered by oncologists skilled in the administration of these toxic agents. The use of methyl-CCNU with its toxic effects remains problematic, and research should be directed toward finding effective drug combinations that do not use this agent.

What Are the Directions for Future Research?

The history of adjuvant treatment for colon cancer is confusing in part because of conflicting data from small, poorly controlled trials with inadequate followup. This experience makes it likely that major advances will require large, prospective randomized trials with well-balanced populations, carefully stratified by known prognostic factors of significance. There has also been little supportive biochemical or immunologic data generated from recent trials to support or reject the biological rationale on which the trial was based. Future trials hopefully should build in laboratory studies to confirm or reject the principal underlying hypothesis.

A review of existing clinical trials served to emphasize the need to continue efforts to improve the quality of trial data and the need to apply appropriate quality-assurance measures. For example, future trials will need to use such measures to document adherence to preestablished surgical resection margins, staging, and compliance with adjuvant therapy.

Although several adjuvant 5-FU containing combinations now show disease-free and overall survival benefits for patients with colon cancer, a wide variety of doses, schedules, routes of administration, and duration of therapy has been used. It is impossible to conclude what dose, schedule, and duration of 5-FU is optimal. Future trials should standardize drug dose and schedule, and link dose, dose intensity, and duration to some biological or biochemical end point. Likewise, the potential mechanism of levamisole effect is presently undefined. Levamisole drug dose and schedule have been selected empirically, and the extent of immunomodulation achieved or even what is desirable has not been established. Although lack of rationale for the activity of the combination should not preclude acceptance of its demonstrated benefits, efforts to build subsequent clinical trials on the provocative results of the 5-FU/levamisole trial are hampered by the absence of data on the immunomodulatory effect, if any, or on the mechanism of action of the combination. Future clinical trials should include sufficient laboratory investigation to address these questions of mechanism of action and biological rationale.

The highest priority for future adjuvant clinical trials in colon cancer remains the search for optimal regimens that improve disease-free survival and overall survival. At present, the 5-FU/levamisole regimen is the standard to which new therapies should be compared. Issues that remain at high priority are the study of other modulators of 5-FU, which include leucovorin, phosphonacetyl-aspartate (PALA) , and others. Crucial for the understanding of these trials will be the biochemical determination of successful modulation of 5-FU effect to be done in concert with the ongoing clinical trial. Other combinations active in advanced disease, such as 5-FU/interferon, have merit for study provided they are built into prospective trial design.

Adjuvant therapy is most conclusively established for patients with Stage III disease. However, other groups of patients, such as those with Stage II disease, possess 5-year disease-free and overall survival outcomes of 80 percent or less and might therefore be legitimate candidates for inclusion into subsequent prospective clinical trials with an untreated arm. Patients with early disease such as Stage I patients have an excellent 5-year survival (>80 to 90 percent) with surgery alone and are not likely to benefit from adjuvant chemotherapy unless the development of newer prognostic markers allows one to select poor prognostic subsets. Newer prognostic markers such as DNA content, proliferative activity, surface glycoprotein, gastrin receptor, oncogenes/tumor suppressor genes, and allelic deletions may allow the refinement of prognostic groups further than presently possible with stage alone.

Although local relapse is not a common problem in colon cancer, there are certain groups (i.e., TNM T4, N1, N2) that have significant local failure rates and should be included in separate clinical trials testing radiation-containing combined modality therapies.

Two recent clinical trials suggest a disease-free and survival benefit from the direct portal administration of chemotherapy, although the magnitude of the effect is less than that seen in the systemic therapy trials with 5-FU/levamisole. Furthermore, neither trial reduced the frequency of relapse in the liver. Subsequent clinical trials will require the direct comparison of effective systemic adjuvant chemotherapy with a similar regimen given by regional infusion before intraportal drug administration can be a recommended alternative to systemically administered adjuvant chemotherapy.

As with colon carcinoma, the prospective clinical trial will be the major tool for defining future effective therapy in rectal carcinoma. Future trials must define the relative merits of combination chemotherapy, including 5-FU/levamisole; 5-FU, methyl-CCNU, and vincristine; and also introduce newer combinations of promise, including 5-FU/leucovorin and other biochemical techniques for 5-FU modulation.

Current evidence indicates that combined modality therapy can significantly reduce the incidence of symptomatic local recurrence in the disease, and the next series of clinical trials must define the proper dose, sequence, and integration of these modalities. The impact on local recurrence, disease-free survival, and overall survival must be measured against any increased toxicity inherent in the combined modality approach.

Adjuvant therapy for colon and rectal carcinoma potentially affects 35,000 to 40,000 patients each year. These therapies, while bringing improved disease-free survival and overall survival, do entail longer and more complex treatments, and there is presently little information to answer questions regarding either physiologic or financial burdens experienced by patients undergoing adjuvant therapy either within or outside the clinical trials setting. Resources need to be allocated to incorporate these important questions into the design of future colorectal adjuvant therapy trials. In addition, differences in disease incidence and outcome observed in various ethnic and socioeconomic groups suggest a need to perform adequate adjuvant trials to address these questions.

The cost to the patient should be considered as an integral part of adjunctive therapy. Ability to pay should never be a factor in a patient's decision to receive treatment. New protocols should always consider cost to the patient. Cost is not only considered in dollars. Cost can also mean quality of life. Decisions affecting the quality of a patient's life require an understanding between the patient and his or her doctor. Basic qualities for all people should be hope, comfort, and freedom from pain.

Conclusions and Recommendations

In answer to the question, "Who is at risk for recurrence after colon and rectal cancer resection?," the consensus panel recommends the following:

- The TNM system based on a complete pathological description can effectively describe risk groups for recurrence and should be used in clinical trials research and clinical practice.

- Patients with colon and rectal cancer should be studied separately when defining adjuvant strategies.

- Patients with Stage III colon cancer or Stage II/III rectal cancer are at high risk for recurrence and warrant adjuvant therapy.

- Anatomic or biologic features may define subsets of patients with Stage II colon cancer at intermediate risk of recurrence sufficient to merit testing of adjuvant treatment compared to observation only controls. These features include:

  – T4 N0 M0

  – T3 N0 M0 plus one or more of the following:

    –Pre-op CEA > 5 ng/ml.

    –Aneuploid DNA content.

    –High S phase.

–Colloid, signet ring, or poorly differentiated histology.

–17p or 18q deletion.

- Patients with Stage I lesions are at low risk for recurrence and should not receive adjuvant treatment.

- Correlation of laboratory observations and clinical data must be pursued to define the biological and clinical significance of these cellular and molecular characteristics.

In answer to the question "Is there effective adjuvant therapy for patients with colon cancer?" we conclude that:

- Optimal adjuvant therapy for Stage II and III colon cancer has not yet been devised. Continued clinical trials in this disease are essential to discover more active adjuvant therapies.

- Based on current clinical trial data, Stage III patients unable to enter a clinical trial should be offered adjuvant 5-FU and levamisole as administered in the intergroup trial unless medical or psychosocial contraindications exist.

- The panel cannot recommend any specific adjuvant therapy at this time for Stage II patients outside of clinical trials.

In answer to the question "Is there effective adjuvant therapy for patients with rectal cancer?" we conclude the following:

- No adjuvant therapy is recommended for Stage I patients; in contrast to Stage II colon cancer, we recommend adjuvant treatment of Stage II rectal cancer.

- Combined postoperative chemotherapy and radiation therapy improves local control and survival in Stage II and III patients and is recommended.

- At the present time, the most effective combined modality regimen appears to be 5-FU plus methyl-CCNU, and high-dose pelvic irradiation (45 to 55 Gy) but chronic toxicity considerations of methyl-CCNU mitigate against using this regimen outside ongoing clinical trials.

- Current clinical trials of combined modality therapy are designed to improve the prognosis of Stage II and III patients. Entry of patients into these clinical trials is highly encouraged.

The following directions for future research are suggested:

- The highest priority for future adjuvant trials in colon cancer should build on the results achieved with 5-FU/levamisole using modulators of 5-FU, modulators of host response, and new regimens of proven efficacy in advanced disease.

- The highest priority for future adjuvant trials in rectal cancer will be to integrate radiation therapy with newer 5-FU modulated regimens such as 5-FU/ levamisole, 5-FU/leucovorin, or other combinations with demonstrated activity in advanced disease.

- There is a need to identify new determinants of risk to be used to select early stage patients likely to benefit from adjuvant therapy.

- There is a need to incorporate into intergroup trials the appropriate basic laboratory investigations required to define mechanisms of drug action, especially in trials involving modulators of host immune response.

- There is a need to address issues of quality of life and the cost benefit of such therapies.

- There is a need to initiate trials to address questions of differences in disease and outcome observed in various ethnic and socioeconomically disadvantaged groups.

§ 10.40   Adjuvant Therapy of Rectal Cancer: National Cancer Institute (March 1991)

The National Cancer Institute wants to bring to the attention of clinicians the benefits that may be achieved with adjuvant therapy of rectal cancer. The data, presented here for your review, suggest that a sequential regimen of 5-fluorouracil (5-FU) based chemotherapy and radiation therapy can reduce overall tumor recurrence rates, substantially reduce local recurrence, and prolong patient survival. Such a regimen may be recommended as therapy for individuals with resected, TNM stage II (Dukes' $B_{2,3}$) and III (Dukes' C) rectal cancer. While previous clinical trials have utilized a combination of postoperative radiation therapy to the pelvis plus 5-FU and the investigational drug, methyl-CCNU (semustine), current preliminary information suggests that substantial treatment benefits may be achieved using irradiation and standard doses of 5-fluorouracil. This combination avoids the potential risks of leukemia and chronic renal insufficiency associated with protracted administration of methyl-CCNU.

The intent of this announcement is to supplement the recent NIH Consensus Development Conference statement on adjuvant therapy of rectal cancer and to provide data to assist you in treatment planning for your patients.

Carcinoma of the rectum is one of the more common malignant diseases in the United States, afflicting an estimated 45,000 individuals a year. The clinical course of patients treated with surgery alone has been characterized by a high death rate (55% of patients die within 5 years) and also by the pain and disability associated with pelvic recurrence of tumor. Therapy that simply reduces local relapse would be a meaningful advance for many patients. Radiation alone, given in doses of 45 to 50 Gy, has produced a modest reduction in local recurrence but has not been shown to have an influence on survival (1).

In April 1990, the NIH Consensus Development Conference on "Adjuvant Therapy for Patients with Colon and Rectal Cancer" stated that:

Combined postoperative chemotherapy and radiation therapy improves local control and survival in stage II and III patients [with rectal cancer] and is recommended;

At the present time, the most effective combined modality regimen appears to be fluorouracil plus methyl-CCNU and high dose pelvic irradiation (45 to 55 Gy), but chronic toxicity considerations of methyl-CCNU mitigate against using this regimen outside ongoing clinical trials (2).

Newly available information, presented here, reinforces the observation that adjuvant therapy benefits patients with rectal cancer and suggests that a regimen of 5-fluorouracil plus pelvic irradiation without methyl-CCNU may well be the optimal combination.

Appearing in the March 14 issue of the New England Journal of Medicine is the final report of one major study that served as the basis for the Consensus Conference recommendations (3,4). The NEJM-reported trial was conducted by the North Central Cancer Treatment Group (NCCTG 794751) from 1980 to 1986 and involved the participation of about 200 patients. Beginning four to ten weeks after curative intent surgery for stage II or III rectal cancer, patients were randomized to receive either combined modality radiation plus chemotherapy, or radiation therapy alone. In both treatment regimens, radiation therapy consisted of 45 Gy to the pelvis delivered over four and one-half weeks followed by a 5.4-Gy boost to the tumor bed. In the combined modality treament, patients received an initial nine-week cycle of 5-FU and methyl-CCNU. This chemotherapy was followed by radiation plus concurrent 5-FU. Patients then received another nine-week cycle of 5-FU and methyl-CCNU.

With further follow-up, the results of this study show a clear advantage for the combined modality treatment in all parameters of evaluation, including reduced overall recurrences (p=0.0016), reduced local recurrences (p=0.036), reduced distant metastases (p=0.011), and improved survival (p=0.026). There is a 46% reduction in pelvic recurrence, a 37% reduction in distant tumor spread, and a 29% reduction in patient deaths. Survival data are summarized in the table below. Acute, severe toxicity was infrequent. Delayed, severe reactions, usually bowel obstruction requiring surgical intervention, occurred in about 6.5% of all patients and were comparable in incidence whether patients received radiation therapy alone or radiation plus chemotherapy.

RESULTS OF COMPLETED CLINICAL TRIALS OF
ADJUVANT THERAPY IN RECTAL CANCER

Trial	Regimen	N	Five-Year Survival Disease-Free	Overall
NCTG	RT	100	42%	47%
794751	MeCCNU/FU + RT/FU	104	63%*	58%*
GITSG	Surgery Only	58	47%	43%
7175	MeCCNU/FU	48	55%	56%
	RT	50	55%	52%
	MeCCNU/FU + RT/FU	46	71%*	59%*
NSABP	Surgery Only	184	30%	43%
R-01	RT	184	33%	41%
	MeCCNU/VCR/FU	187	42%*	53%*
GITSG	RT/FU + MeCCNU/FU	95	54%**	66%**
7180	RT/FU + FU	104	69%**	76%**

*p<0.05   **three-year data

This study confirms for the first time that the benefit achieved with chemotherapy when combined with irradiation is superior to that produced by radiation therapy alone, which many clinicians regard as a standard adjuvant therapy for rectal cancer.

The NCCTG trial design evolved from earlier work, such as the Gastrointestinal Tumor Study Group study (GITSG 7175) that used a combined modality regimen in which radiation (40 to 44 Gy) plus 5-FU was given initially, followed by cycles of 5-FU and methyl-CCNU given for one and one-half years (5,6). That study demonstrated the superiority of chemo-radiation therapy when compared to surgery alone. A reduction in local recurrence was also noted when compared to radiation therapy alone. The NCCTG trial now convincingly confirms that post-surgical, combined modality therapy can improve control of tumor relapse and patient survival not only when compared to surgery alone but also when compared to full dose postoperative radiation therapy.

The new and confirmatory evidence of effective surgical adjuvant therapy for rectal cancer has stimulated a search for safer and still more effective approaches. Important questions remain.

1. Is methyl-CCNU a necessary component of the chemotherapy or is 5-FU as a single agent sufficient?

Methyl-CCNU is an investigational agent that currently can be obtained only from the NCI. No long-term bone marrow or renal toxicities were observed after limited methyl-CCNU treatment on the NCCTG trial. However, after chronic administration, this drug has been associated with a 12-fold increased risk for secondary leukemia or preleukemia (7) as well as with chronic renal toxicity. One clinical study of adjuvant therapy in rectal cancer (GITSG 7180) showed no superiority for combined modality therapy that included methyl-CCNU when compared to treatment with radiation and 5-FU (8). An intergroup trial, led by the Northern Central Cancer Treatment Group (NCCTG 864751), with 453 rectal cancer patients entered between 1987 and 1990, tested combined modality therapy with or without methyl-CCNU administered in a manner identical to the treatment in the superior regimen of the trial reported in the New England Journal of Medicine (NCCTG 794751). The protocol specified an interim analysis after 50% of the predicted tumor recurrences had occurred. That preliminary analysis of the study, which will be presented at the annual meeting of the American Society of Clinical Oncology (ASCO) in May 1991 (9), reveals a rate of recurrence 1.2 times higher for patients receiving methyl-CCNU, statistically ruling out the likelihood that the addition of methyl-CCNU actually confers a 25% or greater advantage in disease control. Severe thrombocytopenia was seen only in patients receiving methyl-CCNU, affecting 12.4% of these individuals. To date, there are not sufficient data to compare survival rates. But based on increased toxicity and lack of evidence for improved effectiveness, the NCI agrees with the study's investigators that methyl-CCNU, delivered in this manner, is probably not a necessary component of multi-modality adjuvant therapy for rectal carcinoma. This conclusion is provisional while we await further maturation of the intergroup sudy (NCCTG 864751). However, the data have been found to be sufficiently convincing that the currently active, NCI-supported, Intergroup study (INT 0114) utilizes 5-FU alone and radiation as the control treatment.

2. Do 5-FU/levamisole, 5-FU/leucovorin, or other promising therapies have a role in adjuvant therapy of rectal cancer?

The demonstration that 5-FU/levamisole can be effective adjuvant therapy of colon cancer (10) and the acceptance that 5-FU/leucovorin combinations are superior to 5-FU alone for metastatic colorectal tumors have produced hope for further improvement in the systemic component of adjuvant treatment of rectal cancer. Both of these combinations are currently being evaluated in protocols sponsored by the National Cancer Institute and are available to eligible, rectal cancer patients throughout North America. In these trials, all patients receive active, postoperative, systemic therapy. Continued accrual of patients to these trials is essential to define further advances in care.

For patients with resected rectal cancer with transmural extension (TNM stage II or Dukes' B_{2-3}) or with positive regional lymph nodes (TNM stage III or Dukes' C) who would be appropriate candidates for adjuvant care but who lack access to or who decline participation in clinical trials, it would be reasonable to consider the following treatment regimen based on available evidence. This regimen is the control arm for the currently active Intergroup study (INT 0114) mentioned above.

Treatment should be initiated from one to two months after surgery if the patient is fully recovered from the operative procedure, maintaining a reasonable state of nutrition, and has normal hematologic parameters.

Week 1 and 5:	5-FU 500 mg/M^2/day x 5 days
Week 9:	Radiation therapy to tumor area and regional node distribution, 45 Gy over 4–6 weeks, followed by 5.4-Gy boost in 3 fractions to the tumor bed. Give 5-FU 500 mg/M^2/day x 3 days during the first and last week of irradiation.
4 and 8 weeks after radiation:	5-FU 450 mg/M^2/day x 5 days
	5-FU should be given by rapid IV injection for all courses. Appropriate adjustments in 5-FU dosage should be made based on toxicity to previous courses. Careful and experienced radiation therapy treatment planning is required with special attention to avoid small bowel injury (11).
	With regard to averting these toxicities, the critical role of the surgeon must be recognized. At the time of surgery, consideration must be given to the possibility that radiation therapy may be a part of postoperative treatment planning. Delineation of the limits of resection with radio-opaque clips and incorporation of one of the surgical techniques for exluding small bowel from the pelvis may minimize some of the treatment related sequelae.

Other doses and schedules of radiation and/or chemotherapy may be of equal efficacy. It is the responsibility of the individual physician, in concert with the individual patient, to develop the most appropriate plan of therapy.

Additional information about the studies cited in this Announcement and about other clinical trials is available from the NCI's Physician Data Query (PDQ) database. PDQ can be accessed through a medical library or by calling NCI's Cancer Information Service at 1-800-4-CANCER. The NIH Consensus Development Conference Statement from the April 1990 Conference on Adjuvant Therapy in Colon and Rectum Cancer is available by writing to:

Consensus Development Statement: Colon/Rectum
Adjuvant Therapy
Office of Medical Applications of Research
Building 1, Room 260
National Institutes of Health
Bethesda, MD 20892

Some physicians may conclude that the currently available data support a contributory role for methyl-CCNU in an adjuvant regimen. Further information about methyl-CCNU or other NCI sponsored investigational agents may be obtained by calling NCI's Drug Management and Authorization Section of the Investigational Drug Branch at 301-496-5725.

REFERENCES

1. FISHER B, WOLMARK N, et al. Postoperative adjuvant chemotherapy or radiation therapy for rectal cancer: results from NSABP protocol R-01. J Natl Cancer Inst 80:21–29, 1988

2. NIH Consensus Conference on Adjuvant Therapy for Patients with Colon and Rectal Cancer. JAMA 264: 1444–1450, 1990

3. KROOK JE, MOERTEL CG, et al. Effective surgical adjuvant therapy for high risk rectal carcinoma. N Engl J Med 324: 709-175, March 14, 1991

4. KROOK J, MOERTEL C, et al. Radiation vs sequential chemotherapy-radiation-chemotherapy, a study of the North Central Cancer Treatment Group, Duke University, Mayo Clinic Proc ASCO 6:92, 1987

5. GASTROINTESTINAL TUMOR STUDY GROUP. Prolongation of disease free interval in surgically treated rectal carcinoma. N Engl J Med 312: 1465–1472, 1985

6. DOUGLASS HO, MOERTEL CG, et al. Survival after postoperative combination treatment of rectal cancer (letter) N Engl J Med 315: 1294, 1986

7. BOICE JD, GREEN MH, et al. Leukemia and preleukemia after adjuvant treatment of gastrointestinal cancer with semustine (methyl-CCNU). N Engl J Med 309: 1079–1085, 1983

8. WEAVER D, LINDBLAD AS, et al. Radiation therapy and 5-fluorouracil (5-FU) with or without MeCCNU for the treatment of patients with surgically adjuvant adenocarcinoma of the rectum. Proc ASCO 9: 106, 1990

9. O'CONNELL M, WIEAND H, et al. Lack of value for methyl-CCNU (MeCCNU) as a component of effective rectal cancer surgical adjuvant therapy: interim analysis of intergroup protocol 86-47-51. Proc ASCO 1991, in press

10. MOERTEL CG, FLEMING TR, et al. Levamisole and fluorouracil for adjuvant therapy of resected colon cancer. N Engl J Med 322: 352–358, 1990

11. GUNDERSON LL, RUSSELL AH, et al. Treatment planning for colorectal cancer. Int J Radiat Oncol Biol Phys 11: 1379–1393, 1985

CHAPTER 11

EXOCRINE PANCREAS NEOPLASMS

§ 11.1   Staging and Classification

TNM: American Joint Committee on Cancer.[1]

The TNM system is not usually utilized except to establish the fact that a tumor 2 cm or less (T1a) has a better prognosis than a tumor over 2 cm (T1b). Extension of the neoplasm into surrounding structures or the presence of metastases indicated a poor prognosis.

Staging of Cancer of the Pancreas[2]

Stage I: Confined to pancreas

Stage II: Involving only neighboring structures such as the doudenal wall

Stage III: Involving lymph nodes

Stage IV: Involving liver or other distant spread.

---

[1] American Joint Committee on Cancer, Manual for Staging of Cancer 110 (3d ed. 1988).

[2] A.S. Hermreck et al., *Importance of Pathologic Staging in the Surgical Management of Adenocarcinoma of the Exocrine Pancreas*, 127 Am. J. Surgery 653 (1974).

Classification of Benign Neoplasms of the Pancreas[3]

Epithelial origin

  Duct, ductular, or centroductular (Centroacinar) cell

    Polyp

    Papilloma, papillomatosis, villous

    Papilloma, papillomatosis, villous papilloma

    Adenoma

      Solid

        Duct (ductule)

        Centroductular (centroacinar)

    Cystadenoma

      Serous: Simple

              Papillary

      Mucinous: Simple

                 Papillary

    Carcinoid

    Oncocytoma

    Ciliated cell

  Acinar cell

    Adenoma

    Cystadenoma

  Mixed epithelial cells

    Duct-islet

    Duct-acinar

    Duct-acinar-islet

    Acinar-islet

    Carcinoid-islet

  Connective tissue origin

    Fibroma

    Leiomyoma

---

[3] A.L. Cubilla & P.J. Fitzgerald, *Tumors of the Exocrine Pancreas, in* Atlas of Tumor Pathology, Second Series, fascicle 19 at 98 (1974).

   Neurilemoma

   Fibrous histiocytoma

   Vascular

    Lymphangioma

    Hemangioma

   Miscellaneous

Mixed epithelial-connective tissue origin

   Fibroadenoma.

    Primary Malignant Neoplasms of the Nonendocrine Pancreas[4]

  Duct (ductule) cell origin

  Duct cell carcinoma

  Giant cell carcinoma

  Giant cell carcinoma (osteoclastoid type)

  Adenosquamous carcinoma

  Adenosquamous (spindle cell) carcinoma

  Microadenocarcinoma (solid microglandular)

  Mucinous ["colloid"] carcinoma

  Cystadenocarcinoma (mucinous)

  Papillary cystic tumor

  Mucinous-carcinoid carcinoma

  Carcinoid

  Oncocytic carcinoid

  Oncocytic carcinoma

  "Oat-cell" carcinoma

  Ciliated cell carcinoma

 Acinar cell origin

  Acinar cell carcinoma

  Acinar cell cystadenocarcinoma

 Mixed cell type

  Duct-islet cell

---

[4] *Id.* at 110.

Duct-islet-acinar cell

Acinar-islet cell

Carcinoid-islet cell

Connective tissue origin

Leiomyosarcoma

Malignant fibrous histiocytoma

Malignant hemangiopericytoma

Osteogenic sarcoma

Rhabdomyosarcoma

Malignant neurilemoma

Liposarcoma

Uncertain histogenesis

Pancreaticoblastoma

Unclassified

Large cell

Small cell

Clear cell

Malignant lymphoma

Histiocytic

Plasmacytoma.

§ 11.2   Etiology

Tobacco

Cigarette smoke has known carcinogenic properties. Smokers have twice the risk of developing cancer of the pancreas than nonsmokers.[5]

---

[5] L.S. Krain, *The Rising Incidence of Carcinoma of the Pancreas: Real or Apparent?* 25 Surgical Oncology 115 (1970); J.R. Malageda, *Pancreatic Cancer; an Overview of Epidemiology, Clinical Presentation and Diagnosis,* 54 Mayo Clinic Proc. 459 (1979); E.Z. Wynder, *An Epidemiological Evaluation of the Causes of Cancer of the Pancreas,* 35 Cancer Res. 2228 (1975).

Pancreatitis

Chronic calcareous pancreatitis is associated with a high incidence of pancreatic malignancy. Pancreatic exocrine insufficiency is occasionally present in patients with cancer of the pancreas, but causation factors are unknown.[6]

Diabetes

Preexisting, long-standing diabetes has been noted in some patients with pancreatic cancer.[7] Most patients with diabetes in association with cancer of the pancreas have had the diabetes for only a few months. This can be due to the malignancy as the cause of the diabetes.

Diet

Coffee has been implicated as a cause of cancer of the pancreas,[8] although not proven.[9] There might be an association between cholesterol and various steroid hormones and pancreatic malignancy, because various endocrinopathies have been reported in women with cancer of the pancreas.[10]

Toxic Agents

There is increased risk of pancreatic cancer in workers in the metal, coal, and gasoline industries. Betanaphthylamine and benzidine have been postulated as offending agents.

§ 11.3   Clinical Manifestations

Epigastric discomfort or pain at times radiating into the back most often occurs. Indigestion is an insidious symptom that can occur early in the disease. Weight loss and decrease in appetite can occur. Jaundice appears when the head of the pancreas is involved, and the common bile duct is obstructed. Cancer of the tail of pancreas can appear as a palpable abdominal mass.

---

[6] D. Mainz & P.D. Webster, *Pancreatic Carcinoma—A Review of Etiologic Considerations,* 19 Am. J. Digestive Diseases 459 (1974).

[7] A.R. Moossa, Tumors of the Pancreas 432 (1980).

[8] B. MacMahon et al., *Coffee and Cancer of the Pancreas,* 304 New Eng. J. Med. 630 (1981).

[9] A.R. Feinstein et al., *Coffee and Pancreatic Cancer,* 246 JAMA 957 (1981).

[10] H.B. Soloway & S.C. Sommers, *Endocrinopathy Associated with Pancreatic Carcinomas: Review of Host Factors, Including Hyperplasia and Gonadotropic Activity,* 164 Annals Surgery 300 (1966).

Associated disorders include steatorrhea, migratory phlebitis, and long-standing recurrent pancreatitis. A history of heavy coffee intake and/or cigarette smoking can be noted.

§ 11.4   Diagnosis

Cancer of the head of the pancreas causes elevation of the alkaline phosphatase and serum bilirubin when the common bile duct is obstructed. Other liver function enzymes can be elevated.

Carcinoembryonic antigen (CEA) can be elevated, although this also can be found in other conditions such as cholangitis, pancreatitis, and hepatitis. Human tumor-associated antigens can be elevated.[11] Pancreatic oncofetal antigen was found to be abnormally high in gastrointestinal malignancies, especially pancreatic cancer.[12] Elevated galactosyl transferase isoenzyme II (GT II) can help differentiate pancreatitis from pancreatic malignancy.[13]

Evocative tests have been used to help distinguish pancreatitis from cancer of the pancreas. The *secretin stimulation test*[14] is a test of pancreatic function by injecting secretin. If there is pancreatic duct obstruction, benign or malignant, the secretin is depressed, making a diagnosis difficult. The secretin is analyzed according to **Table 11–1**.

Table 11–1

Pancreas Secretion Analysis

	Pancreatitis	Pancreatic Cancer
Volume	Normal	Down
Bicarbonate	Down	Normal
Amylase	Normal	Normal

The *cholecystokinin stimulation test*[15] also stimulates pancreatic function and is less than normal in the presence of pancreatitis. The *Lundh test meal*[16]

---

[11] C.R. Mackie et al., *Prospective Evaluation of Some Candidate Tumor Markers in the Diagnosis of Pancreas Cancer,* 25 Digestive Diseases & Sci. 161 (1980).

[12] F.B. Gelder et al., *Studies on Oncofetal Antigen POA,* 42 Cancer 1635 (1978).

[13] D.K. Podolsky et al., *Galactosyltransferase Isoenzyme II in the Detection of Pancreatic Cancer,* 304 New Eng. J. Med. 1313 (1981).

[14] D.A. Dreiling, *The Early Diagnosis of Pancreatic Cancer,* 6 Scandinavian J. Gastroenterology 115 (Supp. 1970).

[15] A. Csendes et al., *Pancreatic Protein Secretion in Response to Secretion plus C-Terminal Octapeptide of Cholecystokinin,* 60 Gastroenterology 770 (1971).

[16] O. James, *The Lundh Test,* 14 Gut 582 (1973); A. Mottaleb et al., *The Lundh Test in the Diagnosis of Pancreatic Disease: A Review of 5 Years' Experience,* 14 Gut 835 (1973).

requires duodenal aspiration following a special meal. Decrease in trypsin output is a positive test. The *glucose tolerance test*[17] can be abnormal in patients with cancer of the pancreas.

Upper gastrointestinal X-ray series at times shows effacement of the medial surface of the second portion of the duodenum from a mass in the head of the pancreas, and the duodenal loop may be enlarged. Ultrasound or computerized tomography (CT) are fairly accurate in visualizing a tumor in the pancreas. Dilated biliary ducts can be seen when the malignancy obstructs the common bile duct, lymph node enlargement might be evident, and hepatic metastases are visualized. CT- or ultrasound-guided needle biopsy can be used to aspirate tissue from the pancreatic mass.

Endoscopic retrograde cholangiopancreatography (ERCP) examines the biliary and pancreatic ducts. Ductal aspiration with cytologic examination discloses malignant cells,[18] although it does this somewhat better for cancer in the pancreatic head than for in the body or tail.

Arteriography helps identify pancreatic masses, but it is more useful to define vascular abnormalities that can be useful when planning a surgical resection.

Isotope scanning of the pancreas with selenomethionine has been used, but it does not seem to add anything to the accuracy of diagnosis.

§ 11.5   Surgical Treatment

Diagnosis, if not made preoperatively by cytology, should be made at the time of exploratory laparotomy. A mass can be open biopsied or needle biopsied. A tumor in the head of the pancreas is best approached by a transduodenal needle biopsy. Open biopsy should be reserved for a mass that cannot be diagnosed by needle biopsy or when the tumor is unresectable. Skinny needle cytology can be used if a competent experienced cytologist is available.

Resectability is determined by examining the liver, hepatoduodenal ligament structures, portal vein by rotating the duodenum medially (Kocher maneuver), and superior mesenteric artery. If any lymph nodes are involved by biopsy, most surgeons would not attempt a curative resection.

Malignancies involving the body or tail of the pancreas can be resected by distal or partial pancreatectomy, and most cancers of the body or tail are far advanced by the time of diagnosis.

---

[17] A.R. Moossa, Tumors of the Pancreas 432 (1980).

[18] L. Bowdon & G.N. Papanicolau, *Exfoliated Pancreatic Cancer Cells in the Duct of Wirsung,* 150 Annals Surgery 296 (1959); R.L. Goodale et al., *Cytological Studies for the Diagnosis of Pancreatic Cancer,* 47 Cancer 1652 (Supp. 1981); S. Kameya et al., *The Diagnosis of Pancreatic Cancer by Pancreatic Juice Cytology,* 25 Acta Cytology 354 (1981); R.G. Rosen et al., *Cytologic Diagnosis of Pancreatic Cancer by Ductal Aspiration,* 167 Annals Surgery 427 (1968).

The Whipple procedure (pancreaticoduodenectomy) is the preferred procedure for cancer of the head of the pancreas. High gastrectomy or antrectomy with vagotomy prevents postoperative bleeding ulcers.[19] **Figure 11–1** illustrates anastomoses following the Whipple procedure. Reconstruction requires choledochojejunostomy, pancreaticojejunostomy, and gastrojejunostomy. Total pancreatectomy is used by some surgeons to avoid the precarious anastomosis of pancreas to jejunum. A portion of the portal vein can be resected in continuity with the tumor resection if involved by tumor extension.

Complications of the Whipple procedure include anastomotic ulceration with gastrointestinal bleeding, anastomotic breakdown, peritonitis, pancreatic fistula, sepsis, wound infection, intrabdominal abscess, pneumonia, and pulmonary embolus. Operative mortality is 3 to 15 percent. Decrease in enzyme secretion by the pancreas results in steatorrhea. Diabetes mellitus always follows total pancreatectomy.

Palliative procedures include choledochojejunostomy to relieve or prevent jaundice and gastrojejunostomy to prevent symptomatic duodenal obstruction.

§ 11.6 Chemotherapy Treatment

Pancreatic cancer is usually detected at an advanced stage in most patients. The median survival from the time of diagnosis to death is less than six months in untreated patients. Chemotherapy alone or in combination with radiation therapy has resulted in only moderate responses.

Initially, single drugs were used, and the most frequent single agent in pancreatic cancer was 5-fluorouracil (5-FU). Most studies of 5-FU used a single agent, and reported a wide range of response rates ranging from minimal to 67 percent with an average response of 20 percent.[20] Other single agents with activity similar to that of 5-FU in the 20-percent range were Mitomycin-C,[21] adriamycin or doxorubicin,[22] and streptozotocin.[23] In view of the encouraging results with the combination of 5-FU, adriamycin, and mitomycin (FAM) in gastric carcinoma,

---

[19] C.S. Grant & J.A. Van Heerden, *Anastomotic Ulceration Following Subtotal and Total Pancreatectomy*, 190 Annals Surgery 1 (1979); H.W. Scott et al., *The Role of Vagotomy in Pancreaticoduodenectomy*, 191 Annals Surgery 688 (1980).

[20] S.K. Carter & R.L. Comis, *The Integration of Chemotherapy into a Combined Modality Approach for Cancer Treatment. VI. Pancreatic Adenocarcinoma*, 2 Cancer Treatment Rev. 193 (1975).

[21] L.H. Manheimer & J. Vital, *Mitomycin C in the Therapy of Far-Advanced Malignant Tumors*, 19 Cancer 207 (1966).

[22] P.S. Schein et al., *Radiomized Phase II Clinical Trial of Adriamycin, Methotrexate and Actinomycin D in Advanced Measurable Pancreatic Carcinoma*, 42 Cancer 19 (1978).

[23] R.W. Dupriest et al., *Streptozotocin Therapy in 22 Cancer Patients*, 25 Cancer 358 (1975).

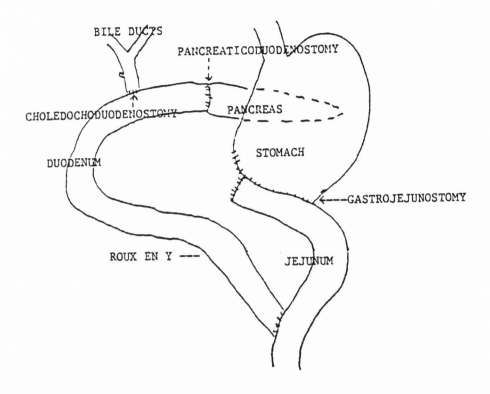

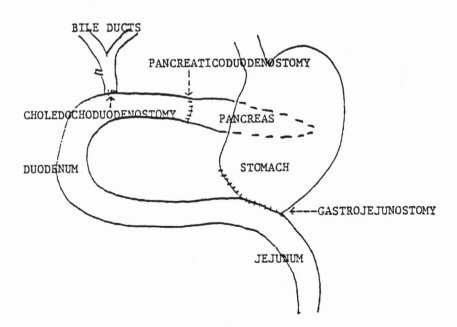

Figure 11–1. Anastomoses following the Whipple procedure (pancreaticoduode-nectomy).

this regimen was utilized in treating pancreatic carcinoma with objective responses ranging from 37 percent to 40 percent.[24]

Streptozotocin, a methylnitrosourea, is toxic for the pancreatic islet beta pancreatic cells in animals and was felt to be effective in treating pancreatic tumors. Objective responses had been reported.[25] With these promising results, streptozotocin was added to mitomycin and 5-FU (SMF regimen) with response rates ranging from 32 percent to 43 percent.[26] Streptozotocin also was added to the FAM-regimen (FAM-S) and produced an objective response rate of 48 percent.[27] The median survival of all patients was 6.75 months, and 7 of the 25 patients survived more than 12 months.

Hexamethylmelamine, a nitrosourea, is less toxic and produced similar results as streptozotocin or adriamycin. It was added to mitomycin and 5-FU, and this resulted in a median survival of nine months for 45 patients with either metastatic Stage III or unresectable Stage II carcinoma of the pancreas. Fifteen percent survived two years, 31 percent showed objective responses, and 44 percent had stable disease. Response was associated with a median survival of 17 months.[28] A regimen combining chemotherapy and radiotherapy for locally unresectable carcinoma of the pancreas compared the survival of patients treated with the standard SMF regimen (streptozotocin, mitomycin, and 5-FU) versus radiation combined with 5-FU followed by the same three-drug SMF combination. The median survival for the combined modality therapy group was 42 weeks compared to 32 weeks for the group treated with chemotherapy alone. The overall survival following the combined modality treatment program was 41 percent at one year compared to 19 percent for the SMF therapy alone.[29]

Recent animal studies demonstrated that caffeine has a synergistic effect with chemotherapeutic agents due to its interference with the repair of DNA damage by cytoxic drugs. A current study underway at the Memorial Sloan-Kettering

[24] J.D. Bitran et al., *Treatment of Metastatic Pancreatic and Gastric Adenocarcinomas with 5-Fluorouracil, Adriamycin and Mitomycin C (FAM)*, 63 Cancer Treatment Rep. 2049 (1979); F.P. Smith et al., *5-Fluorouracil, Adriamycin and Mitomycin-C (FAM) Chemotherapy for Advanced Adenocarcinoma of the Pancreas*, 46 Cancer 2014 (1980).

[25] L.E. Broder & S.K. Carter, Streptozotocin: Clinical Brochure (National Cancer Institute 1975); R.W. Dupriest et al., *Streptozotocin Therapy in 22 Cancer Patients*, 25 Cancer 358 (1975).

[26] R.M. Bukowski et al., *Phase II Trial of Streptozotocin, Mitomycin-C and 5-Flourouracil in Adenocarcinoma of the Pancreas*, 3 Cancer Clinical Trials 321 (1980); R.G. Wiggans et al., *Phase II Trial of Streptozotocin, Mitomycin-C and 5-Fluorouracil (SMF) in the Treatment of Advanced Pancreatic Cancer*, 41 Cancer 387 (1978).

[27] R.M. Bukowski et al., *Phase II Trial of 5-Fluorouracil, Adriamycin, Mitomycin C and Streptozotocin (FAM-S) in Pancreatic Carcinoma*, 50 Cancer 197 (1982).

[28] H.W. Bruckner et al., *Primary Treatment of Regional and Disseminated Pancreatic Cancer with Hexamethylemelamine, Mitomycin C and 5-Fluorouracil Infusion*, 46 Oncology 366 (1989).

[29] Gastrointestinal Tumor Study Group, *Treatment of Locally Unresectable Carcinoma of the Pancreas: Comparison of Combined-Modality Therapy (Chemotherapy plus Radiotherapy) to Chemotherapy Alone*, 80 J. Nat'l Cancer Inst. 751 (1988).

Cancer Center compares the standard SMF treatment regimen to cis-platinum, cytosine arabinoside, and caffeine. This study is in progress and the results should be meaningful, because 80 patients were entered in this study.[30]

Presently, combination chemotherapy with the FAM, SMF, and FAM-S regimens results in a 30-percent response rate with an average median survival of eight months. Clinical trials with these regimens or investigational drugs with or without radiation therapy under the auspices of the National Cancer Institute and the cooperative chemotherapy groups can serve as appropriate treatment for the newly diagnosed patient to determine more successful treatment regimens.

§ 11.7 Radiation Therapy Treatment

The large majority of pancreatic carcinomas, whether resectable or unresectable, are incurable. The role of radiation is to relieve symptoms, especially pain, and to increase longevity for a number of months. Occasional cures do occur, but they are very rare.

Computerized tomography has made it possible to direct radiation fields accurately from multiple directions to give the required high doses of radiation without undue injury to the surrounding normal tissues. Total doses of external radiation range from 4000 to 6000 cGy. Split courses of radiation with two-week rest periods between the 2000 cGy courses of radiation reduce the risk of intestinal injury. Daily increments of radiation can range from 160 to 180 cGy. To avoid renal failure, be careful to exclude most of the renal tissue from the fields of irradiation.

Other techniques of radiation employ injecting radioactive gold-198 or iodine-125 seeds into the tumor followed by external radiation. Radioactive seeds safely can deliver over 10,000 cGy (because of rapid dosage fall-off short distances from the seeds) and improve local control of tumors. Survival rates are not increased in this method because of the lack of control over metastases, the main reason for treatment failure.

An alternative to seed implantation is intraoperative radiation therapy (IORT) given directly into the tumor when the abdomen is open during surgery. A single dose of 1500 to 2000 cGy is given followed by conventional external radiation in the same manner as with seeds.

External radiation and chemotherapy, usually 5-fluorouracil, are often given in combination. The most promising results in operable tumors have been achieved with postoperative 5-fluorouracil and 4000 cGy of radiation given in a split course. This regimen has increased the two-year survival rate. Combined radiation and chemotherapy also is the most effective regimen with inoperable tumors.

---

[30] J. Dougherty et al., *Advanced Pancreas Cancer: A Phase I Trial of Cisplatin, High-Dose Cytosine Arabinoside, and Caffeine,* 81 J. Nat'l Cancer Inst. 1735 (1989).

Complications of radiation for pancreatic carcinoma include duodenal ulcers, gastrointestinal bleeding, pancreatic insufficiency, and, from seed implantations, abscesses and anastomotic leaks.

§ 11.8   Commentary and Significant Cases

Malignancy of the pancreas is a difficult diagnosis to make because of the vague symptoms that can occur in the early course of the disease. Obstructing the common bile duct by the tumor results in jaundice, which will lead to the proper diagnosis. When pain and weight loss are present, the disease is usually not curable. About 25 percent of patients survive five years when the pancreas is resected in an attempt to cure the disease. The morbidity and mortality in pancreatioduodenectomy is significant, and patients must be forewarned of the possible complications.

Gray v. Hicks.[31]   The 54-year-old decedent was seen by the defendants in the summer of 1985 for complaints of right upper quadrant abdominal pain and feeling tired and run down. No problems were noted, and she was told to return. In November 1985, she saw one of the defendants with the same complaints. She was diagnosed as having psychiatric problems. Pancreatic cancer was found in October 1986, and she died one month later. The defendants contended that pancreatic cancer is very difficult to diagnose, and her symptoms indicated other problems that were appropriately treated. A defense verdict resulted.

Jacobs v. Horton Memorial Hospital.[32]   The physician and hospital were found liable to the patient's wife for the emotional distress she allegedly suffered on being informed of the patient's incorrect diagnosis of pancreatic cancer with a prognosis of six months to live. The court held that a doctor or hospital cannot be held liable for emotional distress suffered by members of patient's family as a result of malpractice in treating patient. Recovery is limited to those directly injured by act of malpractice.

---

[31] No N39232 (San Diego Super. Ct. Feb. 1990), *reprinted in* 6 Med. Malpractice Verdicts, Settlements & Experts No. 6, at 16 (1990).

[32] 130 A.D.2d 546, 515 N.Y.S.2d 281 (1987).

CHAPTER 12

LIVER AND BILIARY TRACT NEOPLASMS

LIVER

§ 12.1   Staging and Classification

TNM: American Joint Committee on Cancer.[1]
   The TNM system is not ordinarily used for liver cancers.
   Following are four different classifications of liver tumors.

Tumors of the Liver and Intrahepatic Bile Ducts[2]

Tumors of the liver

   Epithelial

     Benign

        Adenoma

        Adrenal rest tumor

     Malignant

        Hepatocellular carcinoma (hepatoma)

        Combined liver cell and bile duct carcinoma (cholangiohepatoma)

        Hepatoblastoma

        Carcinoid

   Mesodermal

     Benign

        Hemangioma

        Capillary angioma

        Cavernous hemangioma

        Hemangioendothelioma

---

[1] American Joint Committee on Cancer, Manual for Staging of Cancer 88 (3d ed. 1988).

[2] H.A. Edmondson, *Tumors of the Liver and Intra-Hepatic Bile Ducts, in* Atlas of Tumor Pathology, § VII, fascicle 25 at 18 (1958).

Lipoma

Myxoma

Fibromatosis

Malignant

Hemangioendothelial sarcoma (angioblastic sarcoma)

Malignant mesenchymoma

Rhabdomyosarcoma

Mixed elements

Hepatic mixed tumor (teratoid tumor)

Teratoma

Carcinosarcoma

Tumors of the bile ducts

Benign

Adenoma

Cystadenoma

Papilloma

Malignant

Bile duct carcinoma (cholangiocellular carcinoma).

Mesenchymal Tumors of the Liver[3]

I.   Tumors of fibrous tissue

  A.   Benign

    1.   Fibroma

  B.   Malignant

    1.   Fibrosarcoma

II.   Tumors of adipose tissue

  A.   Benign

    1.   Lipoma

    2.   Myelolipoma

    3.   Angiomyolipoma

    4.   Hibernoma

---

[3] K.G. Ishak, *Mesenchymal Tumors of the Liver, in* Hepatocellular Carcinoma 247 (K. Okuda & R.L. Peters eds., John Wiley & Sons, Inc., 1976).

     B. Malignant
        1. Liposarcoma

III. Tumors of muscle tissue
     A. Benign
        1. Leiomyoma
        2. Epitheloid leiomyoma
     B. Malignant
        1. Leiomyosarcoma
        2. Rhabdomyosarcoma

IV. Tumors of blood vessels
     A. Benign
        1. Hemangioma
        2. Infantile hemangioendothelioma
     B. Malignant
        1. Malignant hemangioendothelioma

V. Tumors and tumorlike lesions of lymph vessels

VI. Tumors of mesothelial tissues
     A. Benign
        1. Benign mesothelioma
     B. Malignant
        1. Malignant mesothelioma

VII. Tumors of pluripotenial mesenchyme (mesenchymomas)
     A. Benign
        1. Benign mesenchymoma
     B. Malignant
        1. Malignant mesenchymoma

VIII. Tumors of disputed or uncertain histogenesis
     A. Benign
        1. Granular cell tumor
        2. Myxoma
     B. Malignant

Classification of Primary Liver Tumors[4]

A. Epithelial tumors
     1. Malignant
        Hepatocellular carcinoma

---

[4] M.M. Schonland et al., *Hepatic Tumours, in* Liver and Biliary Disease: Pathophysiology, Diagnosis, Management 887 (R. Wright et al., eds., 1979). Reprinted with permission of W.B. Saunders Company.

Cholangiocarcinoma

Combined carcinoma

Cholangiolocellular carcinoma

Carcinoid tumour

Squamous carcinoma

Hepatoblastoma

B.   Mesodermal tumours

   1.   Malignant

      Malignant haemangio-endothelioma

      Malignant mesenchymoma

      Other sarcomas

C.   Mixed tumours

   1.   Malignant

      Malignant mixed hepatic tumour

      Carcinosarcoma

   2.   Benign

      Liver cell adenoma

      Focal nodular hyperplasia

      (Adenomatous hyperplasia)

      (Partial nodular transformation)

      Bile duct adenoma

      Biliary cystadenoma

      Microhamartoma

      Heterotopic rest tumours

      Cavernous haemangioma

      Infantile haemangio-endothelioma

      Mesenchymal hamartoma

      Other benign tumours

      Benign teratoma.

Benign Epithelial Tumors of Liver[5]

Benign epithelial tumors

   Liver cell adenoma

   Bile duct adenoma

   Bile duct cystadenoma

   Adrenal rest tumor

[5]H.A. Edmondson, *Benign Epithelial Tumors and Tumorlike Lesions of the Liver, in* Hepatocellular Carcinoma 310 (K. Okuda & R.L. Peters eds., John Wiley & Sons, Inc., 1976).

Tumorlike lesions

Adenomatous hyperplasia

Focal nodular hyperplasia

Mixed hamartoma (mixed adenoma)

Solitary and multiple nonparasitic cysts

Congenital hepatic fibrosis and polycystic disease

Mesenchymal hamartoma

Anoxic necrosis.

Hepatocellular-Cholangiocarcinoma Classification[6]

Hepatocellular carcinoma

Intrahepatic cholangiocarcinoma

Combined tumors

Type I: Collision tumors

Type II: Transition tumors

Type III: Fibrolamellar tumors.

§ 12.2   Etiology

Adenomatous Hyperplasia

A definite transition of adenomatous hyperplasia of the liver to hepatocellular carcinoma has been shown.[7] This connection helps explain the association of cirrhosis and liver cancer, because the overgrowth of undamaged liver cells in the repair process in cirrhotic livers is a form of adenomatous hyperplasia.

---

[6]Z.G. Goodman et al., *Combined Hepatocellular-Cholangiocarcinoma: A Histologic and Immuno-Histochemical Study,* 55 Cancer 124 (1985). Reprinted with permission of J.B. Lippincott Company.

[7]M. Arakawa et al., *Emergence of Malignant Lesions Within an Adenomatous Hyperplastic Nodule in a Cirrhotic Liver: Observation in Five Cases,* 91 Gastroenterology 198 (1986); T. Takayama et al., *Malignant Transformation of Adenomatous Hyperplasia to Hepatocellular Carcinoma,* 336 Lancet 1153 (1990).

Aflatoxin

Aflatoxins are produced by a food spoilage fungus (aspergillus flavus). The carcinogenic effect of aflatoxins is most prominent in the liver.[8] Primary hepatocellular carcinoma is more common in geographical areas with a higher intake of aflatoxin.[9]

Alcohol

Alcohol is a liver toxin and can lead to a fine granular cirrhosis (Laennec's cirrhosis or portal cirrhosis). Perhaps some of the liver damage is due to nutritional deficiencies in the chronic alcoholic.

Alpha 1 Antitrypsin

Isolated patients with hepatocellular carcinoma have been reported with aberrant pi genotypes (alpha-1-antitrypsin).[10]

Androgenic Steroids

Some patients treated with oxymetholone, an alkylated testosterone derivative, have been noted to develop hepatocellular carcinoma.[11] None of the cases have developed metastases.

Budd-Chiari Syndrome

The Budd-Chiari syndrome is an obstructive disorder of the hepatic veins from a variety of possible causes such as stricture, neoplasm, trauma, liver disease, plant toxins, systemic infections, and hematologic disorders. Cirrhosis occurs

---

[8] R.W. Detroy et al., *Aflatoxin and Related Compounds, in* Microbial Toxins 4–178 (A. Ciegler et al. eds., 1971); G.N. Wogan, *Aflatoxin Carcinogenesis, in* Methods in Cancer Research 309–44 (H. Busch ed., 1973).

[9] R.C. Schank et al., *Dietary Aflatoxins and Human Liver Cancer. IV. Incidence of Primary Liver Cancer in Two Municipal Populations of Thailand,* 10 Food & Cosmetics Toxicology 171 (1972).

[10] N.O. Berg & S. Eriksson, *Liver Disease in Alpha-1-Antitrypsin Deficiency,* 287 New Eng. J. Med. 1264 (1972); W. Rawlings et al., *Hepatocellular Carcinoma and Partial Deficiency of Alpha-1-Antitrypsin,* 81 Annals Internal Med. 771 (1974).

[11] M.S. Bernstein et al., *Hepatoma and Peliosis Hepatitis Developing in a Patient with Fanconi's Anemia,* 284 New. Eng. J. Med. 1135 (1971); F.L. Johnson et al., *Association of Androgenic-Anabolic Steroid Therapy with Development of Hepatocellular Carcinoma,* 2 Lancet 1273 (1972); A.T. Meadows et al., *Hepatoma Associated with Androzentherapy for Aplastic Anemia,* 84 J. Pediatrics 109 (1974).

with ascites and splenomegaly. This disease is often associated with hepatocellular carcinoma.[12]

Cholangiocarcinoma

Cholangiocarcinoma associated with liver cirrhosis is rare and almost always restricted to biliary cirrhosis, which is due to obstruction or infection of the major extrahepatic or intrahepatic bile ducts. Primary biliary cirrhosis is a disorder without obstruction or infection and is at times caused by certain drugs (chlorpromazine, arsenicals). Infection by flukes such as Clonorchis sinensis or Opisthorchis viverrine, although rarely causing biliary cirrhosis, has been reported in association with cholangiocarcinoma.[13]

Cirrhosis

Cirrhosis of the liver is a known cause of hepatocellular carcinoma found in 80 to 90 percent of cases. Liver fibrosis appears to be an abortive form of cirrhosis and also can be associated with hepatoma.

Familial Cirrhosis and Hepatocellular Carcinoma

The combination of chronic hepatitis, cirrhosis of the liver, and hepatocellular carcinoma occurring in families has been reported.[14] Hepatitis B antigen (HbAg) has been identified in such families.[15] Susceptibility to persistence of HbAg is thought to be by autosomal recessive inheritance with maternal transmission.[16]

---

[12] I.W. Simpson & B.D. Middlecote, *The Budd-Chiari Syndrome in the Bantu, in* Liver 257 (S.J. Sanders & J. Terblanche eds., 1973).

[13] T. Shikata, *Primary Liver Carcinoma and Liver Cirrhosis, in* Hepatocellular Carcinoma 69 (K. Okuda & R.L. Peters eds., John Wiley & Sons, Inc., 1976).

[14] Y. Morimoto et al., *Familial Cirrhosis with Hepatoma,* 58 Japanese Soc'y Internal Med. 89 (1969); K. Yuta et al., *Cirrhosis with Hepatoma in Two Uterine Brothers,* 10 Acta Hepatology Japanese 592 (1969).

[15] E.K. Denison et al., *Familial Hepatoma with Hepatitis-Associated Antigen,* 74 Annals Internal Med. 391 (1971); A. Ohbayashi et al., *Familial Clustering of Asymptomatic Carriers of Australia Antigen and Patients with Chronic Liver Disease or Primary Liver Cancer,* 62 Gastroenterology 618 (1971); M. Velasco et al., *Australia Antigen and Primary Carcinoma of the Liver,* 60 Gastroenterology 729 (1971).

[16] B. Blumberg et al., *Hepatitis and Australia Antigen: Autosomal Recessive Inheritance of Susceptibility to Infection in Humans,* 102 Proc. Nat'l Acad. Sci. 1108 (1969); A.I. Satnick, *Australia Antigen and the Immune Response in Human Diseases,* 55 J. Allergy & Clinical Immunology 42 (1974).

Familial Hepatocellular Carcinoma Without Cirrhosis

Although hepatocellular carcinoma without cirrhosis has been known to occur in families,[17] the incidence is very rare. The genetic susceptibility is unknown.

Hemochromatosis (Hemosiderosis)

Hepatocellular carcinoma has been noted in association with hemochromatosis.[18] Classic idiopathic hemochromatosis is a hereditary iron metabolism disorder with excess deposit of iron in the tissues, cirrhosis, and diabetes mellitus. The exogenous, nonhereditary form is a result of iron over lead from excessive intake of iron compounds or blood transfusions.

Posthepatitis

Posthepatitis or postnecrotic cirrhosis originates from the hepatitis virus (HBAg) and forms a macronodular liver. HBAg has been detected in the serum of 40 percent of patients with hepatoma.[19] The initial viral infection can be subclinical.

§ 12.3   Clinical Manifestations

Liver cancer can grow to a large size with metastases without producing any symptoms. Upper abdominal pain or discomfort can occur. There can be tenderness in the palpable edge of an enlarged liver under the right costal margin. Malaise, weight loss, anorexia, nausea, fever, and jaundice are not uncommon. Ascites with abdominal distention and discomfort can be the presenting symptom. Vascular nevi, distended abdominal surface veins, palmar erythema, and gynecomastia can be seen. Occasionally, a patient can present with hematemesis (vomiting of blood), hemoperitoneum (intraabdominal bleeding), or a moribund condition.

---

[17] R.M. Hagstrom & T.D. Barker, *Primary Hepato-Cellular Carcinoma in Three Male Siblings,* 22 Cancer 142 (1968); L. Kaplan & S.L. Cole, *Fraternal Primary Hepato-Cellular Carcinoma in Three Male, Adult Siblings,* 39 Am. J. Med. 305 (1965).

[18] S. Warren & E.L. Drake, *Primary Carcinoma of the Liver in Hemachromatosis,* 27 Am. J. Pathology 573 (1951).

[19] K. Nishioka, *Report of WHO Associated Workshops of Hepatitis B Antigen* (World Health Organization 1973).

Paraneoplastic Syndromes: Erythrocytosis

Erythrocytosis, an increase in red blood cell mass, and erythroid hyperplasia can occur in hepatoma,[20] hypernephroma,[21] and hemangioblastoma.[22] Erythropoietin can be the origin of the erythrocytosis.[23] Erythropoietin is postulated to be an enzymatic interaction between renal erythropoietic factor (REF) and a globulin substrate secreted by the liver.[24] The possible mechanisms for stimulating erythrocytosis in hepatoma include increased globulin substrate production, direct secretion of erythropoietin, and decreased activation of erythropoietin.

Hypercalcemia

Excessive elevation of serum calcium in malignancies is most often due to skeletal metastases. Hypercalcemia can occur in hepatocellular carcinoma without the presence of metastases to bone,[25] and it also has been reported in association with cholangiocarcinoma.[26] The tumor can secrete parathormone, a precursor or intermediate form of parathormone, or a substance with parathormone-like activity.

Hypoglycemia

Hypoglycemia occurs in 24 to 30 percent of patients with hepatoma.[27] There can be multiple reasons for developing low blood sugar in the presence of hepatocellular carcinoma. There is the possibility of producing a substance with insulin-like activity, but this substance has not been identified,[28] nor is there evidence

---

[20] M.H. Brownstein & H.S. Ballard, *Hepatoma Associated with Erythrocytosis,* 40 Am. J. Med. 204 (1966); A.J.S. McFadzean et al., *Polycythemia in Primary Carcinoma of the Liver,* 13 Blood 427 (1958).

[21] J.S. Hewlett et al., *Hypernephroma with Erythrocytemia. Report of a Case and Assay of the Tumor for Erythropoietic-Stimulating Substance,* 262 New Eng. J. Med. 1058 (1960).

[22] T.A. Walmann et al., *The Association of Polycythemia with a Cerebellar Hemangioblastoma: The Production of an Erythropoiesis Stimulating Factor by the Tumor,* 31 Am. J. Med. 318 (1961).

[23] E.B. Thorling, *In Paraneoplastic Erythrocytosis and Inappropriate Erythropoietin Production—A Review,* 17 Scandinavian J. Haematology (Supp. 1 1972).

[24] A.S. Gordon et al., *A Possible Mechanism for the Erythrocytosis Associated with Hepatocellular Carcinoma in Man,* 35 Blood 151 (1970).

[25] D.J. Becker et al., *Hepatoma Associated with Hypercalcemia,* 186 JAMA 1018 (1963).

[26] W. Naide et al., *Cholangiocarcinoma Causing Hypercalcemia and Hypophosphatemia Without Skeletal Metastases (Pseudohyperparathyroidism),* 13 Am. J. Digestive Disorders 705 (1968).

[27] A.J.S. McFadzean & T.T. Yeung, *Hypoglycemia in Primary Carcinoma of the Liver,* 98 Archives Internal Med. 720 (1956); O.B. Urteaga et al., *Cancer Primario del Hidago y de la Vias Biliares,* 3 Arch. Peru Patol. Clin. 3 (1949).

[28] A. Schonfeld et al., *Hypoglycemia and Polycythemia Associated with Primary Hepatoma,* 265 New Eng. J. Med. 231 (1961).

of stimulating pancreatic insulin release.[29] Increased glucose utilization by the tumor is possible,[30] or there can be a reduction in glucose production by the liver.[31]

In the case of hypoglycemia in a rapidly growing and poorly differentiated tumor, it is likely that the tumor requirement for glucose exceeds the gluconeogenesis production of the normal portions of the liver. With hypoglycemia in a slow-growing and well-differentiated tumor, there is probably defective glycogenolysis from abnormal enzymes.[32]

Sexual Precocity

Precocious puberty can be seen in children over five years of age with hepatocellular carcinoma.[33] This consequence occurs from the secretion of ectopic chorionic gonadotropin by the tumor.[34] The symptoms include deepening of the voice, development of pubic hair, enlargement of the penis, and accelerated growth.

Gynecomastia

Breast enlargement in the male has been reported[35] in association with hepatoma, as well as mammary hypertrophy, amenorrhea, and galactorrhea in the female[36] with hepatoma.

---

[29] D.R. Miller et al., *Hypoglycemia due to Nonpancreatic Mesodermal Tumors,* 150 Annals Surgery 684 (1956).

[30] H.B. Chandalia & B.R. Boshell, *Hypoglycemia Associated with Extrapancreatic Tumors,* 129 Archives Internal Med. 447 (1972).

[31] R.A. Kreisberg & L.F. Pennington, *Tumor Hypoglycemia: A Heterogenous Disorder,* 19 Metabolism 445 (1970).

[32] M. Cochrane & R. Williams, *Humoral Effects of Hepatocellular Carcinoma, in* Hepatocellular Carcinoma 340 (K. Okuda & R.L. Peters eds., John Wiley & Sons, Inc., 1976).

[33] K.G. Ishak & P.R. Glinz, *Hepatoblastoma and Hepatocarcinoma in Infants and Children: Report of 47 Cases,* 20 Cancer 396 (1967).

[34] W. Hung et al., *Precocious Puberty in a Boy with Hepatoma and Circulating Gonadotropin,* 3 J. Pediatrics 895 (1963).

[35] M.O. Williams, *Gynecomastia,* 34 Am. J. Med. 103 (1963).

[36] C. Couinaud et al., *Hepatome Malin avec Amenorrhee et Galactorrhee. Disparition du Syndrome Endocrinien après Hepatectome Droite,* 27 An. Chir. C151 (1973).

Hyperlipidemia

High levels of cholesterol and triglycerides have been noted in hepatoma[37] and in cholangiocarcinoma.[38] There can be a defect in the negative feedback mechanism in which dietary cholesterol inhibits the enzyme necessary to reduce cholesterogenesis.

Dysfibrinogenemia

An increased fibrinogen level can be found in patients with hepatocellular carcinoma,[39] and it is probably due to the release of an antifibrinolytic agent from the tumor. Cryofibrinogenemia has been reported, but it is very rare.[40]

Porphyria Cutanea Tarda

Excessive production of porphyrins by hepatoma can result in cutaneous porphyria and photosensitivity.[41] Porphyrin excess also can be seen in the presence of cirrhosis, possibly from decreased liver breakdown of porphyrin.

Hypertrophic Pulmonary Osteoarthropathy

Hypertrophic osteoarthritic changes can be seen in patients with primary and secondary biliary cirrhosis, portal cirrhosis, and hepatocellular carcinoma.[42] The only consistent finding in these patients is vasodilatation with increased blood flow to the affected areas.

---

[37] M.E. Alpert et al., *Primary Hepatoma in Uganda. A Prospective Clinical and Epidemiologic Study of Forty-Six Patients,* 46 Am. J. Med. 794 (1969); A.E. Hansen et al., *Disturbance of Osseous and Lipid Metabolism in a Child with Primary Carcinoma of the Liver,* 17 J. Pediatrics 9 (1940).

[38] A. Viallett et al., *Primary Carcinoma of the Liver and Hyperlipaemia,* 86 Can. Med. Ass'n J. 1118 (1962).

[39] W. Bell et al., *Cryofibrinogenemia, Multiple Dysproteinemias and Hypervolemia in Patient with Primary Hepatoma,* 64 Annals Internal Med. 658 (1966); H.C. Kwan et al., *Antifibrinolytic Activity in Primary Carcinoma of the Liver,* 18 Clinical Sci. 251 (1959).

[40] W.C. Levin et al., *Secondary Cryofibrinogenemia Associated with Cryopathy. Proceedings of the Ninth Congress of the International Society of Hematology, Vol. 3.* 239 (Universidad Nacional Autonoma de Mexico 1964).

[41] J. Berman & A. Braun, *Incidence of Hepatoma in Porphyria Cutanea Tarda,* 8 Rev. Czech. Med. 290 (1962); R.P.H. Thompson et al., *Cutaneous Porphyria due to a Malignant Primary Hepatoma,* 16 Gastroenterology 779 (1970).

[42] A.G. Morgan et al., *A New Syndrome Associated with Hepatocellular Carcinoma,* 63 Gastroenterology 340 (1972).

Carcinoid Syndrome

Primary carcinoid tumors can arise from the liver,[43] and carcinoid syndrome can occur.[44] The syndrome results from elevated 5-hydroxyindole acetic acid (5HIAA), 5-hydroxytryptophan, and serotonin, causing flushing and explosive diarrhea.

Alkaline Phosphatase Isoenzyme

An isoenzyme of alkaline phosphatase normally found in the serum has been noted in hepatocellular carcinoma and cholangiocarcinoma as well as secondary hepatic tumors (metastases to the liver).[45]

§ 12.4   Diagnosis

Alkaline phosphatase, glutamic oxaloacetic transaminase (SGOT), glutamic pyruvic transaminase (SGPT), serum bilirubin, serum albumin, and lactic acid dehydrogenase (LDH) are liver function tests that can be abnormally elevated in the presence of liver cancer.

Alphafetoprotein (AFP, alpha-1 globulin) is fairly specific for carcinoma arising from the hepatocyte (hepatocellular carcinoma), but has been found elevated in patients with embryonal cancers or teratomas of the gonads. The AFP level reflects response to chemotherapy or recurrence after surgery.[46]

The presence of hepatitis-associated antigen (HbAg, Australia antigen) indicates recent or past infection with the virus. The liver cancer can be due to the chronic liver injury leading to cirrhosis or the carcinogenic effects of the virus.

Carcinoembryonic antigen (CEA) can be elevated in benign or malignant conditions of the liver. Primary liver carcinoma can be associated with increased CEA.[47] Recurrence can be detected early by following the CEA level. Many other malignant tumors also can have elevated CEA.

---

[43] H.A. Edmonson, *Tumors of the Liver and Intrahepatic Bile Ducts, in* Atlas of Tumor Pathology, § VII, fascicle 25, at 105 (1958).

[44] A. Primack et al., *Hepatocellular Carcinoma with the Carcinoid Syndrome,* 27 Cancer 1182 (1971).

[45] M.L. Portugal et al., *Serum Alpha-fetoprotein and Variant Alkaline Phosphate in Human Hepatocellular Carcinoma,* Int'l J. Cancer 383 (1970); M. Warnock & R. Reisman, *Variant Alkaline Phosphatase in Human Hepatocellular Cancers,* 24 Clinica Chimica Acta 5 (1969).

[46] Y. Matsumoto et al., *Response of Alpha-fetoprotein to Chemotherapy in Patients with Hepatoma,* 34 Cancer 1602 (1974); L.C. Parks et al., *Alpha-fetoprotein: An Index of Progression or Regression of Hepatoma and a Target for Immunotherapy,* 180 Annals Surgery 599 (1974); K. Sugahara et al., *Serum Alpha-fetoprotein and Resection of Primary Hepatic Cancer,* 106 Archives Surgery 63 (1973).

[47] E.W. Martin et al., *Carcinoembryonic Antigen, Clinical and Histological Aspects,* 37 Cancer 62 (1976).

To differentiate cirrhosis from hepatic malignancy (hepatoma and cholangio-carcinoma), measuring the serum copper and plasma fibrinogen has been proposed.[48] The copper and fibrinogen levels are higher in the presence of liver malignancy than with cirrhosis.

Chest X-ray and thoracic tomograms or computerized chest tomography detects pulmonary metastases. Abdominal X-rays, liver ultrasound, and computerized tomography (CT scan) of the abdomen are used to determine the presence of a liver mass. A liver scan (radioactive scan) is more useful for detecting diffuse liver disease.

Selective arteriography of the liver can aid in detecting liver masses and vascular anomalies. Arteriographic changes of the left lobe of the liver are more difficult to see than those of the right lobe.[49] Angiography is 69 percent accurate in determining location and size of liver lesions.[50] Splenoportography (venogram) also is a method of demonstrating tumors,[51] but it is more valuable in showing portal vein thrombi.

Needle biopsy is the most effective means of establishing the diagnosis. The needle can be guided by ultrasound or computerized tomography to reach almost any liver lesion. A core biopsy is better than aspiration with a thin needle, but there is a greater risk of bleeding. The patient must be forewarned of the possibility of bleeding and of the possible necessity for surgical exploration and for controlling the bleeding.

Peritoneoscopy can be useful in visualizing the left lobe of the liver and the anterior surface of the right lobe. The presence of cirrhosis can be determined, and the needle can be directed for liver biopsy.[52]

§ 12.5   Surgical Treatment

In accessible areas, partial resection of a liver lobe can be done for peripheral localized tumors. When the neoplasm is large or near the medial portion of the lobe, a total lobectomy is necessary. The decision as to the necessity and extent of hepatic resection is almost always made at the time of surgical exploration. Contraindications to radical surgery include tumor not localized to one lobe or evidence of intraabdominal metastatic disease. A thoracoabdominal incision is

---

[48] O. Miatto et al., *Diagnostic and Prognostic Value of Serum Copper and Plasma Fibrinogen in Hepatic Carcinoma,* 55 Cancer 774 (1985).

[49] R.C. Watson & H.A. Baltaxe, *The Angiographic Appearance of Primary and Secondary Tumors of the Liver,* 101 Diagnostic Radiology 539 (1971).

[50] D.K. Kim et al., *Tumors of the Liver as Demonstrated by Angiography Scan and Laparatomy,* 141 Surgery, Gynecology & Obstetrics 409 (1975).x

[51] G.B. Ong & C.H. Leong, *Surgical Treatment of Primary Liver Cancer,* 14 J. Royal College Surgeons 42 (1969).

[52] G.P. Jori & C. Peschle, *Combined Peritoneoscopy and Liver Biopsy in the Diagnosis of Hepatic Neoplasm,* 63 Gastroenterology 1016 (1972).

usually required to mobilize the complete liver lobe and to gain access to the hepatic veins and vena cava. The porta hepatis is explored, the right hepatic artery and duct are visualized, and they are then ligated and transected. If the gallbladder is present, and a right hepatic lobectomy is planned, the cystic artery and duct also are ligated and transected. Hepatic vessels and ducts are ligated by simple ties or suture ligatures as the dissection proceeds through the liver. Hepatoma is almost always associated with cirrhotic liver changes.

Even though preoperative hepatic function tests are normal, the cirrhosis can be well advanced and can make liver suturing and ligating vessels extraordinarily difficult. Vascular clamp control of the hepatic veins and/or vena cava is helpful early in the procedure. The Pringle maneuver (placing a vascular clamp on the vessels in the porta hepatis) can help diminish bleeding.

Postoperative problems are relatively frequent and include bleeding, wound infection, intra-abdominal abscess, bile leakage, sepsis, pneumonia, pulmonary embolus, wound dehiscence or evisceration, and hepatic failure. Drains frequently are left in the hepatic space and are removed after a few days unless there is evidence of prolonged bile leakage.

§ 12.6   Chemotherapy Treatment

Chemotherapy for hepatocellular carcinoma has had disappointing results. Occasional long remissions have been reported, but no significant survival benefits have been conclusively demonstrated.[53] The combination of surgery, chemotherapy, and radiotherapy can be used for a dominant hepatic mass associated with small amounts of multifocal tumor involvement. Systemic chemotherapy with 5-fluorouracil and doxorubicin can be administered as well as hepatic artery infusion with methotrexate, 5-fluorouracil, nitrogen mustard, mitomycin C, and cisplatin. Hepatic artery occlusion can be attempted with chemotherapy, but hepatic failure or hepatorenal syndrome can ensue.

§ 12.7   Radiation Therapy Treatment

External beam radiation with or without chemotherapy is used for palliation, but the tolerance of the liver to radiation is the limiting factor. Exposing most of the liver to doses in excess of 3000 cGy results in hepatic dysfunction. Small radiation fields to limited areas of the liver are well tolerated. With small fields, the

---

[53] T.K. Choi et al., *Chemotherapy for Advanced Hepatocellular Carcinoma*, 53 Cancer 401 (1984); G. Falkson et al., *Chemotherapy Studies in Primary Liver Cancer*, 42 Cancer 2149 (1978); C.L.M. Olwen et al., *Further Experiences in Treating Patients with Hepatic Cellular Carcinoma in Uganda*, 46 Cancer 2717 (1980).

radiation hepatitis and fibrosis in small areas resulting from 4000 to 5000 cGy does not produce any problems.

Hemangiomas, a benign condition of the liver, can be arrested quite successfully with easily tolerated doses of 1500 to 3000 cGy given in two to four weeks.

Complications of hepatobiliary radiation are usually limited to gastrointestinal bleeding. Liver dysfunction due to radiation (as distinguished from liver dysfunction due to progressive cancer), and renal failure should be avoided by paying attention to the field size and field direction as well as determining in advance that the opposite left kidney is indeed functioning.

GALLBLADDER

§ 12.8　Staging and Classification

TNM: American Joint Committee on Cancer.[54]

The TNM system is not ordinarily used for gallbladder cancers.

Tumors of the Gallbladder[55]

Benign tumors

  Epithelial

    Adenoma

    Mixed tumor

  Mesenchymal

    Leiomyoma

    Hemangioma

    Lipoma

  Paraganglioma

  Ganglioneurofibromatosis

Malignant tumors

  Epithelial tumors

    Adenocarcinoma

      Well-differentiated

---

[54] American Joint Committee on Cancer, Manual for Staging of Cancer 94 (3d ed. 1988).

[55] J. Albores-Saavedra & D.E. Hanson, *Tumors of the Gallbladder and Extrahepatic Bile Ducts,* in Atlas of Tumor Pathology, Second Series, fascicle 22, at 17 (1986).

Papillary

Intestinal type

Pleomorphic giant cell

Poorly differentiated, small cell

Signet ring cell

Clear cell

Colloid

With choriocarcinoma-like areas

Squamous cell carcinoma

Adenosquamous carcinoma

Oat cell carcinoma

Others

Mesenchymal tumors

Embryonal rhabdomyosarcoma (sarcoma botryoides)

Leiomyosarcoma

Malignant fibrous histiocytoma

Angiosarcoma

Kaposi's sarcoma

Others

Miscellaneous

Carcinosarcoma

Carcinoid tumor

Malignant lymphoma

Malignant melanoma

Others.

§ 12.9   Etiology

Hereditary

There appears to be a genetic predisposition for carcinoma of the gallbladder in Native Americans. Hispanic Americans have a high incidence of gallbladder cancer, probably from genetic intermixing with Native Americans.[56] There are other reports of familial occurrence.[57]

Gallstones

Over 80 percent of patients with carcinoma of the gallbladder have associated gallstones.[58] It has been suggested that elective cholecystectomy for gallstones reduces the incidence of gallbladder cancer.[59] It is assumed that chronic irritation from gallstones promotes developing malignancy. Cholesterol-type stones are the type usually present.[60]

Calcification

Diffuse calcification of the gallbladder is found in a significant number of gallbladder cancers.[61] Fibrosis is present and can be a cause of the neoplasm.

Infection

Chronic carriers of Salmonella typhi have a high incidence of hepatobiliary cancer.[62] Other bacterial infections of the gallbladder do not appear to cause malignancy.

§ 12.10   Clinical Manifestations

Gallbladder cancer symptoms are nonspecific with early signs and symptoms consistent with cholecystitis (inflammation of the gallbladder). Mild to severe intermittent or persistent pain in the right upper quadrant of the abdomen is most common. As the tumor invades the liver and local structures and metastasizes to

---

[56] E.J. Dever & R.W. Buechley, *Gallbladder Cancer in Hispanic New Mexicans*, 45 Cancer 1705 (1980).

[57] H.L. Trajber et al., *Adenocarcinoma of the Gallbladder in Two Siblings*, 50 Cancer 1200 (1982).

[58] J. Hart et al., *Cholelithiasis in the Aetiology of Gallbladder Neoplasms*, 1 Lancet 1151 (1971).

[59] E.V. Graham, *The Prevention of Carcinoma of the Gallbladder*, 93 Annals Surgery 317 (1931).

[60] R.D. Soloway et al., *Geographic Differences in the Operative Incidence and Type of Pigment Gallstones and in the Non-Cholesterol Components of Cholesterol Gallstones*, 11 Hepatology Rapid Literature Rev. 1637 (1981).

[61] R.N. Berk et al., *Carcinoma in the Porcelain Gallbladder*, 106 Radiology 29 (1973).

[62] L. Axelrod et al., *Typhoid Cholecystitis and Gallbladder Carcinoma after Interval of 67 Years*, 217 JAMA 217 (1971); J.C. Welton et al., *Association Between Hepatobiliary Cancer and Typhoid Carrier State*, 1 Lancet 791 (1979).

the local regional nodes, there can be a palpable abdominal mass, liver enlargement, jaundice, nausea, vomiting, anorexia, and weight loss.[63] Pruritus (itching) can occur with the jaundice. Ascites and duodenal obstruction can appear.[64]

Paraneoplastic Syndromes

There have been rare reports of Cushing's syndrome from production of ACTH by the tumor,[65] acanthosis nigricans,[66] bullous-type pemphigoid skin lesions,[67] and the Zollinger-Ellison syndrome.[68]

§ 12.11 Diagnosis

X-rays of the abdomen can show a calcified gallbladder. Endoscopic retrograde choledochopancreatography can disclose an irregular filling defect of the gallbladder.

Carcinoembryonic antigen (CEA) is frequently elevated. There are three types of CEA-related macroglobulins found in the bile tract epithelium. Types II and III occur in inflammatory conditions.

Frequently, the diagnosis is made after removing the gallbladder for cholelithiasis. The surgeon should palpate the gallbladder at the time of surgery before excising the gallbladder; however, this task cannot be done at laparoscopic cholecystectomy.

§ 12.12 Surgical Treatment

If the tumor has not penetrated the gallbladder wall, a simple cholecystectomy cures the neoplasm. When the tumor is located on the posterior wall of the gallbladder in the bed of the liver, resection of the liver is necessary. Because the gallbladder is located at the junction of the left and right lobes of the liver,

---

[63] R.E. Hamrick, Jr., et al., *Primary Carcinoma of the Gallbladder,* 194 Annals Surgery 270 (1982).

[64] L.B. Pemberton et al., *The Surgical Significance of Carcinoma of the Gallbladder,* 122 Am. J. Med. 381 (1971).

[65] R.W. Spence & C.J. Burns-Cox, *ACTH-Secreting "Apudoma" of Gallbladder,* 16 Gut 473 (1975).

[66] L. Werko, *Acanthosis Nigricans Associated with Carcinoma of Gallbladder and Plantar Hyper-keratosis,* 26 Acta Dermato-Venereologica 70 (1945).

[67] B. Post et al., *Bulloses Pemphigoid als Cutanes Paraneoplastiches Syndrom bei Einem Gallenblasen Carcinom,* 24 Hautarzt 193 (1973).

[68] S. Nakamura et al., *An Autopsied Case of Malignant Zollinger-Ellison Syndrome due to Gastrinoma of the Gallbladder Accompanied by Giant Intrahepatic Metastasis,* 24 Gan. no Risho. 152 (1978).

hepatic lobectomy is not possible for a large tumor invading the liver, so wide hepatic resection to encompass all the tumor is done.

§ 12.13   Chemotherapy Treatment

Because gallbladder cancer is so rare, there have been no adequate studies to evaluate chemotherapeutic agents. When response has been documented, the duration is very short, usually only weeks. Mitomycin C, 5-fluorouracil, BCNU, adriamycin, and neocarzinostatin have been utilized.

§ 12.14   Radiation Therapy Treatment

Postoperative doses of 5000 cGy by external beam radiation given in six weeks add to the short-term control of gallbladder carcinoma and in some instances contribute to long-term survival. Intraoperative radiation therapy also has been used, but its value is not established.

Superficial carcinomas are sometimes discovered incidentally on the surface of the gallbladder wall during surgery for other conditions. These tumors have a high cure rate with surgery alone and do not benefit from additional therapy.

EXTRAHEPATIC BILIARY DUCTS

§ 12.15   Staging and Classification

TNM: American Joint Committee on Cancer.[69]

The TNM system is not ordinarily used for extrahepatic biliary duct malignancies.

Tumors of Extrahepatic Bile Ducts[70]

Benign

  Adenoma (papillary or tubular)

  Cystadenoma

  Granular cell tumor

  Paraganglioma

---

[69] American Joint Committee on Cancer, Manual for Staging of Cancer 100 (3d ed. 1988).

[70] J. Albores-Saavedra & D.E. Henson, *Tumors of the Gallbladder and Extrahepatic Bile Ducts, in* Atlas of Tumor Pathology, Second Series, fascicle 22, at 153 (1986).

    Mesenchymal tumors

    Papillomatosis

Malignant

  Adenocarcinoma

  Pleomorphic giant cell adenocarcinoma

  Adenosquamous carcinoma

  Oat cell carcinoma

    Colloid carcinoma

  Carcinosarcoma

    Embryonal rhabdomyosarcoma

    Leiomyosarcoma.

§ 12.16 Etiology

Congenital Cysts

Congenital cystic dilation (choledochal cyst) has an incidence of extrahepatic bile duct carcinoma more than 20 times the normal population.[71] Possibly a mixture of bile and gastroduodenal contents promotes the development of carcinoma, especially following internal drainage of the cyst.

Infection

Chlonorchis sinensis (a liver fluke that is a trematode worm) infestation has been reported in association with carcinoma of the extrahepatic bile ducts.[72]

Ulcerative Colitis

Carcinoma of the extrahepatic ducts can develop in patients with ulcerative colitis with or without sclerosing cholangitis. Usually there is a long history of colitis before malignancy occurs.

---

[71] P.A. Blaustein, *Association of Carcinoma with Congenital Cystic Conditions of the Liver and Bile Ducts,* 67 Am. J. Gastroenterology 40 (1977); D.P. Flanigan, *Biliary Carcinoma Associated with Biliary Cysts,* 40 Cancer 880 (1977).

[72] J. Koo et al., *Mucoepidermoid Carcinoma of the Bile Duct,* 196 Annals Surgery 140 (1982).

§ 12.17   Clinical Manifestations

Progressive obstructive jaundice is almost always present, and pain is a common feature. Symptoms of cholangitis (inflammation of the bile ducts) can occur with fever associated with the pain and jaundice.[73]

§ 12.18   Diagnosis

Ultrasound or computerized tomography (CT scan) can be helpful in examining the biliary duct system. Endoscopic retrograde cholangiopancreatography (ERCP) enables the ducts to be visualized if obstruction is not complete. Biopsy can be possible with ERCP. Transhepatic cholangiography is sometimes necessary for diagnosis, but if obstruction is present, a tube should be left in place to drain the bile. Leakage of bile is possible, and can necessitate early surgical exploration.

The serum bilirubin is elevated in the presence of jaundice. Alkaline phosphatase rises with partial obstruction. Other liver function studies can be abnormal.

§ 12.19   Surgical Treatment

It is rare that a bile duct malignancy can be totally resected, but if removal is possible, the attempt should be made. Pancreatoduodenectomy is usually necessary, because the distal common bile duct is surrounded by the head of the pancreas. The proximal duct system can be anastomosed to a defunctionalized Roux-en-Y bowel limb. At times, the intrahepatic duct system has to be utilized for the repair.

Palliation can be achieved by inserting a stent in the duct through the transhepatic approach at the time of cholangiography or transduodenally during ERCP. Compression of the stent by the tumor with obstruction or fever from cholangitis may occur. The stent can also work itself loose and enter the lumen of the bowel, but this development does not present any danger.

§ 12.20   Chemotherapy Treatment

Results of radiotherapy for unresectable disease can be improved by using radiation sensitizers such as hyperthermia, chemotherapy, or radiosensitizing drugs. Studies are progressing on using 5-fluorouracil, doxorubicin, and mitomycin for

---

[73] R.L. Rossi et al., *Management of Cancer of the Bile Duct,* 65 Surgical Clinics N. Am. 59 (1985).

unresectable tumor. Mechanical relief of biliary obstruction with a stent gives adequate palliation for short periods of time. Chemotherapy has not appeared to improve survival.

§ 12.21   Radiation Therapy Treatment

The extrahepatic bile duct carcinomas tend to be localized, so radiation therapy can be effective both for palliation and sometimes for cure with external radiation doses of 4000 to 5000 cGy. The treatment is given with increments of 160 to 180 cGy through fields set up from multiple directions to reduce the risk of damage to surrounding normal tissues. Portions of the total dose can be delivered with intraoperative radiation therapy (IORT) or with intracavitary radioisotope applications. IORT is given in the dosage range of 2000 to 3000 cGy. For intracavitary radiation, the bile duct is catheterized. Radioactive iridium-192 seeds implanted in a ribbon are threaded into the bile duct through the catheter. A dose of 3000 cGy is an appropriate therapy by this method.

AMPULLA OF VATER

§ 12.22   Staging

TNM: American Joint Committee on Cancer.[74]
    The TNM system is not ordinarily used for tumors of the ampulla of Vater.

§ 12.23   Clinical Manifestations

Ampullary carcinoma is difficult to differentiate clinically from periampullary malignancies of the duodenum. Obstructive jaundice and pain are most commonly encountered. Bleeding can occur with hematemesis (vomiting of blood) and/or melena (black, tarry stools), but this is seen more often with duodenal cancers or with a large ampullary carcinoma invading the duodenum.

---

[74] American Joint Committee on Cancer, Manual for Staging of Cancer 106 (3d ed. 1988).

§ 12.24   Diagnosis

Serum bilirubin and alkaline phosphatase are usually elevated. There can be other abnormal liver function studies.

Upper gastrointestinal X-ray studies can show an abnormality in the ampullary region. Endoscopic retrograde cholangiopancreatography (ERCP) can disclose the presence of an ampullary tumor, and biopsy is possible.

§ 12.25   Surgical Treatment

Pancreaticoduodenectomy is the procedure of choice because the ampulla of Vater is in the wall of the duodenum and surrounded by the head of the pancreas. Cure is more likely with ampullary cancers than with malignancy of the pancreas.

§ 12.26   Chemotherapy Treatment

Local recurrence or metastases following surgical resection of ampullary neoplasms respond poorly to chemotherapy. Treatment is similar to that for extrahepatic biliary tract carcinoma (see § 12.20).

§ 12.27   Radiation Therapy Treatment

Radiation therapy for carcinoma of the ampulla follows the same principles as radiation therapy for biliary duct carcinoma (see § 12.21).

§ 12.28   Significant Cases

Chambers v. Rush-Presbyterian-St. Luke's Medical Center.[75]   Awards of $800,000 for a survival action, and $1.5 million on a wrongful death claim were affirmed. The decedent, in July 1980, complained to the defendant gastroenterologist of abdominal pain. X-rays disclosed a partial obstruction of the common bile duct with a normal ampulla and pancreas. The decedent was placed on hyperalimentation on August 12, 1980, despite a blood sugar level of 449 on the previous day, of which the defendant was unaware. On August 13, 1980, the decedent became lethargic, and he lapsed into hyperosmolar nonketotic coma with a blood sugar level of 1104 on August 14, 1980. Permanent brain damage

---

[75] 155 Ill. App. 3d 458, 508 N.E.2d 426, *cert. denied,* 515 N.E.2d 102 (Ill. 1987).

resulted, and he died four months later. The court held that overall survival rate of 33 percent for bile duct cancer did not preclude finding that the negligence of the physician and hospital was the proximate cause of decedent's death.

Grey v. Hicks.[76]   A defense verdict was entered for alleged failure to diagnose cancer of the biliary tract and liver. The decedent complained of back and abdominal pain in August 1985. She was diagnosed as suffering from psychological difficulties. The decedent developed jaundice four months later, and she was diagnosed as having adenocarcinoma of the biliary tract and liver. There was no evidence the decedent complained of abdominal pain after her initial visit in August 1985.

Rathje v. Radisavljevic.[77]   There was a verdict for $152,100 offset by $75,000 settlement by other defendants. The 69-year-old decedent underwent exploratory laparotomy for suspected gallbladder disease, at which time a tumor mass was detected that suggested a rare bile duct cancer. The biopsy report was equivocal, but radiation therapy was administered. The original slides were reread and reported as negative for cancer. Five months later, because of depression, the decedent committed suicide. The defendant claimed it was reasonable to rely on the biopsy report.

---

[76]No. N39232 (L.A. County Super. Ct.), *reprinted in* 6 Med. Malpractice Verdicts, Settlements & Experts No. 11, at 14 (1990).

[77]No. SOC75359/75505 (L.A. County Super. Ct. Feb. 1990), *reprinted in* 6 Med. Malpractice Verdicts, Settlements & Experts No. 6, at 54 (1990).

CHAPTER 13

GENITOURINARY NEOPLASMS

TESTICULAR TUMORS

PROSTATE

§ 13.1   Staging and Classification

TNM: American Joint Committee on Cancer (AJCC).[1]
The TNM system is not ordinarily used for prostate cancer.

American Urologic Association
Staging of Prostate Cancer[2]

Stage A   No palpable lesion

   A1   Focal

   A2   Diffuse

Stage B   Confined to prostate

   B1   Small, discrete nodule

   B2   Large or multiple nodules or areas

Stage C   Localized to periprostatic area

   C1   No involvement of seminal vesicles, <70g

   C2   Involvement of seminal vesicles, >70g

Stage D   Metastatic disease

   D1   Pelvic lymph node metastases or urethral obstruction causing hydro-
        nephrosis

   Pattern 1:   Well-differentiated, small, closely packed glands in essentially circumscribed masses.

---

[1] American Joint Committee on Cancer, Manual for Staging of Cancer 178 (3d ed. 1988).

[2] G.E. Hanks et al., *Cancer of the Prostate, in* Cancer: Principles and Practice of Oncology 1087 (V.T. DeVita et al. eds., 1993).

Pattern 2:   Masses of well-differentiated glands more variable in size and shape and less sharply circumscribed margins than in pattern 1.

Pattern 3:   Well-differentiated glands with diffuse penetration of the stroma by tiny glands or single cells, cribriform pattern, or some differentiation with cords and masses of cells.

Pattern 4:   Some glandular differentiation with areas of closely packed, large, pale polygonal cells growing diffusely through the stroma.

Pattern 5: Undifferentiated with little or no evidence of glandular differentiation.

D2   Bone or distant lymph node or organ or soft tissue metastases.

Mostofi System[3]

This system considers both cytologic features and glandular architecture.

Grade I   — Well-differentiated glands with nuclei that show slight nuclear anaplasia.

Grade II — Gland formation is present, but the nuclei show moderate nuclear anaplasia.

Grade III — Glands with marked nuclear anaplasia and tumors that are undifferentiated (do not form glands).

Gleason System[4]

This system is based on the degree of glandular differentiation and the growth pattern of the tumor in relation to prostatic stroma.

Gaete System[5]

This system evaluates glandular architecture and cytologic features.

---

[3] F.K. Mostofi, *Grading of Prostatic Carcinomas,* 59 Cancer Treatment Rep. pt. 1, at 111 (1975); F.K. Mostofi, *Problems of Grading Carcinoma of Prostate,* 3 Seminars Oncology 161 (1976).

[4] D.F. Gleason, *Classification of Prostatic Carcinomas,* 50 Cancer Treatment Rep. 125 (1966); D.F. Gleason & G.T. Mellinger, *The Veteran's Administration Cooperative Urological Research Group: Prediction of Prognosis for Prostatic Adenocarcinoma by Combined Histological Grading and Clinical Staging,* 111 J. Urology 58 (1974).

[5] J.F. Gaeta et al., *Histologic Grading of Primary Prostatic Cancer: A New Approach to an Old Problem,* 123 J. Urology 689 (1980); J.F. Gaeta, *Glandular Profiles and Cellular Patterns in Prostatic Cancer Grading. National Prostatic Cancer Project System,* 17 Urology 33 (March Supp. 1981).

Table 13–1

Gaete System

Grade	Glands	Cells
I	Well-defined and separated by scant stroma	Uniform and normal size: nucleoli not conspicious; chromatin dark and dense
II	Medium and small, scattered and infiltrating prostatic stroma	Slightly pleomorphic; nucleoli conspicious and small
III	Small, irregular or poorly formed acini combined with areas devoid of organization	Significant pleomorphism; nuclei vesicular and show large, often acidophilic nucleoli
IV	Round and solid masses of cells or diffuse infiltration of small cells with no glands	Small or large, uniform or pleomorphic with significant mitotic activity (> 3 per high-power field)

Mayo Clinic System[6]

This system assesses histologic architecture and cytology for grading, evaluating in particular the following:

Acinar structure

Individual cellular structure

Nuclear characteristics

Presence of nucleoli

Cytoplasmic characteristics

Mitotic activity

Degree of invasiveness.

Whitmore System[7]

Stage A1—Clinically occult carcinoma, well-differentiated, focal

Stage A2—Clinically occult carcinoma, poorly differentiated, multifocal

Stage B1—Palpable tumor, involving less than one lobe

---

[6]G.P. Murphy & W.F. Whitmore, Jr., *A Report of the Workshops on the Current Status of the Histological Grading of Prostate Cancer,* 44 Cancer 1490 (1974); D.C. Utz & G.M. Farrow, *Pathologic Differentiation and Prognosis of Prostatic Carcinoma,* 209 JAMA 1701 (1969).

[7]W.F. Whitmore, Jr., *Cancer of the Prostate,* 21 Am. J. Med. 697 (1956).

Stage B2 — Palpable tumor, involving more than one lobe

Stage C — Extraprostatic extension (including seminal vesicles)

Stage D1 — Metastases confined to pelvis (including positive pelvic nodes)

Stage D2 — Distant metastases.

Histopathologic Types[8]

Epithelial

　　Peripheral tuboalveolar adenocarcinoma

　　Ductal adenocarcinoma

　　Ductal transitional cell carcinoma

Nonepithelial

　　Embryonic myosarcoma

　　Leiomyosarcoma

　　Lymphoma

　　Malignant neurilemmoma.

§ 13.2   Etiology

Environmental factors such as occupation,[9] cadmium exposure,[10] or smoking[11] have not shown an association with prostate cancer. Sexual activity or associated factors and benign prostatic hypertrophy can increase the risk of prostate cancer, but no definite conclusions have been reached.

§ 13.3   Clinical Manifestations

Early prostate cancer is asymptomatic and can be noted on a routine rectal examination or in the specimen from transurethral prostatic resection (TUR) performed for benign prostatic hypertrophy, As the tumor gets larger, there can

---

[8] K.M. Cameron, *Pathology of the Prostate,* 11 Brit. J. Urology 348 (1974).

[9] P. Greenwald et al., *Physical and Demographic Features of Men Before Developing Cancer of the Prostate,* 53 J. Nat'l Cancer Inst. 341 (1974).

[10] L.N. Kolonel, *An Epidemiological Investigation of Cadmium Carcinogenesis* (1972) (doctoral thesis, University of California).

[11] R.R. Williams & J.W. Horn, *Association of Cancer Sites with Tobacco and Alcohol Consumption and Socioeconomic Status of Patients: Interview Study from the Third National Cancer Survey,* 58 J. Nat'l Cancer Inst. 525 (1977).

be slowing of the urinary stream, hesitancy, intermittency, incomplete emptying, incontinence, frequency, nocturia, and dysuria. Hematuria is uncommon.

Local pelvic pain occurs when there is extension of the tumor to pelvic structures. Nerve involvement causes perineal aching and pain along the distribution of the sciatic nerves.

Metastatic disease can cause bone pain in involved sites, especially the low back or pelvis. Cerebral metastases can result in mental confusion. Nodules can appear subcutaneously, or there can be lymph node enlargement.

§ 13.4 Diagnosis

For the early detection of cancer of the prostate, the American Cancer Society advises a yearly rectal examination for asymptomatic males over the age of 40.[12] The presence of irregularity, induration, or nodularity of the prostate is an indication for open biopsy, needle biopsy, or aspiration biopsy, either transperineally or transrectally, and biopsy is an accurate means of establishing the diagnosis, especially when guided by prostate sonography. Transrectal sonogram is extremely useful in visualizing prostatic abnormalities.

Cystoscopy with transurethral resection of the prostate (TUR) obtains tissue for histopathology. Cystourethrography can show a rigid, constricted urethra. Lymphangiography can be used to establish the presence of pelvic lymph node metastases, but at times, it can be difficult to interpret.

Serum acid phosphatase and prostate specific antigen (PSA) determinations can be very useful because they can be elevated in prostate cancer, PSA being more specific. Chest X-rays, bone scans, and bone X-rays are used to establish the presence of metastases.

§ 13.5 Surgical Treatment

A focal, well-differentiated Stage-A tumor can be monitored carefully with frequent examinations and repeat biopsies. Progressive tumor spread occurs in 6.8 percent of these patients.[13]

Radical prostatectomy by perineal or retropubic approach is used when the cancer is diffuse but confined to the prostate. Impotence almost always occurs, and temporary incontinence of urine is common. Strictures of the urethra and

---

[12] *Guidelines for the Cancer-Related Checkup: Recommendations and Rationale,* 30 CA-A Cancer J. for Clinicians 196 (1980).

[13] D.P. Byar, *Veterans Administration Cooperative Urological Research Group: Survival of Patients with Incidentally Found Microscopic Cancer of the Prostate: Result of a Clinical Trial of Conservative Treatment,* 108 J. Urology 908 (1972).

local sepsis can be seen.[14] More recently, preservation of the periprostatic nerves, when feasible, has resulted in a lower incidence of impotence. The extended radical prostatectomy involves the electrocoagulation or cryosurgical destruction of tumor extension beyond the prostate.[15]

Radical pelvic lymphadenectomy can be used as a staging procedure before radical prostatectomy. The morbidity of this procedure includes infection, sepsis, hematoma, lymphocele, and pulmonary embolus.

Pelvic exenteration has been used for locally extensive tumors that have not metastasized.[16] This procedure can be best utilized in highly selected younger patients because of the increased risk in morbidity and mortality.

§ 13.6   Hormonal Therapy Treatment

Tumor regression occurs with hormonal manipulation by orchiectomy, estrogens (diethylstilbestrol), progestational agents (cyproterone acetate), luteinizing hormone-releasing hormone (LHRH) antagonists (leuprolide goserelin, and buserelin), aminoglutethimide, ketoconazole, spironolactone, and flutamide.[17] These agents act through inhibition of androgens. Orchiectomy, diethylstilbestrol, and LHRH antagonists are the most common initial hormonal therapy. Second hormonal manipulation after initial termination of response is usually not successful. Adrenalectomy or hypophysectomy is rarely used. Extraprostatic cancer is an indication for hormone therapy.

§ 13.7   Chemotherapy Treatment

The natural course of metastatic prostate carcinoma varies considerably with many older patients dying of intercurrent disease rather than the tumor. Single chemotherapeutic agents result in regression in up to 20 percent of patients.

---

[14] H.J. Jewitt, *The Present Status of Radical Prostatectomy for Stages A and B Prostatic Cancer,* 2 Urology Clinic N. Am. 105 (1975).

[15] S.A. Loening, *Prostatic Neoplasms: B. Clinical, Diagnostic and Therapeutic Features, in* Genitourinary Oncology 452 (D.A. Culp & S.A. Loening, eds., 1985).

[16] D.L. McCullough & W.F. Leadbetter, *Radical Pelvic Surgery for Locally Extensive Carcinoma of the Prostate,* 108 J. Urology 939 (1972); W.F. Whitmore, Jr., *The Rationale and Results of Ablative Surgery for Prostate Cancer,* 16 Cancer 1119 (1963).

[17] E.D. Crawford et al., *A Controlled Trial of Leuprolide With and Without Flutamide in Prostatic Carcinoma,* 321 New Eng. J. Med. 419 (1989); P. Iverson et al., *Zoladex and Flutamide Versus Orchiectomy in the Treatment of Advanced Prostatic Cancer: A Combined Analysis of Two European Studies,* EORTC 30853 and DAPROCA 86, 66 Cancer 1067 (5 Supp. 1990); W.W. Scott et al., *Hormonal Therapy of Prostatic Cancer,* 45 Cancer 1929 (1980); R. Sharifi & M. Soloway, *Clinical Study of Leupromide Depot Formulation in the Treatment of Advanced Prostate Cancer,* 143 J. Urology 68 (1990).

Doxorubicin, extramustine phosphate, 5-fluorouracil, methotrexate, dacarbazine, cyclophosphamide, and amacrine have shown response. Combination chemotherapy with cytoxan, doxorubicin, and 5-fluorouracil; cytoxan, methotrexate, and 5-fluorouracil; or cytoxan plus doxorubicin are effective.[18]

§ 13.8   Radiation Therapy Treatment

Aside from the medical problems that hinder prostatectomy in the great number of men who develop prostatic carcinoma after the age of 70, the principal considerations for radiation therapy are the greater likelihood of maintaining potency and avoiding incontinence. There are two major therapeutic approaches: external radiation and interstitial radiation with or without supplemental external radiation. External radiation can be used to treat the prostate and adjacent tissues or treat the prostate and all the pelvic lymph nodes. The dichotomy exists because the effectiveness of lymph node irradiation is unsettled.

To avoid genital edema and to avoid submitting the entire rectum to the full course of radiation, megavoltage radiation is given with more than anterior and posterior fields. The supplemental fields can be lateral fields, a perineal field, oblique fields, or arcing fields. A minimum of two fields a day is treated. If the pelvic nodes are being irradiated, they receive doses of 4500 to 5000 cGy in 160 to 200 cGy fractions from the initial fields. If gross lymph node metastases are present, a small field boost to 6000 cGy is made if it can be done without irradiating the small bowel. The total dose to the prostate itself and the paraprostatic tissues vary with the size of the tumor. For sizes ranging from T1 to T4, the dose can range from 6000 to more than 7000 cGy. Radiation is not given in Stage A1 tumors unless the patient is young and the tumor is undifferentiated.

If interstitial brachytherapy is chosen, 125-iodine seeds can be implanted in the prostate retropubically or by the transperineal route. Retropubic implantation is accompanied by staging lymphadenectomy. The transperineal route also can be used to implant 192-iridium ribbons. The dose to the prostate can be 6000 to 8000 cGy. With 125-iodine, the dose can be 12000 cGy by the end of a year. The dose to the bladder and rectum should not exceed 5000 to 6000 cGy. Interstitial brachytherapy is not indicated in the presence of bladder neck obstruction, gross lymph node metastases, or following a transurethral resection of the prostate

---

[18] G.E. Carter et al., *Results of Local and/or Systemic Adjuvant Therapy in the Management of Pathological Stage C or D1 Prostate Cancer Following Radical Prostatectomy*, 142 J. Urology 1266 (1989); R.T. Chlebowski et al., *Cyclophosphamide Versus the Combination of Adriamycin, 5-Fluorouracil, and Cyclophosphamide with Treatment of Metastatic Prostate Cancer: A Randomized Trial*, 42 Cancer 2546 (1978); H.B. Muss et al., *Cyclophosphamide Versus Cyclophosphamide, Methotrexate, and 5-Flourouracil in Advanced Prostatic Cancer: A Randomized Trial*, 47 Cancer 1949 (1981); R.V. Smalley et al., *A Phase II Evaluation of a 3-Drug Combination of Cyclophosphamide, Doxorubicin, and 5-Fluorouracil in Patients with Advanced Bladder Carcinoma or Stage D Prostatic Carcinoma*, 125 J. Urology 191 (1981).

(TURP). A conservation approach also limits interstitial therapy to T1 and 2 and Grade I and II tumors.

Postoperative radiation following radical prostatectomy can be given when the tumor involves the seminal vesicles, extends beyond the capsule of the prostate, or the PSA remains measurable for at least three weeks postoperatively. Radiation starts after complete recovery from the operation, which can be four weeks. Some defer radiation until there is an obvious tumor recurrence, but the larger tumor volume following the delay requires a higher dose of radiation with a greater risk of complications and reduced chance of tumor control. Postoperative radiation is given with small fields to the prostatic bed and surrounding tissues. Doses range from 4500 to 6500 cGy. The patient must be aware that lymphedema of the leg is a possible complication of combining radiation with lymphadenectomy.

Radiation has a valuable role in the palliation of incurable tumors. Excellent relief of pain from bone metastases can be obtained with doses as little as 1000 cGy before prolonged exposure to estrogens. Higher doses can be required later. Pain, hematuria, and bladder neck obstruction from massive pelvic tumors can be relieved with 4000 to 5000 cGy. 32-phosphorus can be used to relieve generalized pain from widespread bone metastases.

Painful gynecomastia from estrogen therapy can be prevented or relieved with three treatments of 300 cGy to the breasts with electrons or kilovoltage X-rays.

§ 13.9   Significant Cases

Beatty v. Morgan.[19]   The court reversed in part a directed verdict for the defendant. The plaintiff was seen for symptoms of pain, urinary frequency, and urgency in January 1980. A transurethral resection (TUR) of the prostate was performed in February 1980. Five months later, another physician diagnosed bladder cancer and removed the bladder. The court held that there remained a conflict in the evidence as to material issues and that failure to diagnose the bladder cancer in February 1980 resulted in five months of pain and other symptoms as well as an unnecessary TUR.

Jones v. Schulman.[20]   The plaintiff had been having routine prostate examinations over a period of eight years by the defendant. Changes were noted in the prostate during this time period, but no workup was performed to rule out prostate cancer. Two years later, another physician diagnosed prostate cancer with metastases to pelvic and vertebral bones. The defense maintained that

---

[19] 170 Ga. App. 661, 317 S.E.2d 662 (1984).

[20] No. 90-143-RCL (D.D.C.), *reprinted in* 7 Med. Malpractice Verdicts, Settlements & Experts No. 1, at 14 (1991).

because there was no discrete nodule palpated, a diagnosis of benign disease was appropriate. The verdict was for $1 million.

Kirby v. Spivey.[21]   The decedent was examined by the defendant for urinary tract problems. A malignancy of the bladder or prostate was suspected, but the decedent did not want to be referred to a specialist and "did not want to have any diagnostic tests respecting the suspected cancer." The defendant failed to note such discussion in the medical record. The decedent ultimately died from a kidney condition. The court affirmed the summary judgment for the defendant holding that despite a genuine issue of fact as to whether the decedent was told of the possible cancer, the failure to diagnose prostate cancer was not a proximate cause of death from kidney disease.

BLADDER

§ 13.10   Staging and Classification

TNM: American Joint Committee on Cancer (AJCC).[22]
    The TNM system is not ordinarily used for bladder cancer. Depth of invasion has prognostic significance.

Jewett-Strong Staging[23]

Stage 0 — Limited to the mucosa

Stage A — Not beyond the submucosa

Stage B1 — Not more than halfway through the muscle layer

Stage B2 — Beyond the halfway level of muscle layer but not into fat

Stage C — Beyond the muscle layer into perivesicle fat

Stage D1 — Metastatic to pelvic lymph nodes and/or invading the substance of adjacent organs

Stage D2 — Metastatic beyond the pelvis.

---

[21] 167 Ga. App. 751, 307 S.E.2d 538 (1983).

[22] American Joint Committee on Cancer, Manual for Staging of Cancer 194 (3d ed. 1988).

[23] H.J. Jewett & G.H. Strong, *Infiltrating Carcinoma of the Bladder. Relation of Depth of Penetration of the Bladder Wall to Incidence of Local Extension and Metastases,* 55 J. Urology 366 (1946).

Marshall Staging[24]

Stage 0   — No tumor definition specimen
            Carcinoma in situ
            Papillary tumor without invasion

Stage A   — Invasion of lamina propria

Stage B1 — Superficial muscle invasion

Stage B2 — Deep muscle invasion

Stage C   — Invasion of perivesical fat

Stage D1 — Invasion of contiguous viscera
            Pelvic nodes

Stage D2 — Distant metastases
            Nodes above aortic bifurcation.

The histopathologic types are:

Urothelial carcinoma

Papillary carcinoma

Transitional cell carcinoma.

The predominant cancer is a transitional cell cancer.
The histopathologic grades (G) are:

GX   — Grade cannot be assessed

G1   — Well differentiated

G2   — Moderately well differentiated

G3–4 — Poorly differentiated or undifferentiated.

§ 13.11   Etiology

Benzidine and 2-naphthylamine found in the dye manufacturing industry are urinary tract carcinogens.[25] Other industrial carcinogens include xenylamine

---

[24] V.F. Marshall et al., *Survival of Patients with Bladder Carcinoma Treated by Simple Segmental Resection: 123 Consecutive Cases 5 Years Later,* 9 Cancer 568 (1956).

[25] L. Rehn, *Blasengeschwaelste bei Analinarbeitern,* 50 Arch. Klin. Chir. 588 (1895); W.W. Scott & H.L. Boyd, *Carcinogenic Effect of Beta-Naphthylamine in Normal and Substituted Isolated Sigmoid Loop Bladder of Dogs,* 70 J. Urology 914 (1953); R.G. Wendel et al., *Benzidine: A Bladder Carcinogen,* 111 J. Urology 607 (1974).

(4-aminodyshenyl),[26] ortho-aminophenols (also found in phenacetin),[27] and 4-nitrodiphenyl.[28] Development of bladder cancer after exposure to industrial carcinogens has a latency period of 10 to 40 years.[29]

Metabolites of tryptophan, such as 3-hydroxyanthranilic acid and 3-hydroxy-kynurenine, have carcinogenic potential.[30] The relationship of these substances to the production of bladder cancer is unclear.

Cigarette smoking has been associated with an increased risk of bladder cancer, although the causal mechanism is unknown.[31]

Carcinogenicity of dietary sweeteners, such as cyclamates and saccharin, has been shown experimentally,[32] but the association with human bladder cancer has had conflicting results.[33]

Although a causal relationship has not been firmly established, there are reports of an apparent increase risk of bladder cancer in persons who regularly drink coffee.[34]

---

[26] W.F. Melick et al., *The First Reported Cases of Human Bladder Tumors Due to a New Carcinogen: Xenylamine*, 74 J. Urology 760 (1955); A.L. Walpole, *Aromatic Amines as Carcinogens in Industry*, 14 Brit. Med. Bull. 141 (1955).

[27] V. Bengtsson et al., *Transitional Cell Tumors of the Renal Pelvis and Analgesic; Abusers*, 2 Scandinavian J. Urology & Nephrology 145 (1968); R.A.M. Case, *Tumours of the Urinary Tract as an Occupational Disease in Several Industries*, 39 Annals Royal College Surgeons Eng. 213 (1966); S. Johansson et al., *Uroepithelial Tumors of the Renal Pelvis Associated with Abuse of Phenacetin-Containing Analgesics*, 33 Cancer 743 (1974).

[28] R. Hoover & P. Cole, *Populating Trends in Cigarette Smoking and Bladder Cancer*, 94 Am. J. Epidemiology 409 (1971).

[29] R.A.M. Case, *Tumours of the Urinary Tract as an Occupational Disease in Several Industries*, 39 Annals Royal College Surgeons Eng. 213 (1966); R. Hoover & P. Cole, *Population Trends in Cigarette Smoking and Bladder Cancer*, 94 Am. J. Epidemiology 409 (1971).

[30] D.M. Wallace, *The Natural History and Possible Cause of Bladder Tumors*, 18 Annals Royal College Surgeons Eng. 366 (1956).

[31] E.L. Wynden & R. Goldsmith, *The Epidemiology of Bladder Cancer, a Second Look*, 40 Cancer 1246 (1977); J.M. Weir & J.E. Dunn, Jr., *Smoking and Mortality: A Prospective Study*, 25 Cancer 105 (1970).

[32] E. Friedman et al., *Toxic Response of Rats to Cyclamates in Chow and Semisynthetic Diets*, 49 J. Nat'l Cancer Inst. 751 (1972); R.N. Hoover & P.H. Strasser, *Artificial Sweeteners and Human Bladder Cancer, Preliminary Results*, 1 Lancet 837 (1980); J.M. Price et al., *Bladder Tumors in Rats Fed Cyclohexylamine or High Doses of a Mixture of Cyclamate and Saccharin*, 167 Science 1131 (1970).

[33] G.R. Howe et al., *Artificial Sweeteners and Bladder Cancer*, 2 Lancet 578 (1977); R.W. Morgan & M.G. Jarm, *Bladder Cancer: Smoking, Beverages and Artificial Sweeteners*, 111 Can. Med. Ass'n J. 1067 (1974).

[34] P. Cole et al., *Smoking and Cancer of the Lower Urinary Tract*, 284 New Eng. J. Med. 129 (1971); J.F., Fraumeni, Jr., *Coffee-Drinking and Bladder Cancer*, 2 Lancet 1204 (1971).

The use of cyclophosphamide (Cytoxan®) in the treatment of malignant diseases has resulted in some patients developing squamous cell carcinoma of the bladder.[35]

There is a high incidence of squamous cell carcinoma of the bladder involvement from schistosoma haematobium (schistosomiasis or bilharzia).[36] The mechanism of causation is unknown.

Identification of a virus in the urinary tract resembling RNA oncogenic viruses has been reported as a possible viral etiology of bladder cancer.[37]

§ 13.12   Clinical Manifestations

Microscopic hematuria can be found on incidental urine examination, but most often, gross hematuria is present. Bladder irritability with dysuria and frequency of urination can occur with or without pyuria. Pain appears with an associated bladder infection or invasion of the bladder neck or ureteral orifice. Abdominal or rectal mass can be noted with very large tumors.

§ 13.13   Diagnosis

Cystoscopy allows visualization of abnormalities of the bladder lining. Deep biopsies are taken from the tumor area and superficial biopsies are taken from the lateral walls, midposterior bladder wall, and areas adjacent to the tumor to evaluate for possible associated carcinoma in situ. Bladder urine, bladder washings, and bladder brushings allow cytologic examination.

The extent of the tumor can be determined by bimanual examination, excretory urography, cystography, chest X-rays, skeletal X-ray surveys, bone scans, and liver function studies. Lymphangiography is not very useful, because the primary bladder drainage to the obturator and internal iliac nodes is poorly visualized.[38] Arteriography of pelvic vessels can demonstrate the extent of tumor. Pelvic ultrasound and pelvic computerized tomography (CT scan) can delineate bladder tumors quite well.

---

[35] R.L. Wall & K.P. Clausen, *Carcinoma of the Urinary Bladder in Patients Receiving Cyclophosphamide,* 293 New Eng. J. Med. 271 (1975).

[36] E.M. Chevlen et al., *Cancer of the Bilharzial Bladder,* 5 Int'l J. Radiation Oncology, Biology & Physics 921 (1979); M. Gelfand et al., *Relation Between Carcinoma of the Bladder and Infestation with Schistosoma Hematobium,* 1 Lancet 1249 (1967).

[37] A.Y. Elliott et al., *Isolation of an RNA Virus from Transitional Cell Tumors of the Human Urinary Bladder,* 74 Surgery 46 (1973).

[38] S.A. Loening et al., *A Comparison Between Lymphangiography and Pelvic Node Dissection in the Staging of Prostatic Cancer,* 117 J. Urology 752 (1977).

Carcinoembryonic antigen assay (CEA) is frequently elevated in patients with bladder cancer,[39] but might not parallel the changes in clinical status. Blood group surface isoantigens can be an indication of malignant potential.[40] The absence of antigens on the surface of bladder tumors is associated with a poor prognosis.[41]

§ 13.14   Surgical Treatment

Therapy of bladder malignancies varies according to the stage and grade of the lesion.

Carcinoma in situ can appear as normal mucosa or patchy, velvety mucosal inflammation. Endoscopic fulguration or electroresection has been beneficial, but there is a high rate of recurrence. The recurrent tumor is usually more aggressive,[42] and because the disorder is diffuse and multifocal in nature, radical cystectomy or radical prostatocystectomy with urinary diversion is frequently done, especially in patients with severe symptoms.[43] The ureters and urethra should be checked for carcinoma in situ to avoid recurrence. Some surgeons excise the regional lymph nodes as a part of the staging procedure.[44]

Superficial low-grade lesions (Stage A) are best treated transurethrally with resection and/or fulguration. Tumor recurrence is frequent.[45] Intravesical thiotepa[46] or other chemotherapy can be administered prophylactically in patients

---

[39] P. Grunan et al., *The CEA Test in Urologic Cancer: An Evaluation and a Review,* 32 Oncology 158 (1975); E.P. Ornellas et al., *CEA in Urogenital Carcinomas, in* National Bladder Cancer Project (Miami 1976).

[40] J. Alroy et al., *Blood Group Isoantigens in Carcinoma in situ of the Human Urinary Bladder,* 38 Laboratory Investigation 331 (1978); A.J. Newman et al., *Cell Surface A, B or O(H) Blood Group Antigens as an Indicator of Malignant Potential in Stage A Bladder Carcinoma,* 124 J. Urology 27 (1980).

[41] S. Bergman & N. Javadpour, *The Cell Surface Antigen A, B or O(H) as an Indicator of Malignant Potential in Stage A Bladder Carcinoma: Preliminary Report,* 119 J. Urology 49 (1978); P.H. Lange et al., *Tissue Blood-Group Antigens and Prognosis in Low Stage Transitional Cell Carcinoma of the Bladder,* 119 J. Urology 52 (1978).

[42] M. Tannenbaum & N. Romes, *The Pathobiology of Early Urothelial Cancer* 232, *in* Genitourinary Cancer (D.G. Skinner & J.B. deKernion eds., 1978).

[43] G.M. Farrow et al., *Clinical Observations on 69 Cases of in situ Carcinoma of the Urinary Bladder,* 37 Cancer Res. 2794 (1977); D.C. Utz & J.H. De Weerd, *The Management of Low-Grade, Low-Stage Carcinoma of the Bladder, in* Genitourinary Cancer 256 (D.G. Skinner & J.B. deKernion eds., 1978).

[44] J.B. deKernion, *Bladder Cancer, in* Cancer Treatment 383 (C.M. Haskell ed., 1980).

[45] S.A. Loening et al., *Urinary Cytology and Bladder Biopsy in Patients with Bladder Cancer,* 11 Urology 591 (1978); S.A. Loening et al., *Analysis of Bladder Tumor Recurrences in 178 Patients,* 16 Urology 137 (1980).

[46] National Bladder Cancer Collaborative Group A, *The Role of Intravesical Thiotepa in the Management of Superficial Bladder Cancer,* 37 Cancer Res. 2916 (1977).

with a high risk of recurrence. Diffuse or multiple tumors requiring frequent extensive bladder resection can be best treated by total cystectomy to avoid a scarred, irritable, and poorly functioning bladder. Approximately 10 percent of patients with superficial tumors develop more aggressive malignancies.[47]

High-stage, high-grade malignancies are treated by radical cystectomy or prostatocystectomy with bilateral pelvic lymphadenectomy.[48] The urethra should be excised in those male patients who have a high risk of recurrence in that area. It is possible to perform segmental bladder resection when the lesion is confined to the dome of the bladder.

Palliation of irritative bladder symptoms in patients with advanced bladder cancer can be obtained by supravesical urinary diversion. Cutaneous ureterostomy can occasionally be helpful.

§ 13.15   Chemotherapy Treatment

Transitional cell carcinoma of the bladder, ureter, renal pelvis, or urethra responds to chemotherapy. In the presence of advanced disease, neoadjuvant (before surgery) or adjuvant (after surgery) chemotherapy can improve local control, allow preservation of the bladder, or prevent distant metastases. Metastatic or recurrent disease can respond to combination chemotherapy. Agents showing tumor regression include: cisplatin; doxorubicin; methotrexate, gallium nitrate; carboplatin; 10-deazaminopterin; 5-fluorouracil; vinblastine; mitomycin C; and vincristine. Combination therapy is usually better than single agents and includes: cisplatin and doxorubicin; methotrexate, vinblastine, doxorubicin, and cisplatin (M-VAC); cisplatin, doxorubin, and 5-fluorouracil; cisplatin, doxorubicin, 5-fluorouracil, and teniposide (VM-26); cisplatin plus teniposide; cisplatin, vinca, and bleomycin; cistaplatin and dichloromethotrexate; cisplatin, methotrexate, and vinblastine; doxorubicin, 5-fluorouracil, teniposide, and mitomycin C; doxorubicin plus bleomycin; methotrexate and vinblastine; methotrexate and mitomycin C; and methotrexate, cyclophophamide, doxorubicin, bleomycin, vincristine, and mitomycin C.[49]

---

[47] L.F. Greene et al., *Benign Papilloma or Papillary Carcinoma of the Bladder?*, 110 J. Urology 205 (1973).

[48] S.P. Dretler, *The Value of Pelvic Lymphadenectomy in the Surgical Treatment of Bladder Cancer*, 109 J. Urology 414 (1973).

[49] M. Al-Sarruf et al., *Phase II Trial of Cyclophosphamide, Doxorubicin and Cisplatin (CAP) Versus Amsacrial in Patients with Transitional Cell Carcinoma of the Urinary Bladder: A Southwest Oncology Group Study*, 69 Cancer Treatment Rep. 189 (1985); J. Carmichael et al., *Cisplatin and Methotrexate in Treatment of Transitional Cell Carcinoma of the Urinary Tract*, 57 Brit. J. Urology 299 (1985); W.G. Harker et al., *Cisplatin, Methotrexate and Vinblastine (CMV): An Effective Chemotherapy Regimen for Metastatic Transitional Cell Carcinoma of the Urinary Tract. A Northern California Oncology Group Study*, 134 J. Clinical Oncology 1118 (1985); H. Scher et al., *Neo-Adjuvant Chemotherapy for Invasive Bladder Cancer: Experience*

§ 13.16   Immunotherapy Treatment

Intravesical (in the bladder) immunotherapy with BCG (bacillus Calmette-Guerin) is used for patients with Stage 0 or Stage I as a prophylactic measure after transurethral resection of the tumor. Subcutaneous BCG also is effective.[50]

Intravesical interferon alpha 2B can be useful as primary treatment of papillary tumors and carcinoma in situ or as secondary treatment after failure of other intravesical agents.[51]

§ 13.17   Radiation Therapy Treatment

The objective of definitive radiation therapy either alone or in multimodality regimens is to save the bladder while equalling the success of the more radical surgical procedures. Combinations of external and interstitial radiation, external radiation alone, and combinations of external radiation and chemotherapy in selected cases achieve this success.

In the earliest stages, radiation is not considered until conservation treatment with transurethral resections (TUR) and intravesical chemotherapy have failed. Radiation is used in Stages 0, Tis, and Ta when there is extensive recurrent multifocal carcinoma with undifferentiated histology. Preoperative external radiation may be combined with radical cystectomy. Doses of 5000 cGy through fields just covering the bladder can be given in five weeks with two, three, or four fields, depending on the energy of the megavoltage radiation, although 5000 cGy has not been adopted across the whole spectrum of bladder carcinoma as the only preoperative dose. Doses can be encountered ranging down to as little as 1600 cGy. Segmental resections that preserve most of the bladder have a high local recurrence rate and should receive preoperative radiation in the 4500 to 5000 cGy range.

For Stage Ta less than 3 cm in diameter, 3000 cGy of intraoperative radiation can be given with 4 to 6 meV electrons followed by a three- or four-week 3000 to 4000 cGy course of megavoltage external radiation.

---

with the M-VAC Regimen, 64 Brit. J. Urology 250 (1989); W.U. Shipley et al., *Treatment of Invasive Bladder Cancer by Cisplatin and Radiation in Patients Unsuited for Surgery,* 258 JAMA 931 (1987).

[50] D.E. Coplen et al., *Long-Term Followup of Patients Treated with 1 or 2, 6 Week Courses of Intravesical Bacillus Calmette-Guerin: Analysis of Possible Predictors of Response Free of Tumor,* 144 J. Urology 652 (1990); H.W. Kerr et al., *Bacillus Calmette-Guerin Therapy Alters Progression of Superficial Bladder Cancer,* 6 J. Clinical Oncology 1450 (1988); D.L. Lumm et al., *BCG Immunotherapy of Bladder Cancer: Inhibition of Tumor Recurrence and Associated Immune Response,* 48 Cancer 82 (1981); M.F. Sarosky & D.L. Lamm, *Long-Term Results of Intravesical Bacillus Calmette-Guerin Therapy for Superficial Bladder Cancer,* 142 J. Urology 719 (1989).

[51] F.M. Torti et al., *Alpha-Interferon in Superficial Bladder Cancer: a Northern California Oncology Group Study,* 6 J. Clinical Oncology 476 (1988).

The preceding regimens can be used in Stage T1 and T2 tumors. Interstitial radiation also can be used in these stages being applied to tumors less than 5 cm in diameter by way of a cystostomy, usually combined with external radiation. The interstitial application is made following a preparatory TUR that reduces the bladder wall to normal thickness so that a single plane implant will be effective. The isotopes currently favored are 137-cesium needles, 192-iridium ribbons or wires, and 182-tantalum wires. The dosage from the radioisotope can be 3000 to 6000 cGy. The preceding external radiation ranges from 1000 to 4000 cGy. 137-cesium, 60-cobalt, and radium tubes in balloon catheters have been placed in the bladder through a cystostomy. The intracavitary brachytherapy can give 1500 to 3000 cGy preceded by 4000 to 5000 cGy of external radiation. Another intracavitary method involves filling intravesical balloons with liquid 32-phosphorus or 198-gold colloids.

Definitive interstitial radiation, without external radiation supplementation, requires 6000 to 6500 cGy in six or seven days.

Tumors can be treated with external radiation alone. The radiation is more effective if all the gross tumor first can be removed by TUR. The 5000 cGy in five weeks is considered to be a satisfactory preoperative dose. It is considered a successful definitive dose if given in four weeks with 250 cGy fractions. Fractions of 160 to 225 cGy require higher total doses ranging to 700 cGy. In dosage plans exceeding 5000 cGy, a dose in excess of 5000 cGy is given as a boost to small fields covering only the bladder. In the lower megavoltage energies, the boost can be given with lateral fields or with arcing fields. The regression of the tumor should be followed closely. It may take six months. Premature salvage surgery should be avoided. Scarring of the bladder as a result of long-standing conservative therapy can lead to the complication of a contracted bladder following radiation.

Despite the advantage of superior staging when radiation is given postoperatively, it is not used extensively because of the complications when combined with radical cystectomy. When used in cases in which residual tumor is suspected, the dose is 4500 cGy. A dose of 5000 cGy can be given if a barium examination shows the small bowel is not in the field of radiation.

In T2 tumors, treatment with external radiation alone, followed by salvage surgery when necessary, is considered as successful as preplanned radical cystectomy, especially in patients over 60 years of age.

In T3a and T3b tumors, the options are the same as in T2 tumors, except that brachytherapy is limited to interstitial implants. Managing the lymph nodes becomes a consideration in T3 tumors. There is a wide range of preoperative dosage in current use. Those who observe improved cure rates with the irradiation of pelvic lymph nodes treat the entire pelvis to doses of at least 4000 cGy in four weeks. The good prognostic signs are a normal intravenous pyelogram, the absence of microscopic vascular invasion, and down-staging the tumor as a result of preoperative radiation. Preoperative radiation and surgery in combination are deemed superior to either modality alone.

Combined radiation and chemotherapy regimens are used to reduce the requirement for salvage surgery and preserve more bladders. Various chemotherapy schedules are combined with whole pelvis radiation of 4500 cGy to 5000 cGy using 180 cGy to 200 cGy fractions. Boosts to the bladder alone bring the final bladder dose to 5500 cGy to 6500 cGy.

T4, N1–N3 tumors can be treated with combined preoperative radiation and surgery, external radiation alone, or combined radiation and chemotherapy.

Incurable cases can be palliated with doses of 4000 cGy to 5000 cGy given to bone metastases, which respond more slowly than other bone metastases, and to the pelvis for hematuria and pain.

§ 13.18   Significant Litigation

Silvers v. Wesson.[52]   A new trial was ordered following a plaintiff's judgment for $30,000. The plaintiff was treated by the defendant in June 1947 for a prostate condition. A bladder tumor was diagnosed in an incurable condition in June 1949. The plaintiff claimed failure to diagnose and treat an incipient cancer of the bladder before it became incurable. The court held that there was insufficient evidence to prove that any treatment might have been done that would in all probability have prevented the development of the bladder tumor into an incurable cancer.

RENAL CELL CARCINOMA (GRAWITZ'S TUMOR)

§ 13.19   Staging and Classification

TNM: American Joint Committee on Cancer (AJCC).[53]
The TNM system is not ordinarily used for malignancies of the kidney.

Robson Staging[54]

Stage A — Small primary with minimal distortion or large primary with renal distortion

No nodes

---

[52] 122 Cal. App. 2d 902, 266 P.2d 169 (1954).

[53] American Joint Committee on Cancer, *Manual for Staging of Cancer* 200 (3d ed. 1988).

[54] C.J. Robson, *Radical Nephrectomy for Renal Cell Carcinoma,* 89 J. Urology 37 (1963).

Stage B — Involves perirenal tissues

      No nodes

Stage C — Involves renal vein with or without involving inferior vena cava or involves superior vena cava

      Single or multiple involved regional or juxtaregional nodes or fixed regional nodes

Stage D — Invading adjacent structures and/or distant metastases.

§ 13.20   Clinical Manifestations

Gross or microscopic hematuria (blood in urine) with or without pain is the most common symptom. Abdominal mass or pain in the flank can be present. The classic triad of hematuria, abdominal mass, and pain is seen in a small number of patients and occurs with advanced disease, indicating a poor prognosis.[55]

The erythrocyte sedimentation rate can be elevated particularly in metastatic disease.[56] A hypochromic, normocytic anemia can appear, possibly due to decreased erythropoietin production or a circulation hemolysin.[57] Temperature elevation can be noted and can be related to increased levels of plasma fibrinogen.[58]

Hepatic dysfunction in the absence of liver metastases occurs in 40 percent of patients. Elevated alkaline phosphatase levels, hypoalbuminemia, hyperglobulinemia, prolonged prothrombin time, and elevated serum haptoglobin levels can be found. These changes can be caused by a toxic substance produced by the tumor. Most of these patients die within five years.[59]

The acute onset of a varicocele, almost always on the left side, can indicate a renal tumor with tumor thrombosis of the main renal vein, involving the gonadal vein.

Amyloidosis and neuromyopathy have been described. These are reversible following nephrectomy.[60]

---

[55] G.P. Murphy & H.K. Schirmer, *The Diagnosis and Treatment of Hypernephroma,* 18 Geriatrics 354 (1963).

[56] L.E. Bottiger, *Prognosis in Renal Carcinoma,* 26 Cancer 780 (1970).

[57] A. Gellhorn & J.L. Harvey, *Studies of Anemia of Disseminated Malignant Neoplastic Disease. Study of Life Span of Erythrocyte,* 11 Blood 618 (1956).

[58] G. Sufrin et al., *Coagulation Factors in Renal Adenocarcinoma,* 119 J. Urology 727 (1978).

[59] R.J. Boxer et al., *Non-Metastatic Hepatic Dysfunction Associated with Renal Carcinoma,* 119 J. Urology 468 (1978).

[60] B. Fallon, *Renal Parenchymal Tumors. B. Clinical and Diagnostic Features, in* Genitourinary Oncology 208 (D.A. Culp & S.A. Loening eds., 1985).

§ 13.21   —Paraneoplastic Syndromes

Hypertension

Elevated blood pressure can be caused by elevated renin levels produced by compressing the renal tissue near the tumor.[61] Essential hypertension also can be seen concomitantly with renal malignancies.

Erythrocytosis

Increased red blood cell mass and count can occur with bone marrow erythroid hyperplasia. Elevated levels of erythropoietin have been noted as the probable cause of the erythrocytosis.

Hypercalcemia

Although elevated serum calcium can be due to extensive bone metastases, a large number of patients have increased immunoreactive parathormone (parathyroid hormone). This condition indicates ectopic parathormone production.[62] Releasing prostoglandins A and E also can cause hypercalcemia.[63]

§ 13.22   Diagnosis

Excretory urogram (IVP) discloses a renal mass. Calcifications in the mass are indicative of malignancy in 50 percent of patients.[64] Tumor calcifications tend to be punctate, mottled, and located centrally. Nephrotomograms should be performed when a renal mass is noted. Ultrasonography can be helpful in distinguishing cyst from tumor. Retrograde pyelogram is indicated when excretion urogram results in nonvisualization of the kidney.

Computerized tomography and renal angiography are accurate diagnostic procedures. Renal scan with 99m-technetium labeled dimercapto succinic acid or I labeled goat antibody against human renal cell carcinoma[65] occasionally can be

---

[61] G. Sufrin et al., *Hormones in Renal Cancer,* 117 J. Urology 433 (1977).

[62] R.C. Benson, Jr., et al., *Radioimmunoassay of Parathyroid Hormone in Hypercalcemic Patients with Malignant Disease,* 56 Am. J. Med. 821 (1974); R.M. Buckle et al., *Ectopic Secretion of Parathyroid Hormone by a Renal Adenocarcinoma in a Patient with Hypercalcemia,* 4 Brit. Med. J. 724 (1978).

[63] K.B. Cummings & R.R. Robertson, *Prostaglandin: Increased Production by Renal Cell Carcinoma,* 118 J. Urology 720 (1977).

[64] J.N. Krieker et al., *Calcified Renal Cell Carcinoma: A Clinical, Radiologic and Pathologic Study,* 121 J. Urology 575 (1979).

[65] P. Belitsky et al., *Radionuclide Imaging of Primary Renal Cell Carcinoma by I-Labeled Antitumor Antibody,* 19 J. Nuclear Med. 427 (1978).

helpful. Venacavography and renal venography can aid in planning the surgical approach.

Needle aspiration of a suspected renal cyst with analysis of the fluid for cancer cells, blood, fat, protein, and lactic dehydrogenase is a relatively safe procedure. Renal cystography can be performed at the same time. Needle biopsy or needle aspiration of the tumor occasionally can be indicated, but seeding of tumor in the needle tract has been reported[66] and hemorrhage or perforation of adjacent viscera can occur.

§ 13.23 Surgical Treatment

Radical nephrectomy, which includes resection of Gerota's fascia and the adrenal gland, is the procedure of choice. Gross tumor should be removed from the renal vein and vena cava. Nephrectomy is performed in the presence of a solitary metastasis and also when there is severe or prolonged hematuria in a nonterminal patient with Stage 4 (multiple metastases present) renal cell carcinoma.

Solitary metastasis to lung, brain, or bone should be resected wherever possible. Some of these patients can still be cured or effectively palliated.[67]

§ 13.24 Chemotherapy Treatment

One of the first agents used in treating renal cell carcinoma was a hormonal agent, progesterone. Initially, an objective response of approximately 15 percent[68] was noted in patients with metastatic renal carcinoma. However, in a larger controlled series of patients, no noticeable effect was noted.[69]

In general, single-agent chemotherapeutic drugs have been used with poor results. However, Velban or vinblastine was noted to have an objective response. Vinblastine is the most effective single chemotherapeutic agent, with a 25-percent objective response rate.

Recombinant Interferon has had a moderate success with response rates varying from 17 to 26 percent[70] in a large series of eases. The Interferon was given

---

[66] J.T. Ferrucci, Jr., et al., *Malignant Seeding of the Tract after Thin-Needle Aspiration Biopsy*, 130 Radiology 345 (1979); R.P. Gibbons et al., *Needle Tract Seeding Following Aspiration of Renal Cell Carcinoma*, 118 J. Urology 865 (1977).

[67] B.M. Tolia & W.F. Whitmore, Jr., *Solitary Metastasis from Renal Cell Carcinoma*, 114 J. Urology 836 (1975).

[68] H.J.G. Bloom, *Hormone-Induced and Spontaneous Regression of Metastatic Renal Cancer*, 32 Cancer 1066 (1973).

[69] W.J. Hrushesky, *What's Old and New in Advanced Renal Cell Carcinoma?*, 18 Proc. Am. Soc'y Clinical Oncology 318 (1977).

[70] *Id.*

either intravenously or subcutaneously for three to five days per week. Interferon is a substance produced by a clone of the E. coli genetically engineered to possess a plasmid DNA, hybridized with a human IFN-producing gene derived from human leukocytes.

Interleukin-2 (IL-2), another biologic response modifier, has shown promising results in treating renal cell carcinoma. IL-2 has been reported to produce tumor regression, and the combination of IL-2 with lymphokine-activated killer (LAK) cells has lead to durable response rates of 15 to 30 percent.[71] Other biologic response modifiers, tumor infiltrating lymphocytes (TIL), and tumor necrosis factor (TNF) have been discovered and are being used in combination with LAK and IL-2.

Numerous studies are under way to evaluate the combination of the above agents, because some studies have shown that Interferon can increase the efficacy of certain chemotherapeutic drugs. Other studies are attempting to decrease the toxicity of the combination therapy. Although many of these agents are still investigational and are being given in research centers, these agents have produced significant antitumor responses of significant duration. It is hoped that the ongoing studies will produce promising results for those patients with renal cell cancer and for kidney cancer.

§ 13.25   Radiation Therapy Treatment

Radiation is used as an adjunct to surgery and for palliation. Radiation used alone does not cure carcinoma in the kidney. No benefit has been established from preoperative radiation.

Postoperative radiation is the regimen for which there is a role, although opinions differ as to its value. Disagreement could arise from a shortage of precisely analyzable cases in various collections. Postoperative radiation increases the survival rate when tumor extension beyond the kidney is limited to transcapsular spread. When lymphatic or venous spread exists, radiation can improve local tumor control, but survival is not improved.

Megavoltage radiation is given to the entire renal bed and adjacent paraaortic lymphatics through anterior, posterior, and oblique fields that are reduced to

---

[71] R.A. Figlin et al., *Recombinant Interferon Alfa-2a in Metastatic Renal Cell Carcinoma: Assessment of Antitumor Activity and Anti-Interferon Antibody Formation,* 6 J. Clinical Oncology 1604 (1988); R.A. Fisher et al., *Metastatic Renal Cancer Treated with Interleukin-2 and Lymphokine-Activated Killer Cells: A Phase II Clinical Trial,* 108 Annals Internal Med. 518 (1988); B.M. Hyman et al., *Recombinant Alfa Interferon in Renal Cell Carcinoma: A Randomized Trial of Two Routes of Administration,* 5 J. Clinical Oncology 286 (1987); S.A. Rosenberg et al., *A Progress Report on the Treatment of 157 Patients with Advanced Cancer Using Lymphokine-Activated Killer Cells and Interleukin-2 or High-Dose Interleukin-2 Alone,* 316 New Eng. J. Med. 889 (1987); T. Umeda & T. Nijima, *Phase II Study of Alpha Interferon on Renal Cell Carcinoma: Summary of Three Cell Abortive Trials,* 58 Cancer 1231 (1986).

appropriate levels of radiation to avoid spinal cord, hepatic, and bowel complications. Doses of 4500 to 5000 cGy are given in 160 to 180 cGy fractions.

Unusual phenomena can occur with carcinoma of the kidney. Elimination of a solitary distant metastasis by surgery, radiation (4500 to 5000 cGy), or both can result in a cure.

Similar dosage levels to bone and soft tissue metastases that are not solitary can give good palliation. Inoperable primary tumors also can be palliated.

Postoperative radiation therapy is used for transitional cell carcinoma of the renal pelvic just as with renal cell carcinoma. The histology of renal pelvis carcinoma is the same as the transitional cell carcinoma of the bladder, making combined radiation and chemotherapy an additional option.

§ 13.26   Significant Litigation

Ealy v. Sheppeck.[72]   Summary judgment for the defendant on the statute of limitations was affirmed. The defendant radiologist interpreted a urogram of the decedent taken in March 1978 as normal. Another urogram taken in January 1979 showed a tumor of the right kidney. The tumor was removed, and the patient died in July 1979. An application alleging malpractice was filed with the New Mexico Medical Review Commission in July 1981 and a court suit was instituted in November 1981. The court held that no continuous medical services were rendered by the defendant after March 1978, and the filing of the action was untimely.

TESTICULAR TUMORS

§ 13.27   Staging and Classification

TNM: American Joint Committee on Cancer (AJCC).[73]

Depth of invasion has prognostic significance, as does the presence of lymph node or distant metastases. The histologic characteristics of the tumor are highly significant in reference to prognosis.

International Union Against Cancer System[74]

T1   Tumor occupying less than half of testis, surrounded by palpably normal gland

---

[72] 100 N.M. 250, 669 P.2d 259 (Ct. App., *writ quashed,* 100 N.M. 259, 669 P.2d 735 (1983).

[73] American Joint Committee on Cancer, Manual for Staging of Cancer 184 (3d ed. 1988).

[74] E.E. Fraley et al., *Staging of Early Nonseminomatous Germ Cell Testicular Cancer,* 145 Cancer 1762 (1980).

T2   Tumor occupying half or more of testis with no enlargement or deformity

T3   Confined to testis causing enlargement or deformity

T4a   Extension to epididymis

T4b   Invasion of other local structures

N0   No deformity of regional lymph nodes on lymphangiography

Nx   Not possible to assess regional nodes (a + or − can be added later to indicate presence or absence of tumor on histologic examination)

N1   Regional lymph nodes deformed on lymphangiography

N2   Fixed, palpable abdominal lymph nodes

M1   Metastases to nodes outside abdomen or to viscera.

Maier and Mittenmeyer Staging[75]

IA.   Confined to testis

IB.   Microscopic tumor in lymph nodes

IIA. N1—Nodes that are grossly negative but microscopically positive

N2—Nodes that are grossly positive

N2A—Nodes that are grossly and microscopically positive; all nodes are less than 2 cm, and fewer than five nodes are involved, all without extranodal extension

IIB. N2B—Six or more nodes are positive and/or the largest node is greater than 2 cm and without extranodal extension

N3—Extranodal extension is present.

Boden and Gibb Staging (spermatic cord)[76]

Stage I or I A—Tumor limited to testis and spermatic cord

Stage II B—Includes tumors with metastases to regional lymph node

Stage III C—Metastases above diaphragm or wide dissemination.

Surgical-Pathological Staging[77]

Stage I: Local spread

P1   Confined to testis

P2   Involves testicular adnexa

---

[75] J.G. Maier & B. Mittemeyer, *Carcinoma of the Testes,* 39 Cancer 981 (1977).

[76] G. Boden & R. Gibb, *Radiotherapy and Testicular Neoplasms,* 2 Lancet 1195 (1951).

[77] N. Javadpour, *Testicular Germ Cell Tumors,* 18 Urology Dig. 19 (1979).

P3   Involves scrotal wall

Stage II: Confined to retroperitoneal lymphatics

N1   Microscopic

N2   Gross involvement without capsular invasion

N3   Gross involvement with capsular invasion

N4   Massive involvement of retroperitoneum

Stage III: Beyond retroperitoneum

M1   Solitary metastases

M2   Multiple metastases

Weinstein and Ross Staging[78]

Stage I   — Tumor limited to the testis without extension through the capsule or to the spermatic cord

Stage II   — Clinical or radiographic evidence of extension beyond the testis but not beyond the regional lymphatic vessels below the diaphragm

Stage IIA — Microscopic retroperitoneal metastases (or extension through the tunica albuginea or to the spermatic cord)

Stage IIB — Gross retroperitoneal disease

Stage IIC — Massive retroperitoneal disease

Stage III   — Distant metastases

Stage IIIA — Extension above the diaphragm but still confined to the mediastinal or superaclavicular lymphatic vessels

Stage IIIB — Extranodal metastases.

Staging System for Testicular Carcinoma[79]

Stage A   — Tumor is confined to the testicle. There is no evidence of spread beyond the confines of the scrotum.

Stage B1 — Evidence of minimal retroperitoneal lymph node metastases, determined either by retroperitoneal lymph node dissection or lymphangiogram (less than six positive nodes, well encapsulated).

---

[78] W.L. Gerber, *Testicular Neoplasms. B. Clinical, Diagnostic, and Therapeutic Features, in* Genitourinary Oncology 361 (D.A. Culp & S.A. Loening eds., 1985).

[79] D.G. Skinner & R.B. Smith, *Testicular Carcinoma, in* Cancer Treatment 412 (C.M. Haskell ed., 1980).

Stage B2—Evidence of moderate retroperitoneal lymph node spread (more than six nodes).

Stage B3—Massive retroperitoneal lymph node involvement, usually a palpable mass on physical examination but without evidence of spread above the diaphragm (can directly invade contiguous structures).

Stage C —Metastatic tumor noted above the diaphragm or to solid visceral organs (liver, brain, or bone).

World Health Organization Histologic Classification[80]

I. Germ cell tumors
   A. Tumors of one histologic type
      1. Seminoma (classic)
      2. Spermatocystic seminoma
      3. Embryonal carcinoma
      4. Yolk sac tumor (embryonal carcinoma, infantile type; endodermal sinus tumor)
      5. Polyembryoma
      6. Choriocarcinoma
      7. Teratoma (mature, immature, with malignant transformation)
   B. Tumors of more than one histologic type
      1. Embryonal carcinoma and teratoma (teratocarcinoma)
      2. Choriocarcinoma and any other type (specify type)
      3. Other combinations (specify)
II. Gonadal stromal tumors
   A. Tumors of specialized gonadal stroma
      1. Leydig (interstitial) cell tumors
      2. Sertoli cell tumors
      3. Undifferentiated or primitive tumors
      4. Combination of the above
   B. Tumors with both germ cell and gonadal stromal elements
      1. Gonadoblastoma

Mostofi and Price Pathologic Classification[81]

A. Tumors showing a single cell type
   1. Seminoma
   2. Teratoma

---

[80] F.K. Mostofi & L.H. Sobin, *International Histological Classification of Tumors of the Testis (No. 16)* (World Health Organization 1977).

[81] F.K. Mostofi & E.B. Price, Jr., *Tumors of the Male Genital System, in* Atlas of Tumor Pathology, Second Series, fascicle 8 (1973).

   3. Embryonal carcinoma

   4. Choriocarcinoma

   B. Tumors showing more than one histologic pattern

      1. Teratocarcinoma (embryonal plus teratoma)

      2. Embryonal cell plus seminoma

      3. Embryonal plus teratoma plus seminoma

      4. Teratoma plus seminoma

      5. Any combination with choriocarcinoma

Dixon and Moore Classification of Germ Cell Tumors[82]

Seminoma

Teratoma

Embryonal carcinoma

Choriocarcinoma

Teratocarcinoma.

§ 13.28   Clinical Manifestations

A painless testicular mass and discomfort or heaviness in the scrotum are the most common presenting symptoms. Pain or tender swelling can occur. Sudden onset of enlargement of a hydrocele can be seen initially.

There is a relatively high incidence of malignancy in an undescended testis, even in those treated by orchiopexy. These patients should be followed carefully with frequent examinations. A cryptorchid testis present after puberty is best treated by removing the testis.

§ 13.29   Diagnosis

The diagnosis is usually obvious on physical examination. Biopsy of the testis can be performed after control of the blood supply of the spermatic cord at the internal ring through an inguinal incision.

Staging of the disease is important to determine treatment. Chest X-rays and lung tomograms, abdominal ultrasound or computerized tomography, intravenous pyelogram, and bilateral pedal lymphangiography can be useful. Angiograms are necessary when bulky retroperitoneal disease is present. Liver scan or sonogram should be obtained if liver function studies are abnormal.

---

[82] F.J. Dixon & R.A. Moore, *Testicular Tumors: A Clinicopathological Study*, 6 Cancer 427 (1953).

Lymph node biopsy is reserved for patients with lymphadenopathy. Routine scalene node biopsy has been suggested.[83]

§ 13.30 —Tumor Markers

Human chronic gonadotropin (HCG) can be elevated in choriocarcinoma and in trophoblastic elements of other testicular tumors.[84]

Radioimmunoassay of alphafetoprotein (AFP) can be present in embryonal carcinoma. AFP is not present in the normal adult.

Elevated serum levels of calcitonin have been reported in patients with germ cell tumors as well as other benign and malignant conditions.[85]

Potential tumor markers include serum lactic dehydrogenase[86] (LDH) and pregnancy-specific beta-1-glycoprotein (SP-1).[87]

§ 13.31 Seminoma Treatment

Surgery

Orchiectomy is performed following high ligation of the spermatic cord. Retroperitoneal lymph node dissection has been recommended,[88] but seminoma is highly sensitive to radiation.

---

[83] A.S. Buck et al., *Supraclavicular Node Biopsy in Malignant Testis Tumors*, 107 J. Urology 619 (1972).

[84] G.D. Braunstein et al., *Ectopic Production of Human Chorionic Gonadotropin by Neoplasms*, 78 Annals Internal Med. 39 (1973); J.S. Cochran et al., *The Endocrinology of Human Chorionic Gonadotropin Secreting Testicular Tumors: New Methods in Diagnosis*, 114 J. Urology 549 (1976).

[85] M. Lee et al., *Elevated Serum Calcitonin Associated with an Extragonadal Seminoma*, 128 J. Urology 392 (1982).

[86] G. Lieskovsky & D.G. Skinner, *Significance of Serum Lactic Dehydrogenase in Stages B and C Nonseminomatous Testis Tumors*, 123 J. Urology 516 (1980); M. Lippert et al., *Role of Lactic Dehydrogenase Isoenzymes in Testicular Cancer*, 18 Urology 50 (1981).

[87] N. Javadpour, *Radioimmunoassay and Immuno-Peroxidase of Pregnancy-Specific Beta-1-Glycoprotein in Sera and Tumor Cells of Patients with Certain Testicular Germ Cell Tumors*, 123 J. Urology 514 (1980); S.A.N. Johnson et al., *Pregnancy-Specific Beta-Glycoprotein in Plasma and Tissue Extract in Malignant Teratoma of the Testis*, 1 Brit. Med. J. 951 (1977).

[88] C.M. Lindsey & J.F. Glenn, *Germinal Malignancies of the Testis: Experience, Management and Prognosis*, 116 J. Urology 59 (1976).

Chemotherapy

Bulky Stage II and Stage III disease can be improved with combination chemotherapy using bleomycin, etoposide (VP-16), and cisplatin (BEP); etoposide and cisplatin (EP); cisplatin, vinblastine, plus bleomycin (PVB); vinblastine, dactinomycin, bleomycin, cyclophosphamide, and cisplatin (VAB VI); platinum, vincristine, methotrexate, bleomycin, dactinomycin, cyclophosphamide, and etoposide (POMB/ACE); or vinblastine, cisplatin, and etoposide (VPV).[89]

Primary extragonadal germ-cell tumors originating in the mediastinum, retroperitoneum, pineal gland, prostate, stomach, or thymus are responsive to radiation therapy and chemotherapy in a similar manner as testicular seminoma.

Radiation Therapy

Seminomas are extremely radiosensitive and are curable with low doses of radiation. Cures begin with doses as low as 1000 cGy, although in practice, at least twice that amount is needed for optimum results.

In Stage I, orchiectomy is followed by megavoltage radiation to the lymph nodes. The iliac and inguinal lymph nodes can be irradiated either unilaterally or bilaterally. The paraaortic lymph nodes are irradiated up to the diaphragm with doses of 2000 to 2500 cGy given through anterior and posterior fields. Fractions are 160 to 200 cGy. Most oncologists do not irradiate the mediastinum and supraclavicular lymph nodes, but those who do give 2000 cGy.

In Stage II, there is greater consensus in favor of irradiating the mediastinum and supraclavicular nodes. The areas in the pelvis and retroperitoneum in which identifiable metastases are present are boosted to 3000 cGy. If the metastases are bulky, the dose is boosted to 4000 cGy. It can be advisable in these cases to irradiate the entire abdomen with gradually shrinking fields using daily fractions of 100 to 150 cGy. The kidneys are shielded after 1500 cGy.

Stage III tumors can be irradiated like Stage II tumors. Preservation of fertility is never guaranteed following radiation in any of these stages. A lead shield over the scrotum does not protect against scattered radiation coming through the pelvic floor. Patients might wish to bank their sperm.

---

[89]D.F. Bajorin et al., *Two-Drug Therapy in Patients with Germ Cell Tumors*, 67 Cancer 28 (1991); G.J. Bose et al., *VAB-6 an Effective Chemotherapy Regimen for Patients with Germ-Cell Tumors*, 4 J. Clinical Oncology 1493 (1986); L.H. Einhorn & S.D. Williams, *Chemotherapy of Disseminated Seminoma*, 3 Cancer Clinical Trials 307 (1980); P.J. Loehrer et al., *Chemotherapy of Metastatic Seminoma: The Southeastern Cancer Study Group Experience*, 5 J. Clinical Oncology 1212 (1987); S.D. Williams et al., *Treatment of Disseminated Germ-Cell Tumors with Cisplatin, Bleomycin, and Either Vinblastine or Etoposide*, 316 New Eng. J. Med. 1435 (1987).

§ 13.32   Nonseminoma Treatment

Surgery

Following orchiectomy, retroperitoneal lymph node dissection is performed for Stage A and B tumors (excluding Stage B tumors, which have advanced retroperitoneal disease). Debulking Stage B and C tumors can aid in subsequent treatment of these patients.[90] Resection of residual retroperitoneal disease or even localized pulmonary metastases after initial chemotherapy can increase response to further therapy.

Chemotherapy

Adjuvant chemotherapy in Stage II nonseminoma is essential in patients whose biologic markers (AFP, HCG, and LDH) do not return to normal following orchiectomy and retroperitoneal lymph node dissection. Useful regimens include: cisplatin, vinblastine, and bleomycin (PVB); vinblastine, dactinomycin, bleomycin, cyclophosphamide, and cisplatin (VAB VI); bleomycin, etoposide and cisplatin (BEP); etoposide and cisplatin (EP); or etoposide plus cisplatin.[91]

Advanced or metastatic tumors also are amenable to combination chemotherapy.

Radiation Therapy

Radiation is seldom used in treating nonseminomatous tumors and has been replaced by chemotherapy. Prior to the advent of chemotherapy, irradiation of the iliac and paraaortic lymph nodes in Stage I was as curative as lymphadenectomy due to the effectiveness of radiation when the metastases were microscopic. The required dosage is in the range of 4500 cGy in 180 cGy fractions. This regimen could be quite acceptable in present day treatment plans.

In metastatic disease that is unresponsive to chemotherapy and nonresectable, radiation can be used in doses of 4500 to 5500 cGy.

---

[90] J.P. Donohue et al., *Improved Management of Nonseminomatous Testis Tumors,* 42 Cancer 2903 (1978); D.G. Skinner, *Considerations for Management of Large Retroperitoneal Tumors: Use of the Modified Thoracoabdominal Approach,* 117 J. Urology 605 (1977).

[91] C.J. Logothetis et al., *Primary Chemotherapy for Clinical Stage II Nonseminomatous Germ Cell Tumors of the Testis: A Follow-Up of 50 Patients,* 5 J. Clinical Oncology 906 (1987); M.A. Socinski et al., *Stage II Nonseminomatous Germ Cell Tumors of the Testis: An Analysis of Treatment Options in Patients with Low Volume Retroperitoneal Disease,* 140 J. Urology 1437 (1988).

§ 13.33   Significant Cases

Daigle v. St. Paul Fire & Marine Insurance.[92]   A verdict for the defendant was affirmed. The plaintiff was seen by the defendant in January 1972 for a lump on the top side of the left testicle. Epididymitis was diagnosed and treated. The plaintiff was again seen two weeks later and nothing further was done. In March 1972, he was seen by another physician, and the growth had doubled in size from the examination in January 1972. The left testicle was removed in April 1972 for cancer and lymphadenectomy was performed two weeks later. Two of the lymph nodes were positive for metastatic cancer. Lung metastases showed up in October 1972, and the patient died in February 1973. The evidence by experts proved that testicular tumors are extremely rare and epididymitis is very common. The court held that a physician is held to the skill and care ordinarily exercised by members of the profession in good standing in the same area and that the highest degree of skill and care is not required.

Martin v. McEachern.[93]   The plaintiff was examined by the defendant for testicular problems in June 1986. The plaintiff was to return if the condition did not improve. In January 1987, the plaintiff was treated for asymptomatic chlamydia, but the defendant failed to examine a testicular lump. A diagnosis of testicular tumor was made in April 1987, and the testis was removed. Pathologic examination disclosed a mixed teratocarcinoma with embryonal cell carcinoma, which required a radical retroperitoneal lymph node dissection. There was a defense verdict.

---

[92] 323 So. 2d 186 (La. Ct. App. 1975).

[93] No. 88-11953 (Hillsborough County Ct., Fla.), *reprinted in* 6 Med. Malpractice Verdicts, Settlements & Experts No. 10, at 19 (1990).

CHAPTER 14

GYNECOLOGIC NEOPLASMS

PREINVASIVE NEOPLASIA

§ 14.1   Pap Smear (Papanicolaou Smear)

Cervical/vaginal cytology by means of the Pap smear is a screening test that identifies abnormal cells and alerts the physician to possible serious problems of preinvasive or invasive cancer. The Papanicolaou classification of reporting findings on cytology is currently used.

Papanicolaou Classification

Class   I: No abnormal cells seen

Class II: Atypical cells present below the level of cervical neoplasia

Class III: Abnormal cells consistent with mild−moderate dysplasia

Class IV: Abnormal cells present consistent with severe dysplasia or CIS

Class V: Cells present consistent with invasive carcinoma

Unable to evaluate.

Because there can be ambiguity and confusion in reports under the Papanicolaou classification, a conference was held at the National Cancer Institute in 1988 and the Bethesda system was recommended as a guideline for cytopathology reports of cervical/vaginal specimens.[1] The Bethesda system includes a statement on specimen adequacy with an explanation for less than optimal/ unsatisfactory specimen and a general categorization as to whether the findings are within normal limits or a descriptive diagnosis with further action is recommended.

Bethesda System

I.   INFECTION

Fungal

Fungal organisms morphologically consistent with Candida species

Other

Bacterial

Microorganisms morphologically consistent with Gardnerella species

Microorganisms morphologically consistent with Actinomyces species

Cellular changes suggestive of Chlamydia species infection, subject to confirmatory studies

Other

Protozoan

Trichomonas vaginalis

Other

---

[1] National Cancer Institute Workshop, *The 1988 Bethesda System for Reporting Cervical/Vaginal Cytological Diagnoses,* 262 JAMA 931 (1989).

Viral

    Cellular changes associated with cytomegalovirus

    Cellular changes associated with herpesvirus simplex

    Other.

Note: for human papillomavirus [HPV], refer to "Epithelial Cell Abnormalities, Squamous Cell."

II.   REACTIVE AND REPARATIVE CHANGES

    Inflammation

        Associated cellular changes

        Follicular cervicitis

    Miscellaneous (as related to patient history)

        Effects of therapy

        Ionizing radiation

        Chemotherapy

        Effects of mechanical devices (for example, intrauterine contraceptive device)

        Effects of nonsteroidal estrogen exposure (for example, diethyistibestrol)

        Other

III.   EPITHELIAL CELL ABNORMALITIES

    Squamous cell

        Atypical squamous cells of undetermined significance (recommended follow-up and/or type of further investigation: specify)

        Squamous intraepithelial lesion (SIL) (comment on presence of cellular changes associated with HPV if applicable)

        Low-grade squamous intraepithelial lesion, encompassing:

            Cellular changes associated with HPV

            Mild (slight) dysplasia/cervical intraepithelial grade 1 (CIN 1)

        High-grade squamous intraepithelial lesion, encompassing:

            Moderate dysplasia/CIN 2

            Severe dysplasia/CIN 3

            Carcinoma in situ/CIN 3

Squamous cell carcinoma

Glandular cell

Presence of endometrial cells of the following circumstances:

Out of phase in a menstruating woman

In a postmenopausal woman

No menstrual history available

Atypical glandular cells of undetermined significance (recommended follow-up and/or type of further investigation: specify)

Endometrial

Endocervical

Not otherwise specified

Adenocarcinoma

Specify probable site of origin: endocervical, endometrial, extra-
uterine

Not otherwise specified

Other epithelial malignant neoplasm: specify

IV.   NONEPITHELIAL MALIGNANT NEOPLASM: SPECIFY HOR-
MONAL EVALUATION (APPLIES TO VAGINAL SMEARS ONLY)

Hormonal pattern compatible with age and history

Hormonal pattern incompatible with age and history: specify

Hormonal evaluation not possible

Cervical specimen

Inflammation

Insufficient patient history

OTHER.

This method of reporting is more accurate and less confusing. The American
Cancer Society recommends that all asymptomatic women age 20 and over, and
those under age 20 who are sexually active, have a Pap test annually for two negative examinations and then at least every three years until age 65. Those women
at high risk of developing cervical cancer (early age at first intercourse, multiple
sexual partners, or other risk factors) need to be tested more frequently. Pelvic
examination should be done every three years from age 20 to 40 and annually
thereafter. Women at high risk of developing endometrial cancer (history of
infertility, obesity, failure of ovulation, estrogen therapy, or abnormal uterine

bleeding) should have a Pap test, pelvic examination, and endometrial tissue sample at menopause.[2]

CERVICAL INTRAEPITHELIAL NEOPLASIA (CIN)

§ 14.2   Classification

CIN I   Mild dysplasia

CIN II   Moderate dysplasia

CIN III   Severe dysplasia

            Carcinoma in situ.

All of these lesions have the potential to progress to invasive cancer. CIN III tends to progress to invasion more consistently than CIN I or II, which can undergo spontaneous regression to normal epithelium.

§ 14.3   Etiology

Coitus at an early age and multiple sexual partners are associated with an increased probability of developing CIN. There is a high incidence of cervical cancer in prostitutes, whereas it is rare in celibate groups such as nuns.

Herpes simplex virus (HSV-2) is a sexually transmitted infection and has a carcinogenic effect. Patients with cervical cancer have a higher incidence of antibodies to HSV-2 than those without cancer.

Local infections by the human papilloma virus (HPV) result in warty papillary condylomatous lesions. Genital condyloma is caused by HPV-6, which is transmitted sexually. There is a strong association between HPV and the development of CIN.

§ 14.4   Clinical Manifestations

Most patients are asymptomatic. Occasionally, there is the complaint of postcoital bleeding or vaginal spotting.

---

[2] *Cancer of the Cervix, in* Guidelines for the Cancer-Related Checkup: Recommendations and Rationale, 30 Ca-A Cancer J. Clinicians 219 (1980).

§ 14.5   Diagnosis

An abnormal Pap test suggesting dysplasia requires further evaluation to identify intraepithelial neoplasia. Colposcopy is performed allowing magnified visualization of the cervix after cleansing with 3 percent acetic acid. Abnormal
colposcopic areas are biopsied and endocervical curettage (ECC) is performed
to rule out microinvasive carcinoma.

The Schiller staining or lugol solution staining aid in visualizing abnormalities.

§ 14.6   Treatment

Therapy for CIN is determined by the patient's age and desire for subsequent
fertility. Local excision of small areas of abnormality with observation can be
used in some carefully selected patients.

Electrocautery in association with dilation and curettage has been used with a
recurrence rate of 3 percent, most commonly with CIN III.[3] Cryosurgery,[4] laser
surgery,[5] and cold coagulation[6] also are successful means of therapy. Each of
these methods requires very careful prolonged follow-up visits to detect recurrence.

Conization of the cervix is both a diagnostic tool and therapy in those young
patients who desire continued fertility. Early complications of conization include
hemorrhage, uterine perforation, and anesthesia risk. Delayed complications can
include bleeding (10 to 14 days after surgery), cervical stenosis, infertility, incompetent cervix, and increased chance of preterm delivery (low birth weight).

Hysterectomy is appropriate when the patient has completed her childbearing
and is interested in permanent sterilization. The patient must be informed of the
alternatives of treatment and their possible problems and complications. Routine
removal of the upper vagina, as advised in the past, is not necessary to prevent
recurrence.

---

[3] W. Chanen & R.M. Rome, *Electrocoagulation Diathermy for Cervical Dysplasia and Carcinoma in situ: A 15-Year Survey,* 61 Obstetrics & Gynecology 673 (1983); R. Ortiz et al., *Electrocautery Treatment of Cervical Intraepithelial Neoplasia,* 41 Obstetrics & Gynecology 113
(1973).

[4] J.L. Benedet et al., *Cryotherapy in the Treatment of Cervical Intraepithelial Neoplasia,* 58
Obstetrics & Gynecology 72 (1981); D.R. Ostergard, *Cryosurgical Treatment of Cervical
Intraepithelial Neoplasia,* 56 Obstetrics & Gynecology 233 (1980).

[5] H. Burke et al., *Carbon Dioxide Laser Therapy of Cervical Intraepithelial Neoplasia: Factors
Determining Success Rate,* 1 Laser Surgery Med. 113 (1980); B.J. Masterson et al., *The Carbon Dioxide Laser in Cervical Intraepithelial Neoplasia: A Five-Year Experience in Treating
230 Patients,* 139 Am. J. Obstetrics & Gynecology 565 (1981).

[6] K. Semm, *New Apparatus for the "Cold Coagulation" of Benign Cervical Lesions,* 95 Am. J.
Obstetrics & Gynecology 963 (1966).

VAGINAL INTRAEPITHELIAL NEOPLASIA (VAIN)

§ 14.7   Clinical Manifestations

Most lesions are asymptomatic, although postcoital spotting of blood can occur. VAIN has been associated with CIN or prior treatment for CIN and can be an extension of the process or simultaneous development.

§ 14.8   Diagnosis

Suspicion arises when the Pap smear shows an abnormality, especially in the absence of a cervix. Colposcopic examination and biopsies of abnormal vaginal areas establish the diagnosis. Lugol solution can be helpful in delineating lesions. VAIN tends to be multifocal in origin and, therefore, the whole vaginal lining must be carefully inspected.

§ 14.9   Treatment

Local excision of involved areas is usually adequate. If large areas are involved, partial vaginectomy can be necessary.

Topical application of 5-fluorouracil (5-FU) can be effective.[7] Cryosurgery has not been as successful as with CIN. Laser surgery can be curative,[8] but it can require more than one treatment, and it can be associated with pain and bleeding.

With failure of more conservative procedures, total vaginectomy can be necessary.

---

[7] H. Cagler et al., *Topical 5-FU Treatment of Vaginal Intraepithelial Neoplasia,* 58 Obstetrics & Gynecology 500 (1981); E.S. Petrilli et al., *Vaginal Intraepithelial Neoplasias: Biological Aspects and Treatment with Topical 5-Flourouracil and the Carbon Dioxide Laser,* 138 Am. J. Obstetrics & Gynecology 321 (1980).

[8] D.E. Townsend et al., *Treatment of Vaginal Carcinoma in situ with Carbon Dioxide Laser,* 143 Am. J. Obstetrics & Gynecology 565 (1982).

VULVAR INTRAEPITHELIAL NEOPLASIA (VIN)

§ 14.10   Classification

Premalignant Vulvar Disorders

1. Vulvar dystrophy
   Hyperplastic dystrophy with or without atypia
   Lichen sclerosis; kraurosis vulvae
   Mixed dystrophy (lichen sclerosis with epithelial hyperplasia) with or without atypia
2. Vulvar atypia
   Dysplasia, atypical hyperplasia with or without dystrophy
   Squamous cell carcinoma in situ
   Paget's disease of vulva.

§ 14.11   Clinical Manifestations

Although usually asymptomatic, bleeding, discharge, or mass can be present. The lesions are papular or macular and pink or red in color. Hyperpigmentation is present in 10 to 15 percent of patients with lesions that are mahogany to dark brown.

§ 14.12   Diagnosis

Careful vulvar examination is important during a routine gynecologic examination. When VIN is suspected, colposcopic examination of the whole vulva should be carried out.

Lesions can be made more visible with the application of 2 percent acetic acid to the vulvar skin. Another technique is the use of 1 percent toluidine blue that is washed off after two to three minutes with 2 percent acetic acid. This procedure stains suspicious areas a deep blue color.

Biopsies establish the diagnosis, but must include the deeper layers of the dermis to rule out invasive carcinoma.

§ 14.13   Treatment

Wide local excision with primary closure is adequate. Multicentric lesions can be excised, but if large areas are involved, skinning vulvectomy with split thickness skin graft or simple vulvectomy can be done.

The lesions can be treated by cautery or cryosurgery, but ulceration, pain, and prolonged healing can result. Laser surgery can require several treatments.[9]

Topical 5-Fluorouracil has been successful in the therapy of multicentric VIN in 50 percent of patients.[10] Prolonged treatment (up to a month) is necessary, and there can be denudation of the skin and associated discomfort.

CERVICAL CANCER

§ 14.14   Staging and Classification

TNM: American Joint Committee on Cancer.[11]
    Variations of the TNM system can be used.

      International Federation of Gynecology and Obstetrics (FIGO)

    0—Carcinoma in situ

    I—Cervical carcinoma, confined to uterus (extension to corpus should be disregarded)

  Ia—Preclinical invasive carcinoma, diagnosed by microscopy only

Iaa1—Minimal microscopic stromal invasion

 Ia2—Tumor with invasive component 5 mm or less in depth taken from the base of the epithelium and 7 mm or less in horizontal spread

  Ib—Tumor larger than T1a2

  II—Cervical carcinoma invades beyond uterus but not to pelvic wall or to the lower third of vagina

 IIa—Without parametrial invasion

---

[9] M.S. Baggish & J.H. Dorsey, *CO Laser for Treatment of Vulvar Carcinoma in situ,* 57 Obstetrics & Gynecology 371 (1981).

[10] J.D. Woodruff et al., *The Contemporary Challenge of Carcinoma in situ of the Vulva,* 115 Am. J. Obstetrics & Gynecology 677 (1973).

[11] American Joint Commitee on Cancer, Manual for Staging of Cancer 152 (3d ed. 1988). FIGO lists of staging and classification (**§§ 14.14, 14.21, 14.34, 14.42**) are reprinted with permission.

IIb—With parametrial invasion

III—Cervical carcinoma extends to the pelvic wall and/or involves lower third of vagina and/or causes hydronephrosis or nonfunctioning kidney

IIIa—Tumor involves lower third of the vagina, no extension to pelvic wall

IIb—Tumor extends to pelvic wall and/or causes hydronephrosis or non-functioning kidney

IVa—Tumor invades mucosa of bladder or rectum and/or extends beyond true pelvis

IVb—Distant metastasis.

Most cervical cancers are squamous cell carcinoma and a few are adenocarcinoma.

§ 14.15 Clinical Manifestations

Cervical cancer can be revealed by Pap smear in an asymptomatic woman. Early symptoms include blood-tinged watery vaginal discharge, painless metrorrhagia, and spotting of blood postcoitally or after douching. As the neoplasm progresses, the bleeding increases until it is continuous.

Flank or leg pain, dysuria, hematuria, rectal bleeding, or constipation occur when the malignancy involves surrounding structures such as ureters, bladder, pelvic wall, sciatic nerve, or rectum.

§ 14.16 Diagnosis

Examination of the cervix with Schiller staining can disclose abnormalities. Colposcopy should be performed with biopsy of suspicious areas. Endocervical curettage can be necessary to evaluate early malignancies.

To determine the stage of the tumor, studies can include pelvic sonography or computerized tomography (CT scan), proctosigmoidoscopy, sigmoidoscopy, intravenous pyelogram (IVP), and barium enema X-rays.

§ 14.17 Surgical Treatment

Extended or radical hysterectomy can be performed for Stage I and Stage IIA as an alternative to radiotherapy.[12] The radical procedure involves removing the

---

[12] D.W. Currie, *Operative Treatment of Carcinoma of the Cervix,* 78 J. Obstetrics & Gynecology Brit. Commonwealth 385 (1971); J. Zander et al., *Carcinoma of the Cervix: an Attempt to*

uterus, upper third of the vagina, uterosacral and interovesicle ligaments, and the parametrium. A less extensive operation can be performed for CIN with early stromal invasion or postirradiation residual microcarcinoma.[13] Pelvic lymphade-nectomy is included to remove ureteral, obturator, hypogastric, and iliac lymph nodes. The ovaries can be preserved because metastases to the ovaries are unusual.

Pelvic exenteration is reserved for recurrences involving the bladder and rectum limited to the pelvis and no evidence of distant metastases.[14] The bladder and rectum are removed in the exenteration procedure with formation of permanent colostomy and ureteroileostomy with ileal conduit[15] or other urinary cutaneous outlet.

The more radical the surgery is, and if radiotherapy has been given to the pelvis, it is more likely that complications will occur. Ureteral fistula, bladder fistula, hemorrhage, lymph fluid collection, pelvic infection, bowel obstruction, and pulmonary embolus are problems that can be encountered postoperatively.

§ 14.18   Chemotherapy Treatment

Stage III cervical cancer can be treated with neoadjuvant chemotherapy and radiation therapy, and can reduce tumor bulk. Hydroxyurea and misonidazole have been used in this manner.[16]

Stage IV A (invasion into local organs such as the bladder or rectum) and Stage IV B (metastatic) have been treated with some success with cisplatin, 5-fluorouracil, dibromoducitol, dianhydrogalactitol, and ifosfamide.[17] Combination chemotherapy is no more effective than single agent therapy.

Individualize Treatment. Results of a 20-Year Cooperative Study, 139 Am. J. Obstetrics & Gynecology 752 (1981).

[13] M.S. Piver et al., *Five Classes of Extended Hysterectomy of Women with Cervical Cancer,* 44 Obstetrics & Gynecology 265 (1974).

[14] A. Brunschwig, *Surgical Treatment of Carcinoma of the Cervix Recurrent After Irradiation or Combination of Irradiation and Surgery,* 99 Am. J. Roentgenology 365 (1967); R.G. Douglas & W.J. Sweeney, *Exenterative Operations in the Treatment of Advanced Pelvic Cancer,* 73 Am. J. Obstetrics & Gynecology 1169 (1957).

[15] E.M. Bricker, *Bladder Substitution After Pelvic Exenteration,* 30 Surgical Clinics N. Am. 1511 (1950).

[16] M.M. Hreshchyshyn et al., *Hydroxyurea or Placebo Combined with Radiation to Treat Stages III B and IV Cervical Cancer Confined to the Pelvis,* 5 Int'l J. Radiation Oncology, Biology & Physics 357 (1979); F.B. Stehman et al., *A Randomized Trial of Hydroxyurea Versus Misonidazole Adjunct to Radiation Therapy in Carcinoma of the Cervix: A Preliminary Report of a Gynecologic Oncology Group Study,* 159 Am. J. Obstetrics & Gynecology 87 (1988).

[17] D.S. Alberts et al., *Phase II Randomized Trial of Cisplatin Chemotherapy Regimens in the Treatment of Recurrent or Metastatic Squamous Cell Cancer of the Cervix: A Southwest Oncology Group study,* 5 J. Clinical Oncology 1791 (1987); R.E. Coleman et al., *A Phase II Study of Ifosfamide in Advanced and Relapsed Carcinoma of the Cervix,* 18 Cancer

Intraarterial chemotherapy to the tumor area has had limited responses with significant toxicity.

§ 14.19   Radiation Therapy Treatment

Radiation therapy can be used in all stages of carcinoma of the cervix, although in some stages it is more strongly indicated than in others. In the great majority of irradiated cases, external radiation and brachytherapy are combined, but both types of radiation also can be used.

Computerized dosimetry displays the dosage at all points of the exposed volume of tissue, but long-standing custom concentrates on Points A and B. Point A has had a tendency to move around, but a practical definition places it 2 cm lateral and 2 cm cephalad to the cervical os. If the lateral vaginal fornix is deep, Point A ends up in the vagina, so it would be advisable, in those cases, to place it 2 cm cephalad to the fornix. The original concept was to place Point A at a presumed critical junction: the crossing of the uterine artery and ureter. Point B is 3 cm lateral to Point A, at the pelvic side wall lymph nodes.

Carcinoma in situ is treated surgically. It can be treated with radiation if there is a contraindication to surgery or if the carcinoma is multifocal involving both the cervix and vagina. Only intracavitary radiation is needed. An exposure of 5000 mghrs gives a high mucosal dose and about 4500 cGy at Point A.

Stage IA is frequently treated surgically but it also can be treated with intracavitary radiation alone using 6000 mghrs or more (at least 6000 cGy at Point A) in two applications one or two weeks apart. The patient is hospitalized the two days or so of intracavitary irradiation and must lie flat in bed to avoid moving the applicators.

Stage IB is treated with both external radiation to the pelvis and one to three intracavitary implants. External therapy is given first. Tumor regression during external therapy permits a better anatomical alignment of the brachytherapy applications. If the primary tumor is 4 cm in diameter or larger, the external radiation can be extended to cover the paraaortic nodes. External radiation is directed, in general, at the periphery of the volume to be irradiated, namely, the lymph nodes. The intracavitary radiation is directed at the cervix and surrounding central tissues. Because the two types of treatment overlap, they have a reciprocal relationship: the higher the dose from one, the lower the dose is given for the other. In the early stages of tumor, the greater emphasis is on brachytherapy.

Chemotherapy Pharmacology 280 (1986); D. Heaton et al., *Treatment of 29 Patients with Bulky Squamous Cell Carcinoma of the Cervix with Simultaneous Cisplatin, 5-Fluorouracil, and Split-Course Hyperfractionated Radiation Therapy,* 38 Gynecology & Obstetrics 323 (1990); J.T. Thigpen et al., *A Randomized Comparison of a Rapid Versus Prolonged (24 hr) Infusion of Cisplatin in Therapy of Squamous Cell Carcinoma of the Uterine Cervix: A Gynecologic Oncology Group Study,* 32 Gynecologic Oncology 198 (1989).

In advanced stages, the greater emphasis is on external radiation. External radiation can be given in fractions of 160 to 200 cGy, most often 180 cGy, to a total dose of 3500 to 5000 cGy. Megavoltage X-radiation is given through anterior and posterior fields. Lateral, oblique, and arcing fields can be added. Paraaortic radiation is given through narrow anterior and posterior midline fields extending to the diaphragm. Paraaortic treatment can be given concurrently with the pelvic irradiation or afterward. The dose is 4000 to 4500 cGy, but can be increased to 5000 cGy with a boost, using lateral fields to decrease the risk of small bowel injury. Interruptions in external therapy can be unavoidable, but they should not exceed one week, if possible, to avoid losing some biologic effect. Similarly, rest periods before and during brachytherapy should not extend beyond three weeks. To avoid overdosing the central tissues from the brachytherapy, a central shield is added to the pelvic fields at some point in the course of the external radiation. The greater the planned brachytherapy exposure is, the sooner the central shield is placed in the course of external treatment. Brachytherapy exposure ranges from 6000 mghrs to 8000 mghrs. The intensity of radiation at Point A should be 40 to 60 cGy per hour. The intensity depends on the quantity of the radioisotope and the arrangement. The combined total dose at Point A ranges from 6500 to 9000 cGy. The dose at Point B is about 5500 cGy.

If Stage IB is treated surgically, radiation can be given postoperatively only if metastatic lymph nodes or extensive lymphatic permeation have been found or the surgical margin shows tumor. The routine combination of radiation and surgery has not been demonstrated to be of any value, nor has staging laparotomy. Postoperative radiation for metastatic lymph nodes can consist of 5000 cGy to the pelvis or to the pelvis and paraaortic nodes. If tumor has been left at the surgical margin of the central tissues, a midline shield is applied after 2000 to 3500 cGy of external pelvic irradiation. An intracavitary vaginal implant of 1800 to 2000 mghrs delivers a mucosal dose of more than 5000 cGy. Patients must be aware that combined surgery and radiation can result in edema of the legs. Also to be considered are possible complications from adherent small bowel in the pelvis and the closer proximity of the bladder and rectum to the intracavitary sources following surgery. If brachytherapy is anatomically not possible in the postoperative patient, the 5000 cGy pelvic dose can be boosted to 6000 cGy with small external fields.

Diffuse infiltration of the cervix with carcinoma can produce a condition described as *barrel cervix*. Treatment includes a radical hysterectomy six weeks after completing radiation therapy.

Stage IIA is treated like Stage IB, but more often in the higher range of the dose spread for Stage IB.

For Stage IIB and higher stages, interstitial radiation can be given to bulky masses, especially in the parametria, using template-guided hollow needles to implant the radioisotope. The dose to Point B should be 6000 cGy.

Carcinoma of the cervical stump is not seen in younger women because subtotal hysterectomies are no longer done. External and intracavitary radiation are manipulated in cervical stump carcinoma to get the dose distributions already described. The quantity of radioisotopes is reduced, though not as much as it is following radical hysterectomy, because the cervical stump seldom can hold as much radioisotope as the intact uterus. Transvaginal kilovoltage radiation can be substituted for brachytherapy using 3000 to 5000 surface rads, which may be given in two to four weeks.

Carcinoma of the cervix diagnosed during the first trimester of pregnancy can be irradiated in the usual way for its stage. Abortion occurs by the end of the external radiation. The products of conception are removed surgically if they are still retained in the uterus. During the second trimester, the pregnancy is terminated by hysterotomy before starting radiation. In the third trimester, a viable baby is obtained by cesarean section and radiation is started 10 days postpartum. Some oncologists advocate vaginal delivery and claim the prognosis is not affected adversely.

Remote afterloading high dose rate brachytherapy is becoming more prevalent. It represents a departure from traditional radiobiologic principles and introduces new factors into the relative biologic effect formula. It is a treatment given in minutes without hospitalization and eliminates handling and exposure of personnel to radioisotopes. The patient is in a shielded room with the applicators in place in her body and attached to channels connected to the radioisotopes. The radioactive sources are in a safe from which they are moved by a projector through the transfer system into the patient. The procedure is performed from a control panel outside the room.

Techniques are evolving to achieve effects equivalent to low dose rate radiation without an increase in tissue injuries. The isotopes are 60-cobalt, 137-cesium, and 192-iridium. To give treatments in minutes, the activity of the isotopes has to be great. The treatments are given while the external radiation is in progress. Depending on the total external radiation dose with which it reciprocates, the high dose rate brachytherapy can be given in one treatment, or in five treatments at weekly intervals. Doses to Point A with each treatment range from 370 to 1000 cGy.

Stage-for-stage adenocarcinoma of the cervix can be irradiated as successfully as squamous cell carcinomas.

Vaginal patency is a common issue in the irradiation of cervical carcinoma. Patency is maintained by sexual activity. Vaginal dilators also can be used while lubricants handle the dryness.

§ 14.20   Commentary and Significant Cases

With the advent of Pap smears, cancer of the cervix can be diagnosed in the early course of the disease, especially during the period of preinvasive neoplasia. The colposcope magnifies the cervix so that early lesions can be identified and their limits can be defined. There must be accurate interpretation of the cytology in the Pap smear. Colposcopic directed biopsies help to define the lesion. When cervical intraepithelial neoplasia (CIN) is present, the patient, in the childbearing age, must be allowed to decide whether conization with frequent follow-up or a hysterectomy should be the course of therapy.

Lambert v. Michel.[18]   A claim for failure to perform a Pap smear resulted in a verdict for defendant. The court held that there was no malpractice when there was failure to perform a Pap smear on a woman who presented herself with various acute problems, but did not present any symptoms relating to her female organs, even though she subsequently had an advanced stage of cervical cancer that could have been diagnosed earlier if physician had conducted a Pap smear.

Lundberg v. Bay View Hospital.[19]   A judgment for $25,000 against the hospital was affirmed. A biopsy of the plaintiff's cervix in April 1955 was diagnosed as cancer. The plaintiff underwent a hysterectomy in April 1955. Thereafter, it was determined that in fact she did not have cancer, and the biopsy material had been grossly misinterpreted. The court held that the pathologist was in the employ of the hospital. It is a jury question as to whether the hospital was negligent in regard to diagnosis and treatment of the patient whereby her uterus was unnecessarily removed.

Piel v. Gallbol.[20]   A directed verdict for the defendant was affirmed. The plaintiff saw the defendant because of bloody vaginal discharge in 1972. Pap smears were done in May 1972 and in October 1972, both of which were reported as "class 2, slightly active, but benign, no tumor cells." A pelvic exam in October 1972 by the defendant disclosed no tumor. Because the symptoms persisted, the plaintiff saw another physician in December 1972 who diagnosed cancer of the cervix. Three Pap smears were done, two of which showed no cancer, but the third indicated highly suspicious atypia. Subsequent surgery eradicated the cancer. The plaintiff contended that failure to do a biopsy was prima facie negligence. The court held that expert testimony was necessary to demonstrate that the failure to run a Pap smear was negligence.

Snead v. United States.[21]   The plaintiff had a Pap smear taken in November 1978 that was interpreted as Class I, negative. She had excessive and prolonged menstrual bleeding in June 1979, and the physician performed a physical examination, but did not take a Pap smear. The bleeding stopped with the use of Provera, and no further follow-up treatment was recommended. In March 1980,

---

[18] 364 So. 2d 248 (La. Ct. App. 1979).

[19] 175 Ohio St. 133, 191 N.E.2d 821 (1963).

[20] 559 S.W.2d 38 (Mo. Ct. App. 1977).

[21] 595 F. Supp. 658 (D.D.C. 1984).

postcoital bleeding occurred. Biopsy of a lesion of the cervix in July 1980 disclosed adenocarcinoma of the cervix, Stage I-B. A radical hysterectomy, salpingo-oophorectomy, and pelvic lymphadenectomy were performed. Metastases appeared in the lung and mediastinum in March 1983. Radiation therapy and chemotherapy were given. The plaintiff was awarded $1.17 million and her husband was awarded $200,000 for loss of consortium. Applying District of Columbia law, the court held that the plaintiff must show that the defendant's deviation from the standard of care was a *substantial factor* bringing about the defendant's present condition, taking into account both the chances of survival given proper treatment and the extent to which the physician interfered with those chances by departing from the standard of care.

Steele v. St. Paul Fire & Marine Insurance Co.[22]   The plaintiff was awarded $50,000 for breach of duty of informed consent. The plaintiff, in October 1972, had a Pap smear that was interpreted as Class 3, dysplasia or cancer in situ. Dilatation and curettage and conization were performed. Foci of carcinoma in situ were found. Pap smears in March 1973 and October 1973 were Class I, negative. She saw another physician, the defendant, in August 1974 who, on learning of her history of carcinoma in situ treated by conization, advised hysterectomy. The surgery was performed in May 1974 and no cancer was found. The court held that the physician's negligence in failing to disclose to the patient that an alternative effective procedure existed and that her last Pap smear had indicated that she probably did not have cancer was a substantial cause of patient's harm.

Wheat v. United States.[23]   Applying Texas law, the court affirmed the award of $3 million to the patient's estate and $1 million to patient's minor daughter, but vacated the other awards unless the husband accepted a remittitur to $900,000 (from $1.8 million) and the patient's adult daughter accepted a remittitur to $250,000 (from $500,000). In 1978, the patient visited a military physician for a routine Pap smear. The Pap smear revealed minimal dysplasia, an early warning sign of cervical cancer. No further tests were done. The patient returned multiple times with abnormal bleeding and abdominal and pelvic pain. In 1979, another physician performed a hysterectomy that showed cervical cancer, Stage II-B. She was not informed of the cancer nor treated for it. Complaints of increasing pain were treated with pain medications. Renal failure occurred in March 1981, and cervical cancer was diagnosed and treated with radiation therapy and chemotherapy. The patient died in March 1982.

---

[22] 371 So. 2d 843 (La. Ct. App.), *cert. denied,* 374 So. 2d 658 (La. 1979).
[23] 860 F.2d 1256 (5th Cir. 1988).

INVASIVE CANCER OF THE VAGINA

§ 14.21   Staging and Classification

TNM: American Joint Committee on Cancer.[24]
Variations of the TNM system can be used.

International Federation of Gynecology and Obstetrics (FIGO)

0— Carcinoma in situ

I— Tumor confined to vagina

II— Tumor invades paravaginal tissues but not to pelvic wall

III— Tumor extends to pelvic wall

IVa— Tumor invades mucosa of bladder or rectum and/or extends beyond the
true pelvis

IVb— Distant metastasis.

Vaginal malignancies are usually squamous cell carcinoma, but occasionally
they are adenocarcinoma or sarcoma.

§ 14.22   Clinical Manifestations

Most often a vaginal discharge, at times bloody, is present. Irregular or postmenopausal vaginal bleeding can occur. The patient can have urinary frequency
or burning and can complain of dyspareunia (painful intercourse).

§ 14.23   Diagnosis

Careful examination of the vaginal wall is essential. Colposcopy is the best
means of inspection. Suspicious areas should be biopsied.
     If the patient's mother received diethylstilbestrol (DES) during her pregnancy,
it should alert the physician to the possibility of adenocarcinoma of the vagina.

---

[24] American Joint Committee on Cancer, Manual for Staging of Cancer 170 (3d ed. 1988).

§ 14.24   Surgical Treatment

Partial or total vaginectomy can be performed with good results, especially in the elderly patient. Recurrent extensive vaginal carcinoma without distant spread can be treated by exenteration.[25]

§ 14.25   Chemotherapy Treatment

Squamous cell carcinoma of the vagina may be treated with chemotherapy similar to that used for cervical squamous cell carcinoma (see § 14.18). Cisplatin and mitoxantrone have been tried with variable results.[26]

Intraepitheliar carcinoma of the vagina can be successfully treated with topical 5-fluorouracil.

§ 14.26   Radiation Therapy Treatment

Stage-for-stage carcinoma of the vagina is as curable as carcinoma of the cervix. The same principles of radiation apply to both.

In Stage I, the total dose is in the range of 8000 cGy to 9000 cGy. Intracavitary radiation is given with cylindrical applicators with 137-cesium tubes placed in tandem along the center of the cylinders. The doses are measured at the mucosal surface. For tumors of the upper vagina, an intrauterine tandem and vaginal colpostats can be used. If the tumor tends to be thick, a portion of the brachytherapy dose can be given interstitially with 137-cesium or 192-iridium needles. If the tumor is undifferentiated or is infiltrative, the treatment starts with megavoltage external radiation through anterior and posterior pelvic fields for a combined parametrial dose of 5000 cGy (external radiation dose plus the brachytherapy contribution). In this circumstance, a 2000 cGy portion of the total vaginal dose can be contributed by the external radiation prior to midline shielding.

Stage II carcinomas require the same total doses as Stage I, but only the technique that employs all three forms of radiation (external, intracavitary. interstitial) is likely to apply. For carcinomas involving the lower vagina, the external

---

[25] D.L. Barclay, *Carcinoma of the Vagina After Hysterectomy for Severe Dysplasia or Carcinoma in situ of the Cervix,* 8 Gynecologic Oncology 1 (1979); R.A. Lee & R.E. Symmonds, *Recurrent Carcinoma in situ of the Vagina in Patients Previously Treated for in situ Carcinoma of the Cervix,* 48 Obstetrics & Gynecology 61 (1976); B. Phillips et al., *Pelvic Exenteration for Vulvovaginal Carcinoma,* 141 Am. J. Obstetrics & Gynecology 1038 (1981).

[26] H.B. Muss et al., *Mitoxantrone in the Treatment of Advanced Vulvar and Vaginal Carcinoma,* 12 Am. J. Clinical Oncology 142 (1989); J.T. Thigpen et al., *Phase II Trial of Cisplatin in Advanced or Recurrent Cancer of the Vagina: A Gynecologic Oncology Group study,* 23 Gynecologic Oncology 101 (1986).

fields should include the inguinal and femoral lymph nodes. If these nodes are palpably enlarged, additional small fields should be used to boost the dose from 5000 to 6500 cGy.

Stages III and IV are irradiated like Stage II but with appropriate modifications in the distribution of dosage. After the usual 5000 cGy to the parametria, an interstitial boost can be used to bring the total parametrial dose to 6500 cGy in a localized area.

§ 14.27   Significant Cases

Ferguson v. Vest.[27]   The 63-year-old plaintiff was given radiation therapy to the vagina based on a Class V Pap smear without the benefit of a biopsy. It was later discovered that she was free of cancer before radiation therapy had begun. The plaintiff claimed that the defendants knew she had previously received a curative dosage of radiation to the vagina. She developed vaginal necrosis and stenosis, bladder and bowel dysfunction, and mental and emotional distress. She had temporary colostomies twice and had to have the vagina removed. She required dilations of the urethra every three weeks. The verdict was for $2.332 million, including $1.2 million for hedonic damages, or loss of ability to enjoy life's simple pleasures.

Needham v. White Laboratories, Inc.[28]   An action was brought against the manufacturer of dienestrol when it was alleged that the plaintiff's vaginal cancer was caused when her mother took DES while pregnant with the plaintiff. Applying Illinois law, the appellate court reversed the judgment for the plaintiff and remanded the case for a new trial. The court held that a cause of action accrues when the plaintiff knows or has reason to know that he or she has a physical problem and also that someone is or can be responsible for it. It was improper to admit evidence that synthetic estrogen was ineffective in preventing miscarriage, because the jury could have based its verdict solely on that fact. The district court abused its discretion in admitting a list of medical articles to show that the manufacturer should have known that the drug could cause cancer in the absence of an adequate foundation or evidence to demonstrate that the titles were an accurate summary of the articles.

---

[27] No. 87-L-207 (Madison County, IL Mar. 1989), *reprinted in* 6 Med. Malpractice Verdicts, Settlements & Experts No. 2, at 44–45 (1990).

[28] 639 F.2d 394 (7th Cir. 1981).

INVASIVE CANCER OF THE VULVA

§ 14.28   Staging and Classification

TNM: American Joint Committee on Cancer.[29]

Prognosis of vulvar malignancies is dependent on depth of invasion involvement of contiguous structures, and the presence of nodal or distant metastases.

§ 14.29   Clinical Manifestations

A small nodule, ulceration, warty or cauliflowerlike growths, or actual mass can be present on the vulva. The malignancy is slow growing and metastasizes late. The patient can complain of itching or burning.

§ 14.30   Diagnosis

After thorough inspection of the vulva, which can be more rewarding with the colposcope, all suspicious lesions must be biopsied. The inguinal regions should be carefully palpated for the presence of metastases to the superficial inguinal and deep femoral nodes.

§ 14.31   Surgical Treatment

The main form of treatment is radical vulvectomy with inguinal and pelvic lymphadenectomy.[30] Because of the morbidity that includes major deformity of the vulva and swelling of the legs, lesser procedures have been advocated. Some surgeons perform pelvic lymphadenectomy only if the inguinal nodes are positive.[31] Microinvasive carcinoma (1 cm or less in diameter with invasion to a depth of 5 mm or less) can be treated by radical vulvectomy[32] or wide resection with excision of superficial inguinal nodes.[33]

---

[29] American Joint Committee on Cancer, Manual for Staging of Cancer 174 (3d ed. 1988).

[30] R.L. Byron, Jr. et al., *The Surgical Treatment of Invasive Carcinoma of the Vulva,* 121 Surgery Gynecology & Obstetrics 1243 (1965); G.W. Morley, *Infiltrative Carcinoma of the Vulva: Results of Surgical Treatment,* 174 Am. J. Obstetrics & Gynecology 874 (1976).

[31] S.L. Curry et al., *Positive Lymph Nodes in the Vulvar Squamous Carcinoma,* 9 Gynecologic Oncology 63 (1980).

[32] J.T. Wharton et al., *Microinvasive Carcinoma of the Vulva,* 118 Am. J. Obstetrics & Gynecology 159 (1974).

[33] P.J. DiSaia et al., *An Alternate Approach to Early Cancer of the Vulva,* 133 Am. J. Obstetrics & Gynecology 820 (1979).

§ 14.32   Chemotherapy Treatment

Topical 5-fluorouracil has been used to treat vulvar intraepithelial neoplasia with some success.[34] Immunotherapy with dinitrochlorobenzene (DCNB) has been found useful in treating atypical vulvar dystrophy.[35]

Preoperative mitomycin C and 5-fluorouracil followed by irradiation can result in local tumor shrinkage to improve the chances for successful resection.[36] There is no standard chemotherapy for metastatic vulvar carcinoma.

§ 14.33   Radiation Therapy Treatment

Surgery is the most widely used treatment for carcinoma of the vulva. Radiation can cure vulvar carcinoma, but it is not considered an alternative to be recommended unless there are reasons to forgo surgery.

Radiation therapy for vulvar carcinoma can be similar to treating carcinoma of the skin, except that treatment fractions do not exceed 300 cGy. Kilovoltage X-rays can be given through a direct perineal field or with multiple fields such as right and left oblique and suprapubic fields. The direct perineal field can be circumscribed by a lead cutout that covers the tumor and 2 cm of normal tissue surrounding it. Peak doses of 4500 to 5700 cGy can be given with 200 to 300 cGy fractions. High megavoltage electrons can be used like kilovoltage X-radiation for direct applications to the tumor. Megavoltage X-ray regimens can consist of anterior and posterior fields that cover the primary tumor and the inguinal, femoral, and pelvic lymph nodes. The fractions can be 180 cGy. When the irradiation of the lymph nodes is elective, the total dose to the large fields can be limited to 4500 to 5000 cGy. The dose to the primary tumor can then be boosted to 7000 cGy with kilovoltage X-rays, electrons, or interstitial brachytherapy. Lymph nodes known to contain metastases can be boosted to 6500 cGy with small fields using megavoltage X-rays or electrons.

Primary tumors can be treated entirely with interstitial radioisotopes to doses of 4500 to 6000 cGy over a period of up to seven days.

Postoperative radiation is used when the surgical margin of the primary tumor is questionable or if metastatic lymph nodes have been found. Doses of 4500 to

---

[34]H. Calgar et al., *Topical 5-Fluorouracil Treatment of Vaginal Intraepithelial Neoplasia,* 5 Obstetrics & Gynecology 580 (1981); F.H. Stillman et al., *A Review of Lower Genital Intraepithelial Neoplasia and the Use of 5-Fluorouracil,* 40 Obstetrics & Gynecology Surv. 190 (1985).

[35]D.C. Foster & J.D. Woodruff, *The Use of Dinitrochlorobenzene in the Treatment of Vulvar Carcinoma in situ* 11 Gynecology & Obstetrics 330 (1981).

[36]W. Levin et al., *The Use of Concomitant Chemotherapy and Radiotherapy Prior to Surgery in Advanced Carcinoma of the Vulva,* 25 Gynecology & Obstetrics 20 (1986).

5000 cGy are given to the primary site and/or the lymph nodes with megavoltage X-rays using 180 cGy fractions. Another regimen consists of vulvectomy alone followed by 4500 to 5000 cGy of elective radiation to the lymph nodes. In any of the postoperative regimens, areas of gross residual tumor are boosted to 6500 to 7000 cGy.

Large tumors can be given 4500 to 5500 cGy of preoperative radiation to improve their resectability if it is questionable.

UTERINE CANCER

§ 14.34   Staging and Classification

TNM: American Joint Committee on Cancer.[37]

International Federation of Gynecology and Obstetrics (FIGO)

0 — Carcinoma in situ

I — Tumor confined to corpus

Ia — Uterine cavity 8 cm or less in length

Ib — Uterine cavity more than 8 cm in length

II — Tumor invades cervix but does not extend beyond uterus

III — Tumor extends beyond uterus but not outside true pelvis

IVa — Tumor invades mucosa of bladder or rectum and/or extends beyond the true pelvis

IVb — Distant metastasis.

§ 14.35   Etiology

Factors associated with increased risk of endometrial carcinoma are obesity, nulliparity (no pregnancies), and late menopause (after age 52). Estrogen and ramoxifen administration has been implicated as a cause of endometrial adenocarcinoma.[38]

---

[37] American Joint Commitee on Cancer, Manual for Staging of Cancer 158 (3d ed. 1988).

[38] C.M.F. Antunes et al., *Endometrial Cancer and Estrogens (Report of a Large Case-Control Study)*, 300 New Eng. J. Med. 9 (1979); C.J. Cohen & C. Deppe, *Endometrial Carcinoma and Oral Contraceptive Agents*, 49 Obstetrics & Gynecology 390 (1977); J. Gordon et al., *Estrogens and Endometrium Carcinoma; An Independent Pathology Review Supporting Original Risk Estimate*, 297 New Eng. J. Med. 500 (1977); L.A. Gray et al., *Estrogens and Endometrial Carcinoma*, 49 Obstetrics & Gynecology 385 (1977).

Adenomatous hyperplasia is considered a precursor of endometrial carcinoma. When atypia is present within hyperplasia, there is even a higher propensity for malignancy to develop. Severe atypical adenomatous hyperplasia can be considered carcinoma in situ.[39]

Leiomyosarcoma can originate within a uterine fibroid. Pelvic irradiation precedes the onset of sarcoma in 5 to 10 percent of patients.

§ 14.36   Clinical Manifestations

Suspicion of endometrial carcinoma should be maintained in any patient with abnormal vaginal bleeding. Prolonged and heavy menstrual periods, bloody spotting between menstrual periods, increased bleeding during menopause, and any bleeding in the postmenopausal patient are causes for evaluation.

§ 14.37   Diagnosis

Routine cervical Pap smears will not ordinarily detect endometrial carcinoma. Endometrial cytology or biopsy is helpful, but dilation and curettage (D&C) is the definitive procedure for diagnosis.

Pelvic ultrasound or computerized tomography (CT scan), chest X-ray, intravenous pyelogram (IVP), cystoscopy, barium enema, and sigmoidoscopy can be helpful in staging the disease.

§ 14.38   Surgical Treatment

Total abdominal hysterectomy with bilateral salpingo-oophorectomy is the standard procedure for carcinoma and sarcoma of the uterus. The incidence of ovarian metastases increases with the depth of invasion of adenocarcinoma.[40]

Bilateral pelvic lymphadenectomy is usually included because 11 percent of patients with Stage I and Stage II adenocarcinoma have metastases to pelvic lymph nodes.[41] At times, this procedure is performed for uterine sarcoma.[42]

---

[39] A.T. Hertig & H. Gore, *Tumors of the Female Sex Organs. Part 2. Tumors of the Vulva, Vagina and Uterus, in* Atlas of Tumor Pathology § II, fascicle 33 at 185 (1960).

[40] *Adenocarcinoma of the Uterus, in* Clinical Gynecologic Oncology 160 (P.J. DiSaia & W.T. Creasman eds., 1984).

[41] W.T. Creasman et al., *Adenocarcinoma of the Endometrium; Its Metastatic Lymph Node Potential; a Preliminary Report,* 4 Gynecology & Obstetrics 239 (1976).

[42] *Sarcoma of the Uterus, in* Clinical Gynecologic Oncology 186 (P.J. DiSaia & W.T. Creasman eds., 1984).

§ 14.39   Chemotherapy Treatment

Progestational agents such as hydroxyprogesterone (Delalutin™), medroxy-progesterone (Provera™), and megestrol (Megace™) have produced antitumor response in 15 to 30 percent of patients with high progesterone receptors levels (greater than 100). Highly differentiated tumors respond better than poorly differentiated tumors. The progestational agents are the primary therapy for recurrent or metastatic disease. Tamoxifen and danazol have shown tumor regression.

Single-agent chemotherapy with doxorubicin, hexamethylmelamine, and cisplatin have been effective in 30 to 40 percent of patients. Combination chemotherapy can be more effective than single agents. Doxorubicin and cisplatin; cisplatin, doxorubicin, and cyclophosphamide (PAC); cyclophosphamide, doxorubicin, and cisplatin (CAP); and megestrol, cyclophosphamide, and doxorubicin with or without 5-fluorouracil have shown fairly good responses.[43]

§ 14.40   Radiation Therapy Treatment

Radiation is mainly adjuvant treatment to surgery. When there is a medical contraindication to surgery, radiation becomes the definitive treatment and can be curative. In its adjuvant role, radiation has widespread use both as preoperative and postoperative treatment because of differing perceptions regarding its best use.

Low-grade Stage I carcinomas are not irradiated unless unfavorable prognostic factors are noted in the pathologic specimen, or the initial staging has to be changed to a higher stage because of findings at surgery. The less favorable prognostic findings are invasion of one-half or more of the thickness of the myometrium, vascular invasion, or tumor cells in the peritoneal washings. Postoperative megavoltage external radiation is given to the whole pelvis with 160 to 180 cGy fractions to total doses of 4000 to 5000 cGy. Two fields or a four-field box arrangement can be used. Alternative intracavitary treatment can consist of 137-cesium containing colpostats in the vagina to deliver a surface dose of 6000 cGy. Additional treatment for tumor cells in peritoneal washings can consist of the intraperitoneal infusion of 15 mCi of colloidal 32-phosphorus or of external megavoltage irradiation of the abdomen up to the diaphragm. Doses of 3000 to

---

[43] H.W. Bruckner & G. Deppe, *Combination Chemotherapy of Advanced Endometrial Adenocarcinoma with Adriamycin, Cyclophosphamide, 5-Fluorouracil and Medroxyprogesterone Acetate,* 50 Obstetrics & Gynecology 415 (1977); C.J. Cohen, *Chemotherapy for Patients with Endometrial Carcinoma,* 13 Clinical Obstetrics & Gynecology 811 (1986); M.W. Pasmantier et al., *Treatment of Advanced Endometrial Carcinoma with Doxorubicin and Cisplatin: Effects on Both Untreated and Previously Treated Patients,* 69 Cancer Treatment Rep. 539 (1985); M.M. Turbow et al., *Chemotherapy of Advanced Endometrial Carcinoma with Platinum, Adriamycin, and Cyclophosphamide,* 1 Proc. Am. Soc'y Clinical Oncology 108 (1982).

3500 cGy can be given to the abdomen with shielding to limit the kidney exposure to 1500 to 2000 cGy and to limit the liver exposure to 2600 to 2800 cGy.

A high-grade Stage I tumor can receive either of the above pelvic irradiation regimens by reason of the tumor grade alone. Because the biopsy can disclose the high grade of the tumor prior to hysterectomy, there is the additional option of giving the radiation preoperatively. The same total dose is used for the preoperative pelvic irradiation. The intracavitary brachytherapy is more extensive, and two applications can be made one or two weeks apart. The total dose from the two applications is about 6000 cGy in the uterus at a depth of 1 1/2 cm and 6000 cGy on the vaginal surface.

Another prognostic factor in Stage I, that can be identified prior to hysterectomy so that a choice can be made between preoperative and postoperative radiation, is the length of the uterine canal. Radiation should be given if the uterine canal is longer than 8 cm. Surgery should be delayed four to six weeks following preoperative radiation.

Definitive radiation for a Stage I medically inoperable case or for a patient who refuses surgery consists of a combination of external and intracavitary radiation. The more extensive intracavitary brachytherapy described above is combined with the 4000 cGy to 5000 cGy of external radiation. The central tissues are shielded after the first 3000 cGy of external irradiation to avoid overdosage from the overlap of the external and intracavitary radiation.

In Stage II, external and intracavitary radiation are combined. The involvement of the cervix in Stage II introduces considerations similar to those in treating carcinoma of the cervix. The radiation is given preoperatively. The lymph nodes at the pelvic side wall should receive at least 5000 cGy from the combined contributions. The whole pelvis external radiation is 4000 cGy or greater with central shielding after 2000 to 3000 cGy. The intracavitary radiation is 4000 to 6000 radium equivalent mghrs, which results in a combined paracervical dose well above 5000 cGy.

Sometimes an endometrial carcinoma cannot be classified as Stage II until after the hysterectomy has been performed. In that case, postoperative radiation consists of 5000 cGy external radiation to the pelvis. Transvaginal kilovoltage radiation can be used to give 2000 cGy with seven treatments, or the same dose can be given with intracavitary colpostats containing 137-cesium.

Stage III can be irradiated postoperatively or can be treated with radiation alone if the tumor is fixed to the pelvic wall and is unresectable. As in other situations, external radiation is combined with intracavitary brachytherapy. The pelvic wall receives at least 5000 cGy, while the central target areas receive higher doses. Areas of gross residual tumor marked by clips can be boosted with small fields to 6000 to 6500 cGy or with interstitial implants.

Stage IV, by reason of paraaortic lymph node metastases, deserves thorough treatment. In addition to the usual pelvic irradiation, the paraaortic lymph nodes should be irradiated up to the diaphragm to doses of 4500 to 5000 cGy.

Previously unirradiated recurrent carcinoma limited to the vagina is curable and should receive a full course of external pelvic irradiation and intracavitary or interstitial brachytherapy.

Advanced incurable carcinoma can be effectively palliated with relief of discharge, hemorrhage, and pain by giving doses of 4000 cGy or more. Bone metastases, as with all other types of cancer, also can be palliated.

§ 14.41   Commentary and Significant Cases

Many of the problems encountered with cancer of the uterus are surgical complications. If preoperative radiation therapy has been administered, the complications are more frequent. Besides the possibility of postoperative bleeding or infection, urinary tract injury with accidental ligation of the ureter, urinary-vaginal fistula, or rectovaginal fistula can occur. Ligation of the ureter must be diagnosed as early as possible; otherwise, permanent damage to the kidney occurs. Further surgical repair is frequently necessary in the presence of cysto-vaginal fistula. Prolonged bladder drainage or diverting colostomy are bothersome to the patient.

Frost v. Sylvest.[44]   The pathology report from a dilation and curettage (D&C) was reported as showing cancer. Based on this report, an abdominal hysterectomy and ovarianectomy were performed on the 43-year-old plaintiff. Subsequent pathology indicated no evidence of cancer. The verdict was for $650,000.

Gist v. French.[45]   The defendant examined the plaintiff for complaints of pain in the right side. Removal of a pelvic tumor was advised. Hysterectomy and appendectomy were performed. Postoperatively, the plaintiff developed pelvic bleeding, and surgery was required to ligate the vaginal branch of the uterine artery during which the left tube and ovary were removed. The court affirmed the verdict of $70,000 for negligence and $9000 to the patient's husband for loss of services and consortium. Evidence of the plaintiff's lack of consent to remove organs was admissible. The court held that a surgeon cannot negligently create a pathologic condition and then operate a second time without the patient's consent and without first advising her how it happened.

Nguyen v. Stewart.[46]   The plaintiff had symptoms of cramping and brownish vaginal discharge with elevated human chorionic gonadotropin hormone (HCG)

---

[44]No. CL88000058 (Chesterfield County, VA Sept. 1989), *reprinted in* 6 Med. Malpractice Verdicts, Settlements & Experts No. 5, at 53 (1990).

[45]136 Cal. App.2d 247, 288 P.2d 1003 (1955).

[46]No. 87-CV-1630 (Boulder Dist. Ct., CO), *reprinted in* 6 Med. Malpractice Verdicts, Settlements & Experts No. 10, at 16–17 (1990).

levels that were twice diagnosed as miscarriages. There was no follow-up treatment to see that the plaintiff's elevated HCG level returned to normal. Another physician diagnosed choriocarcinoma with metastasis to the lung. The lung lesion was resected surgically, and the plaintiff underwent triple-agent chemotherapy that resulted in severe nausea and hair loss. The plaintiff alleged that with earlier diagnosis she could have undergone single-agent chemotherapy with virtually no side effects.

Savelle v. Heilbrunn.[47]   The plaintiff had a hysterectomy and bilateral salpingo-oophorectomy for fibroids. The pathology was reported as showing no evidence of malignancy. Approximately one year later, she had back pain that was diagnosed as metastatic uterine leiomyosarcoma. Chemotherapy was started, and there was an excellent response. Following the discontinuation of chemotherapy because of possibility of accumulative adverse affect, the tumor began to grow. Despite radiation therapy, the plaintiff had severe pain, was confined to home, and needed 24-hour-a-day nursing assistance. The defendant settled for $100,000, the limit of liability under Louisiana law. The court found the Louisiana Patient's Compensation Fund liable for $400,000 additional damages for the physician's failure to diagnose the patient's uterine cancer with lost opportunity to receive earlier treatment with an increased chance of survival and better quality of life.

Wallace v. Garden City Osteopathic Hospital.[48]   There was a directed verdict for the defendant when there was no expert testimony on the standard of care required of a pathologist or the breach of that standard. The plaintiff alleged that the pathologist failed to find more extensive cancer than originally diagnosed when he did not mention a uterosacral ligament in his report that the surgeon sent him. There was no evidence by the plaintiff to establish that this failure in any way caused or accelerated the death of plaintiff's decedent.

OVARIAN NEOPLASMS

§ 14.42   Staging and Classification

TNM: American Joint Committee on Cancer.[49]
    The TNM system seldom is used for ovarian malignancies.

---

[47] 552 So. 2d 52 (La. Ct. App. 1989).

[48] 111 Mich. App. 212, 314 N.W.2d 557 (1981).

[49] American Joint Committee on Cancer, Manual for Staging of Cancer 164 (3d ed. 1988).

International Federation of Gynecology and Obstetrics (FIGO)

I—Tumor limited to ovaries

Ia—Tumor limited to one ovary; capsule intact, no tumor on ovarian surface

Ib—Tumor limited to both ovaries; capsules intact, no tumor on ovarian surface

Ic—Tumor limited to one or both ovaries with any of the following: capsule ruptured, tumor on ovarian surface, malignant cells in ascites, or peritoneal washing

II—Tumor involves one or both ovaries with pelvic extension

IIa—Extension and/or implants on uterus and/or tube(s)

IIb—Extension to other pelvic tissues

IIc—Pelvic extension (2a or 2b) with malignant cell in ascites or peritoneal washing

III—Tumor involves one or both ovaries with microscopically confirmed peritoneal metastasis outside the pelvis and/or regional lymph node metastasis

IIIa—Microscopic peritoneal metastasis beyond pelvis

IIIb—Macroscopic peritoneal metastasis beyond pelvis 2 cm or less in greatest dimension

IIIc—Peritoneal metastasis beyond pelvis more than 2 cm in greatest dimension and/or regional lymph node metastasis

IV—Distant metastasis (excludes peritoneal metastasis).

Histopathology[50]

A. Serous cystomas
    1. Serous benign cystadenomas
    2. Serous cystadenomas with proliferating activity of the epithelial cells and nuclear abnormalities, but with no infiltrative destructive growth (low potential malignancy)
    3. Serous cystadenocarcinomas
B. Mucinous cystomas
    1. Mucinous benign cystadenomas

---

[50] World Health Organization.

2. Mucinous cystadenomas with proliferating activity of the epithelial cells and nuclear abnormalities, but with no infiltrative destructive growth (low potential malignancy)

3. Mucinous cystadenocarcinomas

C. Endometroid tumors (similar to adenocarcinomas in the endometrium)

1. Endometroid benign cysts

2. Endometroid tumors with proliferating activity of the epithelial cells and nuclear abnormalities, but with no infiltrative destructive growth (low potential malignancy)

3. Endometroid adenocarcinomas

D. Clear cell (mesonephroid) tumors

1. Benign clear cell tumors

2. Clear cell tumors with proliferating activity of the epithelial cells and nuclear abnormalities, but with no infiltrative destructive growth (low potential malignancy)

3. Clear cell cystadenocarcinomas

E. Unclassified tumors.

§ 14.43   Clinical Manifestations

Ovarian neoplasms are painless tumors and are rarely diagnosed on routine pelvic examination. With tumor enlargement, the patient can have a feeling of heaviness in the pelvis, abdominal enlargement, and vague gastrointestinal symptoms such as abdominal discomfort, dyspepsia, or nausea. Ascites formation increases the abdominal discomfort and abdominal girth.

§ 14.44   Diagnosis

Pelvic examination, most often, discloses an ovarian mass except in the markedly obese patient or in the presence of a large amount of ascites. Abdominal X-rays can show calcification in the pelvic mass sometimes seen in myomas or teratomas. Pelvic sonogram or computerized tomography (CT scan) distinguishes ovarian tumors from uterine or tubal masses. Intravenous pyelogram and barium enemas can give additional information concerning involvement of surrounding structures.

Ascites can be aspirated and the fluid can be evaluated for malignant cells. However, a large, self-contained malignant ovarian cyst can appear similar to ascites, and puncturing the cyst can spread the malignancy into the peritoneal cavity.

§ 14.45   Surgical Treatment

When the tumor is a borderline malignancy (low malignant potential), removing the ovary suffices in patients who desire to maintain childbearing ability and who have Stage IA disease.[51] Stage I disease is best treated by total abdominal hysterectomy with bilateral salpingo-oophorectomy with or without omentectomy.[52] Removal of the omentum should also be performed in Stage II disease even though the value is inconclusive.

In Stages III and IV the uterus, tubes, ovaries, and omentum should be removed if possible. At least the bulk of the tumor should be removed, trying to leave no more than 2 cm of tumor at any focus in the abdomen. This method allows the best potential effect of chemotherapy.

The second look operation[53] can aid in determining further treatment after a period of chemotherapy. Residual tumor can be removed in this procedure.

§ 14.46   Chemotherapy Treatment

Single-agent chemotherapy is effective as initial treatment of advanced ovarian cancer. Drugs that result in tumor regression include melphalan, chlorambucil, cyclophosphamide, thiotepa, hexamethylmelamine, doxorubicin, cisplatin, ifosfamide, etoposide (VP-16), mitomycin-C, carbolatin, and Peptichemio®.[54] There is increased effectiveness with combination chemotherapy compared to single agent therapy. Combinations used include: cyclophosphamide, hexamethylmelamine, doxorubicin (Adriamycin®), and cisplatin (CHAD); cyclophosphamide, hexamethylmelamine, 5-fluorouracil (CHF); Adriamycin and cyclophosphamide (AC); cisplatin, Adriamycin, and cyclophosphamide (PAC);

---

[51] E.W. Munnell, *Is Conservative Therapy Ever Justified in Stage IA Cancer of the Ovary?*, 103 Am. J. Obstetrics & Gynecology 641 (1969); R.T. Parker et al., *Cancer of the Ovary; Survival Studies Based Upon Operative Therapy, Chemotherapy, and Radiotherapy*, 108 Am. J. Obstetrics & Gynecology 878 (1970).

[52] M.J. Webb et al., *Factor Influencing Survival in Stage I Ovarian Cancer*, 116 Am. J. Obstetrics & Gynecology 222 (1973).

[53] K.S. Raja et al., *Second-Look Operations in the Planned Management of Advanced Ovarian Carcinoma*, 144 Am. J. Obstetric Gynecology 650 (1982); M.J. Webb et al., *Second-Look Laparatomy in Ovarian Cancer*, 14 Gynecologic Oncology 285 (1982).

[54] P. Bruhl et al., *Results Obtained with Fractioned Ifosfamide Massive-Dose Treatment in Generalized Malignant Tumors*, 14 Int'l J. Clinical Pharmacology & Biopharmacology 29 (1976); R. Cavetta & S.K. Carter, *Developing New Drugs for Ovarian Cancer: A Challenging Task in a Changing Reality*, 107 J. Cancer Res. & Clinical Oncology 111 (1984); R.H. Creech, *Phase II Study of Low-Dose Mitomycin in Patients with Ovarian Cancer Previously Treated with Chemotherapy*, 69 Cancer Treatment Rep. 1271 (1985); B.L. Hillcoat et al., *Phase II Trial of VP-16-213 in Advanced Ovarian Carcinoma*, 22 Gynecologic Oncology 162 (1985); A. Paccagnella et al., *Peptichemio in Pre-Treated Patients with Ovarian Cancer*, 69 Cancer Treatment Rep. 17 (1985).

cyclophosphamide and cisplatin (CP); hexamethylmelamine, cyclophosphamide, methotrexate, and 5-fluorouracil (Hexa-CAF); cisplatin, etoposide, and bleomycin (BEP); vincristine, dactinomycin, and cyclophosphamide (VAC); cisplatin, vinblastine, and bleomycin (PVB); and cyclophosphamide, hexamethylmelamine, 5-fluorouracil, and cisplatin (CHEX-UP).[55]

Stage I (limited to ovary) dysgerminoma can have optimal chemotherapy after surgical removal. Stage II and III dysgerminoma can have chemotherapy to preserve fertility. Stage IV dysgerminoma is treated with combination chemotherapy.

In treating germ cell tumors of the ovary other than dysgerminoma, Stage I, II, and III tumors are given adjuvant chemotherapy to increase survival. Chemotherapy is more effective when the postsurgical residual tumor is less than 2 cm in diameter. A second look operation after completing a course of chemotherapy helps to determine if further drug therapy is necessary.

§ 14.47   Radiation Therapy Treatment

Postoperative radiation for epithelial carcinomas of the ovary can yield good cure rates in carefully selected cases. Careful selection limits radiation to cases in which all gross evidence of tumor has been resected, or if residual tumor remains, none of it is over 2 cm in diameter in certain stages and histologic types of tumor. All histologic types with no residual tumor masses in Stage II can be irradiated with good results. In addition, successful radiation is possible in well-differentiated serous carcinomas with small residual tumors in Stages II and III and in mucinous and endometrioid carcinomas with small residual tumors in Stage II.

Stage I tumors are not irradiated unless they are high-grade tumors, have strong adhesions to adjacent tissues, and are ruptured during surgery. They also are irradiated if the tumor has grown through its capsule or if there are tumor cells in ascitic fluid or in peritoneal washings.

---

[55] D.M. Gershenson et al., *Treatment of Malignant Germ Cell Tumors of the Ovary with Bleomycin, Etoposide, and Cisplatin,* 8 J. Clinical Oncology 715 (1990); F.A. Greco et al., *Advanced Ovarian Cancer: Brief Intensive Combination Chemotherapy and Second Look Operation,* 58 Obstetrics & Gynecology 199 (1981); K.G. Louie et al., *Long-Term Results of a Cisplatin-Containing Combination Chemotherapy Regimen for the Treatment of Advanced Ovarian Carcinoma,* 4 J. Clinical Oncology 1579 (1986); J.P. Neijt et al., *Randomized Trial Comparing Two Combination Chemotherapy Regimens (CHAP-5 v. CP) in Advanced Ovarian Carcinoma,* 5 J. Clinical Oncology 1157 (1987); R.E. Slayton et al., *Vincristine, Dactinomycin, and Cyclophosphamide in the Treatment of Malignant Germ Cell Tumors of the Ovary,* 56 Cancer 243 (1985); M.H. Taylor et al., *Vinblastine, Bleomycin, and Cisplatin in Malignant Germ Cell Tumors of the Ovary,* 56 Cancer 1341 (1985); S.D. Williams et al., *Cisplatin, Vinblastine, and Bleomycin in Advanced and Recurrent Ovarian Germ-Cell Tumors: A Trial of the Gynecologic Oncology Group,* 111 Annals Internal Med. 22 (1989).

Radiation limited to the pelvis is inadequate treatment. The entire abdomen must be treated extending up to and covering the top of the diaphragm. The two methods of giving abdominopelvic radiation are the open field method and the moving strip method. The open field is single large anterior and posterior fields covering the entire pelvis and abdomen. The moving strip marks the skin with horizontal stripes 2 1/2 cm apart. Treatment starts in the pelvis with a field 2 1/2 cm in vertical length. Another 2 1/2 cm field is added each day until the vertical length of the field reaches 10 cm. Then the 10 cm field moves up the abdomen in 2 1/2 cm steps to the top of the diaphragm where it shrinks 2 1/2 cm daily to its original 2 1/2 cm vertical length.

Megavoltage radiation is used. The open field is treated with 100 to 125 cGy fractions. The total dose may vary 5 percent across the field in relation to the dose in the liver, which is fixed at 2500 cGy. Shielding limits the dose to kidneys to 1800 to 2000 cGy. The open field is then reduced to pelvic fields where the total dose is boosted to 4000 to 5000 cGy in fractions of 160 to 180 cGy.

The moving strip technique delivers a tumor dose of 2800 cGy. The kidneys and liver are shielded so that they receive 1800 cGy. The pelvis is boosted separately with an additional 2000 cGy.

Tumor implants of a millimeter or less have been managed with intraperitoneal infusion of colloidal 32-Phosphorus, in a dose of 15 mCi. The isotope is infused with 200 cc or more of saline for better diffusion in the abdomen. The infusion is made through a catheter that is positioned in the abdomen fluoroscopically with an injection of radio-opaque contrast material to confirm that the flow is satisfactory. Attention to the flow of the isotope reduces the chance of intestinal injury if external radiation also is used.

Radiation therapy can be given following chemotherapy, but myelotoxicity can prevent employment of an optimum regimen.

Dysgerminomas occur in young women. The tumors are extremely radiosensitive, but if the patients wish to retain their fertility, only one ovary is resected, and further treatment consists of chemotherapy.

When radiation is used, the entire abdomen and pelvis are irradiated to 2500 cGy. Paraaortic metastases and bulky masses are given a boost to 4000 cGy. The mediastinum and supraclavicular lymph nodes may be irradiated electively to 2500 cGy when paraaortic metastases are present, but this treatment is controversial.

In the absence of tumor masses, other indications for abdominopelvic irradiation in dysgerminomas are tumor rupture during surgery and dense adhesions of the primary tumor to adjacent tissues.

Dysgerminomas should be checked for alphafetoprotein and beta-chorionic gonadotropin. These markers indicate the presence of other tumor elements that are better treated with chemotherapy.

Granulosa-theca tumors are radiosensitive. Radiation does not have to be limited to residual tumors less than 2 cm in diameter. Larger tumor masses can be irradiated successfully. The open field technique for abdominopelvic irradiation is suitable.

§ 14.48   Commentary and Significant Cases

Ovarian tumors are most often asymptomatic. Neoplasms are large or have spread before the diagnosis is made. Pelvic examination should be performed on an annual basis, and any suspicious enlargement of the ovary must be evaluated by pelvic sonography or computerized tomography (CT scan). Early surgical diagnosis is important.

Jamison v. Lindsay.[56]   The 16-year-old plaintiff had a tumor of the right ovary removed. The pathologist reported the teratoma was benign but did not inform the surgeon that immature elements were present and that the teratoma was potentially malignant. Months later, the tumor recurred retroperitoneally with metastases to the lung. Chemotherapy and radiation therapy were used. The court affirmed the jury finding that the pathologist and gynecologist were not negligent, even though negligent failure to advise a patient to pursue a potentially necessary course of treatment is actionable.

Toney v. Neighborhood Family Practice.[57]   There was a defense verdict. At exploratory surgery in the 36-year-old plaintiff, a 46-pound benign left ovarian tumor was found and removed. Because of the unreliability of frozen section diagnosis, the plaintiff's family history of ovarian cancer, and the difficulty of follow-up monitoring due to patient's obesity, the defendants decided to remove the right ovary and uterus. The plaintiff contended that removing the remaining ovary and the hysterectomy should not have been done.

---

[56] 108 Cal. App. 3d 223, 166 Cal. Rptr. 443 (1980).

[57] No. 117019 (San Diego County Super Ct. Oct. 1989), *reprinted in* 6 Med. Malpractice Verdicts, Settlements & Experts No. 12, at 64 (1990).